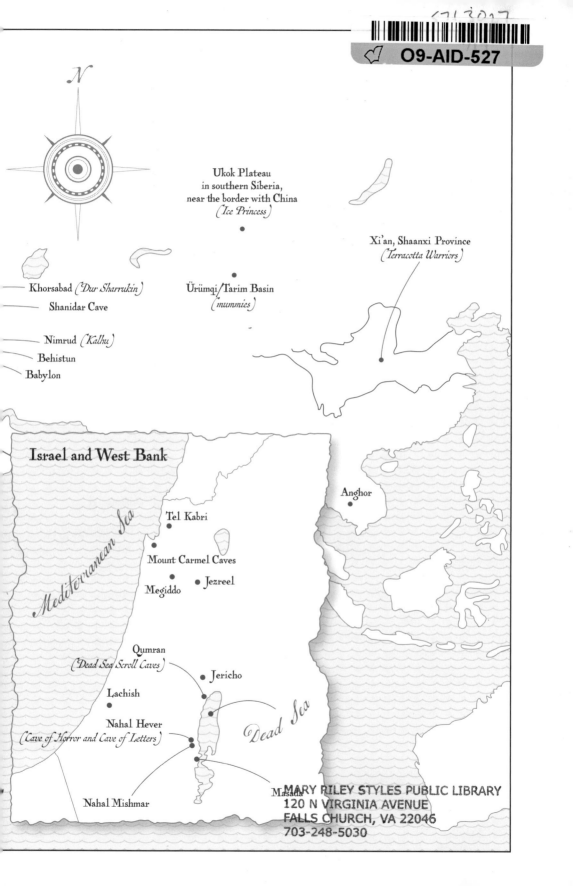

N

Ukok Plateau
in southern Siberia,
near the border with China
(*Ice Princess*)

Xi'an, Shaanxi Province
(*Terracotta Warriors*)

Khorsabad (*Dur Sharrukin*)

Shanidar Cave

Ürümqi / Tarim Basin
(*mummies*)

Nimrud (*Kalhu*)

Behistun

Babylon

Israel and West Bank

Anghor

Tel Kabri

Mount Carmel Caves

Megiddo

Jezreel

Mediterranean Sea

Qumran
(*Dead Sea Scroll Caves*)

Jericho

Lachish

Nahal Hever
(*Cave of Horror and Cave of Letters*)

Dead Sea

Masada

Nahal Mishmar

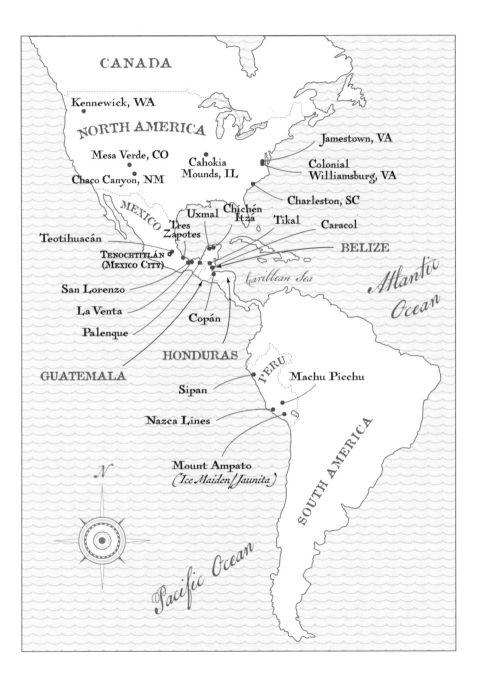

CANADA

NORTH AMERICA

Kennewick, WA

Mesa Verde, CO

Chaco Canyon, NM

Cahokia
Mounds, IL

Jamestown, VA

Colonial
Williamsburg, VA

Charleston, SC

MEXICO

Uxmal   Chichén
         Itzá

Tres
Zapotes

Tikal

Caracol

Teotihuacán

TENOCHTITLÁN
(MEXICO CITY)

BELIZE

Caribbean Sea

San Lorenzo

La Venta

Copán

Palenque

HONDURAS

PERU

Machu Picchu

GUATEMALA

Sipan

Nazca Lines

Mount Ampato
(Ice Maiden/Jaunita)

SOUTH AMERICA

Atlantic
Ocean

Pacific Ocean

N

THREE STONES
MAKE A WALL

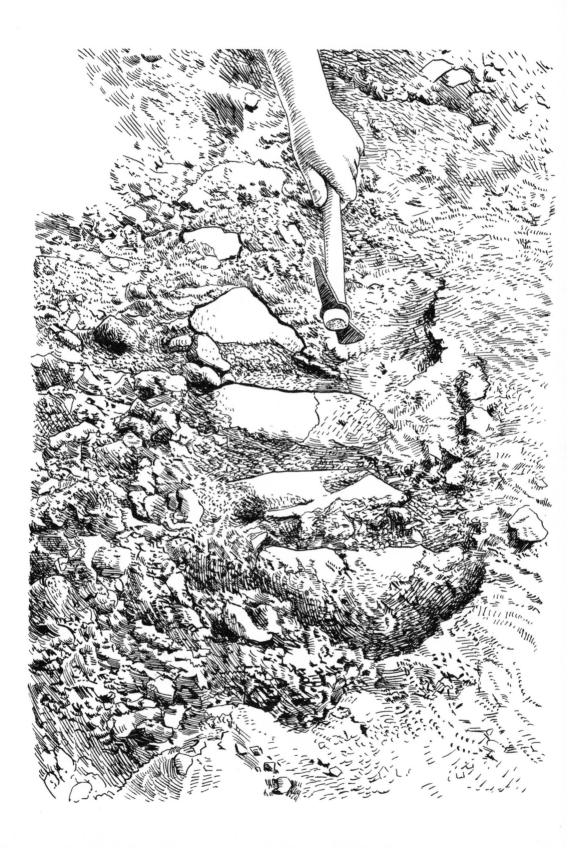

THREE STONES MAKE A WALL

THE STORY OF ARCHAEOLOGY

ERIC H. CLINE

With illustrations by
Glynnis Fawkes

PRINCETON UNIVERSITY PRESS   PRINCETON & OXFORD

Library of Congress Cataloging-in-Publication Data

Names: Cline, Eric H., author.
Title: Three stones make a wall : the story of archaeology / Eric H. Cline.
Description: Princeton : Princeton University Press, [2017] | Includes
bibliographical references and index.
Identifiers: LCCN 2016041435 | ISBN 9780691166407
(hardback : acid-free paper)
Subjects: LCSH: Archaeology—History. | Excavations (Archaeology)—
History. | Archaeologists—Biography. | Archaeology—Methodology. |
Antiquities. | Civilization, Ancient. | BISAC: SOCIAL SCIENCE /
Archaeology. | HISTORY / Ancient / General. | HISTORY / Civilization. |
HISTORY / World.
Classification: LCC CC100 .C55 2017 | DDC 930.1—dc23 LC record
available at
https://lccn.loc.gov/2016041435

British Library Cataloging-in-Publication Data is available
This book has been composed in Sabon Next LT Pro
Printed on acid-free paper. ∞
Printed in the United States of America
1 3 5 7 9 10 8 6 4 2

CONTENTS

List of Illustrations   vii

Preface: A Petrified Monkey's Paw   xi

Prologue: "Wonderful Things": King Tut and His Tomb   1

PART 1 EARLY ARCHAEOLOGY AND ARCHAEOLOGISTS

1   Ashes to Ashes in Ancient Italy   13

2   Digging Up Troy   24

3   From Egypt to Eternity   38

4   Mysteries in Mesopotamia   52

5   Exploring the Jungles of Central America   66

Digging Deeper 1: How Do You Know Where to Dig?   80

**PART 2 AFRICA, EUROPE, AND THE LEVANT:
EARLY HOMININS TO FARMERS**

6   Discovering Our Earliest Ancestors   97

7   First Farmers in the Fertile Crescent   115

PART 3 EXCAVATING THE BRONZE AGE AEGEAN

8   Revealing the First Greeks   131

9   Finding Atlantis?   146

10   Enchantment Under the Sea   157

PART 4 UNCOVERING THE CLASSICS

11   From Discus-Throwing to Democracy   171

12   What Have the Romans Ever Done for Us?   188

Digging Deeper 2: How Do You Know How to Dig?   204

PART 5 DISCOVERIES IN THE HOLY LAND AND BEYOND

13 Excavating Armageddon 221
14 Unearthing the Bible 234
15 Mystery at Masada 245
16 Cities of the Desert 257

Digging Deeper 3: How Old Is This and Why Is It Preserved? 269

PART 6 NEW WORLD ARCHAEOLOGY

17 Lines in the Sand, Cities in the Sky 291
18 Giant Heads, Feathered Serpents, and Golden Eagles 303
19 Submarines and Settlers; Gold Coins and Lead Bullets 314

Digging Deeper 4: Do You Get to Keep What You Find? 326

Epilogue: Back to the Future 333

Acknowledgments 341
Notes 343
Bibliography 383
Index 431

ILLUSTRATIONS

Frontispiece: Excavating at Tel Kabri

Hellenistic bronze figure, Tel Anafa xi

Close-up of wine jars, Tel Kabri xiv

King Tut's gold death mask 1

Howard Carter and assistant, examining King Tut 6

Cave Canem mosaic plus dog in plaster of Paris 13

Mount Vesuvius as seen through Pompeii Arch 16

Street scene, Pompeii 20

Sophia Schliemann wearing Priam's Treasure; depiction
   of the Trojan Horse 24

Wall of Troy VI 25

Rosetta stone hieroglyphics 38

Step Pyramid of Djoser, Saqqara 47

Queen Pu-abi, Ur 52

Man-headed winged bull, Dur Sharrukin (modern Khorsabad) 61

Skull rack at Chichen Itzá 66

Temple of the Grand Jaguar (Temple 1), Tikal 73

Surveyors walking a transect 80

Tractor and ground-penetrating radar, near Stonehenge 88

Laetoli footprints 97

Chauvet cave painting 108

Çatalhöyük figurine: possibly a goddess or queen 115

Plastered skull, Jericho 121

Mycenae: Lion Gate and "Mask of Agamemnon" 131

Lion Gate, Mycenae 133

Akrotiri: miniature wall fresco 146

Eruption of Santorini   147
Uluburun: copper ingots and other artifacts   157
Uluburun diver   160
Delphic oracle   171
Temple of Apollo, Delphi   179
Roman Colosseum   188
Arch of Titus   196
Close-up, Arch of Titus   196
Digging: tools of the trade   204
Stratigraphic layers, Tel Kabri   213
Megiddo: ivory griffin   221
"Solomon's Stables" at Megiddo   226
Dead Sea Scroll fragment   234
Caves at Qumran   235
Masada ostraca   245
Masada   247
Palmyra: distant view   257
Triumphal Arch, Palmyra   261
View of the "Treasury" at Petra   263
Tollund Fen Bog Man   269
Terracotta Warriors   274
Nazca Lines: hummingbird   291
Machu Picchu   299
Pyramid of the Moon, Teotihuacán   303
Olmec colossal stone head, San Lorenzo   306
Aztec Moon Goddess, Tenochtitlán   310
Confederate submarine *H. L. Hunley*   314
Mesa Verde National Park, Colorado   323
Looter digging   326
Looting in Iraq   328
Future artifact   333
Statue of Liberty, head   334

One stone is a stone.
Two stones is a feature.
Three stones is a wall.
Four stones is a building.
Five stones is a palace.
(Six stones is a palace built by aliens.)

—Archaeological axiom

A PETRIFIED MONKEY'S PAW

WHEN I WAS SEVEN YEARS OLD, MY MOTHER GAVE ME A book called *The Walls of Windy Troy*. It was about Heinrich Schliemann and his search for the ruins of ancient Troy, written just for children. After reading it, I announced that I was going to be an archaeologist. Later, when I was in junior high and high school, I read John Lloyd Stephens's *Incidents of Travel in Yucatán* and C. W. Ceram's *Gods, Graves, and Scholars*, which cemented my desire—the stories of finding lost cities in the jungle and uncovering ancient civilizations were mesmerizing. In college, I declared my major in archaeology just as soon as I could and, when I graduated, my mother again gave me the book about Schliemann that had started it all fourteen years earlier. I still have it in my office at George Washington University today.

I'm not alone in being fascinated by archaeology; it's pretty clear that a lot of other people are as well. This is evident by the success of the Indiana Jones movies and in the burgeoning television documentaries that air almost every night on one channel or another. I've lost track of the number of times that someone has said to me, "You know, if I weren't a _____ (fill in the blank with doctor, lawyer, nurse, accountant, Wall Street financier, etc.), I would have been an archaeologist." Most people, however, have little or no idea what's involved. Maybe they imagine searching for lost treasures, traveling to exotic locales, and meticulously digging using toothbrushes and dental tools. It's usually not like that at all, and most archaeologists are nothing like Indiana Jones.

I've been going on archaeological expeditions almost every summer since I was a sophomore in college—more than thirty field seasons in all, over the past thirty-five years. Because of where I've worked—primarily in the Middle East and Greece—most people consider me to be an Old World archaeologist. But I've also excavated in California and Vermont in the United States, which is considered the New World in archaeological terms.

I've been able to participate in a variety of interesting projects, including Tel Anafa, Megiddo, and Tel Kabri in Israel; the Athenian Agora, Boeotia, and Pylos in Greece; Tell el-Maskhuta in Egypt; Palaio-kastro in Crete; Kataret es-Samra in Jordan; and Ayios Dhimitrios and Paphos in Cyprus. Most of those are sites or regions that almost nobody except archaeologists has ever heard of, except perhaps the Agora in downtown Athens and Megiddo in Israel, which is biblical Armaged-don. I can tell you for a fact that digging at those sites is nothing like in the movies.

People often ask me, "What's the best thing you've ever found?" In response, I tell them, "a petrified monkey's paw." It happened on my very first overseas excavation, during the summer after my sophomore year in college. I was digging at the Greco-Roman site of Tel Anafa in the north of Israel on a project run by the University of Michigan.

One day, about mid-morning, it was getting really hot and I was starting to worry about sunstroke. Just then, my little *patish*, or digging hammer, hit an object at such an angle that the piece flew straight up in the air, turning over and over before it landed again. While it was still in midair, I noticed that it was green and thought—in a bit of a daze because of the heat—"hey, it's a petrified monkey's paw!" By the time it landed, I had come to my senses: "What would a petrified monkey's paw be doing in northern Israel?"

Sure enough, when I examined it closely, it turned out to be a Hellenistic bronze furniture piece in the shape of the Greek god Pan—the one with horns on his head who goes around playing on the double pipes. It would probably have been attached to the end of a wooden arm of a chair, but the wood had disintegrated long ago and so only this bronze piece was left where I was digging. It was green because the bronze had turned that color during the two thousand years that the piece had been lying in the ground, waiting for me to find it. We carefully brought it out of the field, drew it, and photographed it, so that it could eventually be published. I didn't see it again for almost thirty years, until I just happened to run across it in a museum at the University of Haifa, where it was on loan from the Israel Museum in Jerusalem.

But then, in 2013, our team digging at the Canaanite site of Tel Kabri in northern Israel found something that trumped even my petrified monkey's paw. I've been codirecting the excavations at the site every other year since 2005 with Assaf Yasur-Landau of the University of Haifa. Each season has brought new surprises, but this was entirely unexpected, for we uncovered what turned out to be the oldest and largest wine cellar yet discovered in the world, dating to about 1700 BCE—nearly four thousand years ago.

It was in June, during the first week of our season, when we came upon a large jar that we nicknamed Bessie. It took us almost two weeks to uncover her completely and find that she was lying on the plaster floor of the room. By that time, she had been joined by what turned out to be thirty-nine of her friends—for we found a total of forty jars, each three feet high, in that room and in the corridor just north of it.

Even though the jars had shattered into dozens of individual potsherds, the soil that had seeped inside had filled up each jar, so that they still had their original shape. We initially thought each jar would have held about fifty liters of liquid. We have since been told by our conservator, when he started to reconstruct them, that each one would actually have held more than one hundred liters, which means four thousand liters in all.

Andrew Koh, our associate director at Kabri, was able to test the sherds, using organic residue analysis to determine what had been in the jars. Most came back positive for syringic acid, which is found in red

Close-up of wine jars, Tel Kabri

wine; a few came back positive for tartaric acid, which is found in both red and white wine. We have little doubt, therefore, that they had all once held wine, with most of it being red wine and some white. That's approximately six thousand bottles of wine, in today's terms. Of course, the wine is now long gone, except for the residue left within the fabric of the jars, but I am often asked what it might have tasted like. Since we don't yet know for certain, I simply answer that it has an "earthy taste" now.

Our discovery, and the article that we subsequently published about it in a peer-reviewed journal, made all the papers, including the *New York Times*, the *Wall Street Journal*, and the *Washington Post*, as well as the *Los Angeles Times*, and *Time*, *Smithsonian*, and *Wine Spectator* magazines. We have since uncovered four more rooms, with seventy additional jars, and are looking forward to more seasons of excavation at this interesting site.

Discovering a wine cellar from ancient Canaan was certainly not what my seven-year-old self ever expected to find when I decided to become an archaeologist. But that's the beauty and excitement of archaeology—you never really know what you are going to find. My nonarchaeologist colleagues at George Washington University think it is the greatest joke in the world to ask *"What's new in archaeology?"*—because, of course, everything we dig up is old. Archaeology keeps surprising us, however, even at sites and places that have long been known. For instance, it now turns out that the site of Troy is at least ten times larger than previously thought; the prehistoric Chauvet cave paintings in France are older than we supposed; a Maya site in Belize completely hidden within the jungle was located using remote sensing; and the site of Tanis in Egypt has been hiding in plain sight all along. In each case, the news was unexpected.

❧❧ ❧❧

Additional announcements of other new finds and hypotheses appear daily, in a pleasurable never-ending deluge that seems to come faster all the time. For instance, on a single day in early June 2016, media reports about archaeology included stories about a new expedition searching for Dead Sea scrolls within the Cave of Skulls in Israel; the discovery of four hundred wooden tablets in London with Latin written on them; two-thousand-year-old military barracks from the time of Hadrian uncovered in Rome; whether a Canadian teenager actually discovered a Maya site in Mexico or not; the opening of an exhibit of five hundred objects from ancient Greece in Washington, DC; new remote sensing being done on the Great Pyramid in Egypt; and the fact that the blade on one of King Tut's daggers is made of iron from a meteorite—which gave rise to the wonderful, although not entirely accurate, headline in the *New York Post*: "King Tut's dagger came from outer space." Within a week, they had been followed by an announcement of new archaeological discoveries beneath the jungle canopy in Cambodia, accomplished with new remote sensing technology.

The good news is that there are lots of new discoveries being made, perhaps more quickly than ever before in the history of archaeology; the bad news is that it means that parts of this book may already be outdated by the time it is published. For instance, all the stories just mentioned plus others relevant to topics that we will discuss later in this book were breaking news as I was finishing up the draft of the book, but others will appear while this book is in press and after it is out.

It is truly an exciting time to be an archaeologist, but I also want to address throughout this book some of the more dubious claims about various finds that are occasionally made in television documentaries, media reports, online personal blog pages, and elsewhere, because it can sometimes be difficult for the general public to distinguish the real discoveries and discussions by professional archaeologists from claims made by pseudo-archaeologists. Each year there are enthusiastic amateurs with little or no training in archaeology who go searching for things like the Ark of the Covenant or places like Atlantis. Their searches can make for compelling stories and good documentary video fodder, but they muddy the water so that real scientific progress is obscured. Some of the claims are so outrageous that in 2007 I published an op-ed article in the *Boston Globe* with the title "Raiders of the Faux Ark." There I warned the general public about being duped and called upon my professional colleagues to investigate such claims when they are made.

Many people, encouraged by pseudo-archaeologists, cannot accept the fact that mere humans might have come up with great innovations such as the domestication of plants and animals or could have built great architectural masterpieces such as the pyramids or the Sphinx all on their own. Instead, they invoke alien, or sometimes divine, assistance to explain how these works came to be, even though there's no need to do so. It's gotten so bad that we've now added to our tongue-in-cheek archaeological axiom, quoted at the front of this book, "six stones is a palace built by aliens."

Perhaps the most compelling reason to write this book now, however, is that the world has been witnessing an assault on archaeological sites and museums during the past several years at a level and pace previously unseen. Deliberate looting and destruction of antiquities has taken place across much of the Middle East, from Iraq to Afghanistan, Syria, Libya, and Egypt, linked in large part to the recent wars and uprisings in those regions. But looting of ancient sites is not limited to that area; it is a worldwide problem, stretching from Greece to Peru, threatening our unique human heritage on a scale never seen before. Already back in 2008, one reporter described the scale of the destruction as "almost industrial," writing: "Looters attack ancient sites with backhoes and small bulldozers, scraping away the top layer of earth across areas the size of several football fields. Then, guided by metal detectors—coins often give away the location of other goods—they sink shafts to extract anything of value." The same wording was used again in 2015, when the head of UNESCO warned of "industrial scale looting in Syria."

Archaeologists have taken an active role in documenting and trying to prevent this ongoing loss of our heritage, but they are not the only ones responsible for taking care of the past. That responsibility lies with everybody. It is up to all of us to help save and preserve the remains and relics of long-lost civilizations. I hope that the material I have included in this book will remind us all of where we have come from and the fascination that it holds and will encourage a wide public audience to help protect our inheritance before it is too late. Not all readers will have the time or freedom to join an archaeological dig, but everyone can raise their voices in support of the archaeological process and our shared heritage.

It also is simply time for a new introductory volume, meant for people of all ages, from youngsters at the age that I once was, back when I read about Heinrich Schliemann for the first time, to adults and retirees who are new to the field of archaeology. In the past few decades, tremendous numbers of discoveries, as well as great advances in archaeology, have been made. These include Lucy, the partial early hominin skeleton at Hadar in Ethiopia, and the 3.6-million-year-old footprints at Laetoli in Tanzania; the spectacular prehistoric cave art at Chauvet Cave in France; the Cape Gelidonya and Uluburun shipwrecks off the southwestern coast of Turkey, with their cargoes of objects made in countries throughout the Bronze Age Mediterranean; the world's oldest temple at Göbekli Tepe and the renewed excavations at the Neolithic site of Çatalhöyük, also in Turkey; the Terracotta Warriors in China; Ötzi the Iceman in the Alps; and the Moche in Peru. All these, and many others as well, are now presented here, in addition to discussions of the archaeologists themselves and the techniques that they have used to excavate those sites and make those discoveries.

In the pages that follow, we will trace the evolution of archaeology from its earliest beginnings to a highly organized, professional, and scientific systematic study of past peoples and cultures. Along the way, we'll meet explorers and archaeologists including Howard Carter, Heinrich Schliemann, Mary Leakey, Hiram Bingham, Dorothy Garrod, and John Lloyd Stephens. These men and women, along with many others, discovered the remains of earlier people and lost civilizations, such as the Hittites, Minoans, Mycenaeans, Trojans, Assyrians, Maya, Inca, Aztec, and Moche. We will examine work that has been done in the Old World (from Europe and the United Kingdom to the Middle East and beyond), as well as in the New World (North, Central, and South America).

These are the archaeologists and discoveries that are the most fascinating to me and that I believe are among the most important in order to understand how archaeology has developed as a discipline over the years as well as to show how it has shed light on some of the long-lost ancient sites and civilizations. Readers will note that there are discussions of sites and artifacts in every chapter, including the "Digging Deeper" sections, and that there are some common threads found throughout, including the current problem of looting around the world; the hard work and physical labor that is involved in doing archaeology; the fact that archaeologists are searching for information rather than gold, treasures, or other rewards; and the improvements in technology that have allowed us to find new sites as well as to increase our knowledge of sites that were initially excavated long ago.

I've also added practical details and advice about how to do archaeology, for I'm frequently asked questions like

"How do you know where to dig?"

"How do you know how old something is?"

"Do you get to keep what you find?"

In answering these questions, I have included a number of examples taken from elsewhere, like Ötzi the Iceman and the Terracotta Warriors, but I also have drawn from my own fieldwork, ranging from Crete to Cyprus to California. In some cases, they can be held up as an example of what *not* to do on a survey or an excavation, including falling down a small cliff while surveying in Greece and, of course, thinking that I had found a petrified monkey's paw on my first dig in Israel. This means, however, that my discussions will occasionally be very location-specific. For instance, we regularly use pickaxes to dig in the Middle East, whereas they are almost never used when digging on the East Coast of the United States, and so I have made an effort to note when the techniques that I am describing might be different in other parts of the world. I also have used BCE and CE ("Before the Common Era" and the "Common Era") when referring to dates, rather than the "BC/AD" system that may be more familiar to some readers. The choice is not meant to offend anyone but simply follows the practice of most modern archaeologists and archaeological reports.

As a whole, the material in this book reflects what I have been teaching in my Introduction to Archaeology class at George Washington University since 2001, with my notes and lectures updated and revised each year to reflect both new discoveries and fresh thoughts on old finds. Another professor or author might well do it differently, as they are welcome to do, but the following discussions reflect my particular love and passion for the field, and some of my favorite stories and examples that I think serve as good illustrations. I hope that readers will find the material interesting enough to continue and read other, more detailed books about specific sites, time periods, and peoples.

At the very least, by the time we're done, those who have read the whole book will know a lot more about a number of famous sites and archaeologists; will realize that there is no need to ever invoke aliens; and will be more knowledgeable about what is involved in doing archaeology. My hope is that it also will become obvious why archaeology matters and why we should care about preserving the past for future generations, for archaeology not only teaches us about the past, it also connects us to a broader sample of human experience and enriches our understanding of both our present and our future.

To be clear, the story of archaeology is really many stories of discoveries from around the globe (and even from space). But these stories and the people in them are united by one goal that links them all—the desire to understand the human story, from its deepest past to the rise (and collapse) of its civilizations. Taken together, they are our story.

PROLOGUE

"WONDERFUL THINGS": KING TUT AND HIS TOMB

ON NOVEMBER 26, 1922, HOWARD CARTER PEERED INTO
the tomb of King Tutankhamen for the very first time. He
squinted, trying to see through the small opening that he had
made, the only light coming from the candle that he was holding in his
outstretched hand. He found himself looking into a room crammed
from floor to ceiling with many kinds of objects, including items of
gold; everywhere there was the glint of gold. The earl of Carnarvon,
who had underwritten the cost of the dig, tugged on Carter's coat and
jumped up and down with impatience. "What do you see? What do you
see?" he demanded. Carter answered, "I see wonderful things."

Carter and his patron Carnarvon had been searching for Tut's tomb
for five years at that point. It turned out to be right underneath where
they had been setting up their camp each season, in the Valley of the
Kings, across the Nile River from modern-day Luxor. They hadn't
known it was there, in part because it was deeply buried underneath a

layer of rock chips that had been dumped by workers when Ramses VI's tomb was being constructed nearby, about two hundred years later.

It took Carter ten years to excavate the tomb. The objects were taken to the Egyptian Museum in Cairo, where they are still on display today. Carnarvon, however, did not live to see any of that, for he died in early April 1923, soon after the opening of the tomb. His death was accidental— the result of blood poisoning that set in after he cut open a mosquito bite while shaving. This promptly led to a rumor that the tomb had been cursed and so whenever anyone who had been present during the opening of the tomb died thereafter, it was widely reported in the media. Carter himself lived for seventeen more years after finding the tomb, and so it seems unlikely that there was ever actually anything to the story. Ironically, it now seems that our best theory about Tutankhamen's death is that he too died from the bite of a mosquito, from which he got malaria.

❧❧❧ ❧❧❧

Tut ruled during the New Kingdom period in Egypt. He was a member of the Eighteenth Dynasty, which began about 1550 BCE and lasted until just after 1300 BCE. Some of the most well-known rulers of Egypt date to this period, including Hatshepsut, the famous female pharaoh, who ruled for twenty years; her stepson Thutmose III, who conquered much of what is now Israel, Lebanon, Syria, and Jordan; Akhenaton, the so-called heretic pharaoh who may have invented what we now call monotheism; and Akhenaton's beautiful wife Nefertiti. The last two were most likely Tut's parents.

Tut came to the throne of Egypt around 1330 BCE when he was only about eight years old. Ten years later, he died unexpectedly and was buried in the Valley of the Kings. His tomb was then covered over and forgotten. It wasn't until thirty-five hundred years later that it was rediscovered.

❧❧❧ ❧❧❧

Carter first went to Egypt when he was just seventeen years old. By 1907, he was already a respected Egyptologist. At the time that Carnarvon first approached him, however, the crusty Carter was out of a job because of an earlier problem involving a group of French tourists that had ended with Carter losing his government position when he refused to apologize. As a result, Carter was spending his days painting water-color scenes. As for Carnarvon, he was under doctor's orders to spend his winters in Egypt, rather than in England, because he had punctured his lung in an automobile accident.

After ten years of working together at various sites, the two men decided to search for Tut's tomb in the Valley of the Kings. Most of the New Kingdom pharaohs of Egypt were buried in this dry and rock-strewn valley, across the river from modern-day Luxor, beginning in about 1500 BCE. Many of the tombs, which were dug into the hillside, had been found and robbed in antiquity centuries earlier, but there were still a few that had not been discovered. King Tut's tomb was one of those.

It was only after five long years, without many finds to report and when Carnarvon began to run out of money and interest, that Carter realized that there was one place in the Valley that they hadn't yet investigated—the spot where they had been establishing their camp each year. They began excavating on the first day of November in 1922. Just three days later, at 10 a.m. on Saturday, November 4, they uncovered the first step leading down to Tut's tomb.

For the rest of that day and all of the next, Carter followed the steps down to the tomb entrance. By the time the sun went down on November 5, he could see the stamp of the Royal Necropolis impressed into the plaster of the sealed doorway, signifying that whoever was buried inside was someone important. Calling a halt to the work, he cabled Carnarvon, who was still in England. In his diary, he recorded precisely what he had written in the telegram:

AT LAST HAVE MADE WONDERFUL DISCOVERY IN THE VALLEY
A MAGNIFICENT TOMB WITH SEALS INTACT
RECOVERED SAME FOR YOUR ARRIVAL
CONGRATULATIONS

What he didn't tell Carnarvon was that he was afraid the tomb would turn out to be empty. Although there were indeed intact seals of the necropolis guards on the door, he could also tell, from the upper part of the sealed doorway, that it had been reopened and reclosed two separate times. He was pretty certain that it had been robbed in antiquity; the question was whether anything remained in the tomb for them to find.

Carnarvon arrived at the dig on November 23. The workers began digging again immediately. By the next day, they were able to confirm that it was Tut's tomb, for seals with his name could be plainly seen, below the seals of the Royal Necropolis.

When they finally opened the heavy stone door on November 25, they encountered a corridor intentionally filled with earth, stones, plaster, and all sorts of other rubble. This entrance corridor was nearly thirty feet long. The next day consisted of clearing endless debris, with the workers building an ever-larger pile outside the entrance of the tomb. By 2 p.m., they reached a second sealed doorway, which led into the room that we now call the Antechamber.

Still they did not know whether they had the find of the century or an empty chamber cleared by tomb robbers in antiquity. What they did know for certain was that Carter had been correct; the tomb had been broken into twice in antiquity. The first time had apparently been soon after the initial burial, when the entrance corridor was still empty, apart from a few objects such as jars of embalming material that had been stored there. The second break-in took place after the corridor had been filled with white stone chips. The robbers had dug a tunnel along the upper left edge, which Carter and Carnarvon could plainly see while removing the rubble, since it had been refilled at some point with dark flint and chert chips.

Looking through the small hole that they had made in the second door, Carter saw with relief that the Antechamber was still full of objects. He later wrote

> At first I could see nothing, the hot air escaping from the chamber causing the candle flame to flicker, but presently, as my eyes grew accustomed to the light, details of the room within emerged slowly from the mist, strange animals, statues and gold—everywhere the glint of gold. For the moment—an eternity it must have seemed to the others standing by—I was struck dumb with amazement, and when Lord Carnarvon, unable to stand the suspense any longer, inquired anxiously, "Can you see anything?" it was all I could do to get out the words, "Yes, wonderful things."

In his diary entry for November 26, Carter expanded on what happened next, which sounds like it could be right out of a Hollywood movie, except that this was real, not fantasy. After enlarging the hole so that both he and Carnarvon could look in at the same time, they gazed into the room by the light of a flashlight as well as another candle, astonished at what they saw. It was a "marvelous collection of treasures," as he put it: "two strange ebony-black effigies of a King, gold sandaled, bearing staff and mace, loomed out from the cloak of darkness; gilded couches in strange forms, lion-headed, Hathor-headed, and beast infernal; . . . alabaster vases, some beautifully executed of lotus and papyrus device; strange black shrines with a gilded monster snake appearing from within; . . . finely carved chairs; a golden inlaid throne; . . . stools of all shapes and design, of both common and rare materials; and, lastly a confusion of overturned parts of chariots glinting with gold, peering from amongst which was a manikin."

Carter ended the entry as if he were still in a daze, stating simply: "We closed the hole, locked the wooden-grill which had been placed upon the first doorway, mounted our donkeys and return[ed] home contemplating what we had seen." It is hard to imagine what those initial moments of discovery must have felt like for both Carter and Carnarvon, especially coming after years of searching and disappointments, but their dreams had been fulfilled beyond expectation.

Later, when Carter and his team were clearing out the contents of this first room, they found the remains of a knotted scarf in which were eight solid gold rings. Carter suggested that one set of tomb robbers had been discovered and the scarf, with the rings inside, had simply been tossed carelessly into one of the boxes either by the intruders or the authorities.

Additional interior rooms, including one now called the Annex and another usually called the Treasury, also had been reached and ransacked by the second set of tomb robbers. Even though they were in better shape than the Antechamber, Carter estimated that the robbers got away with as much as 60 percent of the jewelry that had once been stored in the Treasury.

There were still so many artifacts stuffed into these rooms that it took Carter almost three full months to catalogue and remove them. He finally entered the burial chamber in mid-February 1923. His diary entry for February 15 says simply, "Made preparations for opening sealed doorway to sepulchral chamber." And on the 16th, he wrote simply: "Opened sealed doorway" and recorded the people who were there with him that day.

Those present were witnesses to what the *New York Times* called "the most extraordinary day in the whole history of Egyptian excavation." Carter and others elaborated later, describing especially the huge gilded shrines that surrounded the king's coffin and the innumerable objects that were piled elsewhere in the burial chamber.

Other events subsequently intervened, including much legal wrangling, so that it was nearly two years later—in October 1925—before Carter was able to gaze at Tut's mummy. There he was, interred inside three coffins—one inside the other. The first two were made of wood, covered with gold leaf, but the innermost one weighed nearly two

Howard Carter and assistant, examining King Tut

hundred fifty pounds, because it was made of solid gold. Tut himself was still lying within the coffin, with a gold death mask inlaid with lapis lazuli and blue glass still in place, and with a thick layer of tar (bitumen) covering his body and legs below where the death mask ended.

After trying in vain to get the mummy out of the coffin, including lighting a fire beneath it at one point, Carter finally decided to examine the mummy where it was. The restrained notes that he wrote in his journal entry for November 11, 1925, give us some idea of what that must have been like for him: "Today has been a great day in the history of archaeology, I might also say in the history of archaeological discovery, and a day of days for one who after years of work, excavating, conserving & recording has longed to see in fact what previously has only been conjectural." It took Carter and his assistants nine days to carefully unwrap and study Tut's mummy, including recording all the objects contained within the wrappings.

✦⟶✦ ✦⟶✦

It was clear from his skeleton that Tut was still young when he died, probably somewhere between eighteen and twenty-two years old. In recent years, a number of new studies have been made of the mummy, resulting in new theories about how and why King Tut died while still a teenager. Most of them have involved newer technology, which have helped to shed new light on some aspects of Tut, both in life and in death.

In 2005, Zahi Hawass, the former secretary general of the Supreme Council of Antiquities, led a CT-scan study of Tut's mummy that suggested the presence of a compound fracture of one of Tut's leg bones. This could have led to an infection and eventually his death. If so, perhaps he fell from his chariot and died accidentally, though some have suggested that he was murdered.

That same year, three separate teams of forensic anthropologists were asked to try to reconstruct Tut's facial features. Each of them came up with quite separate suggestions. The French team thought he had rather effeminate features; the Egyptian team believed he was more heavy set; and the US team, who didn't know whose head they were reconstructing, came up with yet another interpretation.

More recently, another CT-scan study was done in 2014 that set off a debate both among scholars and in the media. The participants created a virtual autopsy from approximately two thousand scans that were done. From these, they concluded that Tut had a variety of physical ailments, including buck teeth and a club foot, as well as various genetic disorders. They also suggested that he had suffered from malaria, which might have been the cause of his death, rather than the broken leg that had been suggested previously.

And DNA testing done on Tut's mummy in 2010 has provided more information about his parents and grandparents. Most scholars had assumed that Tut's father was the pharaoh Akhenaton, despite the fact that they were never shown together in the ancient inscriptions. The new DNA studies indicate that this is probably correct, although it is still not clear who his mother was, including perhaps Nefertiti. As technology continues to improve, we may eventually be able to confirm his lineage beyond a doubt.

＊＊＊＊＊＊

A number of other mysteries still surround King Tut and his tomb. Egyptologist Nicholas Reeves and others have pointed out that many of the objects buried with him seem to have originally been intended for someone else, for some bear traces of other royal names. These may even include Tut's famous gold death mask, and it may be that his sudden death at a young age resulted in the need to bury him with grave goods that were not supposed to be his, perhaps even in a tomb that was not originally meant for him.

Reeves's theory jumped into the news in 2015 after a Madrid-based company called Factum Arte, which specializes in replicating art, posted online high-definition photographs of the painted walls inside Tut's tomb, as part of a larger project to create a nearby replica of his tomb specifically for tourists. The original was being damaged by modern visitors, both unintentionally because of moisture from their breathing and from intentional graffiti scratched on the walls, just like in the Paleolithic painted caves at Altamira, Lascaux, and Chauvet in France and Spain, as we shall see in a later chapter. They also scanned the wall surfaces behind those decorated scenes, posting those as well.

Nicholas Reeves took a look at these scans and, like Howard Carter almost a century before him, he thought that he saw "wonderful things." Reeves believed he could see the outlines of two hidden doorways behind the painted scenes on the north and west walls of the burial chamber. This suggested to him that there might still be other chambers left to find, including a whole section of the tomb that might also contain the body of Nefertiti.

Reeves's hypothesis was quickly put to the test by the Egyptian authorities. They asked a Japanese specialist named Hirokatsu Watanabe to scan the areas behind the two walls in the burial chamber, using a high-tech ground-penetrating radar (GPR) system. GPR works like traditional radar but can be used to identify objects under the ground or behind a wall. In early 2016, the initial results came back positive for both locations. There appeared to be an additional chamber behind each of the walls, with both of the chambers possibly having metal and organic objects within them. A second set of scans, however, conducted in March 2016 by a team from the National Geographic Society, "failed to locate the same features," thereby calling the results of the first scans into question. The situation is a good demonstration that even the best remote-sensing tests need to be confirmed through actual excavation, as we will see also in a later chapter on other instances elsewhere in the world. We now await further results and a peer-reviewed publication.

{←→}: {←→}:

The story of the discovery of King Tut continues to resonate even now, almost a century after it was first discovered. It is the best-known example of the fascination and lure of archaeology, as well as the surprises that can be in store. It has been my experience that archaeology contains any number of such surprises, ranging from the mundane to the magnificent, and that new advances in science and technology contribute to such discoveries, as we will see.

PART 1

EARLY ARCHAEOLOGY
AND ARCHAEOLOGISTS

I

ASHES TO ASHES IN ANCIENT ITALY

I N 1752, EXACTLY 170 YEARS BEFORE CARTER DISCOVERED THE tomb of King Tutankhamen in Egypt, archaeologists in Italy found three hundred rolled-up ancient papyrus scrolls. The scrolls were in the remains of a villa that was being excavated within the ruins of a town called Herculaneum, near Mount Vesuvius and modern-day Naples, which had been buried during an eruption on August 24 in 79 CE. They had formed part of a private Roman library kept by their owner in his house, which is now known, appropriately, as the "Villa of the Papyri" and was possibly owned by the father-in-law of Julius Caesar. Although they were excavated more than two hundred fifty years ago, the intact scrolls were saved, though they were carbonized and too fragile to unroll.

For centuries it was believed that the scrolls would remain as mere curiosities, even though they now look like lumps of carbonized wood. But recently, beginning in 2009 and continuing through 2016 so far, papyrologists (scholars who study such scrolls and scraps of papyrus) have been able to discern some of the writing on the scrolls, even without unrolling them. Using a concentrated beam of X rays, they have been able to detect a few individual letters because of the contrast between the carbonized papyrus and the ancient ink, even though the ink is also carbon-based. They are aided in this by virtue of the fact that the ink also seems to contain small amounts of lead, which can be detected. If the techniques continue to improve, we might one day be able to read what is written on all the scrolls. That would be wonderful, since—given the wealthy owner and the fact that they come from his private library—they may well include items like the lost books of Livy's *History of Rome*.

✶⟨◦◦⟩✶ ✶⟨◦◦⟩✶

The ruins at the neighboring town of Pompeii had already been discovered 150 years earlier, in 1594. Workers digging an irrigation trench had accidentally exposed some of the ancient ruins there but then covered them back up and did not investigate them further at that time.

So it was the excavations at Herculaneum that began first, in 1709. To put this in perspective, Benjamin Franklin was only three years old at the time; there were twelve, not thirteen, colonies in what would become the United States (Georgia was not established until 1732); Queen Anne was on the throne of Great Britain, a national entity that had just been created by an act of Parliament uniting England, Wales, and Scotland in 1707; and Captain Cook wouldn't land in Australia for another sixty years or so.

These were the very first archaeological excavations to take place in Europe, or anywhere in the world for that matter. Credit usually goes to a man named Emmanuel Maurice de Lorraine, who was the Duke of Elbeuf. He was living in Italy near Naples at the time and underwrote the first efforts to tunnel into the ground at Herculaneum, after he bought the site specifically because ancient pieces of marble had been recovered from the area.

De Lorraine's workers happened to dig right into the ancient Roman theater at Herculaneum and were able to extract a number of ancient marble statues. Most of them were used to decorate the Duke's estate; others were distributed elsewhere in Europe, some museums included. It wasn't exactly what we would call archaeology—it was more like looting, in that no records were kept and the goal was only to retrieve pretty pieces from antiquity, rather than trying to learn much about the context in which they were found. Proper excavations began a few decades later at Herculaneum, however, and then at neighboring Pompeii. These mark the beginning of what we now call Old World archaeology or, to be more precise in this case, classical archaeology (which is specifically the study of the ancient Greeks and Romans). In large part, methodical archaeology began from the efforts of one man, Johann Joachim Winckelmann, who is widely regarded as the father of classical archaeology and who was the first scholar to study the artifacts from Herculaneum and Pompeii.

The growth of archaeology as a discipline took place during the rest of the eighteenth and into the nineteenth century. It should probably be noted that Winckelmann's work was part of the Age of Enlightenment, which started at about the same time as the earliest excavations at Herculaneum and swept through much of Europe during this period. The sudden but sustained interest in archaeology and antiquity is not surprising when considered in the general context of the times, which saw advances in the various sciences, the growth of national museums and private collections, the eventual rise of Darwinism and social Darwinism, and the European conquest and colonization of much of the rest of the world.

We now know that when Mount Vesuvius erupted in 79 CE, a number of ancient cities were devastated and then buried, including Herculaneum, Pompeii, and Stabiae. More than two thousand people died in Pompeii alone and even more died in Herculaneum and other towns in the area. Some of them were upscale towns by the Bay of Naples, which had a number of houses built by wealthy inhabitants of Rome for use on weekends and during the summer. In some ways not much has changed, for the region is a popular tourist destination today.

There were eyewitnesses to the eruption of Vesuvius. One was a seventeen-year-old known as Pliny the Younger, who was the nephew (and adopted son) of the famous naturalist we call Pliny the Elder. He wrote about the devastation in two letters, which he sent to the Roman historian Tacitus, who had asked him about it.

Pliny wrote that he could see dark clouds, lightning, flames, and dust, lots of dust, in the neighboring town of Misenum. He described

Mount Vesuvius as seen through Pompeii Arch

an utter darkness, like that in a room with no windows in which the lights are off. He said that he could hear women and children crying and men shouting. Soon, he said, it grew lighter, but that was only because of the fire that was rapidly spreading, engulfing the town. And then the darkness came again, along with an unceasing shower of hot ashes. If he and his companions had not constantly shaken the ashes off, they would eventually have been crushed.

This was an interesting—and important—time in Roman history. The changeover from the Roman Republic to the Roman Empire had begun about a hundred years earlier, when Julius Caesar was assassinated in 44 BCE and Augustus came to sole power as the first Roman emperor in 27 BCE, beginning the Julio-Claudian dynasty. When Mount Vesuvius blew up in 79 CE, it was Emperor Titus, of the succeeding Flavian dynasty, who was on the throne.

Excavations began at nearby Pompeii in 1750, at nearly the same time that the carbonized scrolls were found in Herculaneum. Here also time had stopped on that late August morning in 79 CE, with the tables still laid with crockery and food for a meal that would never be eaten. There were also bodies lying in the streets—entire families seeking shelter in some cases and, in other instances, individuals lying alone, some with their jewelry still clutched in their hands.

The catastrophe that enveloped Pompeii quite literally stopped the city and its citizens in their tracks. The ash and pumice mixed with the rain that fell, blending into a cementlike concoction that quickly hardened and resisted attempts by survivors to come back and retrieve their belongings. In addition, dozens of bodies, as well as the rest of the town and all its remains, were entombed. Over time, the perishable materials, ranging from wood to bread to body parts, slowly decayed. Hollow cavities formed, with each cavity bearing the shape of the object, or body, that had once been there.

In 1863 Giuseppe Fiorelli, the Italian archaeologist in charge of excavating Pompeii at that time, figured out what the hollow cavities were, or rather what they had been. He realized that his workers could act as though they were sculptors using what is known as the lost wax method and treat the hollow spaces as if they were molds for making bronze statues.

So, whenever his team came across a cavity while digging, Fiorelli poured plaster of Paris into the opening. When the ash was then excavated away, an exact duplicate in plaster remained of whatever had been there originally. They were able to recover the remains of numerous bodies, including entire families huddled together, as well as everything else organic, such as wooden tables and other furniture, and even loaves of bread. They also recovered some of the pets, including a dog still chained where its owner had left it. It was found upside down in a contorted position, with the impression of his collar still plainly visible in the plaster.

Although Fiorelli's method worked well for things like loaves of bread and wooden objects, it had a major flaw when it came to the human bodies, for his plaster casts made it impossible to see the bones and other artifacts that had remained in the cavity after the body disintegrated, because they were now within the newly created plaster cast. One solution would be to use some sort of transparent material, like resin instead of plaster, but that is a much more expensive process. It has been used for only one victim of Vesuvius, in 1984. This is the so-called Resin Lady, who is still wearing her gold jewelry and hairpin.

Archaeologists also realized that it was possible to restudy the plaster casts themselves, including the bones and other materials that Fiorelli's workers had unintentionally included. In September 2015, a team that included specialists such as radiologists, archaeologists, and anthropologists began doing laser imaging, CT scans, and DNA sampling of the plaster-encased remains. The CT scans especially revealed amazing details, one from a four-year-old boy who was found with his parents and a younger sibling. It is possible to see how scared he must have been just before he died, although it is not clear what killed him. The scans also show that many of the victims had suffered head injuries, perhaps from collapsing buildings or falling rocks, and that they included people of all ages, not just the young, old, and sick city dwellers, as had been previously thought.

✠✦✠ ✠✦✠

Herculaneum, in contrast, was buried in a thirty-foot-high wall of fast-traveling mud that completely engulfed and covered the town. Geologists call such a mudflow a *lahar*; similar events have occurred during volcanic eruptions as recently as 1985 in Columbia and 1991 in the Philippines.

The mudflow preserved large parts of Herculaneum, so that the archaeologists excavating it found it just as it had been back in 79 CE. Some of the houses are still standing to the second story in many places, which is very rare in archaeological excavations, and many of the paintings and decorated tiles are still on the walls. Even wooden objects have been recovered, including roof beams, doors, beds, and a cradle.

It had been assumed that the inhabitants of Herculaneum were able to flee from the city, but in 1981 and then again in additional excavations in the 1990s, at least three hundred bodies were found in what archaeologists think were boathouses by the shore. These were probably people waiting to be evacuated, who were killed instantly when super-heated air from the eruption measuring nearly one thousand degrees Fahrenheit flashed through the area. The heat, and then the hot ash that followed, roasted them alive, incinerating their skin and internal organs and leaving only their skeletons, frozen in positions of agony.

✦⟨←•→⟩✦ ✦⟨←•→⟩✦

Many of the houses in Pompeii also were preserved by the eruption, just like those in Herculaneum, but here they were buried underneath the meters of ash and pumice. One is known as "The House of the Faun" because of the bronze statue that stands within a large basin—used to catch rainwater—in the interior courtyard of the house. The statue is in the shape of a faun—a satyrlike creature with horns on his head and a tail, usually depicted playing the double pipe.

An amazing garden belonged to this house, which was filled with trees and plants. The eruption buried many such house gardens, in both Pompeii and Herculaneum. When modern archaeologists such as Wilhelmina Jashemski, a professor at the University of Maryland, began careful excavations in 1961 specifically in the areas where these gardens once were, they found what are called root cavities from the plants that had once been there. By tracing the roots of various plants, each with a distinctive cavity, they were able to reconstruct what had once been there and, in at least one case, the plan of an entire vineyard.

✦⟨←•→⟩✦ ✦⟨←•→⟩✦

After three hundred years of nearly continuous excavation, archaeologists have unearthed a large amount of ancient Pompeii, though much more remains to be dug. The plan of the city has become clear so that we can tell that prosperous inhabitants lived in some of the areas and middle- or even lower-class inhabitants were the primary residents in other sections. Today it is possible for tourists to see the various quarters of the town and the buildings that went with them: bathhouses, tanneries, shops, and other dwellings. For instance, in 2014 Dr. Steven Ellis and a team of archaeologists from the University of Cincinnati who were digging by the Porta Stabia, one of the main gates into the city, announced that they had found ten buildings with twenty shop-fronts from which food and drink were sold or served. Such an arrangement seems typical in Pompeii, where even the private houses frequently had shops installed on the street side.

So, what did the inhabitants of Pompeii eat and drink? The answer comes from a variety of contexts, which, upon reflection, makes sense. Ellis and his team have excavated a number of drains, latrines, and cesspits. The thought of excavating such places may seem disgusting to some, but the truth of the matter is that the material found within such areas can sometimes be worth more to the archaeologists than gold, if it means being able to reconstruct what life was like for the inhabitants two thousand years ago. In eras before trash collection, the garbage of the city was frequently thrown into the latrines, where it remained for the archaeologists to find it.

This was exactly the case for Pompeii, for in these areas Ellis and his team found the remains of "grains, fruits, nuts, olives, lentils, local fish, and chicken eggs, as well as minimal cuts of more expensive meat and salted fish from Spain." In a drain on a more centrally located property that may have belonged to someone wealthier, they found the remains of "shellfish, sea urchin, and even delicacies, including the butchered

Street scene, Pompeii

leg joint of a giraffe." Not only does this give us clues about what people were eating in Pompeii at the time of the eruption, but it also confirms the unsurprising fact that the different classes ate different types of food.

Ellis's team of archaeologists from the University of Cincinnati also introduced some new archaeological wrinkles into the excavations they conducted at Pompeii. For one thing, they were among the first, if not the first, to use iPads on site, in 2010. They recorded the data; took photographs; employed various off-the-shelf applications, some modified from their original intended use; and then uploaded the data to servers back in Cincinnati, all while still at the site. By contrast, many excavations around the world are still recording their data on paper forms, sometimes in triplicate, and rely on Xerox machines to create copies after the dig season is over.

✛←◦→✛ ✛←◦→✛

In some of the more prosperous houses at Pompeii, there are mosaics embedded in the floors. For example, the House of the Faun has a floor mosaic with a famous scene of Alexander the Great fighting the Persian king Darius III in either 333 or 331 BCE. The House of the Tragic Poet has a floor mosaic in the entryway depicting a black and white dog (of uncertain breed), with a red collar. Beneath the dog's paws is written CAVE CANEM, which is Latin for "beware of the dog."

In other houses, paintings are still preserved on the interior walls. In the Villa of the Mysteries, there is a small room, possibly a dining room, whose four walls are painted with scenes that have been interpreted as depicting the mysteries of Dionysus, possibly including the initiation of a young woman into the religious cult. Other dwellings have painted scenes of dancers, family portraits, and pictures of fruit and other objects. In some ways it is no different from the photos and paintings that hang on the walls of our own houses.

Painted onto the exterior walls of the houses were advertisements and campaign notices—the social media of two thousand years ago. The notices were placed on the outer walls so that the people walking on the streets and shopping in the stores on either side could see them. One advertisement was for a gladiator contest that was to be held on

April 8–12, though it is not clear in what year. Another message gives notice of the open-air market days in each town, occurring in apparent sequence from Saturday in Pompeii to Friday in Rome, with stops in the towns of Nuceria, Atella, Nola, Cumae, and Puteoli in between.

One notice was painted on the wall outside a bar, much like signs that we see today outside drinking establishments. It is a menu of the drinks that were available and their prices. It reads "You can get a drink here for an as [a small coin], a better drink for two, Falernian for four." Another was written outside a shop from which a copper pot had been stolen, offering a reward for either its return or for news of who had taken it.

There also were hundreds of campaign notices. Among the more interesting endorsements is one that says, "I ask you to elect Marcus Cerrinius Vatia to the aedileship. All the late-night drinkers support him." Another, apparently for the same man, says, "The petty thieves support Vatia for the aedileship." We'll never know whether he won.

⁘⁘⁘

Not only were Pompeii and Herculaneum the first sites to be excavated anywhere, but they are still being excavated at the present time, a span of three hundred years. As a result, one could probably study the history of advances in the techniques of excavation and recording just by examining the work done at these two sites. From the initial rudimentary efforts in the beginning that were little more than looting to the use of plaster of Paris to reconstruct the decomposed bodies and wooden furniture to the sophisticated techniques being used today, including CT scans, X rays, laser imaging, DNA analysis, and recording and documenting in the field directly onto iPads with cloud-based storage for the data, the excavations at Pompeii and Herculaneum demonstrate how archaeology has come a long way in the past three centuries.

In addition, the efforts at conservation and preservation have made the sites tourist destinations, which allows all visitors, not just archaeologists, to glimpse a world that existed two thousand years ago and to realize that, in some ways, it is more similar to than different from ours today. Now there may be more advanced technology, like iPads, cell phones, and wireless Internet, but the houses in this region of Italy today are not all that different from theirs back then, and the food is basically similar. There is the same dependence on elected officials, shopping at stores that stock necessary items, drinking at taverns and bars, and frustrations about petty theft and shoplifting. The people keep the same sort of pets and wear jewelry, eat from dishes, and use utensils similar to those their predecessors did back then. Although peacocks' tongues may not be considered a delicacy anymore, and many people do not still clean their clothes using urine, on the whole, the excavations at these sites teach us that the ancient inhabitants of the Mediterranean were not that different from the people today. And if we are ever able to unroll and read the scrolls that are still being investigated from the Villa of the Papyri, we may find out that their private libraries were not so different from ours either.

2

DIGGING UP TROY

H EINRICH SCHLIEMANN WAS WANDERING AROUND THE ancient mound in northwestern Turkey one morning in May 1873, observing his workers' digging. He was certain that they were excavating ancient Troy but had not yet been able to convince all of the doubters.

He suddenly noticed one of the workers unearthing a copper pot, behind which he could see the glint of gold. Dismissing the worker, he and his wife Sophia "cut out the Treasure with a large knife," working quickly because a large section of earth above them looked like it was about to cave in on them at any moment.

Sophia gathered the objects together in her shawl and carried them into their house, where the two of them catalogued the objects and realized what they had just found—a king's treasure of gold necklaces, rings, and earrings, including two diadems, a headband, sixty earrings, and nearly nine thousand smaller ornaments. There were also cups, bowls, and other vessels made of gold, silver, and electrum, including a solid gold sauceboat, which is one of only two that has ever been found, and a golden vessel in the shape of a pomegranate. And there were other objects as well—a copper shield and vase; thirteen spearheads; fourteen battle-axes; daggers, a sword, and other objects of copper or bronze; stone hilts that probably belonged to bronze swords; and a multitude of other items, the like of which has never been found together elsewhere in the world.

They crated everything up, smuggled the treasure onto a boat, and sent it back to their residence in Athens. There, Sophia put on most of the jewelry that they had found. They took a photograph of her, which remains one of the most iconic images in archaeology to this day.

Schliemann announced to the world that they had found Priam's Treasure. The discovery made them world-famous and the story has been repeated in exquisite detail ever since. But is there any truth to it? And had Schliemann really found Troy?

❧❧❧❧

What we know about the story of the Trojan War comes primarily from the *Iliad*, written by the Greek poet Homer. Lesser-known poets, in what is known as the Epic Cycle, provide other details. Although the poems' events are likely to have taken place during the Late Bronze

Wall of Troy VI

Age, probably in the thirteenth or twelfth century BCE, it is important to keep in mind that the story probably wasn't written down until at least five hundred years later.

According to Homer, the Greeks and the Trojans went to war for ten years over a woman named Helen. At the time, Helen was the wife of a man named Menelaus, who was the ruler of a small kingdom or city-state in the southern part of the Greek mainland. His brother was Agamemnon, king of kings, who ruled from the city of Mycenae. It is from this city that we derive the name Mycenaeans, the term that archaeologists use for the Greeks of that time.

A delegation from Troy, the important port city that controlled trade to the east and to the north from its location in northwest Turkey, came to visit Menelaus. Among its members was a man named Paris, sometimes referred to as Alexander. He was a prince of Troy, the son of King Priam. When the delegation returned home to Troy, Helen was among them. The Trojans claimed she had come with them willingly, because she was in love with Paris. The Greeks claimed that she had been kidnapped.

Led by Agamemnon and Menelaus, along with other Mycenaean heroes, including Odysseus and Achilles, the Greeks sent a large fleet of ships and men to besiege Troy and get Helen back. It took ten long years before they were able to do so, and even then it was only by using the trick of the Trojan horse that they were able to succeed. In the end, the Greeks destroyed Troy, burning it to the ground, and returned home with Helen.

Homer's story is rich in detail and yet scholars continue to question it. Was there an actual, historical Trojan War that served as a basis for Homer's epic? And could archaeological evidence for it ever be found? I believe that the answer to both questions is "yes" and that there is now evidence showing that the war was a historical event that took place sometime around 1184 BCE, which—as it turns out—is just about the time when the Mycenaean culture and the entire Late Bronze Age came crashing down. It may be that the Trojan War was part of a much larger catastrophe.

However, the ancient Greeks were divided on whether the Trojan War had taken place, and if so, when it had been fought. Most classical scholars of nineteenth-century Europe were convinced that the Trojan

War had not taken place and that it was completely made up by Homer. Thus, when Heinrich Schliemann, a complete amateur in the field of archaeology, decided that he would search for the site of Troy, he was going against the thinking of most of the scholars of his day.

{←→} {←→}

Despite the opposition, Schliemann was intent on finding Troy and proving that the Trojan War had taken place. Much later, Schliemann claimed that he first decided to do so in 1829, at the age of seven. His father gave him a book for Christmas that included an artist's rendition of Aeneas fleeing from the burning city of Troy, complete with the huge walls that the Mycenaeans had been besieging for ten years. Aeneas was headed for Italy, where his later descendants Romulus and Remus would found the city of Rome, according to tradition. Schliemann said that he decided then and there to find Troy, declaring "Father, if such walls once existed, they cannot possibly have been completely destroyed: vast ruins of them must still remain, but they are hidden away beneath the dust of ages." Eventually, he says, "we both agreed that I should one day excavate Troy." Other scholars question this account because Schliemann mentions this story only much later in his life, despite leaving quite literally volumes of diaries, notes, letters, and other books from early in his career.

Schliemann was in his mid-forties before he had earned enough of a fortune to retire and devote the rest of his life to finding evidence for Troy and the Trojan War. The shenanigans that Schliemann pulled while accumulating this fortune illustrate that he was not a man whose word could be entirely trusted in either his personal or his professional life.

One particular example of his behavior is relevant because it pertains directly to Schliemann's "discovery" of Troy—and one should definitely put "discovery" in quotes. In 1868 Schliemann took a trip to Greece and then proceeded on to Turkey. He says that he traveled around northwestern Turkey with Homer in one hand, looking for a site that was small enough so that Achilles could have chased Hector around it several times and that had both hot and cold springs, to match the description given by Homer.

He looked at a number of sites that had been suggested previously, but none seemed to quite fit the bill. Then he met the US vice consul to Turkey, a man named Frank Calvert. Calvert had also been looking for Troy and thought that he had found it. In fact, he had already bought the ancient mound, which now had the modern Turkish name Hissarlik, meaning "Place of Fortresses."

Calvert had begun some preliminary excavations at the site but didn't have enough money to continue working properly. Schliemann, on the other hand, had plenty of money and was happy to join forces with Calvert. Once they began excavating and Schliemann convinced himself that the mound was indeed the site of ancient Troy, he deliberately left Calvert's name out of all of his subsequent official announcements, lectures, and publications, thereby claiming the fame and glory for himself. It was only in 1999, with a book published by Susan Heuck Allen, that Calvert was restored to his rightful place in history as the true discoverer of the location of ancient Troy.

The first excavation season by Schliemann at Hissarlik began in April 1870. He didn't yet have an official excavation permit from the Turkish authorities, but that didn't stop him. He didn't find much that season, or the next. So, in 1872, with the help of a large team of local workers, he launched his greatest assault on the ancient site. This took the form of a huge trench that his workers dug right across most of the mound and down to a depth of about forty-five feet. Today it is known as Schliemann's Great Trench and is still visible as a huge gash in the middle of the site.

Archaeology was still in its infancy at that time. Even though excavations had been ongoing at Pompeii for more than a century, there wasn't that much digging going on elsewhere in the 1870s. But there were people who were knowledgeable, including Calvert, who warned Schliemann that such reckless digging might result in catastrophe. And sure enough, they were right.

In the Great Trench, Schliemann and his workers went down, down, down; right through all sorts of buildings and stratigraphic levels. It turned out that there were nine cities buried one on top of another in the mound, although Schliemann thought at first that there were only six. He stopped at the second city from the bottom, which he called the "Burnt City." He was convinced that this was the city that Priam had ruled. But he was wrong. We now know, on the basis of pottery analysis and carbon-14 dating, that Troy II dates to about 2400 BCE, during the Early Bronze Age, more than a thousand years before the Trojan War would have been fought.

If one stands at the bottom of the Great Trench today, at the level where Schliemann and his workers stopped digging, and looks straight up, it is possible to see—way high above—a level that contains a building made out of huge blocks of stone. It's just a few feet below the top of the mound, shaded from the sun by the limbs and leaves of a slender tree now growing on the modern surface. This is a building that dates to Troy VI and was reused in Troy VII. It is all that is left of a palace that dates to the Late Bronze Age, the time period for which Schliemann was looking.

Most of that palace, however, is missing. And it's missing because of Heinrich Schliemann. In his haste, Schliemann and his workers dug right through the stone walls of Priam's palace and threw most of it out on their dirt pile. If we were to dig in that spoil heap now, it is highly likely that we would find all sorts of things from the Troy of Priam and Hector, including perhaps clay tablets used by ancient scribes.

So, what was it that convinced Schliemann that Troy II was Priam's Troy? For one thing, he found a huge city gate in that level, which he identified as Homer's Scaean Gate. This was supposedly so wide that two chariots could be driven in side by side. And then came his report of Priam's Treasure.

The story that he told about the day he and Sophia found the treasure has long been repeated in introductory archaeology textbooks, although it is unlikely to be true. Schliemann later admitted that he lied about Sophia's role in his story. She wasn't even at the dig on the day that he claims to have found the treasure. His own diaries and journals show that she was in Athens at the time. Schliemann explained that his intention was to involve her more in his career, in the hopes that she would become more interested in what he did. So he wrote her into the story so that she could share in his triumph. No respectable archaeologist today would dare do what Schliemann did.

Some scholars have also suggested that Schliemann didn't find the treasure all in one place. Instead, they think he gathered the best of his finds from the entire season and announced to a gullible public that he had found them all together as a single treasure. Moreover, since the objects were found in Troy II, they are a thousand years too early to have belonged to Priam. It seems that Priam's Treasure might not be either Priam's or a Treasure.

Soon after he announced his discovery of the objects, Schliemann donated them to the Berlin Museum, perhaps in exchange for being given his doctorate in archaeology at a German university. But the treasure disappeared in the aftermath of World War II and was presumed lost for nearly fifty years. It was only in the early 1990s that the Russians admitted that they had it. They had taken it back to Russia as part of the spoils of war and claimed it as recompense for the losses that they suffered.

Today, Priam's Treasure is on display at the Pushkin Museum in Moscow. It remains there despite the fact that four countries now lay claim to it: Turkey, because that's where Troy is and they say that Schliemann smuggled the treasure out illegally; Greece, because that's where Schliemann first stored the treasure, in his residence in Athens; Germany, because Schliemann gave the treasure to the Berlin Museum and that's where it was until it disappeared in 1945; and Russia, because they took it while liberating that part of Berlin and now claim it as reparation for Nazi aggression. So who really owns it? That still hasn't been resolved and Russia shows no signs of handing it over to anyone else.

What is most interesting about these objects is that they bear a great deal of resemblance to objects found elsewhere, from the islands of the northeast Aegean to the so-called Death Pits of Ur that Leonard Woolley excavated in what is now Iraq. The gold earrings, pins, and necklaces that Schliemann found may not have belonged to Priam, or his wife or daughter, but they did belong to a class of jewelry that was in fashion across much of the Aegean and the ancient Middle East at the end of the third millennium BCE. They may give us clues about ancient trade and interconnections at that time—and *that* makes them even more interesting to archaeologists than their fictional connection to Priam and Homer's *Iliad*.

❊⟨•••⟩❊ ❊⟨•••⟩❊

Schliemann continued to dig at Troy throughout the 1870s and 1880s, though he also was digging at Mycenae at that time, looking for material remains of King Agamemnon. To help him at Troy, he hired Wilhelm Dörpfeld, an architect with some previous archaeological experience, who eventually persuaded Schliemann that he had been wrong and that it was Troy VI or Troy VII at Hissarlik that he should have been investigating all along. Schliemann began to make plans for an additional attack on the mound, focused on these later levels, but on Christmas Day in 1890, he collapsed on a street in Naples and died the next day.

It was left to Dörpfeld to carry on. And so he did, with the financial assistance of Sophia Schliemann, who wanted him to continue her husband's work at the site. He concentrated on excavating the remains that Schliemann had left untouched, mostly around the edges of the mound. As it turned out, those remains were extremely impressive. He unearthed tall stone walls, each several meters thick, that would have stymied any attackers, and large gateways allowing entrance to the interior, but only after one got past the guards.

These were the remains of Troy VI, which seems to have lasted for nearly five hundred years, from about 1700 BCE to 1250 BCE. Dörpfeld found numerous phases of the city, which he labeled "a" through "h." The last phase, Troy VIh, showed signs of an almost-complete destruction of the city. For Dörpfeld, this was the evidence for the Trojan War that they had been seeking. He ended his excavations and published his results.

❈❈❈❈

In the meantime, travelers venturing elsewhere in Turkey, especially to the inland central plateau, had been finding the ruins of another ancient civilization. Back in 1879, while Schliemann was still excavating at Troy, a British Assyriologist named A. H. Sayce suggested a daring hypothesis—that the ruins belonged to the ancient Hittites.

The hypothesis was daring because the Hebrew Bible seemed to place the Hittites in the region of Canaan, if the biblical stories mentioning Uriah the Hittite and other figures were any indication. Sayce's arguments were convincing and were ultimately accepted by other scholars. By 1890, the year that Schliemann died, the second edition of

Sayce's book on the Hittites was already in print. It was entitled *The Hittites: The Story of a Forgotten Empire.*

In 1906 excavations began at what turned out to be the capital city of the Hittites—Hattusa, located by the modern-day town of Bogazköy, 125 miles to the east of Ankara. Within a year, the archives of the city began to be uncovered; thousands of clay tablets that included treaties, records, and royal letters. It turned out that the Hittites had been active across Anatolia from about 1700 to 1200 BCE. They had even held territory in northern Syria, which is why the later biblical writers placed them in that region.

We now know a tremendous amount about the Hittites, thanks in part to the German excavations that have been going continuously at Hattusa for the past century. The decipherment of the Hittite tablets by a Czech orientalist named Bedřich Hrozný, just a decade after their initial discovery, ultimately proved that the Hittites were a major player in the world of the ancient Middle East during the second millennium BCE, both trading and warring with the other powers, especially the Egyptians and the Assyrians.

Among the tablets are a few that document the ongoing troubles that the Hittites had with a small vassal kingdom located in northwestern Anatolia, which they called *Wilusa.* Eventually, sometime early in the thirteen century BCE, probably about 1280 BCE, the Hittites signed a treaty with the king of Wilusa, a man named Alaksandu.

It was not long after this tablet was deciphered that some scholars began suggesting that this was a Hittite reference to the same man whom Homer calls Alexander (Paris) of Ilios and who was responsible for beginning the Trojan War because of his romance with Helen. Philologically, *Wilusa* is close to the Greek name *(W)Ilios*—the original "W" sound in Greek, known as a *digamma*, dropped out over time, so that by Homer's time it was simply *Ilios.* And, of course, *Alaksandu* sounds very much like *Alexander.*

Although it is by no means clear that the two identifications are correct, at the very least these tablets show that the Hittites were involved with an area, and a city, in northwest Anatolia that they called Wilusa. The tablets also record that at least four wars were fought here, the last three of which were all during the thirteenth century BCE, in other words the probable time of the Trojan War. For those scholars who believed that Wilusa is the Hittite name for Troy, this provided additional data that the Trojan War could very well have been an historical event, rather than simply the stuff of myth and legend.

{⋅⋅⋅}{⋅⋅⋅}

Not everyone was convinced, however, by Dörpfeld's argument that Troy VIh was Homer's Troy. Carl Blegen, an archaeologist at the University of Cincinnati, examined Dörpfeld's results and concluded that an earthquake caused the destruction of Troy VIh, not warfare. He decided as he did because a number of walls were found off-kilter, with large stones thrown about, which he thought could have been caused only by Mother Nature. On the other hand, it looked to him as if the first phase of the next level, known as Troy VIIa, was a city that had been besieged and then destroyed by an army. So he reopened the excavations at Hissarlik in the 1930s in an attempt to see whether he was right.

Now there was even less left for him to dig, since Dörpfeld had excavated much of what Schliemann had left untouched. But Blegen found enough to convince himself that Troy VIIa had been destroyed by humans, in a protracted siege. And his evidence is fairly convincing, including arrowheads buried in the walls, bodies left lying in the streets, and other indications that at least one major battle had taken place.

He discovered that the large buildings and palaces of the previous city had been subdivided, so that several families could now live where only one had been previously. He also found that the storage capacity of the city had been increased tremendously, by burying very large jars up to their necks in the ground. To Blegen, all of this indicated a city that was under siege, just as Homer had written. And the timing was still consistent; this city had been destroyed about 1180 BCE or so, which was still within the timeframe suggested by the ancient Greeks.

Moreover, the material culture of the city—that is, the pottery and other artifacts—indicated to Blegen that there was continuity between Troy VIh and VIIa. That is, there was no evidence in Troy VIIa that a new group of people was living there; rather it appeared that the people of Troy VIh had renovated, reconstructed, and rebuilt their city after the earthquake as Troy VIIa. In fact, it was so similar that both Blegen and Dörpfeld, who was still alive, thought that what the archaeologists were calling the first phase of Troy VII was more likely to be the last phase of Troy VI—so Troy VIi, rather than Troy VIIa—but it was too late by that time to change the terminology. And thus Blegen was convinced that an earthquake destroyed Troy VIh, and the Mycenaean Greeks had destroyed Troy VIIa in the process of trying to get Helen back.

{⟶}⟶{⟶}⟶}

Blegen may well have been correct. But fifty years went by, a new generation of archaeologists emerged, and a new team decided to investigate the mound of Hissarlik all over again, beginning in 1988. This time it was an international team of archaeologists, led by two men, Manfred Korfmann from the University of Tübingen, investigating the Bronze Age remains, and Brian Rose from the University of Cincinnati, investigating the post–Bronze Age remains.

Apart from cleaning up and reexamining Schliemann's Great Trench, probably the most important thing that Korfmann's team did was to survey the agricultural fields around Hissarlik. They employed remote sensing devices to peer beneath the surface of the earth without having to excavate first. It took some experimentation to figure out which type of remote sensing worked best, but they eventually realized that a cesium magnetometer was what they needed in that type of soil.

Since human activity, including things like burning, can alter the magnetism of tiny iron particles in the soil, things like pits, ditches, and even walls can sometimes be detected even when buried, especially when burnt or partially burnt materials are present. Preliminary findings need to be interpreted carefully, however, as Korfmann's team found out to their chagrin.

In 1993, more than a century after the legendary excavations at Troy by Heinrich Schliemann, Korfmann announced that their remote sensing images indicated the presence of a huge buried wall that ran around Hissarlik, at a distance of about 1300 feet from the citadel. This, they said, was probably the great wall of the city that had kept Agamemnon, Achilles, and the other Mycenaean Greeks out for ten years during the famous Trojan War immortalized by Homer in the *Iliad* and the *Odyssey*.

When they went to excavate the wall, though, it wasn't there. In its place was a ditch, measuring up to six feet (two meters) deep in places. Over the centuries, the ditch had filled up with all sorts of junk, from broken pottery to stones to random bits of garbage. These had shown up on their remote sensing images as a solid mass running around the city. In the aftermath, the team argued that a ditch would have been as good as a wall in protecting the city, but not everyone agrees with that assessment.

✦←→✦ ✦←→✦

One lesson that Korfmann and the rest of the archaeological world learned was to be wary of holding press conferences to announce remote-sensing findings until some excavating to confirm those presumed discoveries has occurred. Another was that, regardless of their dramatic misinterpretation, it was clear that remote sensing could be successfully used at the site, for Korfmann and his team soon realized that additional images indicated the existence of an enormous Lower City for Troy that lay beneath modern agricultural fields, which nobody had suspected was there.

It turns out that all the previous archaeologists, from Schliemann to Dörpfeld to Blegen, had simply been excavating the citadel—or upper part—of the city, where the king and his direct family and retinue would have lived. The remains that Korfmann's team found increased the size of the city at least tenfold, showing that it covered at least fifty acres with a population of between four thousand and ten thousand inhabitants at the end of the Late Bronze Age, which established it as a city that would indeed have been worthy of a ten-year-long siege, if Homer's story has any truth to it. Korfmann began referring to the city in his scholarly publications as *Troy/Wilusa*—a nod to the Hittite records, which he believed were a reference to this city.

Other findings by Korfmann's team seemed to confirm Blegen's earlier work. For example, in both the citadel and the Lower City, they also found evidence for earthquake destruction in Troy VIh and human destruction—that is, warfare—in Troy VIIa. In one case, they found a house from Troy VIh that had been destroyed by the earthquake and then a house from Troy VIIa that had been built right on top of its ruins, only to be destroyed in war.

Among the evidence for fighting, Korfmann found more unburied bodies, including one of a young girl about age seventeen who was partially burned, as well as arrowheads of an Aegean (or Greek) type. There also was a quantity of what appear to be slingstones, which were gathered together in at least one pile, perhaps ready to be thrown at the attackers by someone inside the walls of the city.

Korfmann's work also confirmed Blegen's earlier findings in other ways. After the Troy VIIa city was destroyed in about 1180 BCE, the next one was occupied by what seem to be a completely new people. In this phase, which archaeologists call Troy VIIb, we see completely new types of pottery, new architecture, and other material culture, including an inscribed seal that has the first writing ever found at Troy.

These are all indications that the inhabitants of the previous city had been completely replaced by a new group. Therefore, it is possible to see the human destruction of Troy VIIa as being evidence of the stories of Homer about the Trojan War. In his story, though, Homer seems to have added in elements from Troy VI, so that he described the beautiful buildings and high walls of the earlier city but the destruction of the later city, thereby compressing the two cities into one, which was his prerogative as an epic poet.

It may even be that the Trojan Horse is a poetic metaphor for the earthquake that leveled Troy VIh, for the Greek god of earthquakes was Poseidon. Just as the goddess Athena was represented by an owl, so a horse represented Poseidon for the Greeks. It is conceivable, at least in the poetic imagination, that "earthquake = Poseidon = the Trojan Horse." At least that's what a German scholar named Fritz Schachermeyer suggested back in the 1950s.

As the Hissarlik digs continued, the post–Bronze Age team, led by Brian Rose of the University of Cincinnati, also found a lot of new material, including a larger-than-life statue of the Roman emperor Hadrian in 1993 and a large marble head of Augustus in 1997. The later Hellenistic Greeks and then the Romans had built upon the citadel and established a nicely gridded city down below, which Korfman had found in addition to the Bronze Age remains in this area.

These later inhabitants were also convinced that this was the site of ancient Troy and, in fact, they gave it the name "New Troy" in both Greek and Latin. Even Alexander the Great came to visit and pay his respects, as did Julius Caesar and others over the centuries. It was initial discoveries from these later periods that first persuaded Frank Calvert, and then Heinrich Schliemann, that they were digging in the right place.

A temple to Athena, and then one to Jupiter, also were later built on top of the mound itself. That explains why Priam's Troy was far closer to the top of the surface today than Schliemann expected it to be. The builders in both the Hellenistic and the Roman periods had shaved off the top of the mound as it stood in their time. This gave them level ground on which to build the temples, theaters, and other structures that went with their cities, now numbered Troy VIII and IX, which were the last to be built at the site.

{←→} {←→}

Manfred Korfmann died suddenly in 2005, but the international excavations continue under new directors. Interest in digging and doing remote sensing in and around the site continues, so perhaps Hissarlik has even more secrets to reveal about the ancient town that inspired one of the greatest epics ever written.

3

FROM EGYPT TO ETERNITY

PYRAMIDS, MUMMIES, AND HIEROGLYPHICS. EGYPTOLOGY seems to be the field of archaeology that is most fascinating to the general public. It also is perhaps the most misunderstood. Everyone, from kindergarteners to grandparents, seems to be enthralled by the ancient Egyptians and knows a little something about them. Or do they? The amount of misinformation about ancient Egypt that is floating around, especially on the Internet, is astounding.

Every year Egyptologists and other archaeologists have to correct misunderstandings—"no, Hebrew slaves did not build the pyramids"— and every year their email accounts are inundated with questions after the airing of any one of the numerous television shows that claim that the pyramids were built by aliens or that they were built to store grain or that the Sphinx is ten thousand years old, or some other nonsense usually dreamed up by amateur enthusiasts. Therefore, in this chapter, we will touch upon aspects of these three topics—pyramids, mummies, and hieroglyphics—so that readers will be in a better position to sift through the often-dubious claims made about these topics.

{←→}{←→}

The first archaeologists who worked in Egypt often weren't really Egyptologists, or at least didn't originally intend to be. Take The Great Belzoni, for example—Giovanni Battista Belzoni, who was born in 1778. He was a strong man in a circus, standing six feet, six inches tall and able to lift twelve men at a time, but he also could be considered an engineer of sorts. He first traveled to Egypt in 1815 to show the Ottoman ruler a new plan for drawing water out of the Nile and ended up becoming one of the first Egyptologists. We should use that term loosely, however, for Belzoni is remembered more for tomb robbing and mummy collecting than he is for any actual science or archaeology, though he was one of the first to explore Ramses II's temple at Abu Simbel.

Karl Lepsius and Auguste Mariette, on the other hand, can rightly be considered giants in Egyptology, even if they were shorter than Belzoni. Lepsius was a Prussian Egyptologist who led an expedition to Egypt in 1842. The mission of the expedition was to record as many monuments as possible, which was done astonishingly well. The resulting twelve huge volumes of drawings and illustrations were published in German over a ten-year period from 1849 to 1859, as *Monuments of Egypt and Ethiopia*. The volumes of written material that accompanied them took another forty years or more to be published and didn't see the light of day until more than a decade after Lepsius himself had died. Taken as a whole, the volumes of texts and plates are considered by many to be the foundations of modern Egyptology.

Auguste Mariette, who was born in France in 1821, started digging in Egypt on behalf of the Louvre in about 1850. Eight years later, he was appointed the first director of antiquities in Egypt. Among other things, he built the first national museum, whose collection still forms the basis of the Egyptian Museum in Cairo today.

Lepsius and Mariette were able to establish their careers in part because of an event that had taken place by 1823, when Mariette was only two years old and Lepsius was thirteen years old. It is one of the most famous events in Egyptology—the decipherment of Egyptian hieroglyphics.

In order to understand how the event took place, we must first go back to 1799 CE, a year or so after Napoleon and his troops invaded Egypt as part of a grand campaign to capture the Middle East. Napoleon had brought along more than one hundred fifty civilians as part of this campaign. Collectively known as the savants, they included scientists, engineers, and other scholars. They were charged with studying and recording the entire country, including the antiquities and monuments. Some today regard their work as really beginning the study of ancient Egypt, setting the stage immediately before Lepsius and Mariette. They also unintentionally set off a frenzy of Egyptomania in Europe, which continues today, as it does in the United States—the Luxor Hotel in Las Vegas being an obvious example.

In any event, the French troops were in the village of Rosetta, in the Delta region, either rebuilding a fort or digging a foxhole—the stories differ. But in the process, they found an inscription that turned out to date from 196 BCE. It had been written to honor Ptolemy V—an Egyptian pharaoh who otherwise is not very memorable. It's extremely important because the text of the inscription is written in three different scripts. At the top of this Rosetta stone, the text is written in Egyptian hieroglyphics. In the middle, the same text is written again, but this time in what is called demotic—essentially Egyptian cursive handwriting. And the bottom third of the stone has the inscription written once again, but this time in Greek.

Using this trilingual inscription, a brilliant French scholar named Jean-François Champollion was able to crack the code of Egyptian hieroglyphics. He did it in part by reading the Greek version, well understood by all scholars of his day, and realizing that two royal names appeared again and again: Ptolemy and Cleopatra. He looked for repetition in the Egyptian hieroglyphics that could represent those two names and was eventually able to use them as keys to his decipherment. Champollion wasn't the only scholar working on this; a British linguist named Thomas Young very nearly beat Champollion to the translation. But it's Champollion who got the credit for doing so in 1823, a mere twenty-four years after the inscription had been found.

It suddenly became clear that all of the "pretty pictures" painted on the walls of the tombs of nobles and inscribed elsewhere were in fact long inscriptions containing their biographies, lifetime achievements, and so on. One set of hieroglyphs that appeared frequently in these contexts is now known to be the symbols for eternity, which makes sense in a tomb setting.

It also turned out that the seven or eight hundred hieroglyphic signs could be read in various directions, but they are always consistent, because the figures always face toward the beginning of the line. The signs also could be read in various ways. For instance, a hieroglyph could be a word-sign and stand for the item being pictured, such as a bird or a bull; or it could stand for a single sound, like of the first letter of the word for the object; or it could be a syllabic sign representing a combination of consonants; or it could be used as a determinative to specify how to read the word next to it. It's no wonder that not many people knew how to read and write in ancient Egypt—probably only about 1 percent of the population. Scribes had a respected position at the royal court, for it is quite possible that even the king and queen did not know how to read or write.

Although many of the inscriptions that we have today have survived because they are carved into stone, such as on the walls of temples and other buildings, the Egyptians more often wrote on sheets of papyrus, flattened reeds that grew along the Nile River, which was their version of paper. Though not as durable as stone inscriptions, thousands of papyrus scrolls have been preserved as a result of Egypt's dry climate.

They used ink created from carbon and other materials. The ink could be black or it could be red, often with both colors used in the same manuscript. In those cases, the word written in red might be the first word of the new sentence, so that it was clear where one sentence ended and another one began, since there was no punctuation as we know it. Red ink also could mark the beginning of a spell, or even just a title or a heading, as determined by the context and the need.

{←→}{←→}

Once Egyptian writing had been deciphered, it became possible for scholars to read the various records left on both stone and papyrus and begin reconstructing the history of ancient Egypt with confidence. In this they were both helped and hindered by the writings left by historians, travelers, and priests from the Greek and Roman periods. One was Herodotus, the Greek historian who lived in the fifth century BCE and reported on his travels in Egypt, including details—many of them highly inaccurate—about how the pyramids were built and bodies were mummified. Another was Manetho, a priest who lived in Hellenistic Egypt during the third century BCE and who attempted to construct a list of the rulers of Egypt from earliest times until his own period.

Manetho divided the history of Egypt into periods, a system that we still use today. Although he mangled many of the pharaohs' names and got some things out of order, on the whole he was reasonably accurate, especially considering that he created this list almost twenty-five hundred years after the foundation of Egypt's First Dynasty. So we say that the Old Kingdom Period began in about 2700 BCE, at the time of the Third Dynasty. The kingdom is known especially for the construction of the pyramids for the pharaohs of the Fourth Dynasty, from about 2600–2500 BCE.

The Old Kingdom lasted for about five hundred years, until approximately 2200 BCE, at which point it collapsed following the ninety-one-year-long reign of Pepi II. The collapse may not have been caused by the long rule of this pharaoh, who came to the throne when he was six years old, for recent studies now suggest that it may have been caused by climate change, in the form of droughts and famine that seem to have devastated both Egypt and much of the ancient Middle East at that time.

A period of anarchy called the First Intermediate Period followed the collapse of the Old Kingdom, with several dynasties vying for control of the whole country and none succeeding. The Middle Kingdom then lasted until about 1720 BCE, at which time Egypt was invaded and taken over by the Hyksos, who came down from the region of Canaan to the north and ruled over Egypt until they were expelled about 1550 BCE by Egyptian forces fighting under the leadership of two brothers, Kamose and Ahmose.

Strangely enough, even though they were brothers, Kamose is considered to be the last king of the Seventeenth Dynasty, while Ahmose is the first king of the Eighteenth Dynasty, which began a new era in

Egypt known as the New Kingdom Period. It is this period that lasted until just after 1200 BCE and included rulers such as the powerful queen Hatshepsut; the militarily aggressive Thutmose III; the monotheist pharaoh Akhenaton; and the boy-king Tutankhamen; as well as ten pharaohs named Ramses. Even though Egypt survived the great collapse of the entire Bronze Age world in the years surrounding 1177 BCE and continued during the Third Intermediate Period, the Saite Renaissance, and then Greek and Roman rule, including by Alexander the Great and later Cleopatra, all dating to the first millennium BCE, it never again reached the heights of power that it had enjoyed during this New Kingdom Period.

❊❀❊ ❊❀❊

With the translation of hieroglyphics in the early nineteenth century, scholars were able to begin reading and studying the other writings left to us by the ancient Egyptians. These range from poems and stories to economic accounts and religious texts. One thing that we frequently find written on papyrus, but also on the walls of the tombs of wealthy people, is the Book of the Dead, otherwise known as the Book of Going Forth by Day. This was essentially a manual to help the deceased person get into the afterlife right after he or she had died, because it contained the answers to the questions that would be asked before one was allowed to enter the afterworld—it was, essentially, a cheat sheet. This went hand in hand with the weighing of the heart ceremony, at which the dead person's heart was placed on one scale and a feather representing truth and justice (*ma'at*) was placed on the other, to see whether the deceased had lived a good and just life. The dead person was allowed entrance to the afterlife only if the heart weighed the same or less than the feather—that is, if it was not heavy with sins and wrongdoing.

In order to stay in the afterworld, the physical body of the dead person had to remain intact, even long after the person had died. This is where the process of mummification enters the picture. Some of the earliest mummies that we have from Egypt seem to have been mummified naturally, but this was obviously not always the case. There also was the problem of making certain that a body remained buried long after its original internment and that jackals, hyenas, or other scavengers didn't maul it later.

Two things developed, therefore. One was the process of mummification. The other was the creation of mastabas, or benches, of mudbrick that were used to protect the burial place. Many scholars suspect that these were the predecessors of the pyramids. Let's look at the two processes one at a time.

First, mummification. Even today, many people try their hand at mummifying things, frequently as a school project in elementary school. This usually involves chickens, rather than a person or a family pet, which is fortunate (unless, of course, the family pet happens to be a chicken).

We know quite a bit about mummification, in part because we have a rather detailed description from Herodotus, who learned about the process during his time in Egypt. He wrote that one should put the body into a type of desiccating salt called natron and then leave it there for seventy days. The natron wicks the moisture out of the body and helps to mummify it. This obviously does not happen overnight, hence the need for a seventy-day-long bath in natron.

But a number of the inner organs also need to be removed. To do this, the mummifier is told to make a slit up the side of the body and reach in to remove the stomach, upper intestines, lower intestines, lungs, and the liver. These are all placed in what we call canopic jars. That's the modern name for them, since they were first identified by early Egyptologists who thought they were associated with the Greek myth of Canopus, a Mycenaean warrior from Greece who fought in the Trojan War but was bitten by a snake and died while visiting Egypt.

Canopic jars were essential equipment for the tomb. Each set could be different, but during the New Kingdom, the lids of the jars depicted the four sons of Horus, who guarded the organs. The stomach and upper intestines would go into a jar that had a jackal head for a lid. The lower intestines were placed in one that had a falcon head for a lid. The lungs would go into a baboon-headed jar, and the liver would go into a jar with a lid shaped like a human head. Then, sweet-smelling herbs and spices would be stuffed into the body cavity where the organs had been and the slit in the side of the body would be sewn up again.

The heart, however, would be left in place within the body, for the ancient Egyptians thought it was the center of intelligence and would be needed in the afterlife. The brain, on the other hand, was not understood and was simply discarded. There were two ways to get it out.

One way to remove the brain was simply to take a long piece of wire, with the end bent into a hook shape. This was shoved up the dead person's nose until the bent end was up in the brain cavity, then it was quickly pulled out, bringing the brain with it. If not all the brain came out the first time, the process was repeated until it was completely removed.

The other way to do it was to tilt the person's head back and put drops into their nose. The drops were made of a powerful acid, so when they ran up into the brain cavity, they melted the brain. When the head was tilted back down, the gray gooey mass would simply run out the person's nose, and voilà—the brain cavity was now empty.

The precise method that the Egyptians used is still debated, even in scientific articles, but it all goes back to Herodotus, who was the first one to tell us that the embalmers pulled most of the brain out through the nostrils using a crooked piece of iron and then cleared out the rest "by rinsing with drugs." In 2012 an object identified as a "brain-removal tool" was found in the skull of a twenty-five-hundred-year-old mummy. It was probably used for both liquefying and removing the brain, or so researchers think.

The embalming was done out of sight of family members, which was probably a good idea, since accidents sometimes did happen. Take, for example, one woman whose cheeks had sunken because of the embalming process. She was a priestess named Henttawy from the Twenty-First Dynasty, and so she lived and died sometime in the tenth century BCE, or about three thousand years ago. The embalmers had stuffed her cheeks with cotton pads, perhaps in an effort to make her appear more lifelike, which seems to have been the custom at the time. But they put in too much and at some point both her cheeks simply ripped off. Of course, she didn't get to stay in the afterlife because her body had not remained intact, but nobody knew that until the mummy was unwrapped in modern times.

Other mummies in the British Museum, and in museums elsewhere in Britain, Germany, and Egypt, have been recently re-examined, using new computerized tomography (CT) scanning and three-dimensional visualization, with a number of interesting things found. The mummies, including both royals and commoners, are from a variety of periods, from 3500 BCE to 700 CE, and are of different ages, from children to adults. Some of them had tattoos, others suffered from various ailments, and almost all of them had dental problems. One investigation, of a female singer named Tamut from Thebes, who was mummified in about 900 BCE, revealed that protective amulets had been hidden inside the wrappings and that she had calcified plaque in her arteries, which may have led to her death from a heart attack or a stroke. Other investigations, of animal mummies, revealed that up to a third of them had little or no actual remains inside the wrappings, leading to speculation about why this might be.

Mummifying the body was one thing that the ancient Egyptians did, but they also had to protect the mummy from the elements. That's why, before about 3000 BCE, we find mastabas, or low benches made out of mudbricks, above the grave into which the mummy was placed. Mastaba means "bench" in modern Arabic; hence the name given to them today. That way, even if a sandstorm hit the cemetery and all of the sand was swept away, the mastaba would remain in place and the mummy would not be exposed to the elements . . . or to the pecking beak of a bird or the jaws of a hyena or some other scavenger.

This may have been what eventually led to the pyramids, several centuries later. It is not clear exactly what triggered the idea of building the first pyramids, but it is unlikely to have had anything to do with ancient aliens. It seems to have been Djoser (or Zozer), a pharaoh who lived during the Third Dynasty, in the years just after 2700 BCE, who was first responsible for asking Imhotep, his vizier (in other words, his right-hand man) to create something a bit more majestic as his burial place. And thus, the Step Pyramid was constructed, which we identify as the first pyramid ever to be built in Egypt. Imhotep seems to have been Djoser's personal physician as well as his architect; he was later hailed as the Father of Egyptian medicine and then eventually deified as a god of healing and, as such, was even later linked to the Greek god Asclepius.

Looking at the Step Pyramid, it appears that Imhotep simply took about six mastabas and placed them one on top of the other, decreasing

Step Pyramid of Djoser, Saqqara

in size as they got closer to the top, so that he ended up with a pyramid built in stages or steps. It was just a short hop from that Step Pyramid to the huge smooth-sided pyramids that we know from outside of Cairo today, because all that needed to be done was to fill in the missing parts and smooth out the sides.

There is a lot more to it than that, of course, and it is still very much a matter of debate how exactly the pharaohs built the pyramids. Many scholars personally favor the idea of using blocks and tackles and pulleys, just as is done when hoisting up heavy stones today, but others like the idea of pulling the blocks up into place via earthen ramps that ran in a spiral around the pyramid. If that method were used, the last thing to do after putting the final blocks into place at the top would be to dismantle the earthen ramps that would have been surrounding the pyramid at that point. There are all sorts of other hypotheses, including the suggestion that there was an internal ramp built within the pyramid that was used and that can't be seen anymore. It is clear from replication studies conducted in recent years that, although the blocks were many and heavy, they were not beyond the technological skill of the Egyptians. There is no need to invoke alien powers.

The other thing to keep in mind, though, is that such big pyramids were not built in isolation; they were normally part of a much larger funerary complex, which also contained ceremonial courts, religious shrines, and other buildings, all dedicated to keeping the king's memory alive. So, there is a funerary complex for Djoser, of which the Step Pyramid is just one part.

The same is true at Giza, outside modern-day Cairo, where the three greatest Egyptian pyramids were built. This is the only one from the original list of the Seven Wonders of the Ancient World that still survives today. They are also one of the few cultural features on Earth that can be seen relatively easily from the International Space Station.

These three pyramids date to the Fourth Dynasty, the so-called Pyramid Age, during the Old Kingdom Period. They were built one after another, by a father-son-grandson combination named Khufu, Khafre, and Menkaure, or—as the later Greeks called them—Cheops, Chephren, and Mycerinus. The first one, built by Khufu (aka Cheops) just after 2600 BCE, is the earliest and largest, so that it is known today as the Great Pyramid. We know that Khufu built this pyramid, in part because graffiti left by the workers inside mention his name. The second pyramid, the one built by Khafre (aka Chephren) is the one to which the Sphinx probably belongs, for the Sphinx sits at what was originally the entrance to the funerary complex for Khafre. The third one is also the smallest, built by Menkaure (aka Mycerinus). Going inside this pyramid is an extremely claustrophobic experience, as I can attest—I'm not the world's biggest person, but even I had to bend my head in order not to hit the ceiling and my shoulders scraped the walls on either side as I walked the length of one of the internal corridors. Moreover, I can clearly remember the oppressive feeling of having tons and tons of rock above me.

The Great Pyramid is the most famous of the three. It probably took ten to twenty years to build, but it is unlikely that it was built by slaves (and it certainly wasn't built by Hebrew slaves, as is sometimes said, because the pyramids were built at least eight hundred years before the date of the biblical story of Joseph that purportedly brought the Hebrews to Egypt).

Herodotus, the same Greek historian who described how to mummify bodies, says that it took one hundred thousand people working in four shifts per year to build such a pyramid. Excavations of the workers' quarters and cemeteries in the vicinity of the pyramids since the 1990s have led to the general conclusion today that the workforce probably consisted of peasants, farmers, and other members of the lower classes who were working for pay during the off season, after the harvest had been brought in, and that they were well treated. In addition to this seasonal work force, there was a permanent contingent of several thousand professional pyramid builders who directed the work and provided the technical expertise. The pyramids were essentially giant public works projects, because building them would have pumped an incredible amount of money back into the economy from royal coffers.

It is clear that a huge workforce was needed, though, because the number of stone blocks used in each pyramid was tremendous. For example, the Great Pyramid was originally probably about 480 feet tall and about 755 feet on each side. There are 2.3 million blocks in the Great Pyramid, some of them weighing several tons. The whole pyramid is estimated to weigh almost six million tons. Originally it would have been finished off with an outer casing of white limestone, but those limestone blocks are long gone, with many of them reused in later buildings both in Cairo itself and in the villages surrounding the pyramids.

Within the Great Pyramid are a series of passageways and chambers. These are still much debated, but it seems that the original entrance and passageway led down to a chamber where the king would have been buried beneath the ground level. It is possible that the plan was changed, however, for another passageway leads upward, to what is called the Grand Gallery and then to the King's Chamber, in which a large granite sarcophagus is still in place.

There are also two narrow shafts leading up from the King's Chamber to either side of the pyramid. These used to be, and sometimes still are, referred to as air shafts, though now some attribute a more ritualistic purpose to them. They have been put to good use in recent years, when it was noticed that the crush of tourists inside the pyramid was creating problems, namely from the moisture in their exhaled breath. Air conditioners (or extractor fans) were placed in the shafts to pull the moist air out and pull in the dry desert air, thereby solving the problem almost immediately. So, if you're in the Great Pyramid and think that you hear the hum of air conditioners, it's not your imagination.

As for the Sphinx, it stands at the entrance to the second pyramid, the one built by Khafre, and Egyptologists have noted the resemblance of its face to statues of Khafre. It's not ten thousand years old, as some amateur enthusiasts have claimed, but rather dates to about 2550 BCE. It sits in one of the quarries from which the Egyptians got the blocks for the pyramids, but it was left because the core of the body was "rotten"— that is, the stone wasn't good enough to be used as building material. So the core was shaped to look like a body and then blocks were added to form the paws as well as the head and face.

It had already been excavated once in antiquity, for the pharaoh Thutmose IV left an inscription claiming that—when he was still a young prince—he had fallen asleep in the shadow of the Sphinx, which was buried up to its neck in sand. This would have been about 1400 BCE. In a dream, the Sphinx told him that if he removed the sand, the Sphinx would make him king over Egypt. He excavated the sand away and fixed the blocks where they were crumbling. When he eventually became king, he left what is now known as the Sphinx Dream Stele between its paws, where modern Egyptologists found it.

Legend has it that the nose of the Sphinx is gone because Napoleon's troops shot it off in 1798 or 1799. That's simply not true. Although his troops did use the Sphinx for target practice, the nose was already long gone by that point. According to the Arab historian al-Maqrizi, who was writing in the fifteenth century, a Sufi Muslim ruler hacked off the nose in 1378 because the Egyptian peasants were making offerings to the Sphinx and treating it as a pagan idol.

{⊷}⁝{⊷}

These days, new technologies are being put to use in Egypt to investigate some of the most famous architectural features, including King Tut's tomb and a number of pyramids, from the Bent Pyramid and the Red Pyramid at Dashur to the Great Pyramid of Khufu at Giza.

For instance, in 2015 Egyptian, Japanese, Canadian, and French scientists used infrared thermography to determine that there were some strange anomalies in several of the pyramids, including differences in temperature between different blocks of stone. The thermal data might indicate the presence of cavities or some sort of internal structure that had not been noted previously.

The scientists are also using muon radiography that might provide additional data about such possible cavities. Muon collectors, or detectors, measure cosmic particles that can pass through solid structures but also can indicate where there are hollows or voids within them. They have also been used previously at a Maya pyramid in Belize in 2013. In late 2015 forty muon detector plates, covering ten square feet, were placed in the lower chamber of the Bent Pyramid at Dashur in Egypt, built a century before the well-known Giza pyramids, and left for forty days. The results, reported in April 2016, were promising, clearly showing the known second chamber within the pyramid and ruling out the possibility of any other undiscovered chambers within the field of view that was covered by the detectors. Next up for investigation is the Great Pyramid. All this means that the pyramids, which have been there since the beginnings of archaeology and Egyptology, are once again coming to the forefront of exploration in the field.

Overall, this excursion into the world of ancient Egypt has attempted to shed some light on the remarkable achievements of this great civilization, as well as some of the recent discoveries that have been made and the new technologies that are now being used to make them. I hope that it will now be easier in the future for readers to judge some of the claims made about the ancient Egyptians—especially when it comes to the big three: pyramids, mummies, and hieroglyphics—whether online, on television, or by well-meaning friends and neighbors. But keep in mind that these popular topics are far from the only things that Egyptologists are working on; interesting papers presented by scholars at the ARCE (American Research Center in Egypt) annual meeting in 2016 included "Kingship during the Third Intermediate Period," "New Kingdom Burial Practices on the Eastern Frontier at Tell el-Borg, Part II," "The Mechanics of Egyptian Royal Rock Inscriptions," and other topics that don't always make it into the television specials.

MYSTERIES IN MESOPOTAMIA

I N 2001 THE BRITISH MUSEUM MOUNTED AN EXHIBIT TITLED "Agatha Christie and Archaeology." Usually known better for her mystery books, including those featuring Hercule Poirot, she reportedly once said, "An archaeologist is the best husband any woman can have. The older she gets, the more interested he is in her."

Agatha Christie knew well of what she spoke. Many people have read one or more of her books, but few realize that she was married to the archaeologist Max Mallowan. He was Leonard Woolley's right-hand man at the site of Ur, in what is now modern Iraq. In 1930, when Mallowan was twenty-six and she was forty, Agatha came to visit the site, for she—along with most of the rest of England at that time—was captivated by the announcements of their finds from the famous "Death Pits of Ur." She had come to see them for herself but found herself even more entranced by Mallowan than she was by the Death Pits. They got married six months later. After she married him, however, Agatha was no longer welcome at the site. As a result, they left Ur soon thereafter, to start their own excavations elsewhere. From then on, she came with him on most of his digs and wrote many of her books while there, when she wasn't helping him process the material that they were finding.

As to why she wasn't welcome at Ur after her marriage to Mallowan, the scuttlebutt is that Woolley's wife, Lady Katharine Woolley, didn't want to share the attention of the men on the dig with anyone else. But Agatha seems to have quickly gotten her revenge, for Lovely Louise, the first person killed off in her book *Murder in Mesopotamia*, is believed by many to be based on Lady Woolley, especially since she is described as a "beautiful but difficult archaeologist's wife." Reportedly, those who were in the know instantly recognized Louise as Lady Katharine, who apparently didn't really mind at all.

꘡꘡ ꘡꘡

The site of ancient Ur is situated on the Euphrates River, just north of where the river empties into the Persian Gulf. This is the region known as Mesopotamia, a name that comes from the Greek words "meso" and "potamia," meaning the area "between the rivers"—namely the Tigris and the Euphrates.

Ur was a site already famous in antiquity. It was continuously inhabited from about 6000 BCE until 400 BCE, when it was finally abandoned after the Euphrates River changed course. During the Bronze Age, from 3000 BCE onward, it had all the typical features of a Mesopotamian city, including religious structures known as ziggurats that reached up to the sky. Woolley identified the site with "Ur of the Chaldees," which the book of Genesis mentions in association with the biblical patriarch Abraham, but it's still anyone's guess whether he was right about that.

Woolley and Mallowan began excavating in 1922, the same year that Carter found King Tut's tomb in Egypt, but it wasn't until the middle of their fifth field season, in 1926–1927, that they began digging the cemetery at the site. Thereafter, between 1927 and 1929, the two archaeologists uncovered the sixteen royal burials that would make them famous. All told, including the later excavations that Woolley conducted without Mallowan after 1931, there were approximately 1,850 intact burials found in the cemetery area. The royal burials thus made up only a small percentage of the graves that they excavated.

The royal burials at Ur date to about 2500 BCE, almost contemporary with the Giza pyramids. And though many of the other burials in the cemetery were very simple, the royal tombs were quite impressive. The royal tombs usually consisted of a stone chamber, either vaulted or domed, into which the royal body was placed. The chamber was at the bottom of a deep pit, with access possible only via a steep ramp from the surface. The precious grave goods were mostly found in the burial chamber with the body, and wheeled vehicles, oxen, and attendants were found in both the chamber and in the pit outside.

There were numerous attendants found in the Death Pits—one had more than seventy bodies of attendants who were killed to go with their master or mistress into the afterlife; another held more than sixty bodies; still another had forty bodies. Most were women, but there were men as well. Woolley assumed that they drank poison after climbing down the ramp into the pit, but CT scans of some of the skulls done in 2009 at the University of Pennsylvania indicate that at least some of those people had been killed by having a sharp instrument driven into their head just below and behind the ear while they were still alive. Death would have been instantaneous.

The grave goods that Woolley and Mallowan found with the royal bodies were amazing, despite the fact that many of the graves had been looted in antiquity. They found gold tiaras, gold and lapis jewelry, gold and electrum daggers, even a gold helmet—which was probably ceremonial, since gold helmets aren't very good at stopping a sword or an ax in battle. There were also delicate sculptures, such as the pair of figures that depict a goat in a tree (frequently referred to as the "ram in a thicket" because of its similarity to the biblical story of the sacrifice of Isaac). One of these lovely sculptures is now in the British Museum; the other is housed at the University Museum of the University of Pennsylvania in Philadelphia.

The excavators at Ur also unearthed the remains of a wooden harp with ivory and lapis inlays, which Woolley later had reconstructed. One of the royal tombs also contained a wooden box with inlays on front and back that Woolley dubbed the Standard of Ur, thinking that perhaps it had been carried on top of a pole into battle in front of the troops, much like the Romans had their banners centuries later. He suggested this because of the scenes that are depicted, which include a possible battle followed by loot presented to the king and then a victory banquet. Among the figures in the banquet scene is a musician holding a harp, which is partially the basis for Woolley's reconstruction. Of course, these scenes could also depict something else entirely and this might be just a simple wooden box rather than a "standard." The discussions and debates about the interpretation of this and some of the other objects still continue today, almost a century after Woolley and Mallowan found the royal graves.

{···} {···}

Woolley and Mallowan were not the first archaeologists to find amazing things in the ancient sites of Mesopotamia. By the mid-1800s, serious excavations were underway at a number of ancient sites in the Middle East, underwritten by institutions like the British Museum and the Louvre, and conducted by people like Austen Henry Layard and Paul Émile Botta. They excavated in what is now Iraq at places like Nineveh and Nimrud, capitals of the Assyrian empire of the eighth and seventh centuries BCE. They shipped magnificent pieces back to the museums, such as the colossal winged bulls, lion friezes, and other pieces currently on display at the British Museum and the Louvre. German and US museums got into the act as well, sponsoring expeditions to the region and excavating at other sites such as Babylon, Uruk, and Nippur.

Aiding the archaeologists were also epigraphers—scholars who study ancient writing—like the British scholar Henry Rawlinson, who helped to decipher cuneiform in the 1830s. Cuneiform is a wedge-shaped writing system—in fact, the very word *cuneiform* means "wedge-shaped." It was used to write Akkadian, Babylonian, Hittite, Old Persian, and other languages in the ancient Middle East, much as we now use the Latin alphabet to write English, French, German, Italian, Spanish, and so on.

Rawlinson, who was a British army officer posted to what is now Iran, cracked the secret of cuneiform the same way that Champollion deciphered Egyptian hieroglyphics, by translating a trilingual inscription. In Rawlinson's case, the inscription was written in Old Persian (a language that had been preserved to modern times), Elamite (another ancient Persian language, but one that had gone out of use long ago), and Babylonian. It had been carved by the imperial order of Darius the Great of Persia in about 519 BCE, four hundred feet above the desert floor into a cliff face at the site of Behistun in Iran.

The story that is often repeated is one originally told by Rawlinson himself. It seems that after spending as many as twelve years, from 1835 to 1847, copying the inscription by climbing up and down rickety ladders and scaffolding, he eventually hired a "wild Kurdish boy" to shimmy down a rope from the top of the cliff in order to copy the final lines of the long inscription. The boy had to swing from side to side and run along the vertical cliff face before somehow clinging to it in order to copy the last little bits.

By 1837, just two years into the project, Rawlinson had already figured out how to read the first two paragraphs of the part that was written in Old Persian. He presented his findings in official papers published in 1837 and 1839, just ahead of others—including an elderly Irish parson named Hincks—who had also been working on deciphering the inscription. It reportedly took Rawlinson another twenty years to decipher the Babylonian and Elamite parts of the inscription and successfully read the whole thing.

𓆏𓆏 𓆏𓆏

Meanwhile, in December 1842, Paul Émile Botta began the first archaeological excavations ever conducted in what is now Iraq. Although Italian-born, in his day job he was the French consul at Mosul, which was a position that essentially left him free to conduct archaeological fieldwork on behalf of the Louvre in Paris. That's what he spent most of his time doing, with the active endorsement of his higher-ups back in France.

Botta's first efforts were concentrated on the mounds collectively known as Kuyunjik, which are right across the river from the city of Mosul. He didn't find much there and quickly abandoned his efforts, prematurely as it turned out. From one of his workers, he learned that some sculptures had been found at a site called Khorsabad, located about fourteen miles to the north. So, in March 1843, he began excavating there instead, with immediate success. Within a week he began to unearth a great Assyrian palace. At first he thought that he had found the remains of ancient Nineveh, but now we know that Khorsabad is the ancient site of Dur Sharrukin, capital city of Sargon II, the Assyrian king who ruled from 721 to 705 BCE.

As for Austen Henry Layard, he did not mean to undertake excavations in Mesopotamia, at least not at first. In 1839, at the age of twenty-two, he had been traveling with a friend to Ceylon (now Sri Lanka), overland from England. They had gone through Turkey and had visited Jerusalem, Petra, Aleppo, and other ancient cities, when they reached Mosul in May 1840. There the archaeology bug bit him, and he became interested in digging the ancient mounds across the river from Mosul, but it was a few years before he was able to return and begin to excavate.

Layard's initial archaeological efforts, beginning in 1845, were at the site of Nimrud, which he first thought was ancient Nineveh. It was located a few miles downstream from Mosul. In order to fool the local ruler, a one-eyed, one-eared despot named Mohammed Pasha, Layard pretended to be going on a hunting expedition, but secretly included some excavating equipment in among his supplies.

When he got to the site, he spent the first night in the hut of a local village chief, dreaming of what he might find. He described it later as "visions of palaces underground, of gigantic monsters, of sculptured figures, and endless inscriptions." That turned out to be more of a premonition than a dream, for he found all that and more in the coming years.

The next morning he began to dig. His team consisted of six local workers, whom he split into two teams. They began digging in two areas, far apart on the mound. Before the first day ended, both groups had uncovered rooms with walls covered in carved inscriptions. But the rooms belonged to two separate palaces—in a single day, Layard had found not one, but two Assyrian palaces. Today they are usually called the Northwest and Southwest Palaces. As a result, he doubled the size of his team—to eleven workers. Later he expanded again, to a total of thirty workers.

From the inscriptions that Layard found, it eventually became clear that a ruler named Assurnasirpal II had built the Northwest Palace. Two hundred years later, another ruler, named Esarhaddon, built the Southwest Palace. There also is a Central Palace at the site, which was discovered only later, built by Tiglath-Pileser III. Shalmaneser III, the son of Assurnasirpal II, also ordered buildings and monuments constructed at the site. In all, these rulers constructed their buildings over a period of more than two hundred years, from 884 to 669 BCE.

Other archaeologists have excavated at Nimrud since Layard, almost up until the present day. It was in the news as recently as March 2015, when videos were released by ISIS militants, showing them taking a bulldozer and a sledgehammer to the ancient remains at the site and also destroying artifacts from Nimrud in the Mosul Museum.

Layard published a book about his amazing discoveries at Nimrud, among which was the Black Obelisk of Shalmaneser III, which is a pillar more than six feet (two meters) tall covered with inscriptions detailing the king's exploits, which includes mention of the biblical Jehu, king of Israel. The book appeared in 1849 and instantly cemented his reputation as an archaeologist, intrepid adventurer, and engaging writer. He called the book *Nineveh and Its Remains*, since that's what he thought he was excavating. This was an unfortunate choice for the title, for when Rawlinson deciphered the inscriptions from the site, it became clear that the ancient city was actually Kalhu, biblical Calah, rather than Nineveh.

Kalhu was the second capital city established by the Assyrians; the first being Assur itself. Kalhu served as their capital for almost 175 years, from 879 BCE until 706 BCE. After that, Sargon II moved the capital to Dur Sharrukin for a brief period, and then Sennacherib moved it to Nineveh. But where was Nineveh? Nobody had yet found it.

⚜⚜

In 1849 Layard returned to Mosul for another round of excavations, which lasted until 1851. This time his primary focus was Kuyunjik, the mound that Botta had abandoned seven years earlier. He now had enough money to hire up to three hundred workers at a time—ten times as many as at Nimrud.

Layard had better luck than Botta. His men immediately began unearthing walls with reliefs and images from what turned out to be a palace built by Sennacherib, who ruled from 704 to 681 BCE. At first, Layard knew it only as the "Southwestern Palace." Within it, he found what is referred to now as the "King's Library." These were two large rooms in which clay tablets were piled a foot deep on the floor. When the translation of them began, the real name of the palace became clear—the "Palace without Rival." And this time, finally, Rawlinson's translation of the tablets found there confirmed that this was the actual site of ancient Nineveh, for Sennacherib had moved the Assyrian capital from Dur Sharrukin to Nineveh after he came to the throne.

Today, Sennacherib's palace is probably most famous for what is called the "Lachish Room." Here Layard found wall reliefs, with both pictures and inscriptions carved into the stone slabs, showing Sennacherib's capture of the city of Lachish in 701 BCE. At that time, Lachish was the second most powerful city in Judah; Senneracherib attacked it before proceeding on to besiege Jerusalem.

The capture of Lachish is described in the Hebrew Bible (II Kings 18:13–14), as is the siege of Jerusalem. Layard's discovery was one of the first times that an event from the Bible could be confirmed by what we call "extra-biblical," or outside the Bible, sources.

Almost thirty years before Layard found Sennacherib's palace, Lord Byron immortalized the biblical account in his poem "The Destruction of Sennacherib," published in 1815: "The Assyrian came down like the wolf on the fold, And his cohorts were gleaming in purple and gold; And the sheen of their spears was like stars on the sea, When the blue wave rolls nightly on deep Galilee."

Subsequent excavations at the actual site of Lachish, in what is now Israel, in the 1930s and again in the 1970s and 1980s, confirmed the destruction of the city in about 701 BCE. They also revealed an Assyrian siege ramp, built of tons of earth and rocks, which looks very similar to ramps depicted in Sennacherib's reliefs.

The Nineveh reliefs also are full of gruesome scenes, including captives having their tongues pulled out and being flayed alive, along with decapitated heads placed on a pole. It is universally accepted that the Assyrians practiced what they preached, and committed such atrocities, but the depiction of them in Sennacherib's palace is most likely meant as propaganda—a means to deter other kingdoms from rebelling against the Assyrians. Foreign ambassadors were probably shown this room in the heart of the palace and then allowed to take the message back home that they shouldn't try to rebel or cross the Assyrians in any way, shape, or form.

{⟨•→}⟩ {⟨•→}⟩

On the excavation of Sennacherib's palace at Nineveh, Layard noted, "in the magnificent edifice I had opened no less than seventy-one halls, chambers, and passages, whose walls had almost without exception been paneled with sculptured slabs of alabaster." He estimated that his workers had dug enough tunnels to expose almost ten thousand feet— or about two miles—worth of such walls, along with twenty-seven doorways formed by colossal winged bulls and lion-sphinxes.

We should note, though, that Layard was a diplomat, not a trained archaeologist; nor was Botta, for that matter. Brian Fagan has said bluntly, "Botta and Layard were appalling excavators by today's standards." In particular, Layard excavated by "chasing walls," which we don't do in archaeology today. His men dug a trench straight down into the mound until they hit a stone wall, and then they followed the wall by digging a tunnel. When that wall met another, they turned the corner and tunneled along that wall, and so on until they had burrowed along all four edges of the room. Botta and his men did essentially the same thing.

By excavating in this manner, Layard uncovered many of the inscribed slabs that made up these walls, as well as the colossal statues. But it also meant that he frequently left the middle of the rooms unexcavated. He also wasn't particularly interested in any of the pottery that his men uncovered during the course of their excavations. Many of the slabs were shipped back to the British Museum, where they can be seen on display today. Others, found both here and at Nimrud and Khorsabad, wound up in museum collections around the world, including some at Dartmouth and Amherst Colleges in the United States.

{⟨•→}⟩ {⟨•→}⟩

It took a tremendous amount of effort to get the pieces back to the British Museum, or the Louvre in the case of Botta and his successor Victor

Place. Botta's finds went on display in the Louvre in May 1847, beating
Layard and the British Museum by a matter of months, since their
pieces didn't go on display until September of that year. In order to get
his finds back to France, at one point Botta had a wagon built, with
wheels that were three feet wide, only to find that it was too heavy to be
moved, even by more than two hundred workers. Layard had similar
problems in transporting his finds back to England.

Victor Place, who replaced Botta at Khorsabad, had the worst misfortune of all. It was on his watch that a major shipment—between two
hundred and three hundred crates filled with antiquities—was lost in
the Tigris River, while being sent to France in May 1855. Bandits inter-
cepted the convoy as it floated down the Tigris after a stop at Baghdad.
When they realized that the cargo wasn't gold, they spitefully capsized

Man-headed winged bull, Dur Sharrukin (modern Khorsabad)

the vessels and killed several of the crewmen. The crates of precious and irreplaceable ancient finds quickly sank straight to the bottom of the river. Nearly one hundred twenty contained antiquities from Khorsabad and another sixty-eight contained sculptures from Sennacherib's palace at Nineveh, which Place had been allowed to take for the Louvre, even though the British team had excavated them. There also was material from elsewhere in Mesopotamia, which had been retrieved by a French expedition to Babylonia. Only seventy-eight of the crates were eventually recovered, leading Seton Lloyd, one of the greatest British archaeologists of recent times, to call this "one of the most appalling disasters in the history of archaeology." The remainder has never been found. Dredging the river in this location using modern remote-sensing technology might still be very worthwhile.

❧❧❧ ❧❧❧

The finds kept coming. Two years before the disaster on the Tigris, in 1853 Hormuzd Rassam, a native archaeologist and Layard's protégé and successor at Nineveh, discovered Assurbanipal's palace at the site, right under the nose of Victor Place, who also was digging there. Assurbanipal was Sennacherib's grandson, ruling from 668 to 627 BCE. Rassam and his workers dug secretly for three straight nights in disputed territory on the mound, and when their trenches first revealed the walls and sculptures of the palace, Place could only congratulate them on their finds.

Within the palace, it was Rassam's turn to find a tremendous library of cuneiform texts, just as Layard had done previously in Sennacherib's palace. It is generally considered that the state archives of Assyria, twenty-five thousand tablets in all, were split between the two palaces, even though they were two generations apart; they are now all in the British Museum.

The texts found by Rassam in Assurbanipal's palace came from what is often called the Royal Library. Apart from the state documents, which provided a comprehensive portrait of the politics, economy, and social conditions of the Assyrian empire, they include religious, scientific, and literary texts that Assurbanipal had instructed his scribes to collect or copy from all over the empire. They formed one of the great libraries of the ancient world, perhaps to be mentioned in the same breath with the much later libraries at Pergamon and Alexandria. Among the tablets were copies of the *Epic of Gilgamesh* and the Babylonian Flood story.

The Flood story was first translated by George Smith, a banknote engraver in London who also moonlighted as an amateur Assyriologist at the British Museum. It was in 1872, nearly twenty years after Rassam first found the tablets, that Smith began piecing together a large fragmentary tablet. He was astonished to realize that it was an account of a Great Flood, very similar to the Deluge account in the Hebrew Bible—the one that Noah had survived. In the account that Smith now held, which turned out to be the eleventh tablet from the *Epic of Gilgamesh*, the survivor was not Noah, but a man named Utnapishtim. When he announced his discovery at a meeting of the Society of Biblical Archaeology in December 1872, all of London was abuzz with excitement.

The problem, though, was that a big piece was missing from the middle of the tablet, right at the part where everything gets interesting. And so, the *Daily Telegraph*, one of the newspapers of the day, promised a thousand British pounds to anyone who would go look for the missing fragment. Smith himself decided to take them up on the offer, even though he had never been to Mesopotamia and had no training as an archaeologist. Within a week after he arrived at Nineveh, he found the missing piece.

How on earth could he have done that? It turns out that it was very simple. He reasoned that perhaps the workers who had found the other fragments had missed this big one. So, rather than digging into the mound again, he searched through the "back dirt pile," as it is called by archaeologists—that is, the huge artificial mound created by archaeologists and their workers when they dump out the earth while excavating a site.

The dirt in these piles should be devoid of ancient objects, but the pile at Nineveh was full of them, because the workers had dug so fast and were frequently careless in picking out the pieces that they came across, whether they were pottery or clay tablets. Not only did Smith find the missing piece that he had come for, but he found something like three hundred other pieces from clay tablets that the workers had also missed and thrown out. When he got back to London, the missing piece fit perfectly into his Flood tablet.

But this was only one of many accounts of a flood. Most recently, an Assyriologist at the British Museum, Irving Finkel, announced in 2014 that he had found another example of a different version of the Flood story. In this version, the survivor is a man named Atrahasis. What is interesting about Finkel's tablet is it appears to describe the ark as being round in shape, as opposed to the way that we usually think of it. The tablet is in a private collection. The owner first brought it to Finkel in 1985 but wouldn't leave it with him long enough for him to translate it. It was only in 2009 that Finkel was able to gain access again and began translating it.

⟨⟨•↠⟩⟨•↠⟩⟩

The nineteenth-century excavations at Nimrud, Nineveh, and Khorsabad, and then at Ur, Babylon, Nippur, Uruk, and other sites, began an era of excavation in the region that continues to this day. The archaeology and textual work done in Mesopotamia has shed light on the origins of Western-complex culture and the way such early beginnings largely shaped how our societies function today, from politics and laws to mathematics, medicine, education, taxes, and everything in between.

Looking back now at these early archaeologists, some scholars have discussed whether they should be considered as having been part and parcel of European colonialism at the time and therefore disparaged as part of a European effort to co-opt the history of nations other than their own, or if they were simply part of a competition or contest sponsored and underwritten by museums for their own gain. Even if those were the underlying motivations, however, the end result is that investigators like Layard, Botta, and others helped bring to light previously unknown, or unexcavated, civilizations such as the Assyrians, Babylonians, and Sumerians and contributed to enlarging our understanding of the origins of Western civilization. The additional question of whether such objects should now be returned to their countries of origin, which is a legitimate one, must also take into consideration the turmoil that has wracked the Middle East since at least the early 1990s and which continues today, from Iraq to Syria.

As recently as 1988, spectacular discoveries were made at Nimrud by local Iraqi archaeologists. There they uncovered the graves of several

Assyrian queens from the time of Assurnasirpal II in the ninth century BCE; the grave goods included incredible gold necklaces, earrings, and other treasures. These disappeared during the Second Gulf War but turned out to be hidden in a bank vault and have since been safely recovered and now published. Work elsewhere in the region has now resumed as well, after being suspended since the early 1990s. It will be interesting to see what the next century of archaeological expeditions uncovers.

5

EXPLORING THE JUNGLES
OF CENTRAL AMERICA

O NE OF THE MOST EXCITING DEVELOPMENTS IN RECENT
years within Maya studies took place in 2009. Using an
advanced LiDAR system installed in a twin-engine airplane, a
team of archaeologists was able to map the hidden Maya city of Caracol
in Belize. In only four days, they were able to successfully demonstrate
that a large area of what looked like impenetrable jungle actually contained buildings, roads, and other parts of a massive city that was completely hidden by the overgrowth.

The name LiDAR stands for "Light Detection and Ranging." It is a
remote-sensing technology that works like radar but uses light from a
laser to produce highly accurate measurements by bouncing the laser
beams off the ground and thereby creating three-dimensional images
with hundreds of thousands of data points. It usually is used from an
airplane and turns out to be especially useful in places like Central
America, because it can map through the trees in a jungle or rain forest
and provide images of lost temples, buildings, and even cities that are
totally overgrown.

The problem at all, or most, of these Maya sites is the forest of trees that grew over them and hid many of them from the outside world for so long. Even today, if the sites are not actively maintained and groomed for the hordes of tourists that visit, the forest would quickly reclaim the ruins. Still other cities remain hidden, which is why as recently as 2014 other research teams have continued to find other Maya cities that were completely overgrown elsewhere in the region. One of the researchers said that "in the jungle, you can be as little as 600 feet from a large site and not even suspect it might be there." LiDAR can change all of that, for not only can it help locate lost cities, but it can map the ones that we know of in a matter of days or even hours, instead of the weeks and months, or even years, that it usually takes.

≬≬

It was in the year 1750 that "a party of Spaniards traveling in the interior of Mexico . . . found, in the midst of a vast solitude, ancient stone buildings, the remains of a city." The Spanish explorers were no doubt stunned to see the huge buildings completely overgrown by vines and with trees growing through what had once been windows. We now know that they had found the Maya site of Palenque.

Although the news spread quickly, little official attention was paid to it. It was not until more than thirty years later, in 1784, that the king of Spain sent another explorer to investigate the rumors. Although additional Spanish expeditions visited the site over the next fifty years, and even though accounts were eventually published in English in 1822 and 1835, still few people noticed. As a result, the discovery of Palenque was overlooked by most of the Western world until 1841, when a US explorer named John Lloyd Stephens published an account of his own travels in the area and introduced it to a broad reading audience, less than a decade before Layard began publishing about the remains he was finding in Mesopotamia.

Stephens was astonished by the lack of attention that had been paid to Palenque before his book *Incidents of Travel* came out. After describing the initial discovery in 1750 and the subsequent investigations by the Spanish, he noted that "If a like discovery had been made in Italy, Greece, Egypt, or Asia, within the reach of European travel, it would have created an interest not inferior to the discovery of Herculaneum, or Pompeii, or the ruins of Paestum." His explorations of Central America with Frederick Catherwood, a British artist and architect, changed all that. Their journeys resulted in best-selling travel books, in which they reported on their discovery of several Maya sites, many of them previously unknown.

Stephens and Catherwood were by no means the first outsiders to have visited these sites, of course, and rather than doing much actual excavation, they explored, cleared away trees and underbrush, surveyed, and drew. But because of the accounts that they subsequently published, they brought the ruins of Central America to the attention of the outside world. In the process, they established the beginnings of what we now call New World archaeology. As one scholar has pointed out, all this was done thirty years before Heinrich Schliemann dug at Troy and more than eighty years before Howard Carter discovered King Tut.

Stephens had been trained in Greek and Latin as a very young student. He went to Columbia University when he was just thirteen years old. A lawyer by the time he was twenty, he didn't practice law for long. Instead, he began traveling across Europe and the Middle East, including Greece, Turkey, Egypt, and Jordan. He published an account of his journeys, which quickly became extremely popular, bringing him fame and fortune.

Catherwood was several years older than Stephens, but having formed a friendship, the two men decided to explore Central America together. Specifically, they wanted to search for ruins belonging to the civilization that we now call the Maya. And so, in 1839, they set off from the United States with a goal of visiting three ancient Mesoamerican sites that they had read about—Copán, Palenque, and Uxmal. They got to those and many more—nearly fifty cities, including one called Chichén Itzá—during two separate voyages of exploration.

The accounts of these expeditions were published as travel volumes in 1841 and 1843. Within them, Stephens described in detail not only the cities and buildings that they saw, but also the various illnesses that they suffered during their trips. Several times he mentioned the mosquitoes that gave them malaria and the burrowing insects that laid eggs under their toenails, as well as other unpleasant ailments, some of which were life-threatening. It seems amazing, after reading through their firsthand accounts, that they ever made it out of the jungle and back to the United States alive, let alone on two separate occasions.

Stephens was an astute observer—someone who could compare and contrast what he had seen in the Old World with what he was now discovering in the New World. From his previous experiences traveling in the Middle East, he was able to conclude—quite correctly—that cities like Copán and Palenque were not built by Egyptians or survivors of Atlantis, both of which had been suggested previously, but rather by the indigenous people of the area, the Maya.

After comparing and contrasting the pyramids, columns, and sculptures that he saw at Copán to those of the Egyptians, he wrote specifically, "unless I am wrong, we have a conclusion far more interesting and wonderful than that of connecting the buildings of these cities with the Egyptians or any other people. . . . Opposed as is my idea to all previous speculations, I am inclined to think that [the ruins] were constructed by the races who occupied the country at the time of the invasion by the Spaniards, or of some not very distant progenitors."

He and Catherwood faithfully recorded the hieroglyphics that were engraved on monuments at Copán and elsewhere. Stephens was convinced that, once they were decoded, these hieroglyphics would reveal the history of the Maya. He wrote, "One thing I believe: its history is graven on its monuments. No Champollion has yet brought to them the energies of his inquiring mind. Who shall read them?" He came back to this point again, writing "I cannot help believing that the . . . hieroglyphics will yet be read. . . . For centuries the hieroglyphics of Egypt were inscrutable, and, though not perhaps in our day, I feel persuaded that a key surer than that of the Rosetta stone will be discovered."

Stephens was referring to Jean-François Champollion, who deciphered Egyptian hieroglyphics by 1823 by studying the trilingual inscription on the Rosetta stone. He was completely correct—when the hieroglyphics engraved on the monuments were finally deciphered, they did turn out to record the history of the Maya, in all its gory detail. It took quite a long time—until just the past few decades in fact—for us to be able to read the inscriptions accurately, but now we know that the Maya were not quite so peaceful as we previously thought and that their history was as full of rivalries and wars as any other ancient civilization.

It took the concerted efforts of a number of individuals to crack the Mayan writing system, including an Englishman named Eric Thompson, a Russian American scholar named Tatiana Proskouriakoff, and a Ukrainian scholar named Yuri Knorosov. Thompson and Knorosov are usually described as bitter rivals, somewhat along the same lines as Jean-François Champollion and Thomas Young, when the French and British scholars were racing to see who would decipher Egyptian hieroglyphics first.

Thompson was the grand old man of Mayan hieroglyphic studies, with a major volume published in 1950. Proskouriakoff was the first to show that the hieroglyphics recorded historical dates and events. She was also able to identify specific women in the texts, as opposed to men. But it is now recognized that it was Knorosov, working in Stalinist Russia during the Cold War, who made the ultimate breakthrough in reading the texts, by making use of a manuscript on the Maya left to us by the sixteenth-century CE Spanish bishop Diego de Landa. Although de Landa's own understanding of Mayan writing was misguided, his manuscript served as an essential key to Knorosov. For that reason, de Landa's text has been called the Rosetta stone of Mayan hieroglyphs. This is especially ironic since de Landa is generally regarded as the man responsible for destroying most of the known Maya bark-fold books, which is why we have so few left today.

Some of the most recent and significant advances in reading Mayan hieroglyphics have been made in the past few decades by a US scholar named David Stuart. Born in 1965, he is the son of Mayanist George Stuart, who worked for the National Geographic Society for nearly forty years. David had been accompanying his parents to Maya ruins since he was a three-year-old toddler. By the age of eight, he was working on the hieroglyphs. By age ten, he was shadowing and helping the great Maya epigrapher Linda Schele during her work at Palenque.

By the time Stuart received his PhD in 1995, he had already published thirteen articles and monographs. He is still the youngest person and one of the few archaeologists ever to be awarded a MacArthur "genius" Fellowship, which he received when he was only eighteen. He's also one of the only people to have won both a MacArthur and a Guggenheim fellowship.

He is probably best known to the general public, however, for a book that he wrote in 2011, during the media frenzy about the supposed Maya prediction that the world would end in 2012 when the current Maya five-thousand-year calendrical cycle completed. He successfully showed that the Maya had not, in fact, been trying to predict when the world was going to end, but rather were simply placing a specific king's reign into a larger context or cycle of time.

It is thanks to all these individuals, and a handful of others, that John Lloyd Stephens's prediction came true. Mayan hieroglyphics have finally been deciphered, and the history of Copán and other Maya cities is indeed, as Stephens put it, "graven on its monuments."

We now know that at Copán, for instance, a UNESCO World Heritage site in Honduras, the Maya listed the names of sixteen of their rulers, covering a period of about four centuries, from 427 CE until a little after 810 CE. They are carved on Altar Q, a fairly small box-shaped stone, six feet wide by six feet long and standing four feet tall, with the rulers depicted four to a side. The founding king of this dynasty was a man known as "Great Sun Green Quetzal-Macaw." Although the site was primarily occupied from about 200–900 CE, these four centuries seem to have been the high point of its existence.

We also know, both from studies of the inscriptions found at various sites and the excavations of those sites themselves, much more about the rise and fall of the Maya. Archaeologists split the history of the Maya into several main periods. The earliest attempts at agriculture and the first villages date to the Archaic period, before 2000 BCE. The Preclassic period lasted from about 2000 BCE to 300 CE, with cities arising by about 750 BCE, and the Classic period stretched from approximately 300 CE to 900 CE. The Terminal Classic period, which saw the collapse of the complex cities of the Maya, makes up the last part of the Classic period, in about 800–900 CE, though the dates vary in different areas. It was followed by the Postclassic period, from about 900 CE until the arrival of the Spanish in the sixteenth century CE.

❦❦❦❦

Copán, which flourished during the Classic period, was one of the three cities that John Lloyd Stephens and Frederick Catherwood initially went looking for in November 1839. (They found all three cities.) Stephens claims to have purchased the entire site of Copán from its local owners for the relatively paltry sum of fifty dollars and thought seriously about how to ship all its monuments home, though he ended up simply having Catherwood draw them instead. However, the original contract has recently been found, and it seems that Stephens didn't really purchase the ancient site, but instead only leased it for a period of three years, which was far more time than Catherwood needed to draw the monuments.

Stephens and Catherwood spent a total of thirteen days at Copán, during which time they found fourteen inscribed standing stones. These are usually called *stelae* (*stele*, in the singular), the Greek word used by archaeologists to refer to an upright standing stone that has an inscription. Catherwood drew all the stelae they found at Copán, as well as Altar Q. Stephens had an inkling of what was depicted on Altar Q, for he describes the sixteen individuals pictured and mentions his suspicion that the hieroglyphics on which they were seated probably gave their name and office, which indeed they do. He was also quite correct in suggesting that the hieroglyphics on the altar "beyond doubt record some event in the history of the mysterious people who once inhabited the city."

Stephens and Catherwood cleared the undergrowth from other ruins at Copán, including the Temple of the Hieroglyphic Stairway and the Sacred Ball Court. The Hieroglyphic Stairway has sixty-three stairs climbing seventy-five feet up to the top of the temple, with at least twenty-two hundred hieroglyphs decorating its length. It is one of the longest Mayan texts known and appears to be a dynastic record. It was started by the unlucky thirteenth king of Copán, who was later captured in battle and beheaded while fighting a rival kingdom. It was doubled in length and completed by the fifteenth ruler in the eighth century CE, who also turned it into an odd bilingual text. The right-hand column contains Maya hieroglyphs, and the left-hand column has strange "Teotihuacán hieroglyphs" that seem to have no real meaning and are apparently more decorative than anything else.

The Ball Court is one of the best examples of its kind ever found at a Maya site, although the rules of the game are still debated. Some say it was played somewhat like soccer. One way to win was by getting the ball through a small ring, but the game ended if the ball touched either the ground or anyone's hands. And although the winners were often treated as heroes, some scholars have argued that the losers were sometimes put to death. Ball courts are found throughout Mesoamerica and were even exported to the US Southwest.

Since Stephens and Catherwood were at the site for less than two weeks, it was left to others to continue the exploration and excavations of Copán. Among them were a well-known amateur archaeologist named Alfred Maudslay, who arrived in the 1880s, and then a team from the Carnegie Institution in the mid-1930s.

After a break in their travels, Stephens and Catherwood went in search of Palenque in April 1840. Along the way, they had a chance to visit a site lost in the Guatemalan rain forest that was probably what we now know to be the major site of Tikal. Although they had heard rumors of its existence, and Stephens had figured out that they could allocate ten days to get there, map it, and get back, they opted instead to head for Palenque without further delay and thus missed visiting the site, which was left for others to discover.

Temple of the Grand Jaguar (Temple 1), Tikal

No doubt they later regretted this decision, especially after the announcement less than a decade later, in 1848, that Tikal had been located, right where they thought it would be. Had they gone when they had the opportunity to do so, they would have received credit for finding one of the largest Maya cities in the region, where as many as one hundred thousand Maya may have once lived. Other archaeologists and explorers came through soon afterward, but it was more than a century before the University of Pennsylvania conducted the first large archaeological project at the site, from 1956–1970.

Approximately three thousand buildings are still visible at the site, although many are still covered by the tropical forest. They include temples and palaces, dating to the Classic period of 200–900 CE, with most built during the final three centuries. George Stuart, the National Geographic archaeologist, estimated that there may be another ten thousand buildings from earlier periods still to be found at Tikal. It is now a national park, in addition to being named as a UNESCO World Heritage Site in 1979.

There are six temple pyramids at Tikal, including Temple 1, called the Temple of the Grand Jaguar. Within the temple, the tomb of the great Maya ruler who built it was found in 1962. His name is frequently translated as Lord Chocolate. He ruled Tikal for fifty-two years, on either side of 700 CE. Within his grave were found pieces of jade, shell ornaments, and ceramic vessels originally filled with food and drink. There were also some unusual carved bones, with scenes that appear to be from a Maya creation story. In addition to all the buildings, ten reservoirs also were found at the site, which provided the city with its drinking water.

Stephens and Catherwood were by no means the first Europeans to look for Palenque, of course. Their entire journey to the region had been sparked by the brief accounts that they had read about that lost city, which had been translated into English from reports filed by various Spanish explorers. Several of the reports attributed the massive ruins to the Egyptians, but at least one—written by the explorer Dupaix, who had also been to Copán during his explorations—concluded that Palenque had been built by people from Atlantis. Such hypotheses began from the erroneous assumption that the poor Maya natives living in small villages nearby could not possibly be the descendants of the same folks who built these magnificent structures; they must have been built by a people known to the Europeans, that is, Egyptians, Romans, Atlanteans, and the like. Stephens was going against such opinions when he declared that Palenque, and the other ruins, had been built by the indigenous Maya, seeing no reason to involve people from elsewhere.

After a difficult journey, Stephens and Catherwood finally reached Palenque, in southern Mexico, in May 1840. They were able to spend three weeks at the site, clearing away the trees and jungle growth in order to draw the standing monuments and buildings, including the so-called Palace, the Temple of the Cross, and the large ball court.

Among the structures that they uncovered was one that we now call the Temple of the Inscriptions, which stood on top of an eighty-foot-tall stone pyramid. The temple is justifiably famous for the three huge tablets with more than six hundred hieroglyphics on them, the second-longest inscription known from the Maya world. Stephens was certain that the hieroglyphics were identical in nature to the ones they had seen at Copán, and so he had Catherwood copy them exactly, in case a future scholar could decipher them, which is precisely what eventually happened.

It wasn't as easy as it sounds. The description that Stephens gave of what they had to do first, in order for Catherwood to produce his drawings, gives us some idea of the effort involved. He says, "When we first saw them, [the tablets] were covered with a thick coat of green moss, and it was necessary to wash and scrape them, clear the lines with a stick, and scrub them thoroughly. . . . On account of the darkness of the corridor from the thick shade of the trees growing before it, it was necessary to burn candles or torches, and to throw a strong light upon the stones while Mr. Catherwood was drawing."

Unbeknownst to them, the eighty-foot-tall pyramid on which the Temple of the Inscriptions stood also served as the burial place for Lord Pacal, who ruled at Palenque for almost seventy years, from 615 to 683 CE. Like King Tut in Egypt almost two thousand years earlier, Pacal also came to the throne as a child; but unlike Tut, he lived and ruled to a ripe old age. Pacal's tomb was not found until 1952, more than a century after Stephens and Catherwood had explored the site, and exactly thirty years after Howard Carter had discovered Tut's tomb.

It was a Mexican archaeologist named Alberto Ruz Lhuillier who discovered the tomb. He became curious about a stone slab in the floor of the Temple of the Inscriptions, at the very top of the pyramid. The slab had a double row of circular depressions with stone plugs in them, which he figured were meant to help remove the slab. He did exactly that, revealing a stairway completely filled with rubble, which led down into the supporting pyramid. It took his team several years to clear the long stairwell and reach the bottom eighty feet below where they had started, where they found Pacal's tomb. Essentially, the tomb is at ground level, but inside the pyramid. It is now thought that the tomb was built first and then the pyramid was constructed around it.

Pacal himself was laid to rest within a limestone coffin or sarcophagus that is thirteen feet long. It has a complicated carving on its lid depicting Pacal descending to the underworld. At first the archaeologists didn't realize that the lid covered a sarcophagus. They thought the whole structure was a solid stone altar, with the carving on the top of the altar. It was only when they drilled a small exploratory hole in the stone that they realized it was hollow, not solid.

Within the sarcophagus, in which Pacal's skeleton rested undisturbed, a jade mask was found still on his face, where it had been placed thirteen hundred years ago. An amazing number of other jade objects also were found, including necklaces, ear ornaments, a diadem and a ring, pectorals, wristlets, two statuettes, and a belt. The skeletons of six other people, who had apparently been sacrificed in order to accompany Pacal into the afterlife, were found with his body.

In 1987 Palenque was declared a UNESCO World Heritage Site. It has been a magnet for more recent explorers and archaeologists as well, including discoveries of new buildings and burials from 1993 to 2000. Among the discoveries is the so-called Red Queen, who was found in 1994 with a tremendous cache of grave goods within an elaborate chamber in Temple XIII. This temple is close to Pacal's burial pyramid and it has been suggested that the Red Queen may have been Pacal's wife, who died about ten years before he did. The Palenque Mapping Project was also busy at the site during 1998–2000, surveying and mapping the buildings, including some that were still hidden in the forest.

From Palenque, Stephens and Catherwood continued to the third site on their list, called Uxmal. Soon thereafter, though, they called a halt to their explorations because Catherwood became quite ill. They had both suffered terribly during the journey, with recurring bouts of malaria for each of them. They had been gone for ten months and it was time to go home to New York. Although this involved another series of adventures, including almost dying on the ship sailing for home, they returned to the United States in July 1840, and Stephens promptly published a two-volume set of their adventures, complete with illustrations by Catherwood. It appeared in June 1841. By that December, twenty thousand copies had been sold, at the relatively affordable price of five dollars for the two-volume set.

Soon they made plans to return for a second time to the Yucatán region, leaving in October 1841, just four months after the release of their book. This time they were gone for eight months, eventually returning to the United States in June 1842, and with the volumes describing this second voyage appearing by February 1843.

The highlight of this second journey was their exploration of the site of Chichén Itzá, near the tip of the Yucatán peninsula. They spent eighteen days there, hiring local workers to help them remove the trees, underbrush, and other debris from a number of buildings at the site, including the Temple of the Jaguars, the Temple of the Warriors, the Pyramid of Kukulkan, and the Platform of Venus. The stairway at Kukulkan, also known as El Castillo, is formed in such a way that the shadow of a giant serpent can be seen at the spring equinox; it is visited by thousands of tourists each year.

Some of these, such as the Temple of the Jaguars and the Temple of the Warriors, contain murals and scenes depicting the conquest of this area by the Toltecs, led by Topiltzin Quetzalcoatl. The Toltecs were a group of newcomers who arrived from Mexico during the last two centuries of occupation at the site, around 1000–1200 CE. The murals indicate that the invaders first arrived by sea and beat the Maya defenders, who came out to meet them in canoes. They then fought a great battle against those same Maya and defeated them again.

At the site is also an astronomical observatory; a long stone "skull rack" featuring a number of skulls carved in stone, undoubtedly to simulate real ones; and a huge ball court, which is the largest in Mesoamerica and which Stephens described at length. Many of these structures date from the time of the Toltec occupation at the site, replacing or built in addition to the earlier Maya structures, for Chichén Itzá flourished later than most of the other Maya sites, reaching its peak in 800–1200 CE, partly because of the arrival of the Toltecs during the midpoint of the period.

Although Stephens and Catherwood visited the site in 1841–1842, and Maudslay came to see it in 1886, it wasn't until Edward Thompson came to the site in 1895 that Chichén Itzá began to be explored systematically. Thompson's excavations covered a period of thirty years. It then took almost another century before it was named a UNESCO World Heritage Site in 1988.

Thompson's excavations included dredging one of the cenotes at the site. For those readers who were unfamiliar with cenotes, Stephens gave a good definition in his book, describing them as "immense circular holes, from sixty to two hundred feet in diameter, with broken, rocky, perpendicular sides from fifty to one hundred feet deep, and having at the bottom a great body of water." There were two at Chichén Itzá, of which he says one was "the largest and wildest we had seen." He describes it as being in the middle of a thick forest, with a "mysterious influence" pervading it. He was well aware of the tradition that human victims had been thrown into it and identified one building right on the edge as "perhaps the place from which the victims were thrown into the dark well beneath."

During the dredging and exploration of this cenote by Thompson and others, human remains were indeed found, including the skeletons of at least fifty victims—young women, men, and a number of children. Objects of jade and gold disks also were found, as were copper bells and other items. It is clear that sacrifices of many kinds were made at this cenote over the years. The sacrifices were not just by the Maya, for many of the objects are of later Toltec manufacture.

꡷꡷꡷꡷

There are numerous other Maya cities, both large and small, that we could also describe, but these four—Copán, Tikal, Palenque, and Chichén Itzá—are fairly representative overall. Although we now know a lot about the Maya and their civilization, what is still a mystery is why it came to an end just after 900 CE, with all or most of the great sites abandoned and subsequently overgrown and lost to the rest of the world. A favorite suggestion has been that they were unable to deal with a century-long drought—that is, climate change—but this is by no means certain. Numerous other hypotheses also have been put forward, including explanations that involve overpopulation and deforestation. But there may not even be a single answer, and it would take an entire book to discuss the various possibilities for the collapse of the Maya. The one thing that is clear at the moment is that, for this mystery to be resolved once and for all, more investigation—and quite possibly more excavation—is definitely needed.

What we can say, though, is that the discovery of the Maya represents the first detection of a previously unknown civilization by archaeologists in the New World. The Spanish already knew about the Inca and the Aztecs, but the Maya were unfamiliar to the general public until the explorations by John Lloyd Stephens and Frederick Catherwood. Their publications challenged the assumption that Native Americans were simply poor villagers deserving of conquest by more advanced Europeans and that they were incapable of achievements along the lines of the Egyptians, Greeks, and Romans. Subsequent investigations have resulted in the successful translation of their extensive written records and have shown that they were as complex (and bloody) politically, militarily, and culturally as the better-known civilizations of the Old World.

DIGGING DEEPER I

HOW DO YOU KNOW
WHERE TO DIG?

HAVING SPENT THE PREVIOUS CHAPTERS DISCUSSING SOME
of the earliest archaeological discoveries made around the
world, from Egypt to Central America, I'd like to change
gears for a moment. This interlude will be the first of several scattered
throughout the book, in which I will address the questions that I am
most frequently asked about how archaeologists do their job. Archaeology is both a technique and a craft and knowing how it is done is part
of its story as well.

For instance, we are often asked, "How do you know where to dig?"
That's a great question that bears on some of the essential tools and
methods archaeologists employ. In this chapter, we'll answer that question by discussing archaeological surveying—that is, the process of
looking for sites on the ground surface, because some are obvious, but
others are not. Surface survey also can help us to figure out where to dig
at an already known site.

First and foremost, though, we need to define what we mean by a site, because they come in all shapes and sizes. For example, the Agora in Athens and huge mounds like Megiddo in Israel, both of which I've excavated at, are clearly ancient sites. But others can be tiny and very hard to find. As Fagan and Durrani point out, a site can be as small as "a tiny scatter of hunter-gatherer artifacts" or as large as the ancient city of Teotihuacán in Mexico; they are simply "places where traces of past human activity are to be found . . . normally identified by the presence of artifacts."

We should also define what an artifact is—and isn't. Quite simply, artifacts make up most of the "good stuff" that is worth writing home about when on an excavation or a survey—they are things made or altered by human beings. Within this category, we include everything from the earliest stone tools to pottery, weapons, jewelry, clothes, and pretty much everything else portable that humans can make. Some artifacts, however, and things associated with them, can't be moved. We call these *features*. And so, something like a ditch is a feature—it's obviously made by a human, but you can't move it without losing it. The same goes for doorways, fire pits, stone altars, and other similar items. Sometimes, though, we also call something a feature when we're just not quite sure yet what it is, but we know it's a "something." That's why we say, "One stone is a stone; two stones is a feature; three stones is a wall."

❈→❈ ❈→❈

There are several ways to find sites, but almost all involve conducting what we call archaeological surveys. Within this broad category are ground surveys, aerial surveys, remote sensing, and sample surveys, most of which we will touch upon in this interlude. In all instances, the goal is to find sites that lie within a specific area, like the region around Pylos in southern Greece, where I once surveyed.

The traditional way to do a ground survey is to have team members physically walk the area in question and see what remains are there. These are frequently called reconnaissance surveys or full-coverage surveys, but they also can be referred to as pedestrian surveys, for obvious reasons. In some areas, however, like regions of the northeastern United

States where it can be nearly impossible to see things because of the vegetation, ground surveys are sometimes conducted by digging small shovel-test pits every few yards, to see whether there is any evidence of artifacts beneath the ground. The density of objects that turn up determines whether these areas can be mapped as a site or not.

Ground surveys first began to be popular in the 1960s and 1970s and then gained traction in the 1980s, in part because they are usually a cheaper alternative to digging and can cover larger areas. They also allow archaeologists to ask and answer different types of questions than when digging a single site, since they frequently involve multiple sites. For instance, someone may want to investigate how intensively a specific area in Greece was occupied during the Bronze Age and later periods—the Dark Ages, Archaic and Classical Greece, Roman and Byzantine periods, and the Turkish Ottoman age. Did the settlement pattern change during the following eras? Can the number of sites and their size tell us the relative population of various time periods? Can changes in where people settled tell us about what resources they were using, how dangerous their environment was, what the political situation was like?

Ground surveys can help provide answers for these kinds of questions. By doing surveys and identifying the various sites from different periods in the area, it is frequently possible to construct a history of the region without ever digging at a single site. Many surveys lead into an excavation afterward, though, especially when the archaeologists decide to concentrate on one of the promising new sites that they have just found and get a permit to dig.

Times have now changed and these days, instead of always beginning with a ground survey, it sometimes makes more sense to start with aerial surveys, at least in areas where the ancient inhabitants erected buildings or otherwise left remains made from durable materials that might still be discernible. This can be as simple as buying aerial photographs or satellite images from specific companies or as complicated and expensive as arranging for overhead flights using LiDAR to survey your area.

If you want to buy imagery, which is by far the easiest way to go, there are a few options. One possibility is to purchase declassified military satellite images like the ones taken by the Corona program. The

Corona program was a surveillance operation conducted by US intelligence agencies from 1960 to 1972. Images from the program were declassified by an executive order in 1995 and are now used for all sorts of purposes, including finding archaeological sites. Sites can sometimes be seen very clearly even in these older images, either with the naked eye, by enlarging it on a computer screen, or by looking at it with a magnifying glass.

Older photos like these can be very valuable. Aerial photos for warfare, spying, or general reconnaissance have been taken for one hundred years. Some of them are useful in part because they were taken before recent economic development or urban expansion destroyed or damaged archaeological sites. One of the earliest examples is that of John Bradford, an archaeologist who was serving in the British army during World War II. In 1943, while studying photographs taken by the Royal Air Force for military purposes, he was able to locate more than two thousand Etruscan burial mounds in northern Italy, simply from the differences in color of the grass or soil visible in the pictures.

Subsequently, Bradford joined forces in 1956 with an Italian engineer from Milan named Carlo Lerici and, from 1957 onward, they explored many of the Etruscan tombs that Bradford had first identified on the aerial photographs by drilling into the earth with a small high-speed auger or drill at these locations. Initially they inserted a hollow pipe with a small spy camera inside and took photographs of the interior of the tombs, but soon they developed what is known as the Lerici periscope, which was specially designed with a powerful light that could fit into the narrow hole that had been drilled. This instrument helped them to quickly look inside the tombs without having to wait for photographic film to be developed, and to identify which tombs had already been looted, in either antiquity or in modern times, and which still contained ancient remains and even frescoes painted on the walls. In this way they were able to investigate several hundred tombs per season without excavating or damaging them in any way.

There is also the option of getting up-to-the-minute high-resolution contemporary color satellite images from companies like DigitalGlobe or images that have been taken from the space shuttle. For example, there's a fairly well-known picture of the ancient city of Angkor in

Cambodia that was taken from the space shuttle *Endeavor*, in which all the buildings that are still standing can be seen very clearly.

My colleague Sarah Parcak, who is a National Geographic explorer and associate professor at the University of Alabama, but is perhaps better known as the "space archaeologist" and winner of the $1 million TED Prize in 2016, surveys using satellite images. The images allow her to use all kinds of fancy techniques, like infrared imaging, to illuminate some features and suppress others. Using these techniques, she found several hundred previously undiscovered sites in Egypt, including seventeen lost pyramids as well as the nearly legendary site of Tanis, all of which were "hiding in plain sight," as she puts it.

Such new techniques with satellite imagery have enhanced our ability to see things that were previously essentially invisible, including ancient paths crisscrossing a desert. That's how the lost city of Ubar in Oman was found in 1992. *Endeavor* had taken a picture of the area and archaeologists noticed where the ancient paths converged. They subsequently excavated there and found the ancient site.

Buried walls, earthworks, and other large constructions associated with settlements often can be seen more easily from the air than they can be seen on the ground, even if one is walking right over them. In a raking light, or if an aerial photograph is taken at a slight angle, shadows cast by buried walls are sometimes visible. More commonly, aerial photos can illuminate "crop marks." Crop marks document the location of buried items precisely, whether they are features like ditches or structures like buildings and walls. The simple reason is that those buried items affect the amount of water absorbed by the soil, and thus the color and height of the vegetation that is growing directly above them. This won't work if there is something built on top of them, like a modern parking lot, but it will work in a field where grass, wheat, barley, or thick weeds are growing.

If there is a buried ditch below the modern surface, the vegetation growing directly above it will be higher and lusher than the surrounding vegetation, because there are more water and nutrients in the soil right there. If there is a buried wall below the modern surface, on the other hand, the vegetation growing directly above it will be lower, less dense, and less lush than the surrounding vegetation, because there are fewer nutrients in the soil at that location.

These differences in height and density might be almost imperceptible at ground level, but from the air they are immediately obvious at certain times of the year. In England and in Europe, especially in Italy, crop marks that are about three feet wide and run straight as an arrow across the fields indicate the presence of buried Roman roads. Others that are round, like the ones that John Bradford saw in the Royal Air Force photographs of northern Italy, may indicate the presence of buried tombs.

I often amuse myself when I'm on a flight that is landing somewhere in Europe by looking out the window of the airplane as we are descending and trying to see if I can discern any crop marks in the fields surrounding the airport. It's amazing how many times I've seen something that I'd love to go back and excavate, in order to figure out what it was.

At one point, in January 2010, Sarah Parcak and I bought some Quickbird satellite imagery of the area surrounding Megiddo in Israel, just as an experiment to see what we might be able to locate by using her new methods of analysis. Almost immediately we saw the outlines of what looked like a large building in a field right next to the ancient mound, precisely where an Israeli archaeologist named Yotam Tepper previously suggested that the Sixth Roman Legion—Legio VI Ferrata (the "Ironclads")—had built their camp in the second century CE.

When we compared the outlines to other known sites and buildings, we found an almost perfect match with other Roman camps, like those that were built around the site of Masada when the Romans besieged it back in 73 or 74 CE. It was clear to us that we must be looking at the site of Legio, where the Sixth Legion had its headquarters, and that Tepper had been correct.

We shared the images with Tepper and Matt Adams, the director of the Jezreel Valley Regional Project, and when they began excavating in that field in 2013 and then again in 2015, after first conducting additional remote-sensing work, including ground-penetrating radar and electromagnetic surveys, they immediately came down upon the remains of ditches and walls, along with Roman period coins, bits of scale armor, and—most important—fragments of roof tiles. The tiles were stamped with the legion's insignia, thus confirming that this was indeed their camp.

As mentioned above, archaeologists have also added LiDAR to their toolkit. It's most useful in places like Central America or Southeast Asia, because it can see through the trees in a jungle or rain forest, by the firing of lasers at the ground, and provide images of lost temples, buildings, and even cities that are completely overgrown and almost inaccessible now, like the Maya city of Caracol in Belize that was found in 2010.

In June 2016 archaeologists working in Cambodia announced that they had found "previously undocumented medieval cities not far from the ancient temple city of Angkor Wat . . . that promise to upend key assumptions about south-east Asia's history." The cities are between nine hundred and fourteen hundred years old and were found by Australian archaeologist Damian Evans, who used LiDAR data captured by an instrument mounted in a helicopter during an aerial survey in 2015 that fully covered 734 square miles. Evans believes that "the colossal, densely populated cities would have constituted the largest empire on earth at the time of its peak in the 12th century." Other archaeologists agree with his assessment, saying that these are the most significant archaeological discoveries in the region in the past century.

LiDAR also is useful in areas without tremendous amounts of vegetation and has been used to map the site of Jezreel in northern Israel and is yet another way to locate Roman roads in England. We've also used it at ground level at our site at Tel Kabri in Israel to quickly and accurately record the wine cellar that we found in 2013, which I described at the beginning of this book.

Most recently, archaeologists have added commercial drones to their toolkit as well, flying the drones much as hobbyists fly model airplanes, both to find and document sites and to detect looting. From them, it is possible to take either low- or high-level photos of a region, sometimes sending the results directly to a computer for future manipulation and analysis.

There are other remote-sensing techniques that are ground-based and can help to figure out whether there is something under the ground where one might want to dig. They include electronic resistivity or conductivity, which basically works by running an electric current through the ground between two poles. If there is something like a buried wall in the way, it will interrupt the current; if there isn't, it won't be interrupted. The end result is a rather fuzzy picture of what is below ground, but often it is not clear exactly how *far* below the surface the ancient remains are or even if the images are being interpreted correctly.

This is where something called "ground truthing" comes in. Ground truthing means double-checking or confirming what has been spotted in the photographs or remote-sensing images to make certain it is real or has been properly interpreted. It frequently involves foot surveys or actual excavation. Thus, at our site of Tel Kabri in northern Israel, electric conductivity images taken in 2003 indicated that there were probably walls in the area that we were interested in, and so in 2005 we went to ground-truth the area by excavating to see whether they were accurate. It took us more than two weeks of digging through totally sterile soil (that is, with nothing in it at all) before we came upon the walls and floors belonging to our Canaanite palace, but they were there—fully six feet below the present surface.

The same principles work with magnetometers, which measure the magnetic field in areas that are of interest to archaeologists. If there are buildings or ditches or other archaeological features that are buried underground, they may show up on a magnetometer reading, because such features affect the magnetic field in the area.

The limitations of these techniques are the same. Although they show anomalies below the surface that stand out from the general soil, it can be difficult to pin down whether the anomalies match certain kinds of subsurface structures. The consistency of soil below the surface can also determine whether the anomalies can stand out against it and the readings don't always let you know how deep the features are located. Different methods might give results that look different. In each case, excavation is needed to confirm what the remote-sensing device identifies.

For some or all of these reasons, our attempts to use a magnetometer at Tel Kabri in Israel failed rather miserably, most likely because of the nature of the soil that we have at the site. On the other hand, at David Schloen's excavations at Zincirli in Turkey, a magnetometer survey worked so well that the results look like a photograph of excavated ruins, except that the ruins are still buried and haven't yet been excavated. As mentioned earlier, the excavators at Troy tried several types of magnetometers before they finally found one kind—a cesium magnetometer—that yielded results. They were then able to map an entire lower town at Troy, buried under the agricultural fields around the mound. Teams had been excavating the mound since the days of Schliemann in the late 1800s, but nobody had thought to excavate in the fields next to it, because it looked like nothing was there. But remember also that in their early days they failed to ground-truth the images of the supposed wall encircling Troy, which turned out to be a large ditch instead.

Troy is not the only place where ground truthing should have been done before releasing reports to the media. Another common remote-sensing technique is ground-penetrating radar, which works exactly as it sounds, by having radar signals bounce back up from buried objects. The newest versions of this technique are extremely powerful and can "see" down nearly four meters (about thirteen feet). This has resulted in some incredible discoveries from the area of Stonehenge in England in 2014 and 2015, including the fact that Stonehenge was apparently once a complete circle.

Here, using ground-penetrating radar, as well as magnetometers and other remote-sensing techniques, archaeologists have been involved in something called the Stonehenge Hidden Landscapes Project. According to media reports, in just a few years of work, they have detected

Tractor and ground-penetrating radar, near Stonehenge

Bronze Age burial mounds, Iron Age shrines, and enclosures for cows and other livestock that date to either the Bronze Age or Iron Age, none of which had ever been noticed before.

Most exciting were the reports in September 2014 that they also had found another monument of standing stones at Durrington Walls, which is less than two miles from Stonehenge and which probably dates to about the same time—that is, forty-five hundred years ago. Apparently dwarfing Stonehenge in size and therefore dubbed Superhenge, it was thought to be a C-shaped enclosure created by more than fifty—and perhaps as many as ninety—giant stones, each about ten to fifteen feet long and five feet in diameter. None was visible, since they appeared to have been deliberately buried horizontally about three feet below the surface, which is why they hadn't been spotted before. It was only through remote-sensing techniques that they were first detected and reported.

Two years later, however, in 2016, additional reports in the media noted that trial excavations had been conducted in the interim, in order to ground-truth the remote-sensing images by digging to reveal two of the huge stones. What the archaeologists found instead surprised them—no giant stones, but rather two enormous pits that may have once held huge timber posts. The posts are no longer present, for they had been removed at some point—if they were ever there—and the pits filled in with chalk rubble. The remote-sensing instruments had registered the rubble as solid rock, giving rise to the original reports of "giant stones" instead of the debris-filled pits that they actually were. If the same is true of all the other reported stones as well, then we have the same situation as at Troy where the "fortification wall" turned out to be a filled-in ditch. Some media reports are now calling Superhenge a timber circle complex five hundred meters in diameter, but note that it was never completed. Whether that is correct remains to be seen, but the sequence of events has become a cautionary tale and we should wait until the archaeologists have completed their work and published their findings in a peer-reviewed journal before further assumptions and hypotheses are made.

Although there have been big advances made in remote sensing in the past couple of decades, sometimes satellite imagery and other high-tech solutions don't help at all in a search for sites. In those cases, archaeologists must resort to the tried-and-true methods of finding archaeological sites on foot. Sometimes this is as simple as taking advantage of the natural erosion that has taken place and keeping a sharp eye out while walking through potential areas. That, for instance, is how Donald Johanson found the first remains of Lucy in 1974, as we shall see.

Other times, it might be a better idea to conduct an organized ground survey, in which sites, structures, features, and artifacts can be seen directly on the ground. These techniques go back to the origins of archaeology and were made more systematic in the 1960s and 1970s. We used these methods on the two archaeological surveys in Greece that I participated in, as well as a survey in Israel, so I can attest to exactly what's involved when doing a site survey in one of these areas. These kinds of surveys are conducted throughout the world, limited only by visibility of materials on the ground and by permission of the landowners.

⁂ ⁂

There are two types of ground surveys that are used in certain areas of the world. As has been mentioned, one type is conducted on a large scale and is intended to cover large areas quickly; this is the reconnaissance or full-coverage survey. The goal of these surveys is to create a map showing the location of possible ancient sites in a large landscape. The other type is an intensive survey that usually involves the examination of a single site or a small area that was initially discovered during the larger survey and flagged as being particularly promising. In this case, the goal is to be able to identify as much as possible about the specifics of the location—its extent, age, cultural affiliation, and range of material objects—often as a prelude to excavation. The archaeologists will do a very detailed investigation of the site or a small area that may involve picking up and bringing back to the camp every single artifact that they find there.

Archaeologists working in an area where no comprehensive map exists of ancient sites from different time periods will start with a general reconnaissance survey. If done systematically and on foot, by having the team members painstakingly walk over every square meter of the area, it is called a full-coverage survey. This is what we did in the region of Boeotia near the city of Thebes in Greece back in the early 1980s, and again near the Mycenaean palace of Pylos in the early 1990s.

At Pylos, we were split into three teams of about six people each. I was in charge of Team A, which we promptly renamed The A-Team. At first we were assigned to survey the mountain heights on one side of the valley, despite my protestations that I was afraid of heights. Sure enough, on the very first day, as we began our survey, I froze. I had to be man-handled back to the car from one sheer drop. It was hardly an auspicious start for the team or the team leader. Later we were able to move lower and I had no problems from then on, but I learned a valuable lesson that I still draw on to this day—listen to your team members, especially if they tell you about a phobia that might affect their duties.

Once we started to get into the swing of things, we got our routine down. First we would find our location on a contemporary map, usually a readily discernible item such as a road. This is much easier today with GPS systems. We would then spread out, about thirty feet (nine meters) apart, so that we covered a total of about one hundred eighty feet (fifty-five meters, give or take). When I shouted or blew a whistle, each person would start walking forward in the designated direction and walk in a straight line until reaching a specific predetermined point, usually another road or a boundary wall that also was marked on the map. This meant walking about the length of an US football field at a time—about a hundred yards or meters—because more than that became complicated.

This is what is known in archaeological surveying terms as walking a transect. And when I say walking in a straight line, I mean quite literally walking in a straight line, regardless of whether that meant fording a stream, rappelling, or falling down a small cliff, or facing down a bull or a local farmer with a shotgun who didn't want us on the land. All those things happened, either to me or to other people on our team, but what was much more frequent was ripping our legs to shreds, even through our pants, because we had to walk right through the under-brush, which in Greece is known as the "macchi." That stuff can be nasty.

While we walked, we scoured the ground, looking for pottery sherds, stone tools and flakes, ancient walls, or anything else that might have marked the remains of an ancient settlement. By the way, it's always easy to identify someone who has just spent several weeks on an archaeological survey, because they're always the ones who spot the pennies and other loose change on the ground when they get back to civilization.

Each team member carries a clicker and clicks once every time they see a pottery sherd, a worked piece of stone, or another type of artifact. Three pieces of pottery get three clicks, five pieces get five, and so on. At the end of every ten steps or so, each team member writes down the number that is on their clicker, which is the number of artifacts they saw during that small section, resets it to zero, and starts walking and counting again. By the time they have reached the end point of the transect, they have a record of the number of the artifacts that they saw during each stage of the hundred-yard walk.

Why is that important? Durable items like pottery, stone, and metal are common on the surface from archaeological structures below the ground, brought there by farming, erosion, rodents, irrigation ditches, pits, and a host of other natural and human processes. When walking across a site that was inhabited in Bronze Age, Iron Age, Roman, and Byzantine times, you will see potsherds and stone tools from all those periods simply lying on the ground. If the numbers are recorded via a clicker, they will increase astronomically as you enter the boundaries of the site. After exiting the boundary of the site on the other side, the numbers will decrease again.

The clicker counts for a team member, again recording the number of pieces of pottery and worked stone seen every ten paces or so, will be something like this: 1, 5, 25, 107, 510, 423, 298, 152, 87, 0. And the numbers for the people immediately adjacent to the team member, on either side, will probably be similar, because they are likely to have walked across that same site. Those further out, however, if their transect did not cross the site, will have normal "background scatter" of artifact counts, for example, 1, 6, 4, 12, 0, 5, 3, 8, 5, 0.

The team members give their numbers to the team leader, who records them in a notebook and marks the probable site on the map, so that the follow-up team can find it again and examine it more thoroughly. And then, the team members spread out again to cover the next section. Again they march a predetermined distance, clicking as they go, repeating the process again and again, until they reach the end of the designated area. They then swing around, spread out once again, and return the way that they came, covering the next segment in the transect, and repeating the process over and over. In this way, a team can traverse and record all of the sites in a square mile or kilometer or whatever they choose each day, until the whole region has been covered.

Back at camp, the results of each day's survey are recorded, and from these results a map of potential sites is developed. The most promising of the new possible sites then receive a visit from a team of experienced surveyors, who are tasked with doing an intensive survey of the newly discovered area. The surveyors record the surface finds more carefully and collect representative objects from the site to document it for future researchers. In our case, the objects consisted mostly of pottery sherds that, because of their size, location on a pot, manufacture techniques, or decoration, helped the pottery experts on the team figure out what periods they came from.

Those are the survey methods that we used near Pylos in the 1990s—and the same methods are often employed today elsewhere in the world. But if the ground is covered with a thick coating of leaves, as in thickly forested areas, or if natural processes have covered the ancient land-scape with more recent soil, or if the ancient people did not construct large structures of durable material, which is the case in the northeast-ern United States, survey techniques will differ. Places where objects were made from wood, fiber, or other perishable materials also don't work for this kind of survey. Thus, although pedestrian surveys are widely employed in the eastern United States along river floodplains where farmers have been plowing the fields, they are not used in heavily wooded areas.

When the size of the region is too large for a full-coverage survey, there are techniques to cover only specific portions, or randomly chosen portions, of an area. Here, the areas to explore are often derived from sampling techniques used in statistics and are called sample surveys.

There is one other type of ground survey to mention. This is a targeted type of survey, which involves only revisiting sites that have been previously discovered. It is the type of survey that we did in the area around Tel Kabri in northern Israel during 2006 and 2007. We had already done some preliminary digging at the site in 2005 and had determined that we wanted to start a long-term multiseason excavation. First, though, we wanted to understand its context—what did the area around Tel Kabri look like before, during, and after its hey-day in the Middle Bronze Age, almost four thousand years ago?

Fortunately, it was easy for us to do such a targeted survey of known sites because the western Galilee, where Kabri is located, has been investigated previously by several teams of archaeologists doing full-coverage surveys in almost every season and under almost every condition imaginable during the past thirty years or more. We already had maps of the area, with all the known Middle Bronze Age sites marked on them. We also had access to the pottery and other artifacts that had been collected and stored by the previous teams of archaeologists.

Maps and survey reports in hand, we drove to the sites that were already known and simply did an intensive survey of each site around Tel Kabri and its hinterland. Our goal was to confirm and refine the dates previously assigned to the sites. We also wanted to recheck how large (or small) each site was. In the end, we were able to produce a map showing the sites that were inhabited in the area just before, during, and after the time that Kabri had flourished as a major center almost four thousand years ago.

And so, the answer to the question posed at the beginning of this interlude, "How do you know where to dig?," boils down to one word—*surveying*—because once an area has been surveyed, it's pretty easy to decide where you want to dig. As to *how* one actually digs, that's a whole different story, which we will discuss in another interlude.

PART 2

AFRICA, EUROPE, AND THE LEVANT: EARLY HOMININS TO FARMERS

DISCOVERING OUR EARLIEST ANCESTORS

I N 2015, THE OCTOBER ISSUE OF *NATIONAL GEOGRAPHIC* magazine featured a story about an exciting discovery made by Lee Berger and his team in a South African cave called Rising Star. After being notified by two recreational cavers that they had seen bones covering a floor deep within the cave, Berger's team began investigating and eventually found more than fifteen hundred bones from at least fifteen individuals, which he thinks belong to a previously unknown hominin species. They have been named *Homo naledi*, after the cave in which they were found. *Naledi* means "star" in the Sesotho language, and *hominin*, a term used throughout this chapter, refers to modern humans, extinct human species, and all of our immediate ancestors.

The bones may be up to 2.8 million years old. They were all found in the almost-inaccessible chamber in the cave in 2013 and 2014, after the two spelunkers showed Berger how to get there. As Jamie Shreeve of *National Geographic* describes it, this required going through a passageway known as Superman's Crawl, which is less than ten inches high and can be traversed only if you hold one arm tight against your body and extend the other above your head, like Superman when he is flying; then climbing up a vertical wall of jagged rock called the Dragon's Back; and then, after a number of other twists and turns, finally squeezing through a passage that at one point narrows to only seven and a half inches wide, before reaching the Dinaledi Chamber in which the bones lie.

The six scientists who subsequently retrieved the bones over a two-year period were all experienced women archaeologists who were small enough to fit through all these passageways. According to Shreeve, Berger advertised on Facebook that he needed "Skinny individuals, with scientific credentials and caving experience" who were "willing to work in cramped quarters." He heard from sixty applicants in just ten days and chose those six, whom he called "underground astronauts."

Their findings are extremely exciting, though not without a certain amount of controversy. If these are deliberate burials, as Berger hypothesizes, it would mean that we may be looking at some of the earliest examples of human self-consciousness, possibly an understanding of past and future, perhaps even a sense of religion going back millions of years—because otherwise the bodies would have been left to lie where the individuals had died, rather than being deliberately brought to this part of the cave. It is, as some have described, a mind-numbing possibility; game changing for those studying human evolution.

Some scholars have taken issue with Berger's use of teams of young anthropologists from around the world to study the body parts and the rapidity with which he publishes the results in open-access journals, including three-dimensional images of the fossils, so that others can download and create their own casts of them. They prefer the slow pace of other researchers who have typically taken decades to analyze and publish a single skeleton, but Berger's approach represents a new way to crowd-source the study of the remains by experts from around the world rather than a single person and may be a harbinger of things to come in this Internet age.

✦←→✦ ✦←→✦

Berger's discoveries are within the subfield of prehistoric archaeology, otherwise known as palaeoanthropology. Archaeologists in this field study a period that covers millions of years—from our earliest hominin ancestors right up until the beginnings of recorded history. Archaeological convention has split this long period of time into several eras:

- The Paleolithic, or Old Stone Age, which extends from about 3.5 million years ago all the way down to anywhere from twenty thousand to twelve thousand years ago; the end point depends upon whether one is talking about Africa, Europe, or Asia
- The Mesolithic, or Middle Stone Age, which continues to about ten thousand years ago
- The Neolithic, or New Stone Age, which lasts until about forty-five hundred years ago

The most famous modern family to work in prehistoric archaeology are the Leakeys. Louis and Mary Leakey are the first generation; their son Richard and his wife Meave are the second generation; and Louise— granddaughter of Louis and Mary—is the third generation.

Louise, who received her PhD from University College London in 2001, reportedly holds the record of being the youngest person ever to find a hominoid fossil. She was only six in 1977 when she found a tooth of a primate ancestor that was 17 million years old. Twenty-two years later, in 1999, she and her mother Meave found a 3.5-million-year-old skull belonging to an early human. Louise also has been involved since 1993 in the Koobi Fora project in northern Kenya, where her father Richard first began working in 1968 and her mother Meave started in 1969.

Meave began her career by working for Louis Leakey, who was first her dissertation adviser and later her father-in-law, after she married Richard in 1970. Richard became well known in his own right, with a long and distinguished career and numerous publications, including the book *Origins*, which was written for the general public. Among the notable discoveries made by his teams was a nearly complete 1.5-million-year-old skeleton. Kamoya Kimeu, a native Kenyan working with Richard and who had worked with Louis and Mary from the 1950s, found the first fragment in 1984; the rest were painstakingly recovered during five seasons of meticulous excavation. "Turkana Boy," as he is known, was probably about eight to eleven years old when he died. He is usually considered to be an example of *Homo erectus*; that is, a direct ancestor of modern humans.

꙳꙳꙳ ꙳꙳꙳

Louis grew up in Kenya and was one of the first people to argue that human origins should be sought in Africa, rather than in Asia, which had been the generally accepted theory until then. He turned out to be correct, though it took a while for others to come around to his point of view. His case was proven by the finds that he and Mary made, beginning in 1948, but then especially from 1959 on. At that time, they were working in a canyon or ravine that was thirty miles long and three hundred feet deep, known as Olduvai Gorge in Tanzania.

Here Louis and Mary found skeletal fragments that they identified as coming from a new species of hominin. Actually, it was Mary who found the first fragment, because Louis was back at the camp with a fever. She went out with their two Dalmatian dogs to check on a site that they hadn't visited since 1931 and promptly found a fragment of skull and two teeth in a hominin jaw. She jumped in the Land Rover and drove back to get Louis. The two of them then found even more bone fragments and were able to reconstruct much of the skull.

Because they were the first discoverers of this species, they got to name it. They initially called it *Zinjanthropus boisei*, after their primary sponsor at the time, Charles Boise, but it was later reassigned to a different genus (according to the taxonoemic ranking system used in biological classifications) and is now called *Australopithecus* (or *Paranthropus*) *boisei*. They also initially thought that it dated to about six hundred thousand years ago, but a dating technique that was new at the time, involving measuring the radioactive decay of potassium into argon in volcanic rock, quickly showed that it was more like 1.75 million years old. At the time, the discovery created a sensation because of its extreme age.

They promptly followed up their discovery the next year by discovering yet another new hominin species, *Homo habilis*. This time they didn't name it after a sponsor. Instead, its name reflects the fact that fossil remains of this species are often found associated with stone tools, for *Homo habilis* translates roughly as "handy man."

It would be hard for us to imagine what it was like for the Leakeys in those early days, except that we have photographs of them working from that period. We see them picking carefully at the dirt, in extremely hot conditions, with a huge umbrella planted for shade and several Dalmatian dogs keeping them company.

It was after Louis died in 1972 that Mary made what is considered to be her most significant discovery—the hominin footprints at Laetoli, which were found in 1978 and 1979. The site is located about forty-five kilometers southeast of Olduvai Gorge. Team members who were throwing elephant dung at each other for fun had found the first footprints at the site a few years earlier, in 1976, but animals had made all of those.

Three individuals who were walking across freshly fallen ash from a nearby volcano about 3.6 million years ago created the famous footprints. It is usually suggested that the footprints were made by hominins that we call *Australopithecus afarensis*. Two of the trails appear to have been made by individuals walking in cadence—that is, walking together—but the third may be unrelated to the first two. In any event, judging from the impressions that were left, all three were less than five feet tall.

We can only imagine what it would have been like for those individuals at the time that they were walking through the area. The volcano would have been erupting in the distance, while ash was falling all around them, perhaps mixed with rain. It is likely to have been overcast, with smoke from the eruption obscuring the sun, but it is conceivable that it was dark as night, as Pliny the Younger reported during the eruption of Mount Vesuvius millions of years later. Animals would have been heading for safety, perhaps oblivious to the short hominins, but it doesn't look like our three were in too much of a hurry. The imprints of their feet indicate that they were walking rather than running, even though it is unlikely that the day was typical for them.

In all, Mary Leakey and her team found about seventy footprints from these human ancestors that go on for almost ninety feet. They are the earliest direct evidence of hominin bipedalism and are now reproduced in the floor of the Hall of Human Origins in the Smithsonian National Museum of Natural History in Washington, DC, as well as at the American Museum of Natural History in New York City.

These are not the only early footprints that have been found. Another series of footprints were found in 2007 and 2008 at Koobi Fora near Lake Turkana. These are *only* about 1.5 million years old, so they are more recent by 2 million years than the ones that Mary Leakey found. Members of *Homo erectus* similar to Turkana Boy probably made the Koobi Fora footprints. They are about a size 9, in terms of today's men's shoes.

꘏꘏꘏ ꘏꘏꘏

All these discoveries have helped to dispel the long shadow that was cast for decades by the so-called Piltdown Man, one of the most famous hoaxes in the history of archaeology. In 1912, long before the Leakeys had begun their explorations, a man named Charles Dawson announced that he had discovered some skull fragments, teeth, and a jawbone in the Piltdown gravel quarry in England. Quickly touted as "the missing link" between humans and apes, the discovery caused a sensation, but it also raised suspicions almost immediately. Partly, the controversy was nationalist—French scholar Boucher de Perthes had found early hominin tools in 1846 near the Sommes River and the Germans had discovered the species Neanderthal in their Neander Valley in 1856; the British had no counterpart until the discovery at Piltdown.

Leading scientists published their doubts within just a few years, but it took until 1953 to prove definitively that Piltdown Man was a fabrication. The skull was human but dated to the medieval period; the fossilized teeth were from a chimpanzee; and the jawbone, which was about five hundred years old, was from an orangutan. Dawson died in 1916, but he has long been suspected of creating the forgery. He is not the only suspect in this unsolved crime, though; the list of possible forgers is pretty long and even includes Arthur Conan Doyle, the creator of Sherlock Holmes.

꘏꘏꘏ ꘏꘏꘏

Real discoveries continued to be made. It was in 1974, soon after Louis Leakey died and just two years before Mary Leakey found the first footprints at Laetoli, that Berkeley paleoanthropologist Donald Johanson made a discovery that ensured his inclusion in the prehistory Hall of Fame.

As frequently happens in archaeology, it was a chance discovery. Johanson and a colleague were surveying near the site of Hadar, in Ethiopia, far to the north of Tanzania where the Leakeys had been working. After a long day in the hot sun with nothing to show for their efforts, they began walking back to where they had parked their Land Rover. Rather than go back the way that they had come, Johanson suggested going a different route, via a gully that they hadn't been through before. As he tells the story, first they spotted a bone from a hominin forearm, then—in rapid succession—a skull fragment, a leg bone, ribs, a pelvis, and a lower jaw. Within two weeks, they had found several hundred pieces of bone, all belonging to a single skeleton.

Lucy, as she is called, died when she was about twenty years old, which was about 3.2 million years ago. She has been identified as an *Australopithecus afarensis* and resembled the individuals who left their footprints at Laetoli five hundred thousand years earlier. It is believed that she would have stood about three and a half to four feet tall and weighed about sixty-five pounds at most. That's just an estimate, though, since we have only about 40 percent of her skeleton, but it was still the most complete hominin skeleton found to that time.

The Beatles' song "Lucy in the Sky with Diamonds" was playing over and over again at the party that night back in the camp when they first returned with the skeletal remains. Sometime that evening they began referring to her as Lucy. She is still called that today.

{←→}{←→}

Lee Berger's discoveries show that caves also can be extremely important sites for prehistoric archaeology, for they play a crucial role in helping us understand our connections to the deep past. Some of the most famous discoveries in caves were made in the 1920s and 1930s by an archaeologist named Dorothy Garrod and several colleagues within a cluster of caves on the slopes of Mount Carmel, south of the modern city of Haifa in what is now Israel. UNESCO recognized the caves as a World Heritage Site in 2012. Most of them are open to the public and can be seen without an appointment—the path for tourists is well maintained, but visitors must be prepared for very hot and dry conditions, especially during the summer.

Garrod is widely recognized as one of the most important early archaeologists. She was the first woman to be named a professor at Cambridge University in England, where she held the Disney Chair of Archaeology from 1939 to 1952. This is a very distinguished professorship that has nothing to do with Walt Disney, but rather was established back in 1851 by a man named John Disney.

Dorothy Garrod's specialty was the Paleolithic period. Her first excavation at Mount Carmel was in Kebara Cave, where she briefly dug in 1928. She then moved on and spent five years, from 1929 to 1934, excavating two other caves, of which the more famous is known as the Tabun Cave; the other is known as el-Wad. She was able to show that the two caves were occupied pretty much continuously for about half a million years. Tabun Cave was occupied first, from about five hundred thousand years ago to forty thousand years ago; the occupation of el-Wad begins just before Tabun is abandoned, about forty-five thousand years ago.

Within Tabun Cave is a burial of a Neanderthal woman, dating to about one hundred twenty thousand years ago. The skull indicates that her brain was about the same size as ours today, but she had no real chin and a very low forehead.

There are also burials in nearby Skhul Cave, which was excavated by Theodore McCown, a US colleague of Garrod's. These burials, however, about fourteen in all, and dating to between one hundred twenty thousand and eighty thousand years ago, are members of our own human species, *Homo sapiens sapiens*, also called anatomically modern people. The burials have generated much discussion among scholars, who include this evidence as support for the proposition that Neanderthals and modern humans were separate species and lived side by side for a time. Recent DNA studies indicate that modern humans and Neanderthals interbred and their European and Asian descendants—including many of us—have genetic markers of each.

From 1982 to 1989, Harvard archaeologist Ofer Bar-Yosef returned to Kebara Cave, where Garrod had dug in 1928. There he and his team found a Neanderthal burial—an adult male who lived about sixty thousand years ago. Nicknamed Moshe, his may be the most complete

Neanderthal skeleton found to date. It caused a great deal of excitement when he was discovered, because even though his head was missing, there were bones from his throat that indicated he may have been capable of speech, which had always been a question about Neanderthals and other premodern hominins, speech being an important event in human evolution.

Moshe would date to about the same time as the Neanderthal burials that have been found at Shanidar Cave in northern Iraq, which Columbia anthropologist Ralph Solecki excavated during several seasons from 1951 to 1961. The ten individuals that Solecki and his team excavated are usually dated to between sixty-five thousand and thirty-five thousand years ago. They have been of intense interest, in part because one of them—called Shanidar 1—was a relatively old man (between forty and fifty years old) at the time of his death and showed evidence of having sustained, and survived, multiple injuries during his lifetime, which means that his group took care of their sick and wounded. Another, an adult male known as Shanidar 4, who died sometime between the ages of thirty and forty-five, was long thought to have been buried with flowers, which was interpreted as some sort of burial ritual, perhaps even an indication of belief in an afterlife or simply just a touching remembrance from a surviving family member. It has also been hypothesized that he might have been some sort of medicine man, since some of the flowers are from plants with medicinal properties, like ragwort and hollyhock. More recently, however, it has been suggested that the flower remains may be the result of later intrusions by a rodent, which is much less interesting and will mean rethinking much of what has been previously written.

{⟶}⟩{⟶}⟩

In Europe—specifically in France and Spain—are other caves that are famous for their wall paintings, including Chauvet and Lascaux in France and Altamira in Spain. Chauvet is by far the oldest, with the first remains there dating to about 35,000 BCE; then comes Lascaux at approximately 15,000 BCE; and then Altamira at about 12,000 BCE.

Altamira may be the youngest, relatively speaking, but it was the first of these three caves to be discovered. It was first noticed by a hunter in 1868 and then visited by a local landowner, Don Marcelino Sanz de Sautuola, in 1876. Two years later, having been inspired by a show about Paleolithic art in Paris in 1878, de Sautuola returned to the cave with his eight-year-old daughter Maria. She spotted the paintings on the wall while he was busy excavating the cave floor, looking for tools and other artifacts. His subsequent announcement of the discovery in 1880 was met with disbelief from the scholarly establishment. How could people this primitive create art that was so evocative, skilled, even artistic? It was only decades later, long after his death, that the scholars admitted he had been right about the antiquity of the paintings.

The paintings in the cave are usually dated to about 12,000 BCE, at the time of the end of the last Ice Age, although some scholars have argued that they could be a good deal older. They certainly are not any more recent, because a rockslide sealed closed the entrance to the cave at that time.

The cave itself is about three hundred meters long, with the usual passages and chambers that we have to come to expect in such caves. Of the animals that are painted or engraved on the walls, the most famous are those on the Polychrome Ceiling, which include a herd of bison and a couple of horses, a deer, and possibly other animals.

By 1979, one hundred fifty thousand annual tourists were visiting Altamira; it was named a UNESCO World Heritage Site in 1985. The huge number of visitors had taken its toll on the paintings, however, because of the humidity from so many people breathing in a small space, as well as graffiti and other vandalism, all of which caused damage. Soon thereafter, the quota of visitors was limited to fewer than ten thousand per year. Eventually the cave was simply closed in 2002 and an exact replica of the cave was built nearby, which most tourists now visit; since 2015, only five randomly selected visitors are allowed in to the original cave for thirty-seven minutes once a week.

As for Lascaux, the story of its discovery is easily told. Four teenage boys and their dog, whose name was Robot for some reason, came upon the cave in 1940. They were walking on a hill above the town of Montignac in the region of Dordogne, near Bordeaux in southern France, and decided to explore a hole that they found—reportedly because their dog started digging in it and they thought it might contain buried treasure. We now know that it did contain buried treasure, but it was a treasure trove of art, not the treasure of gold that the boys were hoping for.

The cave is about six hundred fifty feet long, with at least six hundred paintings and another fifteen hundred engravings on the walls. It was named a UNESCO World Heritage Site in 1979. It is interesting to note that, when Willard Libby was first experimenting with the technique of radiocarbon dating in 1947—which we will discuss in a future chapter—one of the first trials was done on a piece of charcoal that had been found at Lascaux. In part as a result of this technique, the cave is now generally dated to about seventeen thousand years ago, or 15,000 BCE.

The current entrance, and possibly the original entrance as well, leads into the huge Hall of the Bulls, which has four huge bulls painted on the cave wall, covering a total of more than five meters (16 feet). To be precise, these are aurochs, an extinct species of wild cattle. There also are smaller horses and tiny deer painted in the hall.

I'm not sure that it is possible for us to fully appreciate what it would have been like to enter this cave seventeen thousand years ago—no electricity, no tourist path, nothing to prevent you from stumbling into the darkness. We have to imagine grasping some sort of flaming torch and walking gingerly into the dark gaping mouth of the cave. The flickering light reveals new animals on the walls every few feet, but just beyond is inky blackness, terrifying and still. Even if you're one of the artists who is responsible for some of the cave paintings, surely you had at least a small sense of dread each time you entered, placing one foot in front of another, jumping at the shadows of the frightening animals painted on the walls—even the ones that you painted a few years before, but especially those that had been done by the unnamed ones who came before you in the distant past.

From the Hall of Bulls, the path leads straight ahead into the Axial Gallery. This area has paintings of cattle, deer, and horses, including the so-called Chinese horses, which are not Chinese but are called that nevertheless, reportedly because of a vague resemblance to paintings of horses from the Sung dynasty in China (960–1279 CE).

If you turn to the right instead of going into the Axial Gallery, however, there is a passageway that has almost four hundred more engravings, mostly of horses. If you go right again from that point, the Great

Apse appears, which has more than a thousand additional engravings on the walls. Lascaux also features the Chamber of the Felines, which has six large felines among dozens of other engravings.

The cave was never really excavated but was simply prepared for tourism and opened to the public in 1948. Having more than one hundred thousand annual visitors caused the same problems as at Altamira, only they were felt at Lascaux first. By 1963, the cave was closed to the public and only small groups were let in from then on. Problems still abound, though. In 2000, after the installation of a new air conditioning system, fungus began to grow on the walls and the images. In 2006 black mold began to grow as well. The damage is probably irreparable, which is why a replica of the cave has been built nearby, so that the public can visit it instead.

Chauvet is the oldest of the three caves that we are discussing, but it also is the most recently discovered. It is located in the Ardèche region of southern France. The huge cave may be as much as four hundred meters (thirteen hundred feet) long and covers more than eight thousand square meters. It was recently declared a UNESCO World Heritage Site in 2014, just twenty years after it was first discovered and explored in late December 1994 by Jean-Marie Chauvet and a small group of colleagues. Chauvet also has been brought to life by a three-dimensional

Chauvet cave painting

movie produced by the famous director Werner Herzog that was released in 2011.

Nearly four thousand artifacts and animal bones have been found in the cave, as well as a thousand images on the walls. The drawings and paintings in it are simply exquisite. They include some of the earliest and best-preserved cave art in the world, depicting at least thirteen different species, ranging from lions, horses, and woolly rhinos to owls, mammoths, bears, and other animals. They also may include the oldest known images of an erupting volcano.

Discussions about their date have been heated. Until recently, the generally accepted dates from radiocarbon analysis, conducted on thirty to eighty samples over the years, put most of them at about 30,000 BCE, when the cave was thought to be have been first occupied. The cave was then abandoned for several thousand years, before being reoccupied in about 25,000 BCE, at which time dozens more paintings were added. There is also a child's footprint that has been preserved on the soft clay floor of the cave, which probably dates from the second period of occupation. These dates have recently been challenged.

The newest study presents 259 radiocarbon dates, taken from the pigments used in the black paintings as well as bones and charcoal found in the cave, as well as nearly one hundred more dates derived using more esoteric techniques involving uranium-thorium, thermoluminescence, and chlorine-36. These methods suggest that cave bears actually first began using the cave almost fifty thousand years ago, and the earliest paintings were created about 35,000 BCE. This phase ended in about 31,500 BCE, when both the bears and the people stopped using the cave. It was then abandoned for about twenty-five hundred years before being reoccupied by a new group of people, but not bears, from 29,000 BCE to 26,000 BCE. After that, a rockslide closed off the cave entrance so that neither people nor animals could enter from then on, until the cave was rediscovered in 1994.

The discovery of Chauvet Cave was not accidental, though. According to a detailed *New Yorker* article published in 2008, Jean-Marie Chauvet was a park ranger working for France's Ministry of Culture and was actively searching for such caves. This particular cave is located high up on a limestone cliff above the former route of the Ardèche River. It is very close to a natural limestone bridge called the Pont d'Arc. Although the original entrance to the cave had been closed for at least twenty thousand years because of the rockslide, members of Chauvet's group noticed cold air coming from a small opening on the cliff face.

The smallest member of the group, a woman named Éliette Brunel, climbed in after they had removed a few rocks to enlarge the opening. The others quickly followed her and used a chain ladder that they had brought to descend a deep thirty-foot shaft. They found themselves in a huge cavern, with stalagmites and stalactites everywhere. They noticed animal bones on the floor and then the first few paintings on the walls. Brunel yelled out, "They have been here!"—meaning Paleolithic cave painters.

In a *Smithsonian* article published in April 2015, Joshua Hammer reconstructed what happened next, using details from a 1996 memoir published by the explorers:

> The trio moved gingerly across the earthen floor, trying not to tread on the crystallized ashes from an ancient fire pit, gazing in wonder at hundreds of images. "We found ourselves in front of a rock wall covered entirely with red ocher drawings. . . . The panel contained a mammoth with a long trunk, then a lion with red dots spattered around its snout in an arc, like drops of blood. We crouched on our heels, gazing at the cave wall, mute with stupefaction."

There is some debate, and dispute, about exactly who was with Chauvet that day and whom he brought there soon afterward, as well as whether he was even the first to notice the small initial opening. Regardless, inside the cave they saw hundreds of drawings and paintings; some huge and some fairly small; some isolated and others painted as a group, overlapping as needed. They quickly alerted the authorities, who sent Jean Clottes, a specialist in cave paintings and a scientific adviser to the Ministry of Culture. Clottes declared it to be one of the great discoveries of the twentieth century.

Clottes assembled a team of specialists, who have been studying the Chauvet cave paintings ever since 1996. In all that time, the cave has remained closed to the public, in order to avoid the kinds of problems caused by opening the Lascaux and Altamira caves to tourists. In fact, even the research team enters the Chauvet cave only twice a year, for a few weeks in the spring and another few weeks in the fall. At all other times, a four-foot-tall locked steel door prevents anyone from entering. This is the only one of these three caves that has been excavated using modern methods.

The cave has a number of parts. The original entrance chamber, which is now sealed off from the outside by the ancient rockslide, leads into a huge area, named the Brunel Chamber, for Éliette Brunel, the first person to enter the cave in thousands of years. From here you can enter the Chamber of the Bear Hollows, which has a lot of evidence of occupation by cave bears, including hollows that they dug into the soft clay floor.

Two galleries can be reached from the bears' chamber. One is a fairly short gallery called the Cactus Gallery. This one contains the first paint-ing seen by Chauvet and his group—a small red mammoth painted on a rock—which was the painting that Éliette Brunel was looking at when she called out to the others.

The other gallery is much larger and leads to more chambers. This gallery is known as the Red Panels Gallery, since most of the paintings found here are in a series of panels on the eastern wall and are primarily painted in red.

From the Red Panels Gallery, one can go to the left (that is, west) and enter the Candle Gallery, which is the beginning of the second part of the cave system. After the Candle Gallery is the Hillaire Chamber, named for Christian Hillaire, the third member of the original trio who discovered the cave. This chamber is about thirty meters in diameter—so about one hundred feet wide—with a ceiling that is nearly as high. There are numerous wall paintings and drawings in it. Some of them overlap, probably meaning that they were created at different points in time. A natural calcite coating also covers a number of them, meaning that they cannot possibly be fakes, in case anyone was wondering.

From the Hillaire Chamber there are two choices. If you continue heading west, you'll come to the Skull Chamber, where a bear skull was found very carefully placed on a stone that had fallen from the ceiling. Beyond the Skull Chamber is the final gallery in this direction, the Gal-lery of the Crosshatching, where a large horse is drawn on the rock.

If you continue north from the Hillaire Chamber instead of west, though, you enter the Megaloceros Gallery. There are drawings of several rhinoceroses in here, but the gallery gets its name from a drawing of a megaloceros, which is an extinct type of giant deer with huge antlers. The largest member of the megaloceros genus stood far taller than an average human and is known variously as an Irish elk, Irish deer, or giant elk.

French researchers proposed in early 2016 that a spray-shaped image in this gallery, partially covered by the drawing of the megaloceros, is possibly a representation of a nearby erupting volcano. The cave has at least two other, similar sets of images elsewhere, which have always been a mystery to scholars, but it now seems possible that all of them may be depicting the Bas-Vivarais volcanic field, which is only thirty-five kilometers from the cave and which had eruptions that took place between nineteen thousand and forty-three thousand years ago. That would include the time when the cave was occupied. If the researchers' interpretation is correct, these images would be the earliest known representations of erupting volcanoes.

From the Megaloceros Gallery, you can proceed into the so-called End Chamber, where there are images of bison, rhinoceroses, mammoths, and large cats. There are so many here that they make up more than a third of all the images in the entire cave; one group consists of sixteen lions hunting a herd of bison. As in many cases throughout the whole cave, the artist or artists used features in the rock itself to make it look as if the animals were moving and alive.

On one side it is possible to go from the End Chamber into the Belvedere Gallery, which has no paintings but rather a small hole from which you can look back at the left wall of the End Chamber. The other side leads into the Sacristy, which has drawings of a horse, a big bison, a large cat, and a rhinoceros on the walls and lots of animal prints in the soft clay floor. At this point, the cave system comes to an end, at least as it is currently known.

{•••}{•••}

In late April 2015, a replica of the Chauvet cave was opened up nearby. It cost 55 million Euros to build (approximately $63 million), but it allows the general public to finally see the amazing images painted on the walls and rocks of the original cave. Each of the images is an exact replica of the original, created by using three-dimensional models, digital images, and other techniques, ranging from scientific to artistic. The original limestone walls are now reproduced in concrete; the stalagmites and stalactites have been recreated in resin. Reportedly, the results are stunning.

Thus, all three of these caves—Lascaux, Altamira, and Chauvet—are now essentially closed off to the public, but the replicas that have been built at each of them are either attracting, or have the potential to attract, more visitors than the originals ever handled. For example, even at its height, Altamira cave had about one hundred fifty thousand visitors per year, but now the replica is reporting up to two hundred fifty thousand annual visitors.

Perhaps this is incentive to create more such replicas, just as has been done with King Tut's tomb in Egypt, for many popular archaeological tourist destinations face the problem of preservation versus access. Far from "Disney-fying" the site, creating such identical replicas will allow many more members of the general public to enjoy these ancient wonders and leave the originals relatively untouched and able to be further studied by scientists.

Much has already been written about such art, including various hypotheses by scholars about why such Upper Paleolithic paintings were created in the first place, but much more remains to be done. It is clear that humans of thirty-five thousand years ago had enormous manual skills, understood both art and religion, and were more like us than different.

It also is clear that prehistoric archaeology is unique in allowing us to glimpse snapshots of hominin history, ranging from the three individuals who left their footprints in the ash at Laetoli in Tanzania several million years ago to more recent times when our early relatives were painting on cave walls in France and Spain. At this point our image of the human family tree has transformed so that it now looks more like a bush than a tree, with multiple hominin species inhabiting the planet at the same time. For example, we know that fifty thousand years ago there were humans and Neanderthals living together in Europe, as well as others whom we haven't mentioned here, including Denisovans in Asia, "Hobbits" on Flores Island, and even, if the geneticists have it right, some as-yet-unidentified species that also added to the gene pool. It was only twenty-five thousand years ago that we emerged as the sole remaining species, with bits of each of these other species embedded in our DNA. This is a fast-moving field of research, with more discoveries made every year, and so it will be interesting to hear what is found next.

FIRST FARMERS IN THE FERTILE CRESCENT

S OME SITES MAKE HEADLINES AROUND THE WORLD WHEN THEY are discovered. Some sites attract outlandish theories like flies to honey. And some sites do both. In 2007 excavations began at a site in modern Turkey named Göbekli Tepe that dates back more than eleven thousand years ago. By 2010, it was featured on an episode of *Ancient Aliens*.

According to various accounts, a farmer discovered Göbekli Tepe in 1983. He found a carved stone in his field and took it to the local museum. University of Chicago archaeologists had previously conducted an archaeological survey of the site in the 1960s and had already dismissed it as a probable medieval cemetery because of all the broken slabs of stone that they saw, which they identified as possible tombstones. As a result, not much was made of the farmer's discovery, at least initially.

In 1993 Klaus Schmidt, a German archaeologist, saw the carved stone that the farmer had found and reinvestigated the site a year or so later. It took more than a decade to get everything lined up, and excavations at the site did not begin until 2007. Within a short period of time, it became clear that Göbekli Tepe is one of the oldest prepottery Neolithic sites with evidence for religious beliefs that has ever been found, dating to about 9600 BCE. Schmidt led the excavations for seven years, until his unexpected and untimely death from a heart attack while swimming in July 2014.

{↔}{↔}

The Neolithic period, or New Stone Age (from the Greek *neos* meaning "new" and *lithos* meaning "stone"), started about twelve thousand years ago, in about 10,000 BCE in the ancient Near East. During the first part of this period, which lasted for about four thousand years, pottery as we know it hadn't yet been invented, and so it is called the prepottery Neolithic period.

We usually talk about the Neolithic Revolution when we are discussing this period, because it sees the beginning of a whole new way of life. Not only do stone tools change, which is why we call this the New Stone Age in the first place, but this is when we see the first domestication of plants and animals, including wheat and barley, sheep and goats, in an arc of sites running from the top of the Persian Gulf up across to where Turkey meets Syria and then down the Mediterranean coast all the way to modern-day Israel—the Fertile Crescent.

This revolution, in turn, changed everything. Imagine having enough food to be able to settle down and become sedentary, rather than having to be nomadic. Imagine having enough food all year round so that you weren't afraid to have more children and could let your population grow. Imagine having your cluster of huts grow to be a village, then a town, and then a city, and your society to grow more and more complex, so that eventually you needed laws, accounting, writing. All this and more came about because of the domestication of plants and animals, but some claim that other things did as well, including the origins of violence, social inequality, and other injustices.

There are a wide variety of theories about why agriculture and domestication of plants and animals began in this region in the Neolithic period, some of which have been suggested by very well-known scholars such as the Australian archaeologist V. Gordon Childe, the

University of Chicago archaeologist Robert Braidwood, the University of Michigan anthropologist Henry Wright, and a Danish agricultural economist named Ester Boserup. Their suggestions involve possible climate change between ten thousand and nine thousand BCE, which may have led to people settling down in oases; finding the right types of plants and animals that could be domesticated; overpopulation and overuse of natural resources; and other events and occurrences that may have made domestication both necessary and possible.

⊰••⊱ ⊰••⊱

Göbekli Tepe has the oldest known examples of monumental architecture in the ancient Near East. So far archaeologists have uncovered at least five stone circles of various sizes—one of them is sixty-five feet across. They are impressive—even the beautiful photographs that have appeared in various publications so far do not do complete justice to them.

Most of the standing stones have figures or scenes carved on them, including pictures of animals. They have excited the interest of a lot of people, whether professional archaeologists, the general public, or those with far-out theories. The animals include lizards, scorpions, bulls, lions, vultures, and possible dogs or wolves, in addition to other species. Some of them may even be pictographs—that is, images that tell a story five thousand years before the invention of writing—which is a novel suggestion made during summer 2015.

According to Schmidt, there arc at least sixteen other stone circles still buried, which he detected using remote-sensing techniques such as ground-penetrating radar. Each of the circles that have been excavated so far contains a number of standing stones, including two large T-shaped stones in the middle, with smaller standing stones around them. The larger stones can be up to sixteen or eighteen feet tall.

It is not at all clear what the inhabitants of Göbekli Tepe were trying to do here, but Schmidt was convinced that it was a holy place, perhaps the earliest with architecture deliberately built by humans. In 2008, *Smithsonian* magazine published an article wondering whether it is the world's first known temple, and in 2011, *National Geographic* published an article that suggested "the urge to worship sparked civilization."

In that *National Geographic* article, the author pointed out that the builders of Göbekli Tepe were able "to cut, shape, and transport 16-ton stones hundreds of feet despite having no wheels or beasts of burden." He also pointed out that they were living in a world that did not yet have writing, metal, or pottery.

What's important for us is that Göbekli Tepe is located on the northern edge of the Fertile Crescent and seems to be one of the earliest sites from this time period. In fact, it seems to have been inhabited just *before* the inhabitants learned the art of domestication, because the thousands of animal bones that have now been recovered and studied indicate that the inhabitants were hunting and eating wild game, primarily gazelles and birds.

It has long been thought that humans were able to settle down because of the invention of the domestication of plants and animals, as described above, but sites like Göbekli Tepe might indicate the opposite. Because so many people were gathered at a site like this, creating the stone rings, carving the standing stones, and so on, they might have needed to figure out a way to feed them all, if the usual hunting and gathering methods couldn't sustain them. So, Göbekli Tepe is an extremely important site, but the archaeological investigations have really only just begun. We'll see more from this site in the coming years, as the excavations continue under the direction of a new chief archaeologist.

But we should also mention what Göbekli Tepe *isn't*. It's not the Garden of Eden, and Schmidt never claimed that it was, despite some newspaper accounts that said he did. It also probably isn't an ancient site related to Watchers or ancient Nephilim from the Bible, or to a global catastrophe that some think took place after the end of the last Ice Age, as was claimed in a book published in 2014.

It is, plain and simple, one of the most interesting Neolithic sites currently being investigated by archaeologists. It may shed light on the earliest practice of religion and it will definitely shed light on the period when humans began to settle down and domesticate plants and animals. In that regard, it joins two other sites that are extremely fascinating in both regards, which we shall now take a look at: Çatalhöyük, in modern-day Turkey, and Jericho, located in the West Bank near the Dead Sea.

Jericho is a site familiar to many because of the story of Joshua and the Israelites, who invaded Canaan at the end of the Exodus from Egypt, according to the biblical account. There's a whole kettle of fish involved with the archaeology of that story, but in fact, interest in confirming the biblical story led to the discovery of Neolithic Jericho.

Jericho lies in an oasis in the middle of what is otherwise forlorn desert. The water supply is adequate for plentiful drinking as well as irrigation, allowing people to survive and even flourish here. From 1930 to 1936, a well-known British archaeologist named John Garstang conducted excavations at Jericho. As part of his interpretation of what he found, he identified one of the layers within the mound as the city captured by Joshua and the Israelites. His hypothesis came under fire, however, and it was suggested that he had misdated the pottery in the level and therefore had misinterpreted everything.

He eventually invited Kathleen Kenyon, a young archaeologist who had studied with Mortimer Wheeler and had dug at the site of Samaria a bit to the north of Jericho, to reexamine the pottery that he had found. She eventually decided that there was not enough evidence to reach a definitive answer and that she needed to do more excavating at the site, which is a very common decision for archaeologists to make.

And so, she went back to Jericho in 1952 and began her own series of excavations. The stratigraphy at the site, documenting four levels and periods of occupation, turned out to be more complicated than expected. Her drawings of the sections that she made, after she had excavated through an entire part of the mound, show a tangled mess of walls, floors, destructions, and other archaeological remains.

We should mention here that the concept of stratigraphy, which had been adopted from geology, was introduced into Near Eastern archaeology by William Matthew Flinders Petrie and Frederick Jones Bliss when they were excavating at a site called Tell el-Hesi, to the west of Jericho, several decades earlier. They correctly argued that earlier things are usually found lower down than more recent things, especially in the manmade mounds that we call tells and that can be seen throughout the Middle East, including Jericho. They also noted, as Kenyon found to be the case at Jericho, that the stratigraphy of a site can be incredibly complicated.

Kenyon found evidence, particularly more pottery, that indicated to her, and to much of the scholarly world, that the destruction layer found by Garstang actually dated to a thousand years before the time of Joshua—the remains of that city were from the Early Bronze Age, not the Late Bronze Age. Moreover, it looked to her as if the city had already been abandoned by the middle of the second millennium BCE and would have been deserted and empty, if not completely in ruins, by the time that Joshua and Israelites invaded the region.

In any case, while Kenyon was digging at Jericho, she also found Neolithic levels that included walls, buildings, and tombs, and it is on these that we will focus here. At that time, about 7500 BCE, Jericho probably had a population of about two or three thousand people at most. This is about two thousand years after the Göbekli Tepe remains that we just looked at but is still in the prepottery Neolithic period. It was protected by a thick stone wall, giving rise to the notion found in much archaeological literature that Jericho is the first known walled town.

In this same level, Kenyon also uncovered the so-called Jericho Tower. The tower is about twenty-six feet high and thirty feet across at the base. Constructed of unworked medium-sized stones, it is hollow, with an internal staircase leading from top to bottom (and vice versa). It quite possibly served as a storage unit, or ancient grain elevator, to hold their harvested food until needed, but it probably also doubled as a defensive structure to protect the town. Some scholars also have suggested that it could have served a more social function or even an astronomical purpose.

The inhabitants of Jericho buried their dead under the floors of their houses during this period. Kenyon found almost three hundred burials, but what was especially strange was what the inhabitants of Jericho did with the skulls of their dead during the second half of this period, in the prepottery Neolithic B phase, which lasted for another thousand years, down to about 6000 BCE.

During this time at Jericho, and at about a dozen other sites elsewhere in the Near East as well, the inhabitants would remove the skull from the rest of the skeleton, presumably after the body had decayed enough to allow the removal of the skull easily, rather than trying to cut it off. They also removed the lower jaw and then plastered the rest of the skull with clay. In essence, they were basically restoring the flesh of the face. They also put seashells, especially cowrie shells, where the eyes had once been, thereby creating a lifelike appearance. And then they

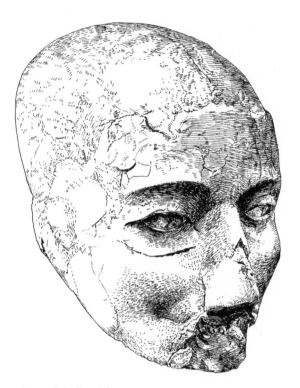

Plastered skull, Jericho

frequently placed the skulls in a prominent place, such as in the living room of their house.

It is generally thought that this reflects some sort of ancestor worship, but we cannot know for certain, since they didn't leave any records telling us why they did it. It is a bit weird, and creepy, at least in my opinion, to think of the head of Uncle Fred, or even a deceased parent, sitting in the corner of the living room, watching everything that is going on. And yet, I have a painting of my late mother in our dining room, which isn't so far removed, is it?

Even today we still have a fascination with skulls, though some people go further than others. When the artist Damien Hirst produced his own version of such a skull, I showed the images side by side to my students—a skull from Jericho and the Damien Hirst skull that he created in 2007. We agreed that they were somewhat similar, but the one that Damien Hirst made was probably a bit more costly, because he created it by using eighty-six hundred flawless diamonds and platinum. The materials alone cost 14 million British pounds (almost 22 million US dollars); it was offered for sale at the bargain price of 50 million British pounds.

Most recently, a joint Italian and Palestinian team of archaeologists excavated at Jericho from 1997 to 2000. They found additional interesting information, including evidence for a large lower city dating to the Middle Bronze Age. Their work temporarily came to a halt when tensions in the region made it unsafe to continue, but they returned to the site in 2008 and have been conducting excavations ever since.

{«»} {«»}

The last site that we will discuss in this chapter also has produced two plaster skulls of the sort found at Jericho, but it is better known for other things. Dating slightly later than Jericho, and flourishing between 6500 and 5600 BCE, during the prepottery Neolithic B period, this is the site of Çatalhöyük in modern-day Turkey.

Excavations at the site began in the early 1960s, under the direction of James Mellaart, a British archaeologist. He uncovered about 160 houses belonging to an amazing village or small town, which had a population that was anywhere from about three thousand to eight thousand people at any one time.

The single-story houses were all interconnected, with party walls serving two houses at a time. All the walls are made of mud brick, but the very strange thing is that none of them has either doors or windows. There are also no streets or alleyways between the houses, since they are all connected.

If there are no windows and no doors and no access from streets or alleyways, then how on earth did they get into their houses? The answer, we think, is ladders. Ladders to get up onto the roof of the house and then ladders to get down into the interior of the house. This has to be the explanation, since it's clear that the people did have access to the interior of their houses. But this is a rather unusual living arrangement. What could possibly have prompted them to build the houses in this way?

The answer is made clear by the discovery of a wall painting that decorated one of the houses. The painting depicts a scene of a very large animal, possibly with horns, that is being hunted by a group of much smaller humans together with a few horses. The artist seems to have had a little bit of a problem with perspective, because otherwise this animal, which looks a lot like a wild pig or—more likely—a bull, would have been incredibly huge. Even if it wasn't as big in reality as it looks in this picture, it still is an indication that there were probably large wild animals roaming around in the area outside this village. It would not be surprising if the villagers were afraid of these wild animals and tried to protect themselves from them, which would also explain why they had no doors or windows in their houses, so the animals could not get in that way. By using ladders, which the animals could not climb, the inhabitants were able to ensure their survival, at least from unwanted predators at night. No other explanation works as well.

Mellaart found this painting during his excavations in the 1960s, but unfortunately he left it unprotected from the elements, so it is not in very good shape now. He found a lot of other wall paintings as well, including one with large-scale men shown running, clad only in loincloths. Another has a rather pleasing geometric pattern above and a number of white hands on a red background below. The hands are reminiscent of paintings that children do in kindergarten, when they trace around their own hand on a piece of paper and then color it in. They've done somewhat the same thing here, in white on red.

Other paintings seem to show other hunting scenes, including one in which lots of little men are surrounding a rather large deer or antelope or some other similar animal with large horns. These hunting scenes, many of which are in the same room within a single house, all have in common that the animals are depicted much larger than the human beings who are apparently hunting them. Again, this may simply be an indication of the importance of the animals that they are hunting, rather than the fact that they were really huge.

On the other hand, the inhabitants do seem to have had a bit of a fixation with bulls. In addition to the paintings showing bulls, there are also what we call plastic, or three-dimensional, sculptures found in some of the rooms. These are primarily clay bulls' heads, complete with horns, or often just the horns themselves.

We've got no clue why they were so fascinated by these bulls. As we shall see, the later Minoans, who lived on the island of Crete in the Aegean about four thousand years later, during the Bronze Age, also had a fixation with bulls. There are some theories that the original settlers of Crete came from ancient Anatolia, but the time span is just too great to try to link the Neolithic bulls of Çatalhöyük with the Bronze Age bulls of Knossos, even if it is tempting.

There is another wall painting that seems to depict a landscape. In fact, it seems to be the view that one sees when gazing out from the village in the direction of a large mountain that rises in the distance. This large mountain—called Hasan Dağı—is actually a volcano, which was the source of much, if not all, of the obsidian fashioned into tools that is found at Çatalhöyük. Lots of little squares are depicted in front of the mountain in the wall painting. This may be the artist trying to depict his or her own village in the foreground; in other words, Çatalhöyük itself. It also may be the case that the volcano is supposed to be erupting in the picture; at least, that is what one team of scholars has recently suggested.

There is yet another scene in which large winged birds that look like vultures seem to be attacking a human figure who is lying prone. This has led some scholars to hypothesize that dead bodies may have occasionally been left out in the open rather deliberately, so that the flesh would be consumed by scavengers before the skeletal remains were buried.

In fact, Mellaart, and now his successor at the site, Ian Hodder of Stanford University, found a number of burials underneath the floor of the houses, just like those Kathleen Kenyon found at Jericho. It is difficult to tell whether they were defleshed before burial here, though the articulated skeletons in at least some of the burials indicate that they were still fully intact when placed in the grave.

Hodder brought all sorts of new ideas with him when he began the renewed excavations at the site in 1993, including basic ones like putting a huge roof over the excavation area, to protect what they were finding rather than leaving everything exposed to the elements as Mellaart had done. He also implemented new creative approaches to raising funds for the excavations, including affiliation with a large local bank, much like the naming of a football or baseball stadium in the United

States, and support from major corporate sponsors such as IBM, Pepsi, British Airways, and Shell, which is virtually unheard of at other sites. He also was involved in the staging of a fashion show in Istanbul in 1997 and again at the 2010 World Expo in Shanghai, which involved building a large replica of Çatalhöyük, so that models could emerge from the replica before proceeding to strut along a catwalk in their Neolithic-inspired outfits.

Hodder had previously been known more for his theoretical archaeological proposals. Before coming to Stanford, he had been a professor at Cambridge University in England. There, he had initiated, along with Michael Shanks and Christopher Tilley, what we call postprocessual archaeology, which can be briefly explained as follows.

{⟶}{⟶}

Starting in the 1960s, a US archaeologist named Lewis Binford developed what's called processual archaeology—frequently just called New Archaeology. Up to that point, archaeology and archaeological publications had been primarily descriptive; that is, describing discoveries, sites, and peoples in terms of what time period they came from, where they were found, what culture they should be assigned to, what the objects looked like, and so on. Binford wanted to make archaeology into more of a science—more anthropological, as it were. In this, he was continuing the trend started by other US archaeologists in the late 1950s, who became famous for saying "archaeology is anthropology or it is nothing."

Binford wanted archaeology to try to explain things, not just to describe them. He wanted archaeologists to come up with universal laws or generalizations of human behavior, as Einstein had done for physics. He also wanted them to use scientific processes and be absolutely neutral and objective in their discussions, which was quite different from what previous archaeologists had been doing.

Binford was extremely influential, especially in the 1960s and 1970s, and he and his students spread the message far and wide. It was mostly US scholars who took to it, however. The Europeans were not quite so enthralled, and by the 1980s they launched a movement reacting to it.

The countermovement is known as postprocessual archaeology, or postprocessualism. Among the leaders was, and still is, Ian Hodder.

Hodder and others rejected, at least to some extent, Binford's reliance on science. The postprocessualists said that there simply aren't any universal laws governing human behavior and that it was ridiculous to try to search for them. They also argued that there shouldn't be as much use of explicit scientific methods, because archaeology is not a "hard science." Hodder and his followers said that trying to pretend to be objective and neutral in our discussions and interpretations was, basically, absurd. Humans are biased animals and it is impossible to remove that bias from our interpretations.

They also said that New Archaeology had essentially "dehumanized" archaeology—and that it wasn't possible to understand the past unless one tried to understand the people and their possible motivations, including the fact that there are multiple voices from the past, such as women and minorities, in addition to the famous dead men like Alexander the Great and Julius Caesar. Hodder is well known for having stated, essentially as a reply to Binford, something like "Archaeology is archaeology and archaeology is history—but archaeology is not anthropology." Ironically, Hodder is now in the anthropology department at Stanford.

Postprocessualism is still very much around today, but its stances have led to some problems, including perhaps being a little too receptive to amateurs, since it holds that everything is relative and open to interpretation, even possibly by nonexperts. In fact, the involvement of nonexperts has led to some interesting activities at Çatalhöyük itself, especially when New Age and Mother Goddess devotees visit the site because of some figurines that have been found there.

These particular figurines at Çatalhöyük are of women. They are usually seated and have rather voluptuous proportions. They fit into a category of female figurines that also are found at many sites in Europe but only during this particular time period. Marija Gimbutas, who was a professor at UCLA from 1963 to 1989, saw them as Mother Goddess figurines, meant to symbolize fertility, motherhood, and the rule of the Mother Goddess over the earth.

It is not clear, however, what these figurines represent at all. Some probably do represent some aspect of fertility or motherhood, but it is not certain whether it is the goddess who is being depicted and for what reason. Would the owner of the figurine have been a woman who wanted to get pregnant or one who was giving thanks for having been pregnant? Or was it neither? Some of the figurines show the woman seated on what looks very much like a throne, including one where she appears to have an animal skin tied around her shoulders. This may indicate that it could be a depiction of a queen or a priestess, rather than the goddess herself. Gimbutas's theories are by no means universally accepted, but Çatalhöyük is nevertheless on the itinerary of many Mother Goddess tours.

{⟶}{⟶}

In any event, the Neolithic is an extremely interesting period, even if one judges it just on the basis of the three sites that we have discussed in this chapter. It was clearly an amazing time of transformation, but it is also clear that we are still very much in the process of learning about it. The finds at Göbekli Tepe from the mid-1990s until today, as well as those at Çatalhöyük and at Jericho, indicate that there is much more still to be found. Future discoveries will undoubtedly change our knowledge and understanding of the Neolithic period, including per-haps a more definitive answer about exactly why it was that agriculture and domestication of plants and animals first began in this particular region known as the Fertile Crescent during that time.

PART 3

EXCAVATING THE BRONZE
AGE AEGEAN

8

REVEALING THE FIRST GREEKS

HEINRICH SCHLIEMANN, THE "DISCOVERER" OF TROY, IS also frequently referred to as the father of Mycenaean archaeology. The reason is simple: after he excavated at the site of Hissarlik in Turkey from 1870 to 1873 and announced to the world that he had found Troy, he decided to go looking for the other side, namely Agamemnon, Menelaus, Odysseus, and the other Mycenaeans who had supposedly fought for ten years against the Trojans.

And so, Schliemann took a break from digging at Hissarlik and tried his hand at excavating Mycenae, the city in the Greek Peloponnese where it was said that Agamemnon, king among kings and leader of the Greek invading force at Troy, had once ruled. It was a lot easier to find Mycenae than it had been to find Troy, because the modern village still had the same name—Mykēnē in Greek—and the remains of the famous Lion Gate entrance to the ancient citadel were partially visible, sticking up out of the ground.

Schliemann thought he knew where to look for Agamemnon at the site. The ancient Greek sources, from Homer down to the later fifth century BCE plays written by Sophocles, Aeschylus, and Euripides, said that Agamemnon had been killed after he returned home from ten years of fighting at Troy. He was murdered by his wife Clytemnestra and her lover Aegisthus, reportedly at the dinner table during a feast, according to Homer (*Odyssey* IV.524–35), but perhaps while taking a bath, according to later accounts. The men that were with Agamemnon were killed as well.

A much-later visitor to the site named Pausanias, who wrote about his travels all over Greece during the Roman period in the second century CE, said that Agamemnon and his men were buried inside the city limits of Mycenae. Pausanias didn't give a specific location for the graves, and so Schliemann had to use his powers of deduction.

{⟷}{⟷}

In February 1874, working without a permit as usual, Schliemann did some exploratory work at the site. He dug, as he put it, "thirty-four shafts in different places, in order to sound the ground and to find out the place where I should have to dig for them." In other words, he was digging test pits at the site—a technique that we have discussed earlier—in order to determine where he should concentrate his efforts once the real excavation started. Several of the test pits produced interesting results, but the most important were two that he dug not far inside the Lion Gate. Here, he says, he found "an unsculptured slab resembling a tombstone" in addition to other finds, including female idols and small figurines.

When he returned in early August 1876 with an initial team of sixty-three workers, he put two-thirds of them to work in an area that was just forty feet inside the Lion Gate. They were instructed to dig in a huge square area 113 feet long and 113 feet wide. Within two weeks, after he had doubled the number of workers to 125, they found a grave circle, with five deep shafts marked at their top by fragmentary tombstones depicting warriors and hunting scenes. This is now known as Grave Circle A.

The shafts that Schliemann found led to graves with multiple burials, an unbelievable number of swords, and a tremendous quantity of

Lion Gate, Mycenae

gold and silver objects, in addition to other grave goods. Among these were gold masks covering the faces of several of the dead men.

According to the story that is now usually told, Schliemann was so certain that he had found whom he was looking for that he immediately sent a telegram to the king of Greece, George I, which read, "I have gazed upon the face of Agamemnon." The king immediately rushed to Mycenae, where Schliemann showed him a marvelous gold mask with a kingly face engraved upon it, complete with mustache and beard. That mask now hangs front and center in a display case in the National Archaeological Museum in Athens.

The problem is, that wasn't the mask at which Schliemann was gazing when he sent the telegram nor was that actually the message that he sent to the king. His telegram to the king was not quite as pithy or punchy, reading (according to one version), "With great joy I announce to Your Majesty that I have discovered the tombs which the tradition proclaimed by Pausanias indicates to be the graves of Agamemnon, Cassandra, Eurymedon and their companions." Moreover, he had been looking at another mask at the time, of a much more cherubic and pleasant-looking fellow. When Schliemann found the more kingly-looking mask before the Greek monarch arrived, however, he showed him the new one instead.

Such a move was fairly typical for Schliemann—remember that he had begun the excavations without a permit to do so. It was only in later telegrams, such as those to the minister of Germany and to members of the news media, that Schliemann began saying that he had gazed upon the face, or into the eyes, of Agamemnon.

The grave goods that Schliemann found in those tombs included marvelous pieces of work: bronze daggers inlaid with hunting and wildlife scenes in silver and gold on the blades; objects of rock crystal and semiprecious stones; and gold, gold, gold—something like eight hundred kilograms of gold objects all told.

Excavations by the Greek archaeologist Panayiotis Stamatakis just a year or so later turned up at least one more grave within Grave Circle A and now, especially with better techniques of dating available, it is considered extremely unlikely that these are the graves of Agamemnon and his men. Their deaths would have taken place sometime between 1250 and 1175 BCE, if they even ever existed rather than being the stuff of myth and legend. We now know that the pottery and other objects in the graves date from 1600–1500 BCE, which means they are from a period three or four hundred years earlier than the time of the Trojan War.

Schliemann probably suspected as much. In his 1880 book on Mycenae, published just a few years after the excavation, he says specifically that the fragmentary tombstones likely dated to the middle of the second millennium BCE, and he even gives them a date of 1500 BCE in the table of contents for chapter 4. And so, he was fairly close to being correct in terms of the date for the tombs and their contents, even if he was completely wrong about whose bodies they contained.

In fact, it is now thought that these are most likely the graves of one of the first dynasties to rule at Mycenae, since the city rose to prominence at about 1700 BCE. These rulers would have lived within a century or two of that rise and were buried outside the city wall. At some point near the end of the Late Bronze Age, however, probably about 1250 BCE, the fortifications of the city were rebuilt to enclose a larger area than previously, which is when the Lion Gate was constructed. It was at that time that Grave Circle A came to be inside the walls.

⊰⊱ ⊰⊱

Just down the hill is Grave Circle B, which was found in the 1950s and is now adjacent to a parking lot for tourist buses and cars. Since the burials here date to 1650–1550 BCE, some of them are earlier than those in Grave Circle A. They may have been the very first kings, and perhaps a queen, to have ruled at Mycenae. In 1995, forensic anthropologists working with the skeletal material found in Grave Circle B attempted to reconstruct what some of the individuals would have originally looked like—it could have been an episode of *CSI: Ancient Greece*. They decided that the remains were from one woman and six men. Even though their end results are just a "best guess," they succeeded in bringing the long-dead people more to life than the bare bones could ever do, for they reconstructed their faces, hair, and, in several cases, beards as well.

Elsewhere on the site are a few very large beehive-shaped tombs, built from huge blocks of stone, known as tholos tombs. Several of them have names given to them in relatively modern times, including the Tomb of Clytemnestra and the Tomb of Agamemnon (also called the Treasury of Atreus). These were built about 1250 BCE, so if Agamemnon is buried anywhere, it could have been in these. They were all found completely looted and empty, however.

⁂ ⁂

Schliemann excavated at Mycenae only in 1874 and 1876. He then went looking for Ithaca, home of Odysseus, after which he returned to Troy for several more seasons of digging. In 1884 he dug at the site of Tiryns, which is only a few kilometers from Mycenae, but never excavated at Mycenae itself ever again. One hundred fifteen years later, Mycenae and Tiryns were jointly named to the UNESCO World Heritage Site list, in 1999.

It was left to later archaeologists to uncover the rest of the site, most of them using much better excavation methods than Schliemann had. The site has been under almost continuous excavation since Schliemann's day, and some very well-known Greek, British, and US archaeologists have spent many seasons there, including George Mylonas, Alan Wace, Elizabeth French, and my own professor, Spyros Iakovides.

Because of their efforts, what was left of the palace at the very top of the citadel has now been completely excavated. It turns out that its interior, and possibly the exterior as well, was covered with brightly colored plaster, with scenes of hunting and other activities garishly painted in blues, yellows, reds, and other colors on the walls. The king would have sat at one side of a large room, surrounded by such painted scenes, while a large fire blazed in a hearth that was set in the middle of the floor. It was dark in there, and smoky, and probably damp as well. Mycenaean palaces seem to have been a bit claustrophobic, with few windows or other openings; they focused inward rather than looking outward.

The rooms around the palace were used for a multitude of things, ranging from what were probably residential quarters for the royal family to workrooms for the craftsmen. There appears to have been a cult center, possibly where religious rituals took place. Some strange idols and figurines have been found there, along with wall paintings.

Texts inscribed on clay tablets also have been found at various places in and around the palace, as they have at other Mycenaean palatial sites. They are written in Linear B, which was deciphered and translated in 1952 by Michael Ventris, an English architect, who proved that it was an early version of Greek. Most of the tablets are simply inventories of goods that were being brought to the palace or sent out from there, but they do include some of the names of their gods, who will be quite familiar to readers, including Zeus, Hera, Poseidon, Artemis, and Dionysus.

There is no doubt that Mycenae was a wealthy city, with international connections. Objects imported from Italy, Egypt, Canaan, Cyprus, Anatolia, and even as far away as Mesopotamia have been found. Some of the most interesting are fragments of Egyptian faience plaques with the name of Pharaoh Amenhotep III on them, which might have been left by an official Egyptian embassy that was sent to Mycenae in the middle of the fourteenth century BCE.

Late in the Bronze Age, possibly about 1250 BCE at the same time as the Lion Gate, a well-constructed tunnel with steps of stone was built, leading down to a water source so that the inhabitants didn't have to venture outside in times of siege. This may be an indication that they could see trouble brewing in the near future.

It is not clear why the city came to an end soon after 1200 BCE, but it did, in the general calamity that ended the whole of the Late Bronze

Age in this region. Mycenae is built directly over a seismic fault line and at least one earthquake, if not more, caused destruction during this period. But it may have been drought and famine, followed perhaps by either internal revolt or external invasion that finally brought down this once-great city. There are some later remains, including a temple dedicated to Hera that was built at the very top of the citadel after the eighth century BCE, during the Archaic period, but Mycenae never regained its lost glory.

Other Mycenaean palaces at Tiryns, Thebes, Pylos, and elsewhere in Greece were destroyed or abandoned at the end of the Late Bronze Age as well. Much remains to be excavated at these and other sites, as shown by the recent discovery of the so-called Griffin Warrior grave at Pylos in 2015 by a team of University of Cincinnati archaeologists led by Jack Davis and Sharon Stocker. Dating to the fifteenth century BCE and located just next to the so-called Palace of Nestor at the site, the tomb contained more than fourteen hundred objects accompanying the single male skeleton—a man who was about thirty to thirty-five years old when he died. Preliminary announcements and media reports list some of the artifacts buried with him: gold rings, necklaces, and other jewelry; gold cups, silver cups, and bronze bowls; a bronze mirror, ivory combs, and carved seal stones; and a long bronze sword with an ivory hilt covered in gold leaf. Between his legs was an ivory plaque inscribed with a carved griffin on it, which has now given its name to the grave and its warrior. The grave was so packed with delicate artifacts that the archaeologists dug with wooden shish kebob sticks instead of metal dental tools, to be sure that no damage was done to them during excavation.

꘎꘎꘎ ꘎꘎꘎

Partway across the Aegean Sea, on the island of Crete, Schliemann also tried to purchase land at a site that he thought might be the capital city of the legendary king Minos. The owner refused to sell it to him, and so it was left to another archaeologist two decades later, Arthur Evans, to excavate the site and bring the other great Bronze Age Aegean civilization, the Minoans, to light. The city that he excavated, beginning in 1900, is now known as Knossos.

Evans was a Victorian gentleman in every sense of the word. In one picture, Evans can be seen clad in a white linen suit and wearing a pith helmet, which is of course not at all the way that we dress when digging today. Born in 1851, he grew up in good circumstances in England, the son of John Evans, who was a respected scholar and a trustee of the British Museum, as well as president of the Society of Antiquaries, the Numismatic Society, the Geological Society of London, and other societies and institutes.

Evans had been searching for this city of Knossos for years, ever since he saw a few items for sale in the marketplace in Athens earlier in the decade. Known as milkstones and sold to pregnant women for help during and after giving birth, these small pieces of semiprecious stone had strange figures and engravings on them. Evans eventually traced them back to Crete, to Kephala Hill on the outskirts of the modern port city of Heraklion, the very land that Schliemann had tried unsuccessfully to buy. Evans had better luck, purchased the mound, and began excavating. Underneath the gentle hill covered by underbrush and trees, his team of workers quickly came across the ruins of what Evans identified as the palace that he was looking for. He spent the rest of his career, and virtually all his family fortune, digging at the site, publishing the results, and reconstructing the remains.

What Evans found at Knossos turned out to be a civilization that was a little older than the Mycenaeans and that had influenced them when they were "growing up." For instance, a number of the objects that Schliemann found in the Shaft Graves at Mycenae were either of Minoan manufacture or bore the stamp of Minoan influence. In fact, Evans thought that the Minoans had conquered the Mycenaeans, though the opposite has turned out to be true.

When we refer to the Minoans, we're using the name that Evans gave to this people, since we don't know what they called themselves, nor do we know where they originally came from. They had flourished at the end of the third millennium BCE and then through most of the second millennium BCE—what we now call the Middle and Late Bronze Age in this region. Around 1700 BCE, a major earthquake hit Knossos, but the inhabitants survived and rebuilt the palace. Probably sometime about 1350 BCE, the Mycenaeans from the Greek mainland seem to have invaded and taken over, bringing with them a new way of writing, new types of scenes for the wall paintings, and a more militaristic way of life that lasted for about a century and a half, until everything collapsed soon after 1200 BCE.

Evans found amazing things at Knossos, but he also made what many consider to be a fatal error, because of the reconstructions that he created from the remains. For example, he imagined that the main part of the palace had three stories, which he inferred from the remains of staircases that he found, and so he reconstructed that part of the palace with three floors. Because he used cement and other permanent materials, it is nearly impossible to undo his reconstruction today. He may well have been correct in part, but not in everything, which is why today such reconstructions are generally not permitted, unless there is a very clear indication of what is original and what has been reconstructed.

What Evans and his team of workers found was a large, essentially open-air palace, with a huge central courtyard. It was light; it was airy; it was open to the elements; it was integrated into the environment. It even had running water and a sewer system. In other words, it was a building belonging to a culture that was very technologically advanced for its time. It served not only as headquarters for the ruler, but also as a center for redistribution. Locals would bring their goods in for storage, like wheat, barley, wine, and grapes, and then the palace would redistribute them as needed. There is, in fact, an entire part of the palace that consists only of corridors packed with large storage jars, including some that are sunk into the ground, in order to keep their contents cold.

Two things remain a mystery, however. One is the fact that there are absolutely no fortification walls around the palace at Knossos. Nor are there any at the other six or seven smaller palaces elsewhere on Crete at this time, despite occasional claims to the contrary. This is strange. Why weren't the people on Crete afraid of being attacked?

Much later, the Greek historian Thucydides said that the Minoans had a thalassocracy—that is, they ruled the sea with their navy. But that explains only why they might not have been worried about invasions by outsiders. It doesn't clarify why they weren't worried about an attack from just down the road. There have been many ideas put forward, but none has been completely satisfactory. One hypothesis is that it was a single family that was ruling Crete at the time, with the father at Knossos, his sons living at other palaces like Phaistos and Kato Zakro, and cousins at still other palaces like Khania. It also has been suggested that perhaps women ruled Crete, as a matriarchy, and that their peaceful rule made fortifications unnecessary. Although this could certainly be true, it still doesn't explain why there are no fortification walls; Zenobia of Palmya, Boudicca of Celtic England, Cleopatra of Egypt, and other female leaders throughout the centuries and elsewhere in the ancient world serve as proof that women are as capable as men of fighting or leading attacks on other cities and regions.

But that brings us to the second mystery, for we have no idea whether it was a king who ruled Knossos. It might have been a queen. It might have been a priest or a priestess. It might have been community rule. We just don't know. The archaeological remains, the artifacts, and even the written texts found at the site are all ambiguous and do not yet allow us to answer the question of who ruled at Knossos. Evans did label one room the "king's throne room" and another the "queen's megaron," but those are just names that he assigned. Someone was in charge, but we're still not sure who it was.

Among the objects brought to light by Evans are two extremely well known figurines of women holding snakes. They are made out of faience and ivory, but they were very fragmentary when found and so were restored by skilled craftsmen hired by Evans. The larger one is frequently called the Snake Goddess and the smaller one the Snake Priestess, but the names also are often used interchangeably and it is not at all clear whether either of them really is a representation of a goddess or a priestess. There are now a number of such figurines in museums around the world. Unfortunately, only a few are likely to be genuine. The rest have been identified as forgeries, probably made by the very men who conserved and reconstructed the real ones for Evans.

The interior walls of the palace were ablaze with color, in the form of many wall paintings. Everywhere the inhabitants looked, there was another elaborate decoration. From these, we can tell a fair amount about the Minoans. For instance, there is one woman depicted who is so beautiful that Evans dubbed her La Parisienne. She is shown with an elaborate hairdo, makeup, jewelry, and a dress of red, white, and blue. Other frescoes show similarly dressed women. Men are pictured too, usually dressed only in a kilt; they too wear jewelry and possibly makeup as well.

There are a few frescoes, though, where the reconstructions of Evans and his team of restorers were downright wrong. One is the well-known Dolphin Fresco; another is the most famous painting at the site, the Priest-King Fresco.

In the Dolphin Fresco, Evans reconstructed a painting with five dolphins and a few flying fish on a wall in the area of the Queen's Megaron. The painting wasn't still on the wall, of course; Evans found the fragments lying in the dirt in front of the wall during his excavations. He only found fragments from two of the dolphins, but the area where he thought the painting had been was large enough that he needed to suggest that there had originally been five dolphins.

The philosophical principle of Occam's razor—that the simplest solution is probably the correct one—comes into play here, though. If Evans found fragments from two dolphins, then he can only state for certain that there were two dolphins originally; everything else is a hypothesis. And since the painting could have come from anywhere in the room, or even from the one above it, we should look around for other possibilities. In 1986 Professor Robert Koehl of Hunter College suggested that the Dolphin Fresco, with only two dolphins, rather than five, was originally on the floor, not on the wall, for there is a space on the floor that is just a perfect size for the existing painting of the two dolphins—and both the Minoans and the Mycenaeans are known to have painted at least some of their floors. It is also conceivable that it was originally inlaid into the floor of a room located directly above the present one and it came crashing down after the palace was abandoned.

The other painting that Evans reconstructed incorrectly is the Priest-King Fresco, which today is reproduced everywhere, from the covers of books to placemats to plaster replicas. Here, Evans and his restorers put together a man whom they called the Priest-King of Knossos—though we should note that the title implies that they were unsure of who was ruling the city, just as we are still uncertain today. They have him walking toward the left side of the painting, with his head and his legs facing to the left, but with his body frontally facing the viewer and twisted toward the right. His right arm is cocked up against his chest, while his left arm goes off to the right, holding a rope (which they said was attached to a bull that isn't shown).

So, what's wrong with this? Well, just about everything. First, the pieces apparently were found in three different rooms in the building, not all together in one. Why Evans thought they were all from the same painting is beyond me. Second, the flesh of the figure is in two different colors; the head, which is facing left and has just a bit of skin visible, is painted white; the chest, which is twisted right, is reddish-brown; and the legs, which are headed to the left, are also reddish-brown. In Minoan art, they used conventions to depict males and females—males are always red or brown; females are white or yellow.

In other words, we have three different figures here, which Evans put together as a single person. We have a woman headed left, of whom we have only the top of her head; a man also headed left, from whom we have only part of his legs; and perhaps a young boy or teenager headed right, for whom we have only the torso, with the right hand cocked against the chest. Moreover, the pose of the torso looks very much like the pose adopted by two boxing boys in a painting found on Santorini. So much for the Priest-King of Knossos, but this serves as a good reminder that archaeology, and archaeological reconstructions, are always open to correction by later researchers.

❋⟺❋ ❋⟺❋

Let's now turn from Evans's reconstructed frescoes and have a quick look at the big central court at Knossos. This was undoubtedly used for all sorts of things, as such big ceremonial areas are throughout the world and in all eras. But the court at Knossos seems to have been where a rather unusual practice took place, if we can believe what is pictured in a small wall painting in one of the buildings, where we see three people—one male and two female—leaping over a bull.

The man is in mid-flight, doing a somersault over the bull's back. One woman is in front of the bull, grasping his horns, perhaps to distract him, while the other is behind the bull and looks poised to catch the man when he lands. It is also possible, however, that all three are leaping over the bull; if so, one woman has just landed, the man is in the process, and the other woman is about to fling herself over. It is unclear which interpretation is the correct one. Either way, this is like doing a routine on the pommel horse at the Olympics, except that the pommel horse is alive, has horns, and is trying to kill you.

Excavators at Knossos also found an ivory figurine, which may be part of a bull-leaping group. The figure is most likely meant to have been positioned flying through the air, for it has pointed toes as well as outstretched arms.

Beyond that, there are several bulls' heads made in stone that have been found at Knossos, some of which appeared to have been deliberately smashed, perhaps after a ritual. These stone heads were hollow, with holes at the nostrils, so that if they were filled with red wine, for instance, and then held at the proper angle, it would look like the participant was holding the head of a bull that had just been sacrificed to the gods and was still dripping blood.

⁂ ⁂

And so, it seems that the Minoans were perhaps doing some bull leaping in their central courtyard as well as some rituals involving bulls in or around the palace. This in turn brings to mind the Greek myth of Theseus and the Minotaur. Back in the Bronze Age, King Minos demanded a sacrifice each year to the Minotaur, the half-man half-bull creature who was living in the basement below his palace at Knossos. The basement was a labyrinth, from which no one had ever gotten out alive. Each year the king of Athens had to send seven young boys and seven girls to King Minos, who then sent them down into the labyrinth.

One year Theseus, the son of the king of Athens, volunteered to go, so that he could try to kill the Minotaur and put an end to the annual sacrifice. His distraught father agreed. Once he got to Knossos, Theseus befriended Ariadne, the daughter of King Minos. She provided him with a sword and a ball of string. As he went through the maze, he unwound the ball of string, so that he could find his way back out. When he got to the Minotaur, he pulled out the sword and cut off the Minotaur's head. He then retraced his steps and emerged victorious.

I have long thought that the story may have been created in an attempt by later occupants of the area to explain the ruins of the palace of Knossos, as well as to account for the vague memories that they had about their ancestors doing something with bulls, and especially the mazelike appearance of the ruined storage areas.

I may be completely wrong about that, however, and there might be another explanation entirely, because in the early 1990s, a huge wall painting was found, depicting multiple bulls and numerous bull leapers in action in front of what can only be described as a maze or a labyrinth. It is a painting that we would understandably expect to find at Knossos, except that's not where it is. It's not even in Crete. It is, in fact, in the Nile Delta region of Egypt, at the site of Tell el-Dab'a. And it dates somewhere between the seventeenth and fifteenth centuries BCE; that is, right in the middle of the second millennium, during the Bronze Age and the height of Minoan culture.

Therefore, it may be that the myth of Theseus and the Minotaur has some kernel of truth in Minoan practice and was not made up later to explain the ruins of Knossos. But the very fact that such a painting is in Egypt, even though it depicts a Minoan motif and was created using techniques that were quite different from those of the Egyptians at that time, is to my mind even more interesting. The excavator of the painting suggested that perhaps a Minoan princess had been brought over for a dynastic marriage. I don't think it is necessary to have such an elaborate explanation, but certainly the presence of the painting shows that Egypt and Crete were in direct contact at that time. I suspect that it was created either by Minoan artists or by local artists who had been trained by Minoans. We already knew from other evidence that such connections existed, but it is fascinating to find such a vivid corroboration of the international connections that were ongoing across the Aegean and eastern Mediterranean during the Bronze Age, more than three thousand years ago.

{••}{••}

Schliemann is usually given credit for discovering the Mycenaeans on mainland Greece, and Evans usually gets credit for discovering the Minoans on Crete, but there is another group that flourished in the Aegean region during the Bronze Age—on the Cycladic islands that lay north of Crete and east of mainland Greece.

These islands, including Naxos, Paros, Melos, Thera, and others, had their own Cycladic culture, albeit with many interconnections with the Mycenaeans and Minoans. They are probably best known for the marble figurines from the Early Cycladic period, during the third millennium BCE, which depict primarily women, but also figures playing musical instruments such as a double pipe and what may be a harp or lyre. At least some of them were involved in the international connections that were ongoing a bit later during the second millennium BCE, including the island of Thera, perhaps better known today as Santorini. We shall discuss those events in the next chapter.

9

FINDING ATLANTIS?

I N 2011 A DOCUMENTARY CALLED *FINDING ATLANTIS* AIRED ON television, in which a team was said to be searching for the remains of the lost island in an area of Spain, just north of Cadiz. Most archaeologists whom I know, and a number of other viewers as well, found the results less than compelling.

It seems that almost every year, there is an announcement made that someone has located the lost island of Atlantis, perhaps in the Bahamas or off the coast of Cyprus. Sometimes a television show results; sometimes a book is published.

Personally, I think the island is in plain sight, and always has been, for I, and many other archaeologists, suspect that if there is any kernel of truth underlying the myth of Atlantis at all, it is probably the volcanic Greek island of Thera, also called Santorini, which erupted during the middle of the second millennium BCE. We'll return to this possible relationship in a bit, but first we should look at the actual excavations and discoveries that have taken place on the island since 1967.

✦⟶✦ ✦⟶✦

Santorini lies about seventy miles north of Crete. The name Santorini is rather recent—it was the Venetians who gave the island that name, after Saint Irene. An older name, frequently used by archaeologists, is Thera, which the Greek historian Herodotus says comes from the name of a Spartan commander named Theras, who was the leader of a colony established there during the first millennium BCE. Even before that, the island was called Kalliste, meaning the "beautiful one" or "fair one," which Herodotus said was the name that the Phoenicians gave to the island (even though *kalliste* is a Greek word). Some suggest that the very first name of the island may have been Strongili, which translates as "the round one" and which makes sense, since it is circular in shape. It is actually a volcano and is still active today.

Sometime during the middle of the second millennium, most likely in either the seventeenth or sixteenth century BCE, the volcano blew its top, scattering ash and pumice primarily to the south and east. This

Eruption of Santorini

would have been during a time when the Minoans were flourishing on Crete and may have dramatically affected their civilization, either for the short or the long term. The explosion is said to have been four or five times more forceful than the most powerful volcanic eruption in modern times, the explosion of Krakatoa in Indonesia, which took place about 130 years ago, in 1883. Archaeologists and geologists have found the pumice from the Santorini eruption in excavations and at the bottoms of lakes in places ranging from Crete to Egypt to Turkey.

The entire middle part of the island is completely gone as a result of the explosion, with only the outer part remaining as an incomplete circle of land. The circle is broken in two places, which is where tons of water rushed in from the Aegean Sea to fill up the caldera that is hundreds of feet deep. That in turn most likely created a tidal wave, or tsunami, that affected places as far away as Crete. Huge blocks of stone can still be seen on the beach by the site of Amnisos, where they had probably been thrown out of place by the disaster. In the middle of the caldera today are several small islands that have popped up just in the last century as a result of the continuing, low-level volcanic activity. Today tourists (and archaeologists) can take a boat out to these little islands and hike on them. I can personally attest that the rocks are so hot that the heat can be felt through the soles of your shoes and everything stinks of sulphur, with an odor of rotting eggs. It is a unique, and not entirely pleasant, experience—but it is memorable.

The eruption also completely buried the Bronze Age city of Akrotiri, which is frequently called the Pompeii of the Aegean because of the deep ash layer that completely covered and preserved it. In some places on the island, the ash layer is so thick that it is quarried today, for use in things like cement. The ash fall filled the houses at Akrotiri, preserving some to the second story. Just as at Pompeii, it is as if life simply stopped here in a single instant, more than thirty-five hundred years ago.

{↔}{↔}

With or without the myth of Atlantis, excavations at the site of Akrotiri have shed very interesting and important light upon life in the Bronze Age Aegean, because the eruption took place at a time when the inhabitants, as well as the Minoans from nearby Crete, were engaged in regular contact and international trade with places like Egypt and Canaan in the eastern Mediterranean.

It is clear from some of the remains found during the excavations that the site may have been nearly abandoned before the time of the final eruption. There are indications that a major earthquake, or perhaps multiple earthquakes, may have hit the island about a decade before the final destruction. At least some of the inhabitants had tried to repair the damage, though many may have already fled at the first sign of trouble. Today we know that earthquakes frequently precede eruptions. The ancients may have known that as well. Because no bodies or other human remains and only a few precious objects have been found despite nearly fifty years of excavation, it is in fact quite likely that most of the inhabitants cleared out before the end finally came, taking their most valuable and easily transportable belongings with them. But they still left behind plenty of things for us to find.

The Greek archaeologist Spyridon Marinatos gets credit for discovering the site, but it wasn't all that hard to find. A portion of the site was in a gully, down which water flowed every time it rained. That water had washed away much of the ash in that area, so that some pieces of the site could be readily seen. The excavations began in 1967.

Marinatos had wanted to start such excavations for nearly thirty years, ever since he published an article in the journal *Antiquity* in 1939. In that article, he had suggested that the Minoan civilization on Crete had been brought to an end, or at least was dramatically and adversely affected, by an eruption of Santorini at some point during the second millennium BCE. It was such a radical suggestion that the editors agreed to publish the article only if they were allowed to add in a note at the beginning, suggesting that he should undertake excavations in order to test his hypothesis.

Marinatos directed the Akrotiri excavations from 1967 until 1974, when he died at the site. The official verdict was that his death was caused by a massive stroke, resulting in him tumbling off the balk into a trench. He is buried at the site, but in true archaeological fashion, I am told that it took several efforts before a proper grave could be dug, because they kept hitting remains from the ancient site. (I should note that there are similar problems when trying to place the supporting posts every time a new roofing system is installed, because they keep hitting ancient remains when digging the holes for the posts.)

Marinatos made discoveries at the ancient site from the very first day that he began digging. The excavations continued after his death and are today led by the well-known archaeologist Christos Doumas. Even though the site has been continuously excavated for nearly fifty years at this point, it is estimated that only a small percentage of the ancient town has been uncovered.

In many places, a situation similar to that seen at Pompeii was encountered, in which the original wood or other organic material had decomposed and otherwise disappeared, leaving an empty space in the now-hardened volcanic ash. Into these spaces, excavators have poured cement or plaster of Paris (just as at Pompeii), which is then colored brown, to imitate the original wood. In this way, the buildings remain preserved up to their second story and sometimes beyond, just as Marinatos and Doumas found them, and are still rendered safe for both the tourists and the archaeologists who wander among them. The architectural continuity of Santorini is such that if the ruins were painted white and blue, the ancient town would be virtually indistinguishable from one of the modern villages on the island.

{⟷}{⟷}

The ash is everywhere at Akrotiri, having gone into every nook and cranny of the site after the eruption. As a result, it has preserved everything as it was at the time of the explosion. Thus, large storage jars remain and can be excavated in place, though often fallen over from their original position. Other large artifacts, like wooden beds, also have been carefully excavated and retrieved, using the lost-wax technique to reconstruct them when they have disintegrated and left empty spaces in the ash.

Quite a bit of pottery has been recovered during the excavations, as well as objects made out of stone and other materials. Some of them, especially the pottery, are painted with marine scenes featuring dolphins and octopi. Others show nature scenes, including flowers, leaves, and long-stemmed grass, and birds in flight that look a lot like the swallows that can be seen on the island today.

Wall paintings adorned the rooms in some of the houses. One of these, which features papyrus plants in a naturalistic scene that covers all four walls of the room, also has two of these little swallows interacting. In fact, the paintings at Akrotiri are among the best preserved that we have found from the Bronze Age Aegean, rivaling those found at Knossos. One is the so-called Nilotic Fresco, which features a scene that might be depicting the Nile in Egypt. It has a leaping feline chasing a duck or goose. On both sides of the river, or stream, are what look like palm trees or perhaps papyrus plants. It was found in a house—the so-called West House—along with several other frescoes that have nautical or perhaps non-Theran scenes. It is possible that the house belonged to a ship captain or to someone who had traveled overseas.

Another rather exotic-looking wall painting shows monkeys swinging from trees and generally hanging about, as monkeys like to do. The only thing is, these monkeys are blue, with white cheeks, which seems a little strange. There is a similar wall painting at Knossos on Crete, also showing blue monkeys, and there are two little blue monkey figurines with yellow cheeks that were found at Mycenae and Tiryns on the Greek mainland.

What is even stranger is that monkeys are not indigenous to the Aegean region. It turns out that there is a species of monkey in Africa called a green guenon, whose fur can be a bluish-green color and who have yellow or whitish cheeks. They are found in areas like Nubia and were prized as pets by the pharaohs of New Kingdom Egypt, who occasionally sent them as gifts to rulers in other countries. So, strange as it may seem, it looks as if these paintings, and the figurines, are correct in their representations of the monkeys. They may represent a group that someone had seen in Egypt or that had been sent over as a gift from Egypt to the rulers of Santorini or Crete.

One painting that seems a masterpiece shows two animals that look like ibexes, or wild goats, as typically found on Greek islands. These two in particular are each painted with a single bold stroke that goes from the tip of the tail all the way up to the neck and then the head of the animal, with the other details then added in as bold lines as well. This masterfully simple painting technique completely captures the two animals.

A number of human figures also are depicted. One shows two young boys who seem to be boxing, which has been mentioned in passing in an earlier chapter, in connection with the Priest-King Fresco at Knossos. They are almost naked, wearing only loincloths, and have shaved heads with clumps of hair hanging down in curls. Where their hair is cut close to the scalp, it is shown as blue rather than black. There also is a painting of a naked young man holding two long strings of fish that he has just caught. This painting shows even more of his hair shaved off and fewer of the tendrils or ringlets. It has been suggested that the young boys had more and more hair shaved each year, perhaps in a ritual, so that by the time they were in their late teens, they had essentially a crewcut.

Other pictures show young women engaged in a variety of activities, including a number who are picking flowers like crocuses and saffron. Some of these young women also have mostly shaved heads, just like the boys. If there was some sort of age-related ceremony related to hair, it apparently extended to the young women as well as the men. Many of the women are depicted wearing earrings and other jewelry and wearing elaborate dresses, so we can easily reconstruct how they adorned themselves back then.

In the West House is another painting in addition to the Nilotic scene, which is known as the Miniature Fresco or the Flotilla Fresco. On one end of the scene, we can see warriors marching off to battle. They are dressed in a fashion like some of the warriors whom Homer describes in the *Iliad*. They wear boar-tusk helmets on their heads and carry what are called Tower Shields, which are long enough to cover a person from the neck down to the lower legs. Behind the warriors is a large building, with women standing on the roof apparently waving goodbye to the warriors. There also are what look like cows and other herd animals, and a herdsman in the distance above them, but below them is a scene with a few boats and men who are sideways or upside-down—which is the way that artists in the Bronze Age depicted dead and drowning people. The scene is usually interpreted as a naval battle, though it also has been suggested that it is a scene of sacrifice.

The fresco continues with a flotilla scene, showing as many as a dozen or more ships departing a port that may or may not be on Santorini. The men row their way across the sea, accompanied by cavorting dolphins, until they reach a second city, at which point they tie up the ships and presumably disembark. This part of the fresco has been the topic of much discussion among archaeologists, with some focusing on the design and depiction of the ships and others focusing on where they might have begun their voyage and where they might have ended it. Suggestions include the possibility that this is a voyage to or from either Egypt or Anatolia (modern-day Turkey), but there has not yet been any consensus on these interpretations.

❊⟨•••⟩❊ ❊⟨•••⟩❊

Santorini also has been at the forefront of a huge debate among Bronze Age Aegean archaeologists ever since 1987, when a radical redating of the volcanic eruption was proposed. It used to be thought that the Santorini eruption took place in about 1450 BCE. Since a certain style of pottery, known as Late Minoan (LM) Ib pottery, was in vogue at the time of the eruption, it used to be thought this type of pottery should also be dated to about 1450 BCE.

As a result of new analysis of radiocarbon dates from the site and nearby, however, it has been proposed that the eruption took place in or around 1628 BCE, rather than 1450 BCE, almost two full centuries earlier. Since the date of the eruption and use of LM Ib pottery are still tied together, that means that any level at any site that contains such pottery actually dates to the seventeenth century BCE, not the fifteenth century BCE. This became known as the high chronology, because it proposes a much earlier date for these historical events.

Sturt Manning, now of Cornell University, has been at the forefront of the discussions about the redating of the eruption since they first began. He has published numerous articles on the subject as well as a book called *A Test of Time*. One of the pieces of evidence that is central to his dating is a piece of wood from an olive tree that had been buried by ash during the eruption. The olive wood dates to about 1628 BCE.

The redating assumes the accuracy of the new radiocarbon dates. But carbon dating is acknowledged to have some problems associated with it, including fluctuations in the ratio of carbon in the atmosphere and the possibility of contamination in the samples, and so not everyone has accepted this change in chronology. Some are willing to accept a bit of a change, but only pushing the date of the eruption back to 1550

BCE, rather than all the way back to 1628 BCE, thereby creating a middle chronology to go with high and low Santorini chronologies.

As an aside, it should be noted that the redating of the eruption, regardless of which date one accepts, means that it cannot be linked in any way, shape, or form to the parting of the Red Sea or any of the Ten Plagues associated with the Exodus of the Israelites from Egypt. Few scholars had ever wished to connect these events anyway—though it is a favorite suggestion of pseudo-archaeologists—since the eruption occurred at least a century, and perhaps as much as four centuries, before the Exodus even possibly took place.

For me, it seems likely that the high chronology is correct, but the debate is ongoing. I highlight this here to show that, even when we have lots of buildings, pottery, and other artifacts from a site, and we know relatively when it was flourishing, we cannot always be certain about the absolute, or chronological, date. We will discuss this issue, as well as radiocarbon dating itself, more in depth in a later chapter.

{↔} {↔}

Santorini and Akrotiri are of great interest to archaeologists because they are central to any discussion about international trade and contact that may have been ongoing between Greece, Egypt, and the Near East more than thirty-five hundred years ago. But they also are of interest to the general public because of the possible connections to the legend of Atlantis.

As mentioned previously, I tend to believe that there is a kernel of truth lying at the bottom of many of the Greek myths and legends, for I think they probably based such tall tales on some aspect of their reality. Thus, I think that something did happen to spark the stories about the Trojan War. I also think that the eruption of Santorini in the seventeenth century BCE (or the fifteenth century, for that matter) may be the real event that underlies the whole story of Atlantis. Here I am dangerously close to being in the realm of the pseudo-archaeologists, hunting for what may be fictional places, but I'll explain briefly why I believe the way I do.

{↔} {↔}

The story of Atlantis comes to us courtesy of the Greek philosopher Plato. In two of his shorter works, called the *Timaeus* and the *Critias* respectively, which were written in the fourth century BCE, more than a thousand years after Thera's eruption, Plato tells us about an incredible civilization and an island that sank, in a day and a night, beneath the waves, never to be seen again. It is in the *Timaeus* that he says specifically, "there occurred violent earthquakes and floods; and in a single day and night of misfortune . . . the island of Atlantis . . . disappeared in the depths of the sea." He never says where Atlantis was located, except that it was "an island situated in front of the straits which are by you called the Pillars of Heracles; the island was larger than Libya and Asia put together."

An Egyptian priest, Plato says, told the initial story of Atlantis to a visiting Greek lawgiver named Solon sometime after 590 BCE. The priest told him that the events had taken place nine thousand years before their time, though—quite frankly—nine hundred years before Solon fits better, since that would put the events back at about 1500 BCE, rather than back at 9600 BCE during the Neolithic Age when there weren't yet any complex cultures (despite what some pseudo-archaeologists claim). The story was then handed down by Solon to his son and then his son's son, and so on, until it reached Plato somewhere around the year 400 BCE.

Plato also gives a very detailed description of what Atlantis looked like, including that it was built of concentric and alternating rings of land and water, with specific measurements of various parts of the city and so on. But since his description of its location is pretty general, people have looked for it in all sorts of places, including the Bahamas, off the coast of Cyprus, and everywhere in between, as has been mentioned.

None of the reported findings has yet panned out. Even when there is a similarity in physical layout, they are either natural formations or show no relationship to Greek culture—or both. Santorini comes closest, but even there the date is way off, as we saw.

One could—and probably should—argue that Atlantis is a mythical place invented by Plato in order to describe what he thinks the perfect city and society might look like. There is, therefore, no reason to believe that we should be able to go out and find it. The eruption of Santorini, however, would have been both heard and felt as far away as Egypt. The Egyptians also would have seen the cloud resulting from the eruption and eventually they would have seen pieces of pumice floating on the water and ending up on the northern shores. There has even been a suggestion by some Egyptologists and other scholars that a well-known Egyptian inscription called the Tempest Stele may be a contemporary account of what they saw and heard during and after the eruption.

Moreover, if the Minoans and the Cycladic islanders, from places like Santorini, stopped coming to Egypt at least temporarily after the eruption, as seems quite likely to have happened, then to the Egyptians it would have seemed as if a great island empire had disappeared. From the point of view of those who had living in Akrotiri, and perhaps elsewhere on the island, their world had indeed come to an end in a single day and night of misfortune.

Thus, the eruption of Santorini could be the basis for Plato's story of Atlantis. But even if it is not, the archaeological finds that have been made at the site of Akrotiri by Marinatos, Doumas, and others have shed wonderful light on the Bronze Age Aegean during the second millennium BCE, which—in my opinion—was among the most fascinating periods of human history.

I O

ENCHANTMENT UNDER
THE SEA

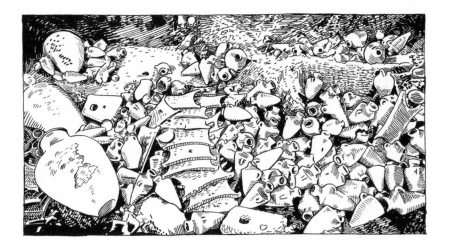

I N 1982, A SEVENTEEN-YEAR-OLD SPONGE DIVER EMERGED FROM
the wine-dark sea off the coast of southwestern Turkey and told his
captain that he had seen a "metal biscuit with ears." When he drew
a picture of it, the captain recognized it as an oxhide copper ingot,
which archaeologists from the Institute of Nautical Archaeology at
Texas A&M University had asked him to keep an eye out for during
their sponge-diving season. He contacted the institute and by the next
summer the archaeologists confirmed that it had come from a shipwreck dating to the Late Bronze Age. They had found what is now
known as the Uluburun shipwreck.

The ship, which sank around 1300 BCE, is—without exaggeration—
one of the most important archaeological discoveries of all time. Shipwrecks always represent a snapshot in time, from the Titanic on back,
but it is unusual to find one from so early and so full of cargo. The
Uluburun wreck was found stuffed with raw materials, including

copper, tin, ivory, and raw glass, as well as finished goods, such as pottery from Cyprus and Canaan, that sheds light on the international trade and relations that took place more than three thousand years ago. It is extremely important as a microcosm of the interconnected world of that time. The fact that it was found in 140–170 feet of water, and that the archaeologists conducted more than twenty thousand dives for a decade without a major accident reported, makes the tale even more unusual.

⁕⟨⟶⟩⁕ ⟨⟶⟩⁕

The story involves George Bass, the father of underwater archaeology, and Cemal Pulak, who was first Bass's student and now is his colleague at the Institute for Nautical Archaeology at Texas A&M University. But it begins in 1959, when Bass was a graduate student at the University of Pennsylvania. He was trying to decide on a dissertation topic when Rodney Young, the curator of the Mediterranean Section of the Penn Museum, called him into his office. A shipwreck had been found off the coast of Turkey and someone was needed to excavate it. Young thought that Bass would be a good choice.

And he was. Bass went out and conducted the world's first underwater excavation, on what is now known as the Cape Gelidonya shipwreck. This is why he is referred to as the father of underwater archaeology. The Gelidonya shipwreck lies reasonably close to the Uluburun shipwreck. Of course, Bass didn't know that at the time. It also dates from almost the same time period, because it sank in about 1200 BCE.

On the Gelidonya wreck, Bass found artifacts that indicated it had been a small ship, and was probably tramping around the Mediterranean—that is, going from port to port, buying and selling goods as it went. It does not appear to have belonged to a wealthy merchant, or a king, but more likely to a private individual trying to earn a living. Among the objects that Bass retrieved were ingots of solid copper—the type that we call oxhide ingots because they are in the shape of a cowhide or oxhide that might hang on a wall or be used on the floor as a rug. These copper ingots each weighed about sixty pounds and are the same as the "metal biscuits with ears" that the young sponge diver would find at Uluburun in 1982.

Bronze is frequently made by combining 90 percent copper and 10 percent tin (arsenic can be used in place of tin, although I wouldn't recommend it). It would make sense, therefore, if there were also raw tin on board the Gelidonya wreck. And indeed there was. Unfortunately, most of it now looked more like toothpaste than raw tin, because of the corrosion caused by saltwater, and some scholars doubted the identification.

Judging from the artifacts that he excavated, Bass also said that the wreck was a Canaanite ship possibly on its way to the Aegean. This went very much against the scholarly thinking of the day, especially since it was generally thought that only the Minoans on Crete might have been sailing the seas—after all, Thucydides talks about the "Minoan thalassocracy" or "rule of the sea." When Bass published his book on the shipwreck in 1967, it was met with derision and disdain in some scholarly quarters. As it turned out, Bass was not only correct on all counts, but he was far ahead of his time in recognizing that others besides the Minoans had been sailing the seas.

{↔}{↔}

Bass was determined to find another wreck at some point that would confirm his conclusions about the Gelidonya shipwreck. In the meantime, he founded the American Institute of Nautical Archaeology in 1972 while still at the University of Pennsylvania and then moved with it to Texas A&M University in 1976, where it—and he—has remained ever since, though they long ago dropped the "American" from their name, to reflect the international nature of their work.

In 1980, the institute purchased a boat and they began doing underwater surveys, searching for other shipwrecks. Underwater surveys can be long and time-consuming, especially back then in the 1980s, when surveys were done as if on land, by following long transects and recording what was seen. At some point, they had the bright idea that instead of doing the surveying themselves, they could simply visit the villages in which the Turkish sponge divers lived and describe to them what they were looking for. That way, they could enlist the help of the professionals who were diving to the bottom of the sea every day, looking for sponges to sell.

And, sure enough, soon thereafter, in 1982, the young sponge diver spotted the "metal biscuit with ears." Bass was on his way toward excavating another wreck that would confirm his conclusions about the Gelidonya shipwreck. What he didn't realize at the time was that the Uluburun shipwreck was far richer and far more important than what he had found previously. The importance of his discovery can be measured by the fact that just a few years later, in 1986, and long before the completion of the excavations, Bass received the Gold Medal Award for Distinguished Archaeological Achievement from the Archaeological Institute of America, the highest honor that his colleagues could bestow.

Uluburun diver

The excavation of the Uluburun shipwreck began in earnest during summer 1984, under Bass's direction. The next year, in 1985, he turned over direction of the project to Cemal Pulak. From then until 1994, excavations were conducted virtually every summer, with a team of professional archaeologists and eager graduate students. They dove on the wreck every day, with each of them diving twice a day, but spending only about twenty minutes on the bottom each time. Decompression was a major physical danger to the divers and decompressing from that depth took a long time. To pass the time, they took to reading novels tied to a rope, once they were close enough to the surface that there was enough light to read by. They collectively worked for more than 6,600 hours while excavating the ship during those ten years, diving more than twenty-two thousand times on the wreck.

It turned out that the top part of the wreck was 140 feet below sea level, but the scatter of remains continued on down to a depth of 170 feet. Even then, they found that the front part of the fifty-foot-long ship had broken off and plunged off a cliff or ledge; it has never been recovered. Bass said that, at that depth, it felt like they had had two martinis before even beginning to work, and so they had to plan out every dive meticulously in advance. They also dove in pairs, using the buddy system, and had an ex–Navy Seal overseeing their safety, which explains the lack of reported accidents even over the course of a decade.

Bass once described, in a *Nova* video, what it was like to be part of the team. As soon as you get to the seabed, he said, you remove the flippers from your feet, so that you don't accidentally excavate anything when swimming or walking close to the sand on the bottom. You grab a vacuum tube coming down from the surface in order to remove a lot of the loose sand, but then—when you move to delicate excavation—you move your hand in a continuous scooping motion in order to remove the sand carefully, because simply waving your hand back and forth does nothing but stir up the sand and cloud your vision. You are helping to map each part of the wreck—and each object found within it—meticulously, because your final plans are to be drawn within millimeter accuracy, as accurately as any plan done at an archaeological site on land. It's hard enough to do that well on land; imagine doing it at 140 feet below the surface after having had a two-martini lunch!

The team ultimately found so many objects that the final report was still being created at the time that I was writing this book and will take up several volumes when it is finally published. In the meantime, either Bass or Pulak has published a preliminary report after the end of each season. They also have presented papers at many conferences, which have since been published.

In order to dive on the wreck, the team lived for several months each summer in wooden buildings that they constructed on the cliff face of the promontory into which the Uluburun ship had probably slammed before it sank more than three thousand years ago. There also was some living space on their dive boat, the *Virazon*, which was permanently moved directly above the shipwreck. With one dormitory for the men and another for the women, plus a building for the kitchen and eating area, another for the conservation and storage of the artifacts, and still one more—hanging out over the water—used as a bathroom, the team truly lived off the grid, a several-hour boat ride away from the nearest town or city.

⭢⭠⭢ ⭢⭠⭢

We know when the boat sank, because of four separate pieces of evidence. First, there is a gold scarab containing the name of Queen Nefertiti that was found on board. She ruled with Pharaoh Akhenaton sometime around 1350 BCE, and so the ship cannot have sunk before that time. Second, some of the wood from the hull of the ship was recovered and dated to about 1320 BCE, using dendrochronology dating, in which tree rings are counted to provide a date for the cutting of the wood used. Third, the Mycenaean and Minoan pottery on board is of a style called Late Helladic IIIA2, which archaeologists date to the last part of the fourteenth century BCE using comparisons from other Greek sites. And fourth, they were able to use carbon-14 to date some of the brushwood that was on board. These all indicate that the ship sank about 1300 BCE, which is about thirty years after the time of King Tut's burial in Egypt and perhaps a few decades before the time of the Trojan War.

We also now know what the ship was carrying. First of all, underneath the rest of the cargo, and spaced out along the length of the hull, were approximately fourteen large stone anchors. These were used as ballast for most of the journey, but as each one was needed, it was put into use. That way, if one of the anchors got stuck on a rock or a reef, the sailors could simply cut the rope and then retrieve another one from down in the cargo hull. Such stone anchors have been found at several sites on land, like Kition or Enkomi on Cyprus and Ugarit in coastal Syria, but none had never before been found still in place within a sunken ship from the Bronze Age.

The main cargo was oxhide ingots, made of 99 percent pure raw copper from Cyprus. There were more than 350 of these ingots on board the ship, stacked row upon row in the hold. We have one letter that was written from the king of Cyprus to the king of Egypt from about 1350 BCE, in which he apologizes for sending "only" 200 copper ingots (or talents, as they were called then); this ship shows that as many as 350 could be shipped at once during this time period. Such ingots may have been used as currency—bullion for international trade.

All told, there is more than ten tons of copper on board this one ship. Some of the ingots were so corroded that the archaeologists had to essentially invent a new type of glue, which they injected into the remains of the ingot and then allowed to harden for the entire year between excavation seasons. Then they carefully picked up each one and floated it to the surface before taking them all back to the museum at Bodrum. There they were conserved and cleaned of the corrosion that had accumulated over the centuries.

As for the tin that Bass had found on the Gelidonya shipwreck—which looked like toothpaste and was doubted by many scholars—the Uluburun shipwreck vindicated him here as well, for it contained more than a ton of tin, in recognizable forms this time, some as fragments of oxhide ingots, others as a smaller type of ingot called a bun ingot, yet others as plates and other vessels made of tin. The tin had traveled a long way already, for its origin was likely the Badakhshan region of Afghanistan, but its voyage wasn't supposed to be over until it had reached the Aegean, most likely, although the sinking of the ship foiled that plan.

Ten tons of copper and one ton of tin will make eleven tons of bronze. Bass once estimated that this would have been enough to outfit an army of three hundred soldiers with swords, shields, helmets, greaves, and other necessary accouterments. Not only did someone lose a fortune when this ship went down, but someone also might have lost a war.

Other raw materials were on board as well, including approximately one ton of terebinth resin, which was used as incense and for making perfume, among other things. It comes from the pistachio tree and has never been found in such quantities in one place before.

The resin was being carried in some of the so-called Canaanite storage jars, of which there were about 140 on board. These are just what they sound like—transportation and storage jars made in Canaan (that is, modern-day Israel, Lebanon, Syria) that could hold any number of things. On the Uluburun ship, they were found to contain not only the resin, but also glass beads—thousands of them in some cases—as well as food such as figs and dates.

One jar held a small folding wooden tablet, with ivory hinges. It probably floated into the jar by accident after the ship sank. Inside the tablet, the two sides, which are recessed, would have originally held wax, colored yellow by terebinth resin. On this wax would have been written some sort of message, for this is what we call a diptych or a wooden writing tablet. Homer talks about such a tablet in book 6 of the *Iliad*, when he mentions a tablet with "baneful signs."

Unfortunately, the wax in the Uluburun tablet is long gone. A second tablet also was found in the excavations, but the wax was gone there too. Thus, we don't know what was originally written in either one. Was it the ship's itinerary? Was it the manifest of the cargo? Was it a message from one king to another? We'll never know.

Among the raw goods being transported on the ship the archaeologists recovered approximately 175 bun ingots of raw glass; most were dark cobalt blue, but others were light blue, and some were an amber color. The chemical analyses of these ingots of raw glass match those from objects of glass found in both Egypt and Greece during this time period, indicating that everyone was getting their raw glass from the same source, possibly in northern Syria or Egypt.

A cache of raw ivory on board the ship included both elephant tusks and hippopotamus canines and incisors. After these were discovered in the wreck, other scholars went back and re-examined ivory objects dating to the Late Bronze Age in various museums around the world. They had previously assumed that most were made from elephant ivory, but to their surprise it seems that most are from hippopotamus ivory. There also was a very small jawbone (mandible) from what seems to have been a Syrian house mouse, a stowaway who climbed on board the ship at some point, perhaps during a stop at the coastal port of Ugarit. And there was ebony wood as well, which comes from Nubia, south of Egypt in northeast Africa.

The cargo also contained many finished goods, some of them secured in a manner that was rather unexpected. The archaeologists were excavating large jars, similar to those that can be seen on the deck of Bronze Age ships, as painted in scenes on the walls of high-ranking Egyptian nobles' tombs. It had always been assumed that these large jars were used to hold fresh water for the crew members to drink. But when the archaeologists began to lift one up and put it into a net, so that it could be floated to the surface, it tilted forward and pottery began to come out—fresh, brand-new, unused pottery. There were plates and dishes and bowls, and big jugs and little juglets, and oil lamps—all from Cyprus and Canaan. It seems that these large jars were not used to hold drinking water but were what we would call china barrels, used to pack and protect new pottery in transit.

There also is one very strange-looking stone item, which has been identified as a mace from the Balkans, as well as several swords. One seems to be Canaanite; one is of Aegean type; and one seems to be Italian. They were probably the personal possessions of the crew members or the captain, but we cannot be certain. The arrowheads and spearheads that were found, as well as various bronze tools, could all be either personal possessions or parts of the cargo.

There are fishhooks and lead weights too, which were undoubtedly used by the crew members to help them catch fresh fish during the voyage. The foodstuffs that have been identified from the Uluburun wreck were all products of the eastern Mediterranean, including olives, almonds, figs, and pomegranates, in addition to fish. These are pretty much the same things that a ship's crew would be eating today in that same area.

But there are also a few fancy drinking cups, made of faience (which is halfway between pottery and glass) in zoomorphic shapes, like a ram's head. They are usually identified as items used by royalty, which may support the idea that the ship was carrying a royal gift from one king to another. We know from textual evidence that rulers did exchange lavish gifts during this period, and so it is not out of the question that we are looking at one here, perhaps being sent from Egypt or Canaan to a Mycenaean king—maybe Agamemnon's ancestor at Mycenae. We shall probably never know for sure.

Among the items that could be construed as worthy of a king is a single gold cup. Although pretty, it is not of much use in determining anything about the ship, its origins, or its date, because it is actually rather generic. There is an iconic photograph, now found in most archaeology textbooks, that was taken before the cup was removed from the seabed. In the picture are the gold cup, a Canaanite jar, a flask made from tin, and a rather plain-looking Mycenaean kylix. When I ask my students what the most important object in the picture is, they invariably point to the gold cup. But this would be wrong—I quote to them from the third Indiana Jones movie, telling them that they "have chosen . . . poorly." Although the Canaanite jar is important for what it contained, and the flask is important because it is one of the few that we have that is made from tin, it is the plain-looking Mycenaean pottery vessel that is the most important piece in the picture, because its distinctive shape helped us to date the wreck.

Bass, Pulak, and their team members also found many pieces of jewelry, ranging from silver bracelets to gold pendants. One of the pendants is a marvelous piece of work, with granulated dots of gold creating a falcon or some other bird clutching a snake in its claws. Another depicts a woman holding a gazelle in each hand. Still another is a type that we can see worn by Canaanite men in Egyptian tomb paintings. There also are cylinder seals from Mesopotamia, including one made from rock crystal with a gold cap on either end, which would have been worn tied around one's wrist or neck, and a small piece of black stone from Egypt that is inscribed "Ptah, Lord of Truth."

Of the scarabs and other small items engraved with Egyptian hieroglyphics, the solid gold scarab of Queen Nefertiti, inscribed with her name in hieroglyphics, Nefer-neferu-aten, is the most important but also one of the smallest. This is a version of her name that she used only during the first five years or so of her reign, when her husband, the heretic Pharaoh Akhenaton, was condemning everything under the sun, except for Aton, who was the god represented by the disk of the sun. This is a rare find and one, as we have noted, that helps us date the ship, for it cannot have sunk before the scarab was made; that is prior to about 1350 BCE.

The one thing that has not been recovered from the shipwreck are bodies, or any partial skeletons at all. It may be that the survivors swam to shore or that their bodies fell victim to the fishes and other sea life while lying underwater for thirty-two hundred years.

{«→}̲ {«→}̲

When the wreck was first found, the excavators thought that the Ulubu-run ship had most likely been going from port to port around the eastern Mediterranean and Aegean regions in a counterclockwise direction, perhaps "tramping" like the Gelidonya ship would do a century later, but with a cargo that was much richer. Since then, other suggestions have been made, including the possibility that it was a cargo meant as a royal gift from one king to another, which we know occurred at the time, and that perhaps it was being sent from Egypt to Greece or from Canaan to Greece or even from Cyprus to Greece.

In every case, though, it is agreed that it was heading to Greece because, although there are objects on board that come from at least seven different cultures and that are clearly meant as cargo, the only objects from Greece are a number of Minoan and Mycenaean ceramic vessels that are used, rather than new, and two personal seals that might have been worn by someone from the Aegean. The objects found on board were probably designed to appeal to a Greek audience.

On its return trip, or perhaps on the continuation of its trip counter-clockwise around the region, the ship probably would have carried a full cargo of typical Mycenaean and Minoan goods, including ceramic vessels full of wine, olive oil, and perfume destined for Egypt, Canaan, and Cyprus. Of course, it never made that return voyage because it sank at Uluburun, despite the presence of what might have been a protective deity on board the ship—a small figurine, made of bronze but covered with gold foil on its head and shoulders, hands, and feet. It was found completely corroded, but "it cleaned up nicely," as we say in the archaeological world. The style of the figurine is typical of votive objects—that is, figures created to express both religious devotion and the desire for divine protection.

If it is the protective deity for the ship, it didn't do its job very well. Their bad luck, though, was our good luck, because we are now able to study this ship and its cargo in its entirety and get a glimpse of what life was like during the international world of the Late Bronze Age more than three thousand years ago.

PART 4

UNCOVERING THE CLASSICS

11

FROM DISCUS-
THROWING TO
DEMOCRACY

A T THE 2016 OLYMPICS IN RIO DE JANEIRO, THERE WERE
competitions in forty-two sporting events, ranging from aquat-
ics and archery to weightlifting and wrestling. But one contest
from the ancient Olympics wasn't held—the race in which the runners
participated while wearing armor, including a helmet on their head,
greaves on their shins, and a shield on their left arm. Similarly,
there weren't any chariot races in Rio nor was there the *pankration*, a
no-holds-barred martial art event akin to today's kickboxing or perhaps
a combination of karate and judo, in which everything was allowed,
except for biting, eye-gouging, and scratching.

The first Olympic Games took place nearly three thousand years
ago, in 776 BCE. They were then held every fourth year, for more than
a thousand years. Athletes came from all over the Greek world to

compete, which is why we refer to the games as Panhellenic (*pan* meaning "all" and *Hellenic* meaning "Greece"). There were 293 Olympiads in all, before the Roman (and Christian) emperor Theodosius declared an end to all pagan festivals in the early 390s CE.

The search for Olympia, the site where the Olympic Games had been held, proved as big a beacon to early explorers and archaeologists as the sites mentioned by Homer. Just as Schliemann searched for Troy, Mycenae, Tiryns, and Ithaca, so too did others search for sites famous in Greek history for other reasons. Close behind the search for Olympia and its games was the hunt for Delphi and its oracle, as well as Athens for its Acropolis and Agora, birthplace of democracy.

The foreign schools of archaeology split up these sites—the Germans were excavating at Olympia by 1875; the French at Delphi by 1892; the Americans in the Agora of Athens by 1931—but Greek archaeologists also were participants in the exploration of their own heritage, just as Stamatakis dug at Mycenae after Schliemann's initial excavations. It is on these sites that we will focus in this chapter.

⁂ ⁂

The site of Olympia was not easy for archaeologists to find. After the last Olympic Games in 393 CE, the sanctuary slowly fell into disuse and was eventually abandoned. The buildings were tossed around and knocked to the ground by earthquakes in the sixth century CE, leaving the column drums from the magnificent temples fallen like parallel toothpicks. Adding insult to injury, the nearby rivers both overflowed their banks—one, the Kladeos River, had done so already in the fourth century CE while the games were still active, but the final ignominy came when the Alpheios River also flooded the area during the Middle Ages, leaving the site covered with a layer of silt and mud more than four meters deep.

It was in 1766 that the English explorer Richard Chandler first successfully located the site. By asking the locals about their discoveries of ancient ruins and using the guidebook written in the second century CE by Pausanias, just as Schliemann would do a century later at Mycenae, Chandler was able to identify the site of the sanctuary, including remains left from the Temple of Zeus, the Greek god to whom the entire sanctuary was dedicated.

When we last visited during March 2015, with a group of George Washington University students, the remains were a pleasure to behold. Small white daisies and wild red poppies mingled with ancient lichen-covered gray stones in a fresh carpet of green grass. Some of the students gave their reports about the individual monuments while wearing tiaras of woven daisy chains on their heads. Springtime in the northwestern Peloponnese region of Greece is beautiful, but the ancient Greeks came for more than just beauty. They came to honor Zeus and to win athletic competitions.

The famous games were part of the festivities that were held to honor Zeus—as much religious as they were athletic—and the temple that Chandler had identified was the most famous building at the site. It also was the largest temple discovered in Greece at the time, measuring sixty-four meters by twenty-eight meters (more than two hundred feet long by ninety feet wide). The pedimental sculptures and the metopes decorating the temple depicted a mythical chariot race, a battle involving centaurs, and the twelve labors of Heracles. It had taken ten years to build it in the mid-fifth century (466–457 BCE).

Most important, it once held the forty-foot-tall gold and ivory statue of Zeus made by the famous Greek sculptor Pheidias, which was one of the Seven Wonders of the Ancient World. Alas, by the time that Chandler found the building, the statue was long gone, having been taken away to Constantinople (Istanbul) in what is now Turkey during the fourth century CE, where it was later destroyed when the building in which it was housed caught fire.

Pausanias reported that there were numerous other statues here as well, but of normal size, some of marble and some of bronze, made by some of the most famous Greek sculptors, including Praxiteles and Lysippus. It was for these famous pieces of ancient art, in part, that the first archaeologists at Olympia came, meaning that the excavations here began for much the same reason as those at Herculaneum in Italy a century earlier.

❊❊❊ ❊❊❊

The French conducted excavations at Olympia in 1829 and recovered fragments of carved metopes from the Temple of Zeus. Alternating with triglyphs (three vertical bars), such metopes were architectural elements that frequently made up part of the decoration of Greek temples between the tops of the columns and the roof. These particular ones, depicting the labors of Heracles, are now in the Louvre in Paris.

It was the Germans, however, who contracted with the Greek government for exclusive rights to excavate the site from 1875 to 1881. Known as the Olympia Convention, the contract established a precedent for all subsequent foreign excavations in Greece. It stated that all the finds discovered during the excavation would remain in Greece, unless the government decided to present duplicates or facsimiles to the excavators, or their government, in thanks for their work. The Germans, in return, were required to publish the results of the excavation for the scholarly community, which they did quite promptly, including inscriptions, sculptures, and buildings. Their investigations have been hailed by Helmut Kyrieleis, a later director, as the first major excavation at a classical site to have "specific scientific objectives." It was their detailed reports, in part, that prompted Baron Pierre de Coubertin, a Frenchman, to initiate the modern Olympic Games, first held in Athens in 1896.

Wilhelm Dörpfeld was associated with these early German excavations at Olympia, serving as an architect and learning the skills of an archaeologist. It was Dörpfeld who gave Heinrich Schliemann a tour of the site in 1881, when he came to see what they had found. Schliemann was so impressed by Dörpfeld that he invited him to come work at Troy, which Dörpfeld did a year later. This was a fortuitous pairing and a great partnership, for the two worked together not only at Troy but then at Tiryns. Dörpfeld subsequently directed excavations at Troy after Schliemann's death, as we have already described in an earlier chapter. Arthur Evans once remarked that Dörpfeld—a meticulous, science-oriented scholar—was Schliemann's greatest discovery.

A new team of German archaeologists resumed excavations at Olympia in 1937, capitalizing on the interest that had been generated by the Berlin Olympics the previous year. This second period of excavation lasted for nearly three decades, though that included a ten-year break (1942–1952) during and immediately after World War II. They too made use of Pausanias's detailed description of the site, without which most of the buildings would probably have remained unidentified. Other

investigations continued thereafter, but it was really only in 1985, under
the direction of Kyrieleis, that the most recent campaign was begun at
the site.

More than a century of excavation has exposed enough that it is now
possible to walk through the site and see the buildings in the central
sanctuary area, including the Great Altar to Zeus; the Temple to Hera;
and buildings such as the Prytaneion and Bouleuterion where the
administrators and council members in charge of the sanctuary and
festival met. The Gymnasium and the Palaistra, where the athletes practiced and trained for a month before the games, are to one side of the
sanctuary area, along with the swimming pool. The Hippodrome,
where the chariot races were held, and the stadium where the foot races
were run are on the other side. It was the excavation of the six-hundred-
foot-long stadium, originally built about 350 BCE, which was the most
expensive and time-consuming part of the project, since it involved the
removal of hundreds of tons of earth. All the efforts by the archaeologists paid off, for they recovered a tremendous amount of information
from inscriptions, statues, and buildings, as well as pottery and other
artifacts. In 1989, Olympia was named a UNESCO World Heritage Site;
nearly half a million tourists now visit it each year.

During the excavation in the 1950s of the dirt embankments on
the sides of the stadium, where upward of forty thousand spectators
would have watched the athletic races, the archaeologists unexpectedly
came upon piece after piece of bronze armor and weapons, including
twenty-two bronze helmets, as well as shields, greaves, and swords.
Originally they were fastened to wooden poles or stakes driven into the
earth of the embankments, in rows above the spectators. Visually it
would have looked like flags flying at the top of the Los Angeles Coliseum or any high school football stadium today, but they were dedications to Zeus made by victorious warriors. The armor and weapons
were placed here so that the citizens from various Greek city-states
could admire the warriors' individual strength and success or collectively give thanks for group endeavors like the Persian War.

Found among the trophies was a bronze helmet dedicated by Miltiades, the general who led the Greeks to victory over the Persians at the
battle of Marathon in 490 BCE. It is a plain helmet, of the common
type that archaeologists call Corinthian. Inscribed along the bottom

edge of the cheek piece are the words "Miltiades presented this to Zeus." There also is a Persian helmet, captured in the same engagement and dedicated afterward, according to the inscription that is engraved upon it: "To Zeus from the Athenians, who took it from the Medes."

Other dedications, usually more valuable objects made of gold and silver, were housed in small buildings known as Treasuries. They were each constructed to look like a miniature temple and were built by the various Greek city-states and colonies to hold the objects sent by their citizens.

Another plain artifact with an inscription from Olympia is equally famous today, but it was not a dedication. Instead, it is a broken ceramic cup or wine jug, inscribed on the bottom with the words "I belong to Pheidias." It is thought to have been the personal drinking cup of the sculptor himself. The Germans found it in 1958, in a building just outside the sanctuary area that must have been the workshop in which Pheidias created the colossal statue of Zeus. The building had later been converted into a Byzantine church, but its proportions exactly match the dimensions of the room in the temple where the statue stood for centuries. Two deposits of waste material excavated by the archaeologists nearby include bits of ivory, metal, and glass, terracotta molds, and tools, among which was a goldsmith's hammer.

The games themselves grew more elaborate over the years, with new events added every so often. When the games first began in 776 BCE, they consisted of a simple footrace. Two longer footraces were added later that same century. Wrestling and boxing followed, as did the pentathlon, which involved competing in five sports—discus, javelin, jumping, running, and wrestling. Chariot races, the race in full armor, and the *pankration* also were added.

Not all these events were conducted as they are today. For instance, the long jumpers competed while holding weights in their hands, which they threw behind themselves while in mid-air in order to propel themselves farther. The German archaeologists unearthed some of these weights, more than two thousand years after the victors dedicated them at the site.

By about 100 BCE (and probably a good bit earlier) there were a full five days of athletics and religious festivities. The winners, of which there was only one in each competition, were each awarded a crown of laurel leaves on the last day of the games. They frequently also received much more elaborate gifts upon returning to their home city, including food and lodging for life for Athenian victors.

The popularity of the games continued even after the Romans conquered Greece in the second century BCE, until Theodosius brought them to an end more than five hundred years later. The Roman emperor Nero was especially enamored of them and even participated in the Olympics of 67 CE. While in the chariot race, he fell off before reaching the finish line but was declared the winner anyway. He also ordered that there be a public musical performance, in which he would participate, and had the town gates shut so that nobody could leave. The Roman biographer Suetonius tells us, with perhaps a bit of exaggeration, that some women faked giving birth while Nero was on stage, and other spectators jumped from the top of the sanctuary walls or pretended to be dead so that they would be carried out for their funeral, in order to get away.

Because other Panhellenic athletic competitions were held in the intervening years, the Olympic Games were held only every fourth year. In between, one per year, the Isthmian Games were held in Corinth and the Nemean Games at Nemea, and the Pythian Games were held at Delphi. At each of these sites, just as at Olympia, temples, treasuries, and athletic facilities were constructed, as were other monuments to the patron deity. At Delphi, that was the god Apollo.

{↔}{↔}

It was the Oracle at Delphi, located in the Temple to Apollo, which brought importance, fame, and wealth to the site in antiquity. Located in Central Greece among the foothills of Mount Parnassus, the oracle was personified by a sacred priestess who reportedly sat on a tripod in an inner room above a crack in the ground. Vapors oozed from this fissure, sending her into a trance and allowing the god to speak through her, giving often enigmatic answers to questions posed by the petitioners.

During the eighth and seventh centuries BCE, the oracle was frequently consulted by Greek city-states wishing to send out colonists to areas from the Black Sea to southern Italy and beyond, including Cyrene in North Africa and Marseilles in southern France. How the oracle knew what to recommend is a very good question, but it seems that most of the colonies were successful, with some eventually surpassing the mother city in prosperity and prestige. The most famous question, according to the Greek historian Herodotus, was reportedly asked by King Croesus of Lydia (in Anatolia), who desired to know whether he should go to war against the Persians, led by Cyrus the Great, in the mid-sixth century BCE. The oracle replied that if he led an army against the Persians, he would destroy a great empire. Croesus took this to be in his favor, went to war, and lost. It was his own empire that was destroyed, thus fulfilling the prophecy.

None of this has left any trace, however, as the French excavators of the site have found. No tripod, no priestess, not even a crack in the ground, although two earthquake fault lines may meet somewhere near here.

The French archaeologists were granted permission to excavate Delphi by virtue of contracts signed with the Greek government in March and May 1891. First, however, they had to move the entire modern village, which was built directly on top of the ancient sanctuary. At a cost of $150 thousand at the time (which would be nearly $4 million in today's money), they moved all three hundred owners into new houses in the fresh village that was created and then commenced digging. Even then they still faced resistance from some of the villagers, who were not happy with the money that they had been paid for their previous houses. Eventually things settled down and the French archaeologists were able to proceed with the excavation. Their results were so remarkable that Delphi, regarded by the ancient Greeks as the navel (*omphalos*) of the world, is today one of the most beautiful and frequently visited tourist destinations in the country. It was named a UNESCO World Heritage Site in 1987.

These French archaeologists were not the first to dig at the site, for attempts had been undertaken from time to time during the previous decades, beginning in the 1820s. Theirs, however, was an officially sanctioned and elaborate expedition, complete with an eighteen-hundred-meter-long railroad track that was set in place to take away the huge volumes of dirt that they were removing. The dig lasted for a bit more than ten years, from October 1892 until May 1903, and was

Temple of Apollo, Delphi

dubbed the "Great Excavation." It was indeed great, both in terms of the discoveries that were made and the number of workers that were employed—up to 220 at one point in 1893.

Since then, nothing on a similar scale has been attempted in terms of excavation at the site, although additional short-term investigations have taken place at various times in the 1920s, 1930s, 1970s, and 1980s–1990s. Thus, there is little to discuss about modern archaeological techniques or advances that have been used at the site. Much has, however, been done in terms of the conservation and preservation of what was found in that decade of excavation more than a century ago, and the publication of what was found has been nothing short of remarkable, with more than sixty volumes published to date about the various buildings, inscriptions, and other finds.

The first season, in 1892, was very brief because they had been delayed by last-minute negotiations with the villagers, and so the first major finds began coming in 1893, with more in 1894 and the years immediately following. It must have been tremendously exciting to be on the French archaeological team during those heady days. Photography was still new at the time, but the archaeologists put it to good use. Some two thousand glass photographic plates still exist at the French School of Athens (École française d'Athènes, founded in 1846), which record some of the spectacular finds at the moment of their discovery.

Several statues, in particular, were nothing short of sensational. The matching set of young men known as Kleobis and Biton of Argos, carved in marble in the Archaic style of the late seventh century BCE, came up one at a time, in 1893 and 1894. The story of these two brothers is known from Herodotus's *Histories*, where he describes how "these dutiful sons" yoked themselves to their mother's wagon and pulled it for five miles so that she could attend a religious festival. In their honor, Herodotus says, the Argives "made and dedicated at Delphi statues of them as being the best of men." Now the proud archaeologists and their workers had recovered these statues; the black-and-white photographs show them clustered around the heads and torsos as the statues emerged from the dirt.

Another statue, perhaps the most famous to be found at the site, is known simply as The Charioteer. Made of bronze, the lower part was uncovered first by the French archaeologists, along with its inscribed stone base, toward the end of April 1896. The upper part, with the head and face still intact, complete with inlaid glass eyes, was found a few days later, in early May. Again, photographs record the moments of discovery. The inscription records the fact that Hieron of Syracuse was victorious in the Pythian Games in 478 (or perhaps 474) BCE. He was the brother (and successor) of the tyrant Gelon and owned the winning chariot—for it was the owner, not the driver, of the chariot who was declared the winner of such races. His other brother Polyzelus (who succeeded him in turn) apparently rededicated the statue later so that he could claim the victory for himself.

Buildings and other structures were uncovered as well. Parts of the treasuries of the Athenians, the Siphnians, the Sikyonians, and the Knidians, among others, came to light, complete with fragments of their elaborate friezes and other decorations scattered in the dirt around them. In these small but beautiful buildings the named city-states stored the precious gold and silver dedications made by their citizens, though these had long since been stolen by the Roman conquerors Sulla and Nero—Nero reportedly took as many as five hundred statues from the sanctuary as well. The remains of the Temple to Apollo also made their appearance. So too did the stadium for the races in the Pythian Games, held once every four years, like the Olympic Games, as well as the site's Gymnasium.

Inscriptions also were found; so many that sometimes dozens appeared in a single day. Among the most famous were fragments of two Delphic hymns to Apollo from the second century BCE. They were found in 1893, inscribed on stones discovered within the Treasury of the Athenians. In between the lines of texts are symbols representing vocal and instrumental notations, so that it was possible to attempt to perform the hymns as originally intended, which was promptly done in mid-March 1894 for the Greek king and queen. Additional performances were held in St. Petersburg and Johannesburg, but it was the one in Paris that same year, at a conference organized by Pierre de Coubertin, that persuaded others to join his movement for the revival of the Olympic Games.

The Sacred Way also was uncovered, winding its way up the mountain from the sanctuary entrance to the stadium like a snake—as befitting the original name for the area, Pytho, before it was renamed Delphi. Today we can all climb the same serpentine path taken by pilgrims and tourists, as described by Pausanias. Taking in the views of the sacred olive groves in the valley and the view of the Peloponnese across the gulf never fails to fill me with a sense of awe and wonder, the two key ingredients for a religious experience in ancient times, and perhaps modern times as well.

Coming up from the terrace of the much-smaller Athena Sanctuary below, where the Gymnasium also is located, we cross the modern road and start out in a paved area just inside the main entrance to the site. We immediately begin walking past statues and other dedications made by individuals as well as city-states, standing on both sides of the Sacred Way. Many of these commemorate military victories, including a dedication by the Athenians marking the victory over the Persians at Marathon in 490 BCE and an entire building commissioned by the Spartans in memory of their victory over the Athenians at Aegospotami in 405 BCE as the final battle of the Peloponnesian War.

As we proceed up the path and sweep around the first bend to the right, we pass by the Treasuries erected by the various Greek city-states. All these are now long gone, as mentioned, along with the riches that they once contained. Only their foundations were left, uncovered by the French archaeologists in 1893–1894, along with pieces of their once richly painted metopes and friezes—depicting battles between gods and giants, the exploits of Theseus, and a variety of other scenes.

As we continue up the hill, we have the sheer wall of the foundations of the Temple of Apollo on our left, for we are still far below the ground level of the temple. Up against this is the Portico of the Athenians. Now bare of offerings, the portico has only an inscription, which reads "The Athenians dedicated the portico and the arms and the figureheads which they took from their enemies." Good detective work by a French scholar in 1948 proved that the inscription refers to cables belonging to a bridge that the Persian king Xerxes had constructed when crossing the Hellespont between Anatolia and Greece during his invasion in 480 BCE. The Athenians retrieved the cables as souvenirs after they defeated Xerxes at Plataea and Salamis that year and dedicated them here in this portico at Delphi.

As we round the next bend, turning to our left, we also come around the corner of the temple and are nearing its front entrance. We can see in the distance where the Tripod of Plataia—sometimes called the Serpent Column—once stood, opposite the Altar of Apollo and the entrance to the temple.

This golden tripod, set on a base of three intertwined bronze snakes, commemorated the Greek victory over the Persians at the Battle of Plataia in 479 BCE. The tripod itself was stolen or destroyed long ago. The bronze base made of the three snakes, on which was inscribed the names of the thirty-one Greek city-states whose men fought in the battle, also was removed, but in its case we know who took it and where it went—it was the Roman emperor Constantine the Great who moved them in the fourth century CE to his new capital city of Constantinople, now better known as modern Istanbul. They are still there today and can be seen in the middle of the Hippodrome, in Sultan Ahmet Square, although their heads (or parts of them) are in the nearby Istanbul Archaeology Museum.

Venturing off the Sacred Way and into the precinct of the Temple of Apollo, we see the reconstructed ruins, with some of the original six pillars standing upright in front; six more would have been at the back. Another fifteen would have been on each side, two more than usual for this type of temple, because it had to be lengthened in order to accommodate extra space for the oracle, the most famous in all of Greece.

Even the present temple itself is reported by Pausanias to be the fifth iteration, though his account might not be entirely believable since he claims that the first three were built from laurel branches, beeswax, and bronze, respectively, before the fourth one was finally built of stone. More dependable, perhaps, are the findings by the archaeologists that there were at least two previous temples in this location. The first one burned down in 548 BCE, and an earthquake in 373 BCE destroyed the second one. The one visible now was built later in the fourth century; the French archaeologists found an inscription listing the benefactors who helped pay for its reconstruction and were also able to ascertain that it took almost forty years to rebuild it, in part because of the attacks on Greece by Philip II of Macedon, father of Alexander the Great, during that period.

Retracing our steps and leaving the temple, we return to the Sacred Way and turn left again, heading around the far side of the temple. Off to our right as we turn this corner are additional statues and other dedications, with a large colonnaded building known as a *stoa* in the distance behind them. Attalos I, a Hellenistic monarch who ruled Pergamon (in what is now Turkey) during the third century BCE, built and dedicated this stoa. His younger son, and eventual successor, Attalos II, built a similar stoa in Athens in the mid-second century BCE.

As we reach the far end of the temple, we see to our right the great theater. We see also, above it all, the stadium, excavated by the French in 1896 and in which the races were run during the Pythian Games. Overall, the same sorts of competitions and races were held here at Delphi as at Olympia, according to Pausanias, with a wreath going to the victor of each competition. These started soon after 591 BCE and were held every four years until the 390s CE, when the entire sanctuary, including the oracle and the Games, was closed by the same order of Theodosius that closed down Olympia.

❖❖❖❖

Athens also has a stadium, but it is modern rather than ancient—used in both 1896 and 2004, the only two times that the modern Olympics have been held in Greece. The city did not play host to any such games in antiquity, though it too had a patron deity—Athena—just as Olympia had Zeus and Delphi had Apollo. Rather, Athens saw the birth of momentous innovations, including the invention of democracy, and was home to philosophical giants such as Socrates, Plato, and Aristotle.

The Acropolis, or high point of the city, is justifiably famous and was named a UNESCO World Heritage Site in 1987. Greek excavators, and Germans as well, including Wilhelm Dörpfeld, uncovered the remains of the buildings here beginning in the 1800s, including the Parthenon, the Erechtheium, and the diminutive Temple of Athena Nike, in addition to numerous marble statues and inscriptions. It is from the Parthenon that the so-called Elgin Marbles came, removed by Lord Elgin and sent to England by 1805, ending up in the British Museum a decade later. The Greeks are still trying to get them back. The archaeologists also uncovered remains on the slopes of the Acropolis, including the theater and the Odeion, some dating from as late as the Roman period but now in use again today for dramatic performances put on by local and visiting artists.

It is the Agora, or marketplace, however, that was daily visited by more Athenians, since it was downtown Athens and the heart of the city. This is where the lawcourts were, as well as some of the most important buildings in the city, including the Bouleuterion, where the senate met, and the Tholos, where the executive committee of the senate met in private; the Metroon, where the archives were kept; various stoas; and other major administrative and legislative edifices. It also was where many commercial shops were located, as appropriate for a marketplace, and served as a meeting place for the citizens, including Socrates, among others. The Hephaisteion, a major temple to Hephaistos (the god of the forge) that was excavated by the Germans in the 1890s, overlooked everything at one end of the Agora. As befits such a major downtown area, it was almost always changing, so that the Agora of the fifth century BCE looked quite different from that of the first century CE, in terms of buildings and layout, though its basic function remained the same throughout.

The Agora has been under almost continuous excavation since 1931 by the American School of Classical Studies in Athens and the activity here reflects changes in techniques and technology during the past eighty-five years. The archaeologists have uncovered all the buildings mentioned in the preceding overview, as well as the streets and paths along which Pericles and Socrates walked, with much more still to be found. The newest excavations now utilize a software program called iDig, for use on the iPad, which was invented by Bruce Hartzler, the technological guru of the excavations. With this specialized program, which moves beyond the off-the-shelf programs used by the excavators at Pompeii several years earlier, the Agora archaeologists can record the excavation data even more quickly, easily, and accurately in real time.

The area is still heavily populated, of course, with modern shops, restaurants, and houses in one of the busiest parts of Athens, at the foot of the Acropolis. Before the archaeologists can excavate anywhere, therefore, they have to purchase the houses and other structures that are currently standing in the area where they intend to dig. Under the successive directorships of T. Leslie Shear Sr., Homer Thompson, T. Leslie Shear Jr., and now John Camp II, some four hundred houses and other buildings have been purchased and demolished, with subsequent excavation done beneath them. The excavators must then proceed carefully through the layers of stratigraphy, working backward through time from the Ottoman period to the Byzantine period and then the Roman period before reaching the levels of Classical Athens and eventually the Bronze Age.

Excavating every summer, the archaeologists have slowly and carefully revealed the history of this most famous marketplace. They have found boundary stones that mark the edge of the area, each inscribed quite literally "I am the boundary of the Agora," as well as buildings known from the writings of ancient authors across the centuries, including the Altar of the Twelve Gods, the Monument of the Eponymous Heroes, the Stoa of Attalos, and perhaps even the house of Simon the Cobbler (where Socrates sometimes taught), and the prison in which Socrates was held during his trial for corrupting the youth and not believing in the gods.

This also is the birthplace of democracy, and so it is not surprising that the archaeologists have found ballot boxes and the actual bronze ballots themselves, which could be held between thumb and forefinger until deposited in the ballot box, so that nobody else could see how you were voting. They also have recovered allotment machines used to choose jurors for trials, water clocks used to time speeches, and inscribed pot-sherds (*ostraca*) that were used when voting to remove someone perceived to have grown too strong and influential in politics, thereby giving rise to our term *ostracism*. Many of these are now housed in the Stoa of Attalos, which was reconstructed in the 1950s, using the same type of materials as the original, and which now serves as the museum for the site.

The Agora also happens to be where I was a young and eager volunteer team member in 1982, during the summer between college and graduate school, for the policy during the past couple of decades has been to use team members who are upper-level college or graduate students intent on a career in archaeology. I didn't know it at the time, but there were at least twelve other volunteer team members working with me that summer who are now also senior archaeologists.

I had the privilege of digging in the Stoa Poikile—the Painted Stoa—which had first been detected and identified a year or so earlier. In antiquity, this building had been famous for the large paintings with which it was decorated—they were still in place when Pausanias came through, six hundred years after they had first been installed, but are now long gone, of course.

I also had the dubious, but literally cool (and wet), thrill of excavating in an ancient well next to the Painted Stoa. This involved stripping down to only shorts and donning a bandana for my head (to keep the mud out of my hair and eyes) and then being lowered via a bucket, as if I were going down for water. Once at the bottom, I stepped out of the bucket into an ooze of muck and began to dig straight down in a very narrow and claustrophobic area into which I barely fit. I, and other similarly small diggers, spent many hours squatting in that soggy environment over the course of the season, carefully excavating intact vessels, sherds, and other artifacts that had either accidentally fallen in or been deliberately tossed in as garbage long ago, and retrieving them from the mire in which they had been preserved.

Excavating in downtown Athens is a novel experience, for at any given moment there are dozens of tourists watching your every move through the chain-link fence high above the excavation area. Revenge comes swiftly, though, for each afternoon we were able to walk through the crowds in the Plaka on our way back home and have them magically part in front of us the entire way, because we were liberally coated with dirt or mud—especially if we had been digging in the well that day. It was a summer that still ranks highly as a unique experience among the more than thirty seasons that I have been in the field.

꒰๑๑꒱ ꒰๑๑꒱

All three sites—Olympia, Delphi, and Athens—are known to anyone who has read about ancient Greece. Because of two centuries of archaeological work, it is possible to wander through the monuments at those sites and get a sense of what it might have been like there in ancient times. Apart from a few select buildings, however, primarily in Delphi and Athens, modern archaeologists have not reconstructed most of the ruined structures, and so the modern tourist must be actively involved and engaged at the sites in order to picture them as they once were.

The three sites discussed here must suffice to represent all the others in Classical Greece. They also represent the development of classical archaeology in this region as well, as it evolved from a search for statues and the location of famous sites to a scientific endeavor focused on asking and answering questions about the lives of ancient Greeks and their accomplishments. Everything else aside, though, it is simply an amazing feeling, sending chills down your spine, to sit in the same theater as did Euripides, stand inside Socrates's jail cell, visit the same Temple to Apollo that held the Delphic oracle and Croesus's representatives, or run a race in the original Olympic stadium. Archaeologists, and archaeology, have made all this possible.

12

WHAT HAVE THE ROMANS
EVER DONE FOR US?

I T MAY SEEM IRREVERENT TO QUOTE MONTY PYTHON AS A
chapter title in an archaeology book, but we've already invoked
Indiana Jones more than once, and—in any event—the answer that
was promptly given in the 1979 movie *Life of Brian* was concise and
reasonably accurate: "sanitation, medicine, education, wine, public
order, irrigation, roads, a fresh water system, and public health."
Although the Romans may not have invented all of these things, they
certainly spread them throughout a large part of the Roman Empire
during the centuries of its existence, especially during the first century
BCE through the fifth century CE. They also brought us large-scale
entertainment and arenas such as the Roman Colosseum in which to
watch them.

Archaeologists have found and excavated Roman ruins not only in
Italy, of course, but also in England, France, Germany, Spain, and elsewhere in Europe, as well as Libya, Egypt, Israel, Lebanon, Jordan, Syria,
and other parts of the Middle East, not to mention Greece, Turkey, and

Cyprus. In 1986, for instance, I was part of a team excavating a Roman villa in Paphos, Cyprus. The villa, which dated to the late second or early third century CE, had been destroyed, apparently during an earthquake. The artifacts that we found attested that it must have belonged to a well-to-do owner. We found the skeleton of what was probably a young girl killed during this event, along with a single leather sandal, in one of the rooms.

The most impressive feature in the house was an intricate and colorful floor mosaic in one room, which depicted Orpheus—a legendary Greek hero known for his musical skills—playing the lyre and surrounded by animals. It has now given its name to the whole house (the House of Orpheus). Our work excavating the mosaic sticks in my mind especially because of the difficulties involved in getting an overhead picture of the entire mosaic once we had finished revealing it, since it was almost ten feet wide and twelve feet long (three by three and a half meters). Because those were the days before drones, or even low-flying kites, were used regularly, our photographer had to climb a ladder and then walk out on a wooden plank that we had attached to the topmost rung, like a gymnast on a balance beam, while we held on to the entire contraption, so that he could be directly above the mosaic and get the desired overhead photographs. Picture yourself on a diving board at a swimming pool, standing on the very end and bouncing on it above the water, but holding a very expensive camera and taking photographs instead of diving in, and you'll get some idea of what it was like for him.

Finds like this villa and mosaic in Cyprus have been discovered everywhere that the Romans established themselves, or where Roman influence was felt, from Europe to the Middle East and beyond. We have already mentioned in earlier chapters Roman-period discoveries in London and at Troy, as well as Athens, Delphi, Pompeii, and Herculaneum. Later in this book we will have additional opportunities on several occasions to comment on the Roman finds at sites such as Masada, Megiddo, and the Dead Sea Caves in Israel, as well as Petra and Palmyra in Jordan and Syria. In this chapter, therefore, we will limit ourselves to a discussion of a few major monuments in Rome itself and muse on some of the problems involved when archaeology is used for nationalistic purposes.

꘏꘏ ꘏꘏

According to tradition, the twins Romulus and Remus founded Rome on April 21, 753 BCE. They were said to be descended from Aeneas, the prince who fled from the burning city of Troy five hundred years earlier, as it was being sacked by the victorious Greeks at the end of the Trojan War sometime around 1250 BCE or a bit thereafter. The Roman poet Virgil tells us Aeneas's story in the aptly named *Aeneid*, which was written in the first century CE during the age of Augustus, Rome's first emperor. Virgil also mentions the twins several times (in books 1 and 8).

It is perhaps not surprising that the story of Aeneas is a bit suspect, since Virgil was trying to create a national epic for the Romans as Homer had earlier done for the Greeks with his *Iliad* and *Odyssey*. The story of Romulus and Remus also is highly suspect. We find the full details in the first book of Livy's *History of Rome*, which was also written during the reign of Augustus and can be seen as part of the same movement to glorify and legitimate Rome's first emperor. Livy said that the twins were abandoned at birth by the Tiber River but were found by a she-wolf who took them back to her lair and raised them as if they were her own pups. Later, a shepherd named Faustulus discovered them, brought them home to his wife, and raised them as his own children. Years afterward, while they were in the process of founding the city, Romulus killed Remus and named the city after himself, or so the legend goes.

Livy's volumes cover Rome's history from its founding to his time. Much of what he says has been corroborated by archaeologists, including the discovery of primitive huts and other remains from the early first millennium BCE on the Palatine Hill in Rome. The story of Romulus and Remus that he relates, however, is a fairly typical rendition of what scholars call a foundation myth, which societies often use to explain how apparently ordinary individuals became rulers or leaders. We see similar tales told about Moses in the Hebrew Bible, as well as about Cyrus the Great of Persia and, much earlier, Sargon of Akkad, who ruled in Mesopotamia during the twenty-third century BCE. All relate events that are open to question.

Livy was not the only person who was enamored of Rome's history and who desired to trace a direct line from antiquity to the present, of course, be it the first century or the nineteenth and twentieth centuries CE. In fact, the archaeological excavations done in Rome during much of the period from 1870 to 1940, and the present state of many of the reconstructed ancient monuments, were undertaken in large part because of a desire to link past and present.

Pope Pius VII initiated a program of excavation and renovation in Rome, beginning in 1803–1804. Work was done to uncover and conserve parts of the Arch of Septimius Severus, the Pantheon, the Arch of Constantine, and the Colosseum. These efforts continued even after Napoleon's conquest of Rome in 1807, with further work in a number of areas, including Trajan's Forum and the interior of the Colosseum.

Work with a nationalistic agenda began in the years after 1870 by order of King Victor Emmanuel II, when the Colosseum and the Roman Forum, as well as a number of other ancient buildings and monuments and some famous sculptures, were either further excavated or simply cleared of rubble. Rome had recently become the capital of a unified Italy, just as it had once been the seat of the Roman Empire, and the king wanted the architecture, both ancient and modern, to reflect its newly reacquired status.

Beyond that, much of what tourists see today was first uncovered by order of Benito Mussolini, the Fascist dictator of Italy who came to power as prime minister in 1922 and who, ten years later, declared, "I . . . am Roman above all." In fact, the very word *fascism*, which Mussolini coined in 1919 to describe his political movement, comes from the Roman *fasces*, which were the bundles of wooden rods with an axhead protruding at one end that were carried around in antiquity to symbolize the power and authority of the Roman magistrates. As a visual representation of his revolution, of Rome's importance in the past and now the present, and of his vision of himself as a new Augustus, Mussolini adopted the image of the fasces as the symbol of his movement, after conferring with an archaeologist to get the image as accurate as possible. When he came to power, Mussolini was intent on re-creating Rome as it had been during the time of Augustus, when that emperor transformed what had been a city of brick into a city of marble.

In order to achieve this, Mussolini ordered that many of the ancient buildings should be excavated and that the various shacks, shops, and other modern or medieval buildings encroaching upon them be torn down. In this manner, under the supervision of an archaeologist named

Corrado Ricci and others during the period from 1924 to 1938, the various additional forums—such as those of Julius Caesar, Augustus, and Trajan—were cleared, as was the Circus Maximus where horse and chariot races had been run. Ancient buildings and monuments were excavated, or further excavated in the case of the Colosseum and the Roman Forum, and some were reconstructed, such as the Ara Pacis—or Altar of Peace—of Augustus, as well as the Mausoleum of Augustus, the Theater of Marcellus, the Pantheon, and various temples. New squares and wide streets, which showcased the newly excavated monuments, also were built. It has been said that the excavations conducted under Mussolini during those fourteen years "added more to our knowledge of Augustan Rome than the previous fourteen centuries had provided."

Mussolini took an active interest in these excavation and construction projects, even posing for a picture swinging a pickax as the demolition of encroaching buildings first began. In other photographs, he is shown with his entourage in front of the Theater of Marcellus on the new Via del Mare ("Avenue of the Sea") and striding though the Piazza Bocca della Verità with the Arch of Janus in the background. Among the most famous is the photograph in which he is riding his horse in full regalia with the Colosseum in the immediate background, during the inauguration of the new Via del Imperio (the "Imperial Way") after its completion in 1932.

The excavation of the Ara Pacis was particularly ingenious. The altar was originally begun in 13 BCE and finished in 9 BCE in order to celebrate Augustus's return after three years of fighting in Spain and Gaul (modern France) and the peace that he had brought to the empire. It was a gorgeous piece of work, freestanding and about ten meters square, with sculptured friezes and relief panels on all four sides, including a personification of the goddess Roma herself, sitting on a pile of armor, and a depiction of the she-wolf suckling Romulus and Remus. Mussolini decided that he wanted it excavated and restored in time for a celebration of the two-thousandth anniversary of Augustus's birth, which was to be held on September 23, 1938.

Ten pieces of the altar had been found accidentally as early as 1568, during the construction of the Palazzo Peretti (later renamed the Palazzo Fiano), with seventeen more fragments recovered in 1859. The latter were scattered in various museums and needed to be retrieved. In addition, the main part of the monument was still below the palace, both underground and underwater—excavations in 1903 had uncovered another fifty-three pieces from the altar but had confirmed that the area was completely flooded.

An archaeologist named Giuseppe Moretti and a hydraulic engineer named Giovanni Rodio led the excavation, in 1937 and 1938. The team first stabilized and reinforced the walls of the palace that were above the ancient monument by injecting liquid concrete into the individual bricks. They then built a huge sawhorse, on which the palace walls could rest, and used hydraulic jacks to lift them up onto the supports. Next, they dug a five-foot-wide trench around the entire area, ending up with a giant circle about two hundred thirty feet around and seventy-five feet across. They placed a pipe into this trench and attached to it fifty-five additional pipes, each 3 inches in diameter, and pushed them into the ground to a depth of twenty-four feet. By pumping carbon dioxide under pressure into the pipes, they were able to create a huge underground refrigerator and freeze solid all the moisture in the earth surrounding each pipe, thereby creating a circular wall of frozen earth twenty-four feet deep and two hundred thirty feet around. This served as a barrier prohibiting any more water from getting in. After pumping out the water that was already present within the area they had isolated, the archaeologists were able to excavate the remains, recovering seventy-five additional large pieces from the altar and hundreds of smaller fragments. They then reconstructed the altar, in a new location near the Mausoleum of Augustus, by combining these new pieces with those that had been recovered earlier and retrieved from the various museums. They finished just in time for the anniversary celebration of Augustus's birth, as Mussolini had wished.

The altar and the area around it have since been renovated, with the most recent version being unveiled in 2006. In addition, several scholars have now called the reconstruction by Mussolini's archaeologists into question, suggesting that it was done hastily and not entirely accurately, with some pieces left out, others improperly joined, and the outer portion potentially being a later addition by Tiberius, the emperor who succeeded Augustus and who may have redone the original structure.

Apart from the Ara Pacis, however, the most famous monuments that most tourists visiting Rome see today date from slightly later in the first century CE and the first half of the second century CE, during the time of the Flavian Dynasty and the period of the Five Good Emperors, respectively. These include the Colosseum built by Vespasian and the arch built by his son Titus, as well as the column built by Trajan and the Pantheon completed by Hadrian.

It was more than eighty years after the construction of Augustus's Ara Pacis that the emperor Vespasian built his own Temple to Peace—the Templum Pacis—in Rome. Commissioned in 71 CE and officially dedicated four years later, it was reportedly ten times as large as the Ara Pacis. It was lost until relatively recently, but archaeologists conducting excavations from 1998 to 2000 uncovered the western corner of the temple, near the Forum of Nerva.

The most famous part of this temple was a much later addition, built sometime between 203 and 211 CE specifically to hold a huge map of Rome inscribed on huge marble slabs, which was attached to the southeastern wall of the temple. Measuring more than fifty feet high and forty feet wide (eighteen meters by thirteen meters), it is known as the Forma Urbis Romae, or, more colloquially, the Severan Marble Plan. It depicted the location of all the major buildings in the city that were present in the early third century CE within an area stretching from the Tiber River all the way to south of the Colosseum, at a scale of about 1:240. It was torn down, and the pieces reused elsewhere in Rome, during the barbarian invasions in the tumultuous fifth century CE. More than a thousand pieces of the map have been found by accident or by archaeologists since 1562, most recently in 2006, but it is still only about 20 percent complete (and only 10 percent of the pieces can be securely placed).

Vespasian had come to the throne as the fourth emperor in a single year, during the aptly named Year of the Four Emperors in 69 CE. At the time, the Roman Empire was engaged in putting down a rebellion in what is now modern Israel—the First Jewish Rebellion, which lasted from 66 CE to 70 CE. Vespasian had been the Roman general in command of suppressing the revolt, leading the Roman troops against the rebels until he was recalled to Rome and installed as emperor. His accession to the throne marked the beginning of the Flavian Dynasty, for his two sons, Titus and then Domitian, succeeded Vespasian. In all, they ruled from 69 to 96 CE, one following the other as emperor.

Because Vespasian had been recalled to Rome, it was actually his son Titus who captured and destroyed Jerusalem in 70 CE. Herod's Temple was burned to the ground and its treasures seized. So many people were enslaved and so much booty was taken as spoils that both the price of slaves and the worth of gold dropped substantially immediately afterward—the ancient historian Josephus says, "in Syria a pound weight of gold was sold for half its former value."

Vespasian's Temple of Peace was constructed in large part to celebrate the successful suppression of the First Jewish Revolt, and it was paid for with the spoils taken during the sack of Jerusalem. Within the temple were placed the looted treasures from Herod's Temple after they had been paraded through the streets of Rome, including the solid gold seven-branched menorah, the Table of Shewbread, and a pair of silver trumpets, according to Josephus. All the items disappeared later, reportedly taken to Carthage during one of the barbarian conquests of Rome in the fifth century CE, possibly at the same time as the huge map was torn down, and subsequently to Constantinople in the sixth century CE. None has ever been found. They are, however, famously depicted on the monumental Arch of Titus, which commemorated the victory over Judea and which was set up and dedicated shortly after Titus's death in 81 CE, at one end of the Roman Forum, near the Colosseum.

The arch was fortuitously preserved because it was incorporated into a fortified tower during the Middle Ages, as part of a fortress built by the Frangipani family, a powerful clan who briefly governed Rome in the twelfth century CE. By 1821, the arch had been freed from the Frangipani additions and restored to its original appearance. It is an impressive monument, towering over the thousands of tourists who now visit the Forum each year. When it was first constructed, it must have been a remarkable sight.

The scene in which these treasures are depicted being carried by Roman soldiers through the streets of Rome, which is on one of the interior faces that would have been visible to people walking or riding through the arch, was the subject of an interesting experiment in June 2012. A team led by Steven Fine of Yeshiva University in New York,

Arch of Titus

Close-up, Arch of Titus

Bernard Frischer of the University of Virginia, and Cinzia Conti of the Soprintendenze Speciale per I Beni Archeologici di Roma utilized a new cutting-edge technique to determine whether the scene had originally been painted, since it is now clear that many architectural features on ancient buildings—such as the Parthenon in Athens and the Temple of Luxor in Egypt, as well as many ancient marble sculptures—were once emblazoned with a profusion of colors.

The Arch of Titus Digital Restoration Project, as it is known, began by conducting high-resolution three-dimensional scans so that the team can eventually create a three-dimensional model of the entire arch as it originally looked. The model will become part of Rome Reborn, a project headed by Frischer, which aims to recreate in three dimensions all of ancient Rome as it looked over time, from 1000 BCE to 500 CE.

The team also employed a noninvasive technique known as UV-VIS spectrometry to determine whether any part of the marble relief had been painted, without having to damage or destroy any part of it. They scanned for the remains of pigment in thirty-two locations, with positive results at twenty of those places. The results were analyzed by Dr. Heinrich Piening, a senior conservator from Germany, who reported that there were "traces of yellow ochre" applied "as a paint layer . . . directly to the stone surface" on one arm and the front of the base of the menorah being carried by one of the soldiers. From a distance, the depiction of the menorah would have appeared golden, as indeed it was in real life. Clearly other parts of the scene were painted as well, but the team has not yet done any work beyond this initial pilot study.

The medieval Frangipani clan also owned, and fortified, the nearby Colosseum, which Vespasian began in 72 CE and which was dedicated, still unfinished, by his son Titus in 80 CE. The original name for this arena was the Flavian Amphitheater, hence the occasional contemporary references to it as simply "the amphitheater." We know, however, that at least by the eighth century it was also called the Colosseum, as it is still known today, possibly because of a huge statue of Nero that once stood nearby, fully 120 feet tall, or perhaps simply because it was indeed colossal—the tallest building in the city, as more than one scholar has remarked.

Vespasian built the amphitheater on top of the remains of a drained artificial lake that had been part of Nero's Golden House (the Domus Aurea). It was a huge palace named for its golden walls, for some of the rooms and possibly the façade were faced with gold leaf. Renowned for the constant dinner parties and feasts that Nero held there, it was built after the Great Fire of 64 CE, of which it is said, "Nero fiddled while Rome burned" (though other sources claim that he actually sang of the sack of Troy while watching the burning fire from a high tower located a safe distance away).

After Nero's suicide just four years later, in 68 CE, the Golden House was abandoned, with portions demolished and covered over by later emperors. It was found by accident as early as 1488, during the Renaissance, when portions of it were reportedly looted for sculptures, perhaps including the famous Laocoön in the Vatican, which may have been found in a room of the palace decorated with scenes from the Trojan War. Raphael, Michelangelo, and other Renaissance painters "lowered themselves on ropes through holes in the ceiling to study the palace's frescoes" and were reportedly influenced in their own art by these ancient wall paintings; a number of them even left their names inscribed on the walls. Modern archaeologists began excavating the remains of this great palace in 1907, with finds coming to light as recently as 2009, and it is now open to tourists.

It has recently been argued, fairly convincingly, that construction of the Colosseum, arguably today the most famous ancient building in all of Rome, may also have been funded by the sudden wealth acquired because of the Roman capture and sack of Jerusalem in 70 CE, just as was Vespasian's Temple of Peace discussed above. Evidence for this comes from an otherwise unassuming piece of marble first seen near the Colosseum in 1813. It has long been known for an inscription upon it dating to the fifth century CE, but it appears to have been hiding, or harboring, an additional ghost inscription.

Professor Géza Alföldy of Heidelberg University made this remarkable discovery in 1995, which was suggested by observations that other scholars had made a few years earlier. The inscription carved into the marble records some restoration work that was done in 443–444 CE, which was paid for by a senator named Rufius Caecina Felix Lampadius. Apparently, this generous Roman had "restored anew at his own expense the arena of the amphitheater together with the podium and platform and rear doors," according to the carved inscription.

Alföldy noticed, however, that a number of holes were drilled into that same face, which had nothing to do with Rufius Lampadius's generous project. He believed that the holes were the remnants of an earlier inscription made of bronze letters that had once adorned the same piece of marble. They had been removed either before or during the carving of the later inscription. Each bronze letter would have had small pegs or protrusions on its back, which were inserted into the holes in the marble face in order to hold the letter in place. All Alföldy had to do was to figure out which letters would best fit the pattern of holes that were left.

Alföldy is one of the world's experts in deciphering such ghost inscriptions, and it didn't take him long to come up with a suggestion. He believed that it had read "The Emperor Caesar Vespasian Augustus ordered the new amphitheater to be made from the (proceeds from the sale of the) booty." Vespasian would have set up such an inscription in 79 CE. The reference to proceeds from the sale of the booty used specific words that meant spoils captured in war. The only war that Vespasian participated in that would have yielded such amounts was the First Jewish Revolt, from 66–70 CE. Alföldy thus suggested that Vespasian used these proceeds to help underwrite the construction costs of the Colosseum, which most scholars now agree is probably correct. But Alföldy wasn't yet done.

He noticed there were still a few holes left unaccounted for, even with this lengthy inscription. In particular, he noticed that the holes seemed to indicate that the original letters in one area had been shifted to the right and an additional letter added in. He determined that this letter was a *T*, which was often used as an abbreviation for *Titus* in such inscriptions, and that it had been inserted before the *C* of *Caesar*. Thus, the altered inscription read, "The Emperor Titus Caesar Vespasian Augustus ordered the new amphitheater to be made from the (proceeds from the sale of the) booty." With the addition of a single letter, Titus—who had been the one to actually capture Jerusalem—claimed the construction of the amphitheater for himself. Such an alteration would have been done in 80 CE, after Vespasian's death, at the time that Titus dedicated the amphitheater.

After its dedication by Titus in 80 CE, just one year after Mount Vesuvius had erupted and covered over Pompeii and Herculaneum, the Colosseum remained a centerpiece of Roman life until the last games were held nearly four hundred years later, in the fifth century CE. The spectacles and entertainments that were held there during those centuries ranged from the notorious gladiator fights to combats involving wild beasts and perhaps even, upon occasion, a naval battle (though naval battles may have taken place here only in the first years of its existence).

Just as the accidental discovery of the Golden House had reportedly influenced Renaissance painters, so too did the Colosseum influence eighteenth- and nineteenth-century Romantic poets and other writers, including Lord Byron, Nathaniel Hawthorne, Charles Dickens, and Mark Twain. In 1817, for example, in the dramatic poem *Manfred*, Lord Byron famously had his main character describe the Colosseum in the moonlight:

> I stood within the Coliseum's wall
> Midst the chief relics of almighty Rome.
> The trees which grew along the broken arches
> Waved dark in the blue midnight, and the stars
> Shone through the rents of ruin . . .
> . . . the gladiators' bloody Circus stands,
> A noble wreck in ruinous perfection!"

As a result of Byron's poem and the writings of the other authors, the Colosseum became a featured tourist attraction, especially for moonlight visits, and remains so to this day (though it is no longer open at night). I think, however, that we would be hard pressed to really and truly imagine the actual scene back in the day, even having seen Russell Crowe and the movie *Gladiator*, because even that would not cover all five senses.

Think of the smells clamoring for priority in your nostrils, from sweat to blood to the stench of fifty thousand unwashed bodies packed into the amphitheater; taste the dust in your mouth, stirred up into the air from the action in the arena; imagine the deafening roar of the crowd, so loud that you can't hear the person next to you; feel the people on either side, packed in so close together that your arms and legs are touching for their entire lengths. You try to ignore the heat of the sun that is beating down on your head and shoulders, despite the large awnings strung up to protect the spectators, while gazing in fascination at the gladiators, the condemned criminals, and the wild beasts imported from Africa and beyond, fighting to the death for your amusement, one after the other, for days on end.

Sensory overload kicks in almost immediately, though, and you become one with the crowd, part of a seething mass focused on the arena below. You turn your head for a split second, and when you look again, a lion is springing toward a hapless zebra, both coming seemingly out of nowhere, but actually brought up from the depths below the arena by an ingenious system that mimics a modern elevator or dumbwaiter, carrying the animals upward to a level just below a trap door that opens and allows them into the arena.

This is what you would have smelled, seen, heard, tasted, and felt when Titus inaugurated the Colosseum with one hundred straight days of such entertainment. Later emperors held them for even longer— Trajan held games that lasted for 123 days and involved ten thousand gladiators and eleven thousand wild animals. But private citizens, vying for prestige in the eyes of their fellow citizens, sponsored most events, so that such spectacles were often a weekly, and sometimes even daily, occurrence.

Although it is debated whether anyone was ever actually thrown to the lions because of their religious beliefs, Pope Benedict XIV declared the Colosseum a shrine to Christian martyrs in 1749. Until then it had been used as a quarry for robbing out the cut stones to be reused in nearby buildings and for the iron clamps that held the stones together, which is why so much of it is now gone.

Of course, Rome was not the only city in the empire with an amphitheater; similar structures were built elsewhere, either by the Romans themselves or by the locals, especially during the first through fourth centuries CE. In fact, there are more than two hundred Roman amphitheaters that can still be seen in countries stretching from Albania to Algeria and Tunisia to Turkey, including nearly forty in France alone. Even today we still use amphitheaters with a similar plan for major sporting events, such as the Coliseum in Los Angeles, although usually the only gladiatorial combats waged there now are between rival football teams.

※←⊷※ ※←⊷※

Nationalism—which by definition includes pride in one's country and, frequently, its past—lay behind the tremendous emphasis on archaeology in Rome during the years of King Victor Emmanuel II and of Mussolini between 1870 and 1940. The connection is worth noting, especially since the link between archaeology and nationalism in Rome is possibly greater than in any other city or region in the world at any other time—including Athens, Jerusalem, Mexico City, and elsewhere. As archaeologist James Packer has said, "For the Fascists, the most important monuments . . . were [used as] . . . tools of propaganda, at once the precedents and justifications for empire."

Unfortunately, one of the great ironies about the rush to excavate the monuments of ancient Rome by both King Victor Emmanuel II and Mussolini is that it resulted in tremendous destruction and demolition of large areas of the city where they wanted to conduct the archaeological work. Large numbers of people had to be moved, businesses were closed, and even churches were adversely affected.

Moreover, the haste in which the teams worked, and the laser focus on the remains from the time of Julius Caesar through the high point of the Roman Empire in the second century CE, also meant that the archaeologists dug through and destroyed the later levels and stratigraphy that covered these monuments, including those of Late Antiquity and the Middle Ages, that is, after the fall of Rome. Most of the objects from these later periods were simply thrown away and many of the rare archaeological notes and plans that were sometimes made in passing were subsequently lost during World War II. There was no attempt at asking and answering key research questions, which is basic to archaeology today—no desire to learn more about the people who had constructed the buildings, attended the games in the Colosseum, and worshipped in the temples.

The link between archaeology and nationalism is not unique to Italy; a recent edited book on nationalism and archaeology in Europe has stated that "it can be seen as a generalized phenomenon, affecting each and every country over the past 200 years." In fact, as the editors point out, it was actually the appearance of nationalism in Germany, Italy, Denmark, and elsewhere that created and institutionalized archaeology as a science, complete with museums in which to store the retrieved artifacts, academic societies for the professionals, journals in which to publish the results of excavations, and university professorships to help teach students about their own recovered history. It also helped cement a belief—crucial to the success of archaeology and still prevalent today—that "the past . . . is of central importance to the present."

Today this importance can be especially seen in the thousands of tourists who visit Rome each year to see the monuments that were unearthed in part as a result of what is sometimes now called fascist archaeology. To the question posed by Monty Python at the beginning of this chapter, "What have the Romans ever done for us?" it would be appropriate to now add tourism to the list.

The connection between nationalism and archaeology also has a dark side, as when the past has been invoked for more than just pride but to support the superiority of one modern group over others, as was seen in both Germany and Italy before and during World War II. It can also be used, and abused, when a modern group wishes to establish a claim to territory using archaeological remains—we see this, for example, in Israel, where both Israelis and Palestinians have claimed their right to the same land on the basis of real or purported links to antiquity. We will revisit this topic in a later chapter, when discussing Yigael Yadin's excavation and interpretation of the archaeological remains at Masada. There is thus a concerted effort among archaeologists today to avoid being unduly influenced by nationalism or other similar sentiments, though that may not always be possible, since we archaeologists are human too, even if we are often excavating in countries other than our own.

DIGGING DEEPER 2

HOW DO YOU KNOW
HOW TO DIG?

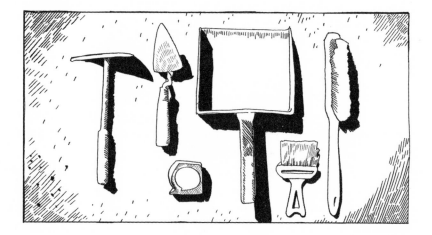

THIS BRINGS US TO OUR SECOND OCCASION WHERE WE ARE able to spend some time digging a little deeper into how one does archaeology. In this case, we are going to do so quite literally, by answering the question "How do you excavate a site?"

The first thing you need to know is that it's possible to learn how to dig in about fifteen minutes. The essential skills are not far different from those necessary for backyard gardening. The specific techniques may vary to a certain extent with the part of the world where one is working, but the tools used are the same in most places. Archaeologists excavating large areas use big tools like picks, shovels, and wheelbarrows. Detail work is done with handpicks and trowels, and dental tools and toothbrushes are used for extremely delicate work, such as excavating skeletons and other organic features that include seeds, nuts, or animal bones. The complications will come when trying to figure out what is being excavated, including deciding whether the area is inside an ancient building or outside; whether a pit or some other feature is present; or addressing some other problem involving stratigraphy.

It may seem surprising that pickaxes are used far more often on excavations than most people imagine, at least in the Mediterranean regions where I have worked. My friend and colleague at Megiddo, Israel Finkelstein, has been known to say on many occasions, "used properly, a pick can be the most delicate instrument on the tell." He is correct, but the secret, even if digging through ten centimeters of fill or soil at a time, is not to raise the pick higher than your hips, and to let the pick head drop down into the soil because of its own weight, rather than raising it high in the air and swinging away wildly. If a team member just starts whacking away at the ground, somebody's going to get hurt. In fact, at one dig that I was on, one of the volunteers swung a pick erratically and knocked her kneecap out of position and halfway up her thigh, or close to it. That meant a full-length cast for the next six weeks or more—so please do be careful.

The rest of the toolkit will consist of a variety of implements, but it will always include a trowel. Archaeologists don't use just any trowel from the local hardware store, however. Marshalltown trowels or WHS trowels are the preferred brands—usually Marshalltowns for US archaeologists and WHS trowels, which are smaller and less flexible, for British or European archaeologists. They aren't expensive; each costs less than $20, even if one purchases a fancy leather holster in which to carry it.

What's amazing to me is that my own trowel is now older than most of the students who come to dig with me these days. It's a Marshalltown, which my mother gave to me when I turned twenty-one. I hate to say it, but if I dropped it by accident at a site now and somebody dug it up, it would probably be considered an artifact itself at this point.

Some people also bring their own hand pick, a smaller version of the pickax. They can be purchased for about $60 from a couple of companies in the United States. The dig will often provide them, however, and I've never really seen the need to have my own, though some of the members of expeditions that I have been on wouldn't be caught dead without one or two hanging from their belts.

The dig also will provide all dustpans, brushes, and measuring tapes. These, along with the trowels and handpicks, will be the instruments of daily use.

I bring dental tools with me every summer as well. My dentist saves the broken ones for me and gives them to me during my annual visit for a checkup and cleaning. Dental tools are usually used only when excavating something that needs to be dealt with very delicately, like a skeleton. I often just leave my case of dental tools in the supply room of whatever dig I'm on, since I use them infrequently.

At many excavations in the Mediterranean region, there will most likely be a color-coded bucket system in place. For instance, at Megiddo and Tel Kabri, we put the excavated dirt into black buckets, pottery into orange buckets, and animal bones into green or blue buckets. Then, every so often, we call for a bucket line and pass the buckets full of dirt all the way down to the dump, where they are emptied. Other times, we simply transfer the dirt from the buckets into wheelbarrows and then trundle them to the same dump and empty them. Sometimes, though, especially when we are carefully excavating on an ancient floor, before dumping the dirt, we will carefully sift all of it through a mesh screen, looking for the smallest objects. By the end of the season, because of carrying all of these dirt buckets around, the team members have grown muscles and shed pounds. We often say that we are probably marketing our digs the wrong way—they should be advertised as health and wellness clinics, where one can lose weight and get in shape, at the same time as uncovering ancient remains.

But don't go to a dig expecting to find skeletons, or gold, or jewelry, buried treasure, tombs, or things like that every day. On excavations in the Mediterranean region, it is pottery, stone tools, and other small objects that are found virtually every hour of every day. In the United States or in Central and South America, or in England or Europe, what one might expect to find may be different. Nevertheless, although most of the finds are mundane objects like pottery and walls of buildings, being the first person to touch those objects in hundreds, if not thousands, of years, is a pretty neat feeling.

✦⟨••⟩✦ ✦⟨••⟩✦

Regardless of where in the world you are digging, a universal rule of thumb is to never yank anything out of the ground when it first starts appearing. It is more important to know where the bottom of an object is than where its top is—because it may be resting on a floor, for instance, which will generate important information about what we call its *context*. And so, after alerting the square or area supervisor and getting permission to continue digging, do so until the object and whatever other artifacts might be related to it are sitting as if they are on top of a table. Only when they can simply be picked up and taken away, like picking up a plate from the table after dinner, should any thought be giving to removal. But, if it is significant enough, the supervisor will probably want to bring over the photographer and perhaps an artist to take a picture and perhaps even draw the objects while they are *in situ*— that is, still in place.

The reason is that every object on an archaeological excavation, or anywhere in the world for that matter, whether it is being excavated by an archaeologist or not, has a context. The context includes an understanding of the other things that are found associated with the object— such as the other grave goods found in King Tut's tomb, for instance—and its physical surroundings, such as whether it is found in sand, mud, water, ice, or ordinary dirt. Knowing an artifact's context can often help us to figure out how it got there. It also will frequently allow the excavator to determine the absolute date of the object.

It is the context of each ancient object that is a large part of what makes it so important and which separates the work of the archaeologist from that of a treasure hunter or a looter. If I am shown, or read an article about, a gold bracelet or some other artifact, the first thing I'm going to say is, "Wow, where did it come from? What was its context?" If we don't know an artifact's context, it loses most of its inherent value for archaeologists, because it means that it's not known where it was found, or when it was found, or what other objects were found with it, or anything about its findspot at all. That's why an object that is looted and then sold on the art market is so sad for an archaeologist to see—an object that could have told us a huge amount is now only being sold because some collector thinks it's pretty or wants something from ancient Egypt or Iraq.

Also, just to add a twist to all of this, an object can be found, even if it's by archaeologists, in a primary context, or a secondary context, or even a tertiary context. If we say that something has been found in a *primary* context, that means that we've found it right where it was originally deposited way back when and that it hasn't been moved or disturbed since.

If we say that an artifact was found in a *secondary* context, that means that we believe it's been moved or disturbed by someone or something after it was first buried. One example of secondary context comes from Jericho, during Kathleen Kenyon's excavations there. As we mentioned, Kenyon found that at Jericho during the Neolithic Period—that is, back about 7500 BCE, or nearly ten thousand years ago—the people would bury the body of a deceased person, or maybe even leave it lying out in the open perhaps, but then, after the flesh had disintegrated, they would take the head, remove it from the body, plaster it with clay, probably to simulate the flesh that had once been there, and then stick seashells, or rather cowrie shells, into the eye sockets where the eyes had once been. They would then put the plastered head on a shelf in one corner of the living room in their house, perhaps as a form of ancestor worship. Therefore, when Kenyon found those skulls, they were in a secondary context.

Does context really matter? Yes, absolutely—because the whole point of realizing that the ancient inhabitants of Jericho were removing the skulls of their dead family members, plastering them, and then putting them in the living room, where the archaeologists found them in a secondary context, means that we can now get some idea of what they were thinking and why they did it. It gives us a glimpse, perhaps, into their thought process, their fears about death or their belief in a life after death, or even the beginning of what we would now call religion.

All in all, an understanding of the concept of archaeological context and its importance is essential because it serves in part to explain why we excavate so carefully and why we need to keep careful records while we do so, because we are destroying the very context that an object is in when we excavate it. Context is everything and recordkeeping is essential. In fact, archaeologists estimate that ancient objects that have been ripped from their archaeological contexts by looters and sold on the art market without any documentation have lost about 90 percent of their value, because so little information is now attached to them. Similarly, fakes and forgeries can irretrievably affect our thought processes about the ancient world.

✦⟨⟶⟩✦ ✦⟨⟶⟩✦

If you're going to dig a site properly, what's involved?

One possibility is called horizontal excavation, which is exposing one entire layer or stratum over an entire site. It is then recorded, drawn, and photographed. Horizontal excavation is often what is done at sites like Colonial Williamsburg in the United States. It's also what was done by the University of Chicago for part of their excavations at Megiddo in the 1920s and 1930s.

A horizontal excavation can help you understand the layout of an entire site—where different activities took place, where people lived, worked, worshipped, were buried. For sites that have only a single level of occupation, horizontal excavation is the obvious strategy. For multi-layer sites, there is a tradeoff to be made, because in achieving this breadth, you sacrifice depth—you know what one level at the site looks like, but you give up learning how the various spots of the site changed over time. At Megiddo, for example, the large excavation team from the University of Chicago worked for almost ten years and still managed to clear off only the top three layers of the site and expose the fourth—leaving the other sixteen layers below unexplored, until they changed their excavation plan.

The other major option is to conduct a vertical excavation—to dig deeply in a few spots in order to get a feel for the chronological sequence or the extent of the site. This can be a good way to get an idea of the stratigraphy that might be encountered if it is later decided to expand the excavations at the site. In that case, just a few limited areas will be selected, and in those places one digs as deeply as possible. This is what the archaeologists from the University of Chicago ended up doing in one area at Megiddo, where they dug a narrow, deep trench all the way down to bedrock, below the occupation levels—that's how we know that there are twenty major levels at the site, going back to at least 3000 BCE.

William Matthew Flinders Petrie—one of the most important of the early archaeologists—was among the first to demonstrate the importance of vertical archaeology while excavating a multilevel site. Petrie originally had no formal schooling at all, though he had already been surveying in England, including at Stonehenge, long before he went to Egypt to measure the pyramids at the age of twenty-six. He learned by experience and eventually became the first professor of Egyptology at the University of London in 1892, when he was about forty years old. He then held that position for the next forty years.

Petrie first dug in Egypt, where he eventually trained a whole group of workers from the village of Quft (or Guft), near modern-day Luxor. To this day, the descendants of those workers, known as guftis, provide much of the skilled labor for archaeological excavations in Egypt. Each gufti does the same task that that gufti's father, grandfather, or great-grandfather was assigned by Petrie—some are the pickmen, some are the trowelmen, some are the overseers. Guftis are a very talented group of workers; I had the pleasure of working with some of them when I was on a dig in the Nile Delta region of Egypt back in the mid-1980s.

Petrie also dug in what is now modern Israel and the Gaza Strip. There he was responsible for the introduction, or in some cases the popularization, of a number of things that we take for granted in archaeology today, including the concept of stratigraphy and superposition—both of which revolve around the idea that earlier things are usually found lower down than more recent things. This is especially true in the tells that are found across much of the Middle East, because tells are composed of one ancient city on top of another, built up over centuries or millennia, and the earliest city is always at the very bottom.

For example, at Megiddo, as just mentioned, the Chicago team found that the seventy-foot-tall mound has no fewer than twenty cities hidden within it. The first one at the bottom dates back to at least 3000 BCE and the most recent one, at the top, dates to about 300 BCE. When looking at a side profile that's been cut into one of these mounds, it is easy to see the different layers, since they are full of dirt, stones, and other materials, with all sorts of different colors, textures, and consistencies. Such a side profile is officially called a stratigraphic section by archaeologists and is usually very carefully drawn and photographed for publication, so that other scholars can see whether the excavation was done properly or if something was misinterpreted.

Petrie is also one of the people responsible for realizing that all the broken pieces of pottery that are found with almost every bucketful of soil while digging can be used to help date the levels of the mound. It turns out that certain types of pottery go in and out of fashion, just like men's and women's clothing and shoes today. The fashions of pottery can be correlated with pretty specific dates and periods, sometimes within a decade or so. Archaeologists call this dating method pottery seriation.

It is frequently these pieces of pottery that give their names to our archaeological periods, so that in Greece, for instance, we talk about Late Helladic IIIA1 pottery, which dates to the first half of the fourteenth century BCE, during the Mycenaean period. Petrie also realized that if the same type of pottery is found at two different sites, the levels in which they are found at the two sites are probably equivalent in time. This has proven to be an extremely important, and useful, point.

Perhaps the oddest thing about Petrie, though, is that when he died in 1942, he willed his head—and his brain—to science. He had died in Jerusalem, and the rest of him is still buried there, but his head was shipped to London. At some point, when it had been stored in a basement for quite a while, the label on the jar fell off, so that for a while nobody knew whose head it was. It was eventually identified and is now reportedly somewhere in a storage room at the Royal College of Surgeons in London, although I haven't gone to look for it personally.

Two other archaeologists who contributed substantially to how we dig today are Mortimer Wheeler and his best-known student, Kathleen Kenyon (later Dame Kathleen Kenyon). Wheeler, who excavated at many sites, including Maiden Castle in England and Harappa in India during the 1930s and 1940s, invented a new excavation method, which he employed during his excavations in both countries.

As Wheeler found, the stratigraphy at a site can get extremely complicated. He therefore decided to excavate in five-meter-by-five-meter squares, but he left a one-meter-wide unexcavated area called a *balk* between contiguous squares. It sounds complicated, but it's not— simply picture a rectangular ice-cube tray like many people keep in their freezers (if they don't have a unit that automatically makes ice for them). The ice cubes, or the squares that you fill with water in order to make the ice cubes, are the squares that you are excavating and the plastic ridge between cubes is the balk. Wheeler's workers could walk and push wheelbarrows on the balk, but more important, leaving a balk also allowed Wheeler to keep track of the stratigraphy, because each square that was being excavated now had four interior sides to it—these were the faces of the balks that had been left in place on all four sides of each square.

If it helps, picture yourself small enough to actually jump down into the square into which you're going to pour water in the ice cube tray and realize that there are four sides that you can look at when you're in there. In the same way, Wheeler could jump down into each square that his workers were excavating and look at the faces of the balks that had been left in place on all four sides, so that he could see what they had already dug through and get a visual idea of the history of the area. It can be quite easy to inattentively dig through a very patchy plaster floor, if there's not much left of it, but afterward it can be seen very plainly as a white line stretching straight across the side of the square in the balk.

Balks are straightened every day, so that a careful eye can be kept on what's happening, including whether someone has accidentally dug through any plaster floors. The balks have to be completely vertical, however, if they are to yield a clear picture of what has already been dug through, and this is where pickaxes can come in handy, for you can use a pick to quickly and easily straighten up the balks.

At the end of each season, most archaeological teams will draw and photograph each section so that they can publish a record of it for others to see and discuss. After all, archaeology is destruction; we destroy the very things that we are studying as we dig through them, and therefore we need to record every little thing as we do so. By publishing detailed drawings and photographs of the excavated sections, other archaeologists can see them too, and they can either agree or disagree with the conclusions reached by the excavators. This is now a standard part of the scientific method for archaeologists working in the Mediterranean, and for many elsewhere as well.

So, for instance, when I was excavating as an area supervisor at Tell el-Maskhuta in Egypt in the mid-1980s, we ended up with a square in which we had dug down about twenty feet, with spectacular balk faces on the interior sides. In these, we could clearly see huge differences in colors between the layers—some were gray and black with ash, from where there had been a fire; others were as sandy as the day is long, from when the site had been abandoned for a period. In still other layers, we could clearly see the outlines of mud bricks from the walls of buildings that had once gone right through our area at different periods. It took us days to properly measure, draw, and photograph each of the balks at the end of the season that year, but we finished with accurate records that we could publish and that other scholars and future archaeologists can consult.

Another time, at Tel Kabri, we found a gorgeous series of white plaster floors with dark brown layers of soil between them. These were from different phases of the palace, as it went through renovations over time. The balks looked like an ice cream layer cake and were easy to measure, draw, and photograph.

In Athens, which is such a tourist destination, the archaeologists and city planners came up with a unique way of showing the stratigraphy that they had to dig through when building the new Metro system in time for the 2004 Olympics. In some of the Metro stations, glass panels were placed on the walls so that the dirt and the stratigraphy could be seen still in situ, as if they were the balks for an ongoing archaeological excavation. The layers of soil can be clearly seen, as well as partial walls of buildings, and drains, and even parts of a road, all of which can be appreciated but not touched.

When recording balks, many archaeologists and excavations now also utilize what is called a Harris matrix, which is a method of representing the stratigraphy graphically. In a Harris matrix, each level is

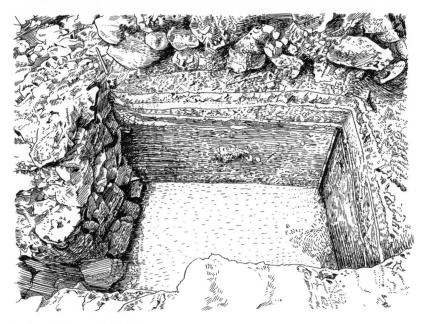

Stratigraphic layers, Tel Kabri

represented by a box placed on the page according to its stratigraphical position, with the lower levels placed lower on the page and the higher levels placed higher on the page. Lines are drawn to connect the boxes, in order to show their vertical and horizontal relationship to each other and thus the stratigraphical history of the square. Frequently one can construct a Harris matrix as a rough working sketch while in the field, which helps trench or area supervisors keep the various levels and their relationships to each other straight in their mind.

Kenyon, who is probably best known for digging at Jericho and Jerusalem, brought Wheeler's method with her when she began excavating at Samaria in what was then Palestine in the 1930s. It is now therefore known as the Wheeler-Kenyon or the Kenyon-Wheeler method.

She and others introduced modifications into this system over the years, however, and it is now frequently combined with having workers or team members physically change the buckets into which they put the pottery and other finds, as well as the labels that go with them, whenever there is a change in the color or texture of the soil, for the change in color may represent the beginnings of a new level or stratum at the site that might become really obvious only later. In this way we are able to detect and record subtle changes in the phases of the remains being excavated. If the digging has been done properly, including changing buckets, tags, bags, labels, and everything else every time a change in soil color or texture is noted, then a mirror reflection of that should be visible in the balks of the area.

With that in mind, once the digging starts in earnest, it would be best to follow the advice that I was given on my very first dig, back when I was a sophomore in college—if there is a change in the color of the soil or the texture of whatever it is that is currently being excavated, stop and alert somebody before continuing to dig, rather than possibly going right through a floor or some other important feature. The supervisor will bring new buckets, tags, labels, and everything else, just in case the different color or texture represents an actual change back in antiquity, like an entirely new level within the mound. If this is the case, that change will also eventually be visible in the balks.

Again, I should emphasize that this is what we do at the sites that I have worked on in the Mediterranean region. Archaeologists excavating in England or in North America will have their own system that they follow, such as bagging artifacts separately by unit and excavation level, as needed.

In addition, the documentation of daily finds and other activities is a necessity, regardless of where in the world you are digging. Such regular chronicles not only help the archaeologists in publishing their results after the season is over but will also aid future researchers coming back to re-examine the data, perhaps in light of new findings elsewhere or new suggestions made by other scholars. These records will include field notes on what was excavated each day; photographs of the structures, features, and artifacts as they were found in the field, as well as back in the laboratory after some have been cleaned and conserved; ceramics and small-find logs, with running inventory lists of what has been found; and other relevant data. In many cases, excavations such as those at Pompeii and Megiddo are now entering some of the records directly onto laptops, iPads, or other devices in the field and then uploading the information daily to servers back home in the United States, England, and elsewhere, so that there is little or no risk of losing data.

❦❦❦

For those who are wondering what a typical day on an excavation consists of, I can speak only about what we do in the Mediterranean region, but a normal workday for us at both Kabri and Megiddo begins with the team out at the site and digging by 5 a.m. We dig for a little more than three hours, until 8:30 a.m., and then stop for half an hour to have breakfast. Then, we continue digging until 11 a.m., at which time we stop for a fifteen-minute break, which usually includes coffee, fruit, and cookies. Returning to work, we continue until 12:30 or 1:00 p.m., at which point we all pile onto the bus and head back to wherever we're staying. By that time of day, most areas around the Mediterranean are too hot to want to be shoveling dirt in a trench.

After a big lunch, most people head for the swimming pool or a long nap in their room during the few hours of down time, before reconvening at 4 p.m. At that point, some team members will wash all the pottery that was found that day and leave it out in the sun to dry, so that the directors can look at it the next day and figure out what time period it comes from. Others will wash the fragmentary animal bones that were found. Still others will enter data into the computer or do whatever other task might have been assigned to them. Square and field supervisors will be writing up their notes for the day and planning the next day's work. That will go on until 6 p.m. or a bit longer, with dinner at 7 p.m., followed by a lecture at 8 p.m.—since many people are doing this work for college credit—and then socializing until lights go out at about 10 p.m.

The whole team then wakes up at 4:30 a.m. the next morning, are out at the site by 5 a.m., and the entire routine begins again, usually for five days per week, and anywhere from four to seven weeks per field season. All this takes place for us in June and July, since that's when most people are able to come as volunteer team members. Most are college students, but many are people from other walks of life, usually ticking off an item on their bucket list—so we have retired doctors, lawyers, nurses, schoolteachers, and so on. The one thing that they all have in common is that they had always wanted to go on a dig, though some are quite surprised at the actual conditions—when digging anywhere in the Middle East, be prepared for it to be very hot, and probably quite dry and dusty as well, unless the site is somewhere near the coast, in which case it can be incredibly humid as well as very hot.

Of course, when excavating elsewhere in the world, such as in England or in North America, one should be prepared for very different situations, including digging in the rain and mud. The time frame involved for an individual day's work can also vary greatly, especially if one is working entirely with professionals, rather than volunteers. This is particularly true when the archaeologists are involved in what is called "cultural resource management"—such as when they are hired to go in just ahead of the bulldozers before a major construction project, in order to make certain that there are no archaeological remains that might be destroyed. In such cases, the workdays can be much longer, possibly from dawn to dusk without a break—except for hastily consumed meals and coffee—for days or even weeks at a time.

❊⟨••⟩❊ ❊⟨••⟩❊

What will be found on a typical day during an excavation? At many sites in the Mediterranean region, from Italy to Israel and beyond, unless one is working at a prepottery Neolithic site, there will broken pieces of pottery turning up with almost every trowelful of dirt. These are called sherds, which is shorthand for potsherds. Think of them as broken dishes thousands of years old. Pottery was in common use for almost all household and industrial activities in most places in the ancient world—made out of local clay, fired en masse, and easily broken when dropped. It was cheaper and easier to gather up the broken pieces, toss them away, and make or obtain a new one than to try to fix it. The same is true of stone tools made of chert, flint, obsidian, or quartz in prehistoric sites—easily made, easily broken, cheaper to replace than repair.

Remember we said earlier that most of the good stuff worth writing home about is going to be what we call artifacts, which are objects manufactured or modified by humans. Sometimes it can be tough to tell a worked stone tool from a stone that just tumbled down the creek bed for a mile or two, but usually it's obvious when something is an artifact. That is, unless it's the first day of the dig—virtually everyone who hasn't been on a dig before comes running up to the square supervisor approximately fifty times on the first morning, waving something and saying "Is this a piece of pottery? Is this pottery?" "No," comes the answer. "It's a rock—but it's a nice rock." After a while, it becomes second nature to tell at a glance a broken piece of pottery from a nice little pebble or rock.

Since pottery and stone are not biodegradable, you'll find lots and lots of such pieces. Remember, pottery and stone also are found during a survey and mark the existence and location of a site; on a dig they are being uncovered still in context, within the site itself.

There also will be animal bones, plenty of dirt, and lots of rocks—lots and lots of small rocks and larger stones. Some of them are just random; others are parts of walls and buildings. The trick is to figure out which is which before picking one up and throwing it away—there's nothing worse than realizing that you've just thrown away half of an ancient wall; that's a rookie mistake.

This also is where the archaeological axiom quoted at the beginning of this book again comes into play—"one stone is a stone; two stones is a feature; three stones is a wall." It is an amazing feeling to start uncovering a line of rocks in an excavation that were clearly set there deliberately by someone long ago.

✠⊷✠ ✠⊷✠

All in all, it will be important to keep in mind that real archaeology is not always as romantic as it is portrayed, especially by Hollywood. Each moment of discovering something remarkable involves many days or weeks of dirt, sometimes blood (and blisters), always sweat, and occasionally tears. The rewards are great, however, whether having a unique experience digging for the first time ever, returning to a dig for the second time, or publishing the results. There is something majestic about an archaeological project, with all the planning that is involved and all the hard work that goes on during and after the season. In a way, it is a bit like a symphony orchestra performing a major piece; it doesn't work unless everyone plays his or her part.

PART 5

═══

DISCOVERIES IN THE HOLY
LAND AND BEYOND

I 3

EXCAVATING ARMAGEDDON

WE HAVE ALREADY MADE A NUMBER OF REFERENCES IN previous chapters to the site of Megiddo in Israel, which is perhaps better known as biblical Armageddon. The very word *Armageddon* comes from *Megiddo* because—in Hebrew—"Har Megiddo" means the mound or mountain of Megiddo. Originally the word was written Harmageddon in Greek. Over time it became Armageddon.

There is nothing quite like walking across the top of a mound like Megiddo, where people lived for three thousand years, wondering what lies beneath your feet. It could be anything—or nothing. I had the pleasure of excavating at Megiddo for ten seasons, digging every other year from 1994 to 2014, and felt that way every morning when walking onto the site each day during the excavation season. What am I walking over? What would I find if I were to stop right where I am and begin digging?

We have already noted several times that the manmade mound at Megiddo towers more than seventy feet above the Jezreel Valley and that it contains at least twenty separate cities, built one on top of another. The earliest dates back more than five thousand years, while the most recent dates to about the time of Alexander the Great in the fourth century BCE.

The valley itself is in the northern part of Israel and is shaped a bit like a triangle on its side—the tip is over by Haifa, on the Mediterranean Sea, and the broad base is over by the river Jordan. It's about twenty or thirty miles from east to west, but only between three and seven miles from north to south. It's a perfect place for a battlefield, which may explain why at least thirty-four battles have been fought here over the past four thousand years. Most were fought for control of Megiddo or nearby areas, since Megiddo looms over the entire valley, through which ran the Via Maris—the road that was called the Way of the Sea and led from Egypt to Mesopotamia and back again. The Egyptian pharaoh Thutmose III once said that the capturing of Megiddo is like the capturing of a thousand cities.

Many famous people have fought at Megiddo or in the Jezreel Valley: Thutmose III in 1479 BCE and Deborah, Barak, Gideon, Saul, Jonathan, and Josiah from the Bible. The Romans fought here too, as did the Crusaders, the Egyptian Mamluks, Mongols from Central Asia, Napoleon, and even British General Allenby in World War I. Only Alexander the Great, of all the invaders of this region, did not fight a battle at or near Megiddo, because the area seems to have simply given in to him. But, of the battles at Megiddo, the most famous is still to come—the battle of Armageddon, described in the Book of Revelation. This is to be the penultimate battle between good and evil, which the forces of good will win; a battle that will be foreshadowed by numerous signs, including an earthquake, plague, hailstones, and a river of blood 180 miles long.

✤⟨•⟩✤ ✤⟨•⟩✤

Probably the two best-known archaeological remains at the site are the water tunnel, which was dug one hundred feet straight down and then three hundred feet straight out from near the edge of the mound, so that the inhabitants could get to the external spring without being subject to attack by enemy forces, and the so-called Solomon's Stables, a set of long stone hallways punctuated with pillars that might not be stables and almost certainly weren't built by Solomon.

It was Gottlieb Schumacher who conducted the first excavations at Megiddo, from 1903 to 1905. He followed the excavation methods current in his day, working at the same time as Flinders Petrie and Howard Carter in Egypt. Since those were still the early days of archaeology, he employed hundreds of workers to dig a huge trench right through the middle of the mound, much like Heinrich Schliemann had done at Troy some thirty years earlier. He also dug smaller trenches at various other places on the top of the mound, but it was the great trench that yielded some of the most interesting finds, including a tomb from the Middle Bronze Age that held the bodies of a number of men and women, along with gold objects and other finery.

Schumacher thought that he had found the bodies of the ruling family of Megiddo from that period, which dates to the middle of the second millennium BCE, and he may well have. Unfortunately, most of the objects cannot be located now.

He also found one of the most famous objects ever to be discovered at Megiddo, namely an oval seal about an inch and a half wide made of a type of stone called jasper. It has a lion inscribed on it, along with the words "Shema, servant of Jeroboam." It's not clear which Jeroboam this is, because there are two kings with this name mentioned in the Bible, but it's definitely one of them. Unfortunately, Schumacher sent it to Istanbul as a gift to the Ottoman Turkish sultan who ruled the area at that time and nobody knows where it is now.

Schumacher's workers also missed things while they were digging, threw them on the back dirt pile, or simply piled them by the sides of their trenches—especially in the case of stones from walls that they took apart. One of these stones turned out to have a cartouche of the tenth century BCE Egyptian pharaoh Sheshonq on it, but the workers didn't notice it.

It was only when the next expedition to Megiddo began that the stone was recognized for what it was—part of a monumental inscription that probably stood about ten feet high. It would have been erected at the site as a victory inscription after Sheshonq captured and then occupied the city. Years or decades later, it was taken down and broken apart and was reused in a wall of a new building. This is where

Schumacher's workers would have found it, but since they missed it and simply piled it on the side of the trench, we don't know from what level or city it comes. If we knew, it would be wonderful, because we could then attach that city to a known person, since Sheshonq is not only known from Egypt but probably also from the Bible, where he is called Shishak.

It was left to a team from the University of Chicago to identify this stone, which they did when they were collecting material to use in building the staff headquarters at the site. The Chicago team dug at Megiddo for approximately fifteen years, from 1925 to 1939; their efforts were halted only by the outbreak of World War II.

They lived at the site for much of the year. The Jezreel Valley was still swampy at that time and so most of them suffered from malaria; finally, the swamps were drained. The overall project was under the direction of James Henry Breasted, founder of the famous Oriental Institute at the University of Chicago, with a series of field directors who included Clarence Fisher, Gordon Loud, and P.L.O. Guy (whose initials were okay for then but mean something entirely different now).

The Chicago expedition was at the forefront of a new type of archaeology, which was more careful and scientific than the type practiced by Schumacher two decades earlier. Courtesy of Petrie, they now knew about stratigraphy and about pottery seriation, that is, the changes in pottery styles over time, as we have discussed in "Digging Deeper 2," so that they could tell one city from another and get a good idea of its date, at least relatively speaking.

Funded by money from John D. Rockefeller, Jr., the Chicago team started out doing what we call horizontal excavation—in which they tried to expose one entire layer over the entire site, record it, draw it, photograph it, and then pick it up and remove it all, so that they could then expose the next layer down. They did that for the very top level, or Stratum I as they called it, dating its end to the mid-fourth century BCE; then also for Stratum II, from the sixth and fifth centuries BCE; and Stratum III, which dates to the Neo-Assyrian period, or the eighth and seventh centuries BCE, before they started to run out of money.

Soon thereafter, they switched to vertical excavation for the rest of their time at the site. And that's how we know that there are at least twenty cities one on top of another within the mound, since they dug all the way to bedrock in what is now known as the Chicago Trench.

The Chicago team also was still prone to using the biblical account to buttress their findings at the site. When they were excavating a series of long parallel rooms that were large enough to have held a bunch of horses, for instance, they turned to the book of I Kings to help with their identification. There they found two passages that they thought were relevant, in 1 Kings 9 and 1 Kings 10.

The first one reads

And this is the account of the forced labor which King Solomon levied to build the house of the LORD and his own house and the Millo and the wall of Jerusalem and Hazor and Megiddo and Gezer. (1 Kings 9:15)

The second one reads

And Solomon gathered together chariots and horsemen; he had fourteen hundred chariots and twelve thousand horsemen, whom he stationed in the chariot cities and with the king in Jerusalem. (1 Kings 10:26)

Combining these two, they decided that Megiddo must have been one of Solomon's chariot cities and that the structures were indeed stables for horses dating back to the time of Solomon in the tenth century BCE. Today, the tour guides still refer to them as Solomon's Stables.

Similar long-roomed structures have been found at other sites. And though it is quite likely that these at Megiddo are indeed stables, it also is possible that they were used as storehouses, or as barracks for soldiers, or even as a suq or marketplace, all of which have been suggested by scholars.

Moreover, later radiocarbon dating and analysis of the pottery found within these structures at Megiddo now indicate that they are unlikely to have been built during the time of Solomon. They are much more likely to date at least a century later, perhaps to the time of Ahab and Omri, kings of the Northern Kingdom of Israel, or even to the time of

"Solomon's Stables" at Megiddo

Jeroboam II, one of their successors. Thus, Solomon's Stables at Megiddo might not be stables and are almost certainly not Solomon's.

The next person to lead an excavation at Megiddo was the famous Israeli archaeologist Yigael Yadin, who came to Megiddo for a few brief seasons in the 1960s and 1970s. Yadin did limited work at the site to investigate a few research questions. He also used it as a training dig for his graduate students, many of whom subsequently went on to become leading archaeologists in their own right.

One of the things that Yadin and his team uncovered was the foundations of what appeared to be a large palatial structure, which he called Palace 6000. Only the foundations remained because the building lay directly underneath the northern set of "stables" that the Chicago team had found. The large blocks from Yadin's Palace 6000 had been reused in the later building to make the troughs that the Chicago team claimed were used to put the food, and perhaps the water, for the horses. It was this palace, Yadin thought, that had been built by Solomon, not the later stables directly above it. But he didn't have any proof for this, except for those biblical passages and the fact that he thought the palace was built at the same time as a large entrance gate to the city itself.

This large gate had six chambers and appeared very similar to one that Yadin had found previously at Hazor. He also figured out that there was another one at the site of Gezer, part of which had been excavated previously but misidentified. Using the same passage from the Bible that mentions Megiddo, Hazor, and Gezer as having been fortified by Solomon, Yadin assigned them all to the tenth century BCE—that is, during the time that Solomon ruled.

This is not the way that archaeology is supposed to work, however, at least in the Mediterranean region. The gates, and the associated buildings, should be dated by the pottery that is found within them, not by biblical passages that may or may not be related to them. Thus, when Israel Finkelstein looked again at the pottery found by both the Chicago team and by Yadin, he said that it dated both the gate and the palace to the ninth century BCE, not to the tenth century and the time of Solomon. If he is correct, then neither of the levels that previous excavators have dated to the time of Solomon is actually from that time period. The details are still being debated, even twenty years after Finkelstein dramatically suggested altering the dating, and so the jury is still out.

Finkelstein has been leading the new set of excavations at Megiddo since 1992, with a series of codirectors, including myself. I started digging with him at the site in 1994. I began as a volunteer team member, even though I already had fifteen seasons of experience, because I wanted to be part of a large-scale expedition to a well-known site in Israel. I rose through the ranks and was appointed associate director in 2006 and then codirector in 2012. I held that position until I retired from the project a few years later.

I was part of the team that was fortunate enough to re-excavate the area in which both Yadin's Palace 6000 and Chicago's northern stables were located, and so I have firsthand knowledge of the issues involved in their redating. I've also dug in most of the other areas at one point or another, each having its own points of interest.

For instance, in the part of the site that we call Area H, the buildings now on the surface are two palaces that date to the Neo-Assyrian period, in the eighth century BCE. The Chicago team exposed them but then didn't dig any deeper in the area. We have excavated what is called a step trench down the side of the mound here, so that we can get a glimpse into the history of the site beneath the Neo-Assyrian level, just like Chicago did on the other side of the site. By the end of the 2014 excavation season, we had dug more than twenty feet down from where we started in 1994 and had reached back into levels dating to the Middle Bronze Age, in the middle of the second millennium BCE (possibly contemporary with the graves found by Schumacher one hundred years ago). Along the way, we encountered several layers of ash, burning, and other signs of destruction, which mark the dramatic end of several of the cities that once occupied the site.

In another area, dating back to the third millennium BCE and the Early Bronze Age, we may have found one of the largest temples ever discovered in the ancient Middle East. It stretches across the entire excavation area that we call Area J, on the eastern side of the mound, where the famous round altar discovered by the Chicago excavators also is located. The large number of bones discovered in this area has led some tour guides to assert that child sacrifice was performed on this altar by the Canaanites. Our excavations yielded thousands of bones from here, which were mostly from sheep and goats, but also from cattle, and even from lions, but none were from any children.

Also on the eastern side of Megiddo, but further south along the edge of the mound, we also dug Area K and reached Middle Bronze Age levels after starting in Neo-Assyrian levels. Here, one of the most interesting cities was destroyed in what was probably the late tenth century BCE, if our dating is correct. When it became clear, back in 1998, that we were digging the remains of a house that had been destroyed at that time, we employed a technique known as fine gridding to help us dig. To my knowledge, this was the first time the technique had been employed at the site and was introduced by Assaf Yasur-Landau—who would later become codirector with me at the site of Tel Kabri, where we use it all the time.

Working with a fine grid simply means taking each square, which normally measures five meters by five meters, and splitting it into smaller squares, each measuring one meter by one meter. By recording which finds, including pottery fragments, come from each of these smaller squares, it is possible to later reconstruct with greater precision exactly what was found and where. I should note that archaeologists in North America do this so frequently that they don't even bother using a separate term for it—and they frequently then divide the one-meter squares into separate quadrants to produce even finer provenience measurements for the materials that are recovered.

As a result of working in this manner at Megiddo, we were able to identify the function of each room of the house with a reasonable degree of precision, from the kitchen to the living room to the bedroom. Several skeletons were found in the house as well, including that of a woman and several children; most were in the area that we had identified as the kitchen.

The big question was, What had caused the destruction of this Canaanite city and of the house? Some thought that invaders, such as perhaps King David or some other group of Israelites, might have done it; others suggested that this might have been the city destroyed or captured by the Egyptian pharaoh Sheshonq when he left his inscription at the site.

The data suggest to me that an earthquake caused the destruction. As an archaeologist, I will be the first to admit that it is frequently hard to tell a destruction resulting from natural causes such as an earthquake from that produced by invaders, but in this case a couple of things stand out to me. First, the walls are tilting and some are out of alignment, an indicator of some strong force moving them. Second, there isn't any evidence of violence accompanying the bodies in the house: no arrowheads, swords, spears, or cut marks on bone. In short, I think Mother Nature caused this destruction, although I cannot prove it for sure.

In another area at Megiddo, at the southern edge of the mound, we do have evidence of a battle, but not from the time period that we initially expected. This too is an example of the surprising curveballs that archaeology can throw when least expected. It was in 2008 that we began to clear away the underbrush from an area where the University of Chicago had excavated in 1925 and 1926. Nobody had been in the area since, or so we thought. We had the photographs and drawings that the Chicago archaeologists had made and we knew that they had found rectangular buildings with small rooms that dated to the Neo-Assyrian period in the eighth century BCE.

When we began clearing the area, which we had renamed Area Q, we found that some of the rooms were now round, rather than rectangular. In and around them, we found a number of bullet casings—that is, the spent remains of bullets that had been ejected from a gun, which we thought at first were the result of weekend hunters or someone doing target practice. As more and more of these bullet casings came to light, we began to realize that perhaps something else had taken place here. And so, we started to collect them, as if they were archaeological artifacts, which indeed it turned out they were.

One of my students, Anthony Sutter, took a number of the bullet casings back with him to the United States for study. When he cleaned off the back of the casings, he was able to read the letters and numbers stamped into the metal, which are known as headstamps. These identify the maker of the bullets and the year in which they were made. I took back others and cleaned them off as well. All of them, both his and mine, said either 1948 or earlier. Not one of the several hundred that we looked at then, or the others that I examined after the 2010 and 2012 seasons, had a later date, and it quickly became clear that we were looking at the material remains of the battle that we knew had taken place at Megiddo during the war in 1948 that resulted in the establishment of the state of Israel.

It also became clear that we were engaging in what is called battlefield archaeology—sometimes called investigations of fields of conflict. Such investigations have been applied in Europe to battlegrounds dating to World War I and World War II. It also has been used in the United States, for instance in the area of the Little Bighorn, in what is now a national park in the state of Montana, where Custer had his last stand. There the archaeologists employed an army of metal-detector enthusiasts to map the bullet casings, which shed new light on how the battle transpired. I've often thought that we could do the same at Megiddo and figure out the route by which the Israeli forces attacked the mound before taking it over.

Now we knew why some of the rectangular rooms originally excavated by Chicago had become round. Someone had moved the rocks of the Neo-Assyrian buildings in 1948 to form foxholes and firing pits in which to crouch and to fire machine guns toward the British police station, now a prison, located across the fields about a kilometer away.

What we didn't know was who had created the foxholes and firing pits, and who had fired the bullets during the battle—the Arab defenders or the Israeli attackers. And this is where things took an unanticipated turn and showed how archaeologists can turn to the most unexpected places to find their answers. Although we never did find out for certain who had created the foxholes, we *were* able to figure out, within a reasonable degree of certainty, who had fired the bullets.

We knew that we had a lot of bullet casings from 8-millimeter (7.93 mm, to be precise) bullets that would have been fired from one or more machine guns, most likely placed in the firing pits. We had even been able to narrow down the type of machine guns that would have been available to shoot the bullets back in 1948 to three specific types: two were German and one was Czech. But then we were stuck. We didn't know anyone who had any of those types of machine guns, let alone all three types, so that we might try a ballistic comparison.

It was only when I happened to mention our interesting finds, and our dilemma, to the chairman of our forensic sciences department at George Washington University, during an administrative retreat, that the breakthrough occurred. He was intrigued enough by my account that he gave me the name of an adjunct instructor whose primary job was at the US Bureau of Alcohol, Tobacco, and Firearms. She, in turn, put me in touch with someone in the bureau who worked at a little-known place where they keep more than six thousand guns, from all time periods and places. When I mentioned to him the three types of machine guns that we thought our bullets were from, he said, "Yep, we've got those." It also turned out that he had been an archaeology major as an undergraduate, and so he was very interested in the challenging problem that I presented—how to identify the type of machine gun(s) that had fired our bullets more than sixty years earlier.

In the end, he fired all three types of machine guns while I watched. We then took those recently fired bullet casings and went back to the original woman whom I had first contacted. She put the new casings and the Megiddo casings side by side into a special microscope; first the ones from one of the German machine guns, and then those from the other type, and then finally the ones fired by the Czech machine gun. The Czech ones matched up perfectly with ours from Megiddo, with the same type of firing pin impressions created and so on. We had a definite identification. We had solved the case: "CSI Megiddo," a cold case from 1948. It was a spectacular moment. Anthony Sutter and I later collaborated on an article about the whole topic in the *Journal of Military History*.

{◦→}{◦→}

The excavations at Megiddo have recently been at the forefront of scientific archaeology in another way. That's because the codirector of the project, Israel Finkelstein, was awarded a large grant from the European Union Research Council in 2009, which allowed him to incorporate newer scientific advances into biblical archaeology. One of the places where he used these techniques was at Megiddo, where he brought in specialists to do microarchaeological studies: for example, to examine the dirt and other material found on floors after they were abandoned, which can yield information about the types of vegetation in the area, the length of time that the building was abandoned before being reoccupied, and so on.

In addition, in 2012 the news media began reporting that a cache of gold jewelry had been found at Megiddo. The cache included eight small gold hoop earrings and a large ornate ring, plus many small beads that had probably once been part of a necklace or bracelet. Stylistically, they all date to about the eleventh century BCE or so, if not a bit earlier, and undoubtedly belonged to a fairly wealthy Canaanite woman who hid, or kept, them in a jar and never retrieved them for whatever reason.

The jewelry was found still in the smallish ceramic jar, but it took a while for the archaeologists to realize that it was inside—nearly two years to be precise. The jar had been discovered completely intact during the 2010 excavation season. It was full to the brim with earth, and so it was sent to the conservation laboratory to be carefully excavated. The conservators had many previous commitments, and so the jar sat on a shelf for quite some time before one of them was able to take a look at it. When she did finally begin to work on it and started to carefully remove the earth inside it, out came the cache of jewelry, much to the surprise—and pleasure—of the conservator and the members of the Megiddo Expedition, who had not anticipated such a discovery.

{◦→}{◦→}

The excavations at Megiddo are continuing. As mentioned in a previous chapter, recent work off the mound by Matt Adams and Yotam Tepper has definitively identified the site of the Roman camp that was established next to the ancient mound in the second century CE.

I still think back to the days when I would walk over the site in the chill of the early morning, wondering what lay beneath my feet. Though I no longer codirect the excavation, along with everyone else I will be watching and waiting to see what else will be uncovered in future seasons at Armageddon.

I 4

UNEARTHING THE BIBLE

A MONG THE DEAD SEA SCROLLS ARE THE OLDEST COPIES OF the Hebrew Bible that we have. Before their discovery, the oldest version of the Bible we had was from a thousand years later, found tucked away in the back room of a synagogue in Cairo, Egypt. Other scrolls contain the basic religious documents and other writings of an apocalyptic sect of Jews, who may or may not have been responsible for the biblical texts.

The earliest of these scrolls dates to the third century BCE; the latest dates to the first century CE. They were hidden in caves on the cliffs by the western side of the Dead Sea, in what is now Israel, most likely during the First Jewish Revolt against Rome, between the years 66 and 70 CE.

Although there is much debate about the scrolls, the majority of scholars subscribe to a two-part theory: first, that the scrolls constituted the library of the nearby settlement called Qumran; and second, that the inhabitants of Qumran hid them in the caves, intending to retrieve them after the revolt was over and the Romans had left. The revolt was

Caves at Qumran

put down, however; the settlement was abandoned; and the inhabitants never came back for the scrolls.

We're not certain who lived at Qumran. Most scholars believe that it might have been the Essenes, who were one of the three main groups of Jews at the time (the others were the Sadducees and the Pharisees). We know a little bit about the Essenes from ancient authors, such as Philo, Pliny the Elder, and Josephus. We are told that they were celibate and didn't have any personal possessions—in other words, almost like monks in a monastery. Since Pliny places them near Ein Gedi, which is right in this area, it has been suggested that Qumran was a monastic settlement and the Essenes wrote the Dead Sea Scrolls. Both of those points are debated, though; for instance, it has been suggested that Qumran may have actually been a Roman villa or a fortress, rather than the equivalent of a monastery.

Whoever lived here, they were inhabiting—literally—one of the hottest, driest places imaginable that they could have chosen, with less than fifty millimeters of annual rainfall. At thirteen hundred feet below sea level, the Dead Sea is the lowest place on Earth. The Jordan River flows into it, but there is no exit for the water. The only way out is through evaporation, which leaves the salts and minerals behind. As a result, the Dead Sea is one of the saltiest bodies of water on the planet, even more so than the Great Salt Lake in Utah, and the entire region is among the hottest places that I have ever been.

{↔} {↔}

The first of these scrolls, of which there are now more than nine hundred, were found in 1947 by three young Bedouin boys, usually reported to have been cousins. They were watering their flocks of sheep and goats at nearby Ras Feshka when one of the boys wandered away from the others, perhaps in search of a stray goat.

Bored, he picked up a stone and tried to throw it into a cave that he could see high up in the cliff. After several attempts, one stone flew straight into the cave and he heard a loud crash and a shattering of pottery.

Since it was getting dark, he went back to their temporary camp and told the other two boys what had happened. But when the boys investigated the cave the next day, they were disappointed that there was no gold to be found. Instead, as they said later, there were ten jars in the cave, one of which was now broken. Most of the jars were filled with dirt, but one had several rolled-up scrolls in it, made of leather. They took the scrolls but left the jars in the cave.

Several weeks later, the Bedouin group to which the boys belonged made their way to the outskirts of Bethlehem and brought the scrolls to the leather and shoe shop of a man named Kando. He also sold antiquities and purchased the scrolls thinking that he could turn them into sandals if he couldn't sell them as ancient artifacts. An alternate version of the story is that Kando bought four scrolls and another Bethlehem antiquities dealer, a man named Salahi, bought three others. In any event, news of the scrolls reached a Jewish scholar in Jerusalem named Eliezer Sukenik. He traveled to Bethlehem by bus and purchased three scrolls—either from Kando or Salahi—and returned to Jerusalem just hours before the 1948 war broke out.

When Sukenik translated the three scrolls, he was startled to find that one of them was a copy of the Book of Isaiah from the Hebrew

Bible. He was the first person to have read this scroll in two thousand years. To his astonishment, it was nearly identical to another copy of Isaiah from the synagogue in Cairo that was dated almost a thousand years later, to the tenth century CE. It differed from our version today only by some thirteen or so minor variants, probably all the result of scribal copying errors over the centuries.

One of the other two scrolls, called the Thanksgiving Scroll, contained the previously unknown hymns and prayers of thanks of a community. The third scroll was also unknown. Called the War Scroll, it records the fact that the inhabitants of Qumran, or whomever the scroll belonged to, were waiting for Armageddon—for a final battle between good and evil. They saw themselves as a fighting force, calling themselves the Sons of Light who would be fighting the Sons of Darkness. The scroll outlines how they were to act and live their lives, all the while planning for this battle. Of course, one could say that the battle never happened, but I would argue that, at least for them it did, if one wants to call the Romans the Sons of Darkness.

Soon thereafter, four more scrolls appeared on the antiquities market. Archbishop Samuel, who was with the Syrian Orthodox Monastery of St. Mark in Jerusalem, was selling them. He had bought them from Kando, the antiquities dealer in Bethlehem, reportedly for $250. And then he offered them to Sukenik, but they were unable to reach an agreement.

So, what to do? In January 1949, the archbishop smuggled the four scrolls into the United States, where they were secretly kept in a Syrian Orthodox church in New Jersey for several years. Then, on June 1, 1954, he placed an advertisement in the *Wall Street Journal* that read "'The Four Dead Sea Scrolls'—Biblical Manuscripts dating back to at least 200 BCE are for sale. This would be an ideal gift for an educational or religious institution by an individual or group. Box F 206, *The Wall Street Journal*."

It just so happened that Yigael Yadin, the preeminent Israeli archaeologist, was in the United States at that time, lecturing at Johns Hopkins University. The advertisement was brought to his attention and, with the help of a middleman from New York, Yadin purchased the four scrolls for the State of Israel for a quarter of a million dollars.

Thus, the seven scrolls were reunited. They are now kept at the Israel Museum in Jerusalem, in their own quarters known as the Shrine of the

Book. But the story gets even better, because Yigael Yadin had changed his original name at some point. His birth name was Yigael Sukenik—he was Eliezer Sukenik's son. The son was able to buy the scrolls that had eluded his father, which seems very fitting.

Of the four scrolls that Yadin purchased from Archbishop Samuel, one was another copy of the Book of Isaiah, in even better shape than the one that his father had purchased. Another was a copy of what is now called the Manual of Discipline. It contains the rules and regulations for the community to which it belonged, which most people assume is the settlement at Qumran.

The third scroll was a commentary on the Book of Habakkuk from the Hebrew Bible. Habakkuk was one of the minor prophets and the book that is attributed to him is not very long, but this commentary is very important. It presents us with three figures—one called the Teacher of Righteousness and his two opponents, who are called the Wicked Priest and the Man of the Lie. None of these figures has been definitely identified, although this scroll has been the focus of much scholarly debate over the years.

As for the fourth scroll that Yadin acquired, it is known as the Genesis Apocryphon. Written in Aramaic, the colloquial language of the Jews of those centuries, rather than in Hebrew, it is an alternate version of the Book of Genesis, different from the version that we have in our current Bibles. The scroll records a supposed conversation between Noah and his father Lamech—which is a conversation that we don't find in our Bibles today.

News of these remarkable documents shook the world of biblical scholarship. It also set off a race between the archaeologists and the Bedouin pastoralists who lived near the Dead Sea, searching for more caves during the 1950s and 1960s. And they found them, one after the other—at least eleven caves in all. By the time that they were done, they had found multiple copies of nearly every book from the Hebrew Bible, except for the Book of Esther. They also found numerous other scrolls that were not religious in nature.

Cave 7 had only scrolls that were written in Greek, the language of commerce and of the occupying Roman forces (along with Latin), rather than in Hebrew or in Aramaic, but it is Caves 3 and 4 that have attracted the most interest. Cave 3 contained a scroll that wasn't written on leather or any other type of parchment, but on sheets of copper. Archaeologists found the scroll in 1952, broken into two parts. In both scholarly and popular literature, it is referred to as the Copper Scroll.

There has been a lot written about this scroll, including a lot of nonsense, because it's a treasure map. Plain and simple, no bones about it, it's a treasure map, like the kind a pirate would leave, with "X marks the spot." Except that it's not an X in each case; instead it's a detailed set of instructions to sixty-four different treasures.

When they first found the Copper Scroll, which is now kept in a museum in Amman, Jordan, the archaeologists could not unroll it by themselves. In fact, they couldn't unroll it using any means that they knew of, and so they simply cut it up. They took it to Manchester, England, where it was cut into twenty-three small sections, using a high-speed saw. The cuts went right through the middle of some of the letters, but on the whole the technique worked, so that the rolled-up scrolls now could be laid flat, albeit looking like pieces in a jigsaw puzzle, but all approximately the same size and shape.

Most of the Copper Scroll is written in Hebrew, but there also are some Greek letters and what appear to be numbers as well. But it is the directions that are most bizarre and that explain, at least to me, why none of the sixty-four treasures listed on the scroll has ever been located.

The first set, for example, says, "In the ruin which is in the valley, pass under the steps leading to the East forty cubits [. . .]: [there is] a chest of money and its total: the weight of seventeen talents. In the sepulchral monument, in the third course: one hundred gold ingots. In the great cistern of the courtyard of the peristyle, in a hollow in the floor covered with sediment, in front of the upper opening: nine hundred talents." But which ruin? Which valley? Which cistern? Which peristyle? It's not clear at all which valley, monument, or cistern is meant.

The Copper Scroll continues like this for column after column after column of text. No wonder nobody has ever found any of the treasures. It's also not clear at all where the treasures were from or whether they were even real. If they were real, then they were most likely the annual tithes that people were sending to the Temple in Jerusalem, except that during the First Jewish Revolt it was not safe to send such tithes there, so they were hidden instead. Still, one would think that if such were the case, then something should have been found long ago. That's why other scholars suggest that they *were* found long ago—but back in antiquity, soon after they were buried. It remains a mystery that various amateur archaeologists try to solve from time to time, without any luck.

There was another scroll that was found by the Bedouin in Cave 11. It made its way to Kando's shop in Bethlehem, just like some of the first ones. It was initially offered for sale, apparently via a clergyman in Virginia acting as a middleman, but then it came into Yigael Yadin's hands after the Six-Day War in 1967. The main part of it had been kept in a shoebox, with other fragments in a smaller cigar box. When it was very carefully unrolled and the various fragments reattached, it turned out to be what is now known as the Temple Scroll. It has explicit details about the construction and appearance of a Jewish temple that was never built, complete with regulations about sacrifices and various temple practices. Yadin eventually published the whole story of its acquisition, and the scroll itself remains an object of intense study today.

It was Cave 4, however, that created a real mess in the world of archaeology and scholarship, for the scrolls found in that cave had all fallen from the shelves where they had originally been and had disintegrated into a mass of fragments on the floor. The original scrolls were now in tens of thousands of fragments, some smaller than a fingernail. The original scholarly committee that was formed to piece the fragments back together and publish them worked on them for more than forty years, with few other scholars even allowed to see them. This created all sorts of ill will, not to mention conspiracy theories about what might be contained in the texts that the scholars were painstakingly putting back together.

In the end, the bottleneck was broken from several different directions, almost all at once, in the late 1980s and early 1990s. One involved photographs of the scroll fragments, which were left at one scholar's front door by someone who still remains anonymous. Another involved a professor and his graduate student who reconstructed what was on the scroll fragments by working from a set of index cards that they had been given, each of which had a single word from a scroll on it, along with the word that appeared before that word and the word that appeared after that word in the original scroll. This is known as a compendium, copies of which were given out by the scroll team to trusted scholars. This professor and his graduate student created a computer program that matched the cards up and reconstructed the original contents of the fragments with about 90 percent accuracy.

The most important revelation was that other photographs of all the fragments had been taken at one point, unbeknownst to most people, and were stored in a vault for safekeeping at the Huntington Museum Library in Los Angeles. Once this fact was revealed and the Huntington declared in 1991 that anyone with proper scholarly credentials could access the microfilm copies of them, the floodgates opened. A new group of scholars was assembled to work on the fragments and volume after volume has since appeared in rapid succession. Some of the most interesting developments came about because women and Jews were among the new scholars working on the texts; the original team had been all male and all Christian. The new scholars brought new backgrounds and new approaches to the study of the scrolls. New techniques also were used on the scroll fragments, such as taking infrared photographs, which allowed for much clearer reading of some of the writing.

Studying the Dead Sea Scrolls, ranging from the whole ones to the completely fragmentary, has become a cottage industry within academia. An immense number of publications have now appeared, from the most scholarly to the most popularizing. And the intense study has yielded some remarkable observations—for example, that the earliest fragment dates to the late third century BCE and is from the Book of Samuel.

There is another fragment from the Book of Samuel that contains a passage that was missing from our copies of the Bible. Here, in 1 Samuel 10–11, two paragraphs in a row begin with the same person's name—Nahash, king of the Ammonites. Most likely a scribe recopying the manuscript looked up after writing the first paragraph and then, when looking down again, saw the same man's name at the beginning of the second paragraph and, thinking that he had already copied that paragraph, went on to the next paragraph. In fact, he had only copied the first paragraph, not both. As a result, our modern Bibles were missing that second paragraph. Many versions today have now restored that missing paragraph, on the basis of this discovery in the Dead Sea Scrolls.

❧❧ ❧❧

The archaeologists found other caves in the region of the Dead Sea that had remnants of scrolls and ancient writing, as well as other objects, but they are probably unrelated to the main body of the Dead Sea Scrolls, since the remains found in them are from other periods.

One of the best known is a cave in a wadi, or canyon or valley, called Nahal Mishmar. In what is now known as the Cave of the Treasure, archaeologists found a tremendous hoard of about four hundred copper objects dating to the Chalcolithic period, about 3500 BCE. A number of them were maceheads, more likely ceremonial than functional; others look like crowns and scepters, though it is not clear whether this is how they were actually used.

Two other caves are even more famous. Located in a wadi called Nahal Hever, which is about twenty-five miles south of Qumran, they are called the Cave of Horrors and the Cave of Letters. One is located in the cliff face that makes up the northern side of the wadi, the other is in a similar location on the southern side. Both had a Roman siege camp built on the top of the cliff directly above them and both are on such a steep slope that it is best to reach them now by precarious rope ladders.

Both caves were first discovered in 1953, but were not truly investigated and excavated until 1960 and 1961, as part of an effort by teams led by four distinguished Israeli archaeologists, including Yadin.

The first one, the Cave of Horrors, is called that because of the grisly discoveries that the archaeologists made in there. They found forty skeletons in the cave, all dating to the time of the Second Jewish Revolt against Roman rule, known as the Bar Kokhba Revolt. The rebellion lasted from 132 to 135 CE and was unsuccessful. The bodies found in this cave are thought to have been refugees or rebels who were unable to get out or escape from the cave because of the Romans camped directly above them, no doubt very deliberately. They may well have starved to death, since there was no evidence of trauma, but we may never know the real story of what happened in the Cave of Horrors.

In contrast, we know an amazing amount about the Cave of Letters. Yadin was in charge of exploring this cave in 1960 and 1961, although it had already been fairly thoroughly examined by archaeologists in 1953. It turned out to be extremely rich, with finds from three periods. One period was the Chalcolithic, from about 3500 BCE, contemporary with the Cave of the Treasure in Nahal Mishmar. A second period was the first century CE, perhaps during the time of the First Jewish Revolt when all the scrolls had been hidden in the caves closer to Qumran. The third period was the second century CE—that is, the time of the Second Jewish Revolt.

The cave has two narrow entrances, both leading into what is called Hall A. In the hall, archaeologists found a fragment from a scroll with part of the Book of Psalms, reading "O Lord, who shall sojourn in thy tents?" (Psalms 15:1–2). Using a metal detector, they also found a number of additional objects, including metal vessels and coins. From Hall A, a narrow tunnel leads to Halls B and C. It's in Hall C that the most important, and grisly, finds were made, including a basket of human skulls found in a crevice along with a skeleton wrapped in a blanket and a child buried in a box lined with leather. In the farthest reaches of the hall, they found correspondence written by Bar Kokhba (in which he is called by his real name, Bar Kosiba). There also were metal keys and a basket made of palm fronds, which was filled with objects such as a mirror, keys, leather sandals, wooden bowls, bronze jugs, and—perhaps most important—an archive of letters wrapped in a bundle of rags belonging to a woman named Babatha, also dating to the time of Bar Kokhba and the Second Jewish Revolt.

It turned out that there were at least three men, eight women, and six children whose skeletons were found in Hall C within the cave. The correspondence written by Bar Kokhba was on wooden slates all wrapped up in papyri; one of them read "Simeon bar Kosiba, President [or prince] over Israel." There is an unconfirmed story that when Yadin went to the president of Israel to personally tell him of the discovery, he saluted and said, "Message from your predecessor, sir."

The material in Babatha's archive included thirty-five papyrus rolls, which were mostly legal documents regarding property that she had inherited from her father and the guardianship of her son. David Harris, a photographer who was there on the day that they were discovered, later wrote, "as Yadin checked to make sure he had missed nothing, his hand touched a bundle of rags. When he brought it out, he could see a hoard of papyrus rolls wrapped together, what we now call the Babatha archive, describing everyday life during the Bar Kosiba period. Thirty-five years later I remember that wonderful and exciting experience as the greatest in my life as a photographer."

The discoveries in the Cave of the Treasure, the Cave of Horrors, and the Cave of Letters contributed dramatic new material to the field of biblical archaeology. It was the discovery of the Dead Sea Scrolls, however, that absolutely revolutionized the field of biblical studies by shedding light on the Hebrew Bible according to texts that date more than two thousand years ago. From their accidental discovery, to the intrigue of their trade on the antiquities market, right through to the academic controversies they have ignited, all these elements make the Dead Sea Scrolls one of the most enthralling archaeological finds of the twentieth century.

15

MYSTERY AT MASADA

I N 73 OR 74 CE, 960 JEWISH ZEALOTS—MEN, WOMEN, AND children—committed suicide on top of the mountain of Masada by the Dead Sea in Israel rather than be captured by the Romans. The story, told to us by the Roman historian Josephus, is one of the most famous from antiquity. But did it actually happen? Yigael Yadin, the Israeli archaeologist from the Hebrew University of Jerusalem who excavated the site in the mid-1960s, said that it did. Moreover, he also said that the objects found during his dig proved it. The book that he subsequently published, *Masada: Herod's Fortress and the Zealots' Last Stand*, was a best seller.

It was no secret that Yadin's excavations at various sites in Israel, such as at Hazor in the 1950s and at Masada in the 1960s, were in part undertaken in the hope of reinforcing Jewish claims to the land by linking them to biblical stories and other famous events, including the story that Josephus tells. Some have long felt that this desire may have affected his interpretations of the finds made during his excavations. In 1995 and 2002, Nachman Ben-Yehuda, a sociologist also at the Hebrew University of Jerusalem, published his own interpretation of the finds from Masada in two separate books—*The Masada Myth* and *Sacrificing Truth*. He concluded that Yadin had been incorrect in many of his interpretations, perhaps deliberately so, in the interest of creating a nationalist narrative out of the remains that he found at Masada and helping the young state of Israel create an identity for itself and its citizens that was based on archaeology.

Subsequently, in 2009, Amnon Ben-Tor, who is now the Yigael Yadin Professor of Archaeology at the Hebrew University of Jerusalem and who had excavated with Yadin at Masada, published a spirited defense of Yadin and his findings, titled *Back to Masada*. In it, Ben-Tor went through the archaeology again, dismissing each of Ben-Yehuda's points and basically confirming Yadin's interpretations and conclusions.

The debate involves the trustworthiness of Josephus's account; the credibility of Yadin, perhaps the most famous of all Israeli archaeologists; and the influence of nationalism on the interpretation of archaeological discoveries. Who do we believe?

{→→}{→→}

Masada is a tall mountain with a flat plateau on top, longer than it is wide, rising high above the surrounding dry and arid desert. It has been a tourist attraction ever since Yadin's excavations in the mid-1960s. Hundreds of tourists a day now roam around the ruins on top of the mountain—half a million visit every year. It is the second most popular tourist site in Israel, after Jerusalem, and was named a World Heritage Site by UNESCO in 2001.

It lies at the southern end of the Dead Sea, far to the south of Qumran and most of the caves in which the Dead Sea Scrolls were found. The top is accessible on foot only via a narrow winding track known as the Snake Path that leads four hundred meters (thirteen hundred feet) up the front face of the massif and the Roman siege ramp still in place on the western side. It gets so hot here that rules have been put into place instructing tourists that they may begin the climb only if it is before 9:30 in the morning. There's too much chance of getting dehydrated during the ascent after that. Those who begin climbing before dawn are rewarded with one of the most spectacular sunrises that they

Masada

will ever see, but most tourists opt to ride up in the cable cars that have been installed, gliding above the Snake Path and waving to those below.

The work that Yadin conducted at Masada over two excavation seasons, from October 1963 to May 1964 and again from November 1964 to April 1965, was a milestone for archaeology in several ways. For example, Yadin was the first to use international volunteers to help dig the site. He recruited participants by placing ads in newspapers, both in Israel and in England, and wound up with volunteers from twenty-eight countries.

Nowadays it is rare for a dig in Israel *not* to have participants from all over the world, but at that point in time, it was a novelty. The sheer numbers that took part is also amazing—Yadin claims to have had no fewer than three hundred volunteers digging at Masada at any given moment during his excavations. Those included volunteers from the Israel Defense Forces, high school students, and kibbutz members, in addition to the international participants.

The logistics of running the dig were staggering. Archaeologists active today, who were graduate students at the time, talk about helicopters sometimes being commandeered to fly tools and equipment up to the top of the mound, though the more usual route was to carry everything up the western side of the mound, via the Roman siege ramp, which provided the best access to the mountaintop for heavily laden volunteers. In the case of heavier equipment, a cable system next to the ramp was used. The tents in which the expedition members lived were pitched at the foot of this same Roman ramp, for logistical reasons. All this Yadin confirms in his book.

The excavation itself has become the stuff of legend. Yadin says that when they first began planning the excavation, they couldn't see any structures with a recognizable plan on top of Masada. The entire area, he says, seemed to be covered with "mounds of stone and rubble." In actuality, many of the buildings could be seen quite plainly, once the team took aerial photographs so that they knew where to dig in many cases.

By the time they finished the excavations, they had discovered that Masada was an elaborate palatial settlement, originally built by King Herod after his successful journey to Rome in 40 BCE, in case he ever had to flee Jerusalem and seek refuge elsewhere. It was later taken over and occupied by the Sicarii rebels fighting Rome in the aftermath of the First Jewish Revolt more than seven decades later.

Masada actually boasted two palaces. One was at the northern end of the rock plateau. It had three levels embedded in the side of the cliff and was placed to grab summer breezes in the intense heat of the Judean desert. The other palace was on Masada's western side. In addition to the two palaces, Yadin's team found rooms and buildings that served as tanneries, workshops, and even a synagogue. They also found numerous storage areas to hold food and other provisions, some of which had jars that still contained charred grain from the final destruction, and many cisterns for holding rainwater, for there was no fresh water to be had in the arid desert region that surrounded Masada.

Some of the walls were covered in plaster painted with images in deep blues, brilliant reds, yellow, and black, of which only fragments now remain. A few of the floors were inlaid with mosaics featuring elaborate designs like those found more commonly in Greece or Rome. Presumably artisans hired by Herod the Great created these, perhaps to emulate what he had seen in Rome. Only parts of them now remain.

Yadin reconstructed some of the original buildings from the fallen stones that they found. The best example of this at Masada was the large complex of storerooms that were in the northeastern part of the site. Here just the lower portions of the walls were left, but the stones from higher up in the walls were all lying right where they had fallen. Yadin and his team reconstructed the walls and rooms, using every available stone to rebuild the walls, which turned out to be eleven feet high. In order to show what they had done, and what they had reconstructed, they painted a black line to separate the lower part that they had excavated from the upper part that they had reconstructed. This is still done at some sites in Israel today; for instance, something similar can be seen at Megiddo on a walk through the Late Bronze Age gate when entering the ancient city.

Yadin says they put "every grain of earth . . . through a special sieve." Nearly fifty thousand cubic yards of dirt was sifted. It was the first time that every single bucket of dirt had been sifted at an excavation in Israel. As a result, they found numerous small items that would probably otherwise have been missed, including hundreds of coins, pieces of pottery with inscriptions on them, and small pieces of jewelry like rings and beads. The coins allowed him to date very precisely the remains that they were uncovering—particularly the coins that had been made just a few years earlier, during the First Jewish Revolt. They included coins from all five years of the revolt, including several very rare ones from the revolt's last year.

Yadin's excavations at Masada have been the subject of much debate in recent years, however, especially over his interpretation of the remains and his use of them in reconstructing the ancient narrative of what happened at the site. His publication appeared just a year after the dig ended, as a large coffee-table book, in one of the first excavation reports ever aimed at a popular audience. In contrast, the official publications of the results have taken up eight additional volumes and the efforts of dozens of scholars working for decades, with the most recent volume appearing in 2007, more than forty years after the original excavation ended.

The story of Masada is therefore more than just a story of the archaeological excavations. It is an example of how archaeologists use historical information to supplement what they find during their excavations and to flesh out the bare details provided by the archaeological discoveries. Yadin made particular use of the writings of Flavius Josephus—the Jewish general turned Roman historian who wrote two books about the Jews in the first century CE and who is the primary source for what may have taken place on top of Masada nearly two thousand years ago. But the relationship between archaeology and the historical record cuts both ways. In other words, since we cannot be certain that Josephus's discussions are 100 percent accurate, we can use archaeology to corroborate—or to challenge—the ancient text. But the event also serves as a cautionary tale about using (or misusing) archaeological evidence to support a nationalistic agenda, as some scholars have suggested Yadin did in this case.

⊁⊱⊁⊱

It was in 73 or 74 CE that the Romans mounted a siege against a small group of Jewish rebels at Masada. Josephus is our only historical source for information about that siege. The story that he tells, of a mass suicide by the Jewish defenders, had long been known . . . and in fact, Yadin was using the archaeology to try to corroborate the details that Josephus gives.

That story is briefly told. As we have previously noted in the chapter on Rome, the First Jewish Rebellion began in 66 CE, when the Jews in what is now Israel rose up against the Romans who were occupying their land. The revolt lasted until 70 CE, at which point the Romans captured Jerusalem and burnt most of it to the ground, including the Temple that had been built there by Herod the Great to replace the original one constructed by King Solomon, which had been destroyed by the Neo-Babylonians centuries earlier. It is said that both the First and Second Temples, that is, those built by Solomon and Herod, respectively, were destroyed on the same day of the year, which is today a Jewish day of mourning known as Tisha B'Av.

When the rebellion ended, a group of rebels managed to escape the destruction of Jerusalem and settled at Masada. Led by a man named Eleazar ben Ya'ir, these were the Sicarii, or Dagger Men. They took over the fortified buildings and palaces that Herod had originally built on top of Masada as a place of last refuge for himself and his family, should he ever need it.

In his account of what happened, though, Josephus got some of the details wrong, and so we suspect that perhaps he wasn't ever there himself, but was using someone else's notes. For instance, he says that Herod "built a palace . . . at the western ascent . . . but inclined to its north side." In actuality, as noted, the archaeologists found two palaces, not one—at the west and at the north—on top of Masada.

Some of the other details that Josephus gives, though, are quite correct—for instance, he describes the baths that were built there, the fact that the floors in some of the buildings "were paved with stones of several colors," and that many pits were cut into the living rock to serve as cisterns. Josephus must be referring to the sort of mosaics that Yadin found still partially intact on some of the floors. As to the cisterns that he mentions, some that were dug into the rock on top of Masada were simply enormous. Yadin estimated that they each had a capacity of up to one hundred and forty thousand cubic feet of water; added together, they could hold almost 1.4 million cubic feet, or more than ten million gallons, of water.

In the end, the rebel group held out for three years, raiding the surrounding countryside for food, until the Romans decided to put an end to them and the final remnants of the rebellion.

Josephus says that the Romans, led by General Flavius Silva, surrounded Masada with a wall that went the entire way around the mountain on the desert floor, with separate garrisons or fortresses built at spaced intervals along the wall, so that no one could escape. Today, eight of Flavius's fortresses can still be seen from the top of Masada when looking down at the surrounding countryside.

Next, the Romans began constructing a long ramp built of earth and stones, making use of a natural ridge that reached from the desert floor to within "300 cubits" of the top of Masada. Once the ramp was constructed, siege engines, like a battering ram and catapults that flung large stones and ballistae that shot huge arrows, could be wheeled upon its length and used against the walls of Masada. Josephus notes: "There was . . . a tower made of the height of sixty cubits, and all over plated with iron, out of which the Romans threw darts and stones from the engines, and soon made those that fought from the walls of the place to retire, and would not let them lift up their heads above the works."

Today, full-size replicas of some of these siege engines can be seen at the site. They were left there after ABC filmed a miniseries about Masada that aired in 1981. Yadin and the other archaeologists uncovered other objects during their excavations in the 1960s that also can still be seen at the site, including what look like catapult balls that were flung up by the Romans and possibly slingstones that were thrown back down by the Jewish defenders.

After the Roman siege engines were set up, the real siege began. Josephus tells us that General Silva ordered the battering ram to be dragged up the ramp and set against the wall. Several men grabbed the rope that was tied to the great piece of pointed wood that formed the battering ram and pulled it back, back, back. When they let go, the ram smashed against the fortification wall with a huge crash. It wasn't going to be long before they had breached the wall.

The Jewish defenders, however, had created their own wall just inside, which was made of wood and earth, so that it would be soft and yielding, as Josephus tells us. He says that they laid down great beams of wood lengthwise right next to the inside of the wall, then did the same about ten feet or so away, so that they had two large stacks of wooden beams. In between the two stacks, they poured earth, so that in the end, they had an extremely thick wall with wood on both sides and an earthen core. This second wall, set up against the stone fortification wall, helped to absorb the blows of the battering ram, spreading the impact. Thus, it took the Romans far longer than they expected to knock a hole in the wall. And even when they did punch a hole in the outer wall, they were still faced with this thick wood-and-earth wall.

In the end, they simply set fire to it, Josephus says, and then made preparations to enter the city. By the time the flames had died down, night had fallen, and Josephus says that the Romans returned to their camps for the night and prepared to overrun the defenders the next morning.

This brief respite from the Roman attack provided the Jewish defenders the time and opportunity to decide to kill themselves rather than be killed or taken prisoner and enslaved by the Romans. Josephus says that Eleazar ben Ya'ir, their leader, asked each family man to kill his own wife and children, declaring "[I]t is still in our power to die bravely, and in a state of freedom, which has not been the case of others, who were conquered unexpectedly."

The men then drew lots, choosing ten of their number to kill all the others. The ten then drew lots and selected one to kill the other nine. He then killed himself, thereby becoming the only person to commit suicide, technically speaking, which is against Jewish law. In effect, though, it was a mass suicide and when the Romans entered the next morning, they were greeted by a vast silence. Only when two women and five children emerged from their hiding place in a cistern did the Romans learn the truth of what had happened, for the women told them of Eleazar's speech, repeating it word for word. According to Josephus, 960 people died that night.

✦⟶✦ ✦⟶✦

The dramatic story has reverberated down through the ages until the present day. In fact, after Yadin's excavations at the site, the Israeli army used to hold its induction ceremonies for new recruits up on top of Masada, making them swear at a dramatic nighttime ritual in front of a blazing bonfire that "never again; never again" would they allow such a thing to happen.

Problems with Josephus's story remain, not least of which is the fact that if the two women and five children really had been hiding in the cistern, there is no way that they would have been able to hear Eleazar ben Ya'ir's speech, and hear it so clearly that they were able to repeat it and Josephus could quote it word for word.

A larger problem is the fact that, if the Romans had punched a hole in the wall even as night was falling, they would never have returned to their camps for the evening. Roman military tactics at the time called for them to press the advantage whenever and wherever they had it, regardless of the time of day or night. Thus, they would have gone straight through the breached and burning wall, leaving no time for a discussion of the plan and a vote on it, ben Ya'ir to make his speech, for successive lots to be drawn, no time for the husbands to kill their wives and families, no time for the ten men to kill the others, and no time for the last man to kill the other nine. In short, it couldn't have happened as Josephus has described it.

More likely what happened was exactly what we might have expected. When the Romans breached the wall, they poured in and massacred the Jewish defenders. It was not a mass suicide, but a mass slaughter. Josephus, writing later back in Rome and using notes and daybooks from the commanding officers who were present, probably was asked to whitewash the whole thing. In fact, Josephus took the story that he tells about the men killing their families, ten men killing the others, and then one man killing the rest, from his own experience.

Several years earlier, in 67 CE, during the initial rebellion against Rome, Josephus had been a Jewish general fighting the Romans at a site called Jotapata. They managed to hold off the Romans for forty-seven days, but in the end he and forty others took refuge in a cave, where they decided to commit suicide, with each man killing another, rather than surrender. In the end, only Josephus was left alive with one other man, whom he persuaded to surrender with him. The story Josephus tells us of what happened at Masada seems to be the story of what happened to him at Jotapata.

✦✦✦ ✦✦✦

It was with some of these Josephus-related problems in mind, including the story of the women and children hiding in the cistern while the rest of the people committed suicide, that Yadin decided to go to Masada. He wanted to excavate, to see what he could find and either prove or disprove the story.

Some of what he found, and how he interpreted it, remains a matter of great debate. The architecture and the objects themselves are not debated; the question lies in how they should be *interpreted*. For instance, among the objects that Yadin found were belt buckles, door keys, arrowheads, spoons, rings, and other items made of iron, in addition to much pottery and numerous coins. He interpreted these as belonging to the Jewish defenders of Masada, as indeed they might have, but some may have belonged to the Roman besiegers or even to later inhabitants or squatters at the site.

He also found fragments of scrolls, including scraps from the Book of Psalms, one containing portions of Psalms 81 to 85 and another from the last chapter in the book, Psalm 150, which reads "Praise ye the Lord. . . . Praise Him with the sound of the trumpet." Other very important but fragmentary nonbiblical texts also were in place, including a fragment from a scroll whose lines of text are identical to one found in the Dead Sea caves at Qumran, which led Yadin, and many other scholars since then, to wonder whether there was any connection between the defenders of Masada and the inhabitants of Qumran.

Perhaps most important, Yadin also found bodies at the site, though fewer than thirty in all (and certainly not anywhere near the 960 that Josephus reported), some with hair still intact and leather sandals nearby. It is these that have generated the most debate in recent years. Twenty-five of them were in a cave near the top of the southern cliff face; they were given a state funeral in 1969, though over Yadin's objections, since he said they couldn't be sure whether they were the Jewish defenders of Masada, the Roman attackers, or some other group of people, perhaps from a different period altogether.

Three other bodies were found near a small bathhouse on the lower terrace of the northern palace. Amnon Ben-Tor, the current director of the excavations at Hazor, says that he was the one who excavated these three skeletons and that it was the most thrilling day in his professional life. In the book that he published, Yadin made the most out of these three bodies, stating that when they first came across the remains, "Even the veterans and the more cynical among us stood frozen, gazing in awe at what had been uncovered."

One of the bodies, Yadin said, was "that of a man of about 20—perhaps one of the commanders of Masada." Next to him were armor scales, dozens of arrows, an inscribed potsherd, and fragments of a prayer shawl. Nearby, on a plaster floor stained with what looked like blood, was the skeleton of a young woman. Her hair was still preserved, "beautifully plaited . . . as if it had been just been freshly coiffeured." Her sandals also were preserved, next to her body. The third body, Yadin said, "was that of a child."

Yadin believed that they formed a family group who died in close proximity to each other. This has been the focus of much debate over the years, as have the pottery sherds with names written on them in ink that he found, including one that says "ben Ya'ir." To Yadin, these bodies and the sherds confirmed Josephus's story and the existence of Eleazar ben Ya'ir.

Unfortunately for Yadin, more recent forensic analysis indicates that the members of the so-called family group that he wrote about were only a few years apart in age and couldn't possibly have been a "family." The man was more likely about twenty-two years old, the woman was eighteen, and the "child" was a boy about eleven years old.

There are other problems as well, including the fact that there were eleven inscribed sherds found instead of ten; pig bones were mixed in with some of the burials; and so on. These were duly listed in the books written by Ben-Yehuda and then dismissed in turn by Ben-Tor.

{↔} {↔}

Regardless of whether one follows Ben-Yehuda or Ben-Tor in reviling or revering Yadin, Ben-Tor's concluding remarks in the book that he wrote in defense of Yadin still ring true. As he said, "Placing Masada on the scientific agenda . . . on the one hand, and in the public consciousness as a tourist site on the other, are both the proper expression and a true monument to the two aspects of Yadin's personality: the scholar and the public figure."

Overall, Yadin's excavations at Masada served as a milestone for archaeology in Israel, especially for use of multinational volunteers and numerous other aspects of the logistics of the operation. They remain significant today for tourism, of course, but also because they are at the heart of recent discussions on the nature of interpretations made by archaeologists, especially those who may or may not have a nationalist agenda beyond a simple reading of the data that they have uncovered.

16

CITIES OF THE DESERT

ALTHOUGH SITES IN MODERN ISRAEL AND PALESTINE ARE perhaps better known to the general public because of their biblical connections, they are not necessarily the most extensive or impressive archaeological sites in the Middle East. Other ruined cities and ancient tells abound farther north and east in Syria, Jordan, and Iraq, though western tourists visit them less frequently because of their remoteness and because of political instability in the past several decades. We have already touched on a number of the sites, including Ur, Nimrud, and Nineveh in Iraq. Here we will briefly describe three more—Ebla and Palmyra in Syria and the desert entrepôt of Petra in Jordan.

Ebla (modern Tell Mardikh) first made headlines around the world in the 1970s. Paolo Matthiae from the Sapienze University of Rome and his team began digging at the site in 1964 and continued almost until the present—nearly fifty years in all. It has taken that long to excavate because the site is absolutely huge, covering about 140 acres. The earthen ramparts that protected the city can still be seen clearly, though there is now a road through them, on which one can drive in order to gain entrance to the rest of the site. There is a huge lower city and then a citadel—a higher mound—right in the middle of the site. On the citadel are the royal palaces and administrative buildings.

Four years after starting the excavation, Matthiae's team found a statue that had been dedicated nearly four thousand years earlier by a local man named Ibbit-Lim. In the inscription, this man said he was the son of the king of Ebla. This was quite a revelation, since previous scholars had thought that Ebla was located farther north in Syria, not here at Tell Mardikh. After further digging, they were able to confirm that they had indeed found ancient Ebla. As it turns out, we now know that Ebla is an extremely important site with a long history dating all the way back to the third millennium BCE and continuing until it was destroyed in about the year 1600 BCE.

Matthiae and his team spent the first nine years working on the portion of the mound and the buildings that dated to the second part of its occupation, from about 2000 to 1600 BCE. They were interested in this period in part because it was the time of the Amorites, who are known from the Bible, and the time of Hammurabi of Babylon, who ruled just after 1800 BCE.

It was only after 1973 that Matthiae's team began to work on the earlier phase of occupation, which dates from about 2400 to 2250 BCE. The very next year they made a discovery that catapulted Ebla, and themselves, into the history books. That was the year when they found the first clay tablets at the site. They found more in 1975 and still more in 1976.

There may be as many as twenty thousand tablets in total, most of which were found in two small rooms within so-called Palace G, still lying on the floor where they had fallen after the shelves on which they were placed had burned and then collapsed. They mostly date between 2350 BCE and 2250 BCE. Finding this large a library from the Early Bronze Age led to headlines around the world. Soon thereafter they made headlines again, and a controversy was ignited, because the initial decipherment by the original epigrapher of the expedition, Giovanni Pettinato, suggested that Sodom and Gomorrah were mentioned, as well as figures from the Bible, such as Abraham, Israel, David, and Ishmael.

It's hard to recall now just how excited people got, but the euphoria many felt soon dissipated when subsequent research by epigraphers showed that the tablets said nothing of the sort. No Sodom or Gomorrah; no Abraham, Israel, David, or Ishmael. The mistake in interpretation had been made because the tablets were written in a previously unknown language, now called Eblaite, which made use of Sumerian cuneiform signs. Pettinato thought he could read it, since he knew Sumerian, the earliest known written language of southern Iraq a thousand miles away, but he ended up completely mistranslating it.

Subsequently, Pettinato cut his ties with Matthiae and also resigned from the international committee that Matthiae had appointed to translate and publish the tablets. He continued to publish about them, however, in several books and articles, even though a new chief epigrapher, named Alfonso Archi, from the University of Rome, had replaced him.

The Ebla tablets are extremely important historically, even though they contain no biblical references at all. They *do* include lists of kings who ruled at Ebla; treaties; place names; evidence of international trade; and confirmation of the existence of a scribal school, where students learned how to read and write. They also proved that Ebla was a major center, ruling over a kingdom that we previously had no idea existed. This is an extremely good example where the textual evidence found by the archaeologists supplements and amplifies the other archaeological data that have come to light over the years.

As to the archaeological data, a number of the palaces and buildings at Ebla were destroyed by fire, which was terrible for them, but very good for the archaeologists, because it preserved the ruins and some of the artifacts within them. The smaller objects include a human-headed bull figure made of gold and steatite and fragments of ivory that once adorned pieces of wooden furniture. The furniture is now long gone and most of the ivory fragments were burnt black by the fire, but the fragments do survive and can be somewhat reconstructed. There's also a fragment from the lid of a stone bowl that has the name of the Old Kingdom Egyptian pharaoh Pepi I (circa 2300 BCE) inscribed on it, which implies some sort of connection, even if indirect, between Egypt and Ebla.

Matthiae and his team stopped digging at the site in 2011 because of the Syrian civil war. Since then, it has been damaged and looted mercilessly. Tunnels have been dug; burial caves full of skeletons have been ransacked, with the bones thrown away; and incalculable harm has been done. Only when the current violence racking the country has been reduced and it is deemed safe to return to the area again will we know the extent of the looting and damage.

{⟶}{⟶}

But Ebla is not the only ancient site in Syria—or elsewhere in the Middle East—to have been affected by recent violence in the region. The desert site of Palmyra also suffered damage as a result of mortar fire and other actions during the Syrian civil war, especially in 2012 and 2013. It was again in the news in May and June 2015 and suffered even more damage, when the forces of ISIS overran the site, and then again in August 2015, when ISIS killed Dr. Khaled al-Asaad, the former director of Palmyra Antiquities. Later, they also blew up two of the most famous temples as well as other monuments at the site, including the Triumphal Arch that had been standing for nearly two thousand years, sparking a worldwide outcry against their actions. They were finally dislodged and ousted from the site by Syrian forces in March 2016.

The Triumphal Arch had stretched across the main street of the city, near its eastern end. The Roman emperor Septimius Severus built it around the year 200 CE, possibly to celebrate his victory over the Parthians in Mesopotamia, an area not too far from Palmyra. Just six months after ISIS blew up the arch, it was recreated in Trafalgar Square in London, using three-dimensional technology and Egyptian marble, at two-thirds its original size. After being on show for three days, the replica was sent to be displayed in other cities around the world, including New York and Dubai.

As much of the world now knows, the ancient site of Palmyra is located in an oasis deep in the Syrian desert, to the northeast of Damascus. It is also a UNESCO World Heritage Site, having been given that designation in 1980. Known as Tadmor in antiquity, the city was active already during the Bronze Age in the second millennium BCE, but had its real heyday during the time of the Roman Empire, especially during the first through third centuries CE, when it was a major Nabataean city.

Triumphal Arch, Palmyra

Although the Nabataeans themselves are still a bit of a mystery, we know that they were major players in the international trade routes that connected the Roman Empire to India and even to faraway China. Palmyra was one of their cities, serving as a major stop on the caravan routes leading across the desert. Its architecture reflected foreign influences, especially Greco-Roman and Persian. The city rebelled against the Romans in the early 270s CE, in what is known as the rebellion of Queen Zenobia.

Zenobia was married to the King of Palmyra. He was assassinated in 267 CE, when their young son was only a year old, and so Zenobia assumed the throne as regent. Soon afterward she initiated a revolt against Rome that lasted for five years or more. Initially, she and her army had a great deal of success—capturing Egypt, taking over the rest of Syria and what today we would call Israel and Lebanon, and even portions of modern-day Turkey.

It was only in 273 CE that the Roman army crushed the Palmyrene army and put down her rebellion, after which the Roman emperor Aurelian destroyed the city. The city was rebuilt, but it was never the same again. According to some ancient sources, Zenobia herself was taken to Rome as a prisoner and was marched through the streets in golden chains the following year as part of the triumphal parade that Aurelian staged to celebrate his victory. What happened to her after that is open to debate—marriage to a Roman, execution, and suicide are all various tales of her final days that have come down to us from ancient authors. Still, along with Boudicca, who had led a revolt against the Romans in Britain two centuries earlier (in 60–61 CE), Zenobia remains one of the best-known female military leaders from antiquity.

The first major excavations at the site, especially of the Roman-period ruins, began in 1929 by French archaeologists. The remains that they uncovered, including the Temple of Bel and the Agora, or marketplace, are very impressive, especially the parts that have been partially reconstructed. Both Swiss and Syrian archaeologists also have excavated there, but the most consistent presence has been that of Polish archaeologists, who were excavating right up until 2011, when they were forced to leave at the beginning of the civil war in Syria, before ISIS invaded the area.

In calmer and safer times, Palmyra is an amazing place to visit, especially at sunrise and sunset. A favorite shot for photographers at either dawn or dusk is the four pylons, known collectively as the Tetrapylon, which was built at an intersection about halfway down the main street, half a kilometer or so from its eastern end. Septimius Severus erected them at the same time as he erected the Triumphal Arch. Of the pylons now visible, one is original and the others are replicas of concrete that were raised in 1963 by the Syrian antiquities department.

The street itself is colonnaded and stretches for more than a kilometer, from the Triumphal Arch and the Temple of Bel at its eastern end, past the Roman theater that could seat thousands of people, to a huge funerary temple at the western end. On the columns, about two-thirds of the way up, are little ledges or pedestals on which stood statues of people. These were the donors who had paid for the construction of the street and the colonnade. The inscriptions just below the statues include details about their names and families, from which we have learned quite a bit about the inhabitants of Palmyra.

As for the huge Temple to Bel, or Ba'al, who was originally a Canaanite god from the second millennium BCE, the altar within the temple was consecrated in 32 CE. The temple as it looked until fairly recently was probably completed about a hundred years later, in the second century CE. Unfortunately, this is one of the temples that ISIS blew up in

late August 2015, thereby destroying a beautiful monument that, like
the Triumphal Arch, had been standing for nearly two thousand years.

Also among the ruins at Palmyra is the camp that the Roman
emperor Diocletian built for his soldiers at the end of the third century
and beginning of the fourth century CE, which has been a focal point
of archaeological excavations. There is also a castle that a local Arab
emir built high up on the hill overlooking the city in the seventeenth
century CE, which is still there today and worth a visit, provided that
the situation in Syria permits.

✸✸

Palmyra is only the second-most-famous Nabataean site now, thanks in
part to Indiana Jones. Even though he is not an accurate portrayal of a
real archaeologist, the third film of the series, *Indiana Jones and the Last
Crusade*, managed to bring the UNESCO World Heritage site of Petra
to the world's attention.

View of the "Treasury" at Petra

Located in the Jordanian desert a few hours' drive south from the modern capital city of Amman, Petra was named one of the New Seven Wonders of the World in an Internet poll conducted in 2007. It is on the bucket list of many people as a place to visit, especially now that there are huge five-star hotels with air conditioning in which one can stay. The Jordanians have been careful to protect this site, which now stands in tremendous contrast to the damage done at Palmyra, where the violence in Syria made such protection of the ancient site impossible.

Although people were living in the area perhaps as early as the fifth century BCE, the city rose to prominence with the Nabataeans beginning in the fourth century BCE. It continued to flourish for more than five hundred years, including and especially during the time when the Romans were in this area, from the early second century CE on. Then, after an earthquake destroyed nearly half of Petra in the mid-fourth century CE and a second one hit in the sixth century CE, everything came to a halt—no more building activities, no more minting of coins.

Petra seems to have been the center of the Nabataean confederation of cities, which were focused on controlling the lucrative trade in frankincense, myrrh, spices, and other luxury goods across the Arabian peninsula, connecting Asia to Egypt. They are known for their hydraulic engineering, which allowed them to bring water from the occasional flash floods in to Petra through a series of dams, canals, and cisterns.

After the city was essentially abandoned later in the seventh century CE, it was basically lost to history and remembered only by the locals living in its immediate vicinity. It was not until 1812 that Petra was "rediscovered" by the western world. That year, a Swiss explorer named Johann Burckhardt came through the area. He was dressed in the Arab garments of the day and called himself Sheikh Ibrahim Ibn 'Abd Allah. In this getup, and with an excellent command of Arabic, he was able to travel throughout the Middle East from 1809 until his death from dysentery in 1817. He was just thirty-two years old when he died.

Others followed in his footsteps, including the first US archaeologist. This was John Lloyd Stephens, who emulated Burckhardt in 1836 by dressing as a merchant from Cairo, renaming himself Abdel Hasis and riding down the Wadi Musa into Petra.

John Burgon's 1845 poem "Petra" describes the buildings as "from the rock as if by magic grown, eternal, silent, beautiful, alone!" It ends with the rather immortal lines "a rose-red city half as old as time." In fact, Burgon had never seen Petra himself. He wrote his poem solely from descriptions he had read about the site, especially the travel account published by Stephens a few years earlier, before Stephens headed off to the Yucatán and his famous Maya discoveries.

The cliff faces into which many of the remains at Petra are carved do turn rose-red at certain times of the day, but they also turn many other colors as well, at various angles of the sun. It is a veritable photographer's paradise, in addition to being a wonderful archaeological site.

Excavations at the site first started in 1929 and are still ongoing today. Philip Hammond, from the University of Utah, led the initial US expedition to Petra, which started in the 1960s. Hammond, who died in 2008 and is usually described as a colorful character, reportedly used to ride around on a white horse during the excavations.

Riding horses, donkeys, or camels is still one of the primary ways to enter the site today. The first view of the site, after a half-hour or more of riding down the Siq, or canyon, is absolutely amazing—as anyone who has seen the Indiana Jones movie can attest, even if they haven't yet been to the site themselves.

The formal name of the Siq is the Wadi Musa. It's the way that most tourists enter Petra, just as Stephens did a century and a half earlier. It's a very narrow canyon, which twists and turns through sheer rock that towers high above on both sides.

This was probably not the main entrance to the city, but rather more of a ceremonial entrance. The final view, featured on postcards and photographs everywhere, is absolutely breathtaking, for the narrow canyon walls suddenly open up onto a huge plaza or open space in front of what we now call the Treasury, which is more formally known as the Khaznah. As Stephens later wrote, "the first view of that superb façade must produce an effect which could never pass away. . . . Even now [a year later] . . . I see before me the façade of that temple; neither the Colosseum at Rome, grand and interesting as it is, nor the ruins of the Acropolis at Athens, nor the Pyramids, nor the mighty temples of the Nile, are so often present in my memory."

The Khaznah was the focus of the *Indiana Jones* film. The Nabataeans carved it out of the soft sandstone of the cliff face, as they did with many other buildings and structures at Petra. Don't believe the film, though; the interior rooms of the Khaznah, or Treasury, are actually very small and there isn't space for too many people to be inside at any one time, even if they include a penitent man. It was probably built to serve as a tomb and was never meant to hold many people. It is called the Treasury because of local folklore that there was gold or other valuables hidden in the large urn on the façade, but the urn is solid stone— although it is now riddled with bullet marks from efforts to blast it apart and collect the treasure.

Near the heart of Petra is the Street of Façades, which are actually tombs carved into the cliff face, and then the remains of the Roman theater, which could hold more than eight thousand people in thirty-three rows of seats. A little further on are the so-called royal tombs, which are again carved into the cliff face. The original occupants of these tombs are debated—we don't really know whether they were royal. Even the names don't help, since they are mostly modern designations, like the Urn Tomb, the Silk Tomb, the Corinthian Tomb, and the Palace Tomb. The only tomb whose occupant may be known is the Tomb of Sextus Florentinus, who was the governor of the Roman province of Arabia in the second century CE.

Farther down the Colonnaded Street, which gets this name from the columns lining it, is the so-called Great Temple. It might not be a temple at all, but it has been called the Great Temple ever since 1921 or so. Some think that it might be the major administrative building for the city, but nobody knows for certain. There are elephant heads on the tops of some of the columns in this structure, but they do not help in figuring out the purpose that it served.

Archaeologists from Brown University have been excavating the Great Temple, as well as other parts of Petra, for the past several decades, first under the direction of Martha Joukowsky and most recently under the codirection of Susan Alcock and Chris Tuttle. In 1998 a huge pool measuring about one hundred fifty by seventy feet and up to eight feet deep, as well as an elaborate system for filling it with water, was found and subsequently excavated by Leigh-Ann Bedal, who was a PhD student at the University of Pennsylvania at the time and now teaches at Penn State Erie, the Behrend College. She was leading a team of international, but mostly US, archaeologists. They also found the remains of what was probably an elaborate garden built in conjunction with the pool, which would have been an amazing sight in antiquity, in this dry desert region.

On the hill opposite is the Temple of the Winged Lions that—no surprise—has statues of winged lions in it. It was probably built in the early first century CE and then destroyed in an earthquake a little more than three hundred years later. It was first found in 1973 using remote sensing and has been excavated by US teams ever since.

In the nearby church, which is built over Nabataean and Roman ruins and dates to the end of the classical period—the fifth and sixth centuries CE—mosaics were found, including one that depicts the seasons. In 1993, while in the process of building a shelter to protect the mosaics and the remains of the church, archaeologists from ACOR (the American Center for Oriental Research) uncovered at least 140 carbonized papyrus scrolls within a room in the church.

Dating from the sixth century CE, the scrolls had been caught in a fire that, ironically, ended up preserving some of them, although most are now illegible. Papyrologists, experts at deciphering ancient texts, have been able to read a few dozen of them and to determine that they are written in Greek. Most of them have to do with various economic matters, such as real estate, marriages, inheritances, and divisions of property, one of them detailing a case involving stolen goods.

From this part of Petra, it is possible to proceed on a long stairway to the upper reaches of the site, where the huge temple known as the Monastery lies. It is every bit as monumental as the Treasury far below, but the climb to visit it is so arduous that it doesn't get as many visitors. Like the Treasury, the façade of the Monastery is carved into the living face of the rock. It is approximately 130 feet high, just like the Treasury, but fully sixty feet wider.

From here, there is a commanding view over the entire area. Even though most of the guidebooks say to climb up to the Monastery in the late afternoon, I would argue that the hour-long climb is best undertaken in the early morning, before the temperature rises too high. I once was able to stay overnight in the old excavation dig house right in the heart of all these ruins and was able to wake up and begin hiking before dawn. My arrival at the top before daybreak guaranteed an amazing vista as the sun appeared over the horizon—a view that I will never forget. I was able to stop and reflect in utter silence on the long history of the region, and the remarkable city that was lost for hundreds of years to the outside world, before starting the descent back down.

❊❊

Palmyra, Petra, and Ebla are just three of the incredible ancient cities that have been excavated in Jordan and Syria. I equally could have spent time describing the wonders of Jerash and Pella in Jordan, Mari and Ugarit in Syria, and a dozen other remarkable sites. The tragic consequences of the ongoing conflict in the Middle East should serve to remind us of just how precious—and fragile—these fragments of the past can be.

HOW OLD IS THIS AND WHY IS IT PRESERVED?

A JOURNALIST RECENTLY ASKED ME DURING AN INTERVIEW, "All of what you excavate, study, and write about took place so long ago. How can you be so certain of your dates?" My short answer to him was "radiocarbon, Egyptian texts and other written records, synchronisms, dendrochronology, pottery typology, a plus/minus factor, and a willingness to acknowledge that none of it is fixed in stone." I was a bit surprised at his question, which was asked in a rather aggressive manner, but then it occurred to me that maybe this is something that a lot of other people wonder about as well but are afraid to ask.

In fact, one of the questions that I am asked most often at social gatherings is simply a variation of the question that I was asked by the journalist, "How do you know how old the things are that you find?" I'm also frequently asked, "How can things that old still be preserved? Why haven't they crumbled to dust?" So here, let's address the topics of how archaeologists date ancient artifacts and what kinds of conditions it takes for such things to be preserved.

The first question is probably easier to answer—how do we know how old something is? As I said to the journalist, it can be as simple as reading an Egyptian text, especially if it says something like "year 8" of a particular pharaoh and we know from other sources what the dates of his rule were. Other times we have synchronisms between cultures or civilizations that interacted, so that we know, for example, from a letter found in the Amarna archive in Egypt that Amenhotep III lived at the same time as Tushratta of the kingdom of Mitanni (in northern Syria) because they are writing letters back and forth . . . and we know from other evidence that Amenhotep lived during the early fourteenth century BCE, so Tushratta must have as well. And in that manner, we can often put together chronological lists of rulers, events, and so on, often using the king lists and astronomical observations left to us by the ancient peoples themselves in Babylonia, Egypt, Assyria, and elsewhere.

There also are a variety of scientific dating methods that are now available to the archaeologist. Common methods used to date ancient objects are radiocarbon dating, thermoluminescence, and potassium-argon analysis. They are what we use to determine the "absolute date" of an object—in other words, its date in calendar years, like 2015 CE or 1350 BCE. It's not always possible to do this, and so sometimes we have to settle for a relative date—for example, Level 3 lies below Level 2 at the site and is therefore older. The archaeologist might not yet know the absolute date for either level, especially at an early stage in the excavations, but he or she already knows where they are relative to each other.

Probably the most commonly used dating method is radiocarbon dating, otherwise known as carbon-14 dating (C-14 for short). This, like all the chemical methods, has a "plus-minus" factor, as in "1450 BCE plus or minus twenty years," and a statistical probability that the date will fall into the suggested range. Because of this, C-14 dating isn't particularly useful for things that are relatively close to us in age, but it is good for dating objects that are at least several hundred years old; several thousand years is even better.

The basic idea, discovered by a scientist named Willard Libby who won a Nobel Prize for his work, is that all living things ingest, either through breathing or eating, a small percentage of a radioactive isotope of carbon while they are alive, along with all the normal carbon. C-14 is constantly being created from radiation in the atmosphere. It combines with oxygen to form a radioactive version of carbon dioxide.

Plants incorporate this C-14 into their system during photosynthesis; animals and humans then ingest it by eating the plants. Since it is radioactive, C-14 decays, as do all radioactive materials. It has a known half-life of a bit more than 5,700 years—that is, half of the original amount will have decayed and disappeared in a bit more than 5,700 years. Since it is fairly easy to determine how much carbon would have originally been in a particular sample, and since the ratio of C-14 atoms to normal C-12 atoms is fairly constant, one can measure the amount of C-14 that is still left in a sample and thereby figure out the date when that organism died (in the case of a human or animal) or was chopped down (in the case of a tree that became a piece of wood) or otherwise ceased to exist (as in short-lived plants and weeds).

Organic materials like human skeletons, animal bones, pieces of wood, and burnt seeds can be C-14-dated. Burnt seeds are especially good, because they usually had a very short shelf life before essentially ceasing to exist. Similarly, short-lived brushwood is good, which is what the Uluburun excavators used to help date their shipwreck. Radiocarbon dating is relatively cheap to do, at least compared to other dating procedures.

The technique can't be used to directly date stone tools or pottery, since those items never ingested C-14. It can, however, be used to date organic items that might have been found in the same context as such stone tools or pottery, thereby helping to date stone and pottery by association.

There also are some known difficulties and problems associated with the technique, including the fact that it requires the destruction of at least part of the object in order to sample it and that the amount of C-14 in the atmosphere has not always been constant, but has fluctuated. Calibration curves accounting for such fluctuations have been created, as have other means of correction, and so radiocarbon dating has been one of the most frequently used methods to date ancient sites. We use it at both Kabri and Megiddo, the sites where I have worked most recently.

In addition, if a large fragment of wood is discovered, like a beam that was once used in a ceiling or wall or even as part of a ship, there is something else that can be done with it besides C-14 dating. This is dendrochronology, or tree-ring dating, which involves counting the rings that can be seen in the wood. This technique may be familiar to those who have visited places like Yosemite or Sequoia National Park, where often a very large stump of a tree is on display, with little markers attached to some of the rings, saying things like "1620: Pilgrims land at Plymouth Rock" and "1861: Start of the Civil War." The rings in those trees have been fit into a master sequence that has been constructed painstakingly by scientists over the years. If a piece of wood with visible rings is discovered during an excavation, it is sometimes possible to fit it into such a sequence and determine its probable date, but even such master sequences do not extend back in time more than ten thousand or twelve thousand years.

The same basic principles can be used to date other materials with various chemical methods, if the age of the site being excavated is appropriate for them. For instance, when trying to date a stone tool from Olduvai Gorge, which is a crucial site for understanding human origins, potassium-argon dating can be useful. This method measures the difference between the amount of potassium in the rock and the amount of argon in it, because potassium decays and becomes argon over time. But it takes a very long time for the decay to happen, and so this method is best used when something is between two hundred thousand and five million years old. In such cases, it would also be impossible to use radiocarbon dating, which works on organic remains but not stone tools and is useful only for dating things within the last fifty thousand years.

Thermoluminescence might be used on certain objects found at sites with a "younger" age. Thermoluminescence can measure the absolute age of something made from clay, like a storage pot, by measuring the amount of electromagnetic or ionizing radiation still in it. Specifically, it can indicate how long it has been since the object was baked or fired in a kiln. Researchers have found that the object has to have been heated up above 450 degrees centigrade or the technique won't work.

A similar, but newer and still experimental, method is something called rehydroxylation, which measures the amount of water that is in a piece of pottery. I first heard about it in 2010, at a miniconference that was held at Megiddo during our summer excavations that year, and I thought it was a really interesting—and promising—procedure. It seems that, when a piece of pottery is fired in a kiln, all the water in the clay evaporates during the process. As soon as the piece of pottery is taken out of the kiln and cools off, it begins to absorb water from the atmosphere again at a constant, slow rate, regardless of the environment of the vessel. Thus, by measuring the amount of water in a sherd, it is possible to determine the last time that it was fired . . . and thus probably its age.

There can be problems with measuring rehydroxylation—and we were told the story of the original researchers being given a medieval brick from Canterbury and trying this method on it, only to get results again and again saying that it was only about sixty-six years old, according to the rehydroxylation analysis. And yet, they knew it had to be much older than that. It eventually turned out that the brick had been in an area of Canterbury that had been bombed during World War II and was caught in the ensuing incendiary fire. The fire had reset the water content of the brick back to zero as of the 1940s, and so the dating method clearly worked, but it no longer measured the date of the brick's original firing back in the medieval period.

It also is possible to do something similar with a piece of obsidian, which is called obsidian hydration. Obsidian is volcanic glass that was highly prized in antiquity for its sharpness, and in fact is still used in some surgical scalpels today. It also absorbs water at a constant and well-defined rate once it is exposed to air, and so measuring the amount of water in a particular piece of obsidian can be used to date obsidian tools.

Stratigraphy, pottery seriation, and object association also can all be used as relative dating methods, especially if it is not possible to generate a precise absolute date otherwise. We have discussed all these in a previous chapter, and so here it is simply worthwhile remembering that one way to date something can be as simple as seeing what was found with it, in other words, in association with it or in the same context, like a stone tool found with a datable organic object.

For example, if an excavator finds a coin minted by the Roman emperor Vespasian in a grave, clearly the grave cannot date from before Vespasian's time. Thus, everything in the grave along with the coin should be from about the same period, unless it was an heirloom at the time that it was buried, which does happen. Similarly, if an Egyptian scarab with the cartouche of Amenhotep III is found on the floor of the room in an ancient house or palace that is being excavated, then everything else on the floor probably dates to the fourteenth century BCE, when Amenhotep III was ruling Egypt.

At Tel Kabri, for instance, on the floor of one of our rooms in the palace, we found a type of scarab that dates specifically to the Hyksos period, that is, the seventeenth to sixteenth century BCE. This gave us an indication of the date for that room, which was then confirmed by the radiocarbon dates that we got from some of the charcoal samples that we submitted for analysis.

As we discussed in chapter 10 on the Uluburun shipwreck, the excavators were able to use no fewer than four ways to date their ship: radiocarbon dating; dendrochronology; the type of Minoan and Mycenaean pottery on board; and the fact that they found a scarab of Nefertiti. All these combined to point to a relative date in the Late Bronze Age and an absolute date of about 1300 BCE for the time that the boat sank. Each dating method has its own limitations and uncertainties, and so when four separate methods point to the same approximate date, the archaeologist can offer that date with a great degree of certainty.

Terracotta Warriors

One of the best examples of using association to date an entire group of objects when they are all in the same approximate context, or grouped around one major central element, are the large pits containing the Terracotta Warriors in China, which were all associated with one emperor's tomb. It was near Xi'an, the capital city of China's Shaanxi Province, that farmers digging a well in 1974 first came across what they thought was a rock. It turned out to be the head and body of a fully armed and life-size warrior made from terracotta. In the decades that have gone by since, archaeologists have uncovered at the site thousands of warriors, as well as terracotta horses and chariots. Together, they are commonly referred to as the Terracotta Army or the Terracotta Warriors.

The soldiers, horses, and chariots that make up the army were buried more than two thousand years ago, in 210 BCE. They were meant to accompany the first emperor of China, Qin Shihuang (pronounced "chin shuh hwang"), into the afterlife. Qin, who ruled from 221 to 210 BCE, was able to unify China for the first time, bringing the period of the Warring States to an end. He died suddenly while on a tour with the army. His tomb and the related pits may well have served as a memorial to his importance in Chinese society, even though his dynasty did not last much longer than he did, for it was overthrown by the Han dynasty just four years later, in 206 BCE. The Han emperors then ruled for the next four centuries, until 220 CE.

So far, Emperor Qin's Terracotta Warriors have been found in three large pits, with much more still to be uncovered. There are estimated to be between six thousand and eight thousand warriors, as well as several hundred horses and perhaps dozens of chariots in these pits, which were constructed near Qin's mausoleum. There's a fourth pit as well, but it was found almost completely empty.

About a mile from the pits is Emperor Qin's tomb itself. It hasn't been excavated yet, though it's pretty obvious where it is, since the huge mound that covers it is about 140 feet tall. According to the writings of the Grand Historian of China, which date to about a century after the death of the emperor, it took more than seven hundred thousand workers working for about thirty-six years to construct the tomb. Although we might not be able take this figure at face value, it probably did require a tremendous number of workers to build the tomb, and probably the pits as well, just as it did for the construction of the pyramids in Egypt more than two thousand years earlier. The interior of the tomb is supposedly magnificent, with a three-dimensional map that includes flowing rivers made of mercury. It is also supposed to contain all sorts of traps for the unwary tomb robber—one ancient source says specifically that "craftsmen were ordered to fix up crossbows so that any thief breaking in would be shot."

Someday archaeologists will excavate the tomb, but in the meantime, the surrounding pits are amazing enough. The first pit to be discovered, which is now appropriately referred to as Pit number 1, has about six thousand terracotta warriors, all life-size. They are standing in rows, as if at attention in a parade drill. The weapons they hold are real ones. They are quite spectacular, even though most of the paint that originally colored their faces, mustaches, beards, and uniforms is now gone—possibly because of a fire that seems to have affected much of the pit or because of the type of soil in which they were buried, but most likely because of exposure to the air after they were excavated.

Pit number 2 has at least a thousand more warriors, as well as horses and chariots. Pit number 3 has fewer than a hundred warriors, some horses, and a chariot, as well as some intact weapons. Some scholars have interpreted this last pit as the headquarters for the army commanders, in part because the figures are taller and are drawn up in battle formation, but that is just a working hypothesis.

Overall, each of the figures in these pits appears to be an individual, distinguished by facial hair, a uniform, or something that they are holding, like a spear, a sword, a shield, or a crossbow. In reality, though, it seems that there are only about eight different facial types, though there are as many as twenty-five different styles of mustaches and beards.

It now seems that the warriors were constructed as if they were on an assembly line, with the head, arms, legs, and body all made separately and then attached. There are areas in the pits where broken pieces can be seen, and even bodies that don't yet have the heads attached, which might indicate that they were made right on site. It took skilled craftsmen to make these; according to one report, the names of eighty-five sculptors have been found on various parts of the figures.

In 2010, 114 additional warriors were discovered in Pit number 1. Many of them were brightly painted, and our technology had advanced enough since 1974 that this time the archaeologists were able to conserve the paint quickly enough that it stayed attached to the figures and did not flake off.

In 2014 researchers announced that they had discovered more about the colors that were once painted on the warriors, including the binding agent that helped the paint adhere to the life-sized figures. It turns out that several layers of lacquer were placed on the terracotta, with a layer of polychrome (paint) applied on top of that. Within the polychrome was animal glue that helped bind this outer layer of paint to the layers of lacquer below.

Interest in the Terracotta Warriors has led to other discoveries in Shaanxi Province. In fact, about twenty-five miles from Emperor Qin's tomb, more pits with different types of terracotta warriors were found in 1990, when a new airport was being built to handle the masses of tourists that began arriving. These warriors are associated with two tombs belonging to the later Han Emperor Jin and his wife, who lived circa 188–144 BCE. Warriors in this group are solid rather than hollow like the warriors in Qin's pits and they're also much smaller—less than two feet high.

They also are completely naked, with no arms. They may have originally been draped with clothing and had arms inserted, perhaps of precious metals that were later robbed, but right now they look very, very strange. Paul Bahn reports that the estimates for the number of these figures in the pits associated with these two tombs range anywhere from ten thousand to a million.

Other pits near Qin's tomb also have been excavated. They contained figures of acrobats and of musicians playing various instruments. There also are courtiers and officials, as well as what appears to be a miniature version of the imperial stables.

In 2014 the tomb of Emperor Qin's grandmother was discovered and excavated. Within it were the skeletons of twelve real horses and the two carriages that they were originally pulling.

As for the mound containing Qin's tomb itself, as mentioned, it has not yet been excavated, in part because we are waiting for our technology to get even better. Some remote sensing has been done, indicating that there are chambers inside the mound, but it has been hypothesized that the emperor's burial chamber may be as much as one hundred feet below the top of the mound. We hope to someday see what lies within.

❧❧ ❧❧

The second question is a bit more complicated to answer—"How can things that old still be preserved? Why haven't they crumbled to dust?" The answer is that a lot of ancient things *have* crumbled to dust or have been otherwise destroyed. Only a small percentage of what once existed has survived to the present. Inorganic materials like stone and metal frequently survive, though silver will turn purple in the ground, bronze will turn green, and so on. It's only gold that stays the exact same color. I've only found gold a few times in my career, but I've found a lot of bronze, including my petrified monkey's paw.

Other items that are made of organic or perishable goods are not as durable, and it can be rare to find things like textiles or leather sandals at most archaeological sites. Happily, though, sometimes such items, and human bodies, are preserved, usually in conditions of moisture and temperature extremes—in other words, places that are very dry, very cold, very wet, or without oxygen. A few very interesting examples from each such location can be readily discussed.

For example, perishable objects have survived in the very dry conditions within King Tut's tomb in Egypt, where all the wooden furniture and boxes and chariots were found, still completely intact. The wooden boats buried by the pyramids also have survived for the same reason, as have so many mummy coffins and pieces of papyrus from ancient Egypt.

Other mummies preserved by dry conditions in a desert come from much further away, in China. These, some as much as four thousand years old, were first reported to the rest of the world by a professor of Chinese studies at the University of Pennsylvania named Victor Mair. He spotted them in a museum in the city of Ürümqi, in a remote part of China north of Tibet, known as the Tarim Basin. He began to study them, as did Professor Elizabeth Barber of Occidental College in California. Mair and Barber have both published books about the mummies, which were extremely well preserved because of the very dry conditions of the desert environment where they were buried.

What is unique about some of the mummies is that, even though they are found in China, they have Causcasoid or European features, including brown hair and long noses. They also were buried with textiles and cloth that looks a lot like plaid. Their DNA suggests that they may be of western origin, with links to Mesopotamia, the Indus Valley, and possibly even Europe.

Studies of these mummies are still ongoing, but perhaps we should not be particularly surprised by these initial findings. The Silk Road, which connected China in the east to the Mediterranean on the west from the second century BCE on, is known to have run through the Tarim Basin, and in fact some of the mummies were brought to the United States in 2010, as part of a traveling exhibition on the Silk Route in antiquity.

In contrast, the bodies of Ötzi the Iceman, found in the Alps in 1991; the Siberian princess discovered in 1993; and Juanita the Ice Maiden, discovered in Peru in 1995, were all found preserved in extremely cold conditions. Ötzi especially has been the subject of much analysis and discussion since he was accidentally discovered by hikers in the Alps, on the border between Austria and Italy. He spawned a worldwide craze, especially in the region where he was found, where one can now purchase Ötzi wine, Ötzi chocolate (think Easter egg bunnies, but in the shape of Ötzi), and, perhaps most relevant of all, Ötzi ice cream.

At first it was thought that Ötzi was a murder victim and so the police were called in. This was most definitely a cold case, though, since not only was Ötzi encased in ice, but it turns out that he had been lying there for more than five thousand years. In fact, it now looks like Ötzi died in about 3200 BCE, which is more than six hundred years before the pyramids in Egypt were built.

Ötzi's body lay wedged in a hollow formed by some rocks. A glacier creeping down the slope swept right over the rocks and his body, so that he was preserved under many feet of ice and snow for thousands of years. In 1991, a sandstorm in faraway North Africa sent sand up into the atmosphere that eventually settled on the ice above Ötzi. The sand, absorbing the sun's rays, melted the ice and exposed Ötzi's head, shoulders, and upper body.

The police, unaware that this was an ancient body, hacked Ötzi out of the ice, damaging his body as well as his belongings, which were scattered around him. Once scientists realized this was not a wayward hiker but was far more ancient, scientific archaeological excavations were carried out in 1992. These retrieved additional artifacts, including his bearskin cap. Ever since then, detailed studies have been made of Ötzi and his belongings, including a complete workup of his DNA.

As it turned out, Ötzi had indeed been murdered, as the police who were called to the scene had first thought, though it had taken place several thousand years earlier. It took ten years before murder could be proven, but the evidence was eventually quite obvious. Even though it hadn't been noticed before, in 2001 an alert radiologist examining X-rays and CT scans that had been taken of Ötzi saw a foreign object embedded in his back, just below his left shoulder. It turned out to be an arrowhead, with a corresponding entry wound several inches below, which means whoever shot him was standing below Ötzi and shooting upward.

It was subsequently determined that the arrowhead had severed an artery, meaning that Ötzi had probably bled to death. It also means that he was shot in the back, which implies murder rather than an accident. The fact that he has a defensive cut on his hand as well indicates that some sort of fight had taken place and that he may have been fleeing from the battle when he was fatally shot.

Ötzi has turned out to be incredibly important. The scientific discoveries, which came one after the other, have been published in a series of peer-reviewed and prestigious journals, including *Science*, the *Journal of Archaeological Science*, and *The Lancet*, among others.

Among the discoveries that were made, scientists determined that Ötzi had brown hair and deep-set brown eyes, a beard, and sunken cheeks. He was probably about five feet, two inches tall and weighed about 110 pounds at the time of his death, which occurred when he was between forty and fifty years old. The strontium isotopes in his tooth enamel, which can be used to determine where someone lived during their childhood years, indicate that he probably lived his whole life near where he died, within a sixty-kilometer radius and most likely in a nearby valley in Italy.

Ötzi's lungs were blackened, probably from inhaling smoke from campfires, either inside caves or outdoors. He suffered from tooth decay and had been ill several times in the months just before he died.

Scientists and archaeologists were able to analyze the contents of his intestine, including pollen, which indicated that he had probably died in late spring or early summer. His last meal included red deer meat, bread made from einkorn, and some plums. In addition, his second-to-last meal included ibex meat, cereals, and various other plants.

In 2016 scientists who were continuing to study the contents of Ötzi's stomach also announced that they had mapped the genome of the oldest known pathogen, a bacterium named *H. pylori* that can cause ulcers. The bacterium may provide a clue to human migration patterns, for it is an Asian strain, and not the more usual Asian-African hybrids present in today's European population. This discovery suggests that the additional migrations that brought African strains to Europe had not yet taken place by Ötzi's time. More and more such genetic studies are taking place, ranging from investigation of King Richard III's body, discovered under a parking lot in England, and King Tut's mummy. It is likely that such studies will become even more important to archaeology in the future.

Ötzi also had sixty-one tattoos, which were made by rubbing charcoal into cuts made in his skin. These are the oldest tattoos yet known, but they are mostly lines and crosses rather than designs or images. In an interesting, and unexplained, related piece of trivia, the actor Brad Pitt now reportedly has a tattoo of Ötzi on his left forearm—Hollywood meets archaeology? Personally, I would have thought that a tattoo of Achilles would have made more sense, since it would be relevant to his starring role in the 2004 movie *Troy* (Pitt, not Ötzi).

Ötzi was quite the well-dressed man, with three layers of clothing. Underneath everything, he wore undergarments made from goatskin. He had leggings made of fur, a coat of leather, and a grass cape over it all, plus a hat made of fur from a brown bear. On his feet, he had leather shoes insulated with straw. In 2004 a professor in the Czech Republic made a pair just like them and went hiking; he said that he didn't get blisters and that they were more comfortable than his normal hiking shoes. All this has now been re-created in several places, including the South Tyrol Museum of Archaeology in northern Italy, which is Ötzi's current home.

Among his other possessions and equipment were a number of objects that shed additional light on Ötzi and his environment and way of life. He had two arrows with flint tips and a kit to repair them, plus a quiver full of half-finished arrows; a partly finished long bow; a dagger with a flint blade; and an ax with a copper blade. Archaeologists also recovered a firestarter kit; a birchbark container that had embers from his fire; and a bone needle. And Ötzi had a backpack in which he carried many of these possessions.

Ötzi is not the only ancient person to have been found on ice. In 1993 a mummified body known as the Siberian princess or Ice Maiden was found on the Ukok Plateau in southern Siberia, near the border with China. Dating to the fifth century BCE, she was about twenty-five years old when she died, perhaps from breast cancer. She was buried with six horses, all saddled and bridled, probably meant to accompany her into the afterlife. This perhaps makes a great deal of sense, because it is thought that the princess was a member of the Pazyryk people—a nomadic group described by the Greek historian Herodotus in the fifth century BCE—who spent most of their lives on horseback.

She is best known for her numerous tattoos, which put Ötzi's to shame, even though his are nearly three thousand years older. Her tattoos, primarily on her left shoulder and arm, include a mythological animal, which looks like a deer with a griffin's head and antlers that also have griffin's heads at the ends. Other bodies buried nearby, of men identified as warriors, some of whom were dug up decades earlier, have similar tattoos; one has them on both arms, his back, and his lower leg.

Two years later, in 1995, anthropologist Johan Reinhard found a mummy of a twelve- to fourteen-year-old Inca female on Mount Ampato in Peru. She also is occasionally called the Ice Maiden, but since that causes confusion with the mummy from Siberia, more usually she is simply Juanita.

Reinhard found her near the peak of the mountain, at a height of more than six thousand meters (eighteen thousand feet) above sea level, where she had been buried more than five hundred years ago. He had climbed the mountain to photograph a nearby volcano that was erupting, thinking he could get a good picture from there. It didn't seem to be a likely place for an Inca sacrifice, and yet there she was, exposed to the elements because the ash from the volcano had melted some of the ice that had protected her. In his book, *The Ice Maiden*, Reinhard describes carrying her down the mountain in his backpack, since she weighed only eighty pounds.

She is not the only such Inca mummy, for others have been discovered as well, including two more that Reinhard also found on Mount Ampato, a boy and a girl located a thousand feet below the summit, when he returned with a full team to explore the mountain systematically. One television show, broadcast by PBS, estimated that there may be hundreds more such Inca children encased in what are now ice tombs on top of peaks in the Andes, where more than 115 Inca sacred ceremonial sites have been found. The question of who these children were and why they were left to die on mountaintops still engages anthropologists and archaeologists working in the region today.

As for finding objects and bodies that have been preserved in waterlogged conditions, a small wooden writing tablet that dates back to the eighth century BCE was found submerged in a well at the site of Nimrud in Iraq. Pieces of two more were found in the Uluburun shipwreck, as we have mentioned, where they had been preserved 140–170 feet below the surface of the Mediterranean Sea for more than three thousand years. The so-called bog bodies, which have been found in places like Denmark and England, are among the best-known examples of organic material that has been preserved in a waterlogged environment.

These bog bodies have been so well preserved that it is possible to see individual whiskers in a beard and the strands of the rope around a victim's neck. Several hundred such bodies have been uncovered in a variety of places in England and Europe within once-swampy areas, called bogs or fens. Bogs contain peat that is a deposit of dead and decayed plant material, usually moss. Peat can be used as fuel or as insulation on cottage roofs. The workers who dig in these bogs occasionally find human remains, of which the soft tissues have been almost completely preserved because of the acidic conditions and the lack of oxygen in the bogs, even though the bones themselves are long gone.

One such body, known as Lindow Man, was found in northwestern England in 1984, in the Lindow Moss bog. The autopsy indicates that he was about twenty-five years old when he died. He had been hit twice on the head with a heavy object, then strangled by a thin cord, which also broke his neck, and finally had his throat cut for good measure. It is not clear whether he was murdered or ritually sacrificed. This is definitely what we would consider a cold case, because he was killed about two thousand years ago, sometime during the first or early second century CE.

Because of the conditions in which he lay for all those centuries, his skin and hair are very well preserved, including his beard and moustache. His fingernails are also so well preserved that we can tell they were manicured. Some of his internal organs also are preserved; they contain parts of what was probably his last meal, including a piece of unleavened bread made from wheat and barley, which had been cooked over a fire.

A similarly preserved body was found in 1950 by two workers cutting peat in a bog in Denmark, not far from the town of Silkeborg. Known as the Tollund Man, he dates to the fourth century BCE, and so he is about five hundred years older than Lindow Man. In his case, we can see every detail of the leather cap that is still on his head and the belt that is around his waist, as well as the stubble on his face and the rope around his neck that was used to hang him.

The two workers who found him thought that he was a murder victim, and he may well have been, but again his death occurred nearly twenty-five hundred years ago, and it is unclear why he was killed. He was probably about forty years old at the time of his death. Because his stomach and intestines were preserved, the archaeologists who were called in to examine him were able to do analyses and determine that his last meal had been a sort of porridge.

If we turn to examples of artifacts and bodies preserved in areas with little or no oxygen, obviously such places are pretty rare in the world, but they do exist in regions like deep in the Black Sea, below two hundred meters (650 feet), where the water is very still and oxygen doesn't circulate to the bottom. Since there's really no oxygen, there's no reason for anything to disintegrate, because there's nothing alive there even at the microscopic level that could damage the artifacts. This is why Bob Ballard found amazing things when he sent a remotely operated vehicle down into the depths of the Black Sea in 1999 and again in 2007.

Most people may know Ballard as the discoverer of the Titanic, but in archaeology he is perhaps better known for his discoveries in the

Black Sea. He found a Neolithic settlement, an ancient shoreline, and a beach that are now far below the current surface of the sea—meaning that the whole area probably flooded sometime in antiquity; two Columbia University professors suggest that such a cataclysmic event may have taken place about seventy-five hundred years ago, ca. 5500 BCE. Ballard also has found several shipwrecks from the Roman and Byzantine periods, dating between one thousand and fifteen hundred or more years ago. In at least one of them, the wood of the boat is so well preserved that the tool marks on the individual pieces of wood from when the boats were being built are still visible. And one of the jars that they brought up had the original beeswax still sealing the top closed.

Not all ships have been as well preserved as the one that Ballard found in the Black Sea or the Egyptian ships by the pyramids. Other ships, such as the Anglo-Saxon ship found at Sutton Hoo in England and a Viking ship recently found in Scotland have left only negative impressions in the soil. Their poor state of preservation is far more typical of artifacts that have been found simply buried in the earth rather than in extreme environmental conditions, but these examples also show how even those badly preserved remains can be interpreted by savvy archaeologists working from the pattern of what has been left behind.

Take, for instance, the Sutton Hoo ship in Suffolk, England. It is twenty-seven meters long and was found in 1939 by an archaeologist named Basil Brown. The owner of the property had invited Brown to excavate a large mound, one of many on her land, in southeastern England. Within the mound, he found the remains of this ship.

There are many interesting things about the ship, which probably dates to sometime between 620 and 650 CE. This was an era during the Anglo-Saxon period, which began about 450 CE after the end of Roman occupation, when new immigrants arrived from continental Europe and lasted until the Norman Conquest in 1066 CE.

Perhaps most interesting is that the ship isn't actually there anymore, and yet its remains can still be seen perfectly well. That is because, although the wood of the ship is completely gone, it is very clear where it once was. The dirt had stains where the wood has disintegrated; there are raised ridges in the soil running the width of the ship, spaced just a few feet apart for its entire length; and there are rusted iron nails, which once held the pieces of wood together. What Brown discovered is the shadow of the boat, rather than the boat itself.

So, why bury a boat on land and not sink it in the water? Most archaeologists think that the boat was buried with its owner; that is, it served as a final resting place for a warrior, or a king, or someone else deserving of such an honor. But, perhaps strangely enough, there's no remains of the body in the boat or anywhere near it—at least that has been found so far. That seems a bit strange: If this was a burial, where is the body? One possibility is that the body and the bones have decomposed so much that they have simply vanished, just like the wood of the ship. If so, they left no mark at all. That's the scenario that most people believe.

Another possibility is that there never was a body. If that's the case, then this is what is known as a cenotaph—that is, a monument to someone who is buried elsewhere. A lot of war monuments today are basically cenotaphs and it might be that the Sutton Hoo ship is an ancient war monument—perhaps a commemoration of a battle fought by the Anglo-Saxons in this part of England.

But even if it didn't yield a body, the Sutton Hoo ship proved to be a treasure trove in other respects. The center of the boat held a number of objects: shoulder clasps made of gold and with enamel inlays, which were probably attached to a cloth tunic or shirt that has perished; a solid gold belt buckle with an intricate design and a metal lid with enamel inlays, which is all that remains of what was once probably a purse, with the cloth or leather part now gone; drinking horns inlaid with fancy designs. These artifacts again indicate that this is no ordinary burial and one can only imagine the parties and celebrations at which they were once used.

One of the objects that has stirred the most interest is an iron helmet, complete with a face plate with holes for the eyes and both a nose and a mouth made of metal. Parts of it are overlaid with gold, as decoration. It must have been very expensive back in the day and probably belonged to someone either wealthy or powerful or both.

In 2011 a similar discovery of a phantom ship was made on the western coast of Scotland, on the Ardnamurchan peninsula. Here, in a burial that dates to the tenth century CE, is what appears to be a Viking warrior buried in his boat. At that time, this region was located along a primary north–south sea route between Ireland and Norway, and Viking houses have been found on the nearby Hebrides Islands.

The grave is five feet wide and about seventeen feet long, which is just enough to hold the entire boat. Just like the Sutton Hoo boat, the wood of this boat has decayed and is now completely missing, apart from a few remnants here and there. Again, the archaeologists found the iron rivets that had once held the boat together—about two hundred of them—and they could easily see the shape of the boat because of the impression it left in the earth.

In this case, we do know for certain that there once was a body here, because the archaeologists found a few teeth and some fragments from an arm bone. They also found the remains of his iron sword and parts of his shield—which had been placed on his chest. The boat contained the Viking's spear, a bronze pin, and a bronze piece from what may have been a drinking horn.

❧⟨•◦•⟩❧ ⟨•◦•⟩❧

In this chapter I have elaborated upon my answer to the journalist who asked how we archaeologists can be so certain of our dates. I hope it is now a bit clearer how we date things, but it also should be clear that we aren't always able to pin something down to a specific year and why there is frequently some wiggle room, especially in radiocarbon dating, in which dates are always given with a plus-or-minus factor and a statistical probability. New techniques are being invented and applied fairly often, and so I suspect that our ability to date things from the past will continue to get more accurate in the future.

I have also touched briefly upon how some things have been preserved for us to find, especially in terms of organic materials that may require extreme conditions in order to survive. It will almost certainly also be possible to improve our methods in the excavation of organic objects or materials, including those that do not take kindly to being exposed by archaeologists after centuries or millennia of burial. Such improvements can already been seen, for example, in the most recently excavated Terracotta Warriors in China, where the brilliant paint that decorated them is still visible and has been successfully preserved and investigated by the archaeologists.

PART 6

NEW WORLD ARCHAEOLOGY

LINES IN THE SAND,
CITIES IN THE SKY

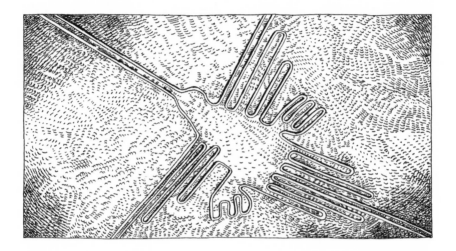

I N THE 1920S, WHEN AVIATORS FIRST STARTED FLYING OVER A high desert region in inland Peru, they noticed long straight lines and huge figures drawn in the dry desert soil. Now known worldwide as the Nazca Lines, the figures technically are geoglyphs and include a spider, a dog, birds, monkeys, a tree, and a strange figure that looks like an ancient astronaut.

Nearly half a century later, in 1968, Erich von Däniken published a book called *Chariots of the Gods?* In it, he suggested that the Nazca Lines must have been created for, or by, ancient astronauts. He argued that only people who could see the figures from the air could have drawn them, because they can't really be recognized at ground level. He also suggested that the long straight lines were landing strips for ancient aircraft or spaceships. As he wrote, "What is wrong with the idea that the lines were laid out to say to the 'gods': 'Land here! Everything has been prepared as you ordered!'"

What's wrong with that, he asks? Well, pretty much everything. To begin with, invoking ancient aliens to explain the Nazca Lines is a conclusion with which almost all archaeologists completely disagree. And yet a considerable portion of the general public takes von Däniken's theories seriously—so much so that his books have sold millions over the years (65 million, according to his webpage).

In 2003 von Däniken even opened up a theme park in Switzerland, called Mystery Park. One of the seven pavilions at the park was devoted to a display and discussion of the Nazca Lines. Unfortunately for von Däniken, even though there was an initial burst of enthusiasm, attendance at the amusement park quickly dropped. Although the one-millionth visitor came through in October 2006, the park closed down just a month later.

In any event, the Nazca Lines are very real and are well worth a visit, even if ancient astronauts didn't build them. They are now a protected site, and most tourists can't walk through the area. It is best to arrange for a low-flying airplane, helicopter, or hot-air balloon, for the lines really are best seen from the air.

They were in the news again in August 2014, when new images were spotted after sandstorms and high winds hit the area. They also made headlines around the world later that same year, in December 2014, when Greenpeace volunteers laid out a huge message saying "Time for Change. The Future Is Renewable." The Greenpeace people came under heavy criticism for damaging the ancient site in their zeal to protect the future, which is, quite frankly, rather ironic.

❧❧ ❧❧

The Nazca Lines are in the high desert of southern Peru, about two hundred miles from Machu Picchu, which we will discuss later in this chapter. As mentioned, they were *not* made by ancient astronauts. Instead, they were made by the local indigenous group known as the Nazca, who lived in this area between 200 BCE and 600 CE and whose graves and other ancient settlement remains are near the lines.

We know this in part because of the similarity with the designs found on Nazca pottery, which include designs of animals, birds, and humans in red, white, and black paint on the vessels. In addition, carbon-14 dating on the wooden stakes that were found at the end of some of the lines indicates a date of about 525 CE, plus or minus eighty years—so, somewhere between 445 CE and 605 CE, which matches well with the known date for the Nazca presence in this area.

It is not generally known outside the profession, but the Nazca culture was not the first to create geoglyphs in this region. An earlier culture known as the Paracas, from which the Nazca might have evolved, also created geoglyphs in the desert just a bit further to the north, near the modern town of Palpa. These date hundreds of years earlier, in some cases. They are mostly found on the sides of hills rather than on the desert floor and include enigmatic human figures as well as more of the "landing strips" to which von Däniken refers. Both sets of figures, Paracas and Nazca, were collectively declared a UNESCO World Heritage Site in 1994.

The Nazca Lines drawn in the desert are huge—and there are hundreds of them, ranging from basic lines that go for miles to very complex and stylized depictions of creatures. Simply moving the oxidized rocks that form the top layer here in the desert to reveal the lighter-colored sand that lies underneath created the lines and pictures. By doing this as a series of narrow lines, either straight or curved, it is possible to create a picture that is very easily seen from above, even if it isn't always easily identifiable what it is.

In fact, in some cases, it's not clear at all what is being portrayed. There's one animal that looks a bit like a cross between a scared cat and some sort of weird dog. It is very cartoonish, with completely straight legs and only three or four digits on each foot.

Another one is most definitely a monkey, but without any eyes or nose and with four digits on one hand but five on the other. Speaking of hands, one of the Nazca figures is simply called The Hands, though it actually looks more like another monkey, but unfinished. It also doesn't have any eyes or nose and again has four digits on one hand and five on the other.

There is also a very convincing—though not particularly scary—spider that is 150 feet long. One of its hind legs goes far past the bounds of the picture, not to mention reality. It might represent the silken thread that the spider is attached to, but they've done it very strangely by making it an extension of one of the legs.

There's also a huge stylized tree and a similarly large stylized birdlike figure known as the Heron, as well as a three-hundred-foot-long hummingbird, with a beak that is about the same length as its body. Another bird is known as the Condor and a fourth bird is called the Parrot, though it doesn't look much like one to me.

Finally, there is the figure sometimes called the Astronaut, who was created on the side of a hill, much like the earlier Paracas drawings that are further to the north. This figure is almost one hundred feet tall, with a bubblehead and big owl-like eyes. Archaeologists more usually call him the Owl-Man, a nickname acquired back in 1949. One of his arms is pointing up; the other is pointing down. He doesn't look much like an astronaut, and many reasonable explanations have emerged for what he might be doing, including perhaps holding a fishing net and wearing a traditional poncho.

A lot of people have made suggestions about the Nazca Lines since they were noticed in the 1920s, ranging from pseudo-archaeologists working on their own to scientists sponsored by the National Geographic Society and other institutions. One of the very first archaeological studies, and systematic description of the lines, was conducted by Berkeley anthropologist Alfred Kroeber in 1926, though his findings would not be published for another seventy years. Theories to explain the existence of the lines and other designs include von Däniken's ancient aliens using the region as landing strips; Paul Kosok's and Maria Reiche's ideas about the figures representing constellations in the form of an astronomical calendar; anthropological hypotheses involving the identification and tracking of underground water sources in this dry desert; and suggestions that they were ceremonial paths for performing religious rituals of the Paracas and Nazca cultures.

Most recently a joint German-Peruvian expedition has been documenting and studying the geoglyphs in both the Nazca area and the Palpa region to the north. They are finding the ruins of many Nazca villages, with glyphs near virtually every settlement. The findings suggest a long history of such glyphs in the region, and some are even superimposed upon others. It also is now clear that the earliest were created on hillsides, from where they could be seen from the plain below, rather than necessitate a view from the air. Even the more complex ones, like the hummingbird, have now been shown to be single-line drawings—in which one can start walking at a specific point and walk along the line without ever having to cross another line. Thus, it is quite possible that these were used as ceremonial processions, as has been suggested.

In any case, there is simply no need to invoke extraterrestrial visitors in order to explain the amazing Nazca Lines. The phenomenon of building these geoglyph figures on the ground has a long tradition over many centuries in many places in Peru, most of which were very visible to the people for whom they were made. It seems to be a regional form of artistic, religious, and cultural expression, not landing strips for extraterrestrials. Nor were they outside the skill level of our predecessors on this planet, who were advanced enough not to need outside assistance in such building projects.

✦❀✦ ✦❀✦

Elsewhere, in northern Peru, the spectacular discovery of a royal tomb made worldwide headlines in 1987. Dating to about 250 CE, it was found in the area of Sipan and was excavated by a Peruvian archaeologist named Walter Alva. This was the region where the Moche culture flourished from 100 to 800 CE.

The kingdom of the Moche was large by Andean standards, located in a north–south strip by the coast. It was an area of about three hundred fifty miles long by fifty miles wide, covering a dozen narrow valleys descending out of the Andes toward the Pacific coast and separated by desert. The Moche traded widely with regions along the coast and over the Andes in the Amazon rainforest, in what is now modern Chile and Ecuador, for goods including lapis lazuli and spondylus shells, as well as boa constrictors, parrots, and monkeys. They supported themselves using irrigation canals to grow crops such as corn, avocados, potatoes, and peanuts; from the ocean they got fish, shrimp, crabs, and other seafood.

Their society seems to have been highly stratified, with arts such as textile weaving, impressive ceramics, and items crafted from precious metals, though they had no writing system and apparently didn't use money as we know it. They also worked hard at construction projects—not only the irrigation canals, but also pyramids, temples, and elaborate burial mounds. One pyramid, near the capital city on the Moche River by the modern city of Trujillo and called the Pyramid of the Sun, was built from more than 130 million mudbricks. It covered more than five hectares, which is about twelve acres. An administrative structure, it is thought to be the largest construction ever built in South America. The other side of the capital city featured the slightly smaller Pyramid of the Moon, which was highly decorated and used for ceremonial purposes.

The Moche civilization suddenly collapsed about 800 CE. We don't know exactly why it happened; theories range from a devastating earthquake to a severe drought caused by an El Niño weather system. By the time the Spanish arrived in the area centuries later, all they found were the weather-beaten and melted remains of the mudbrick pyramids and other buildings that the Moche had left behind.

It was in 1987 that Walter Alva got a call from the local police station near Sipan. Several tomb robbers had had a falling out after finding a wealthy tomb and were fighting over the objects that they found. Rather ironically, one of them called the police for help. The police confiscated the objects and called Alva. When he arrived at the police station, one of the officers reached into a paper bag and then pulled a small gold mask out of it. Alva nearly fell off his chair in surprise.

He took a team of archaeologists back to where the robbers said they had found the tomb, which turned out to be located in an absolutely huge pyramid made of mudbricks. The pyramid, which is one of several at the site, was so damaged by erosion and other mostly natural forces that it almost looked more like a natural mountain than something constructed by humans.

Alva hoped that there might be other tombs that the looters had missed, so he and his team began a proper excavation. Soon they did indeed find several other tombs, including one that turned out to be what *National Geographic* has called "the New World's Richest Unlooted Tomb"—this is Tomb 1, the tomb belonging to the Lord of Sipan, as he is called.

In the tomb, which is basically a large room measuring about five meters by five meters, they first found the body of a man whose feet had been cut off. This was possibly to prevent him from walking away in the afterlife, so that he had to stay to protect the other occupants. He was buried in the upper right corner of the burial chamber, a few feet above the rest of the bodies.

The Lord of Sipan himself was found in the middle of the chamber, with additional burials on all sides of him. Counting the man whose feet had been cut off, there may have been as many as eleven people in the tomb besides the lord himself—three other adult men, one adult woman, three adolescent boys and three adolescent girls, and one child.

More than 450 objects were buried in this one tomb, many of precious metal, including gold and silver, as well as others of copper or bronze now oxidized to a pleasant green color. Among them are necklaces with beads in the shape of what look like peanuts, including one that has silver peanuts on one side and gold peanuts on the other. Because we know that the Moche cultivated peanuts, we shouldn't be surprised to see them represented in jewelry.

There are also three pairs of earrings, or ear ornaments, including one set with an animal inlaid on them who looks a bit like Rudolph the Red-Nosed Reindeer. Another set has a bird that looks like a cross between a duck and a pelican. A third set has what appears to be a three-dimensional representation of the Lord of Sipan himself, all dressed up and ready to go, complete with spear or scepter, shield, ear ornaments, and a necklace of what look like skulls that goes from shoulder to shoulder. If he wore this last set of ear ornaments as part of his outfit when he was all dressed up, then he'd be wearing a miniature of himself, which is intriguing.

On his chest were hundreds of tiny beads still in place, forming a magnificent pectoral collar of green, brown, and white. These had to be painstakingly preserved and conserved. Often the way to recover such artifacts intact is to put some sort of easily removable glue onto cloth, cardboard, or some other material, and then lay it on top of the beads while they are still in place and allow the whole assembly to dry. Then it is lifted up and the beads come with it, still in their original place and with the original design intact, though it's now a mirror image. It can then be transported safely to a conservation room or elsewhere, where the glue can be dissolved and the original pectoral collar, with all of the beads still in place, can be safely studied and worked on some more.

There was also a huge crescent-shaped helmet or headdress made of gold, with feathers that probably went with it; also possibly a faceplate made of gold, to cover the lower part of the lord's face; and what is probably a scepter or a goblet made of gold. There are also several backflaps made in silver, gold, and bronze or copper. These were worn, as the name suggests, as part of the backside of the outfit, most likely covering the lord's rear end. On several of these the so-called Decapitator God is pictured, standing on what looks like a row of skulls. He is found on other objects in the tomb as well. Although small, this is not a god whom one would want to meet in a dark alley.

Other representations, presumably of other gods, are equally ferocious looking, including some with open mouths and lots of sharp pointed teeth, but there are also small gold beads in the shape of faces with inlaid blue eyes that aren't as scary to look at.

As for who this important person in the tomb was, Moche specialists such as Christopher Donnan, in addition to Walter Alva, have suggested that he may have been the Warrior Priest who is known from pictorial scenes that have been found on Moche pots and painted on murals. One of the most famous themes is the so-called Sacrifice Ceremony.

In this ceremony, sacrificial victims have their throats cut; their blood is poured or drained into goblets; and the priests and other participants then drink it. The Warrior Priest is always shown wearing things like a helmet and headdress, backflaps, and ear ornaments and carrying a large goblet or scepter, just like the Lord of Sipan has in his tomb. If that is the case, then the scenes that are portrayed on the pottery and in the murals apparently represent real-life events and real people.

There are numerous other Moche sites that have been investigated during the past several decades, and they have yielded important artifacts and information. The tomb of the Lord of Sipan remains among the best known, however, which has unfortunately resulted in large-scale attempts at looting by would-be tomb robbers looking for another rich burial nearby. At least one aerial photograph shows that the region by Sipan now looks like a moonscape, with pits dug absolutely everywhere. Obviously this is one of the areas of the world where we have to be proactive in the future to prevent such looting activities.

{⟨••⟩}{⟨••⟩}

Moving now a bit closer to us in time, to about 1500 CE, and back down to the southern part of Peru directly east from the region of the Nazca Lines, we reach Machu Picchu, which was declared a UNESCO World Heritage Site in 1983.

The site of Machu Picchu is spectacular, like few others in the world. It lies at an altitude of 7,972 feet above sea level. The views are quite literally breathtaking, in part because at that altitude, it's literally hard to catch your breath. In fact, many tourists suffer from altitude sickness while they are there, which can adversely affect the visit. By way of comparison, the official elevation of Denver is 5,280 feet above sea level, and so Machu Picchu could legitimately be nicknamed the Mile-and-a Half-High City.

The site dates back to a little more than five hundred years ago. It was first built during the fifteenth century, about 1450 CE, and was abandoned less than a century later, around 1532 CE, at the time of the Spanish Conquest. Built at the direction of one of the Inca emperors as a summer refuge and a secondary palace, it is five days' walk from Cuzco, the Inca capital. It is placed atop a large mountain with lush vegetation and a two-thousand-foot drop to the river below. At one end of the site rises a peak, Wayna Picchu, a popular climb for more adventurous tourists. New scholarly projects are continuing at the site,

Machu Picchu

including one that will be testing the DNA of skeletal remains found there.

Hiram Bingham, who was a professor at Yale, gets credit for the discovery of Machu Picchu, which was first brought to the attention of the world in 1911. As a recent great book by Mark Adams, *Turn Right at Machu Picchu*, points out, Bingham didn't really discover the city, since he was basically just shown it by the locals, who had always known it was there. He might not even have been the first Western explorer to find it. But he claimed credit for it, and that's certainly not the first time such a thing has happened. Heinrich Schliemann did the same thing at Mycenae in Greece about forty years earlier, when the locals took him to the ruins of the Lion Gate at the ancient city, and at Troy, when he took over Frank Calvert's work there.

Bingham returned to the site in 1912, sponsored by both National Geographic and Yale University, and excavated there for about four months, even though he had no real formal training as an archaeologist. In 1913 *National Geographic* devoted their entire April issue to Machu Picchu. Some see that issue, and the National Geographic Society's association with Bingham, as the beginning of its rise to the international prominence that it still enjoys today. In that article, Bingham tried to convey some of the wonder of the initial discovery, writing, "we found ourselves in the midst of a tropical forest, beneath the shade of whose trees we could make out a maze of ancient walls, the ruins of buildings made of blocks of granite, some of which were beautifully fitted together in the most refined style of Inca architecture. A few rods farther along we came to a little open space, on which were two splendid temples or palaces. The superior character of the stone work, the presence of these splendid edifices, and of what appeared to be an unusually large number of finely constructed stone dwellings, led me to believe that Machu Picchu might prove to be the largest and most important ruin discovered in South America since the days of the Spanish conquest."

Additional excavations took place in 1914 and 1915, and then Bingham began writing books and articles about his discoveries, of which probably the most famous is *Lost City of the Incas*. He thought that Machu Picchu might have been the lost Inca city of Vilcabamba, but that is now thought to be located elsewhere.

Looking out over the site itself, one can see that it is split into an upper town and a lower town. There is a residential district, presumably where the regular people lived. There also is what seems to be a royal district, possibly for the nobles or royalty, which is distinctly possible if the whole site was used as a royal retreat—like a Camp David for Inca rulers. And then there are temples, warehouses, channels for water, and lots and lots of agricultural terraces. Within the so-called Temple of the Sun, there is also a massive tower known as the Torreon, which was possibly used as an observatory (but that assertion is still debated). A large stone called the Intihuatana might be a ritual stone used to mark winter and summer solstices, but whether that was its use also is debated.

All these buildings were constructed using the standard—or classic—Inca technique. The stones were cut and fitted together so well that there was no need to use any mortar to bind or seal them together. Most of the doors and windows are neither square nor rectangular, but rather trapezoidal. Obviously this was a deliberate architectural feature and some people have suggested that it was to help prevent the buildings from collapsing during an earthquake, which is an interesting idea.

Bingham brought a lot of artifacts back to Yale from Machu Picchu after his excavations at the site in 1912 and 1914–1915. He was supposed to hold them for only eighteen months so that experts in the United States could study them. In fact, they remained at Yale for the next ninety years. It was only when the wife of the Peruvian president, who was an anthropologist herself, began agitating for their return that anything was done about it. The first few objects were returned in 2006, and by 2012 pretty much all the artifacts had been sent back to Peru, except for those that both sides agreed should stay at Yale for further study.

The objects that were returned are now displayed in a museum and research center in Cuzco, where both local and foreign archaeologists and students can study them. They include ceramic bottles decorated with highly intricate designs, some of which will have been used to hold oil or perfume. One has a human face on the long neck of the bottle, with what looks like a flounced skirt on the body of the vessel; another is in the shape of a hand holding an elongated cup. There also is a pin for a shawl, which is made of bone and features two birds facing each other, as well as various pieces of jewelry and other metal objects, including ceremonial knives.

{↔}{↔}

We'll end our brief survey of archaeology in Peru here, having noted some amazing cultures—the Nazca, the Moche, and the Inca—and covered several thousand years and hundreds of square miles of territory, from the deserts to the mountains. We can clearly see the rise and fall of distinctive civilizations, each occupying the same general region one after the other, here in the New World just like in the Old World. In some ways, though, the developments here in Peru are almost more impressive, set as they are in a landscape of enormous mountains and isolated valleys, coastal streams separated by desert, and the Amazon basin nearby, which combined to make it a much harder place in which to develop a large complex society, garner agricultural surpluses, maintain communication between various parts of the polity, and so on. Regardless, it seems that the cycle of history is not so different, whether studying the Moche or Mesopotamia, the Inca or the Indus Valley, the Nazca or New Kingdom Egypt.

1 8

GIANT HEADS, FEATHERED SERPENTS, AND GOLDEN EAGLES

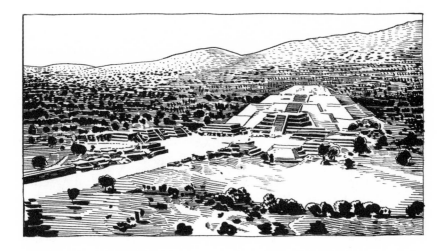

A T THE SITE OF TEOTIHUACÁN, INHABITED FROM ABOUT 100 BCE to about 650 CE in a region approximately fifty kilometers northeast of Mexico City, a secret tunnel was detected in 2003. It led from one of the plazas near the edge of the city to the Temple of the Feathered Serpent and was found after heavy rains opened up a small hole about eighty feet away from the temple. Archaeologists brought remote-sensing devices—specifically radar—and then mapped it. Led by Mexican archaeologist Sergio Gómez, excavation has been going on ever since, using remote-controlled robots in some places and pure hand labor in others.

The tunnel is more than 330 feet long, ending at least forty and perhaps as many as sixty feet directly below the temple. It was sealed about eighteen hundred years ago with at least six walls deployed to block the tunnel at various points along its length. During their meticulous excavations in the tunnel, archaeologists have found more than seventy thousand ancient objects as diverse as jewelry, seeds, animal bones, sea shells, pottery, obsidian blades, vessels with animal heads, rubber balls such as were used in the Mesoamerican ball games, hundreds of large conch shells from the Caribbean, and four thousand wooden objects.

The tunnel ceiling and walls are coated with a glittery powder, perhaps ground-up pyrite or a similar substance, which would have caused them to sparkle and shimmer in the light of torches. At the bottom of the tunnel are three chambers, and offerings that include four large figurines of green stone, remains of jaguars, and jade statues. There are also significant quantities of liquid mercury, which may have represented an underworld river or lake. The area beyond has yet to be investigated and could hold the bodies of the earlier rulers of the city.

{↔}{↔}

We already have discussed a few of the sites found in Central America, namely Palenque and Chichén Itza. In addition to them, some of the most recent and exciting discoveries in New World archaeology have been taking place at the Aztec site of Tenochtitlán, dating to about 1350 CE and located underneath downtown Mexico City, as well as at the site of Teotihuacán that we have just mentioned. Europeans have known about these sites since the Spanish invasion of Mexico in the sixteenth century. But those early Spanish invaders didn't know of the Olmecs.

So, let's start back in the 1930s and 1940s, with the discovery of the Olmec civilization. The Olmecs created the earliest known civilization in what is now modern Mexico, flourishing from at least 1150 BCE (and perhaps as early as 1500 BCE) until about 400 BCE. Ironically, they were the last of the Mesoamerican civilizations to be discovered by modern archaeologists. The general public remembers them now primarily for the seventeen giant stone heads and other sculptures that they have left us. It was Matthew and Marion Stirling, Smithsonian archaeologists, and a *National Geographic* photographer named Richard Stewart who first brought the Olmecs to the attention of the world.

These archaeologists were not the first Westerners to have come across evidence of this civilization. The first known sculpture that can be attributed to the Olmecs was published already in 1869. It had been discovered a few years earlier by a local worker on a farm in Veracruz, on the Caribbean coast of Mexico, near the village of Tres Zapotes (meaning "three sapodillas," after a type of tree found in the region). The name of the village is now also used for the nearby Olmec site where the farmer found the sculpture.

As the story goes, the farmer thought at first the object was an over-turned iron cauldron, but to his surprise it turned out to be a colossal head made of volcanic stone. The face is squat, with large eyes, nose, and lips. A helmet—which looks a lot like an early football helmet made of leather—covers the top of the head and down to the eyebrows. There is nothing below the chin: no neck, no body, no arms, and no legs. There is just the head. Because it looks about as wide as it is tall, it basically resembles a large carved billiard ball, except not quite so round. It was later re-excavated by Matthew Stirling in 1939 and is now known as Tres Zapotes Monument A.

As was often the case, initial discussions—and even some more recent discussions—of these giant heads and of the Olmecs in general sought to link them to Egypt, Phoenicia, people from Atlantis, ancient astronauts, and even China and Japan. They are, of course, not related to any of the above but are indigenous to the region.

The name "Olmec"—or "Olmeca"—means "the people of the rub-ber country." It's not what they called themselves, but rather is what the Aztecs called their archaic descendants who still lived in the same gen-eral region at the time of the Spanish conquest in 1521. Archaeologists have taken to calling this region Olman, meaning the "Rubber Country"—basically, the hot and humid area of the lowlands that stretch from modern southern Veracruz to western Tabasco. At the moment, we have no idea what their name actually was, since the few written records carved on stone left to us by the Olmecs have not yet been translated.

The Stirlings and Stewart were also not the first archaeologists to explore the region. That honor goes to a two-person expedition from Tulane University in New Orleans, Frans Blom and Oliver La Farge, who had set out in 1925 to search for more remains of the Maya. Instead, they found the remains of the Olmecs, including at what is now one of the best-known sites, La Venta, where they discovered another colossal stone head, altars, stelae, and the remains of a pyramid completely over-grown by the jungle. Their findings were published in 1926–1927 as a two-volume set titled *Tribes and Temples*.

{↔}{↔}

The three most important Olmec sites that have been excavated so far are San Lorenzo, Tres Zapotes, and La Venta. In almost every instance, the first archaeologists, and sometimes the later ones retracing their steps, were led to the sites by locals who had uncovered the stone heads, altars, and other remains while farming.

Tres Zapotes was the first of these to be professionally excavated, by a small team led by the Stirlings and including an archaeologist named Philip Drucker, from 1938 to 1940. They re-excavated and thoroughly documented the original Olmec head that had been found by the farm-worker some eighty years earlier. It turned out that the head stands

Olmec colossal stone head, San Lorenzo

nearly five feet high and weighs approximately eight tons. They also found several other carved stone stelae and monuments, including one (Stela C) that had a date inscribed upon it, just like the Maya stelae at various sites like Copan and Palenque, which used a similar dating system. Stirling was able to quickly determine that the date on Stela C was the equivalent of our 31 BCE.

In 1940, during their second season of excavating at Tres Zapotes, the Stirlings went to visit the second Olmec site, La Venta, which they knew from the published volumes of Blom and La Forge. They were looking for the eight monuments that the two earlier archaeologists had been shown by the locals and had documented in a single day, back in 1925. They found them, including the colossal head, which turned out to be eight and a half feet high and twenty-two feet in circumference, plus two stelae, and three "altar-thrones," which generally have a carving of a seated person inside a niche on the front of the altar.

The Stirlings found other remains that the previous explorers had not discovered, including three more huge stone heads and another altar-throne on which the seated man holds a baby on his lap. There are also four more pairs of adults and babies on the same monument, which is why it is usually called the "Quintuplet Altar," although its official name is simply Altar 5.

As a result of all these discoveries during what had simply been a visit to the site, the Stirlings and Drucker decided to return and conduct excavations at La Venta, in 1942–1943. Although World War II was raging at the time, they managed to fit in two short field seasons, during which time they excavated the mounds that could be seen at the site. Some mounds contained tombs with a few grave goods; others were covering mosaic pavements. Subsequent excavations by other scholars have yielded much additional material; La Venta has at least thirty earthen mounds that date between 1000 and 400 BCE, and archaeologist Richard Diehl estimates that approximately ninety stone monuments have now been found at the site.

In 1945, the Stirlings went to visit San Lorenzo, in southern Veracruz. There the locals immediately showed them two colossal stone heads. One was nearly nine feet tall; the other was even taller—9.4 feet tall. Each weighs approximately forty tons. Both were larger than any the Stirlings had seen or found previously at either Tres Zapotes or La

Venta. They also saw about a dozen other stone monuments, all now identified as Olmec. In addition, they were shown two stone jaguars at the nearby village of Tenochtitlán (not to be confused with the larger city underneath Mexico City that we will discuss in a moment). Archaeologists frequently tie these neighboring sites together, referring to them collectively as San Lorenzo Tenochtitlán.

A subsequent field season in 1946 by Stirling and Drucker yielded a few more stone sculptures, but nothing extraordinary, and they never fully published their results. It was left to Michael Coe, of Yale University, to return to San Lorenzo in the mid-1960s and restart the excavations, which were then published. The most recent expedition, led by Ann Cyphers of the National Autonomous University of Mexico, worked at the site from 1990 to 2012.

As a result of his work at the three sites, Matthew Stirling proposed that the Olmec civilization was older than that of the Maya, which initially met with fierce resistance from some of the old-school Mayanists, such as Eric Thompson. After all the debate, however, and with the introduction of radiocarbon dating, it was finally accepted that Stirling was correct and the Olmecs have now been placed in their proper and rightful position among the Mesoamerican civilizations, although there is still much work to be done in elucidating the details.

⟨•••⟩ ⟨•••⟩

In contrast, the discoveries that have been made in downtown Mexico City date to the much later period of the Aztecs. These have revealed previously unknown remains of Tenochtitlán, the Aztec capital city. The Aztecs were composed of a number of groups. Those who settled at Tenochtitlán called themselves the Mexica [meh-SHEE-ka]. The city flourished from about 1325 CE until its destruction by the Spanish conquistadors in 1521. Of course, it's always been known that the Aztec capital lies underneath Mexico City, because the Spaniards destroyed much of it before building their own city right on top of the ruins.

Fortunately, the conquistadors created maps, including one supposedly drawn by Hernán Cortés himself, that show what the city looked like before its destruction. As a result, we know that it was originally built on an island in the middle of Lake Texcoco, with causeways connecting it to the mainland. The space available for living was expanded by creating *chinampas*, or floating gardens, which eventually became firmly enough anchored and covered with enough soil that houses and other structures could be built upon them. It looks like the city was then split into four quarters and may have housed as many as two hundred fifty thousand people.

Because the modern city covers the ancient one, buildings and artifacts are constantly being discovered during various construction projects. For example, the great Calendar Stone, often called the Sun Stone, was discovered in December 1790, when the Mexico City Cathedral was being repaired. This huge stone is almost twelve feet across and weighs about twenty-four tons. It's not quite clear what it was used for, though it may have been a ceremonial basin or altar. On it are depictions of the four periods that the Aztecs thought preceded their own time, lasting a total of 2,028 years. The face in the middle might be the Aztec deity of the Sun, which is why some people call it the Sun Stone.

The great stone was probably originally located on or in the Great Temple, usually called the Templo Mayor. Portions of the Templo Mayor itself were originally found in the mid-1900s, with more accidentally discovered in 1978 when electric cables were being laid in the area. As British archaeologist Paul Bahn notes, the excavation project that was subsequently undertaken was mammoth—several entire city blocks of houses and shops were torn down in the very center of the city so that the archaeologists could investigate the remains. An archaeologist with the wonderfully appropriate name of Eduardo Matos Moctezuma led the team.

The Templo Mayor is actually a double pyramid dedicated to two gods: Huitzilopochtli, god of the sun as well as war and human sacrifice, and Tlaloc, who is the rain and water god. In addition to the remains of the temple pyramid, the archaeologists found artifacts of gold and jade and many animal skeletons, and a rack of human skulls carved in stone. They also found that the Aztecs had buried objects from previous Mesoamerican civilizations.

In 2006 archaeologists found a stone altar depicting Tlaloc that dates to about 1450 CE. They also uncovered a monolith—a stone slab—made of pinkish andesite. The monolith depicts the earth goddess Tlaltecuhtli, originally painted with ocher, red, blue, white, and black.

Aztec Moon Goddess, Tenochtitlán

It was found lying flat, but would have stood eleven feet tall when vertical. It weighs twelve tons and dates to the last Aztec period, 1487–1520. The team that discovered the monolith thought that it might still be in its original position, perhaps at the entrance to a chamber or even a tomb, even though it had broken into four large pieces.

Two years later, in a stone-lined shaft lying right beside the monolith, the archaeologists began finding additional Aztec religious offerings, including sacrificial knives made of white flint; objects made of jaguar bone; and bars of copal, or incense. Beneath the offerings, in a stone box, were the skeletons of two golden eagles, surrounded by twenty-seven sacrificial knives, most of which were dressed up in costumes as if they were gods and goddesses. And beneath these were yet more offerings; by January 2009, the archaeologists had found six separate sets of offerings in this one deep pit, which reached twenty-four feet below street level.

Back up at the eight-foot-deep mark, the archaeologists had found a second stone box. It contained the skeleton of a dog or a wolf that had been buried with a collar made from jade beads. It also had turquoise plugs—like earrings—in its ears and bracelets with little gold bells around its ankles. The archaeologists promptly nicknamed it Aristo-Canine.

The skeleton is covered with seashells and other remains of marine life, like clams and crabs. The lead excavator of the dig, Leonardo López Luján, thinks that the six sets of offerings mark the Aztec cosmology or belief system—for example, the dog/wolf with the seashells would represent the first level of the underworld, "serving to guide its master's soul across a dangerous river," as Robert Draper wrote in the 2010 *National Geographic* story that documented this amazing find. López Luján believes that he may be close to finding the tomb of one of the last, and most feared, Aztec emperors, Ahuitzotl (ah-WEE-tzohtl), who died in 1502 or 1503.

❊❊❊ ❊❊❊

Travel about fifty kilometers northeast of Tenochtitlán and we reach Teotihuacán. The site predates Aztec civilization, although the Aztecs gave the city its name, which may mean "the birthplace of the gods." It was declared a UNESCO World Heritage Site in 1987 and is now one of the most visited tourist sites in Mexico. It's still a matter of debate who lived there and what they called their city. It was inhabited from about 100 BCE to about 650 CE, as noted above, and probably had a population of up to one hundred fifty thousand people when it was at its largest. In an interview published in October 2015, Professor David Carrasco of Harvard University described it as "the imperial Rome of Mesoamerica." By this, Carrasco means that Teotihuacán influenced hundreds of other Mesoamerican communities during its period of greatness and served as a beacon for later civilizations. Extensive evidence of Teotihuacano presence is seen in the Maya regions of southern Mexico and Guatemala hundreds of miles to the south, with many scholars believing that Teotihuacán controlled this region for several centuries.

It used to be thought that the Toltecs built the site, because that's apparently what the later Aztecs told the Spaniards when they arrived, but that doesn't seem to have been factually accurate, because the site is earlier than the time of the Toltecs, who flourished during the tenth through twelfth centuries CE. For the moment, the inhabitants are simply referred to as Teotihuacanos.

A long central avenue dominates the site. Called the Avenue of the Dead, it runs for about a mile and a half. Along it, pyramids and temples were built. These include the Pyramid of the Sun and the Pyramid of the Moon, as well as the Temple of the Feathered Serpent.

The Pyramid of the Sun is the largest of the buildings—more than seven hundred feet wide at the base and more than two hundred feet tall—and has a ceremonial cave right under the pyramid, which was discovered in 1971. The Pyramid of the Moon is not far behind in size; human remains were found there in the renewed excavations that began in 1998, which revealed a burial chamber with rich grave goods, including pyrite mirrors and obsidian blades.

The Temple of the Feathered Serpent is the third-largest building at the site. It gets its name from the heads of the feathered serpents that stick out from the façade of the building, each weighing up to four tons. The building itself probably dates to about 200 CE. Beginning in the 1980s, a series of pits was found in front of the temple, which contained the bodies of nearly two hundred warriors, both male and female, and their attendants. All of them had their hands tied behind their backs and were obviously ceremonial victims, perhaps sacrificed at the time that the building was dedicated or during ceremonies held on various occasions.

It was here that the secret tunnel was detected in 2003, leading from one of the plazas near the edge of the city to the Temple of the Feathered Serpent. As mentioned, investigation of this tunnel continues today; some have suggested that it may lead to a royal tomb, perhaps holding the bodies of the earliest rulers of the city.

Extensive survey work also has been done at the site and surrounding region. Headed by René Millon, the Teotihuacán Mapping Project documented the presence of huge industrial and domestic areas, conscious city planning, and ethnic communities from different parts of Mexico. The maps and other data produced by this project by 1973 provided archaeologists with a broader picture of the city's size, scope, and wealth, beyond just describing the pyramids and other major buildings.

❊❊❊❊

It is not clear why, but Teotihuacán was eventually abandoned, probably sometime in the seventh or eighth century CE. Even so, its location was never forgotten, even after it had been lying in ruins for centuries. We know, for example, that the Aztecs used to come to Teotihuacán and were well aware of the people who had once lived there.

Of course, even these Teotihuacanos are not the oldest inhabitants of the region that we now call Mexico. As we have seen, that designation goes to the Olmecs, who built sites such as San Lorenzo, La Venta, and Tres Zapotes, not to mention the Zapotecs in Oaxaca, who inhabited places like Monte Albán from about 400 BCE to 700 CE. We also mustn't forget the Maya, whom we have discussed in another chapter and who should be placed between the Olmecs and the Aztecs. This region has a rich history, which is only just now beginning to be fully understood and further explored.

19

SUBMARINES AND SETTLERS; GOLD COINS AND LEAD BULLETS

I N 1995 A CONFEDERATE SUBMARINE CALLED THE *H. L. HUNLEY* was discovered just off the coast of Charleston, South Carolina. One hundred thirty years earlier, during the Civil War in February 1864, the *Hunley* had become the first submarine anywhere to sink an enemy ship in battle. The target ship was the USS *Housatonic*. The *Hunley* didn't so much fire its torpedo, but rather rammed the *Housatonic*, piercing its side with the torpedo's sixteen-foot-long metal spar—like a long harpoon—at the front of the sub.

The torpedo was left stuck inside the ship, as designed. It was long thought that the crew then backed off about 150 feet before detonating the torpedo via a rope that pulled a trigger on the attached torpedo. Recent evidence, however, indicates that they may have had difficulty detaching from the *Housatonic* and were only about twenty feet away when the torpedo exploded, so the *Hunley* may have been destroyed in the same detonation. The Confederates also may not have figured on the concussion shock wave caused by the detonation, or else the detonation may have knocked a latch on the forward conning tower loose, since it was found unsecured. In any case, when the torpedo went off, the *Housatonic* promptly sank off Sullivan's Island near Fort Sumter in Charleston Harbor, but so did the *Hunley*, in thirty feet of water and with all eight men still on board. The sub had already sunk twice before, with both crews lost, while practicing for the attack, but this time it was lost for good, at least until 1995.

⁕⟨•⟩⁕⟨•⟩⁕

The excavation of the *Hunley* is a good example of historical archaeology, which is what archaeologists call archaeological work related to events in the modern world since 1500. In most cases there are historical records of these same events. Archaeologists provide a different lens on these incidents, enriching and often contradicting the written records. In the case of the *Hunley*, when the conservation and excavation of the submarine is complete, archaeology may help solve the mystery of why the *Hunley* sank and provide much more information on its construction and operation and a wealth of knowledge about the crew members, little of which was recorded in written records.

The *Hunley* also is a good example of an excavation that was conducted under the Abandoned Shipwreck Act of 1987, which was signed into law in 1988. The act is meant to stop the looting of shipwrecks that sank in either state or federal waters, whether in Lake Michigan, the Potomac River, or off the coast of Florida. It gives authority to the federal government and to the state in which the wreck was found. Thus, the *Hunley* is in the jurisdiction of South Carolina, because the submarine was discovered seven years after the act was signed into law and wasn't raised for another five years after that, in 2000. Credit for finding the sub is usually given to the novelist Clive Cussler and his team.

South Carolina established the Hunley Commission, which serves as the custodian, meaning that it negotiates the details about its recovery, curation, and exhibition. Today, the original submarine is on display in North Charleston, where it is kept in a ninety-thousand-gallon tank of freshwater to help remove salt that has permeated the small spaces between the metal components of the vessel and to prevent additional corrosion.

The forty-foot-long sub was found on its side, at a 45-degree angle, sunken into the silt of the sea floor, thirty feet below the water surface. According to Dave Conlin, the archaeological field director, analysis of the sediments covering the *Hunley* showed that natural processes probably buried it within thirty years of sinking. Raising it involved a lot of people and a neat feat of engineering requiring a hammock of straps below the submarine that was attached to a hoist to bring it to the surface. Once it was safely in the freshwater tank in the laboratory, excavation inside the vessel began almost immediately. The first human remains—three ribs—were found soon after, as were scraps of textile, part of a belt, and a corked glass bottle. The matrix of silt had protected the remains from the currents and the seawater, and the relative lack of oxygen had preserved skeletal material from the bodies as well as other artifacts.

Excavation and investigation of the *Hunley* has continued ever since. By now, the complete skeletons and skulls of all eight men have been recovered. Every one of them was found still sitting at his post, meaning that death might have been fairly instantaneous, or that they might have become incapacitated and drowned in place.

One of the crew members—Joseph Ridgaway of Talbot County, Maryland—has been positively identified through a DNA match made in 2004. Another, the commander, Lieutenant George E. Dixon, also has been identified, though more circumstantially. Dixon was known to have kept an engraved twenty-dollar gold coin with him at all times as a good-luck charm. A young girl had given it to him—some reports say it was his fiancée. It had saved his life earlier, when he had been shot at the Battle of Shiloh in Tennessee and the bullet hit the coin instead of killing Dixon.

The archaeologists excavating the *Hunley* found such a coin, with a deep indentation from a bullet and inscribed with the words "*Shiloh; April 6, 1862; My life preserver. G.E.D.*," near the remains of a crewman. Later they found that the skeleton of that same crew member had a healed bullet wound in the left upper thigh, with pieces of lead and flecks of gold still embedded in his femur. These were most likely from the bullet and the coin, respectively, and it's pretty clear that this must be Dixon's body. They also found his pocket watch, as well as a wallet, a bandana, matches, and tobacco pipes. The remains of Ridgaway, Dixon, and the other crew members were ceremoniously buried in Magnolia Cemetery in Charleston in 2004. As Conlin has noted, the recovery of the *Hunley* "represents a model of federal, state, and private sector united in service to an archaeological resource of extraordinary importance."

UNESCO has now also begun efforts to protect underwater finds around the world by passing the Convention on the Protection of the Underwater Cultural Heritage in 2009. The convention came into play in an interesting way two years later, when the Smithsonian was planning an exhibit that would have displayed objects from an Arab wreck that sank in the Java Sea in the ninth century CE.

The shipwreck contained priceless artifacts from the Chinese Tang dynasty but was not excavated by professional archaeologists. Rather, the artifacts were recovered by a private company and later sold to another company for a reported $32 million. Three different archaeological associations, as well as several members of the Smithsonian's own internal research unit, protested the proposed exhibition, saying that the process by which the artifacts had been recovered was closer to looting than to proper archaeological excavation. In the end, in the face of the protests, the exhibit was first postponed and then finally simply canceled before it ever even opened.

❊❖❊ ❊❖❊

If we now move up the East Coast from South Carolina, we come to the excavations at Jamestown, Virginia. These excavations have been under the direction of William Kelso since the 1990s. They are an excellent example of traditional excavation methodology now enhanced by cutting-edge technology.

Jamestown was the first permanent settlement to be established by British colonists, in what would later become the Commonwealth of Virginia. About one hundred men, who had a very rough time during the first few years, began the settlement in 1607. Reinforcements, including some women, arrived a few years later. It is probably most well known to people today because of Pocahontas, the Native

American woman who reportedly saved the life of Captain John Smith and then married a colonist named John Rolfe. The events are usually pitched as an improbable love story in the face of overwhelming odds, the Disney movie of the same name being one example. When Rolfe later returned to England for a visit, along with a new strain of tobacco that he had developed, he brought Pocahontas with him. The visit had a sad result, for she died while they were in England.

The site of Jamestown had pretty much vanished over the centuries. Before Kelso began his excavations, he had only a little information to work with, mostly gleaned from archives stored in a library. It is the writings of Captain Smith and others—that is, eyewitness accounts—as well as a small sketch of the site by a Spanish spy and a single church tower, made of brick and dating from a later period, that led Kelso to determine where to place the first trenches. His archaeological intuition was excellent, and within hours of beginning their excavations, his team had found the first artifacts and remains of buildings.

What did they find? Right away they came up with weapons and armor, as well as pottery, glass, coins, and other artifacts dating to the seventeenth century. They also found a line of postholes, which was all that remained of the wooden protective palisade wall belonging to the original fort. The wooden posts had long since disintegrated, but the holes in the ground dug to hold the posts were still plainly visible.

As the excavations continued over the years, they found the rest of the outline of the whole fort, as well as the remains of five additional buildings, including the church, the governor's house, the barracks, and a workshop or trading post (which Kelso has also called a factory). By 2007, when Kelso published a brief description of their findings, they also had found numerous graves and skeletons in a variety of places, more than seventy of the interments in a cemetery, and also single graves underneath the church. The skeletal remains indicated that the men had mostly died before the age of twenty-five. The women didn't live much longer than that.

It was four skeletons in particular, though, that caught Kelso's interest. The four bodies had been found in November 2013, in the area of the church where Pocahontas and John Rolfe were married, which Kelso's team had uncovered earlier. The skeletal material was not well preserved, and so the effort to identify them involved the use of chemical testing and high-resolution micro-CT scanning. By late July 2015, the media reported—rather breathlessly—that the remains had been positively identified as belonging to some of the early leaders of the colony.

According to some of those media reports, the skeletons had been taken to the Smithsonian's National Museum of Natural History, where biological anthropologist Doug Owsley worked on them. Owsley, who also teaches classes to some of our George Washington University students, is world famous and has worked on many such cases, including the skeletons from the *Hunley* that we just discussed. Owsley and his team were able to identify the Jamestown skeletons using a combination of forensic analysis and historical records.

The historical records allowed them to determine who had died between January 1608, when the church was constructed, and 1617, when it fell into disrepair and was moved. This narrowed down the list of possible suspects. The forensic analysis gave them the approximate age at death and the gender for the remains of the four skeletons.

They also did chemical testing to determine the diet and such things as the level of lead in the bones. The results indicated that the dead people were most likely English and of high status, because of their high-protein diet and their exposure to things like pewter bowls and glazed pottery, both of which contain lead. Their high status, or at least their importance in the colony, also was indicated by the fact that their graves were found under the chancel of the church—that is, the space around the altar at the eastern end of the church—rather than in the unmarked cemetery located elsewhere.

All four were men. Two were from the original group of immigrants that arrived in 1607. They were Captain Gabriel Archer, who went looking for gold and silver in the hinterland of the settlement before his death at about the age of thirty-five in 1609 or 1610, and Reverend Robert Hunt, the first chaplain of the settlement, who died at the age of thirty-nine after less than a full year at Jamestown. The other two were from the group of reinforcements who arrived in 1610. These are Ferdinando Wainman, who was around thirty-four years old when he died, reportedly of disease, just a few months after arriving, and his relative, Captain William West, who was killed by the Native Americans in 1610, also just a few months after arriving, when he was only about twenty-five years old.

Kelso and his team also uncovered some human bones in 2012 that they thought were unusual and merited further investigation. The bones included fragments from a mutilated and incomplete skull, teeth and the lower jaw, and a severed leg bone—a tibia, to be precise. Kelso found them in the cellar of a Jamestown house, in a context with the discarded bones of butchered horses and dogs, which is a rather unusual and unexpected location, to say the least. He called in Owsley to look at the remains.

Owsley identified the bones as belonging to a young woman, specifically a young English girl about fourteen years old, based on the development of her third molar and the growth stage of her shinbone. They nicknamed her Jane. Although they couldn't determine her identity or her cause of death, because there were so few bones, Owsley and his associates noticed that the bones exhibited unusual cut marks. There were four shallow cuts on her forehead, which the forensic anthropologists identified as an initial attempt to crack open her skull, according to the Smithsonian Insider online newsletter. The back of her head was then hit with a hatchet or a cleaver, in a series of blows. The last one split her head open, presumably providing access to her brain.

They also noticed that the lower jaw, or mandible, had punctures and sharp cuts on its bottom and sides. These, they said, were the result of "efforts to remove tissue from the face and throat using a knife."

From this evidence, Owsley, Kelso, and others have concluded that Jane died during the so-called "Starving Time"—the bleak winter months of 1609–1610 when the colony was ravaged by hunger and disease and almost failed before the reinforcements arrived. They also think that the other colonists ate her after she died. The evidence shows that the colonists were desperate enough at that time to resort to cannibalism.

The forensic scientists also created a reconstruction of her head, using CT scans and other technology. The reconstruction was on display for a while at the National Museum of Natural History in Washington, DC, and the original skeletal remains are presented at Historic Jamestowne, the educational tourist center operated by the Jamestown Rediscovery project on Jamestown Island.

Doug Owsley provides us with a nice connection that takes us from the East Coast all the way across North America to Washington State. That's because Owsley was also responsible for examining the almost-nine-thousand-year-old skeleton of what is known as Kennewick Man to archaeologists and as the Ancient One to the local Native American tribes. The skeleton has been the subject of a great deal of debate since its discovery in 1996, near Kennewick, Washington, by the banks of the Columbia River. In particular, the discovery of Kennewick Man has stoked the controversy that has always surrounded the passage of the Native American Graves Protection and Repatriation Act of 1990 (NAGPRA), which is perhaps the best-known piece of US legislation that has involved archaeology in the past several decades.

NAGPRA requires every federally funded US museum and similar institution to provide an inventory of all their Native American artifacts, including human remains, funerary objects, grave goods, and so on. Each institution with such artifacts or remains had to determine whether any living Native American tribes could claim a relationship with the inventoried objects. If so, then the institution was required to offer to repatriate to the tribe whatever it was.

These included things like Ishi's brain, which belonged to the last known Native American still living in the wilds of California. Ishi, a member of the Yahi tribe, had emerged from hiding in 1911 and was an instant media sensation. Berkeley anthropologist Alfred Kroeber is perhaps best known for his work with Ishi, and Alfred's wife Theodora, also an anthropologist, published a very popular book about him, *Ishi in Two Worlds*.

Ishi also had a lot of interaction with a doctor named Saxton Pope, who was at University of California–San Francisco. Pope was an avid bow hunter. He befriended Ishi, who taught Pope how he made bows and arrows. Pope subsequently wrote and published a book in 1923, entitled *Hunting with the Bow and Arrow*, which is still highly regarded today.

After Ishi's death in 1916, his brain was sent to the Smithsonian warehouse in Suitland, Maryland, where it was kept in a sealed tank. When NAGPRA was passed in 1990, Ishi's brain was repatriated and reunited with his cremated remains in California.

NAGPRA also came to the forefront when Kennewick Man was found in the Columbia River, reportedly by two college students who were wading in the river while watching boat races in late July 1996. The initial discovery was part of his skull, which was found about ten feet from shore. At first it was thought he might have been a murder victim, and so the coroner and a local archaeologist named James Chatters searched for more parts, quickly turning up almost his entire skeleton. It eventually was discovered that he died about eighty-five hundred years ago.

Kennewick Man has been the subject of litigation almost since the moment he was found, with Native American groups arguing that he was Native American and should be repatriated to them, and a number of prominent scholars arguing that he was not Native American, because the remains were too old to be related to any of the current tribes and should be cared for by the federal government because his remains were found on federal land. The case was settled in 2002 and affirmed by an appeals court in 2004, in favor of the scholars. The bones were kept in the Burke Museum of Natural History and Culture, in Seattle, Washington, during the decade-long legal dispute between a group of eight archaeologists, five Native American tribes, and the federal government. They are not on display but were made available for study by scholars after the court decision.

The case is still being debated. Most recently, in 2015, geneticists from the University of Copenhagen and elsewhere published an article in *Nature*, which compared the DNA of Kennewick Man to that of members from the Confederated Tribes of the Colville Reservation and concluded that he is more closely related to modern Native Americans than he is to anyone else. On the basis of that publication, and a subsequent independent validation of those findings by scientists at the University of Chicago, it was decided in late April 2016 that Kennewick Man was to be repatriated and eventually buried by a coalition of five Native American tribal bands, including the Colville.

{↔}{↔}

If we move from the Pacific Northwest to the American Southwest, we find breathtaking Native American sites like Chaco Canyon in New Mexico. The canyon is a National Historical Park near Albuquerque that was named a UNESCO Heritage site in 1987. It has amazing ruins built there by the Ancestral Pueblo people, which date to between 850 and 1250 CE.

At Chaco Canyon are a number of what are referred to as great houses—huge structures with multiple rooms and multiple stories. One of the best examples is Pueblo Bonito, which had between six hundred and eight hundred rooms and was five stories tall. It was built in stages between 850 and 1150 CE. It covers three acres, but scholars are uncertain how many people lived there—estimates range from about eight hundred to several thousand. It is also not completely clear whether it was a ritual center or a thriving village.

The Chacoan culture, as it is now called, covered portions of New Mexico, Colorado, Utah, and Arizona. Imported goods that have been found there, including seashells and copper bells, attest to trade with areas as far away as Mexico. It is unclear, however, why Chacoan culture disappeared by about 1200 CE, although drought and plague, possibly followed by migration, have been suggested.

Mesa Verde National Park, Colorado

Other ruins can be seen at Mesa Verde National Park in southwestern Colorado. Within the park are nearly five thousand individual sites that date between the sixth and thirteenth centuries CE. There are about six hundred cliff dwellings there, which run the gamut from small storage rooms to impressively large villages with as many as 150 rooms. The ruins at Mesa Verde, which include the famous Cliff Palace, Long House, Spruce Tree House, and Balcony House, were named a UNESCO Heritage site in 1978.

Elsewhere, in the Midwest, about ten miles northeast of St. Louis, Missouri, Cahokia Mounds is another UNESCO Heritage site, as of 1982. Built by members of the Mississippian culture between 800 and 1400 CE, and with a population of as many as twenty thousand inhabitants at its peak in about 1100 CE, the site consists of about 120 separate mounds; hence the colloquial name for those who lived here—the Mound Builders. Covering at least two thousand acres, and described as being larger than London was at the time, it is considered to be the largest pre-Columbian archaeological site in the United States.

The biggest of the mounds, known as Monks Mound, is almost one hundred feet tall. It has been estimated that it took 22 million cubic feet of soil to create it. It covers six acres, making it slightly larger than the Pyramid of the Sun by the Moche capital city in Peru and therefore entitled to be dubbed "the largest prehistoric earthen structure in the New World," as it is called on the relevant UNESCO web page. Most of the mounds are much smaller and were originally meant as platforms and foundations for public buildings, as well as for tombs, but still, the early European explorers and settlers could not believe that the local inhabitants built them. The first published report, by Henry Brackenridge in 1811, compared the mounds to the pyramids of Egypt and, just as with the Maya before John Lloyd Stephens's publications, it was thought that foreigners, including possibly Phoenicians or Vikings, if not Egyptians or lost Israelites, must have built them.

It is indeed impressive to consider what must have gone into the building of these mounds and the complex society that they represent. The mounds, of various sizes and shapes, are enduring reminders of a civilization that once stretched across the Mississippi Valley and the southeastern United States. If we had detailed written records left to us by the members of this society, as we do for the Maya and other New

World civilizations, we would undoubtedly be even more impressed by the Native American inhabitants responsible for these remains.

✦◄►✦✦◄►✦

There are also, of course, any number of other North American archaeological sites to visit, including Colonial Williamsburg and George Washington's Mount Vernon, both of which recreate the time period using re-enactors and are aimed at informing the interested visitor. Both also occasionally welcome volunteers to help excavate at the sites.

For those who want to actually participate in a formal excavation in the United States, there are plenty of opportunities. It is relatively easy to learn what's going on and to find a project on which one can volunteer. For instance, there is Crow Canyon Archaeological Center, near Mesa Verde National Park. There it is possible to participate in a number of archaeological programs, whether solo or with the entire family. A similar, well-established program exists at the Center for American Archaeology in Kampsville, Illinois. A variety of other excavations welcome volunteers as participants; most are listed in the Archaeological Fieldwork Opportunity Bulletin that is published online every year by the Archaeological Institute of America on its website.

In any case, the wonderful diversity of the archaeological landscape of North America is clear, even just from our brief survey in this chapter, where our discussion has included a sunken submarine in South Carolina and a lost settlement in Virginia, brief mentions of the ruins in the American Southwest, finds in the Pacific Northwest, and mounds in the Midwest. No matter where on the continent one happens to be, there's something interesting buried in the dirt.

DIGGING DEEPER 4

DO YOU GET TO KEEP WHAT YOU FIND?

I N THIS FINAL "DIGGING DEEPER" SECTION, I WOULD LIKE TO begin by answering another question that I am asked all the time, which has a short answer but is long on associated implications. The question is simply "Do you get to keep what you find?" The answer is very short: "No." Whether you're working in your own country or in a country other than your own, that nation's antiquities department will have a set of rules. The best discoveries might go to a national or regional museum, as has been true throughout the history of archaeology, but most of the material will be put into bags and boxes and stored at the local university, museum, or some other place where graduate students and other scholars can come in and study the material during the months (or even years) after the excavation. A six- or seven-week field season can yield enough material for two years or more of study and published findings.

Not only don't I get to keep what I find, but I don't think that other people should collect such items either. The consensus among scholars is that there is a direct correlation between private collecting and the looting of ancient sites all over the world. Looters wouldn't bother stealing things from archaeological sites if they had no place to sell them.

More complex is the issue of museum collections: whether the British Museum, the Louvre, the Met, and other museums should return items that they obtained in the period of European colonialism in the nineteenth and twentieth centuries to their original countries of origin—like the Elgin Marbles, the bust of Nefertiti, and the Rosetta stone. Museums have become much more careful in the past couple of decades to ensure that the objects they purchase have clear provenance, but many looted objects still are displayed in museums that were obtained decades ago when the rules were not as stringent. It is a moral, ethical, economic, and legal problem that cannot be easily resolved. It may be that case-by-case decisions would be best, but even that remains to be determined.

However, right now we are seeing the greatest prevalence of looting of archaeological sites worldwide that has ever been documented, almost certainly fueled by demand from private collectors. The greatest opportunities for looted objects are places where the policing of ancient sites is difficult because of political instability, like Syria and Iraq at the moment. Of course, looting is nothing new; some of the Egyptian pharaohs' tombs were looted in antiquity, perhaps even immediately after the pharaohs were buried. But now we are seeing an upsurge worldwide in Afghanistan, Egypt, Iraq, Jordan, Syria, and even Peru and the United States. Ancient sites are now pockmarked with looters' pits.

On a small scale, illegal digging for antiquities has always been a way of life in some areas and cultures, usually done by impoverished folks hoping to supplement their meager income in some way. It is hard to blame a Syrian villager who excavates cylinder seals to sell to a middleman in order to feed his family when shops are closed, fields are burned, and travel impossible. But now wholesale looting operations seem to have swung into action, including in Syria, where ISIS reportedly sponsored and actively participated in the antiquities trade, looting entire sites and destroying parts of others, such as Nimrud and the Mosul Museum.

I was part of a delegation of observers who went to Egypt in May 2011, after the January revolution of that year. We went to do some "ground truthing" in order to see whether the fresh holes dug into the ground that my colleague Sarah Parcak thought she had spotted in satellite photographs were looting pits. They were. I know. I was there and have pictures. Results of our study were published in the journal *Antiquity* for others to use.

In fact, looted Egyptian antiquities have shown up in auction houses in London and New York, just as looted Iraqi antiquities have. When the Iraq Museum in Baghdad was looted, some of the most famous pieces in the museum were stolen. Many were returned or have been recovered, but others are still missing. Some ended up on eBay, where I and anyone else could see them, until pressure mounted and such sales were forbidden. Despite this prohibition, some looted objects can still be found for sale on eBay.

One of my favorite stories is of someone who was trying to sell a stolen Iraqi item. When examined closely, it turned out to be one of the replicas that had been for sale in the museum store. Colonel Matthew Bogdanos of the US Army, who was put in charge of recovering the

Looting in Iraq

items stolen from the Iraq Museum, documents many of these stories in his best-selling book *Thieves of Baghdad*, which was published in 2005.

The looting went far beyond the museum and extended to archaeological sites throughout Iraq, with reports of men armed with both shovels and machine guns illegally digging at sites across the country. At least one, the ancient city known as Umma, has been so thoroughly looted that all that can be seen in the photographs are looters' pits, rather than ancient buildings or anything else.

The appearance of one-of-a-kind looted objects can cause a dilemma for archaeologists committed to limiting the trade in illegal antiquities. Such seems to have been the case in 2011, when the Sulaymaniyah Museum in the Kurdistan region of Iraq was advised by an Assyriologist in Britain to buy a group of clay tablets inscribed with cuneiform that he had been shown by an antiquities dealer. In this case, among the tablets was one that turned out to contain a previously unknown section from the *Epic of Gilgamesh*. It fills in a large gap within the fifth tablet in the poem where Gilgamesh and his sidekick Enkidu are heading for the Cedar Forest to get timber; this is usually thought to be the same general region where the famous Cedars of Lebanon mentioned in the Bible were located. The new lines describe the noises that they hear upon entering the forest, including birds, insects, and monkeys.

Lost for three thousand years, this tablet filled in an important piece of one of the classics of world literature. The dilemma for archaeologists, of course, is that we don't want to encourage looting, but also cannot allow such a tablet with valuable information to go into the art collecting market and disappear from public view without making some effort to save it and allow scholars to study it. Discussions on the issue have been prompted by the history of the Dead Sea Scrolls, many of which were purchased from the Bedouin who had illegally found them in the caves around Qumran; it is frequently asked what would happen if such scrolls appeared on the antiquities market today?

In fact, there is something similar that has happened with more than a hundred—or perhaps as many as two hundred—clay tablets that apparently come from an archive that documents the daily life of Jews who were moved to Mesopotamia during the Babylonian Exile in the sixth century BCE and remained there into the fifth century BCE. The tablets appeared on the antiquities market at some point, reportedly after the 1970s, though exactly when is debated. At least half were eventually purchased by a private collector and then published by a pair of scholars, after which they were displayed in an exhibit at the Bible Lands Museum in Jerusalem in early February 2015, from which came a second publication by a different set of scholars.

Even though it is not clear from which site they came, the tablets give its ancient name as "al-yahudu," which, roughly translated, means "Judah-town." They are among the first textual evidence from Mesopotamia confirming that the Babylonian Exile reported in the Bible and elsewhere did take place and what happened to those who were exiled. The tablets are extremely important, but they have no known context and were obviously looted—perhaps from southern Iraq, according to some reports. Should they have been published? Should they have been put on display? In this case, the importance of the texts, like the Dead Sea Scrolls to which they have the best parallel in terms of circumstances of discovery, persuaded at least some scholars that they should be published and displayed, despite the fact that they were apparently looted and acquired illegally. Not all scholars agree; in fact, the Archaeological Institute of America's policy is to refuse to publish articles that describe objects that cannot be clearly demonstrated not to have been looted.

{↔}{↔}

In 1970 UNESCO approved the Convention on the Means of Prohibiting and Preventing the Illicit Import, Export, and Transfer of Ownership of Cultural Property, which was put into effect in April 1972. As a result, any antiquity that is being sold today needs to have valid proof that it was either found before 1970 (or sometimes 1973; that is, after the implementation of the convention) or, if found later, that it was legally exported from its country of origin—in other words, verification that it wasn't looted. Obviously this system is not foolproof and many more objects on the art market are purported to have been found before 1970 than after since the convention took effect, but on the whole, this was a good start (although the convention is now nearly fifty years old and should probably be updated).

Clearly, looting, especially during or in the aftermath of a conflict, is by no means a new problem, but unique situations can sometimes necessitate new laws. Thus, additional legislation is now beginning to be passed, not only about artifacts found in the United States, but also for artifacts found elsewhere and smuggled into the United States.

Lawmakers in the United States have been passing legislation aimed at preserving ancient sites and antiquities for more than a century now. In fact, one of the earliest laws on antiquities was passed during the presidency of Theodore Roosevelt, trying to control the huge trade in looted painted pots and other antiquities illegally dug from graves on Ancestral Pueblo sites in the US Southwest. Known as the American Antiquities Act of 1906, it was aimed at stopping or at least controlling the looting in New Mexico, Arizona, and elsewhere, because sites like Casa Grande in Arizona, which dates to about 1350 CE, were being looted for wooden beams and other ancient remains.

Other laws followed, including the Historic Sites Act of 1935, which gave the National Park Service the right to identify, protect, and preserve cultural property, such as Native American sites or sites from the colonial era. This responsibility of the National Park Service is in part why the National Park Service is the largest employer of professional archaeologists in the United States.

Some of the most important pieces of archaeological legislation have been passed since 1979. These include NAGPRA, which we have discussed in a previous chapter, but also the Archaeological Resources Protection Act (ARPA), which protects archaeological sites on federal land. Anyone who takes artifacts from such a site can be fined up to $20,000 and sent to jail for a year, which will also permanently place a felony on the offender's record. In one instance, federal agents arrested sixteen people in Blanding, Utah, in 2009 for digging Native American artifacts out of nearby federal lands, later charging a total of twenty-four people in the case.

Such legislation has affected everything from the discovery to the excavation to the preservation, conservation, and promotion of archaeological sites. The laws are designed to help, rather than to hinder, archaeologists, and—in fact—along the way they have created innumerable jobs in archaeology, employed by states, cities, and the National Park Service (as we have mentioned) and as cultural resource management archaeologists who often go in just ahead of the bulldozers on construction projects.

Most recently, and looking at current worldwide problems, the US House of Representatives passed legislation in 2015 that makes it illegal in the United States to sell artifacts that have been looted from Syria. That legislation—now referred to as the Protect and Preserve International Cultural Property Act—was approved by the Senate in April 2016 and signed into law by the president on May 9, 2016. Similarly, a memorandum of understanding between the United States and Egypt was signed on November 30, 2016. This will place restrictions on incoming antiquities from Egypt to help curb the ongoing looting in that country.

As far as I am concerned, and I believe that I speak for many of my fellow archaeologists as well, ancient artifacts are part of our collective heritage, and so we can only hope that the new legislation and agreements will help to curtail the looting going on around the world. More can and should be done, from passing legislation to guarding excavated sites and protecting known but unexcavated remains. Those outside the profession can help by not succumbing to the temptation of purchasing an ancient artifact offered in a Middle Eastern market or seen on eBay. Because everything that we excavate, study, and write about took place so long ago, the question that should concern all of us is how we can stem the loss of knowledge about our own shared past before it is too late.

EPILOGUE

BACK TO THE FUTURE

THE CONCEPT OF THE PAST—THAT THERE ARE LAYERS AND layers of civilization and that each culture is in a very real sense built upon the cultures that came before it—is at the very heart of what archaeologists do. As we dig down through layers of dirt, we're not just uncovering objects. We're uncovering our deep connection to the past.

And, of course, someday, *we* will be the past. Our civilization, our culture, will be long gone, and future archaeologists will be uncovering their connections to us. Our iPhones, Barbie dolls, Wal-Mart stores, and McDonald's arches will all be the object of study by future archaeologists. Therefore, I'd like to take this opportunity to look forward into the future and try to address two issues. One is the question of how archaeologists will actually do archaeology in the future—that is, what new tools and techniques they will be using. The other is how archaeologists will interpret us—that is, our society and civilization—in the future. Let's look at this first.

I've been talking about something that I call "future archaeology" ever since I saw two television shows that were made after Alan

Weisman published his best-selling book *The World without Us*. One was shown on the National Geographic Channel and was called *Aftermath: Population Zero*. The other was shown on the History Channel and was called *Life without People*. Both of them looked at what would happen to our cities and monuments in the coming years, if we humans ceased to exist, as did Weisman's original book. The television shows included footage of the Eiffel Tower crumbling, the Space Needle in Seattle coming down, lions roaming the grounds of the White House, and the like.

What would a team of archaeologists find two hundred years from now if all humans (besides the archaeologists themselves) disappeared today? What about in two thousand years? How would they interpret what they find and how would they reconstruct our society?

Leaving aside for the moment all the big administrative buildings, schools, homes, highways, bridges, roads, airports, and so on, what would structures like the Washington Zoo or the Smithsonian museums, or even Starbucks and McDonalds, look like? What would be found in their ruins? Would they be identified properly? That is, would

Statue of Liberty, head

it be obvious that one was once a zoo and one a coffee restaurant? And if they were misidentified, what would archaeologists think that they were?

The zoo might cause a bit of a problem, unless one could still read the signs that were once posted everywhere. It would also depend upon whether all the animals had managed to escape, in which case all the cages would be found empty, or if they had been trapped inside and we found their skeletons. If one found the skeletons and could read the signs, it would be pretty obvious what it once was, but otherwise perhaps not.

The Smithsonian museums, or any large museum for that matter, like the Met in New York City or the Museum of Fine Arts in Boston, will definitely cause problems until it dawns on the archaeologists that they are excavating a museum. Any building that has the Hope Diamond, dinosaurs, and a large whale is sure to cause much confusion and discussion, until they realize that they have been excavating the National Museum of Natural History.

Personally, though, I think it's going to be places like Starbucks and McDonalds that could cause the most confusion. Specifically, I think there is a good chance of misidentifying Starbucks as a religion, complete with a goddess wearing a crown and with flowing locks, and with her shrine or temple located on virtually every block or street corner. The same thing could be said for McDonalds, except in this case the deity being worshipped has a known name—Ronald McDonald—and has red hair and dresses in gaudy clothes. Or maybe we would conclude that these two stand at the head of a pantheon, like Zeus and Hera for the Greeks and Jupiter and Juno for the Romans?

I jest, and yet, if enough relevant records do not survive, those could be the kind of interpretations made by future archaeologists. Already when we're on excavations and find something that we don't immediately understand, we half-jokingly call it cultic or religious.

Future archaeology is interesting to think about, especially since we spend so much time looking at previously vanished cultures and don't usually consider what our culture is going to look like to future archaeologists. Consider, for instance, the fact that so many of our interactions are now online. Most of those interactions will vanish without a trace or will be inaccessible to future archaeologists, and so what will they conclude about our rate of literacy, for instance? And, if they find that things halted suddenly, just like they did in Pompeii back in 79 CE, what will they think about the ubiquitous rectangular blobs of metal, plastic, glass, and circuitry that seem to be associated with every skeleton, including many that are found clutched in someone's hand? Will they have any idea that these once were communication devices?

A similar thought experiment was already undertaken back in 1979, when David Macaulay published a great short illustrated book called *Motel of the Mysteries*. The premise of the book is this: Life in North America is basically extinguished in a single day in 1985. Then, in the year 4022 CE, amateur archaeologist Howard Carson accidentally stumbles upon an ancient site, which turns out to be the Motel of the Mysteries. He then brings in a team to help him, including an assistant named Harriet Burton.

Obviously, "Howard Carson" is based on Howard Carter, and his assistant "Harriet Burton" is based on the real-life Harry Burton, who was an Egyptologist and the photographer during Carter's very real excavation of King Tut's tomb. Macaulay has a lot of fun with references to the discovery of King Tut's tomb, including the famous phrase that Carter, or rather Carson in this case, utters—namely that he sees "wonderful things." As it turns out, though he doesn't realize it, he has not discovered a tomb, although he does find two skeletons. Instead, he has found what we—the knowing readers—recognize is actually a motel room.

The misinterpretations of what they find are hysterical and include many inside archaeological jokes, but it also illustrates what I just said a moment ago—that if we don't know what something is, we often think it might be religious. Thus, in the so-called "Outer Chamber," Macaulay's Howard Carson finds everything facing "the Great Altar," including the body that is still lying on top of the "Ceremonial Platform" and is still holding in its hand "the Sacred Communicator." Of course, we recognize these: the "Great Altar" is none other than a television set; the "Ceremonial Platform" is just a bed; and the "Sacred Communicator" is the remote control for the television set. And yet, in this setting, two thousand years after the fact and with nothing else to go on, Howard Carson interprets all this as religious.

Macaulay tops it all off by having Harriet Burton put on and proudly wear the "Sacred Headband" and "Sacred Collar" that were still in place on the "Sacred Urn" when they found them. The accompanying illustration makes it quite clear that she is, in fact, wearing a toilet seat around her neck as the "Sacred Collar," and it is the strip of paper that says "sanitized for your protection" that is wrapped around her head as the "Sacred Headband." Two toothbrushes are dangling from her ears as "plastic ear ornaments" and she is wearing the rubber stopper for the bathtub drain as an "exquisite silver chain and pendant." Even better, the drawing is a dead ringer for the famous photograph that Heinrich Schliemann took of his wife, Sophia, when she was wearing all the jewelry from Priam's Treasure that he found at Troy.

This is what it may come to when someone in the future excavates Starbucks, McDonalds, museums, zoos, and possibly even motels from our time. All humor aside, it is worthwhile thinking about the fact that our current culture may be wildly misinterpreted by future archaeologists and that we may occasionally, or perhaps even often, misinterpret the past. That is an occupational hazard, but usually—once enough data is found—we come to a scholarly consensus about the proper interpretation of a building or a site or even a civilization.

✣✦✣✦✣

And what about how archaeologists will actually *do* archaeology in the future—that is, what new tools and techniques will they be using? Of course, we have absolutely no way of knowing the answer, just as Heinrich Schliemann and Howard Carter could not have predicted the use of remote-sensing techniques that have now been employed at both Troy and King Tut's tomb.

I suspect that there will continue to be advances in technology, which will allow us to peer even more easily beneath the earth, or beneath the tree canopies in Central America and Cambodia, before we begin digging. For instance, I am absolutely convinced, and have been saying for years, that there must be a better way to conduct remote sensing. Apart from LiDAR, most of the techniques that we are using, such as magnetometers, resistivity, and so on, are now decades old. It is time for new advances. In fact, advances are already beginning to happen in some cases; for example, fluxgate gradiometers and cesium magnetometers have replaced proton magnetometers on some projects. As we have said before, using remote sensing can minimize the need for digging. Since archaeology is destruction, that would allow us to potentially destroy less and to do more work before ever breaking ground.

I wonder, for instance, whether in the future it might be possible to detect things like plaster or other specific materials through a layer of earth, just as we can now detect buried walls and ditches. Could some of the techniques being used by the Transportation Security Administration in airports, for example, to catch drug runners and explosives, be repurposed to detect chemical compounds that would belong to artifacts still buried in the earth? And would it make sense to partner with gas and oil exploration companies, to utilize new techniques that might allow us to peer deeper into the depths of a mound, or to do so in a series of slices, at specific depths? I do think that the time is ripe for another series of technological breakthroughs, but I think it is also a matter of talking to the right engineering people, perhaps someone who would say, "Wait, you want to do what? Oh yeah, we can do that, no problem."

I also think that we will see new analytical techniques coming from chemistry, biology, and especially DNA studies, such as are happening already. Conservation techniques also should continue to improve, so that we can preserve more of what we find. Above all, there should be greater sensitivity to community needs and community goals for archaeology and an increase in collaborative projects between archaeologists and local communities, so that the people whose heritage is being explored have a greater say in what happens to the artifacts of that heritage.

I also think that it is fairly safe to say that the actual process of physically digging—that is excavating with picks, shovels, trowels, and dental tools—will continue as it has since the very first days of archaeology. The number of ways that one can dig carefully and yet quickly, without destroying the remains, is limited. Still, I could be surprised, for some new digging techniques may be invented that I cannot even begin to imagine at the moment. What will not change is the archaeological axiom that the best things on a dig are always found on the last day of the excavation season . . . and almost always in the balk.

※※ ※※

In my office at George Washington University, in addition to the book on Schliemann that my mother gave me twice, I also have two bumper stickers pasted on the wall. The first one says simply "Archaeology: I'd rather be digging." The second one says "Archaeologist. The coolest job on Earth. I save the past, what do you do?" Just as bumper stickers should, they encapsulate my feelings about archaeology in a nutshell—I really *would* rather be digging. But they also issue a challenge to the rest of the world. Archaeology is not only about finding the remains that have been left from past civilizations. It's also about preserving and curating those remains for future generations. I hope that this book lends itself, even in some small way, to that aim.

ACKNOWLEDGMENTS

T HIS BOOK WOULD NOT EVEN BE POSSIBLE WERE IT NOT FOR the efforts of all the archaeologists who have come before me and whose work I am describing here. I am proud to be part of a long and distinguished academic discipline, working in a field that is of interest to so many people.

Along those lines, I'd like to thank all the students who have taken my Introduction to Archaeology course at George Washington University—usually close to 140 every fall semester for each of the past fifteen years—and all the students who have come digging with me over the years at Megiddo and Tel Kabri. This is especially dedicated to all those who have majored in archaeology with me as their advisor—more than 150 so far.

I'd also like to thank a few specific people, first and foremost of whom is Rob Tempio, my editor at Princeton University Press, who suggested that I write this book and provided thoughtful guidance throughout the creative process. Rob is more than my editor; I am proud to call him my friend as well. Second, I'd like to thank Glynnis Fawkes, a superb artist and wonderful archaeological illustrator, whose drawings can be found throughout this book, and Michele Angel, who drew the fabulous maps. I also would like to thank Shaquona Crews, Scot Kuehm, Ryan Mulligan, and everyone else at Princeton University Press who has helped this book to see the light of day. I would especially like to thank Mitchell Allen and Jill Rubalcaba, who individually went through the final drafts of the manuscript with a fine-toothed comb, offering suggestions and erudite edits, as well as Peter Cooper, William Dardis, Randy Helm, Daniel Reynoso, Dan Rubalcaba, Jim West,

Cassandra Wiseman, and several anonymous peer reviewers, all of whom read and made suggestions on all or portions of the manuscript in its various earlier drafts, improving it immeasurably.

Last, but by no means least, I'd like to thank my family—my parents, Martin and Evelyn, for allowing me to indulge my passion while I was growing up; my children, Hannah and Joshua, for allowing me to continue indulging it while they were growing up; and most especially my wife, Diane, for putting up with me and all of this for so long.

NOTES

PREFACE
A PETRIFIED MONKEY'S PAW

xi *When I was seven years old* Braymer 1960.

finding lost cities in the jungle Ceram 1951, 1967; Stephens 1962; see also Ceram 1958, 1966.

xiii *the oldest and largest wine cellar* Assaf Yasur-Landau of the University of Haifa and I are codirectors of the dig; Andrew Koh of Brandeis University is associate director.

xiv *made all the papers* See Jaggard 2014; Lemonick 2014b; Levitan 2013; McIntyre 2014; Naik 2013; Netburn 2013; Wilford 2013. The actual publication of our findings (Koh, Yasur-Landau, and Cline 2014) can be found in the journal *PLoS ONE*, available online: http://journals.plos.org/plosone/article?id=10.1371/journal.pone.0106406.

xv *on a single day in early June 2016* Media reports appearing on June 2, 2016: Hatem 2016; Moye 2016; Rabinovitch 2016; Romey 2016; Smith 2016; Steinbuch 2016; Weber 2016; also http://www.archaeology.org/news/4507-160602-archaeologists-return-to-the-judean-desert; http://www.inquisitr.com/3161047/new-archaeology-discovery-2000-year-old-roman-military-barracks-will-be-viewed-by-subway-riders-video/; http://www.archaeology.org/news/4503-160601-london-writing-tablet; https://www.washingtonian.com/2016/06/02/things-to-do-in-dc-this-weekend-june-2-5/. The actual title of the published scholarly analysis of Tut's dagger was a bit more subdued: "The Meteoritic Origin of Tutankhamun's Iron Dagger Blade"—see Comelli, D'Orazio, Folco, El-Halwagy, Frizzi, Alberti, Capogrosso et al. 2016.

Within a week Dunston 2016.

xvi *I warned the general public* Cline 2007b.

great architectural masterpieces I said this previously in Cline 2015: 620–21; see also Killgrove 2015b. For good discussions debunking such pseudo-archaeology, see Fagan 2006; Feder 2010, 2013; Stiebing 1984.

stretching from Greece to Peru   Curry 2015; Dubrow 2014; Mueller 2016; Romano 2015; Romey 2015; Vance 2015.

the scale of the destruction   Lange 2008.

xvii   *the head of UNESCO*   Neuendorf 2015.

loss of our heritage   Binkovitz 2013; Blumenthal and Mashberg 2015.

xviii   *long-lost ancient sites and civilizations*   Other authors have previously discussed many of the same topics, sites, and archaeologists, of course; I find the various books written or edited by Brian Fagan and by Paul Bahn to be among the most useful and accessible. Relevant volumes are Bahn 1995, 1996a, b, c, 1999, 2000, 2001, 2003, 2007, 2008, 2009, 2014; Bahn and Cunliffe 2000; Bahn and Renfrew 1996; Catling and Bahn 2010; Fagan 1994, 1996, 2001, 2003, 2004a, b, 2007a, b, 2014; Fagan and Durrani 2014, 2016; Renfrew and Bahn 2012, 2015; see also Hunt 2007; Pollard 2007.

PROLOGUE
"WONDERFUL THINGS":
KING TUT AND HIS TOMB

1   *I see wonderful things*   Carter and Mace 1977: 95–96. See also Carter 2010; Pollard 2007: 134–41; Snape in Bahn 1995: 32–35.

2   *seventeen more years*   Shaer 2014; http://www.nbcnews.com/science/science -news/tut-tut-new-view-king-tutankhamun-sparks-debate-n239166.

the bite of a mosquito   On Hatshepsut, see Cooney 2015; Tyldesley 1998. On Thutmose III, see Cline and O'Connor 2006; Gabriel 2009. On Akhenaten, see Aldred 1991; Redford 1987. On Nefertiti, see Tyldesley 2005. See also Dodson 2009 and 2014 on the periods both immediately preceding and following Tut.

most likely Tut's parents   Reeves 1990: 44–46. Many of the details about the tomb and its contents presented below are based on Reeves's excellent book. See also Allen 2006; Reeves and Wilkinson 1996: 122–27. The most recent discussion of the two men and their discoveries is by Fagan 2015.

3   *an automobile accident*   According to Carter's diaries, http://www.griffith .ox.ac.uk/gri/4sea1not.html.

the first step   According to Carter's diaries, http://www.griffith.ox.ac.uk/gri /4sea1not.html.

written in the telegram   See the entry in Carter's diary at http://www.griffith .ox.ac.uk/gri/4sea1not.html; also Reeves 1990: 44–46; Reeves and Wilkinson 1996: 122–27.

4   *the Antechamber*   Ibid. See also Carter's diary at http://www.griffith.ox.ac .uk/gri/4sea1not.html.

dark flint and chert chips   Carter and Mace 1977: 95–96. See also Carter 2010.

Can you see anything?   See Carter's diaries, http://www.griffith.ox.ac.uk/gri/4sea1not.html.

5   *chariots glinting with gold*   See Carter's diaries, http://www.griffith.ox.ac.uk/gri/4sea1not.html.

   ended the entry   Reeves and Wilkinson 1996: 122–27.

   the remains of a knotted scarf   http://www.griffith.ox.ac.uk/gri/4sea1no2.html.

6   *Opened sealed doorway*   http://www.nytimes.com/learning/general/onthis day/big/0216.html#article.

7   *a gold death mask*   http://www.griffith.ox.ac.uk/discoveringTut/journals-and-diaries/season-4/journal.html.

   Today has been a great day   http://www.griffith.ox.ac.uk/discoveringTut/journals-and-diaries/season-4/journal.html.

   a CT-scan study of Tut's mummy   Hawass 2005: 263–72; http://press.national geographic.com/2005/03/07/tutankhamun-ct-scan-results-issued-march-7 –2005-by-the-egyptian-supreme-council-of-antiquities/; http://news.bbc.co.uk /2/hi/science/nature/4328903.stm.

   perhaps he fell from his chariot   King and Cooper 2006.

   Tut's facial features   Handwerk 2005.

8   *a variety of physical ailments*   Shaer 2014; http://www.nbcnews.com/science /science-news/tut-tut-new-view-king-tutankhamun-sparks-debate-n239166.

   new DNA studies   Hawass 2010: 34–59; see also Hawass et al. 2010: 638–47.

   perhaps even in a tomb   See Keys 2015; Martin 2015; Reeves 2014.

   a nearby replica   Reeves 2015b: 1; see http://www.highres.factum-arte.org /Tutankhamun/.

   moisture from their breathing   Del Giudice 2014; Neild 2014.

9   *the body of Nefertiti*   Reeves 2015a, b.

   A second set of scans   See Borger 2016; Ghose 2015; Hessler 2015, 2016a, b; Jarus 2016; Strauss 2015; also http://www.archaeology.org/news/4269–160317 -tutankhamun-tomb-scan.

CHAPTER 1
ASHES TO ASHES IN ANCIENT ITALY

13   *too fragile to unroll*   Wade 2015b.

14   *writing on the scrolls*   Mocella et al. 2015.

   the ink is also carbon-based   Wade 2015b.

   small amounts of lead   Van Gilder Cooke 2016; see also http://popular -archaeology.com/issue/winter-2015–2016/article/metallic-ink-used-in-the -herculaneum-scrolls.

   Livy's History of Rome   Jaggard 2015; Seabrook 2015; Urbanus 2015; Wade 2015b. Similar techniques are now being used on carbonized scrolls that have been found elsewhere, such as at Elephantine in Egypt and En Gedi in Israel. See Estrin 2016; Gannon 2016; Seales, Parker, Segal, Tov, Shor, and Porath 2016.

ancient pieces of marble   Bahn 1995: 122–25; Bahn 1996b: 154–59; Fagan and Durrani 2014: 27; Pollard 2007: 16–21.

15   *artifacts from Herculaneum and Pompeii*   See the entries on Winckelmann in Fagan 2003: 22–25 and Fagan 2014: 42–45. See also Fagan and Durrani 2014: 10–14 for a good discussion, and definitions, of the types of archaeology, including prehistoric, classical, biblical, underwater, forensic, historical, and industrial, as well as Egyptology, Assyriology, and bioarchaeology.

even more died in Herculaneum   There are many, many, many books written about Pompeii and Herculaneum. Among the best are Beard 2010; Berry 2007; Cooley and Cooley 2013; Ellis 2011; Grant 1980, 2005.

16   *they would eventually have been crushed*   Translation available at http://www .gutenberg.org/files/2811/2811-h/2811-h.htm.

17   *the lost wax method*   In the lost wax method, a sculptor creates a statue in wax, then encases it in a harder material and heats it up so that the wax melts and runs out a hole in the bottom. This leaves a cavity in the exact shape of the wax within the harder material, into which molten bronze can then be poured, which creates the same shape in metal as had been originally in wax.

loaves of bread   Stewart 2006.

18   *the so-called Resin Lady*   Clinton 2013; Glover 2013; Griffiths 2015b; Sheldon 2014.

people of all ages   Povoledo 2015; Woollaston 2015.

in the Philippines   http://volcanoes.usgs.gov/hazards/lahar/ruiz.php; http:// pubs.usgs.gov/of/2001/ofr-01-0276/.

doors, beds, and a cradle   http://www.herculaneum.ox.ac.uk/files/newsletters /harchissue1.pdf.

19   *frozen in positions of agony*   Mastrolorenzo et al. 2001.

an entire vineyard   Jashemski 1979, 2014.

the primary residents   See, e.g., Gates 2011: 356–67; MacKendrick 1960: 196–223.

20   *on the street side*   Fuller 2014.

21   *leg joint of a giraffe*   Ibid.

while still at the site   See http://classics.uc.edu/pompeii/index.php/news /1-latest/142-ipads2010.html, http://www.macworld.com/article/1154717/ipad _archeology_pompeii.html, and https://www.macstories.net/ipad/apple-profiles -researchers-using-ipads-in-pompeii/.

the religious cult   Gates 2011: 365–67; see also http://www.stoa.org/diotima /essays/seaford.shtml.

two thousand years ago   The following examples are taken from Lewis and Reinhold 1990: 236–38, 276–78.

23   *clean their clothes*   Kumar 2013.

CHAPTER 2
DIGGING UP TROY

24 *at any moment*   Described by Schliemann in his book, *Troy and Its Remains* (Schliemann 1875); quoted by Traill 1995: 111. I have written about this previously, in Cline 2013: 76–80.

25 *elsewhere in the world*   Schliemann 1881: 453–54, with illustrations and further discussion on subsequent pages. See also the list of items in Traill 1995: 111–12, with quotations from the original notebooks, letters, and other relevant records; and Cline 2013: 76–80.

   repeated in exquisite detail   Ceram 1967: 41–45; see also Mee in Bahn 1995: 98–99; Pollard 2007: 78–83.

   the Epic Cycle   There are many translations of the *Iliad*; see, for instance, Fagles 1991. For a translation of the Epic Cycle, see Evelyn-White 1914. The story is also briefly recapitulated in Cline 2013.

26 *part of a much larger catastrophe*   See discussions in Cline 2013, 2014.

   early in his career   Schliemann 1881: 3. See, e.g., Traill 1985, 1995: 4–5; also Cline 2013: 72–73.

28 *the location of ancient Troy*   Allen 1999.

29 *No respectable archaeologist today*   See the relevant articles on Schliemann's discovery of the treasure in Traill 1993, among other discussions, including Traill 1983 and 1984, but especially Fitton 2012. See also Cline 2013: 76–80; Rose 1993.

30 *all in one place*   See the relevant articles on Schliemann's discovery of the treasure in Traill 1983, 1984, 1993; also discussions in Easton 1981, 1984a, b, 1994, and 1995, as well as Traill 1999, 2000.

   claim it as reparation   See the discussions by Meyer, Rose, and Hoffman in *Archaeology* 46/6 (1993); also Easton 1995; Goldmann, Agar, and Urice 1999; Meyer 1995; and Traill 1995: 300–01.

31 *The Hittites*   Sayce 1890. See also previous brief discussions in Cline 2013: 30–33, 2014: 33–35.

32 *a Czech orientalist named Bedřich Hrozný*   Hrozný 1917.

   especially the Egyptians and the Assyrians   On the Hittites, see especially the overviews by Bryce 2002, 2005, 2012; Collins 2007. See also Ceram 1955.

   the probable time of the Trojan War   See full discussion in Cline 2013: 54–68.

34 *immortalized by Homer*   Wilford 1993a.

35 *not everyone agrees*   Cline 2013: 98; Jablonka 1994; Korfmann 2004: 38; Latacz 2004: 22–37; Wilford 1993b. Note that some of the material in this chapter is similar to that which I have previously published in Cline 2013 and 2014. There also are dozens, if not hundreds, of other volumes available on Troy and the Trojan War; among the best are Bryce 2006; Latacz 2004; Strauss 2006; Thomas and Conant 2005; Wood 1996; and, for young adults, Rubalcaba and Cline 2011.

the Late Bronze Age   Becker and Jansen 1994: 105–14; Bryce 2006: 62; Bryce 2010: 478; Easton et al. 2002: 82; Korfmann 2004: 38; Korfmann 2007: 24; Latacz 2004: 22–24, 73; Shanks 2002: 29.

36   inside the walls of the city   Cline 2013: 99–10; Korfmann 2004.

back in the 1950s   Easton 2010; Schachermeyr 1950.

a large marble head of Augustus   Kunnen-Jones 2002; Reilly 2004; Rose 2014: 226, 249–50.

CHAPTER 3
FROM EGYPT TO ETERNITY

38   by amateur enthusiasts   Recent articles about such claims or beliefs include Kaufman 2016; Killgrove 2015a.

39   often-dubious claims   The following publications also will provide clear and accurate information about the archaeology of ancient Egypt, including further details on the topics discussed in this chapter: Bard 2008; Kemp 2005; Lehner and Wilkinson 1997; Robins 2008; Silverman 2003; Wilkinson 2013.

Giovanni Battista Belzoni   Fagan 2004b: 65–128. On the history of Egyptology up until 1881, see Thompson 2015.

one of the first   Fagan 2004b: 98–104. See the entry on Belzoni by Garry J. Shaw in Fagan 2014: 46–50; also Pollard 2007: 40–43.

the foundations of modern Egyptology   Fagan 2004b: 177–81; Reid 2002: 44–46; Thompson 2015: 198–207; see also the entry on Lepsius by Garry J. Shaw in Fagan 2014: 51–55.

the Egyptian Museum in Cairo   Fagan 2004b: 181–91; Thompson 2015: 223–82; see also the entry on Mariette by Garry J. Shaw in Fagan 2014: 56–61.

40   before Lepsius and Mariette   Fagan 2004b: 47–56; Reid 2002: 31–36; Thompson 2015: 97–103.

after the inscription had been found   Fagan 2004b: 157–70; Reid 2002: 40–44; Robinson 2012; see also Pollard 2007: 44–47; Snape in Bahn 1995: 40–41.

41   did not know how to read or write   Bard 2008: 25–33.

42   pharaohs of the Fourth Dynasty   On Egyptian chronology and dates, see, e.g., Bard 2008: 36–55.

droughts and famine   See, e.g., Weiss 2012.

43   the entire Bronze Age world   Cline 2014.

44   happens to be a chicken   On mummification and the specific details discussed in the following paragraphs, see, e.g., Andrews 1984; Hamilton-Paterson and Andrews 1978.

45   removing the brain   Jarus 2012.

until the mummy was unwrapped   Andrews 1984: 29.

46   *dental problems*   See, e.g., Carrington 2014; Griffiths 2015a; Hawass and Saleem 2015;   also   http://www.historyextra.com/feature/secret-lives-ancient-egyptians -revealed-ct-scans-mummies.

calcified plaque   Griffiths 2015a.

no actual remains   Anyangwe 2015; Morelle 2015; Robinson and Millner 2015.

ancient aliens   On the pyramids and the specific details discussed in the following paragraphs, see especially Lehner and Wilkinson 1997.

47   *built in stages or steps*   Stiebing 2009: 136–37.

can't be seen anymore   Brier and Houdin 2009.

48   *International Space Station*   See   http://www.universetoday.com/93398/can -you-see-the-pyramids-from-space/.

mention his name   See, e.g., http://www.pbs.org/wgbh/nova/ancient/who -built-the-pyramids.html.

49   *four shifts per year*   See also http://www.pbs.org/wgbh/nova/ancient/who -built-the-pyramids.html, where Lehner mentions three, rather than four, shifts.

well treated   See, e.g., Lehner and Wilkinson 1997.

surrounding the pyramids   For more information, see Lehner and Wilkinson 1997 and others, including Bard 2008: 137–40.

50   *modern Egyptologists*   Bard 2008: 141–42.

51   *thermal data*   See Lorenzi 2016a, b.

the Great Pyramid   See Hatem 2016; Lorenzi 2016c. On efforts by University of Texas physicists at a Maya pyramid in Belize, see the home page of the Maya Muon Research Group led by Professor Roy Schwitters: http://www.hep .utexas.edu/mayamuon/.

television specials   See the abstract booklet from the 67th Annual Meeting (2016) at http://www.arce.org/files/user/page157/ARCE_2016_Abstract_Booklet .pdf.

CHAPTER 4
MYSTERIES IN MESOPOTAMIA

52   *the best husband*   See *Time*, "Books: Dame Agatha: Queen of the Maze," January 26, 1976. In that article, she is cited as having pronounced this on the occasion of her twenty-fifth wedding anniversary. Available online for *Time* subscribers at http://content.time.com/time/subscriber/article/0,33009,913961 –2,00.html. For the book that accompanied the exhibit at the British Museum, see Trümpler 2001.

53   *Lady Katharine*   Christie 2011; see also http://bjrichards.blogspot.com /2013/01/more-deadly-than-male-life-of-katharine_4954.html. She also wrote about their life while on excavation, to answer questions posed by friends upon their return; see Mallowan 2012. See also Trümpler 2001.

Ur of the Chaldees   Lloyd 1980b: 43–56; Moorey 1982. See also Larsen 1996; Roux 1992.

54   *a small percentage of the graves*   Zettler and Horne 1998: 14–19, 21–23.

the pit outside   Zettler and Horne 1998: 22–25; see also Edens in Bahn 1995: 142–43; Edens in Bahn 1996c: 68–71; Pollard 2007: 128–33.

some of those people   Zettler and Horne 1998: 22–25; see also Edens in Bahn 1996c: 68–71; Pollard 2007: 128–33.

55   *the British Museum and the Louvre*   See Lloyd 1980a for a good overview, as well as Fagan 2007b and Larsen 1996 for much more detailed, and easily accessible, discussions of early archaeologists in Mesopotamia, to which the following pages owe much; see also http://www.britishmuseum.org/explore /highlights/highlight_objects/me/c/colossal_winged_bull.aspx; and http://www .britishmuseum.org/explore/highlights/highlight_objects/me/c/colossal_statue _of_winged_lion.aspx.

decipher cuneiform   Bahn 2008: 26; Fagan 2003: 55–57; Fagan 2007b: 79–93; Larsen 1996: 79–87, 178–88, 215–27, 293–305, 333–37; Lloyd 1980a: 14, 75–78; and the entry on Rawlinson by Andrew Robinson in Fagan 2014: 183–85.

56   *Rawlinson himself*   Fagan 2003: 55–57; Fagan 2007b: 90–92; Lloyd 1980a: 14, 75–78.

another twenty years   See Bahn 2008: 26; Fagan 2003: 55–57; Fagan 2007b: 79–93; Larsen 1996: 79–87, 178–88, 215–27, 293–305, 333–37; Lloyd 1980a: 14, 75–78; and the entry on Rawlinson by Andrew Robinson in Fagan 2014: 183–85.

back in France   Lloyd 1980a: 94–98; Lloyd 1980b: 35. See also Edens in Bahn 1995: 150–51; Fagan 2007b: 97–107; Larsen 1996: 3–33.

57   *Dur Sharrukin*   Ibid.

other ancient cities   Fagan 2003: 45–46, 51–54; Fagan 2007b: 109–15; Larsen 1996: 34–69; Lloyd 1980a: 15–16, 87–94; Oates and Oates 2001: 2–6; and the entry on Layard by Joan Oates in Fagan 2014: 68–71; see also Edens in Bahn 1995: 150–51; Pollard 2007: 48–53.

among his supplies   Fagan 2007b: 109–23. See also Larsen 1996: 70–78, 88–98, 115–24.

endless inscriptions   Quoted in Lloyd 1980a: 101.

a total of thirty workers   Fagan 2007b: 115–23; Larsen 1996: 88–124; Lloyd 1980a: 101–3.

58   *in the Mosul Museum*   El-Ghobashy 2015.

rather than Nineveh   Fagan 2007b: 131, 134–36; Layard 1849; Oates and Oates 2001: 6.

three hundred workers   Fagan 2007b: 136–44; Larsen 1996: 196–235, 255–74.

59   *moved the Assyrian capital*   Fagan 2007b: 136–44; Larsen 1996: 196–235, 255–74; Lloyd 1980a: 125–29; Russell 1991: 1.

on deep Galilee   Byron 1815, http://www.poetryfoundation.org/poem/173083.

in Sennacherib's reliefs   Ussishkin 1984, 1987, 1988. See also Ussishkin 2014.

60   *any way, shape, or form*   Bleibtreu 1990, 1991.

colossal winged bulls and lion-sphinxes   Quoted in Lloyd 1980b: 33; also in Fagan 2014: 71 and Lloyd 1980a: 125.

today's standards   Fagan 2007b: xi.

61   *two hundred workers*   Fagan 2007b: 106–7; Larsen 1996: 32; Lloyd 1980b: 36; Parrot 1955: 40–41.

back to England   Fagan 2007b: 123–31; Larsen 1996: 125–32.

sent to France   Fagan 2007b: 183–85; Larsen 1996: 344–49; Lloyd 1980a: 98, 130–31, 134, 140; Lloyd 1980b: 32–33, 36; Parrot 1955: 42.

62   *most appalling disasters*   Lloyd 1980b: 32–33, 36.

on their finds   Fagan 2007b: 173–83; Larsen 1996: 315–32; Lloyd 1980a: 138–39.

the British Museum   Fagan 2007b: 181; Lloyd 1980a: 126.

from all over the empire   Lloyd 1980a: 98, 135–39; Lloyd 1980b: 31.

63   *the Epic of Gilgamesh*   A good translation of the *Epic of Gilgamesh* was published by George in 2003.

the missing piece   Lloyd 1980a: 146–47; Oates and Oates 2001: 8–9; Russell 1991: 4.

64   *began translating it*   Finkel 2014a, b; Moss 2014.

everything in between   See, e.g., Kramer 1988; Roux 1992.

other than their own   For an overview and collection of relevant bibliography, see Moro-Abadía 2006: 4–17. See also especially Gosden 2001, 2004; Meskell 1998; Silberman 1989; and Trigger 1984.

65   *safely recovered*   See Hussein 2016; Luhnow 2003; Oates in Fagan 2007a: 66–69. See also http://news.nationalgeographic.com/news/2003/06/photogalleries /nimrud/photo3.html.

CHAPTER 5
EXPLORING THE JUNGLES OF CENTRAL AMERICA

66   *hidden by the overgrowth*   See Chase et al. 2010, 2011, 2012, 2014.

data points   Fagan and Durrani 2014: 136.

67   *or even years*   See Wilford 2010; also http://www.archaeology.org/news/2443 –140818-mexico-yucatan-maya-cities-rediscovered (quote); http://news.national geographic.com/news/2010/05/photogalleries/100520-ancient-maya-city -belize-science-pictures/.

the Maya site of Palenque   Stephens 1949, 2: 245–46. See also the discussion in Stuart and Stuart 2008: 35–63.

68   *the ruins of Paestum*   Stephens 1949, 2: 247.

previously unknown   Stephens 1949, 1962.

New World archaeology   See the introduction in Koch 2013: 1–8. See also the introductions written by Victor Wolfgang von Hagen and published in the reprints of Stephens's volumes by the University of Oklahoma Press (1962; 1970), as well as Glassman 2003; Koch 2013; and von Hagen 1947. See also the recent publication by Carlsen 2016.

discovered King Tut   Koch 2013: 1.

Europe and the Middle East   See the entry on Stephens and Catherwood by Michael D. Coe in Fagan 2014: 63–67; also Pollard 2007: 54–57.

fame and fortune   Republished as Stephens 1970.

life-threatening   See also Carlsen 2016: 158–59, 257–61, 325–26 for comments on, and descriptions of, these various ailments.

69   *not very distant progenitors*   Stephens 1949, 2: 368–74; quotation taken from 2: 373–74. See also Carlsen 2016: x–xi, 231–33, 284–88, 358–62 on Stephens's comments in favor of construction by the local inhabitants both here and at other Maya sites; also the brief discussion of the previous explorers of Copán by Koch 2013: 98–99.

Who shall read them?   Stephens 1949, 1: 123–25.

will be discovered   Stephens 1949, 2: 386. Quoted also in Koch 2013: 6.

70   *bitter rivals*   Coe 2012.

so few left today   See the entry on these three scholars—Thompson, Proskouriakoff, and Knorosov—by Michael D. Coe in Fagan 2014: 191–95; also Stone in Bahn 1995: 218–19.

nearly forty years   See http://www.unc.edu/news/archives/jan07/maya010907 .htm; Stuart and Stuart 1977; Stuart and Stuart 1993.

both a MacArthur and a Guggenheim   See https://www.macfound.org/fellows /214/. See also Coe 2012 and the similarly titled documentary, "Breaking the Maya Code," of which portions are available on YouTube, as well as the entry on Maya writing by David Stuart in Fagan 2007a: 242–43; also Stone in Bahn 1995: 218–19. Note also the bibliography listing for Stuart in Houston, Mazariegos, and Stuart 2001.

71   *cycle of time*   Lyon-House 2012; Stuart 2011.

the high point   Fash 2001; Koch 2013: 129; Stuart 2011: 275–78 and Appendix 5; http://whc.unesco.org/en/list/129.

72   *far more time*   Carlsen 2016: 122–24; Koch 2013: 123–25; Stephens 1949, 1: 98–99.

inhabited the city   Stephens 1949, 1: 110–11.

"Teotihuacán hieroglyphs"   Coe 2005: 115; Fash 2001: 129, 139–50; and Carlsen 57–65 (for a lengthy description and discussion of their entire time at Copan).

73   *put to death*   See http://www.socialstudiesforkids.com/articles/worldhistory /mayanballgame.htm. For a recent scholarly treatment, see Blomster 2012: 8020–25.

in the mid-1930s   Hammond 1982: 46–48; Koch 2013: 130; see also the entry on Alfred Maudslay by Norman Hammond in Fagan 2014: 78–82.

74   *the first large archaeological project*   Koch 2013: 154; Stephens 1949, 2: 163–66.

a UNESCO World Heritage Site   http://whc.unesco.org/en/list/64; http://www.tikalnationalpark.org; Bahn 2009: 136–37; Coe 2005: 122–25; Stuart and Stuart 1977: 52. See also Harrison 1999.

its drinking water   Coe 2005: 124–25; http://www.tikalnationalpark.org; http://www.mayan-traveler.com/tikal-elmirador-flores-copan.php; http://www.utexas.edu/cofa/art/347/maya_tikal.html; http://mesoweb.com/encyc/index.asp?passcall=rightframeexact&rightframeexact=http%3A//mesoweb.com/encyc/view.asp%3Fact%3Dviewexact%26view%3Dnormal%26word%3DI%26wordAND%3DJasaw+Chan+Kawiil.

people from Atlantis   Koch 2013: 82–84, 91–95; Stuart and Stuart 2008: 35–63.

75   *the indigenous Maya*   See Carlsen 2016: x–xi, 231–33, 284–88, 358–62 (on Stephens's arguments against influence from Atlanteans, Egyptians, Phoenicians, or others).

what eventually happened   Carlsen 2016: 245–60; Koch 2013: 162–70; Stephens 1949, 2: 288–90.

while Mr. Catherwood was drawing   Stephens 1949, 2: 288; Stone in Bahn 1995: 216–17.

exactly thirty years after   Koch 2013: 167–68; also Cortez in Bahn 1996c: 126–29; Fagan and Durrani 2014: 333; Stone in Bahn 1995: 216–17.

76   *Alberto Ruz Lhuillier*   Stuart and Stuart 2008: 6–7; also Cortez in Bahn 1996c: 126–29; Fagan and Durrani 2014: 333; Stone in Bahn 1995: 216–17.

Pacal descending to the underworld   This has been featured in an episode of the television show *Ancient Aliens*, which discusses whether this scene shows Pacal piloting a space ship; see episode one of season four (2012).

other jade objects   Stone in Bahn 1995: 216–17; Stuart and Stuart 2008: 11–12, 92–98.

Palenque was declared   http://whc.unesco.org/en/list/411.

new buildings and burials   Stuart and Stuart 2008: 12, 22, 74–105, 182–84.

Pacal's wife   Stuart in Fagan 2007a: 94–97.

77   *the two-volume set*   Koch 2013: 178–81; Stephens 1949, vols. 1–2.

the Yucatán peninsula   Carlsen 2016: 331–39; Koch 2013: 188–244; Stephens 1962, vols. 1–2.

group of newcomers   Coe 2005: 188–89, with references.

78   *earlier Maya structures*   Bahn 2009: 144–45; Coe 2005: 179–90; Koch 2013: 225–30.

almost another century   Bahn 2009: 144–45; http://whc.unesco.org/en/list/483.

the dark well beneath   Stephens 1962: chapters 16 and 17 (also available online at http://www.gutenberg.org/files/33130/33130-h/33130-h.htm#div1_17).

later Toltec manufacture   Coe 2005: 188–89, with references.

79   *overpopulation and deforestation*   Coe 2005: 161; see also (in some cases, with a large grain of salt) Ghose 2014; Mott 2012; Moyer 2014; Stromberg 2012; http://popular-archaeology.com/issue/summer-2015/article/classic-ancient-maya-collapse-not-caused-by-overpopulation-and-deforestation-say-researchers; http://science.nasa.gov/science-news/science-at-nasa/2009/06oct_maya/.

DIGGING DEEPER 1:
HOW DO YOU KNOW
WHERE TO DIG?

80   *an already-known site*   For concise discussions of much of the material covered in this interlude, see Fagan and Durrani 2014: 120–49 (chapter 8). The following also will be of interest to those seeking information beyond what is presented in this chapter: Banning 2002; Collins and Molyneaux 2003; Conyers 2013; Howard 2007; Leach 1992; White and King 2007.

81   *presence of artifacts*   Fagan and Durrani 2014: 92.

We call these features   See Fagan and Durrani 2014: 87 for more on these definitions of artifacts and features, as well for definitions of structures and ecofacts.

where I once surveyed   The following section on surveys and surveying is based on, and indebted to, the discussion in Fagan and Durrani 2014: 126–36.

82   *beneath the ground*   Fagan and Durrani 2014: 126–29, 144–45, 157.

83   *finding archaeological sites*   Casana 2015; Vergano 2014; see also http://www.nro.gov/history/csnr/corona/; http://www.nro.gov/history/csnr/corona/factsheet.html.

visible in the pictures   Bradford 1957.

damaging them in any way   Fagan and Durrani 2014: 145; Lerici 1959, 1962. Lerici's team, including archaeologists from the University of Pennsylvania in the later years, also employed very early versions of proton magnetometers as well as electronic resistivity meters, both of which will be discussed later in this book, to aid them in their detection of additional tombs.

84   *can be seen very clearly*   Fagan and Durrani 2014: 135, fig. 8.10.

as she puts it   Blumenthal and Mashberg 2015; Cronin 2011; Parcak 2009; Said-Moorhouse 2013. For a clip of Sarah Parcak's appearance on *The Late Show* with Stephen Colbert on January 8, 2016, see https://youtu.be/vK2t27FNJmU.

found the ancient site   Maugh 1992.

aerial photos can illuminate   Fagan and Durrani 2014: 133–34.

at that location   Ibid.

85   *built their camp*   Tepper 2002, 2003a, b, 2007.

was indeed their camp   Adams, David, and Tepper 2014; Ben Zion 2015b; Pincus, DeSmet, Tepper, and Adams 2013. See also http://mfa.gov.il/MFA/Israel Experience/History/Pages/Roman-legion-camp-uncovered-at-Megiddo-9 -Jul-2015.aspx.

86   *in the past century*   Dunston 2016.

Roman roads in England   Fagan and Durrani 2014: 136. On LiDAR and Roman roads in England, see Calderwood 2016; Nagesh 2016; Webster 2015. On Jezreel, see http://www.biblicalarchaeology.org/daily/archaeology-today /biblical-archaeology-topics/jezreel-expedition-sheds-new-light-on-ahab -and-jezebel's-city/.

future manipulation and analysis   McNeil 2015.

87   *being interpreted correctly*   Fagan and Durrani 2014: 141–42.

below the present surface   Cline and Yasur-Landau 2006.

the remote-sensing device   Fagan and Durrani 2014.

88   *from buried objects*   Ibid.

a complete circle   See, e.g., Dvorsky 2014a.

89   *been noticed before*   Fagan and Durrani 2014: 130–31; Keys 2014. See also Dvorsky 2014b.

first detected and reported   Keys 2014; Dvorsky 2014b; Moss 2015. See further http://www.usatoday.com/story/news/nation-now/2015/09/07/superhenge -discovery-at-stonehenge/71846436/; http://www.bbc.com/news/uk-england -wiltshire-34156673?ocid=socialflow_twitter%3FSThisFB%3FSThisFB.

never completed   Keys 2016; Knapton 2016.

90   *particularly promising*   Fagan and Durrani 2014: 126.

91   *a full-coverage survey*   Fagan and Durrani 2014: 125–26.

93   *sample surveys*   Fagan and Durrani 2014: 129–30.

94   *almost four thousand years ago*   Yasur-Landau, Cline, and Pierce 2008.

CHAPTER 6
DISCOVERING OUR EARLIEST
ANCESTORS

97   *Rising Star*   Shreeve 2015; see also McKenzie 2016; Wilford 2015; and Williams 2016. For the original scientific publication, see Berger et al. 2015.

our immediate ancestors   Note that *hominin* is now used in place of the previous term, *hominid*, to mean "the group consisting of modern humans, extinct human species, and all our immediate ancestors (including members of the genera *Homo, Australopithecus, Paranthropus,* and *Ardipithecus*)." See http:// australianmuseum.net.au/hominid-and-hominin-whats-the-difference# sthash.bYSSx6yE.dpuf; also http://www.smithsonianmag.com/science-nature /whats-in-a-name-hominid-versus-hominin-216054/?no-ist.

98   *underground astronauts*   McKenzie 2016; Shreeve 2015; Wilford 2015; Williams 2016.

Internet age   See, e.g., Lents 2016; McKie 2015; Pyne 2016; Williams 2016. For a previous announcement by Berger of another discovery of early hominin fossils, from a cave near Johannesburg in South Africa, see Berger et al. 2010, Wilford 2015, Williams 2016, and http://www.sciencemag.org/site /extra/sediba/. These particular fossils were excavated in August 2008, after Berger's nine-year-old son found the first two by accident. They were officially named *Australopithecus sediba* in 2010. Berger dates them to about 1.78–1.95 million years ago.

99   *the third generation*   http://www.nationalgeographic.com/explorers/bios /leakeys/. Many books have been written about the Leakeys, or by the Leakeys themselves. See, for example, Bowman-Kruh 2005; Cole 1975; M. D. Leakey 1979, 1986; R. E. Leakey 1984; Morell 1996.

an early human   Pearson 2003; http://www.nationalgeographic.com/explorers /bios/leakeys/.

father-in-law   http://www.nationalgeographic.com/explorers/bios/leakeys/; http://www.leakey.com/bios/meave-leakey.

the general public   See, e.g., Leakey and Lewin 1979.

100   *a direct ancestor of modern humans*   Thackery in Bahn 1996c: 18–19; Wong 2011; http://www.leakey.com/bios/richard-leakey.

Olduvai Gorge in Tanzania   Cole 1975.

much of the skull   Fagan 2003: 148–52; see also the entry on the Leakeys by Brian Fagan in Fagan 2014: 215–19. A greatly expanded version of the story also can be found in Fagan 1994: 57–78.

associated with stone tools   Bahn 2008: 76–78; Fagan 2003: 148–52; Fagan 2014: 215–19. See also http://www.leakey.com/bios/louis-seymour-bazett -leakey; http://www.leakey.com/bios/mary-leakey; http://www.pbs.org/wgbh /aso/databank/entries/do59le.html.

101   *throwing elephant dung*   http://www.leakey.com/bios/mary-leakey; http:// humanorigins.si.edu/evidence/behavior/footprints/laetoli-footprint-trails; http://www.getty.edu/conservation/publications_resources/newsletters/10_1 /laetoli.html; http://www.pbs.org/wgbh/evolution/educators/course/session5 /engage_a.html.

less than five feet tall   Thackeray in Bahn 1995: 18–19.

in New York City   Fagan and Durrani 2014: 42; Raichlen et al. 2010; Thackeray in Bahn 1995: 18–19.

102   *today's men's shoes*   http://humanorigins.si.edu/evidence/behavior/footprints /footprints-koobi-fora-kenya.

one of the most famous hoaxes   McKie 2012; Millar 1972; Spencer 1990; Walsh 1996.

was a fabrication   "Science: End as a Man," *Time*, November 30, 1953; available online at http://content.time.com/time/subscriber/article/0,33009,823171,00 .html.

103   *a single skeleton*   https://iho.asu.edu/about/lucys-story. See also Johanson and Edey 1981; Johanson and Wong 2010; Pollard 2007: 192–97; Thackeray in Bahn 1995: 17–18; Thackeray in Bahn 1996c: 14–17.

    of her skeleton   https://iho.asu.edu/about/lucys-story. See also Johanson and Edey 1981; Johanson and Wong 2010; Pollard 2007: 192–97; Thackeray in Bahn 1995: 17–18; Thackeray in Bahn 1996c: 14–17.

    still called that today   See https://iho.asu.edu/about/lucys-story; Johanson and Edey 1981.

    recognized the caves   http://whc.unesco.org/en/list/1393.

104   *Disney Chair of Archaeology*   See the entry on Garrod by William Davies in Fagan 2014: 202–5; also Bar-Yosef and Callander 2006: 380–424; Davies and Charles 1999; Fagan 2003: 136–39.

    occupation of el-Wad   Bahn 2008: 44–45; and see the entry on Garrod by William Davies in Fagan 2014: 202–5.

    a very low forehead   http://www.timesofisrael.com/finding-man-israels -prehistoric-caves/.

    anatomically modern people   Bahn 2008: 44–45.

    lived side by side   Choi 2014; Lemonick 2014a.

105   *an important event*   Bahn 2009: 38–39; Bar-Yosef, Vandermeersch, Arensburg, Belfer-Cohen, Goldberg, Laville, and Meignen 1992: 497–550.

    Solecki and his team   Edwards 2010; Solecki 1954, 1971, 1975; Solecki, Solecki, and Agelarakis 2004; Trinkaus 1983.

    previously written   Edwards 2010; Solecki 1954, 1971, 1975; Sommer 1999; Trinkaus 1983.

    and then Altamira   For a good overview of all the cave paintings, see Curtis 2006.

106   *the antiquity of the paintings*   Bahn 1995: 58–59; Fagan and Durrani 2014: 32; Pollard 2007: 74–77; Spivey 2005: 17–20. See also Saura Ramos, Pérez-Seoane, and Martínez 1999.

    entrance to the cave   See, in addition to the references in the previous footnote, also http://whc.unesco.org/en/list/310; http://www.visual-arts-cork.com /prehistoric/altamira-cave-paintings.htm.

    possibly other animals   http://www.visual-arts-cork.com/prehistoric/altamira -cave-paintings.htm.

    visiting Altamira   http://whc.unesco.org/en/list/310.

    thirty-seven minutes   Altares 2015a, b; Rubin 2015. See also http://www .bradshawfoundation.com/news/cave_art_paintings.php?id=The-Spanish -Cave-of-Altamira-opens-with-politics.

107   *treasure trove of art*   Cosgrove 2014. See also Bahn 1995: 60–61; Bahn 2009: 84–85; Bataille 1955.

    fifteen hundred engravings   http://whc.unesco.org/en/list/85.

    now generally dated   Bahn 1995: 60–61; Bahn 2009: 84–85; Hammer 2015; Thurman 2008. See also http://whc.unesco.org/en/list/85; http://www.bradshaw foundation.com/lascaux/index.php.

108   *dozens of other engravings*   Bahn 1995: 60–61; Bahn 2009: 84–85. See also http://www.bradshawfoundation.com/lascaux/index.php.

the public can visit   Cosgrove 2014; Hammer 2015; Rubin 2015. See also http://www.bradshawfoundation.com/chauvet/chauvet_cave_paintings.php.

a three-dimensional movie   Dargis 2011; http://www.bradshawfoundation .com/chauvet/chauvet_cave_paintings.php; http://www.bradshawfoundation .com/chauvet/chauvet_cave_UNESCO_world_heritage_site.php; http://whc .unesco.org/en/list/1426; http://www.metmuseum.org/toah/hd/chav/hd_chav .htm.

109   *an erupting volcano*   Callaway 2016; Chauvet, Deschamps, and Hillaire 1996: 35–70; Clottes 2003; Fagan and Durrani 2014: 16; Lichfield 2016; Nomade et al. 2016.

recently been challenged   Hammer 2015; Morelle and Denman 2015. See also http://www.metmuseum.org/toah/hd/chav/hd_chav.htm; http://www .newworldencyclopedia.org/entry/Chauvet_Cave.

rediscovered in 1994   Daley 2016; Netburn 2016; Quiles et al. 2016.

110   *a small opening*   Thurman 2008; http://www.newworldencyclopedia.org /entry/Chauvet_Cave.

Paleolithic cave painters   Dargis 2011; Thurman 2008. See also http://www .newworldencyclopedia.org/entry/Chauvet_Cave.

crouched on our heels   Hammer 2015; based on Chauvet, Deschamps, and Hillaire 1996: 41.

one of the great discoveries   Hammer 2015; also http://www.newworld encyclopedia.org/entry/Chauvet_Cave.

111   *using modern methods*   Hammer 2015; Thurman 2008; http://www.bradshaw foundation.com/chauvet/chauvet_cave_paintings.php.

a number of parts   See http://www.donsmaps.com/images9/chauvetmap.gif for a useful and detailed map redrawn by Don Hitchcock, after one originally published in Clottes 2003. The succeeding paragraphs follow this map.

called out to the others   Dargis 2011; Rubin 2015.

112   *an Irish elk*   http://www.prehistoric-wildlife.com/species/m/megaloceros .html.

erupting volcanoes   Callaway 2016; Lichfield 2016; Nomade et al. 2016.

moving and alive   Thurman 2008.

113   *recreated in resin*   Hammer 2015; Morelle and Denman 2015; Rubin 2015.

annual visitors   Minder 2014.

at the same time   Williams 2016 uses this same apt analogy—of the family tree turning into a bush—in an article that appeared in *The New Yorker* as the final draft of this manuscript was being completed, writing, "As more fossils surfaced and better research tools allowed for nuanced comparisons, the tree became a bush with many branches, depicting diverse species that overlapped in time."

CHAPTER 7
FIRST FARMERS IN THE FERTILE CRESCENT

115   *an episode of Ancient Aliens* http://occupytheory.org/gobekli-tepe-hoax
-debunked/; http://www.history.com/shows/ancient-aliens/episodes/season-2.
Curry 2008; Fagan and Durrani 2014: 236–37; Mann 2011; Schmidt in Fagan
2007a: 180–83; Spivey 2005: 44–49.

116   *untimely death* http://www.al-monitor.com/pulse/originals/2015/07/turkey
-worlds-oldest-temple-discovered-in-south.html#; http://www.hurriyetdaily
news.com/ancient-gobeklitepe-pioneer-schmidt-passes-away.aspx?pageID=
238&nID=69418&NewsCatID=375.

117   *both necessary and possible*   A dated but still valuable resource that presents
these theories briefly is Redman 1978. See also, e.g., Simmons 2007 with
numerous additional references.

   sixty-five feet across   Curry 2008; Mann 2011; Spivey 2005: 44–49.

   a novel suggestion   Gray 2015; Osborne 2015; http://www.hurriyetdailynews
.com/signs-of-worlds-first-pictograph-found-in-gobeklitepe-.aspx?pageID=
238&nID=85438&NewsCatID=375

   the urge to worship   Curry 2008; Mann 2011; Spivey 2005: 44–49.

118   *in a world*   Mann 2011.

   gazelles and birds   Curry 2008; Mann 2011; Spivey 2005: 44–49.

   couldn't sustain them   Curry 2008.

   some newspaper accounts   See Cline 2012: 42–44.

   claimed in a book   See Cline 2015: 620–21.

119   *Joshua and the Israelites*   Garstang and Garstang 1940; see also Edens in Bahn
1995: 140–41.

   back to Jericho   Kenyon 1957.

   the stratigraphy of a site   Fagan and Durrani 2014: 88, 98–100, 103; see also
Bahn 2008: 56–57; Fagan 2014: 139 (within the entry on Petrie by Garry J.
Shaw); Hallote 2006: 154–55, 181. Max Uhle and Nels Nelson are considered
by New World archaeologists to have done the same in regard to introducing
the concept of stratigraphy into North American archaeology.

120   *invaded the region*   See discussion in Cline 2007a: 93–120.

   an astronomical purpose   See, e.g., Barkai and Liran 2008.

   lifelike appearance   See, e.g., Edens in Bahn 1996c: 42–45.

122   *bargain price*   http://www.damienhirst.com/for-the-love-of-god; http://www
.theguardian.com/artanddesign/video/2012/apr/18/damien-hirst-tate-modern
-skull-video; http://www.tate.org.uk/context-comment/video/tateshots-damien
-hirst-love-god.

conducting excavations Nigro 2006: 1–40. See also the publications posted at https://uniroma1.academia.edu/LorenzoNigro.

site of Çatalhöyük http://www.catalhoyuk.com; see also Edens in Bahn 1995: 68–69; Pollard 2007: 172–75.

122 *at any one time* Fagan and Durrani 2014: 53; Hodder 2006.

123 *works as well* Hodder 2006.

124 *found at Çatalhöyük* See http://maxlab.mcmaster.ca/research-projects-1 /catalhoeyuk-turkey for a list of publications on the analysis of obsidian found at Çatalhöyük.

recently suggested http://www.sci-news.com/archaeology/science-catalhoyuk -map-mural-volcanic-eruption-01681.html; Schmitt et al. 2014.

125 *Neolithic-inspired outfits* Balter 2009; Hodder 2011. See also http://www .catalhoyuk.com/newsletters/04/introduction.html; http://photocollage.topic show.com/PhotoCollage.aspx?Category=events&Title=turkish-catalhoyuk -fashion-show-at-shanghai-world-expo&Mode=Public.

it is nothing Phillips 1955: 246–47; Willey and Phillips 1958: 2.

previous archaeologists Fagan and Durrani 2014: 46–49; Kelly and Thomas 2013: 13–14, 35–38.

126 *remove that bias* Kelly and Thomas 2013: 35–38. See also Fagan and Durrani 2014: 46–49.

archaeology is not anthropology See, e.g., Hodder 1986, 1987, 1999; also Fagan and Durrani 2014: 46–49; Kelly and Thomas 2013: 35–38.

some figurines http://www.catalhoyuk.com/library/goddess.html; http://www .musetours.com/explore-the-land-of-mother-goddess/.

the Mother Goddess See, for instance, Gimbutas 1974, 1991. For a recent discovery, see Kark 2016.

CHAPTER 8
REVEALING THE FIRST GREEKS

131 *famous Lion Gate* Schliemann 1880. See also Castledon 2005; French 2002; Schofield 2007.

132 *inside the city limits* Pausanias, *Description of Greece* 2.16.6–7; translation available online at http://www.theoi.com/Text/Pausanias2B.html.

powers of deduction Schliemann 1880: 60–61.

small figurines Ibid., 61.

a huge square area Ibid., 61–62.

hunting scenes Ibid., 80–99.

133 *gazed upon the face* Harrington 1999; Riley 2015. See also Ceram 1966: 59–60 for a slightly different wording in the telegram, beginning with "I am overwhelmed with joy."

134 *fragmentary tombstones* Schliemann 1880: 86, 99.

135   *reconstructed their faces*   Musgrave et al. 1995: 107–36. See also Brown et al. 2000: 115–19. Similar work has now been done on some of the skeletons from Grave Circle A; see Papazoglou-Manioudaki et al. 2009: 233–77; Papazoglou-Manioudaki et al. 2010: 157–224.

    Mycenae and Tiryns   http://whc.unesco.org/en/list/941

136   *names of their gods*   Robinson 2002.

    an official Egyptian embassy   Cline 1987, 1998.

137   *this once-great city*   See further discussion in Cline 2014.

    wooden shish kebob sticks   Blakemore 2015; Lawler 2015; Wade 2015a, 2016; also http://magazine.uc.edu/issues/0316/pay_dirt.html. See now Davis and Stocker 2016.

    known as Knossos   Castleden 1993; Evans 1921–23; Fitton 2002; see also Mee in Bahn 1995: 92–93; Pollard 2007: 108–13.

140   *made fortifications unnecessary*   Eisler 1988.

    identified as forgeries   Ceram 1966: 31–33; Lapatin 2002.

141   *the Dolphin Fresco*   Koehl 1986: 407–17.

    Priest-King of Knossos   Niemeier 1988; Shaw 2004.

144   *the height of Minoan culture*   Bietak 1992: 26–28.

CHAPTER 9
FINDING ATLANTIS?

146   *north of Cadiz*   Owen 2011; see also the relevant chapter in Adams 2015.

    off the coast of Cyprus   See Adams 2015 for a collection of the claims, which he investigated.

147   *a Spartan commander named Theras*   Herodotus, *Histories*, IV.147; http://www.perseus.tufts.edu/hopper/text?doc=Perseus%3Atext%3A1999.01.0126%3Abook%3D4%3Achapter%3D147%3Asection%3D1.

    kalliste is a Greek word   Herodotus, *Histories*, IV.147; see also Apollonios Rhodius, *Argonautica*, 4.173, 175.

149   *the journal Antiquity in 1939*   Marinatos 1939: 425–39.

150   *archaeologist Christos Doumas*   Doumas 1983.

151   *the paintings at Akrotiri*   Doumas 1993; Marinatos 1984.

    blue monkey figurines   Cline 1991.

152   *their late teens*   Davis 1986.

    a scene of sacrifice   Doumas 1993.

153   *either Egypt or Anatolia*   Morris 1989.

    from an olive tree   Friedrich et al. 2006; Manning et al. 2006; Manning 2014; see also discussions in Warburton 2009.

154   *before the Exodus*   For further discussions, and specific references for additional reading, see Cline 2007a: 85–86, 210.

Greece, Egypt, and the Near East   See discussions in Cline 1994.

why I believe the way I do   See Luce 1969.

155   *larger than Libya and Asia*   Translation by Benjamin Jowett; http://classics
.mit.edu/Plato/timaeus.html.

off the coast of Cyprus   See the amusing recounting in Adams 2015.

156   *after the eruption*   Ritner and Moeller 2014.

CHAPTER 10
ENCHANTMENT UNDER THE SEA

158   *interconnected world*   See discussion in Cline 2014: 73–79, with further references; see also Fagan and Durrani 2014: 328–29; Mee in Bahn 1995: 102–3.

a good choice   http://www.penn.museum/sites/expedition/nautical-archaeology/.

159   *published his book*   Bass 1967.

the international nature of their work   http://nauticalarch.org/about/history/.

160   *the highest honor*   https://www.archaeological.org/awards/goldmedal.

161   *on the wreck*   A sample of the publications to date include Bass 1986, 1987; and Pulak 1998, 1999, 2010. A concise discussion can be found at http://nautical
arch.org/projects/all/southern_europe_mediterranean_aegean/uluburun
_turkey/introduction/.

162   *at many conferences*   See Bass 1986, 1987; Pulak 1998, 1999, 2010.

a few decades before   Numerous citations could be given for all of this from the various scholarly publications, but it is most usefully summarized on the INA's own website at http://nauticalarch.org/projects/all/southern_europe_mediterra-
nean_aegean/uluburun_turkey/continuing_study/dendrochronological_dating/.

163   *between excavation seasons*   Pulak 1998.

164   *from the pistachio tree*   Stern et al. 2008.

from the same source   Jackson and Nicholson 2010; Walton et al. 2009.

165   *the coastal port of Ugarit*   Cucchi 2008.

rather unexpected   For pictures and further description, see especially Bass 1987.

167   *prior to about 1350 BCE*   Manning et al. 2009.

from the Aegean   Cline and Yasur-Landau 2007.

CHAPTER 11
FROM DISCUS-THROWING TO
DEMOCRACY

171   *a combination of karate and judo*   https://www.rio2016.com/en/sports; http://
ancientolympics.arts.kuleuven.be/eng/TC002cEN.html; http://www.bullshido
.org/Pankration.

172   *an end to all pagan festivals*   Andronicos 1992: 18; D. H. Cline 2016: 97; Gates 2011: 245; Pollard 2007: 26; Swaddling 1999: 7; Yalouris and Yalouris 1987: 27.

more than four meters deep   Andronicos 1992: 18; Clayton and Price 1989: 76–77; Gates 2011: 245; Swaddling 1999: 13, 16; Yalouris and Yalouris 1987: 27.

Temple of Zeus   Gates 2011: 245; Kyrieleis 2007: 102; Pausanias, *Description of Greece*, 5.7.1–6.21.7; Pollard 2007: 26–27; Swaddling 1999: 13, 16; translation available online at http://www.theoi.com/Text/Pausanias5A.html#7; http://www.theoi.com/Text/Pausanias5B.html; http://www.theoi.com/Text/Pausanias 6A.html; http://www.theoi.com/Text/Pausanias6B.html.

173   *to win athletic competitions*   D. H. Cline 2016: 99.

caught fire   Andronicos 1992: 18–23, 27; Clayton and Price 1989: 61, 65–67, 76–77; D. H. Cline 2016: 97; Gates 2011: 246–49; Kyrieleis 2007: 108–11; MacKendrick 1979: 165, 220–23; Swaddling 1999: 16–20; Yalouris and Yalouris 1987: 16–17.

a century earlier   Andronicos 1992: 23–27; Kyrieleis 2007: 104–5; MacKendrick 1979: 287–89; Pollard 2007: 29; Swaddling 1999: 8.

174   *the Louvre in Paris*   Kyrieleis 2007: 102–3; MacKendrick 1979: 218, 220; Pollard 2007: 27; Swaddling 1999: 16.

the modern Olympic Games   Ceram 1966: 34–37; Dyson 2006: 82–85; Kyrieleis 2007: 102–3; MacKendrick 1979: 218–20; Pollard 2007: 27–28; Swaddling 1999: 16.

Schliemann's greatest discovery   Schaar 2012: 328, citing Evans 1931: 19. See also MacKendrick 1979: 4.

175   *the most recent campaign*   Dyson 2006: 198; Kyrieleis 2007: 106; MacKendrick 1979: 224; Swaddling 1999: 16.

nearly half a million tourists   Andronicos 1992: 14–18; Gates 2011: 245–46, 249–50; Kyrieleis 2007: 104, 106, 112–13; MacKendrick 1979: 163–64, 223–26, 287–89; Swaddling 1999: 14–36; Yalouris and Yalouris 1987: 10–29; http://whc.unesco.org/en/list/517.

like the Persian War   Andronicos 1992: 30–32; Kyrieleis 2007: 113–14, figs. 28–32; MacKendrick 1979: 164, 225; Swaddling 1999: 30–31.

176   *from the Athenians*   Andronicos 1992: 31; Kyrieleis 2007: 113, figs. 29–30; MacKendrick 1979: 225.

sent by their citizens   Gates 2011: 245–46; MacKendrick 1979: 164–65; Swaddling 1999: 27–29; Yalouris and Yalouris 1987: 11.

a goldsmith's hammer   Andronicos 1992: 27–28; Clayton and Price 1989: 66–67, 70; Kyrieleis 2007: 110–11; MacKendrick 1979: 223; Swaddling 1999: 20.

with new events   See Swaddling 1999: 53–54, 57–89 for more details on the following paragraphs.

177   *food and lodging for life*   D. H. Cline 2016: 96–97, 100; Gates 2011: 250–51; Swaddling 1999: 53–54, 57–89.

pretended to be dead   Suetonius, *Nero*, 23–24; http://www.perseus.tufts.edu/hopper/text?doc=Perseus%3Atext%3A1999.02.0132%3Alife%3Dnero%3A chapter%3D23; and http://www.perseus.tufts.edu/hopper/text?doc=Perseus:abo:phi,1348,016:24.

by the petitioners   Andronicos 1993: 10–12, 17–19; D. H. Cline 2016: 190; Gates 2011: 239–40; MacKendrick 1979: 292–93; Scott 2014: 12–24; Zeilinga de Boer and Hale 2002.

178   *prosperity and prestige*   Andronicos 1993: 7; Scott 2014: 52–63.

fulfilling the prophecy   Gates 2011: 240; Herodotus 1.75.2, 1.91.4; Scott 2014: 83–85; Zeilinga de Boer and Hale 2002; http://www.perseus.tufts.edu/hopper/text?doc=Perseus%3Atext%3A1999.01.0126%3Abook%3D1%3Achapter%3D75%3Asection%3D2; and http://www.perseus.tufts.edu/hopper/text?doc=Perseus%3Atext%3A1999.01.0126%3Abook%3D1%3Achapter%3D91%3Asection%3D4.

earthquake fault lines   See MacKendrick 1979: 293; Scott 2014: 23–24; Zeilinga de Boer and Hale 2002.

commenced digging   Andronicos 1993: 19–20; Dyson 2006: 120–21; MacKendrick 1979: 165; Mulliez 2007: 141; Scott 2014: 267–68; Sheftel 2002; Vogelkoff-Brogan 2014 (citing Amandry 1992). Monetary calculations made according to http://www.davemanuel.com/inflation-calculator.php.

most beautiful and frequently visited   http://whc.unesco.org/en/list/393.

179   *the number of workers*   Dyson 2006: 119; MacKendrick 1979: 166; Mulliez 2007: 134–40, 142–44, 153; Scott 2014: 42, 252–67, 269–73.

more than sixty volumes   MacKendrick 1979: 167–68; Mulliez 2007: 153–56; Scott 2014: 274–84.

180   *spectacular finds*   Mulliez 2007: 151.

emerged from the dirt   Andronicos 1993: 20; Herodotus 1.31 (translation at http://www.perseus.tufts.edu/hopper/text?doc=Perseus:text:1999.01.0126:book=1:chapter=31); MacKendrick 1979: 166–67, fig. 4.6; Mulliez 2007: 144–46, figs. 23–25; Scott 2014: 67, fig. 3.1.

rededicated the statue later   Andronicos 1993: 24–27; Gates 2011: 244, fig. 15.5; MacKendrick 1979: 268–70, fig. 5.18; Mulliez 2007: 147–49, figs. 28–31; Scott 2014: 123.

the Pythian Games   Andronicos 1993: 8–9, 20–21; MacKendrick 1979: 168–69; Mulliez 2007: 144, 147, 150–51; Scott 2014: 158–59, 197–98, 209–11.

181   *revival of the Olympic Games*   Mulliez 2007: 144, 147, 151, fig. 21.

perhaps modern times as well   The following is based on the maps found in a number of publications, including Andronicos 1993: 30–31 (see also discussions on 15–19) and Gates 2011: 239. See also the descriptions in Scott 2014: 233–35, 291–301, and, originally, Pausanias 10.8.6–10.17.1 and 10.18.1–10.24.7; the latter is at http://www.theoi.com/Text/Pausanias10A.html#5.

the final battle   Andronicos 1993: 16; Gates 2011: 243; Scott 2014: 112–13, 128–29, 136–37, 291–92, fig. 6.2; MacKendrick 1979: 172–73.

182   *a variety of other scenes*   Andronicos 1993: 16–17, 20–24; Gates 2011: 241–42; MacKendrick 1979: 168–70, fig. 4.7; Mulliez 2007: 144; Scott 2014: 105–8, 112–13, figs. 5.2–5.4.

portico at Delphi   Gates 2011: 243; MacKendrick 1979: 170–71; Scott 2014: 128.

still there today   Andronicos 1993: 8; D. H. Cline 2016: 137; Gates 2011: 243; MacKendrick 1979: 172–73; Scott 2014: 121–22, 240–41, fig. 11.4.

183   *almost forty years to rebuild*   Andronicos 1993: 17–19; Gates 2011: 238–39; MacKendrick 1979: 171–72, 290–92; Pausanias 10.5.9–13, http://www.theoi .com/Text/Pausanias10A.html#5; Scott 2014: 93–97, 153–57.

closed down Olympia   Gates 2011: 244; Mulliez 2007: 147; Pausanias 10.7.2–8, http://www.theoi.com/Text/Pausanias10A.html#5; Scott 2014: 73, 124–25, 244.

184   *high point of the city*   See Camp 2001; Hurwit 1999; also http://whc.unesco .org/en/list/404.

its basic function   For descriptions and discussions, see especially Camp 1986, 2010. The full publication, but only of the discoveries made before the 1970s, can be found in Thompson and Wycherley 1972.

185   *changes in techniques*   Camp 1986, 2010; Dyson 2006: 188–90; Thompson 1983.

record the excavation data   http://www.ascsa.edu.gr/index.php/news/news Details/bruce-on-idig . On iPads at Pompeii, see http://classics.uc.edu/pompeii /index.php/news/1-latest/142-ipads2010.html, http://www.macworld.com/article /1154717/ipad_archeology_pompeii.html, and https://www.macstories.net/ipad /apple-profiles-researchers-using-ipads-in-pompeii/.

eventually the Bronze Age   Camp 1986: 13; Camp 2010: 30–33; Dyson 2006: 78, 188.

not believing in the gods   Camp 1986: 40–41, 48–57, 77–107, 113–16, 122–50, 156–211. See also Camp 2010: 48–49, 53–61, 66–67, 89–91, 123–28, 176–78; Gawlinski 2014: 13–15, 66–67, 142–43.

186   *the museum for the site*   Camp 1986: 57–59, 107–12; D. H. Cline 2016: 142–43, 185; Gawlinski 2014: 134–42; Thompson 1983.

first been installed   Camp 1986: 66–72; Camp 2010: 95–101; Shear 1984.

retrieving them from the mire   Shear 1984.

CHAPTER 12
WHAT HAVE THE ROMANS EVER DONE FOR US?

188   *Life of Brian*   http://www.imdb.com/title/tt0079470/quotes; http://www .epicure.demon.co.uk/whattheromans.html.

189   *a single leather sandal*   See Stanley Price 1991, with further references in the various footnotes.

a very expensive camera   Stanley Price 1991, esp. 8–9.

190   *Romulus killed Remus*   See, e.g., Gates 2011: 329.

on the Palatine Hill   Coulston and Dodge 2000: 5; Gates 2011: 329; Laurence 2012: 28–29, 31; McGeough 2004: 54–55; Smith 2000: 18–19.

events that are open to question   See, e.g., Gates 2011: 329.

191   *the interior of the Colosseum*   Packer 1989: 138.

its newly reacquired status   Coulston and Dodge 2000: 7–8; Gates 2011: 339; Hopkins and Beard 2005: 171–73; McFeaters 2007: 51; Packer 1989: 138–39; Perrottet 2005; Petter 2000.

a city of marble   Aicher 2000: 119, 134; Connolly and Dodge 1998: 110; Coulston and Dodge 2000: 8; Falasca-Zamponi 1997: 90–99; Fugate Brangers 2013: 125–27; Gates 2011: 340, 349; Guidi 1996: 113–14; MacKendrick 1960: 140, 145–46; McFeaters 2007: 53–54; McGeough 2004: 43–44; Nolan 2005; Olariu 2012; Packer 1989: 139; Painter 2005: xv, 3, 9, 19; Patric 1937; Perrottet 2005.

192   *our knowledge of Augustan Rome*   Aicher 2000: 120–21; Fugate Brangers 2013; Guidi 1996: 113–14; Hopkins and Beard 2005: 173–77; MacKendrick 1960: 140, 145–50; McFeaters 2007: 55–57; McGeough 2004: 43–44; Nolan 2005; Olariu 2012; Packer 1989: 139; Packer 1997: 307; Patric 1937; Painter 2005: xvi, 2–12; Perrottet 2005.

the new Via del Imperio   See, e.g., Hopkins and Beard 2005: 174, ill. 28; MacKendrick 1960: 141, fig. 5.12; Painter 2005: 11–13, 15–16, figs. 1.2–1.8.

anniversary of Augustus's birth   Claridge 2010: 207–12; Connolly and Dodge 1998: 112; Gates 2011: 352–55; MacKendrick 1960: 160–70; Olariu 2012: 360.

193   *the area was completely flooded*   Claridge 2010: 207–8, 213; Fugate Brangers 2013: 130–31; Gates 2011: 352; MacKendrick 1960: 156, 160; Nolan 2005; Olariu 2012: 360.

as Mussolini had wished   Aicher 2000: 124; Claridge 2010: 207–8, 213; Coulston and Dodge 2000: 9; Fugate Brangers 2013: 130–31; MacKendrick 1960: 158–60, 162; Nolan 2005; Olariu 2012: 360, 364; Perrottet 2005.

the original structure   See especially Andersen 2003; Conlin 1997a and b; and Nolan 2005; but also Aicher 2000: 124; Claridge 2010: 207–8, 213; Coulston and Dodge 2000: 9; Fugate Brangers 2013: 130–31; MacKendrick 1960: 158–60, 162; Olariu 2012: 360, 364; Perrottet 2005.

194   *near the Forum of Nerva*   Claridge 2010: 171–74, fig. 64; Hopkins and Beard 2005: 26–28; Kingsley 2006: 203, 205, 216–17.

pieces of the map   Claridge 2010: 173, fig. 65; Coulston and Dodge 2000: 355–57, with further references; Kingsley 2006: 205, 207–208; MacKendrick 1960: 138, 226–30.

195   *half its former value*   Josephus, *Jewish War*, 6.6.317.

near the Colosseum   Claridge 2010: 171–72; Gates 2011: 383–84; Hopkins and Beard 2005: 26–29; Kingsley 2006: xiii, 95, 203, 217–19, 267–69; MacKendrick 1960: 235–36.

a remarkable sight   Claridge 2010: 121–23; MacKendrick 1960: 235–36.

197   *a profusion of colors*   See http://yu.edu/cis/activities/arch-of-titus/; Fine 2013; Povoledo 2012. On polychromy in antiquity, see, e.g., Fine 2013; Gurewitsch 2008; Pazanelli, Schmidt, and Lapatin 2008.

all of ancient Rome   See http://yu.edu/cis/activities/arch-of-titus/; Fine 2013; Povoledo 2012; http://romereborn.frischerconsulting.com.

other parts of the scene   Piening 2013. See also Fine 2013; Povoledo 2012; http://yu.edu/cis/activities/arch-of-titus/.

more than one scholar   Coleman 2000: 231; Connolly and Dodge 1998: 192–93; Dunkle 2008: 256–58; Hopkins and Beard 2005: 2–3, 21, 34–35, 163; MacKendrick 1960: 194, 224, 231–35.

198   *while Rome burned*   Bahn 2009: 71; Connolly and Dodge 1998: 117–18; Gates 2011: 375–77, 386; Hopkins and Beard 2005: 28–31; MacKendrick 1960: 189–94, 224, 230; McGeough 2004: 218, 220.

now open to tourists   Bahn 2009: 71; Binnie 2014; Connolly and Dodge 1998: 117–18; Kington 2009; MacKendrick 1960: 189–94, 224, 230; McGeough 2004: 35–36.

an additional ghost inscription   Feldman 2001: 23–24.

this remarkable discovery   For the discussion in the following paragraphs, see Alföldy 1995 and Feldman 2001. See also Coleman 2000: 229–30; Dunkle 2008: 259; Hopkins and Beard 2005: 32–34; Johnston 2001.

199   *notorious gladiator fights*   Coleman 2000: 231–35, 238–39; Connolly and Dodge 1998: 190–208; Dunkle 2008: 260–63; Futrell 2006: 62, 65–66, 79–80, 113–14, 221; Gates 2011: 385–87; Hopkins and Beard 2005: 2, 12–13, 122–35; MacKendrick 1960: 194, 224, 231–35; McGeough 2004: 218.

200   *A noble wreck*   Quotation from *Manfred*, by Byron, as presented in Hopkins and Beard 2005: 3–5 and Dunkle 2008: 285. See also additional references to the other authors by Hopkins and Beard 2005: 7–12 and Dunkle 2008: 285–87.

201   *a trap door*   Coleman 2000: 234; Connolly and Dodge 1998: 199–202, 207–8; Dunkle 2008: 278–79; Hopkins and Beard 2005: 94, 100, 136–38; MacKendrick 1960: 233–35.

such spectacles   Coleman 2000: 238; Hopkins and Beard 2005: 42–43, 51; McGeough 2004: 218.

the iron clamps   Coleman 2000: 239; Connolly and Dodge 1998: 190, 192; Dunkle 2008: 279–85; Hopkins and Beard 2005: 2–3, 103–5, 160–62, 164–71; MacKendrick 1960: 230.

nearly forty in France alone   Bomgardner 2001; Chase 2002; Welch 2007.

202   *justifications for empire*   Packer 1989: 140. See also Painter 2005: xv.

even churches were adversely affected   Packer 1989: 141; Packer 1997: 307. See also various discussions in Connolly and Dodge 1998; Hopkins and Beard 2005; and MacKendrick 1960.

worshipped in the temples   Guidi 1996: 113; McFeaters 2007: 57–58; Packer 1989: 141; Packer 1997: 307.

a generalized phenomenon   Díaz-Andreu and Champion 1996: 3. For examples, see the various chapters in their edited book as well as the references in the individual chapters' bibliographies.

203   *of central importance*   Díaz-Andreu and Champion 1996: 3.

fascist archaeology   Díaz-Andreu and Champion 1996: 2–4, 7–9, 21; Guidi 1996: 109–10, 113–14; McFeaters 2007: 50–51, 58–59; Painter 2005: 4–5. See also McGeough 2004: 43.

World War II   See discussions in Díaz-Andreu and Champion 1996: 10–11, 14–15; Guidi 1996; McFeaters 2007; and Painter 2005, among others.

purported links to antiquity   See my discussions at the beginning and end of each chapter in Cline 2004.

DIGGING DEEPER 2:
HOW DO YOU KNOW HOW TO DIG?

204 *extremely delicate work*   See also the discussion, with a detailed list of tools, in Fagan and Durrani 2014: 160–61.

207 *an artifact's context*   Fagan and Durrani 2014: 88.

 even a tertiary context   Ibid., 89.

209 *horizontal excavation*   Ibid., 158–60.

 a vertical excavation   Ibid., 156–58.

 the first professor of Egyptology   Bahn 2008: 57; Fagan 2014: 139 (within the entry on Petrie by Garry J. Shaw).

210 *more recent things*   Fagan and Durrani 2014: 88, 98–100, 103; see also Bahn 2008: 56–57; Fagan 2014: 139 (within the entry on Petrie by Garry J. Shaw); Hallote 2006: 154–55, 181.

211 *probably equivalent in time*   Fagan and Durrani 2014: 88, 102–3; see also Bahn 2008: 56–57; Fagan 2014: 139; Hallote 2006: 154–55, 181.

 Royal College of Surgeons   See, e.g., Fagan 2014: 139 (within the entry on Petrie by Garry J. Shaw).

 a new excavation method   Bahn 2008: 61; Fagan 2003: 144–47; Fagan and Durrani 2014: 90; see also the entry on Wheeler by Martin Carver in Fagan 2014: 152–56.

214 *the stratigraphical history*   See http://www.harrismatrix.com/.

 Kenyon-Wheeler method   Bahn 2008: 74–75; Fagan 2003: 140–43; see also the entry on Kenyon by Miriam C. Davis in Fagan 2014: 220–23.

CHAPTER 13
EXCAVATING ARMAGEDDON

221 *the manmade mound at Megiddo*   Davies 1986; Kempinski 1989.

222 *the battle of Armageddon*   See full discussion of all the battles in Cline 2000, including a fuller discussion of the battle described in Revelation.

223 *pharaoh Sheshonq*   See discussion in Cline 2000.

 suggested by scholars   See overall discussion in Cline 2009.

225 *Yigael Yadin*   On Yadin, see Silberman 1993.

227 *a large entrance gate*   See again relevant discussion in Cline 2009.

 a series of codirectors   Finkelstein and Ussishkin 1994; Silberman, Finkelstein, Ussishkin, and Halpern 1999.

 firsthand knowledge of the issues   Cline 2006; Cline and Samet 2013.

229 *identified as the kitchen*   Gadot and Yasur-Landau 2006.

 destroyed or captured   See, e.g., Harrison 2003.

Mother Nature caused this destruction   See Cline 2011, with further discussion and additional references to the other theories and suggestions.

when least expected   Cline and Sutter 2011: 159–90.

230   *how the battle transpired*   See, e.g., Fox 1993; Schofield, Johnson, and Beck 2002; Scott, Babits, and Haecker 2007; also Pollard 2007: 218–22.

232   *the Journal of Military History*   Cline and Sutter 2011: 159–90.

never retrieved them   Hasson 2012; https://english.tau.ac.il/news/tel_megido.

233   *the site of the Roman camp*   Adams, David, and Tepper 2014; Ben Zion 2015b; Pincus, DeSmet, Tepper, and Adams 2013. See also http://mfa.gov.il/MFA /IsraelExperience/History/Pages/Roman-legion-camp-uncovered-at-Megiddo -9-Jul-2015.aspx.

CHAPTER 14
UNEARTHING THE BIBLE

234   *hidden in caves*   On the scrolls, see Cline 2009: 91–97; Davies, Brooke, and Callaway 2002; Fields 2006; Lim 2006; Magness 2002; Pollard 2007: 158–61; Shanks 1992, 1998.

235   *equivalent of a monastery*   On Qumran itself, see, e.g., Cargill 2009; Cline 2009: 93–94; Magness 2002.

236   *turn them into sandals*   Magness 2002: 25–26.

bought three others   See http://www.deadseascrolls.org.il/learn-about-the -scrolls/discovery-and-publication?locale=en_US.; http://gnosis.org/library/dss /dss_timeline.htm. See also the detailed account in Fields 2006, as well as the account in Lim 2006.

237   *The Wall Street Journal*   See http://www.deadseascrolls.org.il/learn-about -the-scrolls/discovery-and-publication?locale=en_US.

239   *the Copper Scroll*   See, e.g., Allegro 1960; McCarter 1992; Wolters 1996.

nine hundred talents   Translation following García Martínez 1996: 461.

240   *various amateur archaeologists*   See, e.g., Neese 2009.

the scroll itself   Yadin 1985; see also White Crawford 2000; Wise 1990.

241   *reconstructed the original contents*   See, e.g., Shanks 2010 and numerous articles in past issues of *Biblical Archaeology Review*.

the floodgates opened   Chandler 1991.

the Book of Samuel   Abegg, Flint, and Ulrich 1999: 213–14.

that missing paragraph   See Vanderkam and Flint 2002: 115–16. See also Abegg, Flint, and Ulrich 1999: 214.

242   *crowns and scepters*   Bahn 2000: 58–59; Moorey 1988.

the Cave of Horrors   Aharoni 1962; Harris 1998; Yadin 1971.

243   *a woman named Babatha*   Freund and Arav 2001; Harris 1998; Saldarini 1998; Yadin 1971, esp. chapters 5–10; see also Freund 2004.

Simeon bar Kosiba   Freund and Arav 2001; Yadin 1971: 124–39.

thirty-five papyrus rolls   Freund and Arav 2001; Harris 1998; Saldarini 1998; Yadin 1971, chapter 16.

wonderful and exciting experience   Harris 1998.

244   *enthralling archaeological finds*   For those who are interested, *The Dead Sea Scrolls Bible* documents alternative readings found in the Dead Sea Scrolls by presenting them in footnotes attached to the traditional text of the Hebrew Bible; see Abegg, Flint, and Ulrich 1999. As of 2012, there also is a website that contains digitized images of virtually all the scrolls and fragments; go to http://www.deadseascrolls.org.il/?locale=en_US. For those who are without Internet access, or who prefer reading physical books, translations of most of the scrolls can be found in García Martinez 1996 or Vermes 1998.

CHAPTER 15
MYSTERY AT MASADA

245   *a best seller*   Yadin 1966. See also summary by Snapes in Bahn 1995: 158–59.

246   *two separate books*   Ben-Yehuda 1995, 2002.

a spirited defense of Yadin   Ben-Tor 2009.

popular tourist site   Ben-Tor 2009: 309; http://whc.unesco.org/en/list/1040.

247   *placing ads in newspapers*   Yadin 1966: 13–14.

international participants   Ibid.

248   *in his book*   Ibid., 19–29.

stone and rubble   Ibid., 37.

arid desert region   Ibid., *passim.*

249   *painted a black line*   Ibid., 88.

coins from all five years   Ibid., 54, 64, 98, 108–9, 168–71.

a popular audience   Yadin 1966.

250   *Jewish rebels at Masada*   Magness 2012: 215.

inclined to its north side   Josephus, *The Jewish War*, 7.8; translation following Whiston 1999: 927.

251   *stones of several colors*   Ibid.

ten million gallons   Yadin 1966: 126.

no one could escape   Josephus, *The Jewish War*, 7.8; translation following Whiston 1999: 926.

darts and stones   Ibid., 928.

252   *dragged up the ramp*   Ibid., 928–29.

a state of freedom   Ibid., 929.

253   *960 people died that night*   Josephus, *The Jewish War*, 7.9; translation following Whiston 1999: 933.

254 *seems to be the story* Josephus, *The Jewish War*, 3.7.3–3.8.9; translation following Whiston 1999: 784–97.

255 *inhabitants of Qumran* Yadin 1966: 171–79.

  leather sandals nearby Yadin 1966: 54, 193, 197; Ben-Tor 2009: 299–307.

  his professional life Ben-Tor 2009: 305.

  gazing in awe Yadin 1966: 54.

  that of a child Ibid.

  names written on them Yadin 1966: 197, 201.

256 *about eleven years old* Ben-Tor 2009: 304.

  a true monument Ben-Tor 2009: 309.

  a nationalist agenda See, e.g., Kohl and Fawcett 1995; Meskell 1998.

CHAPTER 16
CITIES OF THE DESERT

258 *administrative buildings* Eigeland 1978; Matthiae 1981, 2013; see also Edens in Bahn 1995: 148–49.

  found ancient Ebla Eigeland 1978.

  Hammurabi of Babylon Eigeland 1978.

  figures from the Bible Plaut 1978; also Vicker 1979: 1; Bermant and Weitzman 1979: 1–13.

259 *subsequent research by epigraphers* O'Toole 1979: A18.

  a new chief epigrapher Pettinato 1981, 1991; Shanks 1980.

260 *incalculable harm* Chivers 2013.

  finally dislodged Barnard 2015; Hutcherson 2015; Melvin, Elwazer, and Berlinger 2015; Smith-Spark 2015; see also http://www.reuters.com/article/2015/08/18/us-mideast-crisis-archaeology-idUSKCN0QN24K20150818; http://www.huffingtonpost.com/entry/isis-beheads-archeologist-palmyra_55d3a125e4b055a6dab1da13?kvcommref=mostpopular.

  New York and Dubai Turner 2016.

  given that designation http://whc.unesco.org/en/list/23. Major publications on Palmyra include Browning 1979 and Stoneman 1992; and now Smith 2013.

263 *the world's attention* http://whc.unesco.org/en/list/326; the site received its UNESCO designation in 1985. Introductory volumes to the site include Amadasi and Schneider 2002; Browning 1973; and Taylor 2002.

264 *an Internet poll* http://world.new7wonders.com/?n7w-page=new7wonders-of-the-world

  no more minting of coins Lawler 2007; Pollard 2007: 36.

  their hydraulic engineering Pollard 2007: 36.

when he died Pollard 2007: 34–39.

riding down the Wadi Musa Carlsen 2016: 94–106; Stephens 1970: xxxii–xxxiii.

265 *wrote his poem* *Petra*, by John Burgon (1813–1888); Stephens 1970: xl.

started in the 1960s http://www.deseretnews.com/article/25740/U-PROFESSOR
-WILL-LEAD-EXPEDITION-TO-PETRA.html?pg=all

ride around on a white horse http://www.biblicalarchaeology.org/daily
/archaeology-today/archaeologists-biblical-scholars-works/philip-c
-hammond-1924–2008/; http://www.biblicalarchaeology.org/daily/archaeology
-today/biblical-archaeology-topics/scholarship-winners-speak-up/

present in my memory Stephens 1970: xxxiii, 254–56.

266 *collect the treasure* Browning 1973: 118–19.

governor of the Roman province Browning 1973: 90–97.

other parts of Petra http://proteus.brown.edu/483/Home.

an elaborate garden Bohstrom 2016; Lawler 2007; https://petragarden
excavation.wordpress.com/project-history-2/.

267 *carbonized papyrus scrolls* https://acorjordan.wordpress.com/2015/08/01/petra
-papyri/.

the façade of the Monastery Browning 1973: 118–19, 188–89.

DIGGING DEEPER 3:
HOW OLD IS THIS AND WHY
IS IT PRESERVED?

269 *address the topics* For concise discussions of much of the material covered in
this chapter, see Fagan and Durrani 2014: 96–118 (chapter 7).

270 *Common methods* See, e.g., Aitken 1990; Fagan and Durrani 2014: 111–17;
Taylor and Aitken 1997.

carbon-14 dating Fagan and Durrani 2014: 111–12.

271 *a particular sample* See, e.g., the explanation at http://www.physlink.com
/Education/AskExperts/ae403.cfm, which states that it is "fairly simple to
determine how many total carbon atoms should be in a sample given its
weight and chemical makeup."

date their shipwreck Manning et al. 2009.

worked most recently For an example of radiocarbon dating used as part of
academic discussions, see, e.g., Levy and Higham 2014.

272 *tree-ring dating* See Fagan and Durrani 2014: 108–111; also, e.g., Baillie 2014
with earlier references.

273 *begins to absorb water* http://news.bbc.co.uk/2/hi/uk_news/scotland/edinburgh
_and_east/8058185.stm.

the dating method clearly worked Ibid.

274   *the boat sank*   Manning et al. 2009.

275   *made from terracotta*   Bahn 1995: 178–79; Pollard 2007: 199–203.

ruled for the next four centuries   Portal 2007: 15, 18, 21.

almost completely empty   Bahn 1995: 178–79; Portal 2007: 15, 18, and *passim*. See also http://science.nationalgeographic.com/science/archaeology/emperor-qin/.

276   *would be shot*   Quote found at http://www.britishmuseum.org/PDF/Teachers _resource_pack_30_8a.pdf.

just a working hypothesis   Bahn 1995: 178–79.

eighty-five sculptors   Bahn 1995: 178.

277   *conserve the paint*   http://news.bbc.co.uk/2/hi/asia-pacific/8676886.stm; http:// news.nationalgeographic.com/news/2012/06/pictures/120620-terra-cotta -warriors-china-new-army-shield-armor-science/.

layers of lacquer   Yan et al. 2014; http://www.eurekalert.org/pub_releases /2014–08/scp-ss2080114.php.

estimates for the number   Bahn 1995: 179.

the imperial stables   http://www.britishmuseum.org/PDF/Teachers_resource _pack_30_8a.pdf; http://science.nationalgeographic.com/science/archaeology /emperor-qin/.

skeletons of twelve real horses   Russon 2014; http://www.chinadaily.com.cn /china/2006–07/31/content_653375.htm.

the emperor's burial chamber   Moskowitz 2012; http://www.britishmuseum .org/PDF/Teachers_resource_pack_30_8a.pdf.

278   *without oxygen*   See Fagan and Durrani 2014: 62–69.

the desert environment   She subsequently published a book about them (Barber 1999), as did he (Mallory and Mair 2000). See also Hudson in Bahn 1996c: 152–53.

279   *possibly even Europe*   Demick 2010; Wade 2010; see also Hudson in Bahn 1996c: 152–53; http://factsanddetails.com/asian/cat62/sub406/item2567.html.

the Silk Route in antiquity   Demick 2010; Wade 2010; see also Hudson in Bahn 1996c: 152–53; http://factsanddetails.com/asian/cat62/sub406/item2567.html.

on the border   Bahn 1995: 84–85, 1996c: 140–45; Fagan and Durrani 2014: 68, 302–3; Pollard 2007: 232–35; Scarre in Fagan 2007a: 40–41; and http:// www.iceman.it/en/oetzi-the-iceman; see also http://factsanddetails.com /world/cat56/sub362/item1496.html#chapter-0.

before the pyramids   Bahn 1996c: 140–45. For the story of the years immediately following the initial discovery, see Spindler 1995, written by the archaeologist in charge of the initial scientific studies.

280   *standing below Ötzi*   See http://www.iceman.it/en/oetzi-the-iceman, with further references; also http://factsanddetails.com/world/cat56/sub362/item 1496.html#chapter-0.

fleeing from the battle   See http://www.iceman.it/en/oetzi-the-iceman, with further references; also http://factsanddetails.com/world/cat56/sub362/item 1496.html#chapter-0.

a nearby valley in Italy   Bahn 1996c: 140–45. See http://www.iceman.it/en /oetzi-the-iceman, with further references; http://factsanddetails.com/world /cat56/sub362/item1496.html#chapter-0. For an excellent, and brief, explanation of strontium isotope analysis, see http://archive.archaeology.org/0705 /abstracts/isotopes.html.

281   *various other plants*   See again http://www.iceman.it/en/oetzi-the-iceman, with further references; also http://factsanddetails.com/world/cat56/sub362 /item1496.html#chapter-0.

not yet taken place   Barzilay 2016, reporting on an article published in *Science* by Maixner et al. 2016. See also Rosen 2016; http://www.pbs.org/wgbh/nova/next /body/ancient-icemans-h-pylori-genome-hints-at-ancient-migrations-to-europe/; and http://www.eurekalert.org/pub_releases/2016–01/eaob-pfi122915.php.

even more important to archaeology   On European migrations, see, e.g., Cooper and Haak 2015, with references to the original publications in *Science* and *Nature*; for Richard III, see, e.g., Kennedy 2014 and Sample 2015, reporting on the initial publication by King et al. 2014.

his starring role   See Samadelli et al. 2015; Scallan 2015; also http://www .iceman.it/en/tattoos; http://www.celebritytattoodesign.com/brad-pitt-tattoos.

his normal hiking shoes   http://factsanddetails.com/world/cat56/sub362/item 1496.html#chapter-0.

282   *Ötzi had a backpack*   See http://www.iceman.it/en/oetzi-the-iceman, with further references; also http://factsanddetails.com/world/cat56/sub362/item1496 .html#chapter-0.

a nomadic group   Bogucki in Bahn 1995: 156–57; Bogucki in Bahn 1996c: 146–51; Liesowska 2014; Pollard 2007: 236–39; Polosmak 1994; also http:// siberiantimes.com/culture/others/features/siberian-princess-reveals-her-2500 -year-old-tattoos/. See also discussions in Hall 2015; Mayor 2014.

his lower leg   Bogucki in Bahn 1995: 156–57; Bogucki in Bahn 1996c: 146–51; Liesowska 2014; Pollard 2007: 236–39; Polosmak 1994. See also http://siberian times.com/culture/others/features/siberian-princess-reveals-her-2500-year-old -tattoos/.

simply Juanita   http://www.nationalgeographic.com/explorers/bios/johan -reinhard/; Schreiber in Bahn 1996c: 160–61.

283   *weighed only eighty pounds*   Reinhard 2005.

Inca sacred ceremonial sites   Clark 1998; Reinhard in Fagan 2007a: 100–5; Schreiber in Bahn 1996c: 160–61.

bogs or fens   Fagan and Durrani 2014: 63–64; Kaner in Bahn 1996c: 164–69; Tarlow in Bahn 1995: 114–15; see, e.g., Aldhouse-Green 2015 and Glob 2004.

Lindow Man   Kaner in Bahn 1996c: 164–69; Pollard 2007: 212–17; Tarlow in Bahn 1995: 114–15; http://www.britishmuseum.org/explore/highlights/high light_objects/pe_prb/l/lindow_man.aspx.

284   *a piece of unleavened bread*   Kaner in Bahn 1996c: 164–69; Tarlow in Bahn 1995: 114–15; http://www.britishmuseum.org/explore/highlights/highlight _objects/pe_prb/l/lindow_man.aspx.

the rope around his neck   Fagan and Durrani 2014: 63–64; Kaner in Bahn 1996c: 164–69; Tarlow in Bahn 1995: 114–15; http://www.tollundman.dk.

oxygen doesn't circulate   http://abcnews.go.com/Technology/story?id=119824.

a remotely operated vehicle   Ballard 2008; Krause 2000; Søreide 2011. See also http://www.nationalgeographic.com/blacksea/index.html.

285   *the original beeswax still sealing the top*   See Ballard 2008; Krause 2000; Ryan and Pittman 1998; Søreide 2011. See also http://www.nationalgeographic .com/blacksea/index.html.

the remains of this ship   Pollard 2007: 154–57; Tarlow in Bahn 1995: 128–31. For book-length accounts, see, e.g., Bruce-Mitford 1979 and Williams 2011.

many interesting things   Pollard 2007: 154–57; Tarlow in Bahn 1995: 128–31.

286   *the pieces of wood*   Ibid.

the bones have decomposed   Ibid.

a commemoration of a battle   Ibid.

no ordinary burial   Ibid.

an iron helmet   Ibid.

a Viking warrior buried in his boat   Cohen 2011; Kennedy 2011; Ravilous 2012.

287   *the shape of the boat*   Ibid.

a drinking horn   Ibid.

CHAPTER 17
LINES IN THE SAND, CITIES IN THE SKY

291   *Chariots of the Gods?*   Von Däniken 1968.

Land here!   Ibid., 17.

292   *according to his webpage*   http://www.daniken.com/e/index.html.

the park closed down   http://www.swissinfo.ch/eng/closure-of-mystery-park -is-no-enigma/5576928.

sandstorms and high winds   Dearden 2014.

rather ironic   Ruble 2014.

other ancient settlement remains   See Feder 2013; Hall 2010; Pollard 2007: 158–61; Reinhard 1988; Schreiber in Bahn 1995: 208–9.

293   *Paracas and Nazca*   Hall 2010; http://whc.unesco.org/en/list/700.

create a picture   http://science.nationalgeographic.com/science/archaeology /nasca-lines/.

294   *called the Astronaut*   See, e.g., Moran 1998, with a foreword by von Däniken, cited by http://www.jasoncolavito.com/blog/the-nazca-astronaut-a-fishy-story.

the Owl-Man   See http://www.jasoncolavito.com/blog/the-nazca-astronaut
-a-fishy-story, citing Reiche 1949.

wearing a traditional poncho   http://ancientaliensdebunked.com/the-nazca
-astronautowlman-or-fisherman/.

Alfred Kroeber   Kroeber and Collier 1998.

performing religious rituals   Hall 2010; Reiche 1949; http://old.dainst.org/en
/nasca?ft=all.

295   *ceremonial processions*   Hall 2010.

outside assistance   Joe Nickell, previously of the University of Kentucky, created a full-sized experimental reproduction of a Nazca image, using just
string, wooden stakes, and a little mathematics; see http://www.joenickell
.com/NascaGeoglyphRecreator/NascaGeoglyphRec1.html. See also Feder
2013, quoted in Hamilton 2008: 23–26.

the Moche culture   Alva and Donnan 1993; Schreiber in Bahn 1995: 226–27;
Schreiber in Bahn 1996c: 118–21.

and other seafood   Alva and Donnan 1993: 13.

296   *the largest construction ever built*   Alva and Donnan 1993: 13–14, 24.

the mudbrick pyramids   Alva and Donnan 1993: 23–24.

the New World's Richest Unlooted Tomb   Alva 1988: 510–48; see also Alva
1990: 2–15; Alva and Donnan 1993; and http://archaeology.about.com/od
/mocheculture/ig/New-Elite-Moche-Burial/Tomb-of-Lord-of-Sipan-.htm.
Also, regarding later discoveries, Wilford 2006; http://www.nytimes.com
/2001/02/16/science/16reuters-archaeo.html.

297   *eleven people in the tomb*   Note, though, that the number of burials reported
varies; see, e.g., http://www.world-archaeology.com/features/tombs-of-the-lords
-of-sipan.htm, which describes eight people besides the main person buried.

298   *portrayed on the pottery*   http://archaeology.about.com/od/mocheculture/ig
/New-Elite-Moche-Burial/Moche-Sacrifice-Ceremony.htm#step-heading, citing Alva and Donnan 1993, among other sources. On the Moche and their
art, see also Donnan 1978, 1990; Donnan and McClelland 1999; Long 1990.

299   *Machu Picchu*   http://whc.unesco.org/en/list/274.

the time of the Spanish Conquest   See, e.g., Burger and Salazar 2004; Reinhard
2007; see also Pollard 2007: 122–27; Schreiber in Bahn 1995: 238–39.

300   *the DNA of skeletal remains*   See http://www.archaeology.org/news/3730–
151001-machu-picchu-dna.

Turn Right at Machu Picchu   Adams 2011.

the largest and most important ruin   Bingham 1913.

Lost City of the Incas   Bingham 1922, 1979, 2003.

301   *for further study*   http://www.npr.org/2010/12/15/132083890/yale-returns
-machu-picchu-artifacts-to-peru; http://www.carnegiemuseums.org/cmag/bk
_issue/2003/sepoct/feature1.html; http://www.pirwahostelscusco.com/blog
/hostels/new-machu-picchu-exhibit-opens-in-cusco-showcasing-yale-artifacts/;
http://www.cultureindevelopment.nl/News/Heritage_the_Americas/654
/Machu_Picchu,_Yale,_and_the_world_stage.

including ceremonial knives   Ibid.

CHAPTER 18
GIANT HEADS, FEATHERED
SERPENTS, AND GOLDEN EAGLES

303   *pure hand labor*   Cooper-White 2015; Mejia 2015; Shaer 2016; Sullivan 2014; also http://www.thedailybeast.com/articles/2015/05/09/the-mysteries-of-teotihuacan.html.

304   *earlier rulers of the city*   See Cooper-White 2015; Mejia 2015; Shaer 2016; Sullivan 2014; also http://www.bbc.com/news/world-latin-america-29828309; http://www.thedailybeast.com/articles/2015/05/09/the-mysteries-of-teotihuacan.html; http://hds.harvard.edu/news/2015/10/02/exploring-ancient-city-teotihuacan#; http://phys.org/news/2013–04-robot-chambers-ancient-mexico-temple.html. See also videos at https://www.youtube.com/watch?v=iCJM_5dOMSE&feature=youtu.be; https://www.youtube.com/watch?v=C8ZEKp85dwk&feature=youtu.be; https://www.youtube.com/watch?v=kksFtR9dEF4&feature=youtu.be.

    the earliest known civilization   Diehl 2004: 9, 11; Grove 2014: 183; Pool 2007: 7, fig. 1.4; Stone in Bahn 1995: 206–7

    Matthew and Marion Stirling   See especially Stirling 1939, 1940, 1941, 1947. See also the entry on Stirling by Michael D. Coe in Fagan 2014: 115–18; also Stone in Bahn 1995: 206–7.

305   *the nearby Olmec site*   Grove 2014: 1–2, 6; Pool 2007: 1, 35.

    Tres Zapotes Monument A   Grove 2014: 1–2, 6, 21; Pool 2007: 1–3, 250–51, fig. 1.1.

    indigenous to the region   Diehl 2004: 13–15.

    not yet been translated   Diehl 2004: 14; Grove 2014: 2–3, fig. 1.1; Pool 2007: 5, fig. 1.3.

306   *Tribes and Temples*   Blom and La Farge 1926–27; Grove 2014: 5–16; Pool 2007: 36–38; Stone in Bahn 1995: 206–7.

    three most important Olmec sites   See maps in Diehl 2004: 1; Grove 2014: 3, fig. 1.1; Pool 2007: 5, fig. 1.3.

307   *the date on Stela C*   Grove 2014: 17–30; Pool 2007: 40–44; Stone in Bahn 1995: 206–7.

    front of the altar   Grove 2014: 13–16, 31–36; Pool 2007: 44.

    Altar 5   Grove 2014: 33–36 and figs. 4.1–4.2. See Stirling 1940. The Olmec heads have been featured in an episode of the television show *Ancient Aliens*, where it is discussed whether they are wearing flight helmets; see episode 1 of season 4 (2012).

    found at the site   Diehl 2004: 60–82; Grove 2014: 37–49; Pool 2007: 1.

308   *San Lorenzo Tenochtitlán*   Grove 2014: 50–55. On the heads, of which seventeen total have been found at the various Olmec sites, see Pool 2007: 106–7 and fig. 4.3.

    Ann Cyphers   Diehl 2004: 16, 27–28; Grove 2014: 80–89, 104–15, 151–60; Pool 2007: 50–52.

    elucidating the details   Stone in Bahn 1995: 206–7.

    called themselves the Mexica   De Rojas 2012: 5–6; Draper 2010: 110–35; Smith 2003: 4, 36.

on top of the ruins   Bahn 2009: 154–55; Smith 2003: 43–55; Stone in Bahn 1995: 236–37.

309   *split into four quarters*   Bahn 2009: 154–55.

the Aztec deity of the Sun   De Rojas 2012: 56.

Eduardo Matos Moctezuma   Atwood 2014; Bahn 2009: 154–55; de Rojas 2012: 56–62; Stone in Bahn 1995: 236–37.

previous Mesoamerican civilizations   Bahn 2009: 154–55; Stone in Bahn 1995: 236–37.

310   *broken into four large pieces*   Draper 2010: 110–35; Lovgren 2006.

311   *below street level*   Draper 2010: 110–35.

nicknamed it Aristo-Canine   Ibid.

finding the tomb   Ibid.

one of the most visited tourist sites   http://whc.unesco.org/en/list/414.

at its largest   http://science.nationalgeographic.com/science/archaeology /teotihuacan-/. Note that the dates given differ: http://whc.unesco.org/en /list/414.

a beacon for later civilizations   Naughton 2015; see also Bahn 2009: 138–39; Fagan and Durrani 2014: 290–92; Meyer 1973b; http://whc.unesco.org/en /list/414.

312   *right under the pyramid*   http://whc.unesco.org/en/list/414.

pyrite mirrors and obsidian blades   Bahn 2009: 138–39; http://www.utexas .edu/cofa/art/347/teotihuacan.htm.

ceremonies held on various occasions   Stone in Bahn 1995: 228–29; Bahn 2009: 138–39; http://www.utexas.edu/cofa/art/347/teotihuacan.htm.

the earliest rulers of the city   Cooper-White 2015; Mejia 2015; Sullivan 2014; http://www.bbc.com/news/world-latin-america-29828309; http://www.the dailybeast.com/articles/2015/05/09/the-mysteries-of-teotihuacan.html; http://hds .harvard.edu/news/2015/10/02/exploring-ancient-city-teotihuacan#; http://phys .org/news/2013–04-robot-chambers-ancient-mexico-temple.html. See also videos at https://www.youtube.com/watch?v=iCJM_5dOMSE&feature=youtu.be; https://www.youtube.com/watch?v=C8ZEKp85dwk&feature=youtu.be; https://www.youtube.com/watch?v=kksFtR9dEF4&feature=youtu.be.

313   *other major buildings*   Millon 1964, 1973; Millon, Drewitt, and Cowgill, 1973; see http://humanitieslab.stanford.edu/teotihuacan/1497.

once lived there   Bahn 2009: 138–39; Fagan and Durrani 2014: 27, 290–92.

CHAPTER 19
SUBMARINES AND SETTLERS; GOLD COINS AND LEAD BULLETS

314   *at the front of the sub*   Amer 2002: 137–39; Cussler 2011; http://www.hunley.org; http://news.nationalgeographic.com/news/2001/03/0321_hunleyfind.html. Numerous accounts on the *Hunley* are available, including Chaffin 2008; Hicks

2015; Hicks and Kropf 2002; Neyland in Fagan 2007a: 220–23; Ragan 1999, 2006; and Walker 2005.

315   *lost for good*   Gast 2014; http://www.hunley.org; http://futureforce.navylive .dodlive.mil/2014/10/how-did-hunleys-crew-die/.

the wreck was found   Fagan and Durrani 2014: 358; http://www.nps.gov /history/local-law/FHPL_AbndShipwreck.pdf.

Credit for finding the sub   Gast 2014. Note that Amer 2002: 138 gives the date of the recovery of the *Hunley* as August 8, 2001.

the Hunley Commission   Amer 2002: 138; http://www.scstatehouse.gov/code /t54c007.php.

316   *additional corrosion*   Gast 2014.

as well as other artifacts   David L. Conlin (personal communication, July 18, 2016) ; Conlin and Russell 2006; Gast 2014; http://www.achp.gov/docs/Section 106SuccessStory_HLHunley.pdf; http://news.nationalgeographic.com/news /2001/03/0321_hunleyfind.html; http://usatoday30.usatoday.com/news/nation /2001–03–21-hunley.htm.

through a DNA match   http://hunley.org/main_index.asp?CONTENT=press& ID=126; http://www.navy.mil/submit/display.asp?story_id=15458.

317   *his pocket watch*   Amer 2002: 138; Gast 2014; http://www.civilwarnews .com/archive/articles/hunley_study.htm; http://hunley.org/main_index.asp? CONTENT=press&ID=114.

extraordinary importance   See Conlin and Russell 2006; http://www.achp .gov/docs/Section106SuccessStory_HLHunley.pdf.

before it ever even opened   Pringle 2011; Taylor 2011.

318   *while they were in England*   http://www.nps.gov/jame/learn/historyculture /pocahontas-her-life-and-legend.htm.

vanished over the centuries   The following information is based on Kelso's 2007 article on his Jamestown excavations, as published in Fagan 2007a: 172–75. See also Fagan and Durrani 2014: 8; Kelso 2008; Kelso and Straube 2004.

a brief description of their findings   See Kelso in Fagan 2007a: 172–75.

319   *early leaders of the colony*   See Epstein 2015 and O'Brien 2015, from which the following information is derived.

media reports   See Epstein 2015 and O'Brien 2015.

fell into disrepair   http://historicjamestowne.org/july-2015/.

unmarked cemetery located elsewhere   See Epstein 2015 and O'Brien 2015.

less than a full year   http://historicjamestowne.org/archaeology/chancel -burials/founders/gabriel-archer/; http://historicjamestowne.org/archaeology /chancel-burials/founders/robert-hunt/.

a few months after arriving   http://historicjamestowne.org/archaeology/chancel -burials/founders/william-west/; http://historicjamestowne.org/archaeology /chancel-burials/founders/ferdinando-wainman/.

320   *to look at the remains*   http://smithsonianscience.si.edu/2013/05/forensic -analysis-of-17th-century-human-remains-at-jamestown-va-reveal-evidence-of -cannibalism/; https://www.youtube.com/watch?v=FGcN9_Gd5zQ.

access to her brain http://smithsonianscience.si.edu/2013/05/forensic-analysis
-of-17th-century-human-remains-at-jamestown-va-reveal-evidence-of
-cannibalism/; https://www.youtube.com/watch?v=FGcN9_Gd5zQ.

the face and throat http://smithsonianscience.si.edu/2013/05/forensic-analysis
-of-17th-century-human-remains-at-jamestown-va-reveal-evidence-of
-cannibalism/.

after she died https://www.youtube.com/watch?v=FGcN9_Gd5zQ.

on Jamestown Island http://smithsonianscience.si.edu/2013/05/forensic-analysis
-of-17th-century-human-remains-at-jamestown-va-reveal-evidence-of
-cannibalism/; http://historicjamestowne.org; http://anthropology.si.edu/written
inbone/about_exhibit.html.

321 *the Columbia River* Pollard 2007: 240–43; http://nmnh.typepad.com
/100years/2012/10/the-9000-year-old-kennewick-man.html.

repatriate to the tribe Fagan and Durrani 2014: 358; http://www.nps.gov
/nagpra/MANDATES/INDEX.HTM.

Ishi in Two Worlds Kroeber 2011.

still highly regarded today Pope 1923.

repatriated and reunited Bower 2002; the story subsequently became the
subject of a book: Starn 2004.

322 *his entire skeleton* Preston 2014; http://www.burkemuseum.org/kman/. For
overviews of the initial portion of the saga, see Chatters 2002 and Thomas 2001.

made available for study Callaway 2015; http://www.burkemuseum.org/kman/;
http://nmnh.typepad.com/100years/2012/10/the-9000-year-old-kennewick
-man.html.

five Native American tribal bands On the continuing controversy, see Callaway
2015; Gerianos 2016; Mapes 2016a, b; Owsley and Jantz 2014; Preston 2014;
Rasmussen et al. 2015; Zimmer 2016. See also http://www.burkemuseum.org
/kman/.

323 *the Ancestral Pueblo people* http://whc.unesco.org/en/list/353; http://www.nps
.gov/chcu/index.htm; http://www.learner.org/interactives/collapse/chacocanyon
.html. See also Fagan 2005; Fagan and Durrani 2014: 348–50; Lekson 2006,
2007; Vivian and Hilpert 2012.

a thriving village Fagan and Durrani 2014: 348–50; http://www.nps.gov/chcu
/planyourvisit/pueblo-bonito.htm; http://www.nps.gov/chcu/index.htm; https://
www.crowcanyon.org/EducationProducts/peoples_mesa_verde/pueblo_II
_bonito_escalante.asp; https://www.crowcanyon.org/EducationProducts/peoples
_mesa_verde/pueblo_II_overview.asp.

drought and plague http://www.nps.gov/chcu/faqs.htm; http://www.nps
.gov/chcu/planyourvisit/pueblo-bonito.htm. See also Fagan 2005; Fagan and
Durrani 2014: 348–50; Lekson 2006, 2007; Monastersky 2015; and Vivian and
Hilpert 2012.

324 *Mesa Verde National Park* http://www.nps.gov/meve/index.htm.

ruins at Mesa Verde http://whc.unesco.org/en/list/27; http://www.nps.gov
/meve/index.htm; http://www.nps.gov/meve/learn/historyculture/cliff_palace
_preservation.htm; http://www.nps.gov/meve/learn/historyculture/places.htm.

Cahokia Mounds   http://whc.unesco.org/en/list/198.

largest pre-Columbian archaeological site   Hodges 2011; http://whc.unesco .org/en/list/198; http://cahokiamounds.org/explore/.

largest prehistoric earthen structure   http://whc.unesco.org/en/list/198; see also Hodges 2011.

must have built them   Hodges 2011; http://whc.unesco.org/en/list/198.

325   *excavate at the sites*   http://www.history.org; http://www.mountvernon.org /research-collections/archaeology/.

plenty of opportunities   See Fagan and Durrani 2014: 392–93.

Crow Canyon Archaeological Center   http://www.crowcanyon.org.

Center for American Archaeology   http://www.caa-archeology.org.

Archaeological Fieldwork Opportunity Bulletin   https://www.archaeological .org/fieldwork/afob.

DIGGING DEEPER 4
DO YOU GET TO KEEP
WHAT YOU FIND?

327   *case-by-case decisions*   See, e.g., Anderson 2016, Atwood 2006; Cuno 2010, 2012; Felch and Frammolino 2011; Meyer 1973a; Roehrenbeck 2010; Watson and Todeschini 2006; Waxman 2009. See also Bering 2016, as well as http:// content.time.com/time/specials/packages/completelist/0,29569,1883142,00. html for *Time*'s list of "Top 10 Plundered Artifacts"; and http://www. theguardian.com/artanddesign/2016/may/08/greece-international-justice-re- gain-parthenon-marbles-uk for a recent article on the Elgin Marbles.

pockmarked with looters' pits   Fagan and Durrani 2014: 20–22. See also Curry 2015; Dubrow 2014; Mueller 2016; Romano 2015; Romey 2015; Vance 2015.

Nimrud and the Mosul Museum   Casana 2015; http://www.cnn.com /2015/03/09/world/iraq-isis-heritage/.

328   *published in the journal Antiquity*   Parcak et al. 2016.

some of the most famous pieces   Bogdanos 2005. See also Emberling and Han- son 2008; Rothfield 2008a.

329   *Thieves of Baghdad*   Ibid.

illegally digging at sites   See, e.g., Andrews 2003; Emberling and Hanson 2008.

an antiquities dealer   George 2016.

the noises that they hear   Al-Rawi and George 2014; George 2016.

330   *a different set of scholars*   Horowitz, Greenberg, and Zilberg 2015; Pearce and Wunsch 2014; see also Abraham 2011. News reports, reviews, and discussions occur in Baker 2015; Ben Zion 2015a; Hasson 2015; and http://lawrence schiffman.com/wp-content/uploads/2015/03/jews-of-babylon.pdf; http://www .reuters.com/article/us-israel-archaeology-babylon-idUSKBN0L71EK20150203;

http://paul-barford.blogspot.com/2015/02/babylonian-cunies-from-private.html; http://news.cornell.edu/stories/2015/01/new-archive-jewish-babylonian-exile-released; http://www.ancientjewreview.com/articles/2015/2/18/pearce-and-wunsch-documents-of-judean-exiles-and-west-semites-in-babylonia-1.

put into effect http://www.unesco.org/new/en/culture/themes/illicit-traffic-of-cultural-property/1970-convention/; http://portal.unesco.org/en/ev.php-URL_ID=13039&URL_DO=DO_TOPIC&URL_SECTION=201.html.

331 *necessitate new laws* Atwood 2006; Brodie and Tubb 2011; Rothfield 2008b; Rush 2012.

other ancient remains Fagan and Durrani 2014: 355–58; Harmon and McManamon 2006; http://www.nps.gov/archeology/sites/antiquities/about.htm; http://www.georgewright.org/313mcmanamon.pdf.

from the colonial era http://www.nps.gov/history/local-law/fhpl_histsites.pdf.

the offender's record Fagan and Durrani 2014: 358; http://www.nps.gov/archeology/tools/Laws/arpa.htm.

nearby federal lands See http://www.npr.org/templates/story/story.php?storyId=106091937; http://articles.latimes.com/2009/jun/17/nation/na-artifacts-backlash17; http://www.nytimes.com/2009/06/21/us/21blanding.html?_r=0.

332 *signed into law* https://democrats-foreignaffairs.house.gov/news/press-releases/president-signs-engel-bill-stop-isis-looting-antiquities; http://www.al-monitor.com/pulse/originals/2015/06/congress-illegal-isis-looting-syria-artifacts.html; https://www.congress.gov/bill/114th-congress/house-bill/1493/text.

the ongoing looting http://www.theantiquitiescoalition.org/state-department-hearing-on-egypt-antiquities-import-mou/; http://www.state.gov/r/pa/prs/ps/2016/11/264632.htm.

known but unexcavated remains Organizations that are involved in working on such measures include the US Committee of the Blue Shield (www.uscbs.org), SAFE: Saving Antiquities for Everyone (http://savingantiquities.org), the Antiquities Coalition (https://theantiquitiescoalition.org), and the American Schools of Oriental Research Cultural Heritage Initiatives (http://www.asor-syrianheritage.org/about/mission/), among others.

EPILOGUE
BACK TO THE FUTURE

334 *The World without Us* Weisman 2007.

336 *an assistant named Harriet Burton* Macaulay 1979.

the famous phrase Macaulay 1979: 26.

the remote control Macaulay 1979: 30, 52–65.

337 *found at Troy* Macaulay 1979: 32–33, 36–37, 68–81.

proton magnetometers See, e.g., https://archeosciences.revues.org/1781.

338 *artifacts of that heritage* See, e.g., http://www.sfu.ca/ipinch/project-components/community-based-initiatives.

BIBLIOGRAPHY

Abegg, Martin Jr., Peter Flint, and Eugene Ulrich. 1999. *The Dead Sea Scrolls Bible: The Oldest Known Bible Translated for the First Time into English.* New York: HarperCollins.

Abraham, Kathleen. 2011. "The Reconstruction of Jewish Communities in the Persian Empire: The Āl-Yahūdu Clay Tablets." In *Light and Shadows: The Story of Iran and the Jews*, edited by Hagai Segev and Asaf Schor, 261–62. Tel Aviv, Israel: Beit Hatfutsot.

Adams, Mark. 2011. *Turn Right at Machu Picchu: Rediscovering the Lost City One Step at a Time.* New York: Dutton.

———. 2015. *Meet Me in Atlantis: My Obsessive Quest to Find the Sunken City.* New York: Dutton.

Adams, Matthew J., Jonathan David, and Yotam Tepper. 2014. "Excavations at the Camp of the Roman Sixth Ferrata Legion in Israel." *Bible History Daily*, May 1 (originally published October 17, 2013). http://www.biblicalarchaeology.org/daily/biblical-sites-places/biblical-archaeology-sites/legio/.

Aharoni, Yohanan. 1962. "Expedition B—The Cave of Horror." *Israel Exploration Journal* 12, nos. 3–4: 186–99.

Aicher, Peter. 2000. "Mussolini's Forum and the Myth of Augustan Rome." *Classical Bulletin* 76: 117–39.

Aitken, Martin J. 1990. *Science-Based Dating in Archaeology.* Boston: Routledge.

Aldhouse-Green, Miranda. 2015. *Bog Bodies Uncovered: Solving Europe's Ancient Mystery.* London: Thames and Hudson.

Aldred, Cyril. 1991. *Akhenaten: King of Egypt.* London: Thames and Hudson.

Alföldy, Géza. 1995. "Eine Bauinschrift aus dem Colosseum." *Zeitschrift für Papyrologie und Epigraphik* 109: 195–226.

Allegro, John M. 1960. *The Treasure of the Copper Scroll.* Garden City, NY: Doubleday.

Allen, Susan Heuck Allen. 1999. *Finding the Walls of Troy: Frank Calvert and Heinrich Schliemann at Hisarlik*. Berkeley: University of California Press.

Allen, Susan J. 2006. *Tutankhamun's Tomb: The Thrill of Discovery*. New York: Metropolitan Museum of Art.

Al-Rawi, Farouk N. H., and Andrew George. 2014. "Back to the Cedar Forest: The Beginning and End of Tablet V of the Standard Babylonian Epic of Gilgameš." *Journal of Cuneiform Studies* 66: 69–90.

Altares, Guillermo. 2015a. "Altamira Cave Will Open to Visitors." *El País*, March 27. http://elpais.com/elpais/2015/03/27/inenglish/1427469981_303108.html.

———. 2015b. "Altamira Must Be Closed to Visitors, Spanish Scientists Tell UNESCO." *El País*, March 26. http://elpais.com/m/elpais/2015/03/23/inenglish/1427122533_376325.html.

Alva, Walter. 1988. "Discovering the New World's Richest Unlooted Tomb." *National Geographic* (October), 510–48.

———. 1990. "New Tomb of Royal Splendor." *National Geographic* (June): 2–15.

Alva, Walter, and Christopher B. Donnan. 1993. *Royal Tombs of Sipán*. Los Angeles: UCLA Fowler Museum of Cultural History.

Amadasi, Maria G., and Eugenia E. Schneider. 2002. *Petra*. Translated by Lydia G. Cochrane. Chicago: University of Chicago Press.

Amandry, Pierre. 1992. *La redécouverte de Delphes*. Paris: De Boccard.

Amer, Christopher F. 2002. "South Carolina: A Drop in the Bucket." In *International Handbook of Underwater Archaeology*, edited by Carol V. Ruppé and Janet F. Barstad, 127–42. New York: Kluwer Academic–Plenum.

Andersen, Wayne V. 2003. *The Ara Pacis of Augustus and Mussolini: An Archaeological Mystery*. Geneva, Switz.: Fabriart.

Anderson, Maxwell L. 2016. *Antiquities: What Everyone Needs to Know*. New York: Oxford University Press.

Andrews, Carol. 1984. *Egyptian Mummies*. Cambridge, MA: Harvard University Press.

Andrews, Edmund L. 2003. "Iraqi Looters Tearing Up Archaeological Sites." *New York Times*, May 23. http://www.nytimes.com/2003/05/23/international/worldspecial/23LOOT.html.

Andronicos, Manolis. 1992. *Olympia*. Athens, Greece: Ekdotike Athenon.

———. 1993. *Delphi*. Athens, Greece: Ekdotike Athenon.

Anyangwe, Eliza. 2015. "Could Egypt's Empty Animal Mummies Reveal an Ancient Scam?" *CNN*, May 22. http://www.cnn.com/2015/05/22/africa/ancient-egypt-animal-mummies-empty/.

Atwood, Roger. 2006. *Stealing History: Tomb Raiders, Smugglers, and the Looting of the Ancient World*. Repr. New York: St. Martins Griffin.

———. 2014. "Beneath the Capital's Busy Streets, Archaeologists Are Discovering the Buried World of the Aztecs." *Archaeology* 67, no. 4 (June 9):

26–33. http://www.archaeology.org/issues/138–1407/features/2173-mexico-city-aztec-buried-world.

Bahn, Paul G. 1995. *100 Great Archaeological Discoveries*. New York: Facts on File.

———. 1996a. *Archaeology: A Very Short Introduction*. Oxford, UK: Oxford University Press.

———. 1996b. *Bluff Your Way in Archaeology*. West Sussex, UK: Ravette.

———. 1996c. *Tombs Graves and Mummies: 50 Discoveries in World Archaeology*. New York: Barnes and Noble.

———. 1999. *Wonderful Things: Uncovering the World's Great Archaeological Treasures*. London: Seven Dials.

———. 2000. *Lost Treasures: Great Discoveries in World Archaeology*. New York: Barnes and Noble. [NB: This is the US publication of *Wonderful Things*.]

———. 2001. *The Penguin Archaeology Guide*. New York: Penguin.

———. 2003. *Archaeology: The Definitive Guide*. New York: Barnes and Noble.

———. 2007. *The Bluffer's Guide to Archaeology*, rev. ed. London: Oval.

———. 2008. *The Great Archaeologists: The Lives and Legacy of the People Who Discovered the World's Most Famous and Important Archaeological Sites*. London: Anness.

———. 2009. *Legendary Sites of the Ancient World: An Illustrated Guide to Over 80 Major Archaeological Discoveries*. London: Anness.

———. 2014. *The History of Archaeology: An Introduction*. New York: Routledge.

Bahn, Paul G., and Barry Cunliffe. 2000. *The Atlas of World Archaeology*. New York: Checkmark–Facts on File.

Bahn, Paul G., and Colin Renfrew. 1996. *The Cambridge Illustrated History of Archaeology*. Cambridge: Cambridge University Press.

Baillie, Michael G. L. 2014. *Tree-Ring Dating and Archaeology*. Boston: Routledge.

Baker, Luke. 2015. "Ancient Tablets Reveal Life of Jews in Nebuchadnezzar's Babylon." *Reuters*, February 3. http://www.reuters.com/article/us-israel-archaeology-babylon-idUSKBN0L71EK20150203.

Ballard, Robert D., ed. 2008. *Archaeological Oceanography*. Princeton, NJ: Princeton University Press.

Balter, Michael. 2009. *The Goddess and the Bull: Çatalhöyük—An Archaeological Journey to the Dawn of Civilization*. Walnut Creek, CA: Left Coast Press.

Banning, Edward B. 2002. *Archaeological Survey (Manuals in Archaeological Method, Theory and Technique)*. New York: Springer.

Barber, Elizabeth W. 1999. *The Mummies of Ürümchi*. New York: W. W. Norton.

Bard, Kathryn A. 2008. *An Introduction to the Archaeology of Ancient Egypt*. New York: Wiley-Blackwell.

Barkai, Ran, and Roy Liran. 2008. "Midsummer Sunset at Neolithic Jericho." *Time and Mind* 1, no. 3 (November): 273–84.

Barnard, Anne. 2015. "ISIS Destroys Triumphal Arches in Palymyra, Syria." *New York Times*, October 5. http://www.nytimes.com/2015/10/06/world/middleeast/isis-syria-arch-triumph-palmyra.html?_r=0.

Bar-Yosef, Ofer, and Jane Callander. 2006. "Dorothy Annie Elizabeth Garrod." In *Breaking Ground: Pioneering Women Archaeologists*, edited by Getzel M. Cohen and Martha Sharp Joukowsky, 380–424. Ann Arbor: University of Michigan Press.

Bar-Yosef, Ofer, B. Vandermeersch, B. Arensburg, A. Belfer-Cohen, P. Goldberg, H. Laville, L. Meignen, et al. 1992. "The Excavations in Kebara Cave, Mt. Carmel." *Current Anthropology* 33, no. 5: 497–550.

Barzilay, Julie. 2016. "Secrets of 'Iceman': How a 5,300-Year-Old Mummy Sheds Light on Evolution, Migration." *ABC News*, January 7. http://abcnews.go.com/Health/secrets-iceman-5300-year-mummy-sheds-light-evolution/story?id=36146634.

Bass, George F. 1967. *Cape Gelidonya: A Bronze Age Shipwreck*. Philadelphia: American Philosophical Society.

———. 1986. "A Bronze Age Shipwreck at Ulu Burun (Kas): 1984 Campaign." *American Journal of Archaeology* 90: 269–96.

———. 1987. "Oldest Known Shipwreck Reveals Splendors of the Bronze Age." *National Geographic* (December): 692–733.

Bataille, Georges. 1955. *Lascaux: or, The Birth of Art: Prehistoric Painting*. Translated by Austryn Wainhouse. Lausanne, Switz.: Skira.

Beard, Mary. 2010. *The Fires of Vesuvius: Pompeii Lost and Found*. Cambridge, MA: Belknap Press.

Becker, Helmut, and Hans Günter Jansen. 1994. "Magnetic Prospektion 1993 der Unterstadt von Troia und Ilion." *Studia Troica* 4: 105–14.

Ben-Tor, Amnon. 2009. *Back to Masada*. Jerusalem: Israel Exploration Society.

Ben-Yehuda, Nachman. 1995. *The Masada Myth: Collective Memory and Mythmaking in Israel*. Madison: University of Wisconsin Press.

———. 2002. *Sacrificing Truth: Archaeology and the Myth of Masada*. Amherst, NY: Humanity.

Ben Zion, Ilan. 2015a. "'By the Rivers of Babylon' Exhibit Breathes Life into Judean Exile." *Times of Israel*, February 1. http://www.timesofisrael.com/by-the-rivers-of-babylon-exhibit-breathes-life-into-judean-exile/#ixzz3Qq8033Hh.

———. 2015b. "In First, Imperial Roman Legionary Camp Uncovered near Megiddo." *Times of Israel*, July 7. http://www.timesofisrael.com/in-first-imperial-roman-legionary-camp-uncovered-near-megiddo/.

Berger, Lee R., Darryl J. de Ruiter, Steven E. Churchill, Peter Schmid, Kristian J. Carlson, Paul H. G. M. Dirks, and Job M. Kibii. 2010. "*Australopithecus sediba*: A New Species of Homo-Like Australopith from South Africa." *Science* 328, no. 5975 (April 9): 195–204. doi: 10.1126/science.1184944.

Berger, Lee R., John Hawks, Darryl J. de Ruiter, Steven E. Churchill, Peter Schmid, Lucas K. Delezene, Tracy L Kivell, et al. 2015. "*Homo naledi*, a New Species of the Genus *Homo* from the Dinaledi Chamber, South Africa." *eLife*, September 10 (eLife 2015;4:e09560). https://elifesciences .org/content/4/e09560 or http://dx.doi.org/10.7554/eLife.09560.

Bering, Henrik. 2016. "Holding On to the Past." *Wall Street Journal*, May 6. http://www.wsj.com/articles/holding-on-to-the-past-1462563965.

Bermant, Chaim, and Michael Weitzman. 1979. *Ebla: A Revelation in Archeology*. New York: Times Books.

Berry, Joanne. 2007. *The Complete Pompeii*. Repr. London: Thames and Hudson.

Bietak, Manfred. 1992. "Minoan Wall-Paintings Unearthed at Ancient Avaris." *Egyptian Archaeology* 2: 26–28.

Bingham, Hiram. 1913. "In the Wonderland of Peru." *National Geographic* (April): 387–584. Reproduced as "Rediscovering Machu Picchu," http:// ngm.nationalgeographic.com/1913/04/machu-picchu/bingham-text.

———. 1922. *Inca Land: Explorations in the Highlands of Peru*. Boston: Houghton Mifflin.

———. 1979. *Machu Picchu, a Citadel of the Incas*. Repr. New York: Hacker Art Books.

———. 2003. *Lost City of the Incas*. Repr. New Haven, CT: Phoenix Press.

Binkovitz, Leah. 2013. "Q+A: How to Save the Arts in Times of War." *Smithsonian*, January 24. http://www.smithsonianmag.com/smithsonian -institution/qa-how-to-save-the-arts-in-times-of-war-5506188/?no-ist.

Binnie, Isla. 2014. "Nero's Buried Golden Palace to Open to the Public—in Hard Hats." *Reuters*, October 24. http://www.reuters.com/article/us -italy-palace-idUSKCN0ID1WJ20141024.

Blakemore, Erin. 2015. "The Incredible Treasures Found inside the 'Griffin Warrior' Tomb." *Smithsonian.com*, October 28. http://www.smithsonian mag.com/smart-news/heres-what-was-inside-griffin-warriors-grave -180957063/?no-ist.

Bleibtreu, Erika. 1990. "Five Ways to Conquer a City." *Biblical Archaeology Review* 16, no. 3: 37–44.

———. 1991. "Grisly Assyrian Record of Torture and Death." *Biblical Archaeology Review* 17, no. 1: 52–61, 75.

Blom, Frans, and Oliver La Farge. 1926–27. *Tribes and Temples*. New Orleans, LA: Tulane University, Middle American Research Institute.

Blomster, Jeffrey P. 2012. "Early Evidence of the Ballgame in Oaxaca, Mexico." *Proceedings of the National Academy of Sciences* 109, 21: 8020–25.

Blumenthal, Ralph, and Tom Mashberg. 2015. "TED Prize Goes to Archaeologist Who Combats Looting with Satellite Technology." *New York Times*,

November 8. http://www.nytimes.com/2015/11/09/arts/international/ted
-grant-goes-to-archaeologist-who-combats-looting-with-satellite-technology
.html?_r=0.

Bogdanos, Matthew. 2005. *Thieves of Baghdad*. New York: Bloomsbury.

Bohstrom, Phillipe. 2016. "Monumental Forgotten Gardens of Petra Rediscovered After 2,000 Years." *Haaretz*, September 25. http://www.haaretz
.com/jewish/archaeology/1.744119.

Bomgardner, David L. 2001. *The Story of the Roman Amphitheatre*. London:
Routledge.

Borger, Julian. 2016. "Egypt 'Suppressing Truth' over Hidden Chambers in
Tutankhamun's Tomb." *Guardian*, May 13. http://www.theguardian
.com/world/2016/may/12/egypt-hidden-chambers-tutankhamun
-tomb-nefertiti.

Bower, Bruce. 2002. "Ishi's Long Road Home." *Science News*, June 4. https://
www.sciencenews.org/article/ishis-long-road-home?mode=magazine&
context=229.

Bowman-Kruhm, Mary. 2005. *The Leakeys: A Biography*. Westport, CT:
Greenwood Press.

Bradford, John. 1957. "New Techniques and the Archaeologist." *New Scientist* (May 2): 17–19.

Braymer, Marjorie. 1960. *The Walls of Windy Troy: A Biography of Heinrich
Schliemann*. New York: Harcourt Brace.

Brier, Bob, and Jean-Pierre Houdin. 2009. *The Secret of the Great Pyramid:
How One Man's Obsession Led to the Solution of Ancient Egypt's Greatest
Mystery*. New York: Harper Perennial.

Brodie, Neil, and Kathryn Walker Tubb, eds. 2011. *Illicit Antiquities: The
Theft of Culture and the Extinction of Archaeology*. Repr. Boston:
Routledge.

Brown, Terence A., Keri A. Brown, Christine E. Flaherty, Lisa M. Little,
and A. John N. W. Prag. 2000. "DNA Analysis of Bones from Grave
Circle B at Mycenae: A First Report." *Annual of the British School at Athens 95*: 115–19.

Browning, Iain. 1973. *Petra*. Park Ridge, NJ: Noyes Press.

———. 1979. *Palmyra*. Park Ridge, NJ: Noyes Press.

Bruce-Mitford, Rupert. 1979. *Sutton Hoo Ship Burial: A Handbook*. London:
British Museum Press.

Bryce, Trevor R. 2002. *Life and Society in the Hittite World*. Oxford. UK:
Oxford University Press.

———. 2005. *The Kingdom of the Hittites*, new ed. Oxford, UK: Oxford,
University Press.

———. 2006. *The Trojans and Their Neighbors*. London: Routledge.

———. 2010. "The Trojan War." In *The Oxford Handbook of the Bronze Age
Aegean*, edited by Eric H. Cline, 475–82. New York: Oxford University
Press.

———. 2012. *The World of the Neo-Hittite Kingdoms*. Oxford, UK: Oxford University Press.

Burger, Richard, and Lucy Salazar, eds. 2004. *Machu Picchu: Unveiling the Mystery of the Incas*. New Haven, CT: Yale University Press.

Burgon, John William. 1846. *Petra, a Poem: To Which a Few Short Poems Are Now Added*, 2nd ed. Oxford: F. MacPherson.

Byron, George Gordon. 1815. *Hebrew Melodies*. London: John Murray.

Calderwood, Imogen. 2016. "Long-lost Roman Roads Discovered on Flood Maps: Hi-tech Lidar Data Reveals the Route of 2,000-Year-Old Highways across Britain." *DailyMail.com*, January 1. http://www.dailymail .co.uk/news/article-3381432/Long-lost-Roman-roads-discovered-flood -maps-Hi-tech-Lidar-data-reveals-route-2–000-year-old-highways-Britain .html?ITO=applenews.

Callaway, Ewen. 2015. "Ancient American Genome Rekindles Legal Row." *Nature*, June 18. http://www.nature.com/news/ancient-american-genome -rekindles-legal-row-1.17797.

———. 2016. "'Cave of Forgotten Dreams' May Hold Earliest Painting of Volcanic Eruption." *Nature*, January 15. http://www.nature.com/news/cave -of-forgotten-dreams-may-hold-earliest-painting-of-volcanic-eruption -1.19177.

Camp, John M. II. 1986. *The Athenian Agora: Excavations in the Heart of Classical Athens*. London: Thames and Hudson.

———. 2001. *The Archaeology of Athens*. New Haven, CT: Yale University Press.

———. 2010. *The Athenian Agora: Site Guide*, 5th ed. Athens, Greece: American School of Classical Studies at Athens.

Cargill, Robert. 2009. *Qumran through (Real) Time: A Virtual Reconstruction of Qumran and the Dead Sea Scrolls*. Chicago: Gorgias Press.

Carlsen, William. 2016. *Jungle of Stone: The True Story of Two Men, Their Extraordinary Journey, and the Discovery of the Lost Civilization of the Maya*. New York: William Morrow.

Carrington, Daisy. 2014. "Egypt's Mummies Get Virtually Naked with CT Scans." *CNN*, May 1. http://www.cnn.com/2014/05/01/world/meast /mummies-get-virtually-naked-with-ct-scans/.

Carter, Howard. 2010. *The Tomb of Tut-Ankh-Amen: Discovered by the Late Earl of Carnarvon and Howard Carter*, 2 vols. Repr. Cambridge: Cambridge University Press.

Carter, Howard, and Arthur C. Mace. 1977. *The Discovery of the Tomb of Tutankhamen (Egypt)*. Repr. New York: Dover.

Casana, Jesse. 2015. "Satellite Imagery-Based Analysis of Archaeological Looting in Syria." *Near Eastern Archaeology* 78, no. 3: 142–52.

Castledon, Rodney. 1993. *Minoan Life in Bronze Age Crete*. London: Routledge.

———. 2005. *The Mycenaeans*. London: Routledge.

Catling, Christopher. 2012. *Discovering the Past through Archaeology: The Science and Practice of Studying Excavation Materials and Ancient Sites*. London: Southwater.

———. 2013. *A Practical Handbook of Archaeology: A Beginner's Guide to Unearthing the Past*. London: Lorenz.

Catling, Christopher, and Paul G. Bahn. 2010. *The Illustrated Practical Encyclopedia of Archaeology: The Key Sites, Those Who Discovered Them, and How to Become an Archaeologist*. London: Lorenz.

Ceram, C. W. 1951. *Gods, Graves, and Scholars: The Story of Archaeology*. New York: Random House.

———. 1955. *The Secret of the Hittites*. New York: Alfred A. Knopf.

———. 1958. *The March of Archaeology*. New York: Alfred A. Knopf.

———. 1967. *Gods, Graves, and Scholars: The Story of Archaeology*, 2nd rev. ed. New York: Random House.

———, ed. 1966. *Hands on the Past: Pioneer Archaeologists Tell Their Own Story*. New York: Alfred A. Knopf.

Chaffin, Tom. 2008. *The H. L. Hunley: The Secret Hope of the Confederacy*. New York: Hill and Wang.

Chandler, Russell. 1991. "Library Lifts Veil on Dead Sea Scrolls." *Los Angeles Times*, September 22. http://articles.latimes.com/1991-09-22/news/mn-4145_1_dead-sea-scrolls.

Chase, Arlen F., Diane Z. Chase, Jaime J. Awe, John F. Weishampel, Gyles Iannone, Holley Moyes, Jason Yaeger, et al. 2014. "The Use of LiDAR in Understanding the Ancient Maya Landscape." *Advances in Archaeological Practice* 2, no. 3 (August): 208–21.

Chase, Arlen F., Diane Z. Chase, Christopher T. Fisher, Stephen J. Leisz, and John F. Weishampel. 2012. "Geospatial Revolution and Remote Sensing LiDAR in Mesoamerican Archaeology." *Proceedings of the National Academy of Sciences* 109, no. 32: 12916–21.

Chase, Arlen F., Diane Z. Chase, and John F. Weishampel. 2010. "Lasers in the Jungle." *Archaeology* 63, no. 4: 27–29. http://archive.archaeology.org/1007/.

Chase, Arlen F., Diane Z. Chase, John F. Weishampel, Jason B. Drake, Ramesh L. Shrestha, K. Clint Slatton, Jaime J. Awe, et al. 2011. "Airborne LiDAR, Archaeology, and the Ancient Maya Landscape at Caracol, Belize." *Journal of Archaeological Science* 38, no. 2: 387–98.

Chase, Raymond G. 2002. *Ancient Hellenistic and Roman Amphitheatres, Stadiums, and Theatres: The Way They Look Now*. Portsmouth, NH: P. E. Randall.

Chatters, James C. 2002. *Ancient Encounters: Kennewick Man and the First Americans*. New York: Simon and Schuster.

Chauvet, Jean-Marie, Eliette Brunel Deschamps, and Christian Hillaire. 1996. *Dawn of Art: The Chauvet Cave; The Oldest Known Paintings in the World*. Translated by Paul G. Bahn. New York: Harry N. Abrams.

Chivers, C. J. 2013. "Grave Robbers and War Steal Syria's History." *New York Times*, April 6. http://www.nytimes.com/2013/04/07/world/middleeast /syrian-war-devastates-ancient-sites.html?pagewanted=all&_r=1.

Choi, Charles Q. 2014. "Humans Did Not Wipe Out the Neanderthals, New Research Suggests." *Livescience*, August 20. http://www.livescience .com/47460-neanderthal-extinction-revealed.html.

Christie, Agatha. 2011. *Murder in Mesopotamia: A Hercule Poirot Mystery*. Repr. New York: William Morrow.

Claridge, Amanda. 2010. *Rome: An Oxford Archaeological Guide*, 2nd ed. Oxford, UK: Oxford University Press.

Clark, Liesl. 1998. "Ice Mummies of the Inca." *Nova*, November 14. http:// www.pbs.org/wgbh/nova/ancient/ice-mummies-inca.html.

Clayton, Peter, and Martin Price. 1989. *The Seven Wonders of the Ancient World*. London: Routledge.

Cline, Diane Harris. 2016. *The Greeks: An Illustrated History*. Washington, DC: National Geographic Books.

Cline, Eric H. 1987. "Amenhotep III and the Aegean: A Reassessment of Egypto–Aegean Relations in the 14th Century BCE." *Orientalia* 56, no. 1: 1–36.

———. 1991. "Monkey Business in the Late Bronze Age Aegean: The Amenhotep II Figurines at Mycenae and Tiryns." *Bulletin of the British School at Athens* 86: 29–42.

———. 1994. *Sailing the Wine-Dark Sea: International Trade and the Late Bronze Age Aegean*. Oxford, UK: Tempus Reparatum.

———. 1998. "Amenhotep III, the Aegean and Anatolia." In *Amenhotep III: Perspectives on his Reign*, edited by David B. O'Connor and Eric H. Cline, 236–50. Ann Arbor: University of Michigan Press.

———. 2000. *The Battles of Armageddon: Megiddo and the Jezreel Valley from the Bronze Age to the Nuclear Age*. Ann Arbor: University of Michigan Press.

———. 2004. *Jerusalem Besieged: From Ancient Canaan to Modern Israel*. Ann Arbor: University of Michigan Press.

———. 2006. "Area L (The 1998–2000 Seasons)." In *Megiddo IV: The 1998– 2002 Seasons* (2 vols.), edited by Israel Finkelstein, David Ussishkin, and Baruch Halpern, 1: 104–23. Tel Aviv, Israel: Tel Aviv University.

———. 2007a. *From Eden to Exile: Unraveling Mysteries of the Bible*. Washington, DC: National Geographic Books.

———. 2007b. "Raiders of the Faux Ark." *Boston Globe*, September 30, Opinion section, E1–2. http://www.boston.com/news/globe/ideas/articles /2007/09/30/raiders_of_the_faux_ark/.

———. 2009. *Biblical Archaeology: A Very Short Introduction*. New York: Oxford University Press.

———. 2011. "Whole Lotta Shakin' Going On: The Possible Destruction by Earthquake of Megiddo Stratum VIA." In *The Fire Signals of*

Lachish: Studies in the Archaeology and History of Israel in the Late Bronze Age, Iron Age, and Persian Period in Honor of David Ussishkin, edited by Israel Finkelstein and Nadav Na'aman, 55–70. Tel Aviv, Israel: Tel Aviv University.

———. 2012. "Fabulous Finds or Fantastic Forgeries? The Distortion of Archaeology by the Media and Pseudo-Archaeologists, and What We Can Do about It." In *Archaeology, Bible, Politics, and the Media: Proceedings of the Duke University Conference,* April 23–24, 2009, edited by Eric Meyers and Carol Meyers, 39–50. Winona Lake, IN: Eisenbrauns.

———. 2013. *The Trojan War: A Very Short Introduction*. New York: Oxford University Press.

———. 2014. *1177 BCE: The Year Civilization Collapsed*. Princeton, NJ: Princeton University Press.

———. 2015. Review of Andrew Collins, *Göbekli Tepe: Genesis of the Gods; The Temple of the Watchers and the Discovery of Eden* (Bear, Rochester, VT, 2014). *American Antiquity* 80, no. 3: 620–21.

Cline, Eric H., and David B. O'Connor, eds. 2006. *Thutmose III: A New Biography*. Ann Arbor: University of Michigan Press.

Cline, Eric H., and Inbal Samet. 2013. "Area L: The 2006 and 2007 Seasons." In *Megiddo V: The 2004–2008 Seasons* (3 vols.), edited by Israel Finkelstein, David Ussishkin, and Eric H. Cline, 1: 275–91. Tel Aviv, Israel: Tel Aviv University.

Cline, Eric H., and Anthony Sutter. 2011. "Battlefield Archaeology at Armageddon: Cartridge Cases and the 1948 Battle for Megiddo, Israel." *Journal of Military History* 75, no. 1: 159–90.

Cline, Eric H., and Assaf Yasur-Landau. 2006. "Your Career Is in Ruins: How to Start an Excavation in Five Not-So-Easy Steps." *Biblical Archaeology Review* 32, no. 1: 34–37, 71.

———. 2007. "Musings from a Distant Shore: The Nature and Destination of the Uluburun Ship and Its Cargo." *Tel Aviv* 34, no. 2: 125–41.

Clinton, Jane. 2013. "Major Show Reveals Life in Pompeii and Herculaneum." *Express*, March 3. http://www.express.co.uk/news/uk/381414/Major -show-reveals-life-in-Pompeii-and-Herculaneum.

Clottes, Jean. 2003. *Chauvet Cave: The Art of Earliest Times*. Translated by Paul G. Bahn. Provo: University of Utah Press.

Coe, Michael D. 2005. *The Maya*, 7th ed. London: Thames and Hudson.

———. 2012. *Breaking the Maya Code*, 3rd ed. London: Thames and Hudson.

Cohen, Jennie. 2011. "Viking Chief Buried in His Boat Found in Scotland." *History.com*, October 19. http://www.history.com/news/viking-chief -buried-in-his-boat-found-in-scotland.

Cole, Sonia. 1975. *Leakey's Luck: The Life of Louis Seymour Bazett Leakey, 1903–1972*. New York: Harcourt Brace Jovanovich.

Coleman, Kathleen. 2000. "Entertaining Rome." In *Ancient Rome: The Archaeology of the Eternal City*, edited by Jon Coulston and Hazel Dodge, 210–58. Monograph 54. Oxford, UK: Oxford University School of Archaeology.

Collins, Billie Jean. 2007. *The Hittites and Their World*. Atlanta, GA: Society of Biblical Literature.

Collins, James M., and Brian Leigh Molyneaux. 2003. *Archaeological Survey (Archaeologist's Toolkit)*. Walnut Creek, CA: AltaMira Press.

Comelli, Daniela, Massimo D'Orazio, Luigi Folco, Mahmud El-Halwagy, Tommaso Frizzi, Roberto Alberti, Valentina Capogrosso, et al. 2016. "The Meteoritic Origin of Tutankhamun's Iron Dagger Blade." *Meteoritics and Planetary Science* 51: 1301–9. http://dx.doi.org/10.1111/maps .12664.

Conlin, David L., and Matthew A. Russell. 2006. "Archaeology of a Naval Battlefield: *H. L. Hunley* and USS *Housatonic*." *International Journal of Nautical Archaeology* 35, no. 1: 20–40.

Conlin, Diane A. 1997a. *The Artists of the Ara Pacis: The Process of Hellenization in Roman Relief Sculpture*. Chapel Hill: University of North Carolina Press.

———. 1997b. "The Reconstruction of Antonia Minor on the Ara Pacis." *Journal of Roman Archaeology* 5: 209–15.

Connolly, Peter, and Hazel Dodge. 1998. *The Ancient City: Life in Classical Athens and Rome*. Oxford, UK: Oxford University Press.

Conyers, Lawrence B. 2013. *Ground-Penetrating Radar for Archaeology (Geophysical Methods for Archaeology)*, 3rd ed. Walnut Creek, CA: AltaMira Press.

Cooley, Alison E., and M. G. L. Cooley. 2013. *Pompeii and Herculaneum: A Sourcebook*, 2nd ed. Boston: Routledge.

Cooney, Kara. 2015. *The Woman Who Would Be King: Hatshepsut's Rise to Power in Ancient Egypt*. New York: Broadway Books.

Cooper, Alan, and Wolfgang Haak. 2015. "DNA Reveals the Origins of Modern Europeans." *Phys.org*, March 23. http://phys.org/news/2015–03 -dna-reveals-modern-europeans.html.

Cooper-White, Macrina. 2015. "Liquid Mercury Discovered under Ancient Temple May Shed New Light on Teotihuacan." *Huffington Post*, March 28. http://www.huffingtonpost.com/2015/04/28/mercury-royal-tomb_n _7152990.html.

Cosgrove, Ben. 2014. "LIFE at Lascaux: First Color Photos from Another World." *Life*, May 21. http://time.com/3879943/lascaux-early-color-photos -of-the-famous-cave-paintings-france-1947/.

Coulston, Jon, and Hazel Dodge. 2000. *Ancient Rome: The Archaeology of the Eternal City*. Oxford University School of Archaeology Monograph 54. Oxford, UK: Oxford University School of Archaeology.

Cronin, Frances. 2011. "Egyptian Pyramids Found by Infra-red Satellite Images." *BBC News*, May 25. http://www.bbc.com/news/world-13522957.

Cucchi, Thomas. 2008. "Uluburun Shipwreck Stowaway House Mouse: Molar Shape Analysis and Indirect Clues about the Vessel's Last Journey." *Journal of Archaeological Science* 35, no. 11 (November): 2953–59. http://www.sciencedirect.com/science/article/pii/S0305440308001362.

Cuno, James. 2010. *Who Owns Antiquity? Museums and the Battle over Our Ancient Heritage.* Princeton, NJ: Princeton University Press.

———. 2012. *Whose Culture? The Promise of Museums and the Debate over Antiquities.* Princeton, NJ: Princeton University Press.

Curry, Andrew. 2008. "Gobekli Tepe: The World's First Temple?" *Smithsonian*, November. http://www.smithsonianmag.com/history/gobekli-tepe-the-worlds-first-temple-83613665/?no-ist.

———. 2015. "Here Are the Ancient Sites ISIS Has Damaged and Destroyed." *National Geographic*, September 1. http://news.nationalgeographic.com/2015/09/150901-isis-destruction-looting-ancient-sites-iraq-syria-archaeology/.

Curtis, Gregory B. 2006. *The Cave Painters: Probing the Mysteries of the World's First Artists.* New York: Alfred A. Knopf.

Cussler, Clive. 2011. *The Sea Hunters.* New York: Pocket Books.

Daley, Jason. 2016. "New Timeline Zeros in on the Creation of the Chauvet Cave Paintings; Radiocarbon Dates Help Reconstruct the Cave's Long History." *Smithsonian.com*, April 13. http://www.smithsonianmag.com/smart-news/new-timeline-zeroes-creation-chauvet-cave-paintings-180958754/?utm_source=facebook.com&no-ist.

Dargis, Manohla. 2011. "Herzog Finds His Inner Cave Man." *New York Times*, April 28. http://www.nytimes.com/2011/04/29/movies/werner-herzogs-cave-of-forgotten-dreams-review.html?_r=2.

Davies, Graham I. 1986. *Megiddo.* Cambridge, UK: Lutterworth Press.

Davies, Philip R., George J. Brooke, and Phillip R. Callaway. 2002. *The Complete World of the Dead Sea Scrolls.* London: Thames and Hudson.

Davies, William, and Ruth Charles. 1999. *Dorothy Garrod and the Progress of the Palaeolithic.* Oxford, UK: Oxbow Books.

Davis, Ellen N. 1986. "Youth and Age in the Thera Frescoes." *American Journal of Archaeology* 90: 399–406.

Davis, Jack L., and Sharon R. Stocker. 2016. "The Lord of the Gold Rings: The Griffin Warrior of Pylos." *Hesperia* 85, no. 4: 627–55.

Dearden, Lizzie. 2014. "New Nazca Lines Geoglyphs Uncovered by Gales and Sandstorms in Peru." *Independent*, August 4. http://www.independent.co.uk/news/science/archaeology/news/new-nazca-lines-geoglyphs-uncovered-by-gales-and-sandstorms-in-peru-9645983.html.

Del Giudice, Marguerite. 2014. "Tut's Tomb: A Replica Fit for a King." *National Geographic News*, May 20. http://news.nationalgeographic.com/news/2014/05/140520-tutankhamun-egypt-archaeology-cyber-printing-3d/.

Demick, Barbara. 2010. "Cultural Exchange: China's Surprising Bronze Age Mummies." *Los Angeles Times*, October 24. http://articles.latimes.com/2010 /oct/24/entertainment/la-ca-cultural-exchange-mummies-20101024.

De Rojas, José Luis. 2012. *Tenochtitlan: Capital of the Aztec Empire*. Gainesville: University Press of Florida.

Díaz-Andreu, Margarita, and Timothy Champion. 1996. "Nationalism and Archaeology in Europe: An Introduction." In *Nationalism and Archaeology in Europe*, edited by Margarita Díaz-Andreu and Timothy Champion, 1–23. Boulder, CO: Westview Press.

Diehl, Richard A. 2004. *The Olmecs: America's First Civilization*. London: Thames and Hudson.

Dodson, Aidan. 2009. *Amarna Sunset: Nefertiti, Tutankhamun, Ay, Horemheb, and the Egyptian Counter-Reformation*. Cairo, Egypt: American University in Cairo Press.

———. 2014. *Amarna Sunrise: Egypt from Golden Age to Age of Heresy*. Cairo, Egypt: American University in Cairo Press.

Donnan, Christopher B. 1978. *Moche Art of Peru: Pre-Columbian Symbolic Communication*. Los Angeles: UCLA Fowler Museum of Cultural History.

———. 1990. "Masterworks of Art Reveal a Remarkable Pre-Inca World." *National Geographic* (June): 17–33.

Donnan, Christopher B., and Donna McClelland. 1999. *Moche Fineline Painting: Its Evolution and Its Artists*. Los Angeles: UCLA Fowler Museum of Cultural History.

Doumas, Christos G. 1983. *Thera: Pompeii of the Ancient Aegean: Excavations at Akrotiri 1967–1979*. London: Thames and Hudson.

———. 1993. *The Wall Paintings of Thera*. London: Thera Foundation— Petros M. Nomikos.

Draper, Robert. 2010. "Unburying the Aztec." *National Geographic* (November): 110–35. http://ngm.nationalgeographic.com/2010/11/greatest-aztec /draper-text.

Dubrow, Marsha. 2014. "Looting of Peru's Ancient Treasures Is Worse Now Than in Spanish Colonial Era." *Examiner.com*, April 12. http://www .examiner.com/article/looting-of-peru-s-ancient-treasures-is-worse -now-than-spanish-colonial-times.

Dunkle, Roger. 2008. *Gladiators: Violence and Spectacle in Ancient Rome*. Harlow, UK: Pearson Longman.

Dunston, Lara. 2016. "Revealed: Cambodia's Vast Medieval Cities Hidden beneath the Jungle." *Guardian*, June 10. https://www.theguardian.com /world/2016/jun/11/lost-city-medieval-discovered-hidden-beneath -cambodian-jungle.

Dvorsky, George. 2014a. "Archaeologists Confirm That Stonehenge Was a Complete Circle." http://io9.com/archaeologists-confirm-that-stonehenge -was-once-a-compl-1629226053.

———. 2014b. "Archaeologists Have Made an Incredible Discovery at Stone-henge." http://io9.com/archaeologists-have-made-an-incredible-discovery-at-sto-1632927903?utm_campaign=socialflow_io9_facebook&utm_source=io9_facebook&utm_medium=socialflow.

Dyson, Stephen L. 2006. *In Pursuit of Ancient Pasts: A History of Classical Archaeology in the Nineteenth and Twentieth Centuries.* New Haven, CT: Yale University Press.

Easton, Donald F. 1981. "Schliemann's Discovery of 'Priam's Treasure': Two Enigmas." *Antiquity* 55: 179–83.

———. 1984a. "Priam's Treasure." *Anatolian Studies* 34: 141–69.

———. 1984b. "Schliemann's Mendacity—A False Trail?" *Antiquity* 58: 197–204.

———. 1994. "Priam's Gold: The Full Story." *Anatolian Studies* 44: 221–43.

———. 1995. "The Troy Treasures in Russia." *Antiquity* 69, no. 262: 11–14.

———. 2010. "The Wooden Horse: Some Possible Bronze Age Origins." In *Ipamati Kistamati Pari Tumatimis: Luwian and Hittite Studies Presented to J. David Hawkins on the Occasion of His 70th Birthday,* edited by Itamar Singer 50–63. Tel Aviv, Israel: Tel Aviv Institute of Archaeology.

Easton, Donald F., J. D. Hawkins, Andrew G. Sherratt, and E. Susan Sherratt. 2002. "Troy in Recent Perspective." *Anatolian Studies* 52: 75–109.

Edwards, Owen. 2010. "The Skeletons of Shanidar Cave." *Smithsonian,* March. http://www.smithsonianmag.com/arts-culture/the-skeletons-of-shanidar-cave-7028477/?no-ist.

Eigeland, Tor. 1978. "Ebla: City of the White Stones." *Aramco World* 29, no. 2 (March–April): 10–19.

Eisler, Riane. 1988. *The Chalice and the Blade: Our History, Our Future.* New York: HarperCollins.

El-Ghobashy, Tamer. 2015. "Iraq Officials Denounce Islamic State's Destruction of Ancient Site." *Wall Street Journal,* March 7. http://www.wsj.com/articles/nimrud-iraq-officials-denounce-islamic-states-destruction-of-ancient-site-1425653551.

Ellis, Steven. 2011. *The Making of Pompeii: Studies in the History and Urban Development of an Ancient Town.* Portsmouth, RI: Journal of Roman Archaeology Supplemental Series.

Emberling, Geoff, and Katharyn Hanson. 2008. *Catastrophe! The Looting and Destruction of Iraq's Past.* Oriental Institute Museum Publications. Chicago: University of Chicago Press. https://oi.uchicago.edu/sites/oi.uchicago.edu/files/uploads/shared/docs/oimp28.pdf.

Epstein, Marilyn S. 2015. "Jamestown Skeletons Identified as Colony Leaders." *Smithsonian Science News,* July 28. http://smithsonianscience.si.edu/2015/07/jamestown-skeletons-identified-as-colony-leaders/.

Estrin, Daniel. 2016. "Scanning Software Deciphers Ancient Biblical Scroll." *Associated Press,* September 21. http://bigstory.ap.org/article/60785bb2031a478cb71ce9278782c320/.

Evans, Arthur J. 1921–23. *The Palace of Minos: A Comparative Account of the Successive Stages of the Early Cretan Civilization as Illustrated by the Discoveries*, 4 vols. New York: Macmillan.

————. 1931. Introduction to Emil Ludwig's *Schliemann of Troy. The Story of a Goldseeker*, 9–21. London: G. P. Putnam's and Sons.

Evelyn-White, H. G. 1914. *Hesiod, the Homeric Hymns and Homerica*. Loeb Classical Library no. 57. London: W. Heinemann.

Fagan, Brian. 1994. *Quest for the Past*, 2nd ed. Long Grove, IL: Waveland Press.

————. 2001. *The Seventy Great Mysteries of the Ancient World: Unlocking the Secrets of Past Civilizations*. London: Thames and Hudson.

————. 2003. *Archaeologists: Explorers of the Human Past*. Oxford, UK: Oxford University Press.

————. 2004a. *A Brief History of Archaeology: Classical Times to the Twenty-First Century*. Boston: Routledge.

————. 2004b. *The Rape of the Nile: Tomb Robbers, Tourists, and Archaeologists in Egypt*, rev. ed. Boulder, CO: Westview Press.

————. 2005. *Chaco Canyon: Archaeologists Explore the Lives of an Ancient Society*. Oxford, UK: Oxford University Press.

————. 2007a. *Discovery! Unearthing the New Treasures of Archaeology*. London: Thames and Hudson.

————. 2007b. *Return to Babylon: Travelers, Archaeologists, and Monuments in Mesopotamia*, rev. ed. Boulder, CO: University of Colorado Press.

————. 2015. *Lord and Pharaoh: Carnarvon and the Search for Tutankhamun*. Walnut Creek, CA: Left Coast Press.

————, ed. 1996. *Eyewitness to Discovery: First-Person Accounts of More Than Fifty of the World's Greatest Archaeological Discoveries*. Oxford, UK: Oxford University Press.

————, ed. 2014. *The Great Archaeologists*. London: Thames and Hudson.

Fagan, Brian M., and Nadia Durrani. 2014. *In the Beginning: An Introduction to Archaeology*, 13th ed. Boston: Pearson.

————. 2016. *A Brief History of Archaeology: Classical Times to the Twenty-First Century*, 2nd ed. New York: Routledge.

Fagan, Garrett G., ed. 2006. *Archaeological Fantasies: How Pseudoarchaeology Misrepresents the Past and Misleads the Public*, new ed. Boston: Routledge.

Fagles, Robert. 1991. *Homer: The Iliad*. New York: Penguin Books.

Falasca-Zamponi, Simonetta. 1997. *Fascist Spectacle: The Aesthetics of Power in Mussolini's Italy*. Berkeley: University of California Press.

Fash, William L. 2001. *Scribes, Warriors, and Kings: The City of Copán and the Ancient Maya*, rev. ed. London: Thames and Hudson.

Feder, Kenneth. 2010. *Encyclopedia of Dubious Archaeology: From Atlantis to the Walam Olum*. Westport, CT: Greenwood Press.

————. 2013. *Frauds, Myths, and Mysteries: Science and Pseudoscience in Archaeology*, 8th ed. New York: McGraw-Hill.

Felch, Jason, and Ralph Fammolino. 2011. *Chasing Aphrodite: The Hunt for Looted Antiquities at the World's Richest Museum.* New York: Houghton Mifflin Harcout.

Feldman, Louis H. 2001. "Financing the Colosseum." *Biblical Archaeology Review* 27, no. 4: 20–31, 60–61.

Fields, Weston W. 2006. *The Dead Sea Scrolls: A Short History.* Leiden: E. J. Brill.

Fine, Steven. 2013. "Menorahs in Color: Polychromy in Jewish Visual Culture of Roman Antiquity." *Images* 6: 3–25. doi: 10.1163/18718000–123400001. https://www.academia.edu/5102874/_Menorahs_in_Color_Polychromy _in_Jewish_Visual_Culture_of_Roman_Antiquity_Images_6_2013_.

Finkel, Irving. 2014a. *The Ark before Noah: Decoding the Story of the Flood.* New York: Hodder and Stoughton.

———. 2014b. "Noah's Ark: The Facts behind the Flood." *Telegraph*, January 19. http://www.telegraph.co.uk/culture/books/10574119/Noahs-Ark -the-facts-behind-the-Flood.html.

Finkelstein, Israel, and David Ussishkin. 1994. "Back to Megiddo." *Biblical Archaeology Review* 20, no. 1: 26–43.

Fitton, J. Leslie. 2002. *Minoans.* London: British Museum Press.

———. 2012. "'The Help of My Dear Wife': Sophia Schliemann and the discovery of Priam's Treasure." In *Archaeology and Heinrich Schliemann. A Century after His Death. Assessments and Prospects. Myth—History— Science*, edited by George Korres, Nektarios Karadimas, and Georgia Flouda, 421–24. Athens, Greece: Society for Aegean Prehistory.

Fox, Richard A. Jr. 1993. *Archaeology, History, and Custer's Last Battle: The Little Big Horn Reexamined.* Norman, OK: University of Oklahoma Press.

French, Elizabeth. 2002. *Mycenae: Agamemnon's Capital.* Oxford, UK: Tempus.

Freund, Richard A. 2004. *Secrets of the Cave of Letters: Rediscovering a Dead Sea Mystery.* Leiden, The Netherlands: E. J. Brill.

Freund, Richard A., and Rami Arav. 2001. "Return to the Cave of Letters: What Still Lies Buried?" *Biblical Archaeology Review* 27, no. 1: 24–39.

Friedrich, Walter L., Bernd Kromer, Michael Friedrich, Jan Heinemeier, Tom Pfeiffer, and Sahra Talamo. 2006. "Santorini Eruption Radiocarbon Dated to 1627–1600 B.C." *Science* 312, no. 5773 (April 28): 548. doi: 10.1126/science.1125087.

Fugate Brangers, Susan L. 2013. "Political Propaganda and Archaeology: The Mausoleum of Augustus in the Fascist Era." *International Journal of Humanities and Social Science* 3, no. 16: 125–35.

Fuller, Dawn. 2014. "No Scrounging for Scraps: UC Research Uncovers the Diets of the Middle and Lower Class in Pompeii." *University of Cincinnati News*, January 2. http://www.uc.edu/news/NR.aspx?id=19029.

Futrell, Alison. 2006. *The Roman Games: A Sourcebook*. Historical Sources in Translation. Oxford, UK: Blackwell.

Gabriel, Richard A. 2009. *Thutmose III: The Military Biography of Egypt's Greatest Warrior King*. Sterling, VA: Potomac Books.

Gadot, Yuval, and Assaf Yasur-Landau. 2006. "Beyond the Finds: Reconstructing Life in the Courtyard Building of Level K-4." In *Megiddo IV: The 1998–2002 Seasons* (2 vols.), edited by Israel Finkelstein, David Ussishkin, and Baruch Halpern, II: 583–600. Tel Aviv, Israel: Tel Aviv University.

Gannon, Megan. 2016. "X-Rays Reveal the Secrets of Egyptian Scrolls." *Newsweek*, January 17. http://www.newsweek.com/x-rays-reveal-secrets -egyptian-scrolls-papyrus-416719?rx=us.

García Martínez, Florentino. 1996. *The Dead Sea Scrolls Translated: The Qumran Texts in English*, 2nd ed. Grand Rapids, MI: William B. Eerdmans.

Garstang, John, and J. B. E. Garstang. 1940. *The Story of Jericho*. London: Hodder and Stoughton.

Gast, Phil. 2014. "The *Hunley*: Zeroing In on What Caused Civil War Submarine's Sinking." *CNN.com*, February 15. http://www.cnn.com/2014/02/14 /travel/civil-war-submarine-hunley/.

Gates, Charles. 2011. *Ancient Cities: The Archaeology of Urban Life in the Ancient Near East and Egypt, Greece, and Rome*, 2nd ed. London: Routledge.

Gawlinski, Laura. 2014. *The Athenian Agora: Museum Guide*, 5th ed. Athens, Greece: American School of Classical Studies at Athens.

George, Andrew. 2003. *The Epic of Gilgamesh*. New York: Penguin.

———. 2016. "How Looting in Iraq Unearthed the Treasures of Gilgamesh." *Aeon*, February 5. https://aeon.co/opinions/how-looting-in-iraq-unearthed -the-treasures-of-gilgamesh.

Gerianos, Nicholas K. 2016. "Kennewick Man Was a Native American." *U.S. News and World Report*, April 27. http://www.usnews.com/news /science/articles/2016-04-27/corps-determines-kennewick-man-is -native-american.

Ghose, Tia. 2014. "Belize's Famous 'Blue Hole' Reveals Clues to the Maya's Demise." *Livescience*, December 24. http://www.livescience.com/49255 -drought-caused-maya-collapse.html.

———. 2015. "King Tut's Tomb May Hide Nefertiti's Secret Grave." *Livescience*, August 12. http://www.livescience.com/51837-king-tut-tomb-holds -nefertiti.html.

Gimbutas, Marija. 1974. *The Gods and Goddesses of Old Europe, 7000 to 3500 BCE: Myths, Legends, and Cult Images*. London: Thames and Hudson.

———. 1991. *The Civilization of the Goddess: The World of Old Europe*. New York: HarperCollins.

Glassman, Steve. 2003. *On the Trail of the Maya Explorer: Tracing the Epic Journey of John Lloyd Stephens*. Tuscaloosa, AL: The University of Alabama Press.

Glob, P. V. 2004. *The Bog People: Iron Age Man Preserved*. New York: NYRB Classics.

Glover, Michael. 2013. "Pompeii and Herculaneum—British Museum Exhibition Review: Buried Treasure." *Independent*, April 1. http://www.independent.co.uk/arts-entertainment/art/features/pompeii-and-herculaneum—british-museum-exhibition-review-buried-treasure-8548946.html.

Goldmann, Klaus, Özgen Agar, and Stephen K. Urice. 1999. "Who Owns Priam's Treasure?" *Archaeology Odyssey* July–August: 22–23.

Gosden, Chris. 2001. "Postcolonial Archaeology. Issues of Culture, Identity, and Knowledge." In *Archaeological Theory Today*, edited by Ian Hodder, 241–61. Oxford, UK: Polity Press.

———. 2004. *Archaeology and Colonialism. Cultural Contact from 5000 BC to the Present*. Cambridge: Cambridge University Press.

Grant, Michael. 1980. *Art and Life of Pompeii and Herculaneum*. Colchester, UK: TBS Book Service.

———. 2005. *Cities of Vesuvius: Pompeii and Herculaneum*. New Haven, CT: Phoenix Press.

Gray, Richard. 2015. "Is This the Oldest Evidence of Written Language? Pictograms Found in Ancient Turkish City Could Be 12,000-Years-Old." *Daily Mail*, July 21. http://www.dailymail.co.uk/sciencetech/article-3169595/Is-oldest-evidence-written-language-Pictograms-ancient-Turkish-city-12–000-years-old.html.

Griffiths, Sarah. 2015a. "A Glimpse beneath the Bandages: Egyptian Child Mummy Gets a CT Scan in a Bid to Uncover Its Secrets." *Daily Mail*, July 15. http://www.dailymail.co.uk/sciencetech/article-3162711/A-glimpse-beneath-bandages-Egyptian-child-mummy-gets-CT-scan-bid-uncover-secrets.html.

———. 2015b. "Restoration Work Begins on Bodies of Those Who Died When Vesuvius Engulfed Pompeii." *Daily Mail*, May 20. http://www.dailymail.co.uk/sciencetech/article-3089659/Who-petrified-child-Pompeii-Restoration-work-begins-body-boy-House-Golden-Bracelet.html.

Grove, David C. 2014. *Discovering the Olmecs: An Unconventional History*. Austin: University of Texas Press.

Guidi, Alessandro. 1996. "Nationalism without a Nation: The Italian Case." In *Nationalism and Archaeology in Europe*, edited by Margarita Díaz-Andreu and Timothy Champion, 108–18. Boulder, CO: Westview Press.

Gurewitsch, Matthew. 2008. "True Colors." *Smithsonian*, July. http://www.smithsonianmag.com/arts-culture/true-colors-17888/?no-ist.

Hall, Edith. 2015. "Pale Riders: Adrienne Mayor's 'The Amazons' Shows How a Myth Developed." *New Statesman*, January 22. http://www.newstatesman .com/culture/2015/01/pale-riders-adrienne-mayors-amazons-shows -how-myth-developed.

Hall, Stephen S. 2010. "Spirits in the Sand: The Ancient Nasca Lines of Peru Shed Their Secrets." *National Geographic* (March): 56–79.

Hallote, Rachel. 2006. *Bible, Map, and Spade: The American Palestine Exploration Society, Frederick Jones Bliss, and the Forgotten Story of Early American Biblical Archaeology*. Chicago: Gorgias Press.

Hamilton, Sue. 1998. *Ancient Astronauts: Unsolved Mysteries*. Edina, MN: ABDO.

Hamilton-Paterson, James, and Carol Andrews. 1978. *Mummies: Death and Life in Ancient Egypt*. New York: Penguin Books.

Hammer, Joshua. 2015. "Finally, the Beauty of France's Chauvet Cave Makes Its Grand Public Debut." *Smithsonian*, April. http://www.smithsonianmag .com/history/france-chauvet-cave-makes-grand-debut-180954582/?no-ist.

Hammond, Norman. 1982. *Ancient Maya Civilization*. New Brunswick, NJ: Rutgers University Press.

Handwerk, Brian. 2005. "King Tut's New Face: Behind the Forensic Reconstruction." *National Geographic News*, May 11. http://news.national geographic.com/news/2005/05/0511_050511_kingtutface.html.

Harmon, David, and Francis P. McManamon. 2006. *The Antiquities Act: A Century of American Archaeology, Historic Preservation, and Nature Conservation*. Tucson: University of Arizona Press.

Harrington, Spencer P. M. 1999. "Behind the Mask of Agamemnon." *Archaeology* 52, no. 4: 51. http://archive.archaeology.org/9907/etc/mask.html.

Harris, David. 1998. "I Was There!" *Biblical Archaeology Review* 24, no. 2: 34–35.

Harrison, Peter D. 1999. *The Lords of Tikal: Rulers of an Ancient Maya City*. London: Thames and Hudson.

Harrison, Timothy P. 2003. "The Battleground: Who Destroyed Megiddo? Was It David or Shishak?" *Biblical Archaeology Review* 29, no. 6: 28–35, 60–64.

Hasson, Nir. 2012. "Megiddo Dig Unearths Cache of Buried Canaanite Treasure." *Haaretz*, May 22. http://www.haaretz.com/israel-news/megiddo -dig-unearths-cache-of-buried-canaanite-treasure-1.431797.

———. 2015. "Ancient Tablets Disclose Jewish Exiles' Life in Babylonia." *Haaretz*, January 29. http://www.haaretz.com/jewish/archaeology/.premium -1.639822.

Hatem, Ahmed. 2016. "Team Testing New Scanner on Egypt's Great Pyramid." *Associated Press*, June 2. http://bigstory.ap.org/8527da72451e472ca 3925c7e42d7de52#.

Hawass, Zahi. 2005. *Tutankhamun and the Golden Age of the Pharaohs.* Washington, DC: National Geographic Books.

———. 2010. "King Tut's Family Secrets." *National Geographic* (September): 34–59. http://ngm.nationalgeographic.com/2010/09/tut-dna/hawass-text/1.

Hawass, Zahi, Yehia Z. Gad, Somaia Ismail, Rabab Khairat, Dina Fathalla, Naglaa Hasan, Amal Ahmed et al. 2010. "Ancestry and Pathology in King Tutankhamun's Family." *Journal of the American Medical Association* 303, no. 7: 638–47. http://jama.jamanetwork.com/article.aspx?articleid=185393.

Hawass, Zahi, and Sahar Saleem. 2015. *Scanning the Pharaohs: CT Imaging of the New Kingdom Royal Mummies.* Cairo, Egypt: American University in Cairo Press.

Hessler, Peter. 2015. "Radar Scans in King Tut's Tomb Suggest Hidden Chambers." *National Geographic News,* November 28. http://news.nationalgeographic.com/2015/11/151128-tut-tomb-scans-hidden-chambers/.

———. 2016a. "In Egypt, Debate Rages over Scans of King Tut's Tomb." *National Geographic News,* May 9. http://news.nationalgeographic.com/2016/05/160509-king-tut-tomb-chambers-radar-archaeology/.

———. 2016b. "Scans of King Tut's Tomb Reveal New Evidence of Hidden Rooms." *National Geographic News,* March 17. http://news.nationalgeographic.com/2016/03/160317-king-tut-tomb-hidden-chambers-radar-egypt-archaeology/.

Hicks, Brian. 2015. *Sea of Darkness: Unraveling the Mysteries of the* H. L. Hunley. Ann Arbor, MI: Spry.

Hicks, Brian, and Schuyler Kropf. 2002. *Raising the* Hunley: The Remarkable History and Recovery of the Lost Confederate Submarine. New York: Ballantine Books.

Hodder, Ian. 1986. *Reading the Past.* Cambridge: Cambridge University Press.

———. 1987. *Archaeology as Long-Term History.* Cambridge: Cambridge University Press.

———. 1999. *The Archaeological Process: An Introduction.* Oxford, UK: Blackwell.

———. 2006. "This Old House." *Natural History,* June. http://www.naturalhistorymag.com/htmlsite/master.html?http://www.naturalhistorymag.com/htmlsite/0606/0606_feature.html.

———. 2011. *The Leopard's Tale: Revealing the Mysteries of Çatalhöyük.* London: Thames and Hudson.

Hodges, Glenn. 2011. "Cahokia: America's Forgotten City." *National Geographic* (January): 126–45. http://ngm.nationalgeographic.com/2011/01/cahokia/hodges-text.

Hoffman, Barbara. 1993. The Spoils of War. *Archaeology* 46, no. 6: 37–40.

Hopkins, Keith, and Mary Beard. 2005. *The Colosseum*. Cambridge, MA: Harvard University Press.

Horowitz, Wayne, Yehoshua Greenberg, and Peter Zilberg, eds. 2015. *By the Rivers of Babylon: Cuneiform Documents from the Beginning of the Babylonian Diaspora*. Jerusalem: Bible Lands Museum and Israel Exploration Society (Hebrew).

Houston, Stephen, Oswaldo C. Mazariegos, and David Stuart, eds. 2001. *The Decipherment of Ancient Maya Writing*. Norman, OK: University of Oklahoma Press.

Howard, Philip. 2007. *Archaeological Surveying and Mapping: Recording and Depicting the Landscape*, new ed. Boston: Routledge.

Hrozný, Bedřich. 1917. *Die Sprache der Hethiter: ihr Bau und ihre Zugehörigkeit zum indogermanischen Sprachstamm*. Leipzig, Ger.: Hinrichs.

Hunt, Patrick. 2007. *Ten Discoveries That Rewrote History*. New York: Penguin Group.

Hurwit, Jeffrey M. 1999. *The Athenian Acropolis: History, Mythology, and Archaeology from the Neolithic Era to the Present*. Cambridge: Cambridge University Press.

Hussein, Muzahim Mahmoud. 2016. *Nimrud: The Queens' Tombs*. Chicago: Oriental Institute.

Hutcherson, Kimberly. 2015. "ISIS Video Shows Execution of 25 Men in Ruins of Syria Amphitheater." *CNN*, July 4. http://www.cnn.com /2015/07/04/middleeast/isis-execution-palmyra-syria/.

Jablonka, Peter. 1994. "Ein Verteidigungsgraben in der Unterstadt von Troia VI. Grabungsbericht 1993." *Studia Troica* 4: 51–74.

Jackson, Caroline M., and Paul T. Nicholson. 2010. "The Provenance of Some Glass Ingots from the Uluburun Shipwreck." *Journal of Archaeological Science* 37, no. 2 (February): 295–301. http://www.sciencedirect .com/science/article/pii/S030544030900346X.

Jaggard, Victoria. 2014. "Huge Wine Cellar Unearthed at a Biblical-Era Palace in Israel." *Smithsonian*, August 27. http://www.smithsonianmag.com /science-nature/huge-wine-cellar-unearthed-biblical-era-palace-israel -180952495/#igcefjsJmQpfE6vO.99.

———. 2015. "Ancient Scrolls Blackened by Vesuvius Are Readable at Last." *Smithsonian*, January 20. http://www.smithsonianmag.com /history/ancient-scrolls-blackened-vesuvius-are-readable-last -herculaneum-papyri-180953950/#jMhdSfpte7syYFeI.99.

Jarus, Owen. 2012. "Oops! Brain-Removal Tool Left in Mummy's Skull." *Livescience*, December 14. http://www.livescience.com/25536-mummy -brain-removal-tool.html.

———. 2016. "Nefertiti Still Missing: King Tut's Tomb Shows No Hidden Chambers." *Livescience*, May 11. http://www.livescience.com/54708-nefertiti -missing-no-chambers-in-king-tut-tomb.html.

Jashemski, Wilhelmina F. 1979. *The Gardens of Pompeii, Herculaneum and the Villas Destroyed by Vesuvius* (2 vols.). Athens, Greece: Aristide D. Caratzas.

———. 2014. *Discovering the Gardens of Pompeii: Memoirs of a Garden Archaeologist*. Seattle, WA: CreateSpace Independent Publishing Platform.

Johanson, Donald, and Maitland Edey. 1981. *Lucy: the Beginnings of Humankind*. New York: Simon and Schuster.

Johanson, Donald, and Kate Wong. 2010. *Lucy's Legacy: The Quest for Human Origins*. New York: Broadway Books.

Johnston, Bruce. 2001. "Colosseum 'Built with Loot from Sack of Jerusalem Temple.'" *Telegraph*, June 15. http://www.telegraph.co.uk/news/worldnews/1311985/Colosseum-built-with-loot-from-sack-of-Jerusalem-temple.html.

Kark, Chris. 2016. "Archaeologists from Stanford Find an 8,000-Year-Old 'Goddess Figurine' in Central Turkey." *Stanford News*, September 29. http://news.stanford.edu/2016/09/29/archaeologists-find-8000-year-old-goddess-figurine-central-turkey/.

Kaufman, Amy. 2016. "Megan Fox Tackles String Theory, the Truth behind the Pyramids, and the 'Brainwashed' Public." *Los Angeles Times*, June 3. http://www.latimes.com/entertainment/movies/la-ca-mn-megan-fox-ninja-turtles-20160526-snap-story.html.

Kelly, Robert L., and David Hurst Thomas. 2013. *Archaeology*, 6th ed. New York: Wadsworth.

Kelso, William M. 2007. "Jamestown: The Fort That Was the Birthplace of the United States of America." In *Discovery! Unearthing the New Treasures of Archaeology*, edited by Brian Fagan, 172–75. London: Thames and Hudson.

———. 2008. *Jamestown, the Buried Truth*. Charlottesville: University of Virginia Press.

Kelso, William M., and Beverly Straube. 2004. *Jamestown Rediscovery: 1994–2004*. Richmond, VA: APVA Preservation Virginia.

Kemp, Barry J. 2005. *Ancient Egypt: Anatomy of a Civilization*, 2nd ed. Boston: Routledge.

Kempinski, Aharon. 1989. *Megiddo. A City State and Royal Centre in North Israel*. Munich: C. H. Beck.

Kennedy, Maev. 2011. "Viking Chieftain's Burial Ship Excavated in Scotland after 1,000 Years." *Guardian*, October 18. http://www.theguardian.com/science/2011/oct/19/viking-burial-ship-found-scotland.

———. 2014. "Questions Raised over Queen's Ancestry after DNA Test on Richard III's Cousins." *Guardian*, December 2. http://www.theguardian.com/uk-news/2014/dec/02/king-richard-iii-dna-cousins-queen-ancestry.

Kenyon, Kathleen M. 1957. *Digging Up Jericho*. London: Ernest Benn.

Keys, David. 2014. "Hidden Henge: Archaeologists Discover Huge Stone-henge 'Sibling' Nearby." *Independent, UK*, September 9. http://www.sott.net/article/285448-Hidden-henge-Archaeologists-discover-huge-Stonehenge-sibling-nearby.

———. 2015. "Tutankhamun: Great Golden Face Mask Was Actually Made for His Mother Nefertiti, Research Reveals." *Independent, UK*, November 28.   http://www.independent.co.uk/news/uk/home-news/tutankhamun-great-golden-face-mask-was-actually-made-for-his-mother-nefertiti-research-reveals-a6753156.html.

———. 2016. "Remarkable Ancient Structure Found Just Two Miles from Stonehenge." *Independent, UK*, August 15. http://www.independent.co.uk/news/science/archaeology/revealed-remarkable-ancient-structure-found-just-two-miles-from-stonehenge-a7190476.html.

Killgrove, Kristina. 2015a. "Archaeologists to Ben Carson: Ancient Egyptians Wrote Down Why the Pyramids Were Built." *Forbes*, November 5. http://www.forbes.com/sites/kristinakillgrove/2015/11/05/archaeologists-to-ben-carson-ancient-egyptians-wrote-down-why-the-pyramids-were-built/#3339f99613e2.

———. 2015b. "What Archaeologists Really Think about Ancient Aliens, Lost Colonies, and Fingerprints of The Gods." *Forbes*, September 3. http://www.forbes.com/sites/kristinakillgrove/2015/09/03/what-archaeologists-really-think-about-ancient-aliens-lost-colonies-and-fingerprints-of-the-gods/.

King, Michael R., and Gregory M. Cooper. 2006. *Who Killed King Tut? Using Modern Forensics to Solve a 3,300-Year-Old Mystery*. New York: Prometheus Books.

King, Turi E., Gloria Gonzalez Fortes, Patricia Balaresque, Mark G. Thomas, David Balding, Pierpaolo Maisano Delser, Rita Neumann et al. 2014. "Identification of the Remains of King Richard III." *Nature Communications*, December 2. http://www.nature.com/ncomms/2014/141202/ncomms6631/full/ncomms6631.html.

Kingsley, Sean. 2006. *God's Gold: The Quest for the Lost Temple Treasure of Jerusalem*. London: John Murray.

Kington, Tom. 2009. "Rome Archaeologists Find 'Nero's Party Piece' in Dig." *Guardian*, September 29. https://www.theguardian.com/world/2009/sep/29/nero-rome-archaeologists-dining-room.

Knapton, Sarah. 2016. "Huge Ritual Monument Thought to be Buried near Stonehenge Doesn't Exist, Admit Archaeologists." *Telegraph*, August 12. http://www.telegraph.co.uk/news/2016/08/12/huge-ritual-monument-thought-to-be-buried-near-stonehenge-doesnt/.

Koch, Peter O. 2013. *John Lloyd Stephens and Frederick Catherwood: Pioneers of Mayan Archaeology*. Jefferson, NC: McFarland.

Koehl, Robert B. 1986. "A Marinescape Floor from the Palace at Knossos." *American Journal of Archaeology* 90, no. 4: 407–17.

Koh, Andrew J., Assaf Yasur-Landau, and Eric H. Cline. 2014. "Characterizing a Middle Bronze Palatial Wine Cellar from Tel Kabri, Israel." *PLoS ONE* 9, no 8: e106406. doi:10.1371/ journal.pone.0106406.

Kohl, Philip L., and Claire Fawcett, eds. 1995. *Nationalism, Politics, and the Practice of Archaeology.* Cambridge: Cambridge University Press.

Korfmann, Manfred. 2004. "Was There a Trojan War?" *Archaeology* 57, no. 3: 36–41.

——— 2007. "Was There a Trojan War? Troy between Fiction and Archaeological Evidence." In *Troy: From Homer's* Iliad *to Hollywood Epic,* edited by Martin M. Winkler, 20–26. Oxford, UK: Blackwell.

Kramer, Samuel Noah. 1988. *History Begins at Sumer: Thirty-Nine Firsts in Recorded History,* 3rd ed. Philadelphia: University of Pennsylvania Press.

Krause, Lisa. 2000. "Ballard Finds Traces of Ancient Habitation beneath Black Sea." *National Geographic News,* September 13. http://news.national geographic.com/news/2000/12/122800blacksea.html.

Kroeber, Alfred, and Donald Collier. 1998. *The Archaeology and Pottery of Nazca, Peru: Alfred Kroeber's 1926 Expedition,* edited by Patrick Carmichael. Walnut Creek, CA: AltaMira Press.

Kroeber, Theodora. 2011. *Ishi in Two Worlds: A Biography of the Last Wild Indian in North America.* 50th anniv. ed. Berkeley: University of California Press.

Kumar, Mohi. 2013. "From Gunpowder to Teeth Whitener: The Science behind Historic Uses of Urine." *Smithsonian,* August 20. http://www .smithsonianmag.com/science-nature/from-gunpowder-to-teeth -whitener-the-science-behind-historic-uses-of-urine-442390/?no-ist.

Kunnen-Jones, Marianne. 2002. "Archaeologist Brian Rose Makes His Troy Finale." *University of Cincinnati News,* October 14. http://www.uc.edu /profiles/rose.htm.

Kyrieleis, Helmut. 2007. "Olympia: Excavations and Discoveries at the Great Sanctuary." In *Great Moments in Greek Archaeology,* edited by Panos Valavanis, 100–117. Translated by David Hardy. Los Angeles: J. Paul Getty Museum.

Lange, Karen. 2008. "The Stolen Past." *National Geographic* (December): 60–65. http://ngm.nationalgeographic.com/2008/12/palestine-antiquities /lange-text.

Lapatin, Kenneth D. S. 2002. *Mysteries of the Snake Goddess: Art, Desire, and the Forging of History.* New York: Houghton Mifflin Harcourt.

Larsen, Mogans Trolle. 1996. *The Conquest of Assyria: Excavations in an Antique Land, 1840–1860.* New York: Routledge.

Latacz, Joachim. 2004. *Troy and Homer.* Oxford, UK: Oxford University Press.

Laurence, Ray. 2012. *Roman Archaeology for Historians*. London: Routledge.

Lawler, Andrew. 2007. "Reconstructing Petra." *Smithsonian*, June. http://www.smithsonianmag.com/history/reconstructing-petra-155444564/?no-ist=&page=1.

———. 2015. "Rare Unlooted Grave of Wealthy Warrior Uncovered in Greece." *National Geographic News*, October 27. http://news.nationalgeographic.com/2015/10/151027-pylos-greece-warrior-grave-mycenaean-archaeology/.

Layard, Austen Henry. 1849. *Nineveh and Its Remains*. London: John Murray.

Leach, Peter E. 1992. *The Surveying of Archaeological Sites*. London: Archetype.

Leakey, Mary D. 1979. *Olduvai Gorge: My Search for Early Man*. London: Collins.

———. 1986. *Disclosing the Past: An Autobiography*. New York: McGraw-Hill.

Leakey, Richard E. 1984. *One Life: An Autobiography*. Englewood Cliffs, NJ: Salem House.

Leakey, Richard E., and Roger Lewin. 1979. *Origins*. New York: Dutton.

Lehner, Mark, and Richard H. Wilkinson. 1997. *The Complete Pyramids: Solving the Ancient Mysteries*. London: Thames and Hudson.

Lekson, Stephen H. 2007. *The Architecture of Chaco Canyon, New Mexico*. Provo: University of Utah Press.

———, ed. 2006. *The Archaeology of Chaco Canyon: An Eleventh-Century Pueblo Regional Center*. Santa Fe, NM: School of American Research Press.

Lemonick, Michael D. 2014a. "Humans and Neanderthals Were Actually Neighbors." *Time*, August 20. http://time.com/3148351/humans-and-neanderthals-were-actually-neighbors/.

———. 2014b. "What Bronze Age Wine Snobs Drank." *Time*, August 27. http://time.com/3178786/wine-bronze-age-archaeology/.

Lents, Nathan H. 2016. "Paleoanthropology Wars: The Discovery of *Homo Naledi* Has Generated Considerable Controversy in This Scientific Discipline." *Skeptic*, January 6. http://www.skeptic.com/reading_room/paleoanthropology-wars-the-discovery-of-homo-naledi/.

Lerici, Carlo M. 1959. "Periscope on the Etruscan Past." *National Geographic* (September): 337–50.

———. 1962. "New Archaeological Techniques and International Cooperation in Italy." *Expedition*, Spring: 4–10.

Levitan, Dave. 2013. "Archaeologists Uncover 3,700-Year-Old Wine Cellar." *Wine Spectator*, November 25. http://www.winespectator.com/webfeature/show/id/49325.

Levy, Thomas, and Thomas Higham. 2014. *The Bible and Radiocarbon Dating: Archaeology, Text, and Science*. Boston: Routledge.

Lewis, Naphtali, and Meyer Reinhold. 1990. *Roman Civilization: Selected Readings* (2 vols.), 3rd ed. New York: Columbia University Press.

Lichfield, John. 2016. "Chauvet Cave Paintings: A Volcanic Eruption from 36,000 Years Ago—As Captured by Prehistoric Man." *Independent*, January 10. http://www.independent.co.uk/news/world/europe/chauvet-cave-paintings-a-volcanic-eruption-from-36000-years-ago-as-captured-by-prehistoric-man-a6805001.html.

Liesowska, Anna. 2014. "Iconic 2,500 Year Old Siberian Princess 'Died from Breast Cancer,' Reveals MRI Scan." *Siberian Times*, October 14. http://siberiantimes.com/science/casestudy/features/iconic-2500-year-old-siberian-princess-died-from-breast-cancer-reveals-unique-mri-scan/.

Lim, Timothy H. 2006. *The Dead Sea Scrolls: A Very Short Introduction*. Oxford, UK: Oxford University Press.

Lloyd, Seton. 1980a. *Foundations in the Dust: The Story of Mesopotamian Exploration*. London: Thames and Hudson.

———. 1980b. *The Ruined Cities of Iraq*. Chicago: Ares.

Long, Michael E. 1990. "Enduring Echoes of Peru's Past." *National Geographic* (June): 34–49.

Lorenzi, Rossella. 2016a. "Cosmic Ray Tech May Unlock Pyramids' Secrets." *Discovery News*, April 15. http://news.discovery.com/history/ancient-egypt/cosmic-ray-tech-may-unlock-pyramids-secrets-160415.htm.

———. 2016b. "Egyptian Pyramid Scans Reveal New Anomalies." *Discovery News*, January 19. http://news.discovery.com/history/archaeology/egyptian-pyramid-scans-reveal-new-anomalies-160119.htm.

———. 2016c. "Pyramid Interior Revealed Using Cosmic Rays." *LiveScience*, April 28. http://www.livescience.com/54596-pyramid-interior-revealed-using-cosmic-rays.html.

Lovgren, Stefan. 2006. "Aztec Temple Found in Mexico City 'Exceptional,' Experts Say." *National Geographic News*, October 5. http://news.nationalgeographic.com/news/2006/10/061005-aztecs.html.

Luce, J. V. 1969. *End of Atlantis*. London: Thames and Hudson.

Luhnow, David. 2003. "Treasure of Nimrud Is Found in Iraq, and It's Spectacular." *Wall Street Journal*, June 6. http://www.wsj.com/articles/SB105485037080424400.

Lyon-House, Leslie. 2012. "Maya Scholar Debunks World-Ending Myth." *UT News*, December 17. http://news.utexas.edu/2012/12/17/maya-scholar-debunks-world-ending-myth.

Macaulay, David. 1979. *Motel of the Mysteries*. Boston: Houghton Mifflin.

MacKendrick, Paul. 1960. *The Mute Stones Speak: The Story of Archaeology in Italy*. New York: W. W. Norton.

———. 1979. *The Greek Stones Speak: The Story of Archaeology in Greek Lands*. New York: W. W. Norton.

Magness, Jodi. 2002. *The Archaeology of Qumran and the Dead Sea Scrolls.* Grand Rapids, MI: William B. Eerdmans.

——. 2012. *The Archaeology of the Holy Land: From the Destruction of Solomon's Temple to the Muslim Conquest.* Cambridge: Cambridge University Press.

Maixner, Frank, Ben Krause-Kyora, Dmitrij Turaev, Alexander Herbig, Michael R. Hoopmann, Janice L. Hallows, Ulrike Kusebauch et al. 2016. "The 5300-Year-Old *Helicobacter pylori* Genome of the Iceman." *Science* 351, no. 6269: 162–65. http://science.sciencemag.org/content /351/6269/162.

Mallory, James P., and Victor H. Mair. 2000. *The Tarim Mummies: Ancient China and the Mystery of the Earliest Peoples from the West.* London: Thames and Hudson.

Mallowan, Agatha Christie. 2012. *Come, Tell Me How You Live: An Archaeological Memoir.* Repr. New York: William Morrow.

Mann, Charles C. 2011. "The Birth of Religion." *National Geographic* (June): 34–59. http://ngm.nationalgeographic.com/2011/06/gobekli-tepe/mann -text.

Manning, Sturt. 2014. *A Test of Time and A Test of Time Revisited: The Volcano of Thera and the Chronology and History of the Aegean and East Mediterranean in the mid Second Millennium BCE,* 2nd ed. Oxford, UK: Oxbow Books.

Manning, Sturt W., Cemal Pulak, Bernd Kromer, Sahra Talamo, Christopher Bronk Ramsey, and Michael Dee. 2009. "Absolute Age of the Uluburun Shipwreck: A Key Late Bronze Age Time-Capsule for the East Mediterranean." In *Tree-Rings, Kings and Old World Archaeology and Environment: Papers Presented in Honor of Peter Ian Kuniholm,* edited by Sturt W. Manning and Mary Jaye Bruce, 163–87. Oxford, UK: Oxbow Books.

Manning, Sturt W., Christopher Bronk Ramsey, Walter Kutschera, Thomas Higham, Bernd Kromer, Peter Steier, and Eva M. Wild. 2006. "Chronology for the Aegean Late Bronze Age 1700–1400 B.C." *Science* 312, no. 5773 (April 28): 565–69. doi: 10.1126/science.1125682.

Mapes, Lynda V. 2016a. "Five Tribes Will Work Together to Rebury Kennewick Man." *YakimaHerald.com,* April 28. http://www.yakimaherald.com /news/local/corps-of-engineers-says-kennewick-man-is-native-american -will/article_21eba658–0c9b-11e6–9790-b3f1fa7c682f.html?utm_medium= social&utm_source=twitter&utm_campaign=user-share.

——. 2016b. "It's Official: Kennewick Man Is Native American." *Seattle Times,* April 27. http://www.seattletimes.com/seattle-news/science/its -official-kennewick-man-is-native-american/.

Marinatos, Nanno. 1984. *Art and Religion in Thera: Reconstructing a Bronze Age Society.* Athens, Greece: D. and I. Mathioulakis.

Marinatos, Spyridon. 1939. "The Volcanic Destruction of Minoan Crete."
    Antiquity 13: 425–39.

Martin, Sean. 2015. "Was King Tutankhamun's Famous Burial Mask Origi-
    nally Intended for His Stepmother Nefertiti?" *International Business
    Times*, November 26. http://www.ibtimes.co.uk/was-king-tutankhamuns
    -famous-burial-mask-originally-intended-his-stepmother-nefertiti
    -1530646.

Mastrolorenzo, Giuseppe, Pier P. Petrone, Mario Pagano, Alberto Incoro-
    nato, Peter J. Baxter, Antonio Canzanella, and Luciano Fattore. 2001.
    "Herculaneum Victims of Vesuvius in CE 79." *Nature* 410 (April 12):
    79–70. http://www.nature.com/nature/journal/v410/n6830/abs/410769a0
    .html.

Matthiae, Paolo. 1981. *Ebla: An Empire Rediscovered*. Translated by Christo-
    pher Holme. Garden City, NY: Doubleday.

———. 2013. *Studies on the Archaeology of Ebla 1980–2010*. Wiesbaden, Ger.:
    Harrassowitz.

Maugh, Thomas H. II. 1992. "Ubar, Fabled Lost City, Found by L.A. Team:
    Archeology: NASA Aided in Finding the Ancient Arab Town, Once the
    Center of Frankincense Trade." *Los Angeles Times*, February 5. http://articles
    .latimes.com/1992–02–05/news/mn-1192_1_lost-city.

Mayor, Adrienne. 2014. *The Amazons: Lives and Legends of Warrior Women
    across the Ancient World*. Princeton, NJ: Princeton University Press.

McCarter, P. Kyle. 1992. "The Mysterious Copper Scroll: Clues to Hidden
    Temple Treasure?" *Bible Review* 8: 34–41, 63–64.

McFeaters, Andrew P. 2007. "The Past Is How We Present It: Nationalism
    and Archaeology in Italy from Unification to WWII." *Nebraska Anthro-
    pologist*. Paper 33. http://digitalcommons.unl.edu/nebanthro/33.

McGeough, Kevin M. 2004. *The Romans: New Perspectives*. Santa Barbara,
    CA: ABC-CLIO.

McIntyre, Dave. 2014. "Wine Cellaring Runs Deep in Our Judeo-Christian
    DNA." *Washington Post*, April 3. https://www.washingtonpost.com/lifestyle
    /food/wine-cellaring-runs-deep-in-our-judeo-christian-dna/2014/04/02
    /a0469d74-b882–11e3–96ae-f2c36d2b1245_story.html.

McKenzie, Sheena. 2016. "The 'Underground Astronauts' in Search of New
    Human Species." *CNN*, May 4. http://www.cnn.com/2016/05/03/health
    /homo-naledi-human-species-lee-berger/.

McKie, Robin. 2012. "Piltdown Man: British Archaeology's Greatest Hoax."
    Guardian, February 4. http://www.theguardian.com/science/2012/feb/05
    /piltdown-man-archaeologys-greatest-hoax.

———. 2015. "Scientist Who Found New Human Species Accused of Play-
    ing Fast and Loose with the Truth." *Guardian*, October 24. https://www
    .theguardian.com/science/2015/oct/25/discovery-human-species-accused
    -of-rushing-errors.

McMillon, Bill. 1991. *The Archaeology Handbook: A Field Manual and Resource Guide*. New York: Wiley.

McNeil, Sam. 2015. "At Jordan Site, Drone Offers Glimpse of Antiquities Looting: Archaeologists and Criminologists Use New Technologies to Study Global Trade in Stolen Artifacts." *Times of Israel*, April 3. http://www.timesofisrael.com/at-jordan-site-drone-offers-glimpse-of-antiquities-looting/.

Mejia, Paula. 2015. "Liquid Mercury Found in Mexican Pyramid Could Hold Secrets of Teotihuacan." *Newsweek*, March 26. http://www.newsweek.com/liquid-mercury-found-mexican-pyramid-could-hold-secrets-teotihuacan-325450.

Melvin, Don, Schams Elwazer, and Joshua Berlinger. 2015. "ISIS Destroys Temple of Bel in Palmyra, Syria, U.N. Reports." *CNN*, August 31. http://www.cnn.com/2015/08/31/middleeast/palmyra-temple-damaged/.

Meskell, Lynne, ed. 1998. *Archaeology under Fire: Nationalism, Politics, and Heritages in the Eastern Mediterranean and Middle East*. Boston: Routledge.

Meyer, Karl E. 1973a. *The Plundered Past*. New York: Atheneum.

———. 1973b. *Teotihuacán*. New York: Newsweek Book Division.

———. 1993. "The Hunt for Priam's Treasure." *Archaeology* 46, no. 6: 6–32.

———. 1995. "Who Owns the Spoils of War?" *Archaeology* 48, no. 4: 46–52.

Millar, Ronald W. 1972. *The Piltdown Men*. New York: St. Martin's Press.

Millon, René. 1964. "The Teotihuacán Mapping Project." *American Antiquity* 29, no. 3: 345–52.

———. 1973. *Urbanization at Teotihuacán, Mexico*. Vol. 1, *The Teotihuacán Map. Part One: Text*. Austin: University of Texas Press.

Millon, René, R. Bruce Drewitt, and George Cowgill. 1973. *Urbanization at Teotihuacan, Mexico*, vol. 1, *The Teotihuacan Map. Part Two: Maps*. Austin: University of Texas Press.

Minder, Raphael. 2014. "Back to the Cave of Altamira in Spain, Still Controversial." *New York Times*, July 30. http://www.nytimes.com/2014/07/31/arts/international/back-to-the-cave-of-altamira-in-spain-still-controversial.html.

Mocella, Vito, Emmanuel Brun, Claudio Ferrero, and Daniel Delattre. 2015. "Revealing Letters in Rolled Herculaneum Papyri by X-ray Phase-Contrast Imaging." *Nature Communications* 6 (January 20): doi:10.1038/ncomms6895. http://www.nature.com/ncomms/2015/150120/ncomms6895/full/ncomms6895.html.

Monastersky, Richard. 2015. "The Greatest Vanishing Act in Prehistoric America." *Scientific American*, November 14. http://www.scientificamerican.com/article/the-greatest-vanishing-act-in-prehistoric-america/?WT.mc_id=SA_WR_.

Moorey, P. Roger S. 1982. *Ur 'of the Chaldees': A Revised and Updated Edition of Sire Leonard Woolley's Excavations at Ur*. Ithaca, NY: Cornell University Press.

———. 1988. "The Chalcolithic Hoard from Nahal Mishmar, Israel, in Context." *World Archaeology* 20, no. 2: 171–89.

Moran, Sarah V. 1998. *Alien Art: Extraterrestrial Expressions on Earth*. Surrey, UK: Bramley.

Morell, Virginia. 1996. *Ancestral Passions: The Leakey Family and the Quest for Humankind's Beginnings*. New York: Touchstone.

Morelle, Rebecca. 2015. "Egypt's Animal Mummy 'Scandal' Revealed." *BBC News*, May 11. http://www.bbc.com/news/science-environment-32656743.

Morelle, Rebecca, and Stuart Denman. 2015. "Vast Replica Recreates Prehistoric Chauvet Cave." *BBC News*, April 24. http://www.bbc.com/news/science-environment-32403867.

Moro-Abadía, Oscar. 2006. "The History of Archaeology as a 'Colonial Discourse.'" *Bulletin of the History of Archaeology* 16, no. 2: 4–17.

Morris, Sarah P. 1989. "A Tale of Two Cities: The Miniature Frescoes from Thera and the Origins of Greek Poetry." *American Journal of Archaeology* 93: 511–35.

Moskowitz, Clara. 2012. "The Secret Tomb of China's 1st Emperor: Will We Ever See Inside?" *LiveScience*, August 17. http://www.livescience.com/22454-ancient-chinese-tomb-terracotta-warriors.html.

Moss, Stephen. 2014. "Noah's Ark Was Round—So the Ancient Tablet Tells Us." *Guardian*, February 11. http://www.theguardian.com/books/2014/feb/11/noahs-ark-round-ancient-british-museum-mesopotamian-clay-tablets-flood.

———. 2015. "Will We Ever Actually Get to See the 5,000-Year-Old Superhenge?" *Guardian*, September 7. http://www.theguardian.com/uk-news/shortcuts/2015/sep/07/superhenge-standing-stones-near-stonehenge.

Mott, Nicholas. 2012. "Why the Maya Fell: Climate Change, Conflict—And a Trip to the Beach?" *National Geographic News*, November 11. http://news.nationalgeographic.com/news/2012/11/121109-maya-civilization-climate-change-belize-science/.

Moye, David. 2016. "King Tut's Knife Was Made from a Meteorite." *Huffington Post*, June 1. http://www.huffingtonpost.com/entry/king-tut-knife-meteorite_us_574f586ee4b0c3752dcc7014.

Moyer, Justin William. 2014. "More Evidence Mayan Civilization Collapsed Because of Drought." *Washington Post*, December 30. http://www.washingtonpost.com/news/morning-mix/wp/2014/12/30/more-evidence-mayan-civilization-collapsed-because-of-drought/.

Mueller, Tom. 2016. "How Tomb Raiders Are Stealing Our History." *National Geographic* (June): 58–81. http://www.nationalgeographic.com/magazine/2016/06/looting-ancient-blood-antiquities/.

Mulliez, Dominique. 2007. "Delphi: The Excavation of the Great Oracular Centre." In *Great Moments in Greek Archaeology*, edited by Panos Valavanis, 134–57. Translated by David Hardy. Los Angeles: J. Paul Getty Museum.

Musgrave, Jonathan H., Richard A. H. Neave, and A. John N. W. Prag. 1995. "Seven Faces from Grave Circle B at Mycenae." *Annual of the British School at Athens* 90: 107–36.

Nagesh, Ashitha. 2016. "Flood Maps Reveal Long-Lost Roman Roads across England." *Metro*, January 2. http://metro.co.uk/2016/01/02/flood -maps-reveal-long-lost-roman-roads-across-england-5596264/.

Naik, Gautam. 2013. "Very Well Aged: Archaeologists Say Ancient Wine Cellar Found: Discovery in Israel Thought to Date Back 3,700 Years." *Wall Street Journal*, November 22. http://www.wsj.com/articles/SB10001 424052702304337404579213652875322822.

Naughton, David. 2015. "Exploring the Ancient City of Teotihuacan." *Harvard Divinity School News & Events*, October 2. http://hds.harvard.edu /news/2015/10/02/exploring-ancient-city-teotihuacan#

Neese, Shelley. 2009. "Cracking the Code." *Jerusalem Post*, August 19. http:// www.jpost.com/Local-Israel/Around-Israel/Cracking-the-code.

Neild, Barry. 2014. "King Tut Replica Tomb Opens to Public in Egypt." *CNN*, May 2. http://www.cnn.com/2014/05/01/travel/tutankhamuns -replica-tomb-egypt/.

Netburn, Deborah. 2013. "3,700-Year-Old Wine Cellar Held Booze You Might Not Want to Drink." *Los Angeles Times*, November 22. http:// www.latimes.com/science/sciencenow/la-sci-sn-ancient-wine-cellar -found-3700-years-old-20131122-story.html.

———. 2016. "Chauvet Cave: The Most Accurate Timeline Yet of Who Used the Cave and When." *Los Angeles Times*, April 12. http://www .latimes.com/science/sciencenow/la-sci-sn-chauvet-caves-timeline -20160412-story.html.

Neuendorf, Henri. 2015. "UNESCO Head Warns of 'Industrial Scale' Looting in Syria." *Artnet.com*, September 21. https://news.artnet.com/art -world/unesco-warning-looting-syria-333814.

Niemeier, Wolf-Dietrich. 1988. "The 'Priest King' Fresco from Knossos. A New Reconstruction and Interpretation." In *Problems in Greek Prehistory. Papers Presented at the Centenary Conference of the British School of Archaeology at Athens, Manchester, April 1986*, edited by Elizabeth B. French and Ken A. Wardle, 235–44. Bristol, UK: Bristol Classical Press.

Nigro, Lorenzo. 2006. "Results of the Italian-Palestinian Expedition to Tell es-Sultan: At the Dawn of Urbanization in Palestine." *Rosapat* 2: 1–40. https://www.academia.edu/1179527/Results_of_the_Italian-Palestinian _Expedition_to_Tell_es-Sultan_at_the_Dawn_of_Urbanization_in _Palestine.

Nolan, Linda Ann. 2005. "Emulating Augustus: The Fascist-Era Excavation of the Emperor's Peace Altar in Rome." *Archaeology Odyssey* 8, no. 3: 38–47.

Nomade, Sébastien, Dominique Genty, Romain Sasco, Vincent Scao, Valérie Féruglio, Dominique Baffier, Hervé Guillou et al. 2016. "A 36,000-Year-Old

Volcanic Eruption Depicted in the Chauvet-Pont d'Arc Cave (Ardèche, France)?" *PLOS One*, January 8. http://journals.plos.org/plosone/article?id=10.1371/journal.pone.0146621.

Oates, Joan, and David Oates. 2001. *Nimrud: An Assyrian Imperial City Revealed*. London: British School of Archaeology in Iraq.

O'Brien, Jane. 2015. "Remains of English Jamestown Colony Leaders Discovered." *BBC News*, July 28. http://www.bbc.com/news/magazine-33680128.

Olariu, Cristian. 2012. "Archaeology, Architecture and the Use of *Romanità* in Fascist Italy." *Studia Antiqua et Archaeologica* 18: 351–75.

Osborne, Hannah. 2015. "World's Oldest Pictograph Discovered in Göbekli Tepe Shows Decapitated Head in Vulture Wing." *International Business Times*, July 16. http://www.ibtimes.co.uk/worlds-oldest-pictograph-discovered-gobekli-tepe-shows-decapitated-head-vulture-wing-1511137.

O'Toole, Thomas. 1979. "Ebla Tablets: No Biblical Claims; Ebla Tablets Misread, Scholars Report." *Washington Post*, December 9: A18.

Owen, Edward. 2011. "Lost City of Atlantis 'Buried in Spanish Wetlands.'" *Telegraph*, March 14. http://www.telegraph.co.uk/news/worldnews/europe/spain/8381219/Lost-city-of-Atlantis-buried-in-Spanish-wetlands.html.

Owsley, Douglas W., and Richard L. Jantz, eds. 2014. *Kennewick Man: The Scientific Investigation of an Ancient American Skeleton* (Peopling of the Americas Publications). College Station: Texas A&M University Press.

Packer, James. 1989. "Politics, Urbanism, and Archaeology in 'Roma capitale': A Trouble Past and a Controversial Future." *American Journal of Archaeology* 93, no. 1: 137–41.

———. 1997. "Report from Rome: The Imperial Fora, a Retrospective." *American Journal of Archaeology* 101, no. 2: 307–330.

Painter, Borden W. Jr. 2005. *Mussolini's Rome: Rebuilding the Eternal City*. Italian and Italian American Studies. New York: Palgrave Macmillan.

Papazoglou-Manioudaki, Lena, Argyro Nafplioti, Jonathan H. Musgrave, Richard A. H. Neave, Denise Smith, and A. John N. W. Prag. 2009. "Mycenae Revisited Part 1: The Human Remains from Grave Circle A: Stamatakis, Schliemann and Two New Faces from Shaft Grave VI." *Annual of the British School at Athens* 104: 233–77.

Papazoglou-Manioudaki, Lena, Argyro Nafplioti, Jonathan H. Musgrave, and A. John N. W. Prag. 2010. "Mycenae Revisited Part 3: The Human Remains from Grave Circle A at Mycenae; Behind the Masks; A Study of the Bones of Shaft Graves I-V." *Annual of the British School at Athens* 105: 157–224.

Parcak, Sarah H. 2009. *Satellite Remote Sensing for Archaeology*. Boston: Routledge.

Parcak, Sarah H., David Gathings, Chase Childs, Gregory Mumford, and Eric H. Cline. 2016. "Satellite Evidence of Archaeological Site Looting in Egypt: 2002–2013." *Antiquity* 90, no. 349: 185–205.

Parrot, Andre. 1955. *Discovering Buried Worlds*. New York: Philosophical Library.

Patric, John. 1937. "Imperial Rome Reborn." *National Geographic* 71/3 (May): 269–325.

Pazanelli, Roberta, Eike D. Schmidt, and Kenneth D. S. Lapatin. 2008. *The Color of Life: Polychromy in Sculpture from Antiquity to the Present.* Los Angeles: Getty Research Institute.

Pearce, Laurie E., and Cornelia Wunsch. 2014. *Documents of Judean Exiles and West Semites in Babylonia in the Collection of David Sofer.* Bethesda, MD: CDL Press.

Pearson, Stephanie. 2003. "XX Factor: Explorers." *Outside Online*, December 1. http://www.outsideonline.com/1882931/xx-factor.

Perrottet, Tony. 2005. "The Glory That Is Rome." *Smithsonian*, October. http://www.smithsonianmag.com/history/the-glory-that-is-rome-70425698/?no-ist.

Petter, Hugh. 2000. "Back to the Future: Archaeology and Innovation in the Building of *Roma Capitale*." In *Ancient Rome: The Archaeology of the Eternal City*, edited by Jon Coulston and Hazel Dodge, 332–53. Oxford University School of Archaeology Monograph 54. Oxford, UK: Oxford University School of Archaeology.

Pettinato, Giovanni. 1981. *The Archives of Ebla: An Empire Inscribed in Clay.* Garden City, NY: Doubleday.

———. 1991. *Ebla, A New Look at History.* Translated by C. Faith Richardson. Baltimore: Johns Hopkins University Press.

Phillips, Phillip. 1955. "American Archaeology and General Anthropological Theory." *Southwestern Journal of Anthropology* 11: 246–47.

Piening, Heinrich. 2013. "Examination Report: The Polychromy of the Arch of Titus Menorah Relief." *Images* 6: 26–29. doi: 10.1163/18718000–123400002. https://www.academia.edu/5332530/Heinrich_Pienings_Preliminary _Report_of_the_Arch_of_Titus_Digital_Restoration_Project_Images_6 _2013_.

Pincus, Jessie, Tim DeSmet, Yotam Tepper, and Matthew J. Adams. 2013. "Ground Penetrating Radar and Electromagnetic Archaeogeophysical Investigations at the Roman Legionary Camp at Legio, Israel." *Archaeological Prospection* (2013): 1–13.

Plaut, W. Gunther. 1978. "Ancient Tablets Hold Out Promise of Fresh Look at the Bible. *Globe and Mail* (Canada), May 13.

Pollard, Justin. 2007. *The Story of Archaeology: In 50 Great Discoveries.* London: Quercus.

Polosmak, Natalia. 1994. "A Mummy Unearthed from the Pastures of Heaven." *National Geographic* 186/4 (October): 80–103.

Pool, Christopher A. 2007. *Olmec Archaeology and Early Mesoamerica*. Cambridge: Cambridge University Press.

Pope, Saxton. 1923. *Hunting with the Bow and Arrow*. Berkeley: University of California Press.

Portal, Jane. 2007. *The First Emperor: China's Terracotta Army*. Cambridge, MA: Harvard University Press.

Povoledo, Elisabetta. 2012. "Technology Identifies Lost Color at Roman Forum." *International New York Times*, June 24. http://www.nytimes .com/2012/06/25/arts/design/menorah-on-arch-of-titus-in-roman-forum -was-rich-yellow.html?_r=0

———. 2015. "Scientists Hope to Learn How Pompeians Lived, before the Big Day." *New York Times*, October 5. http://www.nytimes.com/2015 /10/06/world/europe/scientists-hope-to-learn-how-pompeians -lived-before-the-big-day.html?_r=0.

Preston, Douglas. 2014. "The Kennewick Man Finally Freed to Share His Secrets." *Smithsonian*, September. http://www.smithsonianmag.com/ history/kennewick-man-finally-freed-share-his-secrets-180952462 /#Bc1CIojqQ1gTGHso.99

Pringle, Heather. 2011. "Smithsonian Shipwreck Exhibit Draws Fire from Archaeologists." *Science Insider*, March 10. http://news.sciencemag.org /2011/03/smithsonian-shipwreck-exhibit-draws-fire-archaeologists

Pulak, Cemal. 1998. "The Uluburun Shipwreck: An Overview." *International Journal of Nautical Archaeology* 27: 188–224.

———. 1999. "Shipwreck: Recovering 3,000-Year-Old Cargo." *Archaeology Odyssey* 2, no. 4: 18–29.

———. 2010. "Uluburun Shipwreck." In *The Oxford Handbook of the Bronze Age Aegean*, edited by Eric H. Cline, 862–876. Oxford, UK: Oxford University Press.

Pyne, Lydia. 2016. "Dear Paleoanthropology, Homo Naledi Just Shifted Your Paradigm." *JSTOR Daily*, January 23. http://daily.jstor.org/homo -naledi-and-paradigm-shift/.

Quiles, Anita, Anita Quilesa, Hélène Valladas, Hervé Bocherens, Emmanuelle Delqué-Količ, Evelyne Kaltnecker, Johannes van der Plicht et al. 2016. "A High-Precision Chronological Model for the Decorated Upper Paleolithic Cave of Chauvet-Pont d'Arc, Ardèche, France." *Proceedings of the National Academy of Sciences of the United States of America* 113, no. 17: 4670–75. http://www.pnas.org/content/113/17/4670.full (by subscription only).

Rabinovitch, Ari. 2016. "Archaeologists vs. Robbers in Israel's Race to Find Ancient Scrolls." *Reuters*, June 2. http://www.reuters.com/article/us -israel-archaeology-idUSKCN0YO17J.

Ragan, Mark K. 1999. *The Hunley: Submarines, Sacrifice, and Success in the Civil War*, rev. ed. Charleston, SC: Narwhal Press.

———. 2006. *The Hunley*. Orangeburg, SC: Sandlapper.

Raichlen, David A., Adam D. Gordon, William E. H. Harcourt-Smith, Adam D. Foster, and William Randall Haas Jr. 2010. "Laetoli Footprints Preserve Earliest Direct Evidence of Human-Like Bipedal Biomechanics." *PLoS ONE*, March 22. http://www.ncbi.nlm.nih.gov/pmc/articles/PMC2842428/.

Rasmussen, Morten, Martin Sikora, Anders Albrechtsen, Thorfinn Sand Korneliussen, J. Víctor Moreno-Mayar, G. David Poznik, Christoph P. E. Zollikofer et al. 2015. "The Ancestry and Affiliations of Kennewick Man." *Nature* 523, no. 7561: 455–58. doi: 10.1038/nature14625.

Ravilous, Kate. 2012. "Viking Boat Burial—Ardnamurchan, Scotland." *Archaeology* 65, no. 1 (January–February). http://archive.archaeology.org/1201/features/topten_scotland.html.

Redford, Donald B. 1987. *Akhenaten: The Heretic King*. Princeton, NJ: Princeton University Press.

Redman, Charles. 1978. *The Rise of Civilization: From Early Farmers to Urban Civilization in the Ancient Near East*. San Francisco: W. H. Freeman.

Reeves, Nicholas. 1990. *The Complete Tutankhamun*. London: Thames and Hudson.

———. 2014. "Tutankhamun's Mask Reconsidered." *Bulletin of the Egyptological Seminar* 19: 511–27. https://www.academia.edu/7415055/Tutankhamuns_Mask_Reconsidered_in_press_corrected_proof_2015_.

———. 2015a. "The Burial of Nefertiti? Addenda and Corrigenda." https://www.academia.edu/15247276/The_Burial_of_Nefertiti_Addenda_and_Corrigenda_2015_.

———. 2015b. *The Burial of Nefertiti?* Valley of the Kings Occasional Paper No. 1. Tucson, AZ: Amarna Royal Tombs Project. https://www.academia.edu/14406398/The_Burial_of_Nefertiti_2015_.

Reeves, Nicholas, and Richard H. Wilkinson. 1996. *The Complete Valley of the Kings: Tombs and Treasures of Ancient Egypt's Royal Burial Site*. London: Thames and Hudson.

Reiche, Maria. 1949. *Mystery on the Desert: A Study of the Ancient Figures and Strange Delineated Surfaces Seen from the Air near Nazca, Peru*. Private printing.

Reid, Donald. 2002. *Whose Pharaohs? Archaeology, Museums, and Egyptian National Identity from Napoleon to World War I*. Berkeley: University of California Press.

Reilly, Mary. 2004. "Brian Rose: Raider of the Lost Art(ifacts)." *University of Cincinnati News*, April 22. http://www.uc.edu/News/NR.aspx?ID=1591.

Reinhard, Johan. 1988. *The Nazca Lines: A New Perspective on their Origin and Meaning*. Lima, Peru: Los Pinos.

———. 2005. *The Ice Maiden: Inca Mummies, Mountain Gods, and Sacred Sites in the Andes*. Washington, DC: National Geographic Books.

———. 2007. *Machu Picchu: Exploring an Ancient Sacred Center*. Los Angeles: UCLA, Cotsen Institute of Archaeology.

Renfrew, Colin, and Paul G. Bahn. 2012. *Archaeology: Theories, Methods, and Practice*, 6th ed. London: Thames and Hudson.

———. 2015. *Archaeology Essentials: Theories, Methods, and Practice*, 3rd ed. London: Thames and Hudson.

Riley, Chloe. 2015. "Dueling Gold Mask(s) of Agamemnon Coming Soon to Field Museum." *Chicago Tonight*, November 6. http://chicagotonight .wttw.com/2015/11/06/dueling-gold-masks-agamemnon-coming-soon -field-museum

Ritner, Robert K., and Nadine Moeller. 2014. "The Ahmose 'Tempest Stela': Thera and Comparative Chronology." *Journal of Near Eastern Studies* 73, no. 1: 1–19.

Robins, Gay. 2008. *The Art of Ancient Egypt*, rev. ed. Cambridge, MA: Harvard University Press.

Robinson, Andrew. 2002. *The Man Who Deciphered Linear B: The Story of Michael Ventris*. London: Thames and Hudson.

———. 2012. *Cracking the Egyptian Code: The Revolutionary Life of Jean-François Champollion*. Oxford, UK: Oxford University Press.

Robinson, Julian, and Jack Millner. 2015. "The FAKE Mummies: Ancient Egyptian Embalmers Wrapped Bandages Round Mud and Sticks Because of Shortage of Animals." *Daily Mail*, May 11. http://www.dailymail.co.uk /news/article-3076642/Scandal-Ancient-Egypt-animal-mummy-industry -s-revealed-EMPTY.html.

Roehrenbeck, Carol A. 2010. "Repatriation of Cultural Property–Who Owns the Past? An Introduction to Approaches and to Selected Statutory Instruments." *International Journal of Legal Information* 38, no. 2: Article 11. http://scholarship.law.cornell.edu/ijli/vol38/iss2/11.

Romano, Nick. 2015. "Strapped for Cash, Some Greeks Turn to Ancient Source of Wealth." *National Geographic News*, August 17. http://news .nationalgeographic.com/2015/08/150817-greece-looting-artifacts -financial-crisis-archaeology/.

Romey, Kristin. 2015. "Ancient Egyptian Artifacts Smuggled into U.S. Are Heading Home." *National Geographic News*, April 22. http://news.national geographic.com/2015/04/150422-ancient-egypt-artifact-repatriation -looting-archaeology-smuggling-antiquities-mummy/.

———. 2016. "Canadian Teen Who 'Discovered' Lost Maya City Speaks Out." *National Geographic News*, June 2. http://news.nationalgeographic .com/2016/06/lost-maya-city-mexico-william-gadoury-satellite-discovery -archaeology/.

Rose, C. Brian. 2014. *The Archaeology of Greek and Roman Troy*. Cambridge: Cambridge University Press.

Rose, Mark. 1993. "What Did Schliemann Find—and Where, When, and How Did He Find It?" *Archaeology* 46, no. 6: 33–36.

Rosen, Meghan. 2016. "The Iceman Tells a New Tale: Infection with Ulcer-Causing Bacteria." *ScienceNews*, January 7. https://www.sciencenews.org/article/iceman-tells-new-tale-infection-ulcer-causing-bacteria.

Rothfield, Lawrence. 2008a. *The Rape of Mesopotamia: Behind the Looting of the Iraq Museum*. Chicago: University of Chicago Press.

———, ed. 2008b. *Antiquities under Siege: Cultural Heritage Protection after the Iraq War*. Walnut Creek, CA: AltaMira Press.

Roux, George. 1992. *Ancient Iraq*, new ed. New York: Penguin Books.

Rubalcaba, Jill, and Eric H. Cline. 2011. *Digging for Troy* (Young Adults). Boston: Charlesbridge.

Rubin, Alissa J. 2015. "The Chauvet Cave's Hyperreal Wonders, Replicated." *New York Times*, April 24. http://www.nytimes.com/2015/04/25/arts/design/the-chauvet-caves-hyperreal-wonders-replicated.html.

Ruble, Kayla. 2014. "Drone Footage Shows Extent of Damage from Greenpeace Stunt at Nazca Lines." *Vice News*, December 17. https://news.vice.com/article/drone-footage-shows-extent-of-damage-from-greenpeace-stunt-at-nazca-lines.

Rush, Laurie, ed. 2012. *Archaeology, Cultural Property, and the Military*. Repr. Suffolk, UK: Boydell Press.

Russell, John M. 1991. *Sennacherib's Palace without Rival at Nineveh*. Chicago: University of Chicago Press.

Russon, Mary-Ann. 2014. "China: Ancient Tomb of First Emperor Qin Shi Huang's Grandmother Discovered in Xi'an." *International Business News*, September 11. http://www.ibtimes.co.uk/china-ancient-tomb-first-emperor-qin-shi-huangs-grandmother-discovered-xi-1465022.

Ryan, William B., and Walter C. Pittman. 1998. *Noah's Flood: The New Scientific Discoveries about the Event That Changed History*. New York: Simon and Schuster.

Said-Moorhouse, Lauren. 2013. "Space Archaeologist Unlocks Secrets of Ancient Civilizations." CNN, September 20. http://www.cnn.com/2013/09/02/travel/space-archaeologist-unlocks-secrets/.

Saldarini, Anthony J. 1998. "Babatha's Story: Personal Archive Offers a Glimpse of Ancient Jewish Life." *Biblical Archaeology Review* 24, no. 2: 28–37, 72–74.

Samadelli, Marco, Marcello Melis, Matteo Miccoli, Eduard Egarter Vigl, and Albert R. Zink. 2015. "Complete Mapping of the Tattoos of the 5300-Year-Old Tyrolean Iceman." *Journal of Cultural Heritage* 16, no. 5: 753–58.

Sample, Ian. 2015. "Richard III DNA Tests Uncover Evidence of Further Royal Scandal." *Guardian*, March 25. http://www.theguardian.com/uk-news/2015/mar/25/richard-iii-dna-tests-uncover-evidence-of-further-royal-scandal.

Saura Ramos, Pedro A., Matilde Múzquiz Pérez-Seoane, and Antonio Bel-
trán Martínez. 1999. *The Cave of Altamira*. New York: Harry Abrams.

Sayce, Archibald H. 1890. *The Hittites: The Story of a Forgotten Empire*, 2nd
ed. London: Religious Tract Society.

Scallan, Marilyn. 2015. "Ancient Ink: Iceman Otzi Has World's Oldest Tattoos." *Smithsonian Science News*, December 9. http://smithsonianscience
.si.edu/2015/12/debate-over-worlds-oldest-tattoo-is-over-for-now/.

Schaar, Kenneth W. 2012. "Wilhelm Dörpfeld: Schliemann's Important Discovery." In *Archaeology and Heinrich Schliemann—A Century after His
Death: Assessments and Prospects; Myth—History—Science*, edited by George
S. Korres, Nektarios Karadimas, and Georgia Flouda, 328–32. https://
www.academia.edu/3210347/Korres_G._Karadimas_N._and_Flouda_G.
_eds._2012._Archaeology_and_Heinrich_Schliemann_A_Century
_after_his_Death._Assessments_and_Prospects._Myth_-_History
_-_Science_Athens.

Schachermeyr, Fritz. 1950. *Poseidon und die Entstehung des griechischen Göt-
terglaubens*. Bonn: Franck.

Schliemann, Heinrich. 1875. *Troy and Its Remains: A Narrative of Researches
and Discoveries Made on the Site of Ilium, and in the Trojan Plain*. New
York: Benjamin Blom.

———. 1880. *Mycenae: a Narrative of Researches and Discoveries at Mycenae
and Tiryns*. New York: Scribner, Armstrong.

———. 1881. *Ilios: The City and Country of the Trojans*. New York: Benjamin
Blom.

Schmitt, Axel K., Martin Danišík, Erkan Aydar, Erdal Şen, İnan Ulusoy,
and Oscar M. Lovera. 2014. "Identifying the Volcanic Eruption Depicted
in a Neolithic Painting at Çatalhöyük, Central Anatolia, Turkey." *PLoS
ONE*, January 8. doi: 10.1371/journal.pone.0084711.

Schofield, John, William G. Johnson, and Colleen M. Beck, eds. 2002.
Matériel Culture: The Archaeology of Twentieth Century Conflict. London:
Routledge.

Schofield, Louise. 2007. *The Mycenaeans*. Malibu, CA: J. Paul Getty
Museum.

Scott, Douglas, Lawrence Babits, and Charles Haecker, eds. 2007. *Fields of
Conflict: Battlefield Archaeology from the Roman Empire to the Korean War*.
Westport, CT: Praeger Security International.

Scott, Michael. 2014. *Delphi: A History of the Center of the Ancient World*.
Princeton, NJ: Princeton University Press.

Seabrook, John. 2015. "The Invisible Library." *New Yorker*, November 16.
http://www.newyorker.com/magazine/2015/11/16/the-invisible-library?
utm_content=bufferd6a5a&utm_medium=social&utm_source=facebook
.com&utm_campaign=buffer.

Seales, William Brent, Clifford Seth Parker, Michael Segal, Emanuel Tov, Pnina Shor, and Yosef Porath. 2016. "From Damage to Discovery via Virtual Unwrapping: Reading the Scroll from En-Gedi." *Science Advances* 2, no. 9 (September): e1601247; DOI: 10.1126/sciadv.1601247

Shaer, Matthew. 2014. "The Controversial Afterlife of King Tut." *Smithsonian*, December. http://www.smithsonianmag.com/history/controversial -afterlife-king-tut-180953400/.

———. 2016. "A Secret Tunnel Found in Mexico May Finally Solve the Mysteries of Teotihuacán." *Smithsonian*, June. http://www.smithsonianmag .com/history/discovery-secret-tunnel-mexico-solve-mysteries-teotihuacan -180959070/?utm_source=twitter.com&no-ist.

Shanks, Hershel. 1980. "Ebla Update: New Ebla Epigrapher Attacks Conclusions of Ousted Ebla Scholar; Professor Archi Disagrees with Professor Pettinato's Biblical Connections." *Biblical Archaeology Review* 6, no. 3 (May–June): 47–59.

———. 1992. *Understanding the Dead Sea Scrolls*. New York: Vintage Press.

———. 1998. *The Mystery and Meaning of the Dead Sea Scrolls*. Washington, DC: Biblical Archaeology Society.

———. 2002. "Greeks vs. Hittites; Why Troy Is Troy and the Trojan War Is Real." *Archaeology Odyssey* 5, no. 4: 24–35, 53.

———. 2010. *Freeing the Dead Sea Scrolls: And Other Adventures of an Archaeology Outsider*. New York: Bloomsbury Academic.

Shaw, Maria. 2004. "The 'Priest-King' Fresco from Knossos: Man, Woman, Priest, King, or Someone Else?" In ΧΑΡΙΣ: *Essays in Honor of Sara A. Immerwahr*, edited by Anne P. Chapin, 65–84. *Hesperia* Supplement 33. Princeton, NJ: American School of Classical Studies at Athens.

Shear, T. Leslie Jr. 1984. "The Athenian Agora: Excavations of 1980–1982." *Hesperia* 53, no. 1: 1–57.

Sheftel, Phoebe A. 2002. "'Sending Out of Expeditions': The Contest for Delphi." In *Excavating Our Past: Perspectives on the History of the Archaeological Institute of America*, edited by Susan Heuck Allen, 105–13. Boston: Archaeological Institute of America.

Sheldon, Natasha. 2014. "Human Remains in Pompeii: The Body Casts." http://decodedpast.com/human-remains-pompeii-body-casts/7532.

Shreeve, Jamie. 2015. "This Face Changes the Human Story. But How?" *National Geographic News*, September 10. http://news.nationalgeographic .com/2015/09/150910-human-evolution-change/.

Silberman, Neil A. 1989. *Between Past and Present. Archaeology, Ideology and Nationalism in the Modern Middle East*. New York: Henry Holt.

———. 1993. *A Prophet from Amongst You: The Life of Yaigael Yadin; Soldier, Scholar, and Mythmaker of Modern Israel*. Reading, MA: Addison-Wesley.

Silberman, Neil A., Israel Finkelstein, David Ussishkin, and Baruch Halpern. 1999. "Digging at Armageddon." *Archaeology* (November–December 1999): 32–39.

Silverman, David P. 2003. *Ancient Egypt*. Oxford, UK: Oxford University Press.

Simmons, Alan H. 2007. *The Neolithic Revolution in the Near East: Transforming the Human Landscape*. Tucson: University of Arizona Press.

Smith, Andrew M. II. 2013. *Roman Palmyra: Identity, Community, and State Formation*. Oxford, UK: Oxford University Press.

Smith, Christopher. 2000. "Early and Archaic Rome." In *Ancient Rome: The Archaeology of the Eternal City*, edited by Jon Coulston and Hazel Dodge, 16–41. Oxford University School of Archaeology Monograph 54. Oxford, UK: Oxford University School of Archaeology.

Smith, Michael. 2003. *The Aztecs*, 2nd ed. Oxford, UK: Blackwell.

Smith, Roff. 2016. "Ancient Roman IOUs Found beneath Bloomberg's New London HQ." *National Geographic News*, June 1. http://news.national geographic.com/2016/05/ancient-rome-London-Londinum-Bloomberg -archaeology-Boudicca-archaeology/#close.

Smith-Spark, Laura. 2015. "Syria: ISIS Destroys Ancient Muslim Shrines in Palmyra." *CNN*, June 24. http://www.cnn.com/2015/06/24/middleeast /syria-isis-palmyra-shrines/.

Solecki, Ralph S. 1954. "Shanidar Cave: A Paleolithic Site in Northern Iraq." *Annual Report of the Smithsonian Institution*: 389–425.

———. 1971. *The First Flower People*. New York: Alfred A. Knopf.

———. 1975. "Shanidar IV, a Neanderthal Flower Burial in Northern Iraq." *Science* 190, no. 4217: 880–81.

Solecki, Ralph S., Rose L. Solecki, and Anagnostis P. Agelarakis. 2004. *The Proto-Neolithic Cemetery in Shanidar Cave*. College Station: Texas A&M University Press.

Sommer, Jeffrey D. 1999. "The Shanidar IV 'Flower Burial': A Re-evaluation of Neanderthal Burial Ritual." *Cambridge Archaeological Journal* 9, no. 1: 127–29.

Søreide, Fredrik. 2011. *Ships from the Depths: Deepwater Archaeology*. College Station: Texas A&M Press.

Spencer, Frank. 1990. *Piltdown: A Scientific Forgery*. Oxford, UK: Oxford University Press.

Spindler, Konrad. 1995. *The Man in the Ice: The Discovery of a 5,000-Year-Old Body Reveals the Secrets of the Stone Age*. New York: Harmony Books.

Spivey, Nigel. 2005. *How Art Made the World: A Journey to the Origins of Human Creativity*. New York: Basic Books.

Stanley Price, Nicholas, ed. 1991. *The Conservation of the Orpheus Mosaic at Paphos, Cyprus*. Los Angeles: J. Paul Getty Conservation Institute.

Starn, Orin. 2004. *Ishi's Brain*. New York: W. W. Norton.

Steinbuch, Yaron. 2016. "King Tut's Dagger Came from Outer Space." *New York Post*, June 2. http://nypost.com/2016/06/02/king-tuts-dagger-came -from-outer-space/.

Stephens, John Lloyd. 1949. *Incidents of Travel in Central America, Chiapas, and Yucatán* (2 vols.). Edited with an Introduction and Notes by Richard L. Predmore. New Brunswick, NJ: Rutgers University Press.

———. 1962. *Incidents of Travel in Yucatán* (2 vols.). Edited and with an Introduction by Victor Wolfgang von Hagen. Norman: University of Oklahoma Press.

———. 1970. *Incidents of Travel in Egypt, Arabia Petraea, and the Holy Land.* Edited and with an Introduction by Victor Wolfgang von Hagen. Norman: University of Oklahoma Press.

Stern, Benjamin, Carl Heron, Tory Tellefsen, and Margaret Serpico. 2008. "New Investigations into the Uluburun Resin Cargo." *Journal of Archaeological Science* 35, no. 8 (August): 2188–2203. http://www.sciencedirect .com/science/article/pii/S0305440308000320.

Stewart, Doug. 2006. "Resurrecting Pompeii." *Smithsonian*, February. http://www.smithsonianmag.com/history/resurrecting-pompeii -109163501/?no-ist.

Stiebing, William H. 1984. *Ancient Astronauts, Cosmic Collisions*. Amherst, NY: Prometheus Books.

———. 2009. *Ancient Near Eastern History and Culture*, 2nd ed. New York: Pearson Longman.

Stirling, Matthew W. 1939. "Discovering the New World's Oldest Dated Work of Man." *National Geographic* 76 (August): 183–218.

———. 1940. "Great Stone Faces of the Mexican Jungle." *National Geographic* 78 (September): 309–34.

———. 1941. "Expedition Unearths Buried Masterpieces of Carved Jade." *National Geographic* 80 (September): 278–302.

———. 1947. "On the Trail of La Venta Man." *National Geographic* 91 (February): 137–72.

Stoneman, Richard. 1992. *Palmyra and Its Empire: Zenobia's Revolt against Rome*. Ann Arbor: University of Michigan Press.

Strauss, Barry. 2006. *The Trojan War: A New History*. New York: Simon and Schuster.

Strauss, Mark. 2015. "Desperately Seeking Queen Nefertiti." *National Geographic News*, August 14. http://news.nationalgeographic.com/2015/08 /150814-nefertiti-tomb-tutankhamun-tut-archaeology-egypt-dna/.

Stromberg, Joseph. 2012. "Why Did the Mayan Civilization Collapse? A New Study Points to Deforestation and Climatic Change." *Smithsonian*, August 23. http://www.smithsonianmag.com/science-nature/why-did-the -mayan-civilization-collapse-a-new-study-points-to-deforestation -and-climate-change-30863026/?no-ist.

Stuart, David. 2011. *The Order of Days: The Maya World and the Truth about 2012*. New York: Harmony Books.

Stuart, David, and George E. Stuart. 2008. *Palenque: Eternal City of the Maya*. London: Thames and Hudson.

Stuart, George E., and Gene S. Stuart. 1977. *The Mysterious Maya*. Washington, DC: National Geographic Books.

———. 1993. *Lost Kingdoms of the Maya*. Washington DC: National Geographic Books.

Sullivan, Gail. 2014. "In Mexican City Teotihuacan, 2,000-Year-Old Tunnel Holds Ancient Mysteries." *Washington Post*, October 30. http://www.washingtonpost.com/news/morning-mix/wp/2014/10/30/in-mexican-city-teotihuacan-2000-year-old-tunnel-holds-ancient-mysteries/.

Swaddling, Judith. 1999. *The Ancient Olympic Games*, 2nd ed. Austin: University of Texas Press.

Taylor, Jane. 2002. *Petra and the Lost Kingdom of the Nabataeans*. Cambridge, MA: Harvard University Press.

Taylor, Kate. 2011. "Shipwreck Show Postponed." *New York Times*, June 28. http://artsbeat.blogs.nytimes.com/2011/06/28/shipwreck-show-postponed/?_r=0.

Taylor, R. E., and Martin J. Aitken, eds. 1997. *Chronometric Dating in Archaeology*. London: Springer.

Tepper, Yotam. 2002. "Lajjun–Legio in Israel: Results of a Survey in and around the Military Camp Area." In *Limes XVIII: Proceedings of the XVIIIth International Congress of Roman Frontier Studies, Amman*, September 2000, edited by Philip Freeman, Julian Bennett, Zbigniew T. Fiema, and Birgitta Hoffmann, 231–42. British Archaeological Reports S1084. Oxford, UK: British Archaeological Reports.

———. 2003b. "Survey of the Legio Area near Megiddo: Historical and Geographical Research" (master's thesis, Tel Aviv University [Hebrew]).

———. 2003a. "Survey of the Legio Region." *Hadashot Arkheologiyot— Excavations and Surveys in Israel* 115: 29*–31*.

———. 2007. "The Roman Legionary Camp at Legio, Israel: Results of an Archaeological Survey and Observations on the Roman Military Presence at the Site." In *The Late Roman Army in the Near East from Diocletian to the Arab Conquest: Proceedings of a Colloquium Held at Potenza, Acerenza, and Matera, Italy* (May), edited by Ariel S. Lewin and Pietrina Pellegrini, 57–71. BAR International Series 1717. Oxford, UK: ArchaeoPress.

Thomas, Carol G., and Craig Conant. 2005. *The Trojan War*. Westport, CT: Greenwood Press.

Thomas, David Hurst. 2001. *Skull Wars: Kennewick Man, Archaeology, and the Battle for Native American Identity*. New York: Basic Books.

Thompson, Homer A. 1983. *The Athenian Agora: A Short Guide*. Meridien, CT: American School of Classical Studies at Athens.

Thompson, Homer A., and Richard E. Wycherley. 1972. *The Agora of Athens: The History, Shape, and Uses of an Ancient City Center.* Vol. 14, *The Athenian Agora.* Princeton, NJ: American School of Classical Studies at Athens.

Thompson, Jason. 2015. *Wonderful Things: A History of Egyptology.* Vol. 1, *From Antiquity to 1881.* Cairo, Egypt: American University in Cairo Press.

Thurman, Judith. 2008. "First Impressions: What Does the World's Oldest Art Say about Us?" *New Yorker,* June 23: 58–67. http://www.newyorker.com/magazine/2008/06/23/first-impressions.

Traill, David A. 1983. "Schliemann's 'Discovery' of Priam's Treasure." *Antiquity* 57: 181–86.

———. 1984. "Schliemann's Discovery of Priam's Treasure: A Re-examination of the Evidence." *Journal of Hellenic Studies* 104: 96–115.

———. 1985. "Schliemann's 'Dream of Troy': The Making of a Legend." *Classical Journal* 81: 13–24.

———. 1993. *Excavating Schliemann.* Illinois Classical Studies Supplement. New York: Scholars Press.

———. 1995. *Schliemann of Troy: Treasure and Deceit.* New York: St. Martin's Griffin.

———. 1999. "Priam's Treasure: The 4,000-Year-Old Hoard of Trojan Gold." *Archaeology Odyssey* 2, no. 3: 14–27, 59.

———. 2000. "'Priam's Treasure': Clearly a Composite." *Anatolian Studies* 50: 17–35.

Trigger, Bruce G. 1984. "Alternative Archaeologies: Nationalist, Colonialist, Imperialist." *Man,* n.s. 19, no. 3: 355–70.

Trinkaus, Erik. 1983. *The Shanidar Neandertals.* New York: Academic Press.

Trümpler, Charlotte, ed. 2001. *Agatha Christie and Archaeology.* London: British Museum Press.

Turner, Lauren. 2016. "Palmyra's Arch of Triumph Recreated in London." *BBC News,* April 19. http://www.bbc.com/news/uk-36070721.

Tyldesley, Joyce A. 1998. *Hatchepsut: The Female Pharaoh.* New York: Penguin Books.

———. 2005. *Nefertiti: Egypt's Sun Queen.* New York: Penguin Books.

Urbanus, Jason. 2015. "The Charred Scrolls of Herculaneum." *Archaeology,* April 6. http://www.archaeology.org/issues/175–1505/trenches/3166-trenches-italy-herculaneum-papyri-scanned.

Ussishkin, David. 1984. "Defensive Judean Counter-Ramp Found at Lachish in 1983 Season." *Biblical Archaeology Review* 10, no. 2: 66–73.

———. 1987. "Lachish: Key to the Israelite Conquest of Canaan?" *Biblical Archaeology Review* 13, no. 1: 18–39.

———. 1988. "Reconstructing the Great Gate at Lachish." *Biblical Archaeology Review* 14, no. 2: 42–47.

———. 2014. *Biblical Lachish: A Tale of Construction, Destruction, Excavation and Restoration.* Washington, DC: Biblical Archaeology Society.

Vance, Erik. 2015. "Losing Maya Heritage to Looters." *National Geographic News*, August 10. http://news.nationalgeographic.com/news/2014/08 /140808-maya-guatemala-looter-antiquities-archaeology-science/.

Vanderkam, John, and Peter Flint. 2002. *The Meaning of the Dead Sea Scrolls: Their Significance for Understanding the Bible, Judaism, Jesus, and Christianity*. New York: HarperCollins.

Van Gilder Cooke, Sonia. 2016. "Lead Ink from Scrolls May Unlock Library Destroyed by Vesuvius." *New Scientist*, March 21. https://www.newscientist .com/article/2081832-lead-ink-from-scrolls-may-unlock-library-destroyed -by-vesuvius?utm_content=buffer72dcc&utm_medium=social&utm _source=facebook.com&utm_campaign=buffer

Vergano, Dan. 2014. "Cold War Spy-Satellite Images Unveil Lost Cities." *National Geographic News*, April 25. http://news.nationalgeographic.com /news/2014/04/140425-corona-spy-satellite-archaeology-science/.

Vermes, Geza. 1998. *The Complete Dead Sea Scrolls in English*. New York: Penguin.

Vicker, Ray. 1979. "Untitled Brief Paragraph on Ebla and Pettinato." *Wall Street Journal*, June 18, p. 1.

Vivian, R. Gwinn, and Bruce Hilpert. 2012. *Chaco Handbook: An Encyclopedia Guide (Chaco Canyon)*, 2nd ed. Provo: University of Utah Press.

Vogelkoff-Brogan, Natalia. 2014. "The American Dream to Excavate Delphi; or, How the Oracle Vexed the Americans (1879–1891)." *From the Archivist's Notebook*, October 2. https://nataliavogeikoff.com/2014/10/02 /the-american-dream-to-excavate-delphi-or-how-the-oracle-vexed-the -americans-1879–1891/.

Von Däniken, Erich. 1968. *Chariots of the Gods?* New York: Berkley Books.

Von Hagen, Victor Wolfgang. 1947. *Maya Explorer: John Lloyd Stephens and the Lost Cities of Central America and Yucatán*. San Francisco: Chronicle Books.

Wade, Nicholas. 2010a. "A Host of Mummies, a Forest of Secrets." *New York Times*, March 15. http://www.nytimes.com/2010/03/16/science/16archeo .html?pagewanted=all&_r=0.

———. 2015a. "Grave of 'Griffin Warrior' at Pylos Could Be a Gateway to Civilizations." *New York Times*, October 26. http://www.nytimes.com /2015/10/27/science/a-warriors-grave-at-pylos-greece-could-be-a-gateway -to-civilizations.html?_r=0.

———. 2015b. "Unlocking Scrolls Preserved in Eruption of Vesuvius, Using X-Ray Beams." *New York Times*, January 20. http://www.nytimes .com/2015/01/21/science/more-progress-made-toward-learning-contents -of-herculaneum-scrolls.html?_r=0.

———. 2016. "In Greek Warrior's Grave, Rings of Power (and a Mirror and Combs)." *New York Times*, October 3. http://www.nytimes.com/2016/10 /04/science/greece-archaeology-pylos-griffin-warrior.html.

Walker, Sally M. 2005. *Secrets of a Civil War Submarine: Solving the Mysteries of the H.L. Hunley*. Minneapolis: Carolrhoda Books.

Walsh, John E. 1996. *Unraveling Piltdown: The Science Fraud of the Century and Its Solution*. New York: Random House.

Walton, Marc S., Andrew Shortland, Susanna Kirk, and Patrick Degryse. 2009. "Evidence for the Trade of Mesopotamian and Egyptian Glass to Mycenaean Greece." *Journal of Archaeological Science* 36, no. 7 (July): 1496–1503. http://www.sciencedirect.com/science/article/pii/S0305440309000934.

Warburton, David, ed. 2009. *Time's Up! Dating the Minoan Eruption of Santorini: Acts of the Minoan Eruption Chronology Workshop, Sandbjerg, November 2007*. Århus: Århus University Press.

Watson, Peter, and Cecilia Todeschini. 2006. *The Medici Conspiracy: The Illicit Journey of Looted Antiquities—From Italy's Tomb Raiders to the World's Greatest Museums*. New York: PublicAffairs.

Waxman, Sharon. 2009. *Loot: The Battle over the Stolen Treasures of the Ancient World*. New York: Times Books.

Weber, Katherine. 2016. "Archaeological Discovery: 2,000-Y-O Military Barracks Found in Rome during Subway Line Dig." *Christian Post*, June 2. http://www.christianpost.com/news/archaeologists-rome-discover-2000-year-old-military-barracks-subway-line-dig-164732/.

Webster, Ben. 2015. "Flood Maps Reveal Lost Roman Roads." *The Times*, December 24. http://www.thetimes.co.uk/tto/news/uk/article4653857.ece.

Weisman, Alan. 2007. *The World without Us*. New York: St. Martin's Press.

Weiss, Harvey. 2012. "Quantifying Collapse: The Late Third Millennium BC." In *Seven Generations since the Fall of Akkad*, edited by Harvey Weiss, 1–24. Wiesbaden, Ger.: Harrassowitz.

Welch, Katherine E. 2007. *The Roman Amphitheatre: From its Origins to the Colosseum*. Cambridge: Cambridge University Press.

Whiston, William. 1999. *Josephus: The New Complete Works*. Translated by William Whiston. New York: Kregel Academic and Professional.

White, Gregory G., and Thomas F. King. 2007. *The Archaeological Survey Manual*. Walnut Creek, CA: Left Coast Press.

White Crawford, Sidney. 2000. *The Temple Scroll and Related Texts*. Sheffield, UK: Sheffield Academic Press.

Wilford, John Noble. 1993a. "Have They Discovered Ancient Walls of Troy?" *Times-News*, February 23. http://news.google.com/newspapers?id=6JVPAAAAIBAJ&sjid=kyQEAAAAIBAJ&pg=5139,5636818&dq=troy+korfmann&hl=en.

———. 1993b. "Outer 'Wall' of Troy Now Appears to Be a Ditch." *New York Times*, September 28. http://www.nytimes.com/1993/09/28/science/outer-wall-of-troy-now-appears-to-be-a-ditch.html.

———. 2006. "A Peruvian Woman of A.D. 450 Seems to Have Had Two Careers." *New York Times*, May 17. http://www.nytimes.com/2006/05/17/world/americas/17mummy.html?ex=1148011200&en=08cced452dd20f1b&ei=5087%0A&_r=0.

———. 2010. "Mapping Ancient Civilization, in a Matter of Days." *New York Times*, May 10. http://www.nytimes.com/2010/05/11/science/11maya .html?pagewanted=all&_r=0.

———. 2013. "Wine Cellar, Well Aged, Is Revealed in Israel." *New York Times*, November 22. http://www.nytimes.com/2013/11/23/science/in-ruins -of-palace-a-wine-with-hints-of-cinnamon-and-top-notes-of-antiquity .html?_r=2.

———. 2015. "Homo Naledi, New Species in Human Lineage, Is Found in South African Cave." *New York Times*, September 10. http://www .nytimes.com/2015/09/11/science/south-africa-fossils-new-species-human -ancestor-homo-naledi.html?_r=1.

Wilkinson, Toby. 2013. *The Rise and Fall of Ancient Egypt*. New York: Random House.

Willey, Gordon R., and Phillip Phillips. 1958. *Method and Theory in American Archaeology*. Chicago: University of Chicago Press.

Williams, Gareth. 2011. *Treasures from Sutton Hoo*. London: British Museum Press.

Williams, Paige. 2016. "Digging for Glory." *New Yorker*, June 27: 46–57. http://www.newyorker.com/magazine/2016/06/27/lee-berger-digs-for -bones-and-glory.

Wise, Michael O. 1990. *A Critical Study of the Temple Scroll from Quran Cave 11*. Chicago: University of Chicago Press.

Wolters, Al. 1996. *The Copper Scroll: Overview, Text, and Translation*. Sheffield, UK: Sheffield Academic Press.

Wong, Kate. 2011. "30 Years after Televised Spat, Rival Anthropologists Agree to Bury the Hand-Ax." *Scientific American*, May 5. http://blogs .scientificamerican.com/observations/30-years-after-televised-spat-rival -anthropologists-agree-to-bury-the-hand-ax/.

Wood, Michael. 1996. *In Search of the Trojan War*, 2nd ed. Berkeley: University of California Press.

Woollaston, Victoria. 2015. "Revealed—What's inside the Pompeii Mummies." *Daily Mail*, September 29. http://www.dailymail.co.uk/sciencetech /article-3253660/Peering-inside-Pompeii-s-tragic-victims-Incredible -CT-scans-reveal-bodies-unprecedented-laying-bare-bones-delicate -facial-features-dental-cavities.html.

Yadin, Yigael. 1966. *Masada: Herod's Fortress and the Zealots' Last Stand*. New York: Random House.

———. 1971. *Bar-Kokhba*. London: Weidenfeld and Nicolson.

———. 1985. *The Temple Scroll: The Hidden Law of the Dead Sea Sect*. London: Weidenfeld and Nicolson.

Yalouris, Athanasia, and Nicolaos Yalouris. 1987. *Olympia: The Museum and the Sanctuary*. Athens, Greece: Ekdotike Athenon.

Yan, Hongau, Jingjing An, Tie Zhou, Yin Xia, and Bo Rong. 2014. "Identification of Proteinaceous Binding Media for the Polychrome Terracotta Army of Emperor Qin Shihuang by MALDI-TOF-MS." *Chinese Science Bulletin 59*, no. 21 (July): 2574–81.

Yasur-Landau, Assaf, Eric H. Cline, and George A. Pierce. 2008. "Middle Bronze Age Settlement Patterns in the Western Galilee, Israel." *Journal of Field Archaeology* 33, no. 1: 59–83.

Zeilinga de Boer, Jelle, and John R. Hale. 2002. "Was She Really Stoned? The Oracle of Delphi." *Archaeology Odyssey* 5, no. 6 (November–December): 46–53, 58. http://www.biblicalarchaeology.org/daily/ancient-cultures/daily-life-and-practice/the-oracle-of-delphi—was-she-really-stoned/.

Zettler, Richard L., and Lee Horne, eds. 1988. *Treasures from the Royal Tombs of Ur.* Philadelphia: University of Pennsylvania Museum of Archaeology and Anthropology.

Zimmer, Carl. 2016. "Eske Willerslev Is Rewriting History with DNA." *International New York Times,* May 16. http://www.nytimes.com/2016/05/17/science/eske-willerslev-ancient-dna-scientist.html?smprod=nytcore-ipad&smid=nytcore-ipad-share.

INDEX

Abandoned Shipwreck Act, 315
ABC (television channel), 251–252
Abraham, 258, 259
absolute dates, 270, 272
Achilles, 27, 34, 281
ACOR (American Center for Oriental
    Research), 267
Acropolis, 172, 184
Adams, Mark, 300
Adams, Matt, 85, 233
advertisements, 21–22
Aegean Sea, 137, 148
Aegisthus, 132
Aeneas, 27, 190
Aeneid (Virgil), 190
aerial surveys, 81, 82–86
Aeschylus, 132
Afghanistan, xvi, 163, 327
Africa: early hominins, 97–103; Ethiopia,
    103; human origins and, Asia vs., 100;
    Kenya, 99–100; Koobi Fora, 99, 102;
    Laetoli, xvii, 101; South Africa, 97–98,
    356n98; Tanzania, xvii, 100
afterlife beliefs: Death Pits of Ur, 54;
    Egyptian mummification and, 43–47;
    Maya civilization, 76; Moche
    civilization, 296–298; Siberian princess,
    282; Terracotta Warriors, 275
Aftermath: Population Zero, 334
Agamemnon, 26, 34, 131–132, 133–134
Agatha Christie and Archaeology exhibit,
    52. *See also* Christie, Agatha
Age of Enlightenment, 15
Agora, Athens, xii, 172, 184–187
Agora, Palmyra, 262
Ahab, 225
Ahmose, 42

Ahuitzotl, 311
Akhenaton, 2, 8, 43, 162, 166–167
Akkad, 190
Akrotiri, 148–153
Alaksandu, 32
al-Asaad, Khaled, 260
Albania, 201
Alcock, Susan, 266
Alexander (*Iliad*), 32
Alexander the Great, 21, 37, 43, 183, 222
Alföldy, Géza, 198–199
Algeria, 201
Allah, Sheikh Ibrahim Ibn 'Abd, 264
Allen, Susan Heuck, 28
al-Maqrizi, 50
Alps, 279–282
Altamira cave paintings, 105–114
Altar 5, 307
Altar of Apollo, 182
Altar of Peace, 192–193
Altar of the Twelve Gods, 185
Altar Q, 71, 72
altars: Aztec, 309–310; classical Greece, 175,
    182, 185; classical Rome, 192–193; as
    features, 81; Maya, 71, 72, 76; Megiddo,
    228; Olmec, 306, 307
Alva, Walter, 295, 296, 298
Amarna archive, 270
Amazon rainforest, 295
Amenhotep III, 136, 270, 274
American Antiquities Act, 332
American Center for Oriental Research
    (ACOR), 267
American Museum of Natural History, 101
American Research Center in Egypt
    (ARCE), 51
American School of Classical Studies, 185

American Schools of Oriental Research
Cultural Heritage Initiatives, 382n332
Amherst College, 60
Amman, 264
Amnisos, 148
Amorites, 258
amphitheaters, 191, 192, 194, 195, 197,
198–201
Anatolia, 32, 124, 136, 182
ancestor worship, 121
ancestors, human, 97–114. *See also*
hominins
Ancestral Pueblo, 323, 332
anchors, stone, 163
ancient alien theories, 291–292, 294, 295
Ancient Aliens (TV series), 115–116, 353n76,
377n307
ancient astronauts, 291–292, 294, 305
Ancient One, 321–322
Andes, 283, 295
Angkor, 83–84
Anglo-Saxon period, 285
animal bones: Chauvet cave, 109, 111;
excavation techniques, 204, 206, 217;
future archaeology, 335; Göbekli Tepe,
118; Jamestown, 320; Masada, 256;
Megiddo, 228; Qin's tomb, 277;
radiocarbon dating, 271; Tenochtitlán,
309, 310–311; Teotihuacán, 304
animals: Akrotiri wall paintings, 151;
Çatalhöyük wall paintings and
sculptures, 123–124; cave paintings, 106,
107–112; domestication of, 116–117, 118,
127; ivory from, 164–165; monumental
architecture, 117–118; mummification
of, 46; Nazca Lines, 291–295; non-
indigenous, in paintings, 151; Olmec
statues, 308; zoomorphic cups, 165–166
anthropology, 126, 135
Antiquities Coalition, The, 382n332
antiquities trade, 327–332
Antiquity, 149, 328
Apollo, 177, 181
Ara Pacis, 192–193, 194
Arabia, 266
Aramaic, 238
ARCE (American Research Center in
Egypt), 51
Arch of Constantine, 191
Arch of Janus, 192
Arch of Septimius Severus, 191

Arch of Titus, 195–197
Arch of Titus Digital Restoration Project,
197
archaeological excavations; careless, 14–15,
28–30, 60, 223–224; delicate artifacts,
58, 61–62, 260, 137, 204, 206; destructive
techniques, 191–193, 201–203; funding,
124–125; "ground truthing," 87, 88–89;
horizontal, 209, 224; illegal, 327, 329;
methods avoiding excavation, 83;
methods overview, 204–218; permanent
reconstructions, 139; permits/
permission for, 132, 134, 178; site
location differences, 204, 205, 206, 210–
211, 214–215, 216, 229; software for, 185;
stratigraphy, 205, 209, 210–214, 224 (*see
also* stratigraphy); test pits, 82, 132;
vertical, 209–210, 224–225; volunteers,
help of, 216, 247–248, 256, 325. *See also*
archaeological sites
Archaeological Fieldwork Opportunity
Bulletin, 325
Archaeological Institute of America (AIA),
160, 330, 325
Archaeological Resources Protection Act
(ARPA), 332
archaeological restorations/reconstructions:
classical Rome, 191–193, 201–203;
digital, 197; facial reconstruction, 7, 135,
280, 320, 361n135; Masada, 249; Minoan
frescoes, 141–143; permanent, 139;
buildings, plaster reconstruction, 150.
See also replicas
archaeological sites: damage caused by
tourism, 8, 106, 108, 111–112; definition
of, 81; deliberate destruction/vandalism
of, 8, 58, 106, 260, 262–263; hidden,
66–67, 76, 84, 303–304, 312–313;
interpretation of, 333–337; locating/
identifying, 80–94; modern buildings on,
185, 309; protection/preservation of, 124,
264, 331 (*see also* artifacts, preservation
of); regional violence and, 259–260;
replicas of (*see* archaeological restorations/
reconstructions; replicas); robberies/
looting of (*see* robberies/lootings); size of,
81; stratigraphy (*see* stratigraphy);
surveying, 80–94; test pits, 82, 132;
underwater, 157–168, 193, 314–317
archaeological techniques: advances in,
22–23, 337–338; "chasing walls," 60;

computed tomography, 7–8, 18, 22, 46, 280, 318–319, 320; dating (*see* dating techniques); DNA testing (*see* DNA testing); electronic resistivity/ conductivity, 86–87, 337, 354n83; excavation methods, 204–218 (*see also* archaeological excavations); fine gridding, 228–229; future archaeology, 333–339; ground-penetrating radar, 9, 88–89, 117; ground truthing, 87, 88–89, 328; infrared thermography, 50–51; iPads, data collection, 21, 22, 185, 215; LiDAR, 66–67, 82, 86, 337; lost wax method, 17–18, 22, 150, 346n17; magnetometers, 87–88, 337; muon radiography, 51; plaster casting, 17–18, 22, 150; remote sensing (*see* remote sensing); remote-controlled robots, 303; site identification and surveying, 80–94; stratigraphy (*see* stratigraphy); tools, 204–218; underwater archaeology, 157–168, 193, 314–317; UV-VIS spectrometry, 197; X-ray, 13–14, 280

archaeology: anthropology and, 126; battlefield, 230–232; biblical, 232; classical (*see* classical archaeology); colonialism and, 64, 327; community collaboration, 338; discipline of, 15; excavation methods, 204–218 (*see also* archaeological excavations); forensic, 7–8, 135, 231–232, 255–256, 319, 320; future, 333–339; historical, 315; history and, 126, 249–250; hoaxes, 102, 208; misinterpretations and, 333–337; mythology and, 154–156; nationalism and, 189, 190–191, 201–203, 245–246, 250, 256; New Archaeology, 126; New World (*see* New World archaeology); objectivity and neutrality in, 126; Old World, 15; papyrology, 13–14; postprocessual, 125–127; prehistoric, 99, 113–114; "space," 84; underwater, 157–168, 193, 314–317. *See also* archaeological techniques

Archer, Gabriel, 319

Archi, Alfonso, 259

architecture: Athens, 184–187; Delphi, 172–184; Olympia, 172–177; classical Rome, 189–203; Greco-Roman, 261; Inca, 301–302; monumental, 117–118; painting of, 197; Palmyra, 261. *See also specific types, e.g.,* temples

Ardèche, 108

Ardnamurchan peninsula, 286

Aristo-Canine, 311

Aristotle, 184

Arizona, 323, 332

Ark of the Covenant, xvi

Armageddon, xii, 221–233, 237. *See also* Megiddo

armor: classical Greece, 175–176; classical Roman, 85; helmets, 54, 286, 297–298; Jamestown, 318; Masada, 255; Moche tombs, 297–298; Terracotta Warriors, 274, 275–278; Viking ships, 287

ARPA (Archaeological Resources Protection Act), 332

arrowheads: Masada, 254; Ötzi the Iceman, 280; Troy/Hissarlik, 33, 36; Uluburun shipwreck, 165

Artemis, 136

artifacts: antiquities trade, 327–332; context, 207–2208; cultural heritage and, 338; dating of (*see* dating techniques); definition of, 81; deliberate destruction of, 327; delicate, excavation of, 58, 61–62, 260, 137, 204, 206; destruction through radiocarbon dating, 271; excavation techniques, 206–207, 217; features vs., 81; hoaxes, fakes, and forgeries, 102, 208; interpretation of, 333–337; museum collections, 327; Native American, 321–322, 332; ownership of (*see* artifacts, ownership of); preservation of (*see* artifacts, preservation of); private collections, 317; recording during site surveys, 91–93; robberies/looting of (*see* robberies/ looting); shipwrecks, 157–159, 162–168. *See also specific types, e.g.,* grave goods, figurines, *and specific materials, e.g.,* gold artifacts

artifacts, ownership of: classical Greece, 174; colonialism and, 327; Machu Picchu, 301; Mesopotamian, 64–65; Native American, 321–322; overview, 326–332; Priam's Treasure, 30

artifacts, preservation of: advances in, 338; beadwork, 297; Egyptian scrolls, 41; Elba, 259; through fire, 259, 267; *Hunley* submarine, 315–316; inorganic materials, 278; organic materials, 278; overview, 278–287; papyri, 13–14, 41;

artifacts, preservation of (*continued*)
Pompeii and Herculaneum, 13–23;
Akrotiri, 146–156; Petra, 267; ships,
285–287; site survey methods and, 91–93
Asclepius, 46
Asia: ancient trade routes, 264; early
hominins, 113; human origins and,
Africa vs., 100; LiDAR, 86
Assur, 58
Assurbanipal, 62
Assurnasirpal II, 58, 65
Assyria, xviii, 32, 55, 57–65
Astronaut, the, 294
astronomical features, 77, 120, 294, 301
Athena, 36
Athena Sanctuary, 181
Athens: Acropolis, 172, 184; Agora, xii, 81;
downtown, xii
Agora, 81, 172, 184–187; Peloponnesian
War, 181; stratigraphy, 213; Theseus and
the Minotaur myth, 143–144
Atlantis, xvi, 146–156
Aton, 167
Attalos I, 183
Attalos II, 183
auction houses, 328
Augustus, 16, 190, 191, 192
Augustus's Forum, 192
Aurelian, 261–262
Australopithecus afarensis, 101, 103
Australopithecus boisei, 100
Avenue of the Dead, 312
Axial Gallery, 107
Ayios Dhimitrios, xii
Aztec civilization, xviii, 308–313

Babatha archive, 243
Babylon, 55, 56, 62, 64, 258
Babylonian Exile, 329–330
Babylonian Flood story, 63
"back dirt pile," 63
Back to Masada (Ben-Tor), 246
Badakhshan, 163
Baghdad, 328
Bahamas, 146, 155
Bahn, Paul, 277, 309
Balcony House, 324
balks, 211–214
ball courts, 72–73, 77
Ballard, Bob, 284–285
Bar Kokhba Revolt, 242

Barber, Elizabeth, 278
Bar-Yosef, Ofer, 104–105
Bass, George, 158–168
Bas-Vivarais volcanic field, 112
Battle of Plataia, 182
Battle of Shiloh, 316
battlefield archaeology, 230–232
beads, 232, 297, 298, 311
Beatles, The, 103
Bedal, Leigh-Ann, 266
Bedouins, 236, 238, 240, 329
beehive tombs, 135
Behrend College, 266
Belize, xv, 51, 66, 86
Belvedere Gallery, 112
Belzoni, Giovanni Battista, 39
ben Ya'ir, Eleazar, 250, 252, 253, 255
Benedict XIV, 201
Bent Pyramid, 50, 51
Ben-Tor, Amnon, 246, 255, 256
Ben-Yehuda, Nachman, 245–246, 256
Berger, Lee, 97–98, 103
Berlin Museum, 30
Berlin Olympics, 174
Bethlehem, 236, 237, 240
Bible, Hebrew: Cedars of Lebanon, 329;
Dead Sea Scrolls, 189, 234–244, 246,
329; *Dead Sea Scrolls Bible*, 370n244;
Elba, 257–260; Exodus, 119, 154; extra-
biblical confirmation of biblical events,
59; Lachish, 59; Flood story, 63, 190;
Hittites, 31–32; Jericho, 119; Megiddo,
xii, 221–233; Masada, 245–256;
Nephilim, 118; Nineveh, 58; Palmyra,
257; Petra, 257, 263–268; Ur, 53;
Watchers, 118
Bible, Hebrew, books of: Esther, 238;
Genesis, 238; I Kings, 225; Isaiah, 236–
237; Psalms, 243, 254; Revelation, 222;
Samuel, 241
Bible Lands Museum, 330
biblical archaeology, 232
Binford, Lewis, 126
Bingham, Hiram, xviii, 300–301
bipedalism, 101–102
Black Obelisk of Shalmaneser III, 58
Black Sea, 284–285
Blanding, Utah, 332
Blegen, Carl, 33–34, 35–36
Bliss, Frederick Jones, 119
Blom, Frans, 305–306, 307

Boeotia, xii, 91
bog bodies, 283–284
Bogdanos, Matthew, 328
Boise, Charles, 100
bones. *See* animal bones; human remains; skeletons; skulls
Book of Going Forth by Day, 43
Book of Habakkuk, 238
Book of the Dead, 43
Bordeaux, 106
Boserup, Ester, 117
Botta, Paul Émile, 55, 56–57, 58, 59, 60–61
Boudicca, 140, 262
Bouleuterion, 175, 184
Brackenridge, Henry, 324
Bradford, John, 83
Braidwood, Robert, 117
Breasted, James Henry, 224
British Airways, 125
British Museum: Assyrian archaeology, 52–53, 54, 55, 60–61, 63, 64; classical Greek artifacts, 184; mummies, 45; provenance and, 327; trustees, 138
bronze: creation of, 159, 163–164; lost wax method and, 17; preservation of, xiii, 278
Bronze Age: Egypt, 43, 144; libraries, Elba, 258; Mesopotamia, 53; shipwrecks, 157–168; site survey methods and, 92; Stonehenge, 89; stratigraphy, 185; Troy/Hissarlik, 34, 36
Bronze Age Aegean: Akrotiri, 148–153; Crete, 124, 137–144, 149, 151, 159, 162; Cycladic islands, 144–145, 146–156; evidence of trade, 136, 144, 149, 154, 157–159, 162–168; Knossos, 124, 137–144, 151; Minoan civilization, 137–144, 149, 151, 157–159, 162–168; Mycenae, 31, 131–137, 138–139, 151, 157–159, 162–168, 300; Theseus and the Minotaur myth, 143–144; underwater archaeology, 157–168
bronze artifacts: Cave of Letters, 243; classical Greece, 173, 175–176, 180, 182, 185–186; classical Rome, 199; Gelidonya wreck, 159, 163–164; Mycenae, 134, 137; Pompeii and Herculaneum, 19; Troy, 25; Uluburun shipwreck, 165, 167
Brown University, 266
Brown, Basil, 285–286
Brunel Chamber, 111
Brunel, Éliette, 110, 111

brushwood, dating methods, 271
bullet casings, 230–232
Burckhardt, Johann, 264
Burgon, John, 264–265
burial sites: Çatalhöyük, 124; cenotaphs, 286; Etruscan, 83; Jamestown, 318–320; Minoan, 138; Moche, 295–298; Mycenae, 132–135; Neanderthal, 104–105; ships and, 286–287; Ur, 53–55. *See also* tombs
Burke Museum of Natural History and Culture, 322
Burnt City, 29
Burton, Harry, 336
Byron, Lord, 59, 200
Byzantine period, 185, 285

Cactus Gallery, 111
Cadiz, 146
Caesar, Julius, 13, 37
Caesar's Forum, 192
Cahokia Mounds, 324
Cairo, 2, 39, 47, 48, 49, 234, 237, 264
Calah, 58
calderas, 148
Calendar Stone, 309
Calvert, Frank, 28, 37, 300
Cambodia, 84, 86
Cambridge University, 104, 125
Camp, John II, 185
campaign notices, 21–22
Canaan: Hittites, 31; Hyksos, 42; Tel Kabri palace and wine cellar, xiii–xiv, 87; trade items from, 136, 149, 157–159, 162–168
Candle Gallery, 111
cannibalism, 320
canopic jars, 44
Cape Gelidonya shipwreck, xvii, 158–159, 160, 163
Caracol, 66–67, 86
carbon dating. *See* radiocarbon dating
Carnarvon, earl of, 1, 2–5
Carnegie Institution, 73
Carrasco, David, 311
Carter, Howard, xviii, 1–9, 68, 223, 336
Carthage, 195
Casa Grande, 332
Çatalhöyük, xvii, 122–125
Catherwood, Frederick, 68–79
Cave of Horrors, 242, 244
Cave of Letters, 242–243, 244

Cave of the Treasure, 242, 244
caves: Dead Sea Scrolls, 189, 234–244;
    Neanderthal burial sites, 103–105; wall
    paintings in, 105–114
Cedar Forest, 329
Cedars of Lebanon, 329
cenotaphs, 286
cenotes, 78
Center for American Archaeology, 325
Central America. See Mesoamerica
Central Palace, 58
Ceram, C. W., xi
ceremonial processions, 294–295
cesium magnetometers, 337
Chaco Canyon, 322–323
Chacoan culture, 322–323
Chalcolithic period, 242
Chamber of the Bear Hollows, 111
Chamber of the Felines, 108
Champollion, Jean-François, 40, 69, 70
Chandler, Richard, 172
Charioteer, 180
Chariots of the Gods? (von Däniken),
    291–292
Charleston Harbor, 315
Charleston, South Carolina, 314, 317
Chatters, James, 322
Chauvet, Jean-Marie, 108, 109–110
Chauvet cave paintings, xv, xvii, 105–114
chemical testing, 318–319
Cheops, 48
Chephren, 48
chert, 217
Chicago Trench, 225
Chichén Itzá, 68, 77–78, 304
Childe, V. Gordon, 116–117
Chile, 295
China, xvii, 261, 274, 275–278
chinampas, 309
Christie, Agatha, 52–53
Circus Maximus, 192
Classic period, Maya, 71, 74
classical archaeology: Atlantis, 146–156;
    classical Greece, 171–187; classical
    Rome, 188–203; development of, 187;
    early Greek civilizations, 131–145;
    underwater archaeology, 157–168
classical Greece: Acropolis, 172, 184; Agora,
    172, 184–187; Athens, 184–187; Delphi,
    172–184; Olympia, 172–177
classical Rome, 188–203. See also Rome/
    Roman Empire

clay tablets. See tablets
Cleopatra, 40, 43, 140
cliff dwellings, 324
Cliff Palace, 324
climate change, 42, 79
clothing: as artifacts, 81; bog bodies, 284;
    Chinese mummies, 279; Hunley
    submarine, 316; Moche tombs, 297–298;
    preservation of, 278, 279, 280, 281;
    reconstruction from paintings, 152
Clottes, Jean, 109
Cloud-based storage, 22
Clytemnestra (Odyssey), 132
Coe, Michael, 308
coins: Cave of Letters, 243; dating methods
    and, 273–274; Hunley submarine, 316–
    317; Jamestown, 318; Masada, 249, 254
Colonial Williamsburg, 209, 325
colonialism, 64, 327
Colonnaded Street, 266
Colorado, 323, 324
colossal stone heads, 305–308, 377n307
Colosseum, 191, 192, 194, 195, 197, 198–201
Columbia River, 321–322
Columbia University, 68, 285
columns, 69, 174
Commonwealth of Virginia, 317
community collaboration, 338
computed tomography (CT): Egyptian
    mummies, 7–8, 46; Jamestown
    skeletons, 318–319, 320; Ötzi the
    Iceman, 280; Pompeii and
    Herculaneum, 18, 22
Condor, the, 294
Confederated Tribes of the Colville
    Reservation, 322
Conlin, Dave, 316, 317
conquistadors, 67–68, 304, 305, 308, 312
Constantine, 182
Constantinople, 173, 182, 195
constellations, 294
context, artifacts and, 207–208
Conti, Cinzia, 197
Convention on the Means of Prohibiting
    and Preventing the Illicit Import,
    Export, and Transfer of Ownership of
    Cultural Property, 330
Convention on the Protection of the
    Underwater Cultural Heritage, 317
copal, 310
Copán, 68, 69, 71–73, 307
copper, 158–159, 163–164

Copper Scroll, 239–240
Corinth, 177
Corinthian helmets, 175–176
Corinthian Tomb, 266
Corona program, 82–83
corporate sponsorship, 125
Cortés, Hernán, 308
cosmology, 311
creation stories, 74
Crete, 124, 137–144, 149, 151, 159, 162;
    Knossos, 124, 137–144, 151;
    Palaiokastro, xii
Critias (Plato), 155
Croesus, 178, 187
crop marks, 84, 85
Crow Canyon Archaeological Center, 325
Crowe, Russell, 200
Crusaders, 222
CT (computed tomography). *See* computed
    tomography (CT)
cultic objects, 136, 335, 336
cultural heritage, 338
culture, future archaeology and, 333–339
cuneiform, 55–56, 62–63, 329
Cussler, Clive, 315
Cuzco, 299, 301
Cycladic islands, 144–145, 146–156
Cyphers, Ann, 308
Cyprus: 136, 146, 155, 163, 165, 167, 188–
    189; Ayios Dhimitrios, xii; Paphos, xii
Cyrene, 177–178
Cyrus the Great, 178, 190

Dagger Men, 250
Daily Telegraph, 63
Damascus, 260
Darius the Great, 56
Darius III, 21
Dartmouth College, 60
Darwinism, 15
Dashur, 50, 51
dating techniques: Chauvet cave, 109;
    dendrochronology, 162, 272, 274;
    hominin fossils, 100; Jericho, 119–120;
    Kabri, 271; Lascaux cave, 107; Masada,
    249; Megiddo, 225–226, 227, 271;
    Mycenae, 134, 135; Nazca Lines, 292–
    293; object association, 273–274;
    obsidian hydration, 273; Olmec
    civilization, 308; overview of, 269–278;
    potassium-argon analysis, 270, 272;
    pottery, 211, 224–226, 227, 271, 273–274;

radiocarbon dating (*see* radiocarbon
    dating); rehydroxylation, 272–273;
    Santorini explosion, 153–154; seriation,
    224, 273–274; stratigraphy, 273–274 (*see
    also* stratigraphy); thermoluminescence,
    270, 272; Uluburun shipwreck, 162, 162,
    166–167, 271, 274
David, 258, 259
Davis, Jack, 137
Dawson, Charles, 102
de Coubertin, Baron Pierre, 174, 181
de Landa, Diego, 70
de Perthes, Boucher, 102
de Sautuola, Don Marcelino Sanz, 106
de Sautuola, Maria, 106
Dead Sea Scrolls, 189, 234–244, 246, 329
Dead Sea Scrolls Bible, 370n244
Dead Sea, 236, 246
death, investigating cause of: Death Pits of
    Ur, 54; Egyptian mummies, 7–8, 46;
    Jamestown, 319, 320; Juanita the Ice
    Maiden, 280–281; Kennewick Man, 321–
    322; Lindow Man, 283–284; Masada,
    255–256; Mycenae, 135; Ötzi the Iceman,
    279–280; Pompeii and Herculaneum, 18;
    Siberian princess, 282; Tollund Man, 284
Death Pits of Ur, 30, 52–55
Decapitator God, 298
Delphi, 172–184
democracy, 184, 185–186
dendrochronology, 162, 272, 274
Denmark, 283, 284
dental tools, 206
"Destruction of Sennacherib, The" (Byron),
    59
Dickens, Charles, 200
diet, reconstruction of, 20–21, 118, 165, 281,
    284, 319
DigitalGlobe, 83
Dinaledi Chamber, 98
Diocletian, 263
Dionysus, 21, 136
diptych, 164
Disney Chair of Archaeology, 104
Disney, John, 104
Disney, Walt, 104
Dixon, George E., 316
Djoser, 46–48
DNA testing: advances in, 338; Chinese
    mummies, 279; *Hunley* submarine, 316;
    Kennewick man, 322; King Richard II,
    281; King Tut, 8, 281; Machu Picchu

DNA testing (*continued*)
    remains 299–300; Neanderthals, 104;
    Pompeii and Herculaneum, 18, 22
documentation, 212–215
Dolphin Fresco, 141
Domitian, 195
Domus Aurea, 197–198, 200
Donnan, Christopher, 298
Dordogne, 106
Dörpfeld, Wilhelm, 31–34, 174, 184
Doumas, Christos, 150
Doyle, Arthur Conan, 102
Dragon's Back, 98
Draper, Robert, 311
drones, 86
droughts, 42, 79, 137, 296, 323
Drucker, Philip, 306, 307
Dur Sharrukin, 57, 58, 59, 61
Durrington Walls, 89

Early Bronze Age, 29, 120, 228
Early Cycladic period, 145
earthquakes: Akrotiri, 149; Cyprus, 189;
    Delphi, 183; Megiddo, 229; Mycenae,
    137; Petra, 267; Troy, 33–34, 35–36
earthworks, 84
eBay, 328
Ebla, 257–260
ebony, 165
Ecuador, 295
Egypt: Atlantis myth and, 156; biblical
    Exodus from, 119, 154; Bronze Age
    trade, 136, 144, 149, 151, 154, 157–159,
    162–168; Bronze Age wall paintings,
    144; Cairo, 2, 39, 47, 48, 49, 234, 237,
    264; Carter in, 1–9; Dead Sea Scrolls,
    234, 237; early archaeology, 1–9, 38–51;
    Elba and, 259; excavation techniques,
    210; hieroglyphics, 38, 39–41, 43;
    historical periods, 2, 3, 42–43; Hittites
    and, 32; John Lloyd Stephens, 68; King
    Tut's tomb, 1–9, 43, 113, 207, 278, 281,
    336; Maya ruins and, 74–75; Megiddo
    and, 222; recent discoveries, 84;
    robberies/looting, xvi, 332, 327–328;
    Roman ruins in, 188; Tel el-Maskhuta,
    xii; texts of, dating methods and, 270;
    trade routes, 264; wall paintings, 8–9,
    41, 43, 144, 165
Egyptian Museum, 2, 39
Egyptology, 38–52

Egyptomania, 40
Eighteenth Dynasty, 2, 42–43
Ein Gedi, 235
El Castillo, 77
El Niño weather system, 296
Elamite, 56
electronic resistivity/conductivity, 86–87,
    337, 354n83
electrum, 24
Elgin Marbles, 184, 327
Elgin, Lord, 184
Ellis, Steven, 19–20
el-Wad, 104
embalming process, 44–45
End Chamber, 112
Endeavor space shuttle, 84
engines, 251–252
England: bog bodies, 283–284; Celtic, 140;
    crop marks, 85; excavation techniques,
    205, 206, 211, 214–215; hominin fossils,
    102; LiDAR, 86; Maiden Castle, 211;
    Roman ruins in, 188; Stonehenge,
    88–89; Sutton Hoo, 285–286
Enkidu, 329
Enkomi, 163
Epic Cycle, 25
Epic of Gilgamesh, 63, 329
epigraphy, 55, 258–259
Erechtheium, 184
Esarhaddon, 58
Essenes, 235
Ethiopia, 103
Etruscan civilization, 83
Euripides, 132, 187
Europe: Age of Enlightenment, 15; bog
    bodies, 283–284; colonialism, 64, 327;
    crop marks, 85; early archaeology in,
    14–15; early hominins, 105–114;
    excavation techniques, 205, 206; female
    figurines, 126–127; John Lloyd
    Stephens, 68; nationalism and
    archaeology, 202–203; Roman ruins in,
    188, 189
European Union Research Council, 232
Evans, Arthur, 137–144, 174
Evans, Damian, 86
Evans, John, 138

Facebook, 98
facial reconstruction, 7, 135, 280, 320,
    361n135

Factum Arte, 8–9
faience artifacts, 136, 240, 165
fakes, 208
famine, 42, 137
fasces, 191
fascism, 191, 202, 203
Faustulus, 190
features: artifacts vs., 81; astronomical, 77, 120, 294, 301; buried, detecting, 84–85, 86–88; excavation techniques (*see* archaeological excavations); intentional destruction of, 260; recording during site surveys, 91–92
female figurines, 126–127, 132
Fertile Crescent civilizations: Çatalhöyük, xvii, 122–125; Göbekli Tepe, xvii, 115–118; human ancestors, 115–128; Jericho, 118–122, 208, 214
fertility symbols, 126–127
fields of conflict, investigation of, 230–232
figurines: Çatalhöyük women, 126–127; Cycladic islands, 145; Elba, 259; Minoan, 140, 143; Mycenae, 132, 136; Teotihuacán, 304; Uluburun shipwreck, 167–168
Finding Atlantis, 146
fine gridding, 228–229
Fine, Steven, 195
Finkel, Irving, 64
Finkelstein, Israel, 205, 227, 232
Fiorelli, Giuseppe, 17
fire: evidence of, 212, 259, 282; preservation of artifacts, 259, 267; rehydroxylation dating and, 273
First Dynasty, 42
First Intermediate Period, 42
First Jewish Revolt, 194–195, 199, 234–235, 239, 243, 248, 249, 250
First Temple, 250
Fisher, Clarence, 224
Five Good Emperors, 194
Flavian Amphitheater, 197
Flavian dynasty, 16, 194–195
flint, 217, 310
Flood stories, 63–64
Florentinus, Sextus, 266
Flores Island, 113
Flotilla Fresco, 152–153
fluxgate gradiometers, 337
foods, diet reconstruction, 20–21, 118, 165, 281, 284, 319

footprints, hominin, xvii, 101–102, 109, 113
forensic archaeology, 7–8, 135, 231–232, 255–256, 319, 320. *See also* death, investigating cause of
forgeries, 208
Forma Urbis Romae, 194
Fort Sumter, 315
Forum of Augustus, 192
Forum of Caesar, 191, 192
Forum of Nerva, 194
Forum of Trajan, 191, 192
fossils, hominin: early hominins, 356n98; Africa, 97–103; Europe, 105–114; France, 105–114; hoaxes, 102; Iraq, 105; Israel, 103–104; Spain, 105–114
foundation myths, 190
Fourth Dynasty, 42, 48
France, 102, 105–114, 188
Frangipani family, 195, 197
French, Elizabeth, 135
French School of Athens, 180
frescoes: Akrotiri, 151–153; classical Roman, 198; Minoan, 140–143
friezes, 182, 192
Frischer, Bernard, 197
full-coverage surveys, 81, 90–94
funding, archaeological excavations, 124–125
funerary complexes, 48
funerary masks, 133
future archaeology, 333–339

Galilee, 94
Gallery of the Crosshatching, 112
garbage, diet reconstruction and, 20–21
gardens, 19, 266–267, 309
Garrod, Dorothy, xviii, 103–104
Garstang, John, 119–120
Gaza Strip, 210
Gelon, 180
Genesis Apocryphon, 238
genetic testing. *See* DNA testing
geoglyphs, 291–295
Geological Society of London, 138
geology, 119
George I, 133
George Washington University, xi, xv, xix, 173, 231, 319, 339
Germany, 102, 188, 203
Gezer, 227
ghost inscriptions, 198–199
Gilgamesh, 329

Gimbutas, Marija, 126–127
Giza, pyramids of, 48–51
Gladiator, 200
glass ingots, 164
Göbekli Tepe, xvii, 115–118
goddess figurines, 140
Gods, Graves, and Scholars (Ceram), xi
gold artifacts: Aztec, 309, 311; classical
    Greece, 173, 176, 180–181, 182; classical
    Rome, 195, 197–198; Ebla, 259;
    Egyptian, 1, 4, 5, 6–7, 8; Maya, 78;
    Megiddo, 223, 232; Mesopotamian, 65;
    Moche, 297–298; Mycenae, 132–134,
    137; Pompeii and Herculaneum, 18;
    preservation of, 278; Sutton Hoo, 286;
    Troy, 24–25, 30; Uluburun shipwreck,
    162, 166–167; Ur, 54
Gold Medal Award for Distinguished
    Archaeological Achievement, 160
Golden House, 197–198
Gómez, Sergio, 303
Gomorrah, 258, 259
GPR (ground-penetrating radar), 9, 88–89,
    117
Grand Gallery, 49
Grand Historian of China, 275
Grave Circle A, 132, 134, 135, 361n135
Grave Circle B, 135
grave goods: Assyrian, 65; King Tut, 8;
    Maya, 76; Moche, 296–298; Mycenae,
    132–135; Native American, 321–322;
    Olmec, 307; Pylos, 137; Teotihuacán,
    312; Ur, 54
grave sites. *See* burial sites; tombs
Great Altar to Zeus, 175
Great Apse, 107–108
Great Excavation, 179
Great Fire, Rome, 198
Great Pyramid, xv, 48–51
Great Salt Lake, 236
Great Sun Green Quetzal-Macaw, 71
Great Temple, 266, 309
Great Trench, 28–29, 34
Greco-Roman architecture, 261
Greece/Greek civilization: Athenian Agora,
    xii; Atlantis, 146–156; Boeotia, xii;
    Classical era, 171–187; early civilizations,
    131–145; Egypt and, 41–42, 43; Pylos,
    xii, 81, 91, 93, 137; Roman ruins in, 188;
    robberies/looting, xvi; site survey in,
    90–94; Trojan War and, 25–28;

underwater archaeology, 157–168. *See
    also* Bronze Age Aegean; classical
    archaeology
Greek historians, 42, 44, 45, 48–49, 139, 147,
    159, 178, 180, 282
Greenpeace, 292
Griffin Warrior, 137
ground-penetrating radar (GPR), 9, 88–89,
    117
ground surveys, 81–82, 90–94
ground truthing, 87, 88–89, 328
Guggenheim Fellowship, 70
Guy, P.L.O., 224
Gymnasium, 175, 181, 181

H. L. Hunley, 314–317
H. pylori, 281
Habakkuk, 238
Hadar, xvii, 103
Hadrian, xv, 194
Haifa, 103, 222
Hall of Bulls, 107
Hall of Human Origins, 101
Halls A–C, Cave of Letters, 243
Hammer, Joshua, 109
Hammond, Philip, 265
Hammurabi, 258
Han dynasty, 275
hand picks, 205
Hands, The, 293
Harappa, 211
Harris matrix, 213–214
Harris, David, 243
Harvard University, 311
Hasan Dağı, 124
Hasis, Abdel, 264
Hatshepsut, 2, 43
Hattusa, 32
Hawass, Zahi, 7
Hawthorne, Nathaniel, 200
Hazor, 227, 255
headstamps, 230
Hebrew Bible. *See* Bible, Hebrew
Hebrew University of Jerusalem, 245–246
Hebrides Islands, 287
Hector, 27
Heidelberg University, 198
Helen, 26, 32, 34
Hellenistic era, xiii, 36
Hellespont, 182
helmets, 54, 286, 297–298. *See also* armor

Henttawy, 45
Hephaisteion, 184
Hephaistos, 184
Hera, 136, 137, 335
Heracles, 173, 174
Heraklion, 138
Herculaneum, 13–23
Herod the Great, 248, 250
Herod's Temple, 195
Herodotus, 42, 44, 45, 48–49, 147, 178, 180, 282
Heron, the, 293
Herzog, Werner, 109
hieroglyphics: Egyptian, 38–41, 43, 69, 70; Maya, 69–71, 72, 75; Teotihuacán, 72
Hieron, 180
high chronology, 153–154
Hillaire, Christian, 111
Hillaire Chamber, 111
Hippodrome, 175, 182
Hirst, Damien, 121–122
Hissarlik, 28–37, 131. *See also* Troy
Historic Jamestowne, 320
Historic Sites Act of 1935, 332
historical archaeology, 315
Histories (Herodotus), 180
history (discipline), archaeology and, 126, 249–250
History Channel, 334
History of Rome (Livy), 14, 190
Hittite civilization, xviii, 31–33, 35
Hittites: The Story of a Forgotten Empire, The (Sayce), 31
hoaxes, 102, 208
Hobbits, 113
Hodder, Ian, 124–127
Holy Land: Dead Sea Scrolls, 189, 234–244, 246, 329; Elba, 257–260; Masada, 189, 203, 245–256; Megiddo, 189, 206, 209, 210, 215, 221–233, 249; Palmyra, 189, 257, 260–263; Petra, 189, 257, 263–268. *See also* Middle East
Homer, 25–28, 34, 36, 132, 152, 164
hominid, 355n97
hominins: Africa, 97–103; Europe, 105–114: footprints, xvii, 101–102, 113; France, 105–114; Iraq, 105; Israel, 103–104; Lucy, xvii, 90, 103; South Africa, 356n98; Spain, 105–114; terminology, 355n97; Turkana Boy, 99–100, 102
Homo erectus, 100, 102

Homo habilis, 100
Homo naledi, 97–98
Homo sapiens, 104
Honduras, 71
horizontal excavation, 209, 224
House of Orpheus, 189
House of the Faun, 19, 21
House of the Tragic Poet, 21
houses: Çatalhöyük, 122–123; Chaco Canyon, 323; Megiddo, 228–229; Mesa Verde, 323, 324; Nero's Golden House, 197–198, 200; Roman villas, 189; Viking, 287
Hrozný, Bedřich, 32
Huitzilopochtli, 309
human ancestry: earliest ancestors, 97–114; Fertile Crescent civilizations, 115–128
humain remains: bog bodies, 283–284; *Hunley* submarine, 316–317; Juanita the Ice Maiden, 280–281; Kennewick Man, 321–322; Lindow Man, 283–284; Native American, 321–322; Ötzi the Iceman, xvii, 279–280; preservation of, 278–284; Siberian princess, 282; Tollund Man, 284. *See also* skeletons; skulls
human sacrifice, 78, 298, 312
Hunley Commission, 315
Hunt, Robert, 319
Hunter College, 141
Hunting with the Bow and Arrow (Pope), 321
Huntington Museum Library, 241
Hyksos, 42
Hyksos period, 274

Iakovides, Spyros, 135
Ibbit-Lim, 258
IBM, 125
Ice Age, 106, 118
Ice Maiden, 279, 282–283
Ice Maiden, The (Reinhard), 282–283
iDig, 185
idols, 136
Iliad (Homer), 25–28, 34, 152, 164, 190
Imhotep, 46–47
Inca civilization, xviii, 282–283, 299–302
Incidents of Travel (Stephens), xi, 67
India, 211, 261
Indiana Jones, xi, 166, 188, 263
Indiana Jones and the Last Crusade, 263, 265
Indonesia, 148
infrared thermography, 50–51

inorganic materials, preservation of, 278
Institute of Nautical Archaeology, 157, 158, 159
International Space Station, 48
international trade. *See* trade
Internet interactions, future archaeology, 335
Intihuatana, 301
iPads, 21, 22, 185, 215
Iran, 56
Iraq: artifact ownership and, 64–65; Assyrian Empire, 56–65; Death Pits of Ur, 30, 52–55; early hominins, 105; Nimrud, 55, 57–58, 60, 64–65, 283, 327; robberies/looting, xvi, 327, 328–329; Umma, 329
Iraq Museum, 328, 329
Ireland, 287
Iron Age, 89, 92
Ishi, 321
Ishi in Two Worlds (Kroeber), 321
Ishmael, 258, 259
ISIS militant group, 58, 260, 262–263, 327
Israel: Cave of Skulls, xv; Dead Sea Scrolls, 189, 234–244, 246, 329; early hominins, 103–104; excavation techniques, 210–211; Gezer, 227; Hazor, 227, 245; Israeli–Palestinian conflict, 203; Jerusalem (*see* Jerusalem); Jezreel, 86; Jezreel Valley, 86, 221, 222; Lachish, 59; Masada, 189, 203, 245–256; Megiddo, xii, 81, 85, 189, 206, 209, 210, 215, 221–233, 249; nationalism, 245–246, 250; Roman ruins in, 188; statehood of, 230–232; Tel Anafa, xii, xviii; Tel Kabri (*see* Tel Kabri)
Israel (Bible character), 258, 259
Israel Defense Forces, 247
Israel Museum, xiii, 237–238
Israelites, biblical Exodus, 119, 154
Istanbul, 125, 182
Istanbul Archaeology Museum, 182
Isthmian Games, 177
Italy: Classical Rome, 188–203; crop marks, 85; nationalism and archaeology, 191–193, 201–203; Ötzi the Iceman, xvii, 280; Pompeii and Herculaneum, 13–23; Rome (*see* Rome/Roman Empire); Troy, 24–37, 87–88, 131–132, 174, 300
Ithaca, 135
ivory artifacts: Elba, 259; Minoan, 140, 143; Mycenae, 137; Uluburun shipwreck, 164–165

jade artifacts: Chichén Itzá, 78; Palenque, 76; Tenochtitlán, 311; Teotihuacán, 304; Tikal, 74
Jamestown, 317–320
Jamestown Island, 320
Jamestown Rediscovery project, 320
Jashemski, Wilhelmina, 19
jasper, 223
Java Sea, 317
Jericho, 118–122, 208, 214
Jericho Tower, 120
Jeroboam II, 226
Jerusalem: Dead Sea Scrolls, 236, 237–238; excavation methods, 214; Roman Empire and, 195, 198; tourism, 246; temples, 195, 239–240, 250
jewelry: as artifacts, 81; Assyrian Empire, 65; Machu Picchu, 301; Masada, 249, 254; Maya, 76; Megiddo, 232; Mesopotamian, 54; Moche, 297; Pompeii and Herculaneum, 17, 18; Pylos, 137; trade and, 30; Troy/Hissarlik, 25, 30, 337; Uluburun shipwreck, 166
Jews: Babylonian Exile, 329–330; Dead Sea Scrolls, 234–244; First Jewish Revolt, 194–195, 199, 234–235, 239, 243, 248, 249, 250; Masada, 245–256
Jezreel, 86
Jezreel Valley, 86, 221, 222
Jezreel Valley Regional Project, 85
Johannesburg, 356n98
Johanson, Donald, 90, 102–103
Johns Hopkins University, 237
Jordan, 68, 188, 189, 257, 263–268, 327; Kataret es-Samra, xii
Jordan River, 236
Josephus, 195, 235, 245, 246, 250–251, 252, 253–254
Jotapata, 254
Joukowsky, Martha, 266
Journal of Archaeological Science, 280
Journal of Military History, 232
Juanita the Ice Maiden, 279, 282–283
Judea, 195
Julio-Claudian dynasty, 16
Juno, 335
Jupiter, 335

Kabri, Tel. *See* Tel Kabri
Kalhu, 58
Kalliste, 147

Kampsville, Illinois, 325
Kando, 236, 237, 240
Kataret es-Samra, xii
Kato Zakro, 140
Kebara Cave, 104–105
Kelso, William, 317–320
Kennewick, Washington, 321–322
Kennewick Man, 321–322
Kenyon, Kathleen, 119–120, 124, 208, 211, 214
Kenyon-Wheeler method, 214
Kephala Hill, 138
Khafre, 48, 50
Khania, 140
Khaznah, 265–266
Khorsabad, 57, 60, 61–62, 64
Khufu, 48
Kimeu, Kamoya, 99
King Minos, 143–144
King Tut, 1–9, 43, 113, 207, 278, 281, 336; iron dagger, xv. *See also* Tutankhamen
King's Chamber, Great Pyramid, 49
King's Library, 59
Kition, 163
Kleobis and Biton of Argos, 180
knives, sacrificial, 310
Knorosov, Yuri, 70
Knossos, 124, 137–144, 151
Koehl, Robert, 141
Koh, Andrew, xiii
Koobi Fora, 99, 102
Korfmann, Manfred, 34–37
Kosok, Paul, 294
Krakatoa, 148
Kroeber, Alfred, 294, 321
Kroeber, Theodora, 321
Kurdistan Region, 329
Kuyunjik, 56–57, 58–60
kylix, 166
Kyrieleis, Helmut, 174, 175

La Farge, Oliver, 305–306, 307
La Venta, 305–308
labyrinths, 143–144
Lachish, 59
Lachish Room, 59
Laetoli, xvii, 101
lahar, 18
Lake Texcoco, 308–309
Lamech, 238
Lampadius, Rufius Caecina Felix, 198–199

Lancet, The, 280
Laocoön, 198
lapis lazuli, 7, 295
Lascaux cave paintings, 105–114
laser imaging, 18, 22
Late Antiquity, 202
Late Bronze Age: end of, 136–137; Jericho, 120; Megiddo, 249; Mycenae, 134, 136–137; shipwrecks, 157–168; Troy, 25–26, 35; Uluburun shipwreck, 274. *See also* Bronze Age Aegean
Late Helladic IIIA1 pottery, 211
Late Helladic IIIA2 pottery, 162
Layard, Austen Henry, 55, 57–60, 62
lead testing, 319
Leakey, Louis, 99–102
Leakey, Louise, 99
Leakey, Mary, xviii, 99–102
Leakey, Meave, 99
Leakey, Richard, 99
Lebanon, 188
Legio, 85
Legio VI Ferrata, 85
legislation: Abandoned Shipwreck Act of 1987, 315; Native American Graves Protection and Repatriation Act of 1990 (NAGPRA), 321, 332; anti-looting, 330–331; Archaeological Resources Protection Act (ARPA), 332; Historic Sites Act of 1935, 332; Protect and Preserve International Cultural Property Act, 332
Lepsius, Karl, 39–40
Lerici periscope, 83
Lerici, Carlo, 83
Lhuillier, Alberto Ruz, 76
Libby, Willard, 107, 270–271
libraries: Alexandria, 63; Assyrian, 62–63; Elba, 258; Pergamon, 63
Libya, xvi, 188
LiDAR (Light Detection and Ranging), 66–67, 82, 86, 337
Life of Brian, 188
Life without People, 334
Light Detection and Ranging (LiDAR), 66–67, 82, 86, 337
Lindow Man, 283–284
Linear B, 136
Lion Gate, 131, 132, 134, 300
liquid mercury, 276, 304
Little Bighorn, 230

Livy, 14, 190
Lloyd, Seton, 62
London, xv, 260
Long House, 324
Lord Chocolate, 74
Lord of Sipan, 296–298
Lord Pacal, 75, 353n17
Lorraine, Emmanuel Maurice de, 14–15
Lost City of the Incas (Bingham), 300
lost wax method, 17–18, 22, 150, 346n17
Louvre, 39, 55, 56, 61, 174, 327
Lower City, Troy, 35–36
Lucy, xvii, 90, 103
Luján, Leonardo López, 311
Luxor, 210
Luxor Hotel, 40
Lydia, 178
Lysippus, 173

MacArthur Fellowship, 70
Macaulay, David, 336
Macedon, 183
maceheads, 242
Machu Picchu, 292, 299–302
magnetometers, 87–88, 337
Magnolia Cemetery, 317
Maiden Castle, 211
Mair, Victor, 278
Mallowan, Max, 52–55
Man of the Lie, 238
Manfred (Byron), 200
Manning, Sturt, 153
Marathon, 175, 181
Mariette, Auguste, 39–40
Marinatos, Spyridon, 149–150
Marseilles, 178
Marshalltown trowels, 205
Maryland, 316
Masada, 189, 203, 245–256
Masada: Herod's Fortress and the Zealots' Last Stand (Yadin), 245
Masada Myth, The (Ben-Yehuda), 246
mastabas, 46–47
material culture. *See* artifacts; pottery
matriarchy, 140
Matthiae, Paolo, 257–260
Maudslay, Alfred, 73
Mausoleum of Augustus, 192, 193
Maya civilization: Belize, 51; Caracol, 66–67, 86; Chichén Itzá, 68, 77–78, 304;

Copán, 68, 69, 71–73, 307; demise of, 78–79; general, xviii; Olmec civilization and, 308; Palenque, 67–68, 69, 70, 73–76, 307; Tikal, 73–74; Uxmal, 68, 76–77; Teotihuacán and, 311
McCown, Theodore, 104
McDonalds, 335
Mediterranean, excavation techniques, 206, 211–213, 214–216
Megaloceros Gallery, 111–112
Megiddo, xii, 81, 85, 189, 206, 209, 210, 215, 221–233, 249. *See also* Armageddon
Mellaart, James, 122–123
Melos, 145
Menelaus, 26, 131
Menkaure, 48
mercury, liquid, 276, 304
Mesa Verde National Park, 323, 324
Mesoamerica: Aztec civilization, 308–313; early archaeology, 66–79; excavation techniques, 206; LiDAR and, 86; Maya civilization (*see* Maya civilization); Olmec civilization, 304–308; Teotihuacán and, 311; Toltec civilization, 77–78, 312
Mesolithic period, 99
Mesopotamia: Babylonian Exile, 329–330; early archaeology, 52–65; foundation myths, 190; trade evidence, 136
Met, 327, 335
metopes, 173–174, 182
Metroon, 184
Mexica civilization, 308–311
Mexico City, 303, 304, 308
Mexico City Cathedral, 309
Mexico. *See* Mesoamerica
Michelangelo, 198
Middle Ages, 202
Middle Bronze Age: Jericho, 122; Megiddo, 223, 228; Minoan civilization, 138; Tel Kabri, 94
Middle East: Afghanistan, 163, 327; climate change, 42; excavation techniques, 209, 210–211, 216; experience in, xii; Fertile Crescent civilizations, 115–128; Holy Land (*see* Holy Land); looting and destruction of antiquities, xvi; Mesopotamia, 52–65; Napoleon in, 40; Roman ruins in, 188, 189; stratigraphy, 119. *See also* individual countries
Middle Stone Age, 99

military intelligence images, 82–83
milkstones, 138
Millon, René, 312
Miltiades, 175–176
Miniature Fresco, 152–153
Ministry of Culture, France, 109, 110
Minoan civilization, xviii, 124, 137–144, 149, 151, 157–159, 162–168
mirrors, pyrite, 312
Mississippi Valley, 324
Mississippian culture, 324
Missouri, 324
Mitanni, 270
Moche civilization, xvii–xviii, 295–298
Moctezuma, Eduardo Matos, 309
Monastery, Petra, 267
Mongols, 222
Monks Mound, 324
monoliths, 309–310
Montana, 230
Monte Albán, 313
Montignac, 106
Monty Python, 188, 203
Monument of the Eponymous Heroes, 185
monumental architecture, 117–118
Monuments of Egypt and Ethiopia, 39
Moon Goddess, 309–310
Moretti, Giuseppe, 193
mosaics: Cyprus villa, 189; Masada, 248, 251; Olmec, 307; Petra, 267; Pompeii and Herculaneum, 21
Moshe, 104–105
Mosul Museum, 58, 327
Motel of the Mysteries (Macaulay), 336
Mother Goddess beliefs, 126–127
motherhood symbols, 126–127
Mound Builders, 324–325
Mount Ampato, 282, 283
Mount Carmel, 103–104
Mount Parnassus, 177
Mount Vernon, 325
Mount Vesuvius, 13–23, 101
mudflows, 18
mummies: Chinese, 278–279; Egyptian, 6–7, 38–39, 43–46; Inca, 282–283; mummification process, 43–47; preservation of, 278–279
muon radiography, 51
murals, 77, 298
Murder in Mesopotamia (Christie), 53
Museum of Fine Arts, 335

museums: antiquities market and, 327; future archaeology and, 335
musical instruments, 54–55, 145, 195, 277
Mussolini, Benito, 191–193, 202
Mycenae, 31, 131–137, 138–139, 151, 157–159, 162–168, 300
Mycenaeans, xviii, 26–27, 131, 138, 141, 144–45
Mycerinus, 48
Mylonas, George, 135
Mystery Park, 292
mythology: Atlantis, 146–156; Egyptian, 44; factual basis of, 154–156; foundation myths, 27, 190; Theseus and the Minotaur, 143–144; Troy and Schliemann, xi, 24–37

Nabataeans, 260, 261, 264, 265–266, 267
NAGPRA (Native American Graves Protection and Repatriation Act of 1990), 321, 332
Nahal Hever, 242
Nahal Mishmar, 242
Nahash, 241
Napoleon, 40, 50, 191, 222
National Archaeological Museum, 133
National Autonomous University of Mexico, 308
National Geographic: archaeologist, 74; Channel, 334; explorer, 84; magazine, 97–98, 117–118, 296, 300, 311; photographer, 304; Society, 9, 70, 294, 300
National Museum of Natural History, 320, 335
National Park Service, 332
nationalism, 189, 190–191, 201–203, 245–246, 250, 256
Native American Graves Protection and Repatriation Act of 1990 (NAGPRA), 321, 332
Native Americans: Chaco Canyon, 322–323; colonial America; 317–318, 319; legislation protecting artifacts and sites of, 321–322, 332; Mound Builders, 324–325
Nature, 322
Naxos, 145
Nazca Lines, 291–298
Neander Valley, 102
Neanderthals, 102, 104–105, 113

Near East: Bronze Age trade, 136, 144, 149, 154; monumental architecture, 117–118; plastered skulls, 120–122; stratigraphy, 119
Nefertiti, 2, 8, 9, 162, 166–167, 274, 327
Nemea, 177
Nemean Games, 177
Neo-Assyrian period, 224, 227, 228, 229, 230
Neo-Babylonians, 250
Neolithic period: Atlantis myth and, 155; Black Sea settlement, 285; Çatalhöyük, xvii, 122–125; Göbekli Tepe, xvii, 116–118; Jericho, 118–112, 120–122, 208; time era of, 99
Neolithic Revolution, 116
Nephilim, 118
Nero, 177, 181, 197–198
Nerva, 194
New Age beliefs, 126
New Archaeology, 126
New Kingdom, 151
New Mexico, 322–323, 332
New Seven Wonders of the World, 264
New Stone Age, 99, 116
New Troy, 37
New World archaeology: beginnings of, xviii, 68–69; assumptions about New World, 78–79; Mexico, 304–313; North America, xii, xviii, 314–325; Peru, 291–302; stratigraphy, 359n119
New York Times, 6
New Yorker, 109
Nickell, Joe, 376n295
Nilotic Fresco, 151
Nimrud, 55, 57–58, 60, 64–65, 283, 327
Nineveh and Its Remains (Layard), 58
Nineveh, 55, 57, 59–60, 62, 62, 63, 64
Nippur, 55, 64
Noah, 238
Nobel Prize, 270
Norman Conquest, 285
North Africa, 178
North America. *See* United States
North Charleston, 315
Northern Kingdom of Israel, 225
Northwest Palace, 57–58
Norway, 287
Nova, 161
Nubia, 165
Numismatic Society, 138

Oaxaca, 313
object association, 273–274
obsidian, 124, 217, 312
obsidian hydration, 273
Occam's razor, 141
Occidental College, 278
Odysseus, 131, 135
Odyssey (Homer), 34, 132, 190
Old Kingdom Period, 42, 48, 259
Old Persian, 56
Old Stone Age, 99
Old World archaeology, xii, xviii, 15, 69, 79, 302
Olduvai Gorge, 100, 101, 272
Olman, 305
Olmec civilization, 304–308, 377n307
Olympia, 172–177
Olympia Convention, 174
Olympic Games, 171–177, 181, 213
Oman, 84
Omri, 225
online interactions, future archaeology, 335
Oracle of Delphi, 172–184
organic material, preservation of, 278, 283
Oriental Institute, 224
Origins (Leakey), 99
Orpheus, 189
Ottoman period, 185
Ötzi the Iceman, xvii–xviii, 279–282
Owl-Man, 294
Owsley, Doug, 319, 321

Packer, James, 202
paint, archaeological evidence of: architectural features, 197; Aztec monoliths, 309–310; Palmyra, 261; Terracotta Warriors, 276–277
Painted Stoa, 186
paintings: Akrotiri, 151–153; Çatalhöyük, 123; cave, 105–114; classical Roman frescoes, 198; Mycenae, 136, 151; non-indigenous animals in, 151; Pompeii and Herculaneum, 21; Tiryns, 151; volcanoes, 124. *See also* wall paintings
Palace 6000, 226–227
Palace G, Elba, 258
Palace of Nestor, 137
Palace Tomb, 266
Palace without Rival, 59
palaces: Assyrian, 57–58, 59–60, 62, 62; classical Roman, 198; Elba, 258, 259;

Kato Zakro, 140; Khania, 140; Masada, 248; Megiddo, 226–228; Minoan, 138–144; Mycenae, 135–136, 137; Phaistos, 140; Troy/Hissarlik, 29, 33

palaeoanthropology, 99

Palaiokastro, xii

Palaistra, 175

Palatine Hill, 190

Palazzo Peretti, 192

Palenque, 67–68, 69, 70, 73–76, 307

Palenque Mapping Project, 76

Paleolithic period, 99

Palestine, 203, 214

Palmyra, 189, 257, 260–263

Palmyra Antiquities, 260

Palpa, 293, 294–295

Pan (Greek god), xiii

Panhellenic games, 172, 177

Pantheon, 191, 192

Paphos, xii, 189

papyri: Cave of Letters, 243; Egypt, 41, 43; Petra, 267; Pompeii and Herculaneum, 13–14; preservation of, 278

papyrology, 13–14, 267

Paracas, 293, 294

Parcak, Sarah, 84, 85, 328

Paris (*Iliad*), 26, 32

Paros, 145

Parrot, the, 294

Parthenon, 184, 197

Pasha, Mohammed, 57

patish, xii

Pausanias, 132, 172, 174, 181, 183, 186

Pazyryk civilization, 282

PBS (television channel), 283

peat, 283, 284

pedestrian surveys, 81–82

Peloponnese, 131, 173, 181

Peloponnesian War, 181

Penn Museum, 158

Penn State Erie, 266

Pepi I, 259

Pepi II, 42

Pepsi, 125

Pergamon, 183

Persia, 56, 178, 181, 182, 190, 261

Persian War, 175

Peru: Juanita the Ice Maiden, 279, 282–283; Machu Picchu, 299–301; Moche civilization, xvii, 295–298; Nazca Lines, 291–295; robberies/looting, xvi, 327

Petra, 189, 257, 263–268

"Petra" (Burgon), 264–265

Petrie, William Matthew Flinders, 119, 210–211, 223–224

petrified monkey's paw, xii–xiii, xviii, 278

Pettinato, Giovanni, 258, 259

Phaistos, 140

Pheidias, 173, 177

Philip II, 183

Philo, 235

Phoenician civilization, 147

Piazza Bocca della Verità, 192

pickaxes, 205

pictographs, 117

Piening, Heinrich, 197

Piltdown Man, 102

Pitt, Brad, 281

Pius VII, 191

Place, Victor, 61, 62

plagues, 323

plants: domestication of, 116–117, 118, 127; radiocarbon dating and, 271; reconstruction of, 19, 232

plaster casting, 17–18, 22, 150

plastered skulls, 120–122, 208

Plataea, 182

Platform of Venus, 77

Plato, 155–156, 184

Pliny the Elder, 15, 235

Pliny the Younger, 15–16, 101

Pocahontas, 317–318

Polychrome Ceiling, 106

Polyzelus, 180

Pompeii, 13–23, 215

"Pompeii of the Aegean," 148

Pont d'Arc, 109

Pope, Saxton, 321

Porta Stabia, 19

Portico, 182

Poseidon, 36, 136

Postclassic period, 71

postprocessual archaeology, 125–127

potassium-argon dating, 270, 272

potsherds, 217

pottery: Akrotiri, 150; as artifacts, 81; dating techniques, 210–211, 224–226, 227, 271, 273–274; excavation techniques, 217; Jamestown, 318; Jericho, 119–120; Late Helladic IIIA1, 211; Late Helladic IIIA2, 162; Late Minoan Ib, 153; Masada, 249, 254, 255;

pottery (*continued*)
    Mycenaean, 134, 162, 166; Nazca, 292;
        recording during site surveys, 91–93;
        seriation, 224; Troy/Hissarlik, 29, 33
Praxiteles, 173
Preclassic period, 71
pre-Columbian sites, United States, 324
prehistoric archaeology, 99, 113–114
prepottery Neolithic B period, 120, 122–125
prepottery Neolithic period, 115–116, 117–
        118, 120–122
Priam, 26, 29–30
Priam's Treasure, 29–30, 337
priestess figurines, 140
Priest-King Fresco, 141–142, 162
primary context, 207
propaganda, 59–60
Proskouriakoff, Tatiana, 70
Protect and Preserve International Cultural
        Property Act, 332
proton magnetometers, 337, 354n83
provenance, 327. *See also* artifacts,
        ownership of
Prytaneion, 175
pseudo-archaeology: aliens and pyramids,
        38, 46, 47; Atlantis, xvi, 146; mythology
        and, 154; Nazca Lines, 291–292, 294, 295
Ptolemy, 40
Ptolemy V, 40
Pueblo Bonito, 323
Pulak, Cemal, 158–168
Pushkin Museum, 30
Pylos, xii, 90–94, 137
Pyramid Age, 48
Pyramid of Kukulkan, 77
Pyramid of the Moon, 296, 312
Pyramid of the Sun, 295–296, 312
pyramids: Aztec, 309–313; Egyptian, xvi,
        38–39, 46–51; Maya, 51, 69, 73–77; Moche,
        295–298; Olmec, 306; Teotihuacán, 312
pyrite, 304, 312
Pythian Games, 177, 180, 181, 183
Pytho, 181

Qin Shihuang, 275–278
quartz, 217
Queen's Megaron, 141
Quft, 210
Quickbird, 85
Quintuplet Altar, 307
Qumran, 234–235, 237, 238, 242, 243, 246,
        255, 329

radiocarbon dating: Lascaux cave, 107, 109;
        Megiddo, 225–226; Nazca Lines, 292–
        293; Olmec civilization, 308; overview
        of, 270–271; Santorini eruption, 153–
        154; Tel Kabri, 274; Troy/Hissarlik, 29;
        Uluburun shipwreck, 274
Ramses, 43
Ramses II, 39
Raphael, 198
Ras Feshka, 236
Rassam, Hormuzd, 62, 63
Rawlinson, Henry, 55–56, 59
reconnaissance surveys, 81, 82–83, 90–94
reconstructions. *See* archaeological
        reconstructions/recreations; replicas
recordkeeping, 212–215
Red Panels Gallery, 111
Red Pyramid, 50
Red Queen, 76
Red Sea, 154
Reeves, Nicholas, 8–9
rehydroxylation, 272–273
Reiche, Maria, 294
Reinhard, Johan, 282
relative dates, 270
reliefs: Assyrian Empire, 59–60; classical
        Rome, 193
religious beliefs, early hominins, 98, 113,
        116, 117, 208
religious objects, 136, 168, 310–311, 335, 336
religious rituals, 136, 143, 152, 294
remote sensing: archaeological excavation
        and, 87; Egypt, 9; Göbekli Tepe, 117;
        ground-based techniques, 86–90;
        LiDAR system, 66–67, 82, 86, 337; Maya
        civilization, 66–67; overview of, 81,
        86–90; Petra, 267; proton
        magnetometers, 337, 354n83; Qin's
        tomb, 277–278; Rome, 85; technological
        advances in, 337–338; Teotihuacán, 303–
        304; Troy/Hissarlik, 34–35, 37;
        underwater artifacts, 62
remote-controlled robots, 303
Remus, 27, 190, 192
Renaissance painters, 198, 200
replicas: Altamira cave, 106, 113;
        Çatalhöyük, 125; Chauvet cave, 112–113;
        King Tut's tomb, 8–9, 113; Lascaux cave,
        108, 113; Masada siege engines, 251–252;
        Palmyra, 260, 262
Resin Lady, 18
Ricci, Corrado, 192

Richard III, 281
Ridgaway, Joseph, 316, 317
Rio de Janeiro, 171
Rising Star, 97–98
robberies/looting: aerial surveys and, 86; antiquities trade and, 327–332; classical Rome, 197–198; context of artifacts and, 207, 208; Egypt, 3–4, 5, 332; Egypt, 39; Elba, 259–260; Herculaneum, 14–15; legislation prohibiting, 330–331; Mesopotamia, 54; Moche tombs, 296, 298; museum collections and, 327; Mycenae, 135; political instability and, 327; Syria, 332; shipwrecks, 315
Rockefeller, John D. Jr., 224
Rodio, Giovanni, 193
Rolfe, John, 318
Roman Forum, 191, 192, 195
Roman historians, 15–16, 42, 245, 250
Roman period, stratigraphy, 185
Roman Republic, 16
Romantic poets, 200
Rome/Roman Empire: aerial surveys and, 85, 86; ancient trade routes, 261; Bar Kokhba Revolt, 242; classical era, 188–203; early excavations of, 189–203; Egypt and, 41–42, 43; First Jewish Revolt, 194–195, 199, 234–235, 239, 243, 248, 249, 250; founding of, 27, 190; Masada, 245–256; Megiddo and, 222, 233; military barracks in, xv; Olympics and, 177; Palmyra and, 260–263; Petra and, 264–268; Pompeii and Herculaneum, 13–23; Roman Republic vs., 16; Second Jewish Revolt, 242, 243; shipwrecks, 285; stratigraphy, 202; Troy, 24–37, 87–88, 131–132, 174, 300
Rome Reborn, 197
Romulus, 27, 190, 192
Ronald McDonald, 335
Roosevelt, Theodore, 332
Rose, Brian, 34, 36
Rosetta Stone, 40, 69, 70, 327
Royal Air Force, 83, 85
Royal College of Surgeons, 211
Royal Library, 62

Sacred Ball Court, 72–73
Sacred Way, 181, 183
Sacrifice Ceremony, 298
Sacrificing Truth (Ben-Yehuda), 246
Sacristy, 112

SAFE (Saving Antiquities for Everyone), 382n332
Saint Irene, 147
Saite Renaissance, 43
Salahi, 236
Salamis, 182
Samaria, 119, 214
sample surveys, 81
Samuel, Archbishop, 237, 238
San Lorenzo, 306–308
San Lorenzo Tenochtitlán, 308
Santorini, 145, 146–156
Sapienze University of Rome, 257
Sargon, 190
Sargon II, 57, 58
satellite imagery, 82–85
Saving Antiquities for Everyone (SAFE), 382n332
Sayce, A. H., 31–32
Scaean Gate, 29
scarab artifacts, 162, 166–167, 274
Schachermeyer, Fritz, 36
Schele, Linda, 70
Schliemann, Heinrich: archaeologist, xvii–xviii; Dörpfeld and, 174; Mycenae, 131–137, 300; Troy, xi, 24–37, 68, 131–132, 223, 300, 337
Schliemann, Sophia, 24–25, 29, 31, 337
Schloen, David, 87
Schmidt, Klaus, 115–116, 117, 118
Schumacher, Gottlieb, 223–224
Science, 280
scientific processes, 126
Scotland, 285, 286–287
scrolls: Dead Sea Scrolls, 234–244, 255; Egyptian, 41; Herculaneum, 13–14, 17, 23; Masada, 254–255; Petra, 267
sculptures: Çatalhöyük, 123; classical Greece, 173; classical Rome, 191, 197; Maya, 69; Mesopotamian, 54, 57, 62; Olmec, 304–308; painting of, 197. See also statues
seals: Egyptian, 4; Megiddo, 223; Mesopotamian, 166; Minoan, 167; Mycenae, 137, 167; Troy, 36
Seattle, Washington, 322
Second Jewish Revolt, 242, 243
Second Temple, 250
secondary context, 208
seeds, dating methods, 271
Sennacherib, 58, 59, 62
Sequoia National Park, 272

seriation, 224, 273–274
Serpent Column, 182
Seven Wonders of the Ancient World, 48, 173
Seventeenth Dynasty, 42
Severan Marble Plan, 194
Severus, Septimius, 260
Shaanxi Province, 275, 277
Shaft Graves, 138
Shalmaneser III, 58
Shanghai, 125
Shanidar Cave, 105
Shanks, Michael, 125
Shear, T. Leslie Jr., 185
Shear, T. Leslie Sr., 185
Shell, 125
shell artifacts: Chaco Canyon, 323; Jericho,
    120–121, 208; Tenochtitlán, 311;
    Teotihuacán, 304; Tikal, 74
sherds, 217, 255–256
Sheshonq, 223–224, 229
ships/shipwrecks: Cape Gelidonya, xvii,
    158–159, 160, 163; *Hunley*, 314–317;
    preservation of, 285–287, 315–316;
    Sutton Hoo, 285; Uluburun xvii, 157–
    168; Viking, 286–287; Shishak, 224
Shreeve, Jamie, 97–98
Shrine of the Book, 237–238
Siberia, 282–283
Siberian princess remains, 279, 282
Sicarii, 248, 250
siege engines, 251–252
signs/notices, 21–22
Silk Road, 279
Silk Tomb, 266
Silkeborg, 284
Silva, Flavius, 251
silver artifacts: classical Greece, 176, 180–
    181; classical Rome, 195; Moche, 297–
    298; Mycenae, 133–134, 137;
    preservation of, 278; Troy, 24; Uluburun
    shipwreck, 164, 166;
Simon the Cobbler, 185
Sipan, 296
Siq, 265
Six-Day War, 240
Sixth Roman Legion, 85
skeletons: Cave of Horrors, 242; Cave of
    Letters, 243; excavation techniques, 204,
    206; *Hunley* submarine, 316–317;
    Jamestown, 318–320; lead testing, 319;
    Machu Picchu, 299–300; Masada,

255–256; radiocarbon dating, 271;
    reconstructions from, 135. *See also*
    animal bones; human remains; skulls
Skhul Cave, 104
Skull Chamber, 112
skulls: Aztec, 309; Cave of Letters, 243;
    Chauvet cave, 111; Death Pits of Ur, 54;
    early hominins, 99, 100, 102, 103, 104;
    facial reconstruction from, 7, 135, 280,
    320, 361n135; *Hunley* submarine, 316–
    317; Jamestown, 320; Kennewick man,
    321–322; Maya, 77; Moche, 297–298;
    mummies, 45; plastered, 120–122, 208
slaves, pyramid building and, 38, 48
Smith, George, 63
Smith, John, 318
Smithsonian, 109, 117
Smithsonian Insider, 320
Smithsonian Institute, 304, 317, 321
Smithsonian National Museum of Natural
    History, 101, 319
Snake Goddess, 140
Snake Path, 246, 247
Snake Priestess, 140
social Darwinism, 15
Society of Antiquaries, 138
Society of Biblical Archaeology, 63
Socrates, 184, 185, 187
Sodom, 258, 259
software, 185
Solecki, Ralph, 105
Solomon, 225–227, 250
Solomon's Stables, 222–223, 225–226
Solon, 155
Sons of Darkness, 237
Sons of Light, 237
Sophocles, 132
Soprintendenze Speciale per I Beni
    Archaeologici di Roma, 197
South Africa, 97–98, 356n98
South America: excavation techniques, 206;
    Inca civilization, 282–283, 299–302;
    Juanita the Ice Maiden, 279, 282–283;
    Machu Picchu, 299–301; Moche
    civilization, xvii, 295–298; Nazca Lines,
    291–295. *See also* specific countries
South Carolina, 314, 315, 317
South Tyrol Museum of Archaeology, 281
Southwest Palace, 57–58, 59
"space archaeology," 84
space shuttles, imagery from, 83–84

Spain: Altamira cave, 105–114; Atlantis, 146; conquest of Mexico, 67–68, 304, 305, 308, 312; early hominins, 105–114; Roman ruins in, 188

Spanish Conquest, 299

Sparta, 147, 181

Sphinx Dream Stele, 50

Sphinx, xvi, 38, 48, 50

Spruce Tree House, 324

stadiums, classical Greece, 175, 181, 184, 187

Stamatakis, Panayiotis, 134

Standard of Ur, 54–55

Stanford University, 125

Starbucks, 335

Starving Time, 320

statues: bronze, 173, 180; classical Greece, 173, 180, 181, 183, 184; marble, 173, 184; Mesopotamian, 61; Olmec, 305–308, 308, 377n307; Palmyra, 262; Terracotta Warriors, xvii, 274, 275–278; Troy/Hissarlik, 36. See also sculptures

Stela C, 307

stelae, 50, 72, 306, 307

Step Pyramid, 46–48

Stephens, John Lloyd, xi, xviii, 67–79, 264, 265, 324

Stewart, Richard, 304

Stirling, Marion, 304, 306–308

Stirling, Matthew, 304, 305, 306–308

Stoa of Attalos, 185, 186

Stoa Poikile, 186

stoa, 183, 185, 186

Stocker, Sharon, 137

stone tablets. See tablets

Stonehenge Hidden Landscapes Project, 88–89

Stonehenge, 88–89

stratigraphic sections, 211

stratigraphy: classical Greece, 185; classical Rome, 202; dating techniques and, 273–274; excavation techniques and, 205, 209, 210–214, 224; introduction of, 119, 359n119; Jericho, 119; Megiddo, 224–225; Troy, 28–29

Street of Façades, 266

Strongili, 147

Stuart, David, 70–71

Stuart, George, 70, 74

submarine wrecks, 314–315

Suetonius, 177

Suffolk, 285

Sukenik, Eliezer, 236–237, 238

Sulaymaniyah Museum, 329

Sulla, 181

Sullivan's Island, 315

Sultan Ahmet Square, 182

Sumerian civilization, 64

Sun Stone, 309

Sung dynasty, 107

Superman's Crawl, 98

superposition, 210

Supreme Council of Antiquities, 7

surveying, 80–94, 159

Sutter, Anthony, 230, 232

Sutton Hoo, 285–286

symbols: Egyptian, 41; fasces, 191; fertility/motherhood, 126–127; vocal and instrumental notations, 181

synchronisms, 270

Syria: artifact ownership and, 64; civil war, 259–260, 262; Ebla, 257–260; Palmyra, 189, 257, 260–263; robberies/looting, xvi–xvii, 327, 332; Roman ruins in, 188; stone anchors, 163

Syrian Orthodox Monastery of St. Mark, 237

Tabasco, 305

Table of Shewbread, 195

tablets: Assyrian, 59, 62–64; Babylonian Exile, 329–330; cuneiform, 329; Elba, 258–259; Hittite, 32–33; Maya, 75; Mycenae, 136; Nimrud, 283; Uluburun shipwreck, 164

Tabun Cave, 104

Tacitus, 15

Tadmor, 260

Talbot County, Maryland, 316

Tamut, 46

Tang dynasty, 317

Tanis, xv, 84

Tanzania, xvii, 100

Tarim Basin, 278, 279

tattoos, 281, 282

Teacher of Righteousness, 238

TED Prize, 84

Tel Anafa, xii

Tel Kabri: digging at, xii; excavation techniques, 206, 209, 213, 215, 228; radiocarbon dating, 274; remote sensing, 86, 87; survey techniques, 93–94; wine cellar, xiii

Tell el-Dab'a, 144

Tell el-Hesi, 119
Tell el-Maskhuta, xii, 212
Tell Mardikh, 257, 258
Tempest Stele, 155
Temple in Jerusalem, 239–240
Temple of Apollo, 179, 181, 182, 183, 187
Temple of Athena Nike, 184
Temple of Bel, 262–263
Temple of Luxor, 197
Temple of Peace, 195, 198
Temple of the Cross, 75
Temple of the Feathered Serpent, 303–304, 312
Temple of the Grand Jaguar, 73, 74
Temple of the Hieroglyphic Stairway, 72
Temple of the Inscriptions, 75, 76
Temple of the Jaguars, 77
Temple of the Sun, 301
Temple of the Warriors, 77
Temple of the Winged Lions, 267
Temple of Zeus, 172, 173–174
Temple Scroll, 240
Temple to Hera, 175
Temple to Peace, 194
Temple XIII, 76
temples: Athens, 184–187; Aztec, 309; classical Greece, 172–187; classical Rome, 194, 195; Delphi, 172–184; Egyptian, 39, 41; future archaeology, 335; intentional destruction of, 262–263; Jerusalem, 195, 239–240, 250; Machu Picchu, 301; Maya, 72, 73, 74–78; Megiddo, 228; Moche civilization, 295–298; monumental architecture and, 117; Mycenae, 137; Palmyra, 262–263; Petra, 267; Teotihuacán, 303–304, 312–313
Templo Mayor, 309
Templum Pacis, 194
Tennessee, 316
Tenochtitlán, 308–311
Teotihuacán, 303–304, 311–313
Teotihuacán Mapping Project, 312–313
Tepper, Yotam, 85, 233
terebinth resin, 164
Terminal Classic period, Maya, 71
Terracotta Warriors, xvii–xviii, 274, 275–278
tertiary context, 207
Test of Time, A (Manning), 153
Tetrapylon, 262
Texas A&M University, 157, 158, 159
textiles. See clothing

thalassocracy, 139, 159
Thanksgiving Scroll, 237
Theater of Marcellus, 192
theatres, 262, 266
Thebes, 91, 137
Theodosius, 172, 177
Thera, 145, 146–156
thermoluminescence, 270, 272
Theseus, 143–144, 182
Thieves of Baghdad (Bogdanos), 329
Third Dynasty, 42, 46
Third Intermediate Period, 43
Tholos, 184
Thompson, Edward, 78
Thompson, Eric, 70, 308
Thompson, Homer, 185
three-dimensional visualization, 46
Thucydides, 139, 159
Thutmose III, 2, 43, 222
Thutmose IV, 50
Tiberius, 193
tidal waves, 148
Tiglath-Pileser III, 58
Tikal, 73–74
Tilley, Christopher, 125
Timaeus (Plato), 155
tin, 159, 163–164
Tiryns, 135, 137
Tisha B'Av, 250
Titanic, 284
Titus, 16, 194, 195, 197, 201
Tlaloc, 309
Tlaltecuhtli, 309
Tollund Man, 284
Tomb 1, Moche tombs, 296–298
Tomb of Agamemnon, 135
Tomb of Clytemnestra, 135
Tomb of Sextus Florentinus, 266
tombs: aerial surveys and, 85; Egyptian, 1–9, 41, 43, 113, 165, 278, 336; Etruscan, 83; Inca, 283; Maya, 74, 75–76; Moche, 295–298; mound, 324; Mycenae, 132–135; Petra, 266; Pylos, 137; Terracotta Warriors, 274, 275–278; Ur, 54–55. See also burial sites
tools: archaeological excavation, 204–218; as artifacts, 81; Çatalhöyük, 124; dating techniques, 271, 272; for excavation, 217; Homo habilis, 100; Neolithic Revolution, 116; Ötzi the Iceman, 282; Uluburun shipwreck, 165

Topiltzin Quetzalcoatl, 77
Torreon, 301
tourism, 8, 106, 108, 111–112, 113, 203
trade: ancient trade routes, 261, 264, 279;
    archaeological evidence of, 136, 144,
    149, 154, 259, 295, 323; jewelry and, 30;
    shipwreck evidence of, 157–159, 162–168
Trafalgar Square, 260
Trajan, 194, 201
Trajan's Forum, 191, 192
Transportation Security Administration, 338
Treasuries: classical Greece, 176, 180–181,
    182; Petra, 263, 265–266, 267
tree-ring dating, 162, 272, 274
Tres Zapotes, 305, 306–308
Tribes and Temples, 306
triglyphs, 174
Tripod of Plataia, 182
Triumphal Arch, 260, 261, 262, 263
Trojan Horse, 36
Trojan War, 25–28, 190
trowels, 205
Troy, xv, 24–37, 87–88, 131–132, 174, 300
Troy, levels of: Troy II, 29, 30; Troy VI, 29,
    31, 34, 36; Troy VIh, 31, 33, 35–36; Troy
    VII, 31, 33–34; Troy VIIa, 33, 34; Troy
    VIIb, 36; Troy VIII, 37; Troy IX, 37
Troy (film), 281
Trujillo, 295
tsunamis, 148
Tulane University, 305
Tunisia, 201
Turkana Boy, 99–100, 102
Turkey: amphitheaters, 201; Cape
    Gelidonya shipwreck, xvii, 158–159, 160,
    163; Çatalhöyük, xvii, 122–125; Göbekli
    Tepe, xvii, 115–116; Roman ruins in,
    188; site survey in, 90–94; Troy and
    Schliemann, xi, 24–37; Uluburun
    shipwreck, xvii, 157–168; Zincirli, 87
Turn Right at Machu Picchu (Adams), 300
Tushratta, 270
Tutankhamen, 1–9, 43, 113, 207, 278, 281,
    336. *See also* King Tut
Tuttle, Chris, 266
Twain, Mark, 200

Ubar, 84
UCLA, 126
Ugarit, 163, 165
Ukok Plateau, 282–283

Uluburun shipwreck, xvii, 157–168, 271,
    274, 283
Umma, 329
underwater archaeology, 157–168, 193,
    314–317
underworld beliefs, 311
UNESCO: Convention on the Means of
    Prohibiting and Preventing the Illicit
    Import, Export, and Transfer of
    Ownership of Cultural Property, 330'
    Convention on the Protection of the
    Underwater Cultural Heritage, 317
UNESCO World Heritage sites: Acropolis,
    184; Altamira cave, 106; Cahokia
    Mounds, 324; Chaco Canyon, 322;
    Chauvet cave, xvii, 108; Chichén Itzá,
    78; Copán, 71; Delphi, 178; Haifa caves,
    103–104; Lascaux cave, 107; Machu
    Picchu, 299; Masada, 246; Mesa Verde,
    323; Mycenae, 135; Nazca, 293;
    Olympia, 175; Palenque, 76; Palmyra,
    260; Paracas, 293; Petra, 263;
    Teotihuacán, 311; Tikal, 74; Tiryns, 135
United States: antiquities preservation
    legislation, 332–333; battlefield
    archaeology, 230; Chaco Canyon, 322–
    323; excavation techniques, 205, 209,
    214–215, 229; Jamestown, 317–320;
    Mound Builders, 324–325; pre-
    Columbian sites, 324; robberies/looting,
    327, 332–333; shipwrecks, 314–317;
    stratigraphy, 359n119; Washington
    Kennewick Man, 321–322
University College London, 99
University Museum of the, University of
    Pennsylvania, 54
University of Alabama, 84
University of California–San Francisco, 321
University of Chicago, 115, 117, 209, 210,
    224, 322
University of Cincinnati, 19–20, 33, 34, 36,
    137
University of Copenhagen, 322
University of Kentucky, 376n295
University of London, 210
University of Michigan, 117
University of Pennsylvania, 74, 158, 159,
    266, 278, 354n83
University of Rome, 259
University of Tübingen, 34
University of Utah, 265

University of Virginia, 197
Upper Paleolithic, 113
Ur, 30, 52–55, 64
Urn Tomb, 266
Uruk, 55, 64
Ürümqi, 278
US Bureau of Alcohol, Tobacco, and
　Firearms, 231
US Committee of the Blue Shield, 382n332
US House of Representatives, 332
US Senate, 332
USS *Housatonic*, 314–315
Utah, 236, 323
UV-VIS spectrometry, 197
Uxmal, 68, 76–77

Valley of the Kings, 1–9
Vatican, 198
Ventris, Michael, 136
Veracruz, 305, 307
vertical excavation, 210, 224–225
Vespasian, 194–195, 198–199, 273
Via del Imperio, 192
Via del Mare, 192
Via Maris, 222
Victor Emmanuel II, 191, 202
Vikings, 285, 286–287
Vilcabamba, 300
Villa of the Mysteries, 21
Villa of the Papyri, 13–14, 23
villas, 189
Virazon, 162
Virgil, 190
Virginia, 317–320
volcanoes/volcanic eruptions: Çatalhöyük
　paintings, 124; cave paintings of, 109,
　112; Cycladic islands, 146–156; Olduvai
　Gorge, 101; Pompeii and Herculaneum,
　13–23
von Däniken, Erich, 291–292, 293, 294
votive objects, 167–168

Wace, Alan, 135
Wadi Musa, 264, 265
Wainman, Ferdinando, 319
wall paintings: Akrotiri, 151–153;
　Çatalhöyük, 123–124; Chauvet,
　Lascaux, and Altamira caves, xvii,
　105–114; Egyptian, 8–9, 41, 43, 144, 165;
　Etruscan tombs, 83; Masada, 248;
　Minoan, 139, 140–143; Mycenae, 136,

139; Nero's Golden House, 198;
　Pompeii, 21–22
Wall Street Journal, 237
walls: buried, detection techniques, 34,
　84–85, 86–87; Çatalhöyük, 120, 122–
　123; "chasing walls," 60; excavation
　techniques, 217, 223; features vs., 81;
　Knossos, 139–140; Masada, 249, 251–
　254; Megiddo, 229; Mesopotamian, 57,
　59, 60, 62; reconstruction of, 193, 249;
　Troy, 25, 27, 29, 31, 33, 34–36
Walls of Windy Troy, The, xi
War Scroll, 237
warfare, archaeological evidence of, 33,
　35–36, 229
Warring States period, 275
Warrior Priest, 298
Washington, George, 325
Washington State, 321–322
Watanabe, Hirokatsu, 9
Watchers, 118
wax tablets, 164
Way of the Sea, 222
Wayna Picchu, 299
weapons: as artifacts, 81; Jamestown, 318;
　Mesopotamian, 54; Mycenae, 132–133,
　134; Olympia, 175; Ötzi the Iceman,
　282; Pylos, 137; Teotihuacán, 312;
　Terracotta Warriors, 274, 275–278; Troy/
　Hissarlik, 36; Uluburun shipwreck, 165;
　Viking ships, 287
Weisman, Alan, 334
West Bank, 118–122
West House, 151, 152
West, William, 319
Wheeler, Mortimer, 119, 211–212, 214
Wheeler-Kenyon method, 214
WHS trowels, 205
Wicked Priest, 238
Wilusa, 32–33, 35
Winckelmann, Johann Joachim, 15
wine cellar, xiii–xiv, 86
wood: dating techniques, 271–272;
　preservation of, 278, 285–287
Woolley, Katharine, 53
Woolley, Leonard, 30, 52–55
World Expo, 125
World War I, 222, 230
World War II, 30, 174, 202, 203, 224, 230,
　273, 307
World without Us, The (Weisman), 334

Wright, Henry, 117
writing, preserved: cuneiform, 55–56, 62–63, 329; dating methods and, 270; hymns to Apollo, 181; Petra, 267; cuneiform, 55–56, 62–63; Egyptian hieroglyphics, 38–41, 43–44, 69, 70; Elba, 258–259; epigraphy and, 55–56; Greek and Roman, 41–42; Linear B, 136; Maya hieroglyphics, 69–71; Mycenae, 136; Olmec, 305; Rosetta stone, 40, 69, 70, 327; Troy/Hissarlik, 36

Xerxes, 182
Xi'an, 275
X-ray techniques, 13–14, 280

Yadin, Yigael, 203, 226–227, 237–238, 240, 243, 245–256

Yahi tribe, 321
Yale University, 300, 308
Yasur-Landau, Assaf, xiii, 228
Year of the Four Emperors, 194
Yeshiva University, 195
Yigael Yadin Professor of Archaeology, 246
Yosemite, 272
Young, Rodney, 158
Young, Thomas, 40, 70
Yucatán peninsula, 77

Zapotecs, 313
Zenobia, 140, 261–262
Zeus, 136, 173, 175, 176, 335
ziggurats, 53
Zincirli, 87
Zinjanthropus boisei, 100
zoos, future archaeology, 335

2017

12/13/23   4 ×   LAD   9/23/19

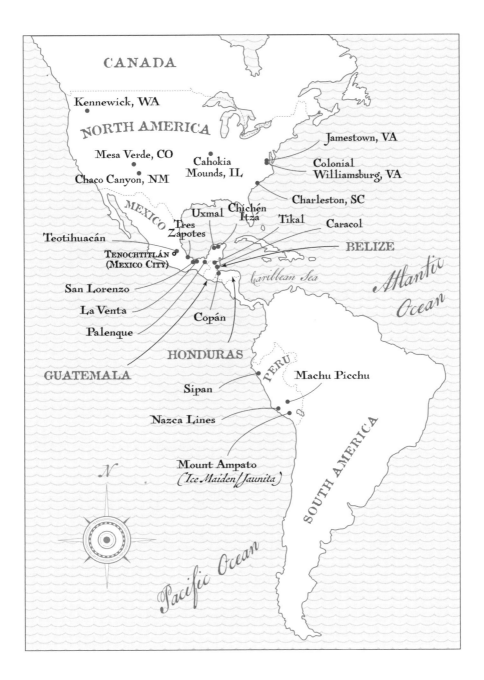

CANADA

NORTH AMERICA

Kennewick, WA

Mesa Verde, CO

Chaco Canyon, NM

MEXICO

Teotihuacán

TENOCHTITLÁN
(MEXICO CITY)

San Lorenzo

La Venta

Palenque

Tres
Zapotes

Uxmal

Cahokia
Mounds, IL

Chichén
Itzá

Tikal

Caracol

BELIZE

Copán

HONDURAS

GUATEMALA

Jamestown, VA

Colonial
Williamsburg, VA

Charleston, SC

Caribbean Sea

Atlantic
Ocean

PERU

Sipan

Nazca Lines

Machu Picchu

SOUTH AMERICA

Mount Ampato
(Ice Maiden / Jaunita)

N

Pacific Ocean

Ardnamurchan peninsula
(Viking boat)

Tollund Fen bog
(near Silkeborg)

Sutton Hoo
(Anglo-Saxon boat)

Lindow Moss bog

Stonehenge

Gelidonya
(shipwreck)

Bogazköy
(Hattusa)

Uluburun
(shipwreck)

Kuyunjik
(Nineveh)

Pompeii

Göbekli
Tepe

Ötzi the Iceman

Lascaux Cave

Mycenae

Rome

Chauvet
Cave

Altamira
Cave

Ziba

Delphi

Troy

Çatalhöyük

Olympia

Athens

Zincirli

Ebla

Knossos

Thera/Santorini

Palmyra

Umma

Rosetta

Ur

Herculaneum

Pylos

Petra

Stabiae

Tiryns

Luxor
(Thebes)

Tanis

Abu Simbel

Giza Pyramids
(Giza/Cairo)

Valley of the Kings
(Tut's tomb)

Hadar

Koobi Fora
(Lake Turkana)

Olduvai Gorge

Laetoli

Atlantic

Ocean

Rising Star Cave